Wisdom With
Understanding
is Better
Than Rubies

Lurine Karon Greenberg
Fine Arts Collection

BEETHOVEN
AS I KNEW HIM

I (*frontispiece*) Beethoven. Engraving by Eduard Eichens after the oil painting by Ferdinand Schimon (1819)

BEETHOVEN AS I KNEW HIM

Anton Felix Schindler

Edited by
Donald W. MacArdle

English Translation by
Constance S. Jolly

Dover Publications, Inc.
Mineola, New York

Copyright

Published in Canada by General Publishing Company, Ltd., 30
Lesmill Road, Don Mills, Toronto, Ontario.

Bibliographical Note

This Dover edition, first published in 1996, is an unabridged
republication of *Beethoven as I Knew Him: A Biography by Anton Felix
Schindler, Edited by Donald W. MacArdle and translated by Constance
S. Jolly*, originally published by The University of North Carolina
Press, Chapel Hill, and Faber and Faber, London, 1966. The 1966
edition was the first English translation, fully annotated, of Schindler's
*Biographie von Ludwig van Beethoven (Dritte, neu bearbeitete und
vermehrte Auflage)*, the author's fully revised third edition, 1860,
originally published in two volumes.
The heading on p. 7 is new; it appeared as "Note on this Edition" in
the original publication. Höfel's engraving of Beethoven, facing p. 168,
faced p. 169 in the 1966 edition.

Library of Congress Cataloging-in-Publication Data

Schindler, Anton Felix, 1795–1864.
  [Biographie von Ludwig van Beethoven. English]
  Beethoven as I knew him / edited by Donald W. MacArdle ;
English translation by Constance S. Jolly.
    p.   cm.
  Translation of: Biographie von Ludwig van Beethoven.
  Originally published: Chapel Hill : University of North Carolina
Press, 1966.
  Includes indexes.
  ISBN 0-486-29232-0 (pbk.)
  1. Beethoven, Ludwig van, 1770–1827. 2. Composers—Austria—
Biography. I. MacArdle, Donald W. II. Title.
ML410. B4S3333 1996
780'.92—dc20   96-22901
[B]   CIP
                                        MN

Manufactured in the United States of America
Dover Publications, Inc., 31 East 2nd Street, Mineola, N.Y. 11501

Note on the Annotated Translation, 1966

Donald MacArdle, whose idea it was to produce this new annotated translation of Anton Schindler's biography of Beethoven, died on 23 December 1964 just after the manuscript had been sent to the printer. He was thus deprived of the pleasure of seeing in print the work to which he had devoted so much time and energy.; and the final editing was carried out in the offices of Faber and Faber, his British publishers. In the supervening stages I have borne in mind the wishes he expressed in our correspondence and done my best to ensure that the work took the final shape that he intended.

Although the main text, notes and biographical sketch of Schindler were complete, Mr MacArdle had decided to wait until the galley-proof stage before adding a number of minor items. Among these were the editor's foreword, the list of abbreviations, and the illustrations. I have made good all the lacunae I have been able to. A general note he did on the work for publicity purposes seemed a possible substitute for his proposed foreword, and so I have included this. I had considerable difficulty in deciphering his innumerable abbreviations, only a few of which were explained in the text. In addition to the illustrations that appeared in the 1860 edition of the biography, I have included reproductions of the Höfel engraving and Danhauser drawing as they have a particular relevance. I trust that Mr MacArdle would have approved of their inclusion.

Had he lived, it is probable that Mr MacArdle would have made a number of revisions and additions in the text and notes, being the vigilant scholar that he was. I hope that at least the minor revisions we have made (some of them on the advice of an expert, to whom we are very grateful), would have been made by him.

It should be mentioned that occasionally Mr MacArdle simply corrected factual slips on Schindler's part and expanded his references without referring to these corrections and expansions in his notes. For example, the date given in the original German for the 'letter of 29 June 1801 to Wegeler' mentioned on p. 61 was 29 June 1800—which is known to be wrong. But corrections and changes of this kind *are* mentioned in the notes if the reasons for making them are complex. Mr MacArdle also sometimes gave the full text of, or corrected, letters that Schindler reproduced in an incomplete or corrupt form, where it seemed desirable (e.g. Beethoven's 'letter of thanks' on p. 168). These amplifications and corrections are mentioned in the notes too. Two other points: (i) Square brackets: insertions in square brackets in the main text are Mr MacArdle's unless they come in the middle of a *quotation*—when they are Schindler's (except in passages in letters added by Mr MacArdle). (ii) American expressions: there is a little inconsistency here. Although Mr MacArdle generally used English expressions where there was a choice, he did sometimes use American ones instead—such as, for instance, 'measure' (=bar) and 'quarter note' (= crotchet). I have left these unchanged as most English readers will probably be familiar with them.

I should like to thank the Trustees of the British Museum for giving us permission to reproduce Plate I and Facsimiles I–IV from their copy of the 1860 edition of the Schindler biography and Plates II and III from the Höfel engraving and Danhauser drawing respectively; and Mr John R. Freeman for providing us with photographs of this material.

Giles de la Mare,
Faber and Faber Ltd.,
London, 1966.

Contents

CONTENTS

CONTENTS

Illustrations

Plates

Facsimiles

List of Abbreviations

(References are in general to volumes (roman) and page numbers; * denotes that references are to letters, † to compositions, and ‡ to portraits.)

ADB   *Allgemeine deutsche Biographie*, Leipzig, 1875–

AmZ   *Allgemeine musikalische Zeitung*, Leipzig, 1798–1848; *Neue Folge* (NF) (*Deutsche Musikzeitung*), Leipzig, 1863–5

*And.   *The Letters of Beethoven*, edited by Emily Anderson, 3 vols., London and New York, 1961

BaF   Stephan Ley, *Beethoven als Freund der Familie Wegeler-von Breuning*, Bonn, 1927

B.&H.   Breitkopf und Härtel (music publisher, Leipzig)

BHdb   Theodor von Frimmel, *Beethoven-Handbuch*, 2 vols., Leipzig, 1926.

BJ   *Beethovenjahrbuch*, edited by Theodor von Frimmel, 2 vols., Munich and Leipzig, 1908–9; also journal edited by Joseph Schmidt-Görg, Bonn, 1954–

Bory   Robert Bory, *Ludwig van Beethoven:His Life and Work in Pictures*, translated (from French) by Winifred Glass and Hans Rosenwald, Zürich and New York, 1960

Brit   *Encyclopaedia Britannica*, 11th ed., Cambridge, 1910–11

BStud   Theodor von Frimmel, *Beethoven-Studien*, 2 vols., Munich and Leipzig, 1905–6

BusV   Max Unger, *Ludwig van Beethoven und seine Verleger S.A. Steiner und Tobias Haslinger in Wien, Ad. Mart. Schlesinger in Berlin*, Berlin and Vienna, 1921

BusZ   Alfred Chr. Kalischer, *Beethoven und seine Zeitgenossen*, 4 vols. (III and IV edited and completed by Leopold Hirschberg), Berlin and Leipzig, 1909–10

CM	Convenzionsmünze (assimilated coinage, official currency: see WW below and And.I xlvii *ff.*)
DM	*Die Musik*, Berlin and Leipzig, 1901–15; Stuttgart, 1922–43
†GA	*Beethovens Werke. Kritische Gesamtausgabe*, 25 vols., Leipzig (B.&H.), 1866–8, 1888 (references are to vol./composition no., e.g. GA 9/71)
GdMf	Gesellschaft der Musikfreunde (Society of the Friends of Music)
Grove	*Grove's Dictionary of Music and Musicians*, London and New York, 5th ed., edited by Eric Blom, 9 vols., 1954
Hanslick	Eduard Hanslick, *Geschichte des Concertwesens in Wien*, Vienna, 1869
†Hess	Willy Hess, *Verzeichnis der nicht in der Gesamtausgabe veröffentlichten Werke Ludwig van Beethovens*, Wiesbaden, 1957
*Kal	See KBr below
KatH	Joseph Schmidt-Görg, *Katalog der Handschriften des Beethoven-Hauses und Beethoven-Archivs Bonn*, Bonn, 1935
KBr	*Beethovens sämtliche Briefe*, edited by Alfred Chr. Kalischer, 5 vols., Berlin and Leipzig, 1906–8
Kerst	Friedrich Kerst, *Die Erinnerungen an Beethoven*, 2 vols., Stuttgart, 1913
KFr	Kalischer-Frimmel: vols. II and III of KBr above revised and enlarged by Theodor von Frimmel, Berlin, 1909–11
KHV	Georg Kinsky, *Das Werk Beethovens. Thematisch-bibliographisches Verzeichnis seiner sämtlichen vollendeten Kompositionen*, completed and edited by Hans Halm, Munich, 1955. See also WoO below
k.k.	kaiserlich und königlich (imperial and royal: of Austrian royalty)
Köchel	Ludwig Ritter von Köchel, *Chronologisch-thematisches Verzeichnis sämtlicher Tonwerke Wolfgang Amadé Mozarts* (Leipzig, 1862), 6th ed., Wiesbaden, 1964

KS	*Beethoven's Letters*, edited by Alfred Chr. Kalischer, translated by J. S. Shedlock, 2 vols., London and New York, 1909
Leitzmann	*Ludwig van Beethoven*, edited by A. Leitzmann, 2 vols., Leipzig, 1921
LvB	See Leitzmann above
M.&L.	*Music and Letters*, London, 1920–
*MM	Donald MacArdle and Ludwig Misch, *New Beethoven Letters*, Norman, Oklahoma, 1957
MMR	*Monthly Musical Record*, London, 1871–
m.p.	manu propria (in his own hand)
MQ	*Musical Quarterly*, New York, 1915–
MR	*Music Review*, Cambridge, 1940–
MT	*Musical Times*, London, 1844–
NB	Gustav Nottebohm, *Beethoveniana*, Leipzig and Winterthur, 1872 (NB I); and *Zweite Beethoveniana*, Leipzig, 1887 (NB II)
NBJ	*Neues Beethoven-Jahrbuch*, edited by Adolf Sandberger, Augsburg and Brunswick, 1924–42
NF	*Neue Folge* (new series). See AmZ above
Nohl	Ludwig Nohl, *Beethovens Leben*, 3 vols., Leipzig, 1867–77
NS	New Style (Gregorian calendar)
NV	Gustav Nottebohm, *Ludwig van Beethoven: Thematisches Verzeichnis* (Leipzig, 1868), new ed., Leipzig, 1925
NZfM	*Neue Zeitschrift für Musik*, Leipzig, 1834–1920; Mainz, 1951–. See also ZfM below
OS	Old Style (Julian calendar)
*‡SBSK	Max Unger, *Eine Schweizer Beethovensammlung: Katalog*, Zürich, 1939 (Br: references to letters; Bi: references to portraits)
Schindler-Moscheles	Anton Schindler, *The Life of Beethoven*, edited by Ignaz Moscheles, 2 vols., London, 1841 (translation of first ed. (1840) of Schindler's *Biographie*)

LIST OF ABBREVIATIONS

SchKH	Georg Schünemann, *Ludwig van Beethovens Konversationshefte*, 3 vols., Berlin, 1941–3
SchwMZ	*Schweizerische Musikzeitung und Sängerblatt*, Zürich, 1861–
SIMG	*Sammelbände der Internationalen Musikgesellschaft*, Leipzig, 1899–1914
SimJB	Nikolaus Simrock, *Jahrbuch*, I–III, edited by Erich H. Müller, Berlin, 1928–34
SJB	Ludwig Schiedermair, *Der junge Beethoven* (Leipzig, 1925), new ed., Bonn, 1947
Sonneck Impr	Oscar Sonneck, *Beethoven: Impressions of Contemporaries*, New York, 1926
TDR	Alexander Wheelock Thayer, *Ludwig van Beethoven's Leben* (von Hermann Deiters neubearbeitet und von Hugo Riemann ergänzt), 3rd ed., 5 vols., Leipzig, 1917–23. Originally written in English, this biography was translated into German by Deiters. Vols. I–III were published in Berlin in 1866, 1872 and 1879. After Thayer's and Deiters's deaths, vols. IV and V were completed by Riemann and published in 1907 and 1908
TF	Alexander Wheelock Thayer, *Thayer's Life of Beethoven*, edited and revised by Elliot Forbes (from the English and the German versions), 2 vols., Princeton, 1964
TK	Alexander Wheelock Thayer, *Life of Ludwig van Beethoven*, edited, revised and amended from the original English MS and TDR above by H. E. Krehbiel, 3 vols., New York, 1921
WoO	Werk ohne Opuszahl (work without opus no.). KHV (above) numbers and lists works not previously given an opus no. as WoO
WW	Wiener Währung (Viennese currency—depreciated currency: see CM above and And. I xlvii*ff*)
ZfM	*Zeitschrift für Musik*, Leipzig, 1921–43. See also NZfM above
ZfMw	*Zeitschrift für Musikwissenschaft*, Leipzig, 1918–35

Editor's Foreword

Anton Schindler is the one author who could appropriately have written a book entitled *Beethoven as I Knew Him.** For most of the last ten years of the composer's life, Schindler was intimately associated with him: as pupil, as scrivener and servant, as factotum, sometimes almost as member of the family. In 1840 he issued a hastily written *Biographie von Ludwig van Beethoven*, that was translated into English the following year by Ignaz Moscheles, the eminent pianist and Beethoven disciple. Schindler's final work on his great friend was the *Biographie* published in 1860, which owes almost nothing to the earlier version.

It is this 1860 edition of Schindler's *Biographie* that is now offered for the first time in an extensively annotated translation. The text is almost exactly as Schindler wrote it, with correction only of typographical errors and slips of the pen ;† but in my annotations I have done much to amplify topical references, to clarify obscure passages, and to incorporate pertinent results of Beethoven research of the past hundred years.

The Beethoven who steps forth from these pages is indeed the Beethoven of the *Eroica* and the last quartets, but he is also the very human man who sputters at poor service in a tavern and rises to the defence of a maligned colleague. Alike for the intensive Beethoven scholar and the general music-lover, this book will give much that cannot be found elsewhere.

---

* The title was the Editor's.
† See also Note on this Edition, page 7, paragraph 4.

Anton Schindler: A Biographical Sketch*

Anton Felix Schindler was born in Meedl (Moravia), about twelve miles north of Olmütz, on 13 June 1795. His father, the local schoolmaster, was also a good amateur musician, and Schindler received early training on the violin and was for a time a *Sängerknabe* at the Mauritzkirche in Olmütz. After instruction at the Gymnasium in Olmütz, he went to Vienna in the autumn of 1813 to study jurisprudence. He continued his musical activities, and in March 1814 he happened to be asked by a musical acquaintance to take a note from his teacher to Beethoven, who received the young man kindly. During the next five years or so the casual acquaintanceship with the great composer gradually became more intimate. From early 1817 Schindler was a clerk in a law office, probably that of Beethoven's cello-playing attorney, Johann Baptist Bach, and three years later he seems to have been employed in the chancellery of Beethoven's patron the Archduke Rudolph; he took his law examinations at the end of 1819, but his heart was in music rather than in the courts. By the autumn of 1822 he had made his decision, and was leader of the violins at the Josephstadt-theater.

About two years before, however, he had entered into what proved to be the principal activity of his life: being factotum for Beethoven. This activity was at its height during the year 1823, when Beethoven was engaged in the ill-fated project of selling manuscript copies of the *Missa Solemnis* to the courts of Europe. During this time, as Thayer says, 'Schindler was called upon to write, fetch and carry as steadily and industriously as if he were, in fact, what he described himself to be—a private secretary.' He seems to have handled almost all of the extensive correspondence involved in this undertaking, and in addition took upon himself many other tasks such as the finding of a lender who would advance money to Beethoven on the security of certain bank shares that he owned, the arranging for Beethoven's occupancy of a summer residence in a suburb of the city, the negotiating with the publisher Diabelli

* A more extended biographical study of Schindler, with many references to the literature, may be found in *Music Review* XXIV (1963) 51.

for editions of the last piano sonata and the *Diabelli Variations*, the routine supervision of the many copyists who were working on the *Missa*, and such lesser but time-consuming tasks as dealing with the many people who wished for favours from Beethoven, picking up monies due to Beethoven and making payments on his behalf, and doing the composer's household shopping. During the summer of 1823 it seems to have been Schindler's practice to hasten from the theatre to Beethoven's summer home at Hetzendorf, some four miles away, as soon as rehearsals were over, and then hasten back for the evening performance.

The spring of 1824, an eventful one for Beethoven because of the preparations for the concert of 7 May in which the ninth symphony and parts of the *Missa* were to receive their first performance, was a busy one for Schindler. The details involved in arranging for this concert were almost beyond counting, and Beethoven's indecision and vacillation on important points, even on the basic one of whether the concert should be given, made his assistant's task more difficult. The concert was an artistic success but a financial failure, and the virulence with which Beethoven accused Schindler of having cheated him over the receipts brought about a breach between the two men that lasted for more than two years, and that was healed only when in December 1826 Beethoven had returned to Vienna to die.

Schindler was tireless in his attendance in the sick-room, and acted as amanuensis when Beethoven's increasing weakness made it impossible for him to write. On the afternoon of 26 March 1827, Beethoven's last day of life, Schindler and Beethoven's boyhood companion Stephan von Breuning left the sick-room and 'went to the cemetery in the little village of Währing [about two miles north-west of the centre of Vienna] and selected a place for Beethoven's grave. When they re-entered the sick-room they were greeted with the words: "It is finished!"' (Thayer). Arrangements for the funeral on 29 March were made by Breuning and Schindler, and as might be expected Schindler was one of the chief mourners at the ceremonies.

After Beethoven's death Vienna held little for Schindler, and he spent most of the next two years with his sister in Pesth. In the spring of 1829 he returned to Vienna as a teacher and writer; in December 1831 he left Vienna to become director of the Musikverein in Münster, and in June 1835 accepted the much more desirable post of director of music in the city of Aachen. As Schindler's biographer Hüffer says, 'Since he possessed real talent as a teacher, he was the ideal man to mark out new paths in his concerts in Münster and Aachen and to establish the correct way to perform the Beethoven symphonies. He also nurtured the Beethoven tradition in the numerous lessons that he gave in these cities.'

The adjective 'ideal', however, is subject to the limitations of Schindler's personality: his talent for making enemies was no less considerable than his talent for teaching, and in May 1840 he requested release from his contract at Aachen. During his years in that city he completed the first edition of his *Biographie von Ludwig van Beethoven*, which was published in Münster in 1840.

In January and February 1841 and again in the following spring Schindler spent some months in Paris, and excerpts from the journal that he kept on these two visits formed the appendix 'Beethoven in Paris' in the second (1845) edition of his *Biographie*. This appendix discusses the growing acceptance of Beethoven's music in the French capital. After his return from Paris he resumed his private teaching in Aachen, but with no other source of income he was forced to consider the idea of selling his collection of Beethoven memorabilia to some library. Negotiations with Berlin, London, and the Belgian Government dragged on for several years, and in the summer of 1845 he accepted the offer from the King of Prussia of a lump payment of 2,000 thalers and an annuity of 400 thalers a year for life. The material that he turned over to the Royal Library in January 1846 included a few autograph scores, sketches, and letters, but the principal item was 136 Conversation Books that Beethoven had used during the period 1819 to 1827. These form a most incomplete record of Beethoven's daily life during that period—they can represent at most only a very few of the conversations that Beethoven had with his associates; but they form a valuable, if often perplexing, and always tantalizing, source of first-hand information about his activities.

Schindler continued his teaching and writing in Aachen, then in Münster and, from 1848, in Frankfurt-am-Main; and in 1856 he moved to his last home in Bockenheim near Frankfurt. During the next few years he worked diligently on the revision of the *Biographie*— actually, a complete rewriting—but for lack of the source material that he had sent to Berlin he was forced to depend largely upon his memory. His health and vigour remained unimpaired until his last illness (probably pneumonia). He died on 16 January 1864 in his sixty-ninth year.

FOREWORD TO THE THIRD EDITION (1860)

A new edition![1] It is generally said that second editions are the joy of the publisher and the pride of the author. For my part, I can honestly say that I feel nothing of pride; on the contrary, I thank Providence with all my heart that I have been granted the life to give this book its present form, for the first edition was on many counts too limited by reason of the circumstances and conditions under which it was prepared. Yet it may not be said that the present edition is completely to my satisfaction; even in this improved version there is so much that I should like to change and improve that I would destroy the whole thing if I felt I could start from the beginning and achieve my desired goal in a sustained frame of mind. The frequently described emotion of a writer so disgusted at the thought of his own completed work that for a time he does not want to see it or hear about it, has come over me with a sharpness that almost completely annihilates any pleasure I might feel at finishing my task.

Moreover, there is a conviction, now more prevalent than before, that no matter how extraordinarily difficult it is to write fully and accurately about Beethoven and his individuality in all things, hypotheses, abstractions, and bold assumptions must be avoided. The writer must act as if he had seen and heard with his own eyes and ears everything he claims. Also, he must not degenerate into wordiness, but must set the matter forth as briefly, concisely, and summarily as possible. These conditions diminish my joy in the undertaking, for I am not always able to comply with them. Even the reassuring knowledge that by far the largest part of what is recorded here was actually experienced through my own senses at the side of the great artist, so that I did not have to have recourse to documents, the hearsay of others interested in these matters, or correspondence with distant persons—this assurance serves only as a palliative.

All the same, the second edition of the book is sold out and a third is requested. Here it is, much expanded and supplemented, and—as the sole source of satisfaction to the author—many dates wrongly given in the other editions, and hence widely spread by other writers, have here been corrected. Nevertheless, I do not pretend that this book exhausts everything that could be said about Beethoven the man and the musician, nor even everything I myself might say, using hitherto untouched documents, at some time in the future. I can, however, state with full conviction that all the important events of the master's life and work are set forth in this book, and that the reader may with ease gain an accurate picture of his character.

In order to put the reader in a position to judge this book not only from the usual critical standpoint but, more importantly, from the standpoint of the author in relation to his task, it is essential for me to relate, as briefly as possible, certain circumstances that governed the preparation of the first edition. I greatly regretted as harmful to Beethoven's interests the omission of this information, which occurred only out of deference for one still alive at that time.

Soon after the master's death, the private government medical adviser, Dr. Wegeler in Coblenz, sent me some notes on Beethoven's youth, especially on the Bonn years, after learning from his brother-in-law, the imperial and royal Hofrat, Stephan von Breuning, of the charge concerning a biography that had been laid on both of us by the dying master. When I visited the worthy gentleman in Coblenz in 1833 he told me of the letter he had just received from Friedrich Rochlitz declining our suggestion that he take part in the preparation of this book, of which further details are given in the Introduction.[2]

Then Wegeler said that the best way to compile a biography of Beethoven, our common friend and teacher, would be for the three of us (Wegeler, Ferdinand Ries, and myself) to collaborate in writing it. He urged me to discuss the plan further with Ries, whom I planned to see a few days later in Frankfurt. I did so, and Ries consented immediately. Yet as soon as I showed him Beethoven's letters and began to tell him some of the events of the master's life that only I could know, it became apparent to me that it would be almost impossible for us to work together according to Wegeler's plan. Ries gave importance to things that were either without interest or of a harmful nature and not appropriate for exposure in the public forum. He bore a long-cherished grudge in his heart against his friend and teacher, and I was not able to persuade him to lay it aside for it was not entirely unjustified. In the proper place in the book I shall have to speak of their relationship in order to be honest with both the teacher and the pupil. At any rate, Ries maintained his position: concerning great men everything may be said, for it does not injure them.

When I returned to the Lower Rhine and told Wegeler of the unhappy outcome of my overtures to Ries, he was not particularly surprised. I then made so bold as to ask him if the two of us might undertake the work alone. Though hesitant at first, he finally agreed on condition that both of us start writing immediately. I gave him my promise. But at our very first attempts to procure certain information on various points by means of correspondence with Vienna, long delays and other obstacles forced us to postpone the work for a time. Wegeler lost patience, and on 28 October 1834 he made known to me his desire to publish his notes forthwith. The publication did not take place then, however, and further negotiations with Ries were held.

The Lower Rhine Music Festival of 1837 in Aachen brought Ries and myself together, and for five whole weeks we collaborated on our notes. We spoke frequently of Wegeler's plan, but the results remained as dubious as ever; in fact, Ries's stubborn holding to his opinion almost caused a rift between us. The very next year, soon after his sudden death, there appeared the *Biographische Notizen über Ludwig van Beethoven*, by Wegeler and Ries.

In Vienna there lived the court lawyer Dr. Johann Baptist Bach, with whom the reader will later become more closely acquainted. All that needs to be said here is that he was one of the foremost juridical authorities of the imperial capital and Beethoven's attorney in legal affairs; moreover, he counselled the master in musical matters of an important nature. The author counts this excellent man, in whose office he was employed during his student years, as one of his special patrons. Because he was eager for the early completion of a description of the master's life, and because it was under his aegis that this work was to be undertaken if Beethoven's dying wish were to be carried out to the letter, I had to acquaint him of the negotiations I had had with Wegeler and Ries.

I was astounded when he replied that I should proceed immediately and alone with the writing of a biography. He offered to assist me in any way possible, and expressed the desire to review and criticize my manuscript. With this encouragement, I sat down at my desk—quite devoid, however, of anything resembling a *furor biographicus*.

With considerable misgivings I sent the manuscript to be censored in Vienna, but nothing was found unacceptable there. On the other hand, I was very surprised at the liberal use my patron made of his red pencil. To this lover of brevity and conciseness of presentation (in contrast to the tendency of most lawyers) much of what I had written seemed too detailed. Factual material having to do with the history of the times was in his opinion liable to put both of us in a dangerous position, even when it served to illustrate certain facets of Beethoven's character. Accordingly, much of what I had written was struck out for no apparent reason and with no regard for inner coherence. Much of the material he deleted has been included in this edition. Dr. Bach shared with many others an attitude towards biographies of artists and scholars that may be formulated in approximately these words:

The accomplishments of a great military leader or a great statesman are usually associated, in general and in detail, with the nation's history. Therefore the story of his life must always be told as it relates to the whole course of events. In the case of an artist or a scholar, however, the situation is quite different. Since his works are in the hands of the public, his biography can and should be restricted to the traits of personality with which the biographer himself is well acquainted, and should mention his works only to the extent that such reference is necessary to an understanding of the total man.

Though this view may be valid in general, it does not apply in Beethoven's case, for here we are dealing not only with the person of the artist and the products of his genius but with an exceptional character who must be considered in purely human terms, a man, too, of deep religious and moral convictions, and even of a scientific and political bent—interests foreign to most musicians. As such, he excites our interest to an uncommon degree.

In short, the first edition appeared—but under the restrictions and limitations that had been agreed upon. The author was safe from the gallows or the wheel, but he was subject to suspicion and intrigue that was sufficient to do considerable harm to his work without his being able to vindicate himself openly. To expose this situation will advance Beethoven's interests and also the interests of the whole music-loving public, as will be seen from the supplementary article, 'Beethoven's Studies'.

Finally, let me address a request to those writing about musical matters.

It is hardly a matter of indifference to the author of any text that his work should be a dependable source for other responsible writers. We must, however, distinguish between books that are out of print and those that are still available in the bookshops. In regard to the latter, my honourable colleagues ought always to observe the maxim: 'Do not unto others what you would not have them do unto you!' Few books can have been so freely copied from as my first edition during its general sale. I am sure that Herr Staatsrat Wilhelm von Lenz in St. Petersburg had no thought of making a disagreeable announcement when, in 1852, after the publication of his book *Beethoven et ses Trois Styles*, he wrote to me: 'I have quoted you 233 times in my book, for you are and continue to be the source for most of the important details.' Two hundred and thirty-three quotations, many of them half a page long! Does not such brotherly co-operation exceed the bounds of scholarly consideration? The Herr Staatsrat's next book, *Beethoven, eine Kunststudie*, has as its first volume *Das Leben des Meisters*, which is nothing but a rehash of the biographical section of my book, a bit of literary reweaving of old threads.

Another Russian, Alexandre Oulibicheff, made quite different use of my book in his work, *Beethoven, ses Critiques et ses Glossateurs,* which has recently been translated into German by Ludwig Bischoff and published under the title, *Beethoven, seine Kritiker and seine Ausleger.* As one hostile to the great composer, Oulibicheff saw fit to give corroboration to many of his remarks and affirmations with statements from my book, which he twisted and distorted until they led to conclusions that could only have been formulated in the head of a bitter, prejudiced adversary.

Another no less comprehensive use of my book was made by A. B. Marx in his work, *Beethoven, Leben und Schaffen,* but not until the edition was almost sold out. It is with real pleasure, however, that I acknowledge the wise use this outstanding scholar and writer has made of just those portions he found necessary. We shall have occasion to cite this Berlin professor's book as being relevant to the matters in hand. His work is of paramount significance in the whole body of Beethoven literature.

My publisher joins me in asking that the honourable writers on musical subjects regard this new edition with the utmost consideration and respect for rights of property.

Anton Schindler

Bockenheim (near Frankfurt-am-Main)
December 1858

EDITOR'S NOTES (1–2)
Foreword to the Third Edition (1860)

[1] The publication history of Schindler's *Biographie* and allied works is as follows:

1840   *Biographie von Ludwig van Beethoven.*

1841   *The Life of Beethoven, edited by Ignace Moscheles, Esq.* (2 vols.). Schindler's name does not appear on the title-page, but the Editor's Preface makes it clear that the work is a translation of the 1840 edition without omissions or alterations, to which are added clearly identified footnotes and an appendix to each volume that are the work of Moscheles.

1842   *Beethoven in Paris, nebst anderen den unsterblichen Tondichter betreffenden Mittheilungen.* This contains excerpts from the Conversation Books (16 pages, mostly entries by Schindler), an extended essay on Beethoven's music in Paris as Schindler found it during his visit to that city in January and February 1841 (viii + 101 pages), and other lesser essays (pp. 102–178).

1845 *Biographie von Ludwig van Beethoven (Zweite, mit zwei Nachträgen vermehrte Ausgabe)*. This is a reprinting in a single volume of the 1840 edition plus the 1842 *Beethoven in Paris*.

1860 *Biographie von Ludwig van Beethoven (Dritte, neu bearbeitete und vermehrte Auflage)* (2 vols.). In this edition the biographical portion has been completely rewritten; the added material includes a discussion of Beethoven's interpretation of some of his sonatas, and much personal and miscellaneous material, most of which had not appeared in the earlier editions. The present volume is an annotated translation of this 1860 publication.

1864 *Histoire de la vie et de l'œuvre de Ludwig van Beethoven*. French translation of the 1860 edition by Albert Sowinski.

1871 Reprinting of third (1860) edition, without change; but identified as 'Vierte Auflage'.

1909 *Anton Schindler's Beethoven-Biographie (Neudruck herausgegeben von Dr. Alfr. Chr. Kalischer)*. A reprint of the 1860 edition with 378 notes by the editor, most of these being references to the composer's letters as they appear in the Kalischer Collected Edition. This reprint is often referred to as the 'Vierte Auflage'.

1927 *Ludwig van Beethoven (Fünfte Auflage)*. A photolithographic reprint of the 1860 edition, with an Introduction (20 pages) and about fifty notes of slight value by the editor, Fritz Volbach.

1949 *Biographie von Ludwig van Beethoven (in verkürzter Form mit berechtigenden Anmerkungen, neu herausgegeben von Stephan Ley)*. As its title indicates, an abridgement of the 1860 edition, with about two hundred notes by the editor.

[2] The Introduction, the first part of which follows closely the Introduction to the 1840 edition of the biography, quotes parts of two letters written by Rochlitz to Schindler in the autumn of 1827 in which Rochlitz states his inflexible decision not to participate in the writing of a life of Beethoven. No further correspondence on this subject, with Schindler or with Wegeler, is known.

INTRODUCTION

One day during the painful four months of Beethoven's last illness, it chanced that he was discussing with Stephan von Breuning and the author of this book the collection of biographies compiled by the Greek writer Plutarch. Breuning took advantage of this long-wished-for opportunity to ask the master, apparently with no particular object in mind, which of his contemporaries he would prefer as his biographer. Without a moment's hesitation Beethoven replied, 'Rochlitz, if he should survive me.' He went on to say that it might be assumed with certainty that after his death many zealous pens would hasten to amuse the world with innumerable anecdotes and fables about him, devoid of all truth, for such is the usual lot of men who have had any influence upon their period. It was thus his sincere wish that whatever might be said about him in the future should in every respect adhere strictly to the truth, even though it might bear hard upon this or that person, or even upon himself.

This statement, uttered at a moment when our friend's death seemed to be near at hand, was too important for us to neglect to follow up. In doing so, however, we were obliged to observe the greatest caution, as was necessary with everything that might even remotely have to do with death, for Beethoven's imagination, more capricious even than in health, swept through the universe developing plans for travel and for great compositions, and the like. In short, he gave no thought to the imminence of death, nor would he be warned of its approach. He was determined to live, for there was still so much for him to create that perhaps no one other than himself had the powers to.

Prudence, therefore, compelled us to await a suitable opportunity to touch again on this topic of conversation. Unhappily, this came only too soon, for as Beethoven recognized the waning of his physical strength he admitted that hope of recovery was vain, and with stoic fortitude faced his death. Plutarch and others of his favourite Greek authors lay around him as one day he made some observations on his much-admired Lucius Brutus, whose statuette was before him. This opened the way for us to resume the interrupted conversation regarding his biographer. Resigned to his fate, Beethoven read with great care a document that Breuning had prepared, and said calmly: 'There is one paper, there another. Take them and make the best use of them. But I charge you both to adhere strictly to the truth in all matters. And write to Rochlitz.'

Our object was accomplished. He gave us the necessary explanations and information regarding some of the papers he had indicated. His wish, as expressed in that momentous hour, was that I should take in my care all letters that were at hand, and Breuning all family documents and similar papers.

After the master's death we had decided to communicate jointly to Hofrat Rochlitz the wish of our departed friend. But Breuning fell ill, and after barely two months followed the friend of his youth to the grave. This tragic occurrence left me in a most difficult situation regarding the task that we had jointly undertaken for Beethoven, since I had lost my only collaborator. Breuning's widow immediately gave me the papers that had been assembled by her deceased husband (except for family documents, which were retained by the executor of the estate, Dr. Bach), and it now lay solely with me to acquaint Rochlitz with Beethoven's wish, which I did under the date of 12 September 1827. On the 18th of that month I received the following reply:

The eccentricities and roughnesses in our revered Beethoven's manner have long failed to conceal from me the greatness and nobility of his character, and although on the occasion of my visit to Vienna in 1822 I was with him only a few times (but then with frankness and confidence), this was only because of the ailment that bore on him so heavily and that made intercourse with him so difficult. This, together with my happy acknowledgement of his genius and his great deserts as an artist, has been the reason why I have to the best of my ability followed the course of his spirit and his entire inner life, as far as these are displayed in his works, from his youth to his death. And since from time to time I had taken every opportunity to acquaint myself with authentic facts concerning his life history, I deemed myself, at the time of his death, not wholly unqualified to become his biographer. This I resolved to do by making Beethoven's life story, like Maria von Weber's, a principal article in the third volume of my book, *Für Freunde der Tonkunst*. Now comes your offer to supply me with material, and the desire of Beethoven himself as conveyed to me by you. From all this you may judge whether I would be inclined to accede to the request expressed by you as well as by other friends of Beethoven.

It is all the more distressing to me that I may not undertake this task. A life devoted from early years to almost unremitting labour has of late been taking its harsh revenge upon me. . . . I am now compelled to adjust myself to an almost complete change from my former activities, and the most important part of this change must be that I sit and write far less than before. Accordingly, so that I may not be forced or enticed into new projects, I refuse to undertake any new work of consequence. And thus I must of necessity renounce the fulfilling of the wish that is both yours and mine. . . . I need not say how much it pains me to give you this answer, but one must bow to necessity. Accept my thanks for your confidence.

INTRODUCTION

Despite this positive refusal I ventured to repeat my request, with the assurance that I would place at his disposal my personal experiences with Beethoven. Under the date of 3 October 1827 Rochlitz honoured me with a reply in which he initially thanked me for the copy of Beethoven's will of 1802 that I had sent him, and continued:

I cannot tell you how much the obvious sincere and childlike goodness of heart that it displays has delighted me, nor how deeply moved I have been by the painful sufferings of his noble soul. Surely this document will have a single effect upon all (unless they be totally insensitive) who become acquainted with it. I do not know what more favourable, more convincing thing can be added here to honour the deceased, not as an artist but as a man. I cannot undertake to comply with the wish that you express to me a second time, and it cannot be of help to either of us if I add: I am sorry!

In view of my earlier decision not to entrust the papers that I had to anyone else if Rochlitz should refuse to act, upon his explanation I took no further steps, awaiting suitable time and circumstances. The Foreword sets forth how these two factors later came into effect; their result is shown in the present work.

The life history of Beethoven, of the artist who constitutes the summit of the latest period of German music, must first of all show the circumstances under which the man achieved the peak of his art and created such great, such immortal works. It must also attempt to delineate a character and a personality that in no way contradicts documents or the accounts of others. In order to write about Beethoven, if the portrait is to consider anything but the purely artistic side of the man, one must have known him personally, watched him for years, seen with one's own eyes the circumstances of his life, and been able to determine their influence on him—in short, one must have shared his joy and his suffering. From the circle of his intimate friends I am the only one still alive, and I am deeply sensitive of the obligation laid upon me to present faithfully and authentically the facts that made up the world of Beethoven.*

The division of the biography into three periods will be retained, though the time included in the second period has been changed. The first division was not the choice of the author but was based on a suggestion that Breuning made at our friend's deathbed, and that Beethoven approved. Because the biography was planned to consider only the external events of his life, the second period was to terminate quite appropriately with October 1813. That was, in the course of events, the moment of the master's deepest preoccupation with his art, his most

* In the interests of this book the author refers the reader to two articles that describe the relationship between Beethoven and himself: AmZ XXIX (1827) 368 and Berliner AmZ IV (1827) 244.

complete obliviousness to material things—and his consequent lack of every physical necessity. It is difficult to determine the influence his state of mind had on his external situation, but certainly these two considerations affected one another. At the appropriate time we shall go into greater detail. The connexion between the external and the artistic life demands a prolongation of this period to the end of 1814, because it was that year that saw our master reach the peak of his artistic glory. But this circumstance is not the only determining factor in my ending the second period at the end of 1814. Changes in his family situation in 1815 and the consequent alteration of his whole life constitute a clear point of separation and dictate to the biographer the logical boundary-marker between the two periods.

The periods are therefore divided as follows: the first begins with Beethoven's birth and extends to the end of 1800, a long space of time but still one that may be termed his period of study and preparation; the second, at the beginning of which Beethoven makes his début as a composer of symphonies and a creator of major works, includes the years 1801 to 1814: 'My youth, yes I feel my youth is now just beginning' (Beethoven to Wegeler, 16 November 1801); and the third period ends with his death in 1827.

For my account of the events of Beethoven's youth I am indebted principally to Wegeler, the companion of the young Amphion until 1796. Beethoven's letters to this friend and Wegeler's notes supplement the following years up to the beginning of the second period. As guarantors of the events of the second period not recorded in letters and documents I had Beethoven's circle of friends, and of course I learned much of these events from the master himself. Many of these men, all of whom the reader will meet, were my close associates for years after the master's death. As for the events of the third period, I witnessed them personally and in one way or another took part in most of them.

A musical portion will consist of directions and aids for a correct understanding and performance of Beethoven's music, particularly the piano music, and will be based not only on tradition but also on fundamental precepts. Digressions on artistic personalities of an earlier time and of the present are necessary to an understanding of the matter. At the close of this portion there will be a summary of the editions of our composer's works to show that a distribution of this extent has never existed in any literature.

Valuable aids in the portrayal of Beethoven's character and religious feelings are the three books from Beethoven's personal library that Stephan von Breuning and the author have selected as worth keeping. They are Homer's *Odyssey* in the Voss translation, Christian Sturm's

INTRODUCTION

Betrachtungen der Werke Gottes im Reiche der Natur, a book of instruction and edification in two volumes, and Goethe's *West-östlicher Divan*.

Our master had acquired in his early years, and retained, the habit of marking, underlining, and even quite frequently copying into his journal passages from his reading that seemed to bear special reference to his thoughts and feelings, to his art, or to his personal circumstances.[3] Thus we have a considerable number of literary excerpts, some of them so appropriate they might have been written by the master himself. Many situations in his life are far more brightly illuminated by these quotations than would otherwise be possible. We also have notes written in Beethoven's own hand in the margins of these interesting relics.

The appendix at the end of the discussion of each period contains the long-desired list of all the principal works (as well as most of the smaller ones) in the order of their composition, with notes on their first performance, their publication, and their first publisher. With the confusion in the present cataloguing, the establishing of these dates has been a particularly difficult part of my task. Perhaps my corrections and suggestions for disposing, in so far as is possible, of this bad situation will be welcome. The composer's life-story will also be accompanied by a description of the musical characteristics of his time, the attitude and training of musicians, the publishing situation, and much more. This book should thus discharge the special function of the biography of a great artist: to be a mirror of its time and also a textbook for those who wish to learn from it.

Critical reviews of various works, written either at the time of their first performance or after their publication, are incorporated into the biographical material. These criticisms, which were lacking in the first edition, serve not only as witnesses to the artistic views of the time but also as demonstrations of the continuing cross-currents opposing Beethoven. They provided the material sought by those who wished to harm the master, a hostility often ignored by the young artist but one that increasingly obstructed him as the years passed and that he had to overcome.

The fortunate fact that today the appreciation of Beethoven's works in all cultivated societies has attained a much higher level, has made it advisable for one to address oneself to a mixed circle of readers. The author therefore hopes that his efforts to present all his material clearly have been successful, and that the critic will not have to repeat his reproachful verdict on the first edition that in his enthusiasm for the great composer the author paid too much homage to the rhetorical phrase. Most of all he hopes that the book may to some degree satisfy the needs of the serious scholar, for the best reward of such a work is the approbation of distinguished artists and scholars of many disciplines and of honourable sentiment.

This time the author has given no thought to the army of musicians notorious at all times for their indifference to books, for avoiding any teaching that might widen their limited horizons and for keeping to the same traditional routines. On the contrary he has allowed himself in the present edition to give an historically accurate account of this class's indifference, past and present alike. It is one of the strangest phenomena of the material world that many things keep their basic character unchanged through many generations while everything around them is striving to alter life's principles and maxims and make them appropriate to the demands of the times, to open the doors to a scientific approach to every discipline, and to wipe out the old German philistinism from our whole environment. Among the circle of musicians this attitude persists in full force (with the exception of the circle, and it is not small, of the autonomous, industrial aristocracy) and distinguishes itself only in the degree to which it preserves itself in the various regions of musical Germany.

EDITOR'S NOTES (3)

Introduction

3 A collection of these marked passages—54 from Homer, 43 from Goethe, 41 from Sturm, 31 from Shakespeare, and others to a total of more than two hundred from a dozen or more authors—may be found in Nohl's *Beethovens Brevier*.

FIRST PERIOD

Beethoven's Birth (1770) to the End of 1800

A single man is all mankind
A. Meissner

[I]

Ludwig van Beethoven was born in Bonn on 17 December 1770.[4] His father, Johann van Beethoven, was a tenor in the Electoral choir, and died in Bonn in 1792. His mother, Maria Magdalena *née* Keverich (or Keferich), came from Ehrenbreitstein near Coblenz, and lived only until 1787. His grandfather, Ludwig van Beethoven, was probably born in Maestricht, where the family name still persists.[5]* He was a bass singer, then director of the Electoral choir in Bonn, and is said to have performed his own operas for the splendour-loving Elector Clemens August.[6] He died in 1773. With the aid of a fine portrait in oils,[7] Beethoven always retained a vivid memory of this grandfather.

The subject of the house in which Beethoven was born has aroused much controversy. Dr. Wegeler says on page 6 of his *Biographische Notizen über Ludwig van Beethoven* (*Biographical Notes on Ludwig van Beethoven*) that, according to all the evidence, the composer was born at No. 515 on Bonngasse. This statement is corroborated by the neighbour across the street, Frau Mertens *née* Lengersdorf, also mentioned by Wegeler. Later a Bonn school-teacher, Dr. Hennes, investigated further and arrived at the same conclusion.

Despite such overwhelming evidence (which is further supported by the baptismal record in the parish church), a heated dispute broke out in 1845 when a statue of the composer was to be unveiled in Bonn. Jealousy and ambition claimed as Beethoven's birthplace No. 934 Rheingasse, a house that the Beethoven family did indeed occupy in the 1780's. Even Wegeler's *Nachtrag zu den biographischen Notizen* (*Appendix to the Biographical Notes*), which came out in the same year declaring that Beethoven was beyond a doubt born in the house on Bonngasse, did not silence the clamorous opponents.

---

* In 1840 the author saw the full name of the composer on the sign plate of a shop in Maestricht selling articles from the Colonies: Louis van Beethoven.[5]

At the written request of Dr. Schildt, owner of the Bonngasse house, the author of this work wrote to Johann van Beethoven, the composer's brother in Vienna, asking him to settle the question. He replied that he could not remember the exact name of the street where the family had lived at the time of Ludwig's birth, but he was sure it was not near the Rhine. The dispute over this insignificant matter, in which even distinguished men of the city took up cudgels in favour of the Rheingasse house, was not to be dismissed on the basis of any new evidence from Vienna. On the contrary, public opinion was so far deceived by the self-interest of the speculators that the truth must remain silent.[8]

The rumour that Beethoven was the illegitimate son of King Friedrich Wilhelm II of Prussia was first circulated by Fayolle and Choron, then published in seven editions of the Brockhaus *Conversations-Lexikon*.[9] Beethoven was deeply mortified, and on 7 December 1826 he wrote to his boyhood friend Wegeler, asking his intercession to 'make known to the world the integrity of his parents, especially of his mother'.[10] That he had not addressed his request to Wegeler many years earlier may be explained by the fact that the *Lexikon* was practically unknown in Austria before this date, having presumably been banned by the censor.[11]

According to page 5 of his *Notizen*, Wegeler believed that no refutation of the libel was necessary, since the Prussian king had not been in Bonn before Beethoven's birth and Beethoven's mother had never once left Bonn after her marriage. The author of this work, however, disagreed, and when the publishers in Leipzig announced the eighth edition of the *Lexikon*, he thought it high time to draw their attention to the falsity of the rumour. On 17 February 1833 he accordingly referred them to Beethoven's letter to Wegeler. The damaging sentence was consequently altered in the new edition.

Wegeler is our only source on Beethoven's upbringing and early education. On page 9 of his *Notizen* he writes: 'Beethoven's education was neither very good nor particularly bad. He learned reading, writing, arithmetic, and some Latin at the public school, and at home his father supervised his musical instruction with relentless severity. The family had no other income than the meagre earnings of the father, a man of no moral or spiritual strength and addicted to drink, who was determined that his eldest son should be trained to help with the education of the other children.'

We know, moreover, that the temperamental boy, who had no love for drudgery, had to be driven forcibly to the piano. He had even less inclination for playing the violin: hence the pretty little fable about the spider, 'which, whenever little Ludwig was playing his violin in his room, descended from the ceiling to sit on the instrument. When his mother discovered her son's companion, she killed it, whereupon the boy smashed his violin to bits'. As an adult, Ludwig could remember no such incident. It was a popular anecdote, however, even before Dr. Christian Müller of Bremen published it in his biographical essay on Beethoven (AmZ XXIX (1827) 346).[12]

Beethoven received more advanced musical training from a conductor and oboist named Pfeiffer, a man noted for his musical talent. Wegeler writes: 'Beethoven owed much to this teacher and was so grateful to him that even after he had gone to Vienna, he continued to make Simrock give him regular sums of money'. It has been established, though Wegeler only supposed it so, that Beethoven learned to master the techniques of organ playing from van den Eeden, organist at the Electoral court. Years later Beethoven recalled several incidents dating from this association, especially in connection with the position of the hands at the keyboard, which he considered very important for an organist and even more so for a pianist, an opinion we shall refer to again in the musical portion of this book. Wegeler continues, 'The composer Neefe, formerly musical director with the Grossmann theatrical company and thereafter Court organist, had little if any influence on the musical instruction of young Ludwig.[13] Beethoven later accused Neefe of criticizing his first experiments in composition with undue severity. In 1785 Elector Max Franz, the brother of Emperor Joseph, appointed Beethoven as organist to the Electoral chapel,[14] a rather undemanding office that he and Neefe discharged by turns. Apparently the Elector appointed a second organist merely as a means of extending assistance.'

In its first year of publication (3 October 1798 to 25 September 1799), the *Allgemeine musikalische Zeitung* (AmZ) printed 'The life of C. G. Neefe, written by himself,' dated 'Frankfurt, 30 September 1782'. Since he had already left Bonn and moved to Frankfurt, he could not have been at the court when Beethoven was engaged as organist.[15] But Neefe's 'criticizing his first experiments in composition with undue severity' is still quite possible, for even at that early age, Beethoven had already committed quite a number of compositions to paper: the *Three Original Quartets for Piano, Violin, Viola, and Violoncello, Composed at the Age of Thirteen*, which Artaria published ostensibly from Beethoven's *Nachlass*,[16] may well have been the subject of harsh criticism from many quarters. But the confusion of dates and facts becomes even greater if, as Wegeler claims, the *Court Calendar* names Christian Neefe and Ludwig van Beethoven as organists for the year 1790, long after Beethoven had finished with 'first experiments'. The *Court Calendar* is not likely to be incorrect in such a matter.*

* In an article about musical events in Bonn, written for the March 1783 issue of C. F. Cramer's *Magazin der Musik* (Hamburg), extracts from which were reprinted in the twenty-fifth issue of the *Niederrheinische Musik-Zeitung* (1858), we read:

For his appointment as organist as well as for his subsequent training and study in Vienna, Beethoven was beholden to Count von Waldstein who, according to Wegeler, was 'his first and in every respect most important Maecenas'.[18] Count von Waldstein was a Knight of the Teutonic Order and the constant companion and favourite of the young Elector. Later he became Commander of the Teutonic Order at Virnsberg and chamberlain to the Emperor. He was not only a lover of music but an accomplished performer as well, and thus was able to exercise a direct influence on the development of the youthful Beethoven's talents. At his suggestion Beethoven perfected his ability to improvise variations upon a theme, an art in which he was not later equalled, let alone excelled, by any of his contemporaries. A letter from Waldstein to his protégé (the text of the letter is given further on) shows how quickly he recognized the young artist's genius and what a brilliant future he predicted for him. Wegeler tells us moreover that this true nobleman, always having the greatest consideration for the young composer's sensitiveness, saw to it that Beethoven received frequent sums of money, which were generally thought to be a small allowance from the Elector. It is fitting to mention here that in 1806,[19] when virtually at the peak of his powers, Beethoven publicly expressed his gratitude to this patron, protector, and fellow artist in the dedication of his great C major sonata, opus 53.

Hardly had the youthful organist assumed his new duties when a characteristic incident occurred, of which Wegeler and Beethoven have each left us an account.[20] The incident is additionally interesting since the two versions differ markedly. This is perhaps the first in the whole series of contradictions and conflicting statements concerning Beethoven's life. The problem places so many pitfalls in the path of the biographer that he is often quite unable to find his way, especially when the composer himself has contributed to his quandary.

'In the Roman Catholic Church,' writes Wegeler, 'the *Lamentations of*

Louis van Beethoven, son of the above-mentioned tenor, an eleven-year-old boy of most promising talent. He plays the piano with strength and authority, sight-reads very well, and plays chiefly the *Well-Tempered Clavier* by Sebastian Bach, which was given to him by Herr Neefe.[17] Anyone familiar with this collection of preludes and fugues in all the successive keys (it might almost be termed the *ne plus ultra*) will know what an accomplishment this is. In so far as his other duties have allowed, Herr Neefe has also instructed him in thoroughbass. He is now supervising the boy's exercises in composition, and to encourage him has had his piano work, *Nine Variations on a March*, printed in Mannheim. This young genius is deserving of assistance so that he may be able to travel. Should he continue to progress at his present rate, he will certainly become a second Wolfgang Amadeus Mozart.

This article disputes the facts of Wegeler's account, Beethoven's age, his famous experiments in composition, and even Neefe's departure from Bonn and residence in Frankfurt. Where is the truth to be found? Wegeler's account and others that fit in with it appear to be the most reliable.

the Prophet Jeremiah are sung on three days of Holy Week. [Author's note: Not everywhere; in fact, they are seldom heard.] The *Lamentations* consist of short verses of four to six lines and were performed like chorales, though in a certain prescribed pattern. The chant consisted of four consecutive notes—for example, C, D, E, F—on the third of which several words or even whole sentences were sung; then a short cadence would carry the melody line back to the first note. Since the organ could not be played during these three days [nowadays it must be silent only on Good Friday] the singer was accompanied by a pianist.' (Obviously on the piano although this procedure is unheard of today and the piano is considered the least suitable instrument for use in a church.)

As an illustration of the principle, the notation of the first versicle of the *Lamentations* follows. I have chosen a five-line staff rather than one of four lines such as is used in the old liturgy books for the *Officium Hebdomadae* (Office for Holy Week). To clarify the rhythm of the chant, I have substituted round notes for the old square symbols.[21]

Ex. 1

To resume Wegeler's account of Beethoven's musical prank:

Once when it was his duty to accompany the *Lamentations*, Beethoven asked the singer Heller, noted for his ability to retain his pitch, for his permission to confuse him; and made use of the permission given perhaps too casually to introduce such extensive modulations into the accompaniment, though persistently striking the reciting note with his little finger, that the singer became confused to the point that he could not find the closing cadence. Father Ries, who was then music director and first violinist of the Electoral chapel, still tells in detail how greatly Kapellmeister Lucchesi was astonished by Beethoven's playing.

Everyone acquainted with the ritual of the Catholic Church knows that the accompanist, to relieve the monotony of the single note held almost constantly throughout the three fairly long *Lectiones* of the *Lamentations*, generally ornaments the line with embellishments and variations in the registration, just as the organ does when accompanying the *Preface* at High Mass, the notation of which is very similar to the *Lamentations*. Harmonic excesses, however, such as Beethoven, according to his own report, was guilty of in Bonn, would obviously be out of place. As for the outcome of the incident itself, the singer, humiliated at the insult to his musical ability, complained to the Elector of the arrogant organist who, as he himself later recalled, 'was most graciously reproached and forbidden to play any more such clever practical jokes in the future'.

Another incident recorded by Wegeler is even more interesting to us, since it shows that even in his earliest attempts at composition Beethoven wrote music that was very difficult to perform, a characteristic that gave rise to a whole series of vigorous protests and objections that survived the composer himself and may still be heard today. Wegeler writes, 'When Haydn first returned from England, the Electoral orchestra entertained him with a breakfast at Godesberg, a resort near Bonn.* Beethoven took this opportunity to show Haydn a cantata he had written. The older composer was much impressed, and urged Beethoven to continue his studies. Later the cantata was to have been performed in Mergentheim,† but several passages were so difficult for the wind instruments that some of the players announced that it could not be played, and the performance was cancelled.'[22]

A similar fate awaited the overture to his opera *Leonore*, which had to be shelved for the same reason, as we shall see in the second portion of this book. Beethoven apparently destroyed the aforementioned cantata, since it has never been heard of.[23] Such drastic self-criticism is indeed surprising, since he preserved other experiments in composition, such as the three quartets for piano, violin, viola, and violoncello mentioned before and a trio in E flat major for piano, violin, and violoncello. Beethoven called the latter 'one of his worthiest experiments in the art of composition', and is said to have written it at the age of fifteen. At any rate, the second movement, the Scherzo, may be considered to contain the germ of all the succeeding scherzos.‡

* This must have occurred in June 1792 and may have been the beginning of Beethoven's plan to study with Haydn, since it was only five months later that he left for Vienna.

† Mergentheim, a small town in Württemberg, was from 1527 the seat of the Grand Master of the Teutonic Order, whose residence was the nearby castle of Neuhaus. The present residence of the *Hoch- und Deutschmeister* is Vienna.

‡ This trio is included in the Breitkopf & Härtel *Thematisches Verzeichnis* (*Thematic Index*) on page 127.[24] Ferdinand Ries was instrumental in having it published in 1830 by Dunst in Frankfurt.

Wegeler lists Beethoven's earliest compositions as follows: the sonatas published in Speyer's *Blumenlese*; next, the song *Wenn jemand eine Reise thut*; and then the music for a carnival ballet to be danced by the nobility. The piano arrangement of this ballet reached the music publisher Dunst, probably through Ferdinand Ries who vigorously supported the Dunst undertaking. Wegeler writes of the ballet: 'It apparently consisted of a *Minnelied*, a German folksong, a drinking song, and other movements. This composition was for a long time considered to be the work of Count Waldstein, since Beethoven did not put his name to it and since Waldstein, in collaboration with Habich, the dance instructor from Aachen, had organized the ballet.'

Then follow the variations on a theme by Righini, *Vieni Amore*, dedicated to the Countess von Hatzfeld. These afforded the young composer an opportunity to demonstrate his extraordinary ability. On the trip just mentioned from Bonn to Mergentheim, the residence of the Elector in his capacity as Grand Master of the Teutonic Order, the whole orchestra stopped at Aschaffenburg. There Beethoven was introduced by Ries, Simrock (who later became a music publisher in Bonn), and the two Rombergs, Anton and Bernhard, to Sterkel, the famous pianist and Kapellmeister at the Electoral court of Mainz. Sterkel, entreated on all sides, as Wegeler tells us, sat down and played. His touch was very light and delicate and, as father Ries expressed it, rather feminine. Beethoven stood near him, excited and very attentive, since Sterkel was the first piano virtuoso he had ever heard. Then Beethoven, too, was invited to play, but he refused until Sterkel said he doubted that Beethoven would be able to play his own composition, the *Vieni Amore* variations. Thereupon Beethoven played not only these variations, as far as he could remember them (since Sterkel was unable to locate a copy), but also a number of others equally difficult. But what amazed the listeners was that he played in exactly the same delicate manner that had so impressed him in Sterkel's performance. He thus demonstrated how easily he could imitate another pianist's style.*

In relating this incident, Wegeler, our Beethoven authority from Coblenz, admits that Beethoven's playing was at that time generally raw and harsh. In the course of this biography we shall frequently mention the development of his style as a pianist; but it is interesting and somewhat startling to compare Wegeler's last remarks with observations on Beethoven's playing made by John Cramer in 1799 and by Cherubini in 1805. These two contend that Beethoven could no more

---

* Both old and new catalogues also include for 1780: *Nine Variations in C Minor on a March Theme by Dressler*; and for 1792: *Thirteen Variations in A Major on a Theme from 'Das rothe Käppchen'*; *Es war einmal ein alter Mann*. ('*Little Red Riding Hood*': *Once there was an old man*). These were published by Simrock.[25]

adopt another pianist's style than he could exchange his whole artistic individuality for another's. Bernhard Romberg, too, whom I had the pleasure of visiting in his native city of Münster in 1834, supported this Cramer-Cherubini opinion. He related to me several other interesting recollections from the time he and Beethoven both lived in Bonn. It was through Romberg that I became personally acquainted with Baroness von Bevervörde, *née* von Böselager, [25a] of that city, who had been a pupil of Beethoven's. We shall hear more about her soon. Beethoven himself blamed the harshness of his touch at that time on his constant playing of the organ. Another equally plausible reason may have been the lack of a really good model for him to imitate.

One peculiarity of Beethoven's was his aversion to giving lessons and playing at social gatherings. Because it explains some of his actions and idiosyncrasies of character in later years, we quote an anecdote from Wegeler: 'Frau von Breuning sometimes used to entreat him to give piano lessons to Count von Westphal, the Austrian ambassador, who lived across the street from her. He would rebel like an obstinate donkey but, because he knew she would be watching from the window, he would go right up to the Count's door, and then often turn and run back to her house, promising to give a double lesson the next day; that day was impossible. Even his financial situation did not induce him to undertake this kind of labour, but only the thought of his family and especially of his beloved mother.'

This reluctance, however, does not seem to have applied to one pupil, the above-mentioned Frau von Bevervörde. She assured me that the regularity of her lessons and Beethoven's instruction in general had never given her grounds for complaint. Teacher and pupil were about the same age, and as a young girl she must have been very beautiful, for the lady I met still possessed traces of beauty. She told me a great deal more about her earnest, pensive young teacher and also spoke at length of the musical life of her native city in the 1790's, and remembered how she had played duets with Bernhard Romberg to the great delight of that veteran of the arts.

But the story of Fräulein von Böselager does not discredit Wegeler's observation that Beethoven detested teaching (that is, regular and systematic lesson-giving), for it was an aversion that remained with him throughout his life. If he occasionally enjoyed a pupil, it was the exception, as with the case of our young lady from Bonn, who was not only unusually pretty but is also said to have played very nicely. Beethoven is not the only teacher who has had his favourite pupils! Ferdinand Ries perhaps suffered the most at that time from his master's dislike of teaching. 'I used to play the piano,' Ries told me, 'and Beethoven would compose or do something else. He would hardly ever sit down and attend to me for a full half-hour.'* During his whole four years of lessons with Beethoven, Ries calculated that he had had barely fifty full hours of instruction, though in his memoirs he speaks differently on this point.

As for not his liking to play at social gatherings, Wegeler writes:

Later when Beethoven was a celebrity in Vienna, his aversion to playing for an audience had become so strong that every time he was urged to play, he would fly into a rage. He often came to me then, gloomy and out of sorts, complaining that they had made him play even though his fingers ached and the blood under his nails burned. Gradually we were able to converse and I would try to divert and calm him. If I was successful, I would let the conversation flag and sit down at my desk, and Beethoven, if he wished to stay and talk with me, would have no choice but to sit on the piano stool. Soon he would play a few random chords, often without even turning to the keyboard, and gradually the loveliest melodies would emerge. Oh, that I could have written them down! Sometimes, as if with no ulterior motive, I would leave music paper lying about on the table, in the hope that he would leave me in possession of a manuscript. But after covering the paper with notes, he would fold it up and stick it in his pocket! All I could do was laugh at my foolish schemes. But I would never say anything about his playing, or would barely mention it in passing. Then, his good spirits restored, he would leave me and I could be sure that he would return to me as a friend. But I could never cure him of his obstinacy, which was often the source of bitter quarrels with his closest friends and patrons.

If it were appropriate to add here some personal reminiscences dating from the period between 1818 and 1821, I could perhaps reflect in some detail on the inducements or conditions under which Beethoven would both play and expound at great length; for sometimes he would interrupt me as I played, drive me from the piano and take my place, crying, 'You frivolous, superficial dilettante!' or scornfully calling me, 'Herr Ignoramus-without-Education';[26] then he would play in part or in full, and explain as he played, the sonata movement that I had been 'maltreating' or 'thumping out' so painfully. But these memories gain significance in respect to Beethoven's piano playing only when they are joined to other more important events. It is enough to say here that Beethoven seldom performed without first losing his temper and sometimes quarrelling openly. Only one of his acquaintances, Count Franz von Brunsvik, who until 1815 was very close to Beethoven, assures us that his own experience was different. We shall frequently have occasion to mention this excellent gentleman's name again.

Wegeler does not refer to Beethoven's short visit to Vienna in the spring of 1787, nor have I been able to learn much about it. But I may rely on the testimony of the young composer's friends who affirm that

* Carl Czerny's pupils complain of similar treatment.

he then met two men who deeply and indelibly impressed themselves on the sixteen-year-old boy's mind: the Emperor Joseph and Mozart. The latter's prophetic words about the young musician's future, pronounced after Beethoven had improvised a fugue on a theme that Mozart had given him, 'This young man will make a name for himself in the world,' have been repeated in substance again and again, but we do not know exactly when and where the 'Monarch of Music' said them. Some claim it was when the Emperor, on the recommendation of the Elector Max Franz, summoned Beethoven to his apartments and listened to him in the presence of Mozart.[27] No one seems to know whether Beethoven met Gluck personally, but it is not very likely, since the older man was seeing very few people at that time and died on 15 November that year. This, like so many other important circumstances, is already too far in the past; eye and ear witnesses are no longer alive. Beethoven himself as a rule did not speak of his early youth, and when he did, he seemed uncertain and confused. And so there remains much from which we cannot remove the cloak of darkness and oblivion. These early events, however, constitute only the short, relatively unimportant prologue to the full drama of Beethoven's life. We need not, therefore, feel too concerned when they are uncertain or even entirely lost.

These few scattered incidents are all that we know of Beethoven's life in his native city. Germany was enjoying a long period of peace that lasted until the early 1790's; musicians were busy with their duties at the courts of princes and noblemen where they occupied a prominent and distinguished position; there were none of those advertisements in the newspapers or any of the other inventions that our glorious generation has found for transforming pupils into accomplished artists; Beethoven himself was concerned about money and at the same time was keenly aware of his need for further training and for the solitude that his budding genius required. These external and internal circumstances help to explain why the youth of the composer who was to give his name to an era of German art seems to offer so few artistically significant anecdotes and to be so devoid of miracles and romance, and why the young Beethoven seems to come off so poorly when compared with our great number of little prodigies who, at the same age, have astounded the world with their operas and symphonies.

Perhaps another reason for this paucity of artistic éclat may be found in the determination that the young pianist, organist, and composer exercised from his earliest years onwards, to be a human being in the fullest sense of the word and to live only by the most fundamental human principles, in utter contrast to the musical demigods of today. He saw in this striving the highest purpose of his life and was never dissuaded from it. A letter to Wegeler written on 29 June 1801 contains the following passage: 'I want to tell you that the next time you see me, I shall be great; not greater as an artist but better, more fully rounded as a man, and if the general prosperity of our country is somewhat improved, then shall the sole purpose of my art be the benefit of the poor. O happy moment! How fortunate I consider myself that I can bring this to pass!'

Until now we have been primarily concerned with Beethoven as a musician. Now it is time to look at another aspect of the man, one which is indispensable to artistic aspiration if art is to be genius rather than routine exercise. I am speaking of culture in a general sense, but particularly of a certain degree of familiarity with classical literature that provides nourishment for the imagination. Beethoven was first introduced to German literature by the Breuning family in Bonn. They encouraged his taste for reading and poetry and saw to his cultural enrichment in various fields. We shall see again and again what rare fruits this initiative was to bear. The same letter of 29 June 1801 shows how early Beethoven turned to ancient literature for satisfaction and peace of mind, for in this letter he tells his friend for the first time of the disquieting trouble he was having over his hearing but softens the despair of his communication with the words, 'Plutarch has taught me resignation.' Plutarch was, in fact, one of the classical writers who accompanied Beethoven through his whole life. From him Beethoven learned the history of Greece, its political institutions, and much more.

It would be fitting to devote a few last words to the Breuning family before we leave Bonn and move with our young hero to the Austrian capital. Until his death, Beethoven showed the warmest gratitude to the members of this family: 'For indebtedness is kindness' recompense.'* Even many years later, Beethoven referred to the Breunings as his guardian angels, and liked to recall the many reprimands he received from the lady of the household. 'She knew how to keep the insects away from the blossoms,' he would say. By 'insects' he meant certain friends who had begun to have a dangerous effect on the natural evolution of his talent and to distort the perspective of his consciousness as an artist by awakening his vanity with their fawning flattery. He almost believed that he was already a great artist, and would sooner listen to those who confirmed this folly than attend to those other friends who wished to show him that he still had to learn everything that distinguishes the master from the apprentice. A letter from Count Waldstein, who perhaps belonged to the former group, shows what hopes he attached to the eminent talents of his protégé:

* *Denn Pflicht ist des Guten Vergeltung.* Quoted by Beethoven from page 459 of Voss's translation of the *Odyssey*.

Dear Beethoven:

At last you are going to Vienna to fulfil a long-delayed dream. Mozart's spirit is still mourning, grieving the death of its young ward. It has found refuge with the inexhaustible Haydn, but it is as yet idle, waiting for a new embodiment and new occupation. Through unremitting hard work you shall receive the spirit of Mozart from Haydn's hands.

Your sincere friend,

Waldstein[28]

This somewhat mystical letter, so confident in the glorious future of the young musician, is particularly valuable to us, for it tells us of the end of his novitiate in Bonn and the date of his departure from that friendly town on the Rhine for the musical world in Vienna, where we shall rejoin him.

[II]

Beethoven's prime motive in travelling to Vienna was to further his musical studies under the direction of Joseph Haydn. To this end the Elector Max Franz continued to pay Beethoven his full salary as Chapel organist, which, though a modest sum, furnished him an assured allowance to meet his basic living expenses.[29] Beethoven's journey to the capital must have followed his reception of the above-quoted letter from Count Waldstein—probably in November 1792—just at the critical period when, as a result of the outbreak of the French Revolution, all southern Germany was mobilizing for war. Troop movements so impeded Beethoven's journey that before he had got half-way his travelling funds were exhausted. He had, however, struck up a friendship with a fellow-traveller who was able to help him out of his difficulties. Besides the assurance of a steady income, the Elector had given Beethoven letters of introduction to various prominent persons in Vienna. And as soon as Beethoven, then almost twenty-two years of age, had seen something of that cultural capital of Europe and had made a few acquaintances there, he resolved to remain for ever, even if it should mean losing the patronage of his benefactors in Bonn.

One of his first and most influential friends was the distinguished Baron Gottfried van Swieten, director of the Imperial library. A biographical sketch of this outstanding man, who died in 1803, reads:

He was a close friend of both Haydn and Mozart, and musical circles in Vienna owe him a great debt of gratitude for his many services, including the formation of a musical society made up of the high nobility for the purpose of performing the words of Bach and Handel. [More of this later.] For Haydn he adapted the text of *The Creation* from the English and wrote the libretto for *The Seasons*. [Correction: He translated the English poem by Thomson.] It was at his request that Mozart enriched and modernized the orchestration of four Handel oratorios (*Messiah, Acis and Galatea, Alexander's Feast,* and *Ode for St. Cecilia's Day*).

Van Swieten himself wrote in AmZ I (1799) 252: 'I belong, as far as music is concerned, to a generation that considered it necessary to study an art form thoroughly and systematically before attempting to practise it. I find in such a conviction food for the spirit and for the heart, and I return to it for strength every time I am oppressed by new evidence of decadence in the arts. My principal comforters at such times are Handel and the Bachs and those few great men of our own day who, taking these as their masters, follow resolutely in the same quest for greatness and truth.'

This patron of the arts, who became the self-appointed cicerone of the newcomer, soon made of Beethoven a frequent companion and house-guest. The evening gatherings at Swieten's home had a marked effect on Beethoven, for it was here that he first became acquainted with the music of Handel and Bach. He generally had to stay long after the other guests had departed, for his elderly host was musically insatiable and would not let the young pianist go until he had 'blessed the evening' with several Bach fugues. We still have a note written in the hand of this whimsical gentleman to Beethoven: 'Herr Beethoven, Alstergasse 24, care of Prince Lichnowsky. If you have no other engagement, I should like to have you at my house next Wednesday with your nightcap in your bag. Please reply immediately, Swieten.'

Among the many associations that Beethoven had with members of the high nobility, the most important was with the Lichnowsky family. This very fortunate circumstance in his life was so significant and had such rich consequences that we must ourselves make their acquaintance. All members of this noteworthy family had the rare gift of being totally receptive to all that is beautiful and great. Theirs was nobility in its purest sense, a dedication to the concept of *noblesse oblige*. They held art and science in equally high esteem, in contrast to those of their peers whose sole interest was the perpetuation of chivalry at a time when this mode of life was fading away. Prince Karl Lichnowsky was a pupil of Mozart, and in piano technique far surpassed most of the noted music-lovers of his generation. His brother, Count Moritz, who had also studied with Mozart, was even more talented. He was to become Beethoven's constant and life-long associate, and as such we shall speak of him often. Princess Christiane, *née* Countess von Thun, was endowed with the same spirit and had received the same musical education.

Beethoven found a haven in this house of humanitarian ideals and practices, and lived there for several years without ever assuming the usual aristocratic prejudices. The prince was a fatherly friend to the young man, and the princess was like a second mother. When Elector Max Franz was driven from Bonn by the French occupation of the left bank of the Rhine and could no longer pay Beethoven his stipend as organist, Prince Lichnowsky undertook to support Beethoven, as we learn from the letter of 1801 to Wegeler that has already been mentioned: 'You ask about my financial situation. Actually it is not too bad. For the past two years Lichnowsky, who, though this may surprise you, has been my dearest friend (we have had our little differences, but haven't they really strengthened our friendship?), has set aside the sum of six hundred florins upon which I may draw until I can find a suitable post.' The great love that this princely family felt for Beethoven was constant and unwavering, even when, according to Count Moritz, their often ill-tempered and apparently ungrateful protégé warranted their severe reprimands, though on Beethoven's account their 'little differences' served merely to strengthen the friendship.

It was mainly the Princess who pardoned as original and lovable the moody and, by conventional standards, unmannerly behaviour of the young artist and defended him against the somewhat less charitably inclined prince. Some years later Beethoven wrote of his protectress: 'They treated me like a grandson. The Princess's affection became at times so over-solicitous that she would practically put me under glass so that no one unworthy could touch me or breathe upon me.' Count Moritz left authoritative accounts of many incidents involving Beethoven and his place within this aristocratic circle. According to the Count's memoirs, the composer's brother, Karl, was even then largely responsible for Beethoven's fits of bad temper and unworthy behaviour.

The inevitable results of such careful handling were not lost upon an explosive young man like Beethoven, who was outspoken in his unorthodox opinions, but who could not help at the same time being impressed by the whispering of strangers. Moreover, his talent had already won wide recognition, making his anti-social stand a difficult one to maintain, so that he would often be the victim of conflicting impulses to which, for all his bravado, he was acutely sensitive. Even Swieten's discreet advice often went unheeded and, although he had been the one to introduce Beethoven into the high circles of society, he had no recourse but to feel gratified when his headstrong and independent young protégé consented to be present at his musical soirées. To remain aloof from the conventions and formalities of salon society seemed almost an obsession with Beethoven and, though he frequented and was accepted by the musical élite, he refused to affect their mannerisms.

In order to throw some light on the reasons for this apparent boorishness, let us turn from the salons of princes to another, equally important, side of Beethoven's life in Vienna, his situation with respect to the musicians of the city. It could hardly be expected that an artist who had made his way upward as rapidly as our Beethoven could remain free from the attacks of his colleagues, even though he moved almost exclusively among the high aristocracy and was to an amazing extent tolerated there. In fact, it was the very brilliance of his genius even more than his social eccentricities and uncouthness that caused a whole army of enemies to array themselves against him. Those who were jealous of his success refused to see his outward behaviour, his irritability, his tendency to be openly critical in the company of other artists, as natural corollaries of great genius. His low opinion of social graces and formalities, his absolute insistence that musicians master every technique of their art, even his Rhenish accent, all prompted his enemies to take their revenge by spreading gossip and slanderous rumours.[30]

We will explore this situation more fully when we come to the second period of Beethoven's life. Let us mention here, however, that by all accounts of Viennese musical life of this period, the musicians were with very few exceptions almost totally lacking not only in musical training but in the basic fundamentals of any education, and that they were, as a group, as thoroughly imbued with professional jealousy as the artisans' guilds of the day. They immediately became suspicious of any foreigner who let it be known that he intended to establish residence in the capital.* During its third year of publication, the *Allgemeine musikalische Zeitung* carried an article on musical life in Vienna. In column 67 we read: 'Should it ever occur to him [the foreign artist] to remain here, the entire *corpus musicum* would rise up in arms against him.' This situation did not improve until the 1830's, and even then the attitude of the artists themselves remained as before—owing probably to the social structure in general. For wherever class distinctions occur, the artist is most often looked upon as being on the same level as the servant. This was clearly the case with Beethoven, who certainly was not happy to be 'as abjectly dependent as a dying old valet'.

These attitudes explain the persecutions which, as we shall see, tormented Beethoven throughout his life. For his own part, he answered his enemies by scorning them and by assuming personal idiosyncrasies— a course of action which, for an artist, may have embarrassing complications, as indeed in Beethoven's case it did. As for the music critics, Beethoven demanded only that they should be moderate in their praise as well as in their censure, though he paid but little attention to them. We shall speak elsewhere of his lifelong indifference to his critics.

* The same was true of Munich, and has been until very recently.

Another characteristic that was equally important to his artistic life was his scorn of wealth and position. He regarded them as mere conventions, accidents of fate and not worthy of special consideration. He respected first of all the human qualities of a man; a prince's title or a banker's position were only secondary attributes. To bow down before Mammon and its guardians was, to Beethoven, foolishness, the deepest possible degradation of a man's spirit. When he did show respect for a highly placed or a wealthy individual, it was because of that person's humanitarian benevolence. Recent critics have attributed Beethoven's social indifference to mere pride, but they have missed the mark. It is, on the contrary, the very manifestation of a genius sure of itself and of its mission. As such, it is consistent with the whole being of the man.

An enumeration of Beethoven's ethical principles should include mention of his political views, but we shall have a better opportunity to examine them later on. Let us for the time being concentrate on purely musical matters.

Apparently when Beethoven began his studies with Haydn, his knowledge of musical science was confined to thoroughbass. If he was able to improvise fugues or fugal passages on the piano at the age of sixteen—and we can infer from Mozart's remarks quoted earlier that he was—this ability had been acquired through frequent playing of contrapuntal piano music added to a precocious talent for improvisation. Moreover, we know that Haydn had given up the systematic teaching of harmony long before 1792 because of his duties as Kapellmeister for Prince Esterházy in Eisenstadt, his continuous preoccupation with composition, and his advancing age. There was probably also a scarcity at that time of truly serious students.

Given these circumstances, it is not difficult to see why any true co-operation between teacher and pupil was doomed even before they met. The pupil was wrong for the teacher; first, because Beethoven was in thought and behaviour already too strictly dominated by his previous experience; secondly, because it was several years too late for him to start a formal course of advanced musical instruction; and finally, because of his apparent wilfulness and his unorthodox views. And the teacher was wrong for the pupil: theory and practice must be integral and inseparable components of mastery itself, and Haydn was out of practice as a teacher. Just as the most gifted mathematician cannot, without years of experience as a teacher, introduce the most able student to the principles of mathematics, so the most learned scholar of counterpoint who has no training as a teacher cannot hope to share with his pupil the secrets of his art. Add to all this an insufficiency of time for regular and systematic teaching, and we will see that the great and learned composer, though well-intentioned and able to give good advice in specific cases, was not a teacher in the strict sense of one who, with patience and devotion, leads his pupil step by step from the elementary to the advanced. Yet Beethoven was Haydn's pupil—we know that this had been arranged by Beethoven's patrons in Bonn—and we can infer that a certain musical superstition that besets us today was even then given credence (though there were no demigods then, and outstanding artists were not yet the object of idol worship). This superstition to which all amateur and many professional musicians adhered was the belief that a renowned composer possesses all knowledge and wisdom, and that there is no artistic period, let alone a particular writer, with whom he is not thoroughly and completely imbued; therefore it follows that he must be an excellent teacher.

But to get back to Haydn and Beethoven. One of Beethoven's most favoured and respected musical contemporaries was Johann Schenk, the composer of the comic opera, *Der Dorfbarbier* (*The Village Barber*), which has enjoyed a great success and has been translated into almost all the European languages. Schenk was a gentle, good-natured man and a competent teacher. One day Schenk met Beethoven as he was coming, with a notebook under his arm, from a lesson with Haydn. Schenk looked at the notebook and noticed a number of mistakes. When he pointed them out, Beethoven answered that Haydn had just corrected that exercise. Schenk turned back through the book and found many more uncorrected violations of the rules of counterpoint. Beethoven immediately became suspicious that Haydn was not being honest with him.[31] He decided then and there to break with his teacher, though he was persuaded to wait until Haydn's approaching second journey to England (January 1794) should afford a convenient excuse. From that day on, however, it was Schenk who corrected Beethoven's exercises and who was in fact his teacher, though Beethoven continued to take his notebooks to Haydn. One can only imagine with what reluctance he went, and it is not surprising that their relationship deteriorated from that moment.

It was Schenk himself who told me of these events. But such a strange, almost incredible circumstance needs corroboration. Ignaz von Seyfried relates the same incident in his biographical essay on Johann Schenk in Schilling's *Lexikon der Tonkunst*:

In 1792 Beethoven came to Vienna, and Schenk heard him for the first time improvising at Abbé Gelinek's. To hear him was a great privilege, reminding one strongly of Mozart. Beethoven, who was eager to learn, would often complain to Gelinek that his studies in counterpoint with Haydn were not progressing, for the teacher seemed too distracted by his many undertakings to give the necessary attention to Beethoven's exercises. Gelinek brought the matter to Schenk's attention and asked him whether he cared to undertake the guidance of Beethoven's studies. Schenk declared that he would be delighted, but with two stipulations: that he would not accept any remuneration and that the whole affair was to be kept a close secret. Beethoven agreed to the conditions and the promise was conscientiously kept. At the beginning of August 1792* the lessons in theory began and continued without interruption until May of the following year. In order to avoid all suspicion of a second master's hand, Beethoven recopied each corrected exercise before presenting it for Haydn's approval. This little-known relationship is documented by a note in Beethoven's hand. One day in early June when Schenk arrived for the usual appointment with his pupil he found the fledgling flown to Hungary to visit Prince Esterházy, leaving this diplomatically penned note: 'Dear Schenk: I did not plan to leave so early for Eisenstadt. I wish I could have spoken to you first. In the meantime, you may be assured of my gratitude for your many kindnesses to me. I shall endeavour with all my strength to express my appreciation to you. I hope to see you and enjoy your companionship again soon. Farewell, and do not altogether forget

Your

Beethoven'

Apparently Ferdinand Ries had no knowledge of the relationship between the two men, or he would certainly have included it in his biographical notes on Beethoven. Could it be that by the time of Ries's connection with Beethoven, from 1800 till 1805, Beethoven had already completely forgotten this strange circumstance? This would be consistent with his easy dismissal of all that lay in the past.

Ries confines his account to a rather moving passage on page 86: 'Haydn had wished Beethoven to put on the title-page of his first published works the words, "Pupil of Haydn". Beethoven refused for, he said, although he had taken a few lessons from Haydn, he had never learned anything from him.' Is not this too strong? Can we not assume that Beethoven received much valuable advice from Haydn, even though the systematic instruction was negligible? Ries continues:

Beethoven also studied counterpoint with Albrechtsberger and dramatic music with Salieri. I was well acquainted with all three teachers. All esteemed Beethoven highly but were of one opinion concerning his studies: all agreed that Beethoven was so headstrong and stubborn that it had required hard experience to teach him all that he had rejected in his formal lessons. Albrechtsberger and Salieri were particularly given to this view of the matter. The truth is that Beethoven could not respond to the pedantic rules that Albrechtsberger applied to counterpoint or to Salieri's equally strict approach to dramatic composition in the Italian style of that day.

We have quoted Seyfried's remarks concerning Beethoven's 'eager-

---

* Unquestionably the date should be 1793, since we know that Beethoven arrived in Vienna only late in the autumn of 1792, and it must have taken him a certain length of time to realize that he was not progressing under Haydn's instruction.

ness to learn', a description for which he must have been indebted to
Schenk. Who can doubt the truth of the statement? We must consider
that the composer's years of study were pursued under a grave handi-
cap, for no greater misfortune can befall a young, talented, and earnest
artist than to be passed from one teacher to another, each with differing
artistic principles and methods (as is generally the case), particularly
when the student has developed criteria of his own that cause him to
question his teachers' theories and methods. Such was the lamentable
situation in which Beethoven found himself. In Bonn his budding talents
had been more or less methodically nurtured first by his father, then
Pfeiffer, van den Eeden, and Neefe, then (in Vienna) by Haydn and
Schenk simultaneously, and Albrechtsberger. He had thus been submitted to the often conflicting methods of no fewer than six teachers, not
counting his father.[32] Too many cooks spoil the broth, as they say.
Beethoven was undoubtedly critical of his own training, for I heard him
say years later that Mozart's genius had been fully realized largely
because of the uniform instruction he had received from his father.

I should like to close my account of Beethoven's thankless student
years by relating an incident involving him and his former teacher in
secret, Schenk. Because of his frequent moves between the city and the
country, and because of his withdrawn nature, Beethoven would often
go for years without seeing his closest friends, even those who lived
within the confines of Vienna. If they did not take it upon themselves to
contact him and tell him of what went on in their lives, or if he had not
met them occasionally by chance, he would have forgotten them entirely. One day in the spring of 1824 when Beethoven and I were walking across the Graben, we encountered Schenk. Beethoven was overjoyed to see once more the old friend of whom he had heard nothing for
several years. He clasped Schenk's hand and drew him into a nearby
tavern, the Jägerhorn. He led him to a back room which had to be
lighted even in broad daylight, and, to avoid being disturbed, closed the
doors; then he began to pour out his heart. After he had bewailed his
misfortunes for a time, he remembered the events of the years 1793–4
and burst out laughing to think how they had fooled Haydn, who never
once had guessed what was going on. It was from this conversation
that I first learned of the strange relationship between Beethoven and
Schenk. Beethoven, then at the very peak of his genius, profusely
thanked Schenk, who only had a meagre income from his compositions,
Der Dorfbarbier, an opera *Achmet und Almanzine*, and various operettas,
for being such a good teacher and devoted friend. Their leave-taking at
the end of this memorable hour was moving, as if they were saying farewell forever, and indeed Beethoven and Schenk never did see one another again after that day.

FIRST PERIOD

We come now to a chapter of Beethoven's life that must be treated with discretion: the matter of his various love affairs. Who would have guessed twenty years ago that one day the world would find this aspect of the composer's life fully as engrossing as his musical works? Yet this is the case. I considered that I had dealt sufficiently with the problem in the previous editions of this book, in which I confined myself to a brief, well-documented account, for with the exception of one affair which deeply affected Beethoven's life and work, I felt that the composer's love-life was worthy of no greater emphasis than other equally interesting chapters of his life.

The literary world disagreed. What I had written was too short and too prosaic for them, and so they distorted the facts, turning the sober musician into a romantic hero crazed with love. For to them any composer whose work is often so wildly passionate—it is on Beethoven's music that these writers based their findings—must be himself a prodigious and passionate lover, certainly no ordinary man with normal emotions! The lamentable fact is that our novelists and writers of magazine stories and articles have found it profitable to choose some well-known figure to write about. They depict his personal idiosyncrasies as signs of madness, arising from unnatural excesses; they clothe him with totally false attributes; they put into his mouth words and critical judgements that are at complete variance with his true feelings and ideas. Beethoven did not escape this sort of commercial treatment. His passions and affairs have been elaborated upon and shamelessly exploited by both French and German writers. I am sorry, but I still cannot devote a great deal of space to Beethoven's loves, for my opinion remains unchanged. We must, however, make note of certain events.

Ignaz von Seyfried, who edited the book, *Beethovens Studien*, published by Tobias Haslinger in 1832 (see page 464 of the present volume for an historical appraisal of this work), says in the biographical appendix, page 13: 'Beethoven never married and, strangely enough, never had a love affair.' Ries seems to have known more about it. On page 117 of his *Notizen* we find: 'Beethoven was very fond of women, especially young, pretty ones. . . . He was often in love, though generally for only a short time.' Wegeler answers, appealing to Stephan von Breuning and Bernhard Romberg for verification. On page 42 of the *Notizen* we read this sentence: 'Beethoven was never out of love; indeed, he was generally very deeply involved with one woman or another.' He then mentions, as Beethoven's first love, a Fräulein d'Honrath of Cologne who often visited the Breuning family in Bonn for several weeks at a time. 'There followed a deep infatuation for a certain very pretty and charming Fräulein von W. Bernhard Romberg told me three years ago of this attachment, whose intensity reminds one of Goethe's *Werther.*' Fräulein von W. was a childhood friend of Beethoven's pupil Baroness von Bevervörde who, in 1834, shared with Bernhard Romberg and me in Munich her reminiscences of their love.[33] Wegeler's authoritative biography sums up the situation thus: 'These affairs were passions of adolescence, and their impression was neither deep nor long-lasting. In Vienna, at least as long as I was there,* Beethoven was perpetually engrossed in a love affair, and among his conquests were some that most lovers would have found extremely difficult if not impossible.'

Let us hear what Beethoven himself had to say in a letter to his friend in Coblenz written on 16 November 1801 when he was almost thirty-one years old:

My life is somewhat happier, now that I have become more sociable. You can hardly imagine how lonely, how wretched I have been for the past two years. My deafness haunted me and made me avoid the company of people so that they must have thought me (Oh so wrongly!) a misanthrope. This change in my life has been brought about by a lovely, enchanting girl who loves me and whom I love. After two years I again know moments of bliss, and for the first time I feel that marriage might bring me happiness. Unfortunately she is not of my class, and anyway I really could not marry now. I have to keep moving about.

Further on in the same letter we read: 'I feel that I could never tolerate a quiet life.' Does this mean that he had decided, already at this early age, never to marry? In examining the next period of his life, we shall find authentic reports covering this delicate subject. It is enough to say here that this 'enchanting girl' who brought 'this change' and 'moments of bliss' into the life of the despairing composer was the same one who very soon afterwards caused him great suffering.

Let us return from this brief look at the joys and pains of love to the realm of music and to those things that affected Beethoven's life and work. When Beethoven arrived in Vienna, he was introduced into two separate musical circles. In the home of Baron van Swieten he found a group of oratorio devotees. Prince Karl Lichnowsky, on the other hand, entertained a smaller and more select circle of musicians and music-lovers dedicated to the art of chamber music. The newcomer from Bonn immediately found a place in this latter society. Among the most influential musicians there, four were particularly notable: the violinist Ignaz Schuppanzigh, the viola-player Franz Weiss, and the two 'cellists Anton Kraft and his son Nikolaus. As we shall see, the first three of these artists had a marked influence on Beethoven's development and especially on a large proportion of his music. It was in this

---

* Dr. Wegeler was in Vienna as a medical student from 1794 to 1796.

company of performing artists that Beethoven learned what he needed to know about the playing of stringed instruments.[34] We should also mention the names of Joseph Friedlowsky, who taught Beethoven the mechanics of the clarinet, the famous horn-player Johann Wenzel Stich (he gave himself the Italian name of Giovanni Punto) to whom Beethoven was indebted for his knowledge of writing for the horn which he demonstrated so brilliantly in his horn sonata opus 17; and Beethoven had Carl Scholl to thank for instruction in the mechanism of the flute, which underwent such great changes in design during the first decades of the nineteenth century.

The present generation of composers has learned from the former how to write idiomatically for all the instruments in the same way that the composers of the previous epoch—those whom music historians call the 'classical' composers—learned, namely by direct association with instrumentalists, or the so-called practical-empirical method. It is by this method that the 'art of orchestration', and the mechanics of art in general, have been taught during the last two hundred years and up to the present time. We may now ask ourselves which method is the surer road to true artistic skill—the old practical-empirical method or the method now in vogue which uses printed texts which the student must unthinkingly copy or imitate. Such a method will destroy altogether or, at the very least, dull the budding creativity of the student. If we, then, ask such a question, we should certainly choose the method our ancestors followed, since it is one applicable to all the arts, and especially since it makes the student think for himself, rather than oversimplifying the whole matter for him as the modern system does. That the older method was necessarily slower is another reason to prefer it, as the pupil was given time for the natural development of his intellectual faculties and could not skip over any of the necessary stages of learning. If we had held to the methods of our ancestors, by which so many musicians achieved the peak of artistic mastery, we would not have today all these musically crippled young composers of symphonies and operas.

To return from this not inappropriate parenthesis to the true matter of our study, I should like to point out how close to Beethoven's own age were many of the musicians named above, and further to indicate that these men, particularly those of the Lichnowsky circle, were largely responsible for bringing about the 'Beethoven era' in music by inspiring almost all the compositions of Beethoven's so-called first period. The reader can imagine what stimulus Beethoven derived from this group and how valuable to him were their advice and criticism, some of it indirect and some directly pertaining to his own compositions—most of which were played for the first time in Lichnowsky's salon. He himself spoke of the progress he made in this atmosphere, specifically in the art of the string quartet, though he derived an intimate and practical knowledge of all instrumental playing from his acquaintance with the musicians of this group and of another which he frequented at the same time and which we shall soon speak of. Without such instruction and the stimulus to try his hand at instrumental forms, he might not have attempted to write quartets, much less symphonies, until much later. For Mozart and Haydn were regarded as the masters of both forms, and any new efforts would have been rejected as those of a presumptuous upstart. This is the reason that Beethoven's earliest quartets enjoyed no success at first, even among the members of his own circle.

It is now time to meet another patron of the arts, one whose influence was not confined to artistic taste in the Austrian capital, but who bore much responsibility for the development of the whole musical trend in the era following Mozart and Haydn. Count Rasumovsky was for more than twenty years Russian ambassador to Vienna, and his name is worthy of its fame.

Count Rasumovsky, himself an accomplished musician and perhaps the person most dedicated to the carrying on of the Haydn tradition in instrumental music, would alternate with Prince Lichnowsky in gathering the aforesaid musicians at his palace to play quartets, in which he himself would take the second violin part. After a while, however, he decided on a different course, one destined to give his circle a preeminent role in the history of music. He engaged a permanent quartet with a lifetime contract, the first and only example of its kind in Austria. He had his imitators, wealthy patrons who hired musicians as permanent members of their households, but no one else followed the Russian Maecenas in providing them with pensions to support them to the end of their days.

Count Rasumovsky's quartet consisted of Schuppanzigh (first violinist), Sina[35] (second violin), Weiss (viola), and Linke (cello). Known as 'The Rasumovsky Quartet', they gained European distinction as well as a place in the history of music. This was in spite of the fact that they never made a single concert tour, which is unfortunate on several counts, for they would have established standards of authenticity in the conception and performance of classical works, standards that are sorely lacking in our time.

We have just called Count Rasumovsky the person most dedicated to the carrying on of the Haydn tradition of the quartet. How is this to be explained? Quite simply: Haydn had discovered in Rasumovsky a fine sensitivity to those particular qualities in his quartets and symphonies that, because they could not be grasped superficially nor conveyed through the usual musical symbols, had escaped other artists. And he undertook to acquaint the Count with his hidden intentions so that Rasumovsky in turn might explain them to the musicians. This circumstance is of the greatest importance in regard to the Rasumovsky Quartet in general, and particularly when we consider Beethoven's string quartets, for the very youth of Rasumovsky's group indicates that their talents were still in a formative stage and that they had to look to older artists for a sense of style and taste.

Count Rasumovsky, one of the first to determine the course of the new direction in music, became, from the moment he engaged a permanent quartet, more closely bound to Beethoven's destiny than any other of the composer's patrons. Indeed, Rasumovsky's quartet became Beethoven's quartet; the musicians were put entirely at his disposal just as if they had been hired expressly for his use. Seyfried tells us just how Beethoven took advantage of this opportunity to further his own artistic mastery as well as to bring out the deeper design in his works. In the biographical sketch of Schuppanzigh that appeared in the *Lexikon der Tonkunst*, he says:

It is well known that Beethoven was as much at home in the Rasumovsky establishment as a hen in her coop. Everything he wrote was taken warm from the nest and tried out in the frying pan. Every note was played precisely as he wanted it played, with such devotion, such love, such obedience, such piety as could be inspired only by a passionate admiration of his great genius. And it was precisely the delving into the most secret depths of the music, the total comprehension of the spirit of the work, that enabled this quartet to gain, through the playing of Beethoven's music, its universal fame. One voice alone, Beethoven's, spoke through the music and through its interpretation.*

Seyfried had the great good fortune of being present at those extraordinary performances, and his words have significance as a scholar's admonition to our generation, not only in connection with Beethoven's music, but in regard to the whole musical period of which he was a part. His warning will, however, fall on deaf ears, for already the traces of that tradition were disappearing; indeed, the whole inner spirit and being of classical music is vanishing while the present generation claims that the only necessary criterion is a mechanical correctness in reproducing the notes.[36]

Let us now take a look at Beethoven's economic situation, a controversial topic that has already received wide attention and one to which we shall need to refer again several times.

---

* In AmZ VII (1806) 534, there appears the following characterization of Schuppanzigh's performance: 'When playing a quartet, Schuppanzigh can penetrate the very spirit of the composition. He knows how to bring out all the fire and strength, and also the refinement, tenderness, humour, love and caprice so expressively that the first violin could hardly be entrusted to better hands.' From this early description we can anticipate the excellence that he and his associates were to attain in maturity.

We know from Beethoven himself that Prince Lichnowsky had promised him a yearly allowance of six hundred gulden until he should find a suitable appointment. In the letter of 29 June 1801 to Wegeler in which Beethoven mentioned this arrangement, he also wrote: 'My compositions pay me very well and I can say that I receive more orders than I can fill. What's more, I have six or seven publishers[37] and could have more if I wanted them. No one bargains with me any more: I state my price and they pay it.' Another letter, this one written on 15 January 1801 to the music publisher Hoffmeister in Leipzig,[38] gives us an idea of the prices Beethoven could command for his compositions at that time. He asked twenty ducats for his septet, opus 20, twenty ducats for his first symphony, ten ducats for his second piano concerto, and twenty ducats for the Great Sonata, opus 22: certainly very considerable sums for those days.

Wegeler writes of the ineptness that Beethoven displayed at that time in his financial affairs. We quote him here because his words serve as a key to the composer's subsequent economic ups and downs and explain many of the apparent paradoxes of word and deed that kept recurring throughout his life. On page 33 Wegeler says:

Beethoven, who was brought up under the most necessitous of circumstances, and who was always financially dependent on some patron or other (sometimes on his friends), had no idea of the value of money and was anything but thrifty. To give an example, the dinner hour at the Prince's (Lichnowsky) was four o'clock. 'Am I supposed', said Beethoven, 'to come home every day at half-past three, change my clothes, shave and all that? I'll have none of it!' And so he would very often eat at a tavern, for in this as in all affairs he had absolutely no appreciation of the value of money or things.

The desire for freedom and independence, on the other hand, was so strong in Beethoven that his lack of financial acumen seems difficult to understand.* Such clearly contradictory traits, constantly at war with one another, must have been the source of many of the fits of moodiness and ill-temper that haunted our master. To this biographer, who for many years witnessed the struggle between the temperamental extremes in Beethoven's nature and who noted with pain its effects on the composer as well as on those who were associated with him, both extremes are like dangerous precipices which can neither be climbed nor circumvented. Only those who stand at a greater distance can hope to undertake the task of reconciling all the aspects of this monumental figure.

* And on the day that one becomes a slave,
  The Thunderer, Jove, takes half his worth away.

This is a passage from the *Odyssey* (Book XVII, lines 392–93) of which Beethoven was particularly fond.

We have already alluded to the symptoms that even then caused our master to fear greatly for his sense of hearing. Now we must learn more of this defect, a matter of tragic importance in the composer's life. Beethoven's much-quoted letter to Wegeler, written in 1801, is again useful in this context. After expressing his satisfaction with his financial situation, he continues:

But that jealous demon, my poor health, threatens to spoil things for me. For the past three years, my hearing has been growing constantly weaker as a result, they say, of my abdominal condition which, as you know, gave me trouble even then and has grown worse here. I have frequent attacks of diarrhoea which always leave me very weak.

Further on he tells what treatment he had received, but to no avail, from the physicians Frank and Vering. He continues:

I can truly say that I am leading a life of misery. For two years now I have ceased to attend any social functions, for I cannot bring myself to tell people, 'I am deaf'. If I had any other profession it would not matter so much, but for a musician, not to be able to hear is a terrible calamity. What would my enemies, whose number is considerable, say of my deafness! To give you some idea of this strange affliction, let me tell you that when I go to the theatre, I have to sit in the very front and lean forward to be able to understand the actors. I cannot hear the higher notes of instruments or singers if I am at any distance from them. As for conversation, it is surprising that there are some people who have not noticed my difficulty; as I have always been easily distracted, they probably think my mind is wandering. Often I can hardly make out what a person with a soft voice is saying: I hear the voice but cannot understand the words, and yet if a person shouts, it is unbearable. What is now to become of me, only Heaven knows. Vering says I will surely improve, though I may not be entirely cured. I have often cursed [my Creator and]* my own existence, but Plutarch has taught me resignation.

There was at that time in the metropolitan church of St. Stephan in Vienna a priest named Father Weiss who concerned himself with the healing of the deaf and who had effected many cures. No mere charlatan, he was familiar with the physiology of the ear, though his treatments employed only the simplest methods. He had gained a wide reputation with the general public, and had even earned the respect of the practising physicians. With the concurrence of his doctor, Beethoven sought help from this priest. The results were at first promising, as long, that is, as the patient was strict in his observance of the cleric's regimen, which consisted not only of dietary precautions but of injunctions to take more rest and to put as little strain on his hearing as possible. But Beethoven was unable to restrict his activities for any length of time, nor could he,

* Editor's note. The words in brackets were omitted by Schindler.

because of his social situation, give his ears the rest they needed. In short, the improvement that was at first apparent was only temporary, for the patient totally lacked the necessary persistence. In the third period, and at other times too, we shall need to refer again to this lamentable subject of Beethoven's deafness and also to the kindly Father Weiss who occupied a real place in the composer's life and whose help he sought again more than twenty years later. I wish to quote here another letter to Wegeler written on 16 November 1801 because it mentions an improvement in his malady and also because it shows how little Beethoven heeded the advice of his doctors:

I feel that my youth is only now beginning.* Wasn't I always a sickly fellow? But for some time now I have been growing stronger both physically and mentally. Every day brings me closer to that goal that I feel but that I cannot describe. Your Beethoven can live only in the accomplishment of that aim. So don't speak to me of rest! I know of none other than sleep and I resent it that I now need more than I used to. I am only half cured of my illness, but when I am again a whole man, I'll come to you and we'll renew our old friendship.

Towards the end of the first period Beethoven undertook a concert tour of northern Germany, where his name had already been much talked of. He visited Prague, Leipzig, and Berlin, and his piano playing —and especially his brilliant improvisations—caused great excitement.[39] This trip took place in 1796, probably in the autumn, as we shall later learn from Beethoven's own account. His stay in the Prussian capital gave him the opportunity of meeting King Friedrich Wilhelm II, himself a music-lover and performer, to whom Beethoven dedicated his two cello sonatas opus 5. This was Beethoven's first and only concert tour,[40] and it is interesting to note that he remembered almost nothing of his experiences or impressions on the trip, as he told Hofrat Rochlitz in 1822. His memory of events of the past was always extremely poor.

---

* It is in this same letter that the composer speaks of his 'lovely, enchanting girl' and his 'moments of bliss'.

APPENDICES TO THE FIRST PERIOD

APPENDIX 1

The Situation of Music in Vienna at the Close of the Eighteenth and the Beginning of the Nineteenth Centuries

In order to describe Beethoven's position in regard to the various factions that comprised the Austrian capital's musical society, we should attempt to draw as accurate a picture as possible of that society as it existed at the end of the first period of his life. This is an important task for the biographer, for the musical world influenced Beethoven the man even more than Beethoven the musician. Such a picture, even though a mere sketch, will also help the reader to understand the musical taste and spirit of the times.

We have already noted Swieten's great contribution to the state of music in Vienna, where he organized a musical society among the high nobility for the purpose of performing the works of Handel, Bach,* and Hasse. Readers may be interested to learn the names of those under whose patronage these concerts were given. A notice in issue No. 34 of the AmZ (1801) of the first performance of Haydn's *The Seasons*, conducted by the composer, names many of them: Princes Liechtenstein, Esterházy, Schwarzenberg, Auersperg, Lobkowitz, Lichnowsky, Trautmannsdorf, and Kinsky, and Counts Czernin, Erdödy, Fries, Apponyi, Zinzendorf, Harrach, and others. Several of these names appear on the title-pages of Beethoven's compositions of the first and second periods. These dedications, which bespeak the respect and familiarity that Beethoven enjoyed among the nobility of that day, were retained in all the subsequent editions of these works in order both to honour the music and to indicate the musical taste predominating at the time among the upper echelons of Viennese society.

The concept of nobility among the German nobles in Austria consisted of a perfect balancing of education and breeding, training in both thought and action, and attention to the development of will, character,

---

* Johann Sebastian Bach's music was practically never performed except for a few motets. The great master's larger works were unknown even in musical circles, and not only Vienna but all Germany was ignorant of their existence. The small body of his religious music that was available was looked upon as 'Lutheran music' and was thus automatically condemned.

and all the aspects of intelligence, all of which made this society worthy
to be called the standard-bearer of German culture and morality.* A
cultured and enlightened upper class that also possesses tremendous
wealth will certainly be in a position to serve both science and the arts.
This state of affairs prevailed among the Viennese nobility who had a
special penchant for music. There was a preference for music without
ostentation—music which, whether performed by four voices or a
hundred, would work its magic on the listener, cultivating his mind and
his senses, ennobling his emotions. It was characteristic of the whole
German people to respond to the unpretentious greatness, true feeling,
and pure human emotions that were inherent in its music. This people
also knew how to derive from the mystery of musical tones their inexpressible meaning and lofty spirit. And yet this was not a time of
philosophical sophistication; it was rather a period of uninhibited enjoyment whose purity lasted well into the first decade of our century.
'Anyone who was not a part of the music in Vienna in those days cannot
know what it is to truly hear and truly enjoy music'—thus the older
musicians later expressed their nostalgia for that time. Fortunately,
there were not yet hundreds of periodicals filled with art criticism!

As for the music-lovers of that time, we know that they were found
almost exclusively among the educated classes, who by inclination and
breeding assigned to music its place among the disciplines. No amateur,
therefore, presumed to usurp the role properly taken by the professional
musician. A quotation from the third year of the AmZ suffices to illustrate the honour accorded by the amateur to the truly deserving and
gifted artist: 'The Viennese art lovers value talent too much to expect
the artist to court their favour; they would respect him far less if he
were to do so.'

A picture of Vienna at the turn of the century would be incomplete
without mention of the orchestral concerts that took place regularly at
the Emperor's court. Emperor Franz almost always played in the first
violin section, and when an opera was performed the Empress Theresia,
a Neapolitan princess, would sing the arias and take part in the ensemble
numbers. She was an accomplished artist.† These court concerts, most
of which took place in the summer before an audience of nobles at

---

* In the third period we shall again have occasion to refer to the Austrian nobility, but we
shall find them much changed.

† A few years later when with the death of the Empress (1807) these concerts were given
up, Emperor Franz organized his own string quartet which is known to have accompanied
him on all his longer journeys, even to Paris in 1815 and to the Congress of Aachen in 1818—
always under the direction of the court composer, Franz Krommer. The Emperor played the
first violin; his adjutant general, Field-Marshal Lieutenant Baron von Kutchera, played
second violin; the Emperor's first valet played the viola; and the chamberlain, Count Rudolph
von Wrbna, played the cello. After the death of the last of these in the early 1820's, his place
was filled by Herr Gottlieb, a member of the Emperor's court orchestra.

Laxenburg, were sometimes conducted by Salieri but more often by Weigl, a disciple of Mozart who had studied with the composer himself. The writer has heard both conductors speak nostalgically of the golden age of Viennese music, for Fate had allowed them to witness the full glory of that time.

Such a combination of circumstances could have none but the most beneficial influence on the development of Beethoven's talent. An age that earned for art and artists in general the name of Golden may also be called Beethoven's own Golden Age. He would have been happy to continue in this way, associated with all that was good and noble, his creative genius encouraged and helped, had not an evil demon stolen into the faculty most essential to his work, embittering his disposition and threatening his whole artistic capacity—and all this largely due to his own negligence! He seems to have realized and admitted that he was to blame for his defect. In his copy of the *Odyssey* the following passage is underlined:

> *No being whom earth nourishes to breathe*
> *Her air and move upon her face is more*
> *The sport of circumstance than Man. For while*
> *The gods give health, and he is strong of limb,*
> *He thinks no evil in the coming days*
> *Will overtake him. When the blessed gods*
> *Visit him with afflictions, these he bears*
> *Impatiently and with a fretful mind.*
>
> .   .   .   .
>
> *Let no man, therefore, dare to be*
> *Unjust in aught, but tranquilly enjoy*
> *Whatever good the gods vouchsafe to give.*
> (Book XVIII, lines 166–73, 181–83)

APPENDIX 2

Introduction to the Catalogue of Works

A few preliminary remarks will help to introduce a listing of the works that belong to the last five years of Beethoven's first period, the time in which his artistic genius began to flower.

A. Beethoven's compositions may be divided into two categories, one designated by opus numbers, the other by a separate series of numbers.[41] The opus numbers were assigned by Beethoven himself and may be considered reasonably authentic up to a certain point, as long, that is, as he maintained his practice of writing a number in his own hand on each manuscript. This category consists mainly of the largest and most important works in each medium. The compositions designated by numbers other than opus numbers were catalogued according to an agreement among the various publishers, at first with the composer's permission, and include such short works as variations, dances, and songs, many of which were not published until after Beethoven's death.[42]

It is only for the last five years of this first period that the cataloguing of Beethoven's works conforms to the chronological order of their publication. The author will be obliged to report a disorder in the listing of subsequent compositions to a degree that probably has never been equalled in the cataloguing of any other composer's works. Beethoven himself was only partly to blame; more guilty are the publishers and also certain persons who were for many years under Beethoven's supervision and whose acquaintance the reader will make in the next chapter.

The publishers' responsibility for the unfortunate disorder resulted largely from their failure to agree among themselves, generally because of mutual distrust and envy. Another source of confusion was the unauthorized, largely arbitrary assignment of opus numbers to a great many arranged works. The originals of these arrangements could have been logically organized if only the arranged versions had been listed in a separate category.

B. The works of the master were not always published in the order of their composition. Some were withheld to await further revision; some lay hidden for years in the publisher's desk for commercial, or rather speculative, reasons. The catalogue that appears in the Appendices to the Third Period contains several such works withheld by the publishers. As for the chronological order of the works, even opus 1 is misleading. The C minor trio that stands third in the collection was actually the first to be completed. It may have been placed after the trios in E flat major and G major to create an effect of increasing tension from one to the next, or perhaps the composer felt that when presenting three works of a kind in one publication he should place the weakest one in the middle. This seems to have been the case with the three sonatas opus 2 and the three sonatas opus 10 that belong to this period. In later compositions the practice was no longer followed.

It has often been claimed by the school of theoretical critics of Beethoven's music now flourishing in Russia and France that certain of the works that appear with others under one opus number differ so widely in style or content from their companion pieces that they must date back to an earlier time. These critics must be vigorously contradicted. If the works in question were written a single year earlier or later, it is of no importance, and there was never an interval of several years. We can be quite sure that none of the works catalogued below were written before 1794. Some of these over-subtle theoretical critics claim, in their zeal to trace a regular progression, or retrogression, in Beethoven's works, that his shorter pieces, bagatelles, small piano pieces, some of the songs, etc., were written during the master's boyhood. They suppose that after *Fidelio* and after the C minor and *Pastoral* symphonies, the composer would no longer be able to write minor pieces like these.

I would remind these impoverished art-gossips who attempt most painstakingly to calculate the growth of Beethoven's genius almost by mathematical formulas, basing their theories only upon opus numbers, that with my own eyes I saw Beethoven write more than a few of these little pieces during the time that I lived with him, and even have in my possession copies of some of them with his own corrections. Is Mont Blanc not surrounded by smaller peaks and even by little hills?

The reader will remember that at thirty years of age Beethoven is known to have exclaimed, 'Don't speak to me of rest!' Twenty years later, however, he realized his need of rest, though it was a kind of active rest, or restful activity, that he sought. In such moments he would produce little pieces, some of them intended as gifts for patrons and friends. Why cannot the art critics, those self-styled philosophers who grub about trying to dig out the earth's very core, see that from time to time Beethoven would consciously revert to a youthful mood, then with renewed spirit and vigour leap forward still further? In the course of the third period we shall hear his designation for these little pieces.

C. One may ask when the various works first appeared. The exact date cannot be ascertained in every case. A difference of a year either way is of no importance, and it is not always possible to say whether a work was submitted to the public at the end of one year or the beginning of the next. As for establishing a chronological order of at least the major works, the present author worked closely with the publishers Artaria and Diabelli while Beethoven was still alive. In this connection I delivered in the year 1819 a letter from Artaria to Beethoven containing many questions. This letter will be quoted in the Appendices to the Second Period as evidence of the disorder in the catalogue of the works. Unfortunately, there seems to be no way out of this labyrinth. The original manuscript of Artaria's letter still exists.

D. In the List of Compositions, the first publisher is named wherever possible as the one most likely to have produced an accurate version. It is important to know that Beethoven himself always proof-read those of his works that were published in Vienna. As far as I know, the only compositions printed elsewhere that he proof-read himself were the last sonatas opp. 109, 110, and 111, published by Schlesinger in Paris.[43] However, it would be wishful thinking to suppose that all the editions corrected or revised by the composer were absolutely flawless. Unfortunately, this was hardly ever the case. Among the older Viennese publishing establishments were some that were all too often guilty of careless work despite all the composer's efforts. In the first and second movements of the *Sonate Pathétique*, for instance, a great number of the execution marks were omitted that are truly necessary not merely for colouring but for accurate performance. This omission was never remedied in subsequent editions. As for the correctness of recent editions, it should be said briefly but frankly that some of the publishing firms merit severe censure.

A publishing house that would search out the original editions of piano works and reproduce them scrupulously would render a truly outstanding service to the Beethoven literature. Merely making cheap editions available is not as great a service as many hold it to be, unless one is willing to place the music publisher on a par with the cotton manufacturer. A 'warning' that appears in the second period will show the honourable publishers what importance Beethoven attached to the correctness of his works and what care he expected of others. Even though most of the old Viennese publishing houses have changed hands, such as the large Bureau des Arts et d'Industrie which, together with Eder and Mollo & Co., was taken over by Steiner & Co. (now Haslinger), and the publisher Cappi which is now Witzendorf, it is hardly likely that all copies of their original editions are lost.

APPENDIX 3

Catalogue of Works Published between 1795 and the End of 1800

[Editor's note. The list given here is taken without correction from Schindler. A corrected list, incorporating the results of research in the hundred years since Schindler prepared his catalogue, may be found in KHV, pp. 755 ff.]

Opus No.	Year of Pubn.	Original Publisher	
1	1795	Artaria	Three Trios (E flat major, G major, C minor) for piano, violin, and cello.

According to Ferdinand Ries (*Notizen*, page 85), Haydn's advice against the publication of the C minor trio after hearing all three played at the home of Prince Lichnowsky aroused in Beethoven the suspicion that Haydn was envious and jealous of him. We know that during most of 1794 and 1795 Haydn was in England. The fact of his absence from Vienna does not tally with the publication date of these trios nor with the remark attributed to him. If in answer to a question from young Ries about the statement he explained that he believed the public would neither understand nor respond favourably to the trio, the remark that Beethoven misunderstood may be dismissed from our minds. Anyone who knows Haydn's own trios, however, will be astonished at this reaction. For my own part, I can only think that this was merely one of the many unfortunate misunderstandings that marked the course of Beethoven's life.

2	1796	Artaria	Three Sonatas (F minor, A major, C major) for piano.
3	1796	(unknown)	Grand Trio in E flat major for violin, viola, and cello.

It has been said that this trio was actually composed before the opus 1 trios, perhaps as early as 1791, but that Beethoven found it too insubstantial to present to the public as his very first work. This is merely an idle rumour.

4	1796	Artaria	Quintet in E flat major for 2 violins, 2 violas, and cello.

Opus No.	Year of Pubn.	Original Publisher	
			This work evolved from Beethoven's first attempt to write for wind instruments. The original was an octet for 2 clarinets, 2 oboes, 2 horns, and 2 bassoons, of which Artaria still possesses the manuscript. The admirable new catalogue of Beethoven's works published by Breitkopf & Härtel has it the other way around, saying that the octet grew out of the quintet.[44] Moreover, the opus number 103 given in this catalogue for the octet is wrong. There is no original work opus 103 or 104: these numberings result from the confusion in the catalogue and among the cataloguers. (See the aforementioned letter of 1819 from Artaria to Beethoven.)
5	1797	Artaria	Two Grand Sonatas in F major and G minor for piano and cello.
6	1797	Eder	Easy Sonata in D major for piano (4 hands).
			The following variations designated by numbers were published in 1797:
			a. Nine Variations in A major on a theme from the opera *Die Schöne Müllerin*; Artaria.
			b. Six Variations in G major on a theme from the same opera, 'Mich fliehen alle Freuden'; Artaria.
			c. Twelve Variations in C major on a theme, a *Menuet à la Vigano*; Artaria.
			d. Twelve Variations in A major; theme from the ballet *Das Waldmädchen*; Artaria.
7	1798	Artaria	Grand Sonata in E flat major for piano.

Opus No.	Year of Pubn.	Original Publisher	
8	1798	Artaria	Serenade in D major for violin, viola, and cello.
9	1798	Artaria	Three Trios (G major, D major, C minor) for violin, viola, and cello.
10	1799	Eder	Three Sonatas (C minor, F major, D major) for piano.
11	1799	Mollo	Grand Trio in B flat major for piano, clarinet (or violin), and cello.
12	1799	Artaria	Three Sonatas (D major, A major, E flat major) for piano and violin.
13	1799	Eder[45]	*Sonate Pathétique* in C minor for piano.
14	1799	Mollo	Two Sonatas in E major and G major for piano.

In the same year the following were published:

    a. Twelve Variations on the theme *Ein Mädchen oder Weibchen*; Traeg.

    b. Eight Variations in C major; theme from *Richard Löwenherz*, 'Mich brennt ein heisses Fieber'; Traeg.

    c. Ten Variations in B flat major; theme from Salieri's *Falstaff*, 'La stessa, la stessissima'; Artaria.

| 15 | 1800 | Mollo | Concerto No. 1 in C major for piano and orchestra. |

This work was first performed in the spring of 1800 by Beethoven himself at the Kärntnerthor Theater and was enthusiastically received.[46] At the same concert, two new works, the Septet and the first symphony in C major, were per-

Opus No.	Year of Pubn.	Original Publisher	

formed; Beethoven also improvised at the piano. The review of the symphony was brief: 'Much art, novelty and richness of ideas, but the wind instruments were used far too much, so that it was more band music than true orchestral music' (AmZ, sixth year, col. 321).

In the same year the following were published:

    a. Seven Variations in F major, theme from the *Opferfest*, 'Kind, willst du ruhig schlafen'; publisher not known.

    b. Eight Variations in F major; theme, *Tändeln und scherzen*; Simrock.

Several more short pieces of this category—variations, dances, and minuets—were also published in 1800. For lack of space, though, let us confine our list to the more important works of the year:

1. The first three quartets (F major, G major, and D major) were published by Mollo. Later they appeared with three other quartets as opus 18, and are therefore listed in the second period.

2. The vocal work *Scena ed Aria: Ah perfido!* belongs to the first period. Aloys Fuchs gives us the date of composition of this work, for on 4 May 1852 he wrote to me: 'I have a manuscript score with the title in Beethoven's own hand: "Une grande Scène mise en Musique par L. v. Beethoven à Prague 1796. Dedicata alla Signora Contessa di Clari". Beethoven's handwriting appears frequently throughout the score, as well as on the title-page where he wrote "Opus 46".' This work is among the first composed by the young master, and the opus numbers assigned to it, '65' by Breitkopf & Härtel and '48' by Hofmeister, are incorrect. The above dedication serves also to confirm the date of Beethoven's journey to Leipzig and Berlin.

Adelaide also belongs to this period. It was composed in 1797 and immediately published by Artaria. The opus number '46' given to it is therefore erroneous. I have a facsimile of the note that Beethoven sent along with the song to the poet, Matthisson, who was then living in Dessau. This historically interesting letter appeared many years ago in a periodical whose name I do not know. It reads:

FIRST PERIOD

Most honoured Sir:

You receive herewith one of my compositions that was published some years ago, and it is to my shame that perhaps you have no knowledge of it. I can give no excuse, nor explain why I have told you nothing of my intentions, though I have dedicated it to you with all my heart. Perhaps it was because I did not at first know where to reach you, and perhaps, too, from my diffidence, since I feared that I might have been presumptuous in dedicating something to you, not knowing whether you would approve of it.

Even now I am fearful as I send you my *Adelaide*. You must know what changes a few years can bring about in an artist who is still growing; the more progress he makes, the less satisfied he is with his earlier works. My most ardent wish would be fulfilled if the musical setting of your heavenly *Adelaide* should not entirely displease you and if it should move you to write a similar poem, not finding me too audacious in asking you to send it to me directly so that I might bend all my efforts to approximating the beauty of your poetry.

The dedication of this composition is a token of gratitude both for the pleasure I took in writing the music for your *Adelaide* and for the great joy your poetry has always afforded me and always will. As you play through my *Adelaide*, please remember from time to time

Your sincere admirer,
Beethoven

Vienna, 4 August 1800

APPENDIX 4

Music Criticism and the Reception of Beethoven's Works

To complete our account of the first period of Beethoven's life, we must learn how the music critics reacted to the young master's first works. The writings of these critics form an integral part of Beethoven's biography, for he introduced even from the very beginning an extraordinary direction in music, which he consistently pursued, thereby incurring their extraordinary opposition. The criticisms of Beethoven's music were therefore something like a sharp spice in his life, or like soldiers-at-arms who accompanied him along his way with only slight changes in uniform. The content is, of course, generally quite informative, and we must therefore include some examples. If the reader feels that these critical pronouncements are in general more significant than those of our day, he has some idea of the role that criticism of the arts played at that time.

In all Germany, nay throughout the whole world of music, there existed only one journal of criticism whose authority was acknowledged by all, the *Allgemeine musikalische Zeitung* (AmZ) published in Leipzig, the business capital of music. The first annual volume goes from October 1798 to the end of September 1799. This pattern was followed for twelve years, after which the publication year was made to conform to the calendar year. The editor was the highly respected writer on musical subjects, Friedrich Rochlitz. The many contributing writers were all competent, experienced, and independent persons thoroughly imbued with a sense of responsibility to art and artists. The most striking characteristic of the paper was the consistency of its judgements; though it must not be assumed that space was not also given to dissenting opinions, especially in respect to works performed in other countries, which sometimes had to be reported upon by less-known reviewers.

This journal exercised great influence on the period, largely because of its unity and adherence to basic principles and its discretion and absolute impartiality as regards the personal position of the artists reviewed. The great respect that it commanded continued to be observed in Vienna even after another musical journal was started there in the second decade, edited first by Ignaz von Mosel and then by F. A. Kanne, a well-written publication but with very little authority or influence. In general the quality of the AmZ remained on a uniformly high plane until the beginning of the thirties, when all artistic endeavours, particularly in music, began to assume a very different character as they succumbed more and more to the influences of commerce.

Permit me to insert a few parenthetical remarks concerning the state of music criticism in our own time. We have today a multitude of musical journals arising out of and depending upon conditions very different from those prevailing at the turn of the century. Music criticism has become mixed up in the papers with belles-lettres and even politics, and most recently we have witnessed the struggle between the faction of the so-called 'music of the future' and the faction of traditional music. All these divergent interests must of necessity give rise to a multiplicity of shallow opinions corrupting the very name of criticism. Hence the irresponsibility and consequent ineffectiveness of all music criticism, for it exists now for the sole purpose of promoting the commercial interests of a few individuals. There is hardly a German city that can boast as many as two independent newspapers conducted solely according to principle and dedicated to nothing but the very best. In the smaller towns unbiased criticism is virtually impossible because of the close social ties between the critics and those whom they criticize, and because of many other visible and invisible factors.

In our time most musicians are artisans and use the journals to further their own ends, while the journals allow themselves to be cheaply compromised and made use of. Moreover, the musical amateurs now force themselves forward, many of them claiming a high degree of musicianship though in point of fact they are innocent of any substantial knowledge of the arts, whereas in earlier days the amateur was influential only when he was content merely to enjoy. We have only to consider the countless number of men's singing clubs, with all their petty jealousies, rivalries, and factions. We are truly in need of a different type of criticism, one free of all influence, independent, able to withstand the buffeting winds, unwilling to act as the maid-servant of any faction.

This contrast explains the great significance of the AmZ to that section of music history with which this book deals. The musicians of our day who seem to reach artistic fame so effortlessly, even if only for a short time, could learn from that paper the conditions by which truly deserved, truly immortal fame is to be achieved, a process in which scholarly, just criticism plays a significant part.

The first year of the AmZ contains reviews of four works by our young hero, three sets of variations and the three sonatas for piano and violin, opus 12.[47] The first review concerns itself with the twelve variations on the theme *Ein Mädchen oder Weibchen* and the eight variations on *Mich brennt ein heisses Fieber*. The critic writes:

That Herr van Beethoven is an accomplished pianist is well known, and even if it were not known, one would be able to surmise it from these variations. Whether he is equally successful as a composer is, however, a question that it would be difficult to answer in the affirmative, judging from these samples of his work. This critic does not mean to say that some of the variations did not have a certain appeal for him, and he is happy to admit that with *Mich brennt ein heisses Fieber* Herr B. succeeded better than Mozart, who likewise made an arrangement of this theme in his youth.[48] But Herr B. was less fortunate with the variations on the first of the themes, which contain clumsy, harsh modulations that are far from pleasing.

As evidence, the critic then cites several passages as examples, and complains emphatically about the 'whole flood of variations that get invented and unfortunately even get printed, while many of the authors seem ignorant of what a good variation really is.' Here was a thorn that must have pricked our Beethoven rather deeply.

The review of the three sonatas, opus 12, is, even for that time, as strange in itself as it is surprising in respect to the music, and we have therefore included it in its entirety. It reads:

This critic, who was not previously familiar with the composer's piano pieces, must admit, after having with great difficulty worked his way through these curious, extraordinarily difficult sonatas, that he felt like a man who expected to take a stroll through an inviting wood with a congenial friend, but who found instead only hostile entanglements, and finally emerged from the thicket exhausted and disheartened. Undeniably Herr van Beethoven is going his own way, but what an eccentric, tortuous way it is! Intellect, intellect, and more intellect, but without nature, without song! Indeed, there is nothing in the music but a mass of learning without even a good method of conveying it. It is dry and uninteresting, a forced attempt at strange modulations, an aversion to the conventional key relationships, a piling up of difficulty upon difficulty until one finally becomes impatient and loses all pleasure in the task. Another critic has already said nearly the same thing, and we can only agree with him completely.

And yet this music cannot be dismissed altogether. It has its value, especially as an exercise for already accomplished pianists. There are always those who like things that are too difficult in concept and presentation, things that seem to go against the natural grain. To play these sonatas precisely as they are written would give such people a certain pleasure as well as a sense of achievement. If Herr v. B. would only assert himself a little less, if he would only consent to the natural idiom, he could certainly, with his talent and his zeal, produce much good music for an instrument which he seems to have mastered exceptionally well.[49]

The review of the variations on *La stessa, la stessissima* is by far the most bizarre of all the early criticisms: 'These variations give one no cause for joy. They have such unmusical passages, where harsh tirades in continuous semitones result in shocking dissonances with the bass, and vice versa! No, Herr v. B. may be able to improvise, but he does not know the first thing about writing good variations.' These words were written of a composer who was already almost thirty years old. What an opportunity they offered his enemies to redouble their opposition!

The three sonatas for piano, opus 10, in C minor, F major, and D major, were accorded a somewhat more friendly reception in the second volume of the AmZ. I quote here only the first part of the article:

It cannot be denied that Herr v. B. is a man of genius, a man of originality, and above all a man of independence. He is sustained by an extraordinarily thorough grounding in the art of composition and by his own phenomenal mastery of the instrument for which he writes. He assuredly ranks as one of the foremost pianists and composers for the piano of our time. His superabundance of ideas, which in most young artists of genius becomes an obsession from which, having found a satisfactory vehicle, they cannot free themselves, leads too often in Beethoven's case to a wild piling up of these ideas, or sometimes to a bizarre grouping of them, so as to produce an effect of gloomy contrivance or perhaps of contrived gloom that is likely to prejudice the listener against the whole work. Imagination, which Beethoven possesses to an unusual degree over and above his excellent knowledge of fundamentals, is precious, nay indispensable, for the composer who wishes to become a great artist, one who refuses to write trivial popular music, striving instead to create something with its own inner strength and life, something that will be played again and again. And yet there can be in all the arts a kind of overburdening that springs from excessive intellectualism and striving for effect, just as there can be a clarity and grace that transcend all the complexities and technicalities of the composition.

The kindly critic goes on to wish that the composer had been more led by instincts of economy, and adds:

Few indeed are the artists to whom one would like to say, 'Spare your treasure and practise thrift!', for not many have a wealth of ideas and the skill to implement them. It is therefore not exactly censure that we direct at Herr v. B., but rather a well-intentioned appeal which, while it may imply a certain criticism, contains much credit and respect.[50]

For the later sonatas we find more praise than censure. The following warning addressed to the composer is interesting: '. . . and we do wish that he would remember in certain passages that he is not writing for the organ'. The critic had perceived the former organist in these sonatas! It would be helpful if he had cited the passages to which he was referring. One could not find them now even with the most powerful microscope, for actually these sonatas have no such passages.

The same volume, covering the final year of the eighteenth century, includes a review of opus 13, the *Sonate Pathétique*. The review must be quoted here because it contains the first, though still very cautious, hint that the critic has penetrated some of the intrinsic poetry rather than stopping at the technical aspects of the work. It is not unlikely that the composer gave the critic his cue in the epithet *'pathétique'*, a title that was at first to have belonged to the sonata in C minor, opus 10, because of the marked similarities between the first and third movements. The name had a powerful effect on artists and the general public alike; it offered them a definite handle by which to grasp the music. What was the criticism of this sonata written in February 1800? It reads as follows:

The admirable sonata is well named *pathétique*, for it is indeed deeply emotional in nature. A noble melancholy is introduced with the effective, smoothly modulated Grave in C minor that recurs from time to time to interrupt the strongly expressive, fiery mood of the Allegro movement. In the A flat major Adagio, whose beautiful flowing melodies and definite rhythm demand that it should not be dragged, the character changes to one of repose and consolation. The feeling as well as the key of the Allegro return with the Rondo, so that the basic mood is maintained throughout the sonata, giving it unity, inner life, and true aesthetic worth. To be able to speak thus warmly of a sonata, provided that all the other requirements of the art of music are fulfilled as they are here, is an indication of its beauty. The only reproach that the critic could make to a Beethoven who is certainly capable of originality (and perhaps this is less a reproach than a wish for absolute perfection)would be that the theme of the Rondo has a slightly familiar ring. The critic himself cannot say just where he has heard it before, but it is not new.

From these few examples of contemporary criticism, the reader can surmise Beethoven's continuing battle with the old, familiar, entrenched musical tastes. They reflect, as would be expected, the spirit of the era, and one must not forget that this was the era that bore the names of Haydn and Mozart.

The criticisms of Beethoven published in the AmZ never over-stepped the bounds of decency and respectability, even in the second period when they were frequently more severe, and they were never as destructive as a recent Beethoven enthusiast claimed they were when he wrote: 'One reads [in the AmZ] strange things about the "imper-tinence" of the "talented young upstart" who "indulges in the wildest eccentricities in derision of the arts".' The criticisms quoted above demonstrate the journal's high standards, which were consistently maintained. We already know Beethoven's own attitude towards critics in general. We would expect none other from an ambitious artist con-fident of his talent. We cannot, however, blame him for being occa-sionally put out when the Leipzig critics were particularly harsh in their judgements, for they thereby lent ammunition to his enemies. He was able to recover quickly, however, as a letter of 15 January 1801 to the publisher Hoffmeister shows, for in one place he rails against the 'Leip-zig O——',[51] but further on says, 'Let them talk; their chatter will cer-tainly never render anyone immortal, any more than it can take away the immortality of a person whom Apollo has chosen'.[52] Hoffmeister, who probably provoked the remark, was thus offered a measure of comfort. In general, though, the 'Leipzig O——' were only doing their duty.

As a final example, here is a description of Beethoven's piano playing written in Vienna for the first volume of the AmZ (1798, col. 525):

Beethoven plays brilliantly, though he sometimes lacks delicacy and clarity. He is at his best in free improvisation. In a truly extraordinary manner he is able to perform impromptu on any given theme a graceful and at the same time closely knit development of ideas, not merely a variation of the figure, which many virtuosi do so well—and so emptily. Since the death of Mozart, who still in my opinion remains unchallenged, I have not heard any playing that has given me so much pleasure.

EDITOR'S NOTES (4–52)

First Period

⁴ The date 17 December 1770 is that of Beethoven's baptism. The exact date of his birth is not known, but 16 December is perhaps the most probable (NBJ VII [1937] 29; see also *Musica Divina* IX [1921] 10). Brother Johann was baptized on 2 October 1776 and died on 12 January 1848.

⁵ Grandfather Ludwig was baptized in Malines on 5 January 1712, married Marie Josepha Poll in Bonn in September 1733, and died in Bonn on 24 December 1773. Father Johann was born in Bonn in 1739 or 1740, married Maria Magdalena *née* Keverich of Ehrenbreitstein (1746–1787), widow of Johann Leym, on 12 November 1767, and died on 18 December 1792 (MQ XXXV [1949] 533). The Beethovens of Maestricht, if related to the composer at all, were an entirely separate branch of the family. Schindler's reference was probably to Ludwig Jakob Dominikus van Beethoven (1790–1853) of this branch (see *Beethoven und die Gegenwart* [1929], pp. 114 ff, espec. p. 150).

⁶ TK I 46 and TF 47 point out that there is 'no proof whatever, certainly none yet made public, that Chapelmaster van Beethoven was an authority on operatic works'.

⁷ A reproduction of this portrait is given in Ley's *Beethovens Leben in Bildern*, p. 5.

⁸ The conflicting contentions that Schindler summarizes here are given *in extenso* in TDR I 477 ff. The house on the Bonngasse has since 1889 been maintained by the Verein Beethoven-Haus as a Beethoven museum.

⁹ Choron and Fayolle, in their *Dictionnaire historique des musiciens* (1810), as quoted in Kastner-Frimmel's *Bibliotheca Beethoveniana* (supplement to NV [1925]), p. 6, say: 'Louis van Beethoven, said to be the natural son of Friedrich Wilhelm II, King of Prussia, was born at Bonn in 1772 [sic]'. This material was borrowed by Brockhaus for his *Conversations-Lexikon*; it appears in the fifth edition (1819), probably the one that Beethoven's friends saw, and is repeated as late as the seventh edition (1827), though not in the eighth (1833). Regarding this and other similar myths, see MQ XXXV (1949) 536–37. Kalischer (BusZ II 46) has pointed out that a similar royal lineage was attributed to Goethe.

¹⁰ Wegeler had referred to this canard in his letter of 28 or 29 (not 20) December 1825 to Beethoven (TK III 214; TF 1019; TDR V 278). Beethoven's reply, quoted in part above, is in And. 1542. Until recently the date of Beethoven's letter was read, '7 October 1826', the date that Schindler used in the text.

¹¹ In February 1820 one of Beethoven's visitors had written in a Conversation Book (SchKH I 242): 'It says in the *Conversations-Lexikon* that you are a natural son of Friedrich der Grosse.'

EDITOR'S NOTES

[12] The spider story had appeared as early as AmZ II (1800) 653. In the first formal biography of Beethoven, that by Johann Aloys Schlosser (1828), p. 7, it is explained that the story was told originally by Disjonval regarding the French concert-director Berthaume, and that by a confusion of names it became applied to Beethoven.

[13] Note, however, the passage in a letter quoted by Neefe as having been written to him a few months after Beethoven had arrived in Vienna: 'I thank you for your advice, which you gave me very often as I was progressing in my divine art. If ever I become a great man, you also share in it.' (MM 7).

[14] 'Beethoven was not appointed assistant organist in 1785 by Max Franz . . . but at the age of 13 in the spring of 1784 by Max Friedrich' (TK I 74; TF 71). He had been Neefe's unpaid deputy since June 1782 (TK I 69; TF 65).

[15] The autobiographical sketch that Schindler refers to, which has been reprinted in vol. XXI of *Beiträge zum Rheinischen Musikgeschichte* and in Nettl's *Forgotten Musicians* (1951), pp. 246–64, was written while Neefe was on leave of absence from Bonn for a musical tour in September and October 1782. He had come to Bonn in the autumn of 1779 and remained in that city, as a member of the Electoral court and then as City Organist and City Clerk, until 1796.

[16] The quartets named are WoO 36, composed in 1785 and published by Artaria & Co. towards the end of 1828. KHV (741–42) lists 37 compositions by Beethoven written before his departure for Vienna at the end of 1792; a similar list by Schiedermair (SJB 106, 116, 149) includes 45 numbers.

[17] Regarding Neefe's statement that it was he who introduced Beethoven to the *Well-Tempered Clavier*, note the statement by Nikolaus Simrock in his letter of 23 March 1828 to Gottfried Weber: 'For more than fifty years I have revered Sebastian Bach as the greatest German. I owned his *Preludes and Fugues* as long ago as 1776. . . . I presented [them] to young Beethoven in the ninth year of his age on the condition that he should be able to play them for me soon. I did not have long to wait: he worked on them every day with all his might' (SIMG X [1909] 494).

[18] This characterization is probably true, in spite of Beethoven's reference to Count Browne-Camus in the dedication in 1798 of his *Three String Trios* opus 9 as the *premier Mécène de sa Muse* (KHV 22). There is reason to doubt, however, that Waldstein played any significant part either in Beethoven's appointment as assistant organist or in his being sent to Vienna to study with Haydn.

[19] The sonata opus 53 was composed in 1803–4 and published in May 1805 (KHV 124).

[20] TK I 88 and TF 82 attribute this prank to 1785. However, a page of sketches, transcribed and discussed in BJ 1957/58, pp. 107–10, is clearly a study that Beethoven made for this occasion, and can with reasonable certainty be assigned to 1790–2. Wegeler's narrative, which Schindler gives in full, is found on p. 14 of the *Notizen*; the comments in square brackets are Schindler's. No account of the incident by Beethoven is known.

[21] The passage as transcribed by Schindler deviates slightly from the presently accepted chant in *Liber Usualis* (edition in Gregorian notation with Introduction and Rubrics in English [1950]), p. 626.

[22] It is known that Haydn visited Bonn on 25 December 1790 on his way to London, and that all the members of the Electoral chapel (thus including Beethoven) were introduced to him after the church service (TK I 110; TF 100). It is far from certain, however, that the second visit in July 1792 actually took place.

'Wegeler's account is the only contemporary record of such a visit, if an account written more than forty-five years after the event can be called 'contemporary'; there are discrepancies and improbabilities in Wegeler's narrative that lead Schiedermair (SJB 145) to the conclusion (to which Deiters [TDR I 254n] also leans) that in all probability the *Cantata on the Death of Joseph II* (WoO 87) was laid before Haydn at the time of his only visit to Bonn in December 1790' (MMR LXXXIX [1959] 204).

Further evidence that the visit of December 1790 was the only time that Haydn was in Bonn is found in Wegeler's statement that '*later* the cantata was to have been performed in Mergentheim'. The visit of the Electoral musicians to Mergentheim was in September and October 1791 (TK I 112); many years later Simrock informed Schindler that during this visit a cantata by Beethoven was rehearsed but not publicly performed (TDR I 274; Kerst I 19).

[23] The *Cantata on the Death of Joseph II*, WoO 87, as well as its companion work, the *Cantata on the Elevation of Leopold II to the Imperial Throne*, WoO 88, were indeed lost from sight for nearly one hundred years until in 1884 copies of the two works appeared at an auction in Vienna (KHV 542).

[24] The reference is to the first (1851) edition. In the second (1868) edition, prepared by Nottebohm, the trio appears on p. 143; it is listed in KHV (480) as WoO 38.

[25] See also Note 16 above.

[25a] See Note 33.

[26] This phrase occurs in the salutation of a note that Beethoven addressed to Schindler in the summer of 1823 (MM 361).

[27] It is most improbable that such an audition took place or, indeed, that Beethoven ever met the Emperor. Beethoven arrived in Vienna on 7 April (ZfMw X [1927] 153), and the Emperor left the city for the Crimea four days later (SJB 121). The recollection that Beethoven carried of the monarch may well have resulted merely from having seen him at some public function.

[28] This was one of the dozen or more entries in the Stammbuch presented to Beethoven by a group of his friends shortly before he left for Vienna early on the morning of 2 November 1792. A facsimile of this memento, with commentary by Gerstinger, was published in 1927 by Velhagen & Klasing (Bielefeld and Leipzig); see also NB I 138 and SJB 160.

[29] 'Records of the exchequer still available in Düsseldorf show that Beethoven continued to receive fifty thalers quarterly until March 1794' (TDR I 348). In addition, during his first year in Vienna the Elector had given him a donation of 500 florins to apply against his expenses in the capital city (NBJ VI [1935] 47).

[30] 'Beethoven's instant achievement of a position as an artist only paralleled by Mozart and of a social rank which Gluck, Salieri, and Haydn had gained

only after making their names famous throughout Europe, together with the general impression that the mantle of Mozart had fallen upon him—all this begat bitter envy in those whom his talents and genius overshadowed; they revenged themselves by deriding him for his personal peculiarities and by condemning and ridiculing the novelties in his compositions; while he met their envy with disdain, their criticisms with contempt; and, when he did not treat their compositions with indifference, he too often only noticed them with sarcasm.' (TK 1 241; TF 231).

[31] 'In *Beethovens Studien* (1873) Nottebohm has made a careful study of the 245 of Beethoven's exercises for Haydn that were still extant. Corrections by Haydn appeared in only 42 of them, and in the others there were at least as many mistakes, on the average, as in those that had been corrected. "Here and there Haydn had changed notes; he marked many places with an "X" or a "NB"; but nowhere had he added a single explanatory word" (NB I 172). Nottebohm concludes (*Studien*, p. 41) that this disregard of mistakes in the elements of musical grammar "can be explained only by the assumption that Haydn did not take the time to look through Beethoven's exercises carefully. . . . Haydn was not a systematic, thorough, or careful teacher' (MMR LXXXIX [1959] 206).

The article from which this quotation was taken discusses the relationship between Haydn and Beethoven in considerable detail.

[32] A more nearly complete list of Beethoven's teachers would also include the following:

Rovantini (violin, viola)	1779?–1781
Zenser (organ)	1780
Friar Koch (organ)	1781
Franz Ries (violin)	1785–1786
Mozart	1787
Salieri (vocal writing)	1793–1802 (1809?)
Schuppanzigh (violin)	1794
Krumpholz (violin)	1795

In addition to these givers of formal lessons, Beethoven was always avid for instruction from virtuosi on the various orchestral instruments, as is pointed out later by Schindler.

[33] Actually, 'Fräulein von W.' (Maria Anna Wilhelmina von Westerholt) and Baroness von Bevervörde were the same person: the Baroness Bevervörde *née* von Böselager referred to on p. 44 above. Of the mass of material that has been written on Beethoven's relationship with women, Walther Nohl's *Beethoven und die Frauen* (Alemannen-Verlag Albert Jauss, Stuttgart, n.d.) is perhaps the most temperate and factual. The two volumes, *Beethovens Frauenkreis*, that form vols. II and III of Kalischer's *Beethoven und seine Zeitgenossen* (Schuster & Loeffler, Berlin and Leipzig, n.d. [1908–10?]) make up in quantity what they lack in discrimination. The subject is also discussed, from another viewpoint, in such considerations of the Immortal Beloved as TK ch. XXI (I 317 ff), Sonneck's *The Riddle of the Immortal Beloved* (G. Schirmer Inc.,

New York, 1927), and Unger's *Auf Spuren von Beethovens 'Unsterblicher Geliebten'* (Hermann Beyer & Söhne, Langensalza, 1910).

[34] In making statements like these, Schindler disregards the fact that for several years during his adolescence in Bonn, Beethoven was a viola player in an orchestra that performed a wide range of operatic and concert music. He never lost his interest in the capabilities and techniques of orchestral instruments, as is shown by his conversation with the bassoonist Mittag in 1825 (Volkmann, *Neues über Beethoven* [1904], pp. 45 ff), but he learned from these virtuosi as a master and not as a pupil.

[35] Schindler, always suspect in the matter of dates, says of Sina in a footnote: 'Geb. 1778, verstorben in Boulogne sur mer den 2. October 1857'. A transcript from the Registry of Deaths in Boulogne-sur-Mer, however, reads: 'Le vingt septembre, mil huit cent cinquante-sept, est décédé . . . Léopold Louis SINA, artiste musicien . . . demeurant en cette ville, domicilié à Paris . . . né en Prusse à Breslaw (Silésie), âgé de soixante-douze ans, célibataire.' If Sina died at the age of seventy-two in September 1857, he must have been born in 1785 or the latter part of 1784. For Sina at the age of nine to have taken part in 1793 in quartet playing with youths of sixteen (Schuppanzigh) and fifteen (Weiss and Nikolaus Kraft), as stated in TK I 170 and TF 156, would have indicated precocity that was unusual but by no means unique.

In listing Sina as a member of the Rasumovsky Quartet, it is possible that Schindler confused the personnel with that of the group that had played at Prince Lichnowsky's palace in 1793. TK II 125 and TF 444, speaking of the formation of the quartet for Count Rasumovsky, say that the Count's 'own skill rendered him amply competent to play the second violin, which he usually did; but the young Mayseder, or some other of the first violinists of the city, was ever ready to take his part when required. Three permanent engagements only were, therefore, necessary.' Hanslick, however, names Sina as violin II of the Quartet (p. 203), and says, 'At first Rasumovsky alternated with Lichnowsky in assembling these artists for the performance of quartets, usually himself taking the second violin part, but he soon gave up this last trace of dilettantish egoism and engaged the four performers as a permanent quartet with contracts for life, an example of princely generosity without parallel.'

In the discussion of the dissolution of the Rasumovsky Quartet in 1816, TK II 337 and TF 640 say, 'So, too, had ended the engagement of Schuppanzigh, Weiss, and Linke with Rasumovsky. The destruction of his palace, the approach of old age, and failing sight induced him now to dismiss them with suitable pensions from his service. Schuppanzigh went to Russia; Linke returned to the Erdödys, and Weiss remained in Vienna.' Sina's name is not mentioned. See, however, pages 216, 501, 503 *infra*.

[36] 'Becker (*Anton Schindler, der Freund Beethovens*, Frankfurt-am-Main, 1939, pp. 26, 106) points out that Schindler neither understood nor tolerated the 'new music' of the 1850's; the Bach revival of those days was to him an unsolved and unpleasant mystery. For years before 1863 Schindler had avoided performances of works by Beethoven and Mozart in order (as he explained) not to contaminate his recollection of their proper performance' (MR XXIV [1963] 69).

[37] Beethoven's statement was not an exaggeration: during the years 1798–1801 compositions by him were published by Artaria, Simrock, Traeg, Eder, Mollo, and F. A. Hoffmeister.

[38] Here and elsewhere, Schindler, like so many writers since his time, confused the Leipzig publisher Franz Anton Hoffmeister (with two *f*'s, not one as Schindler wrote it) with the Leipzig publisher Friedrich Hofmeister (one *f*), with whom Beethoven had no known contact before 1816.

[39] TK I 198 (see also TK I 195) refers to this mention of Beethoven's piano-playing in Leipzig as another item 'in the long list of Schindler's mistakes'. The list is indeed long, but this item does not belong on it. In *Der junge Beethoven* (1st ed., 1925), p. 320, Schiedermair quotes from letters written from Dresden by Baron Clemens August von Scholl to Elector Max Franz:

'Young Beethoven arrived here yesterday. . . . He is going to play at court, and will go from here to Leipzig and Berlin. He has improved tremendously and composes well' (24 April 1796). 'Beethoven was here for about a week. Everyone who heard him play at the piano was entranced. Beethoven had the privilege of playing for an hour and a half, quite alone and without accompaniment, for the Elector of Saxony, who understands music. His Royal Highness was greatly pleased, and made him a gift of a gold snuff-box. Beethoven left from here for Leipzig and Berlin' (6 May 1796).

[40] This is substantially true of Beethoven's years of maturity, but as a *Wunderkind*, probably in the late autumn of 1781, his mother took him to Holland, where he 'played a great deal in great houses, astonished people by his skill, and received valuable presents' (TK I 66; TF 63).

[41] The 'curious and incomplete series' of works bearing what Deutsch refers to as 'opusculum numbers' is discussed in *Notes* IV (1946) 36.

[42] Actually, the only numbered work published after 1810 was the spurious set of variations on *Ich hab' ein kleines Hüttchen nur*, listed in KHV as Anhang 10.

[43] Letters from Beethoven to Breitkopf & Härtel and Hoffmeister & Kühnel in Leipzig, to Simrock in Bonn, and to other publishers in other cities show clearly that he sought to proof-read all his major works, wherever published, and that he struggled in vain with his publishers to bring about an accurate presentation of his music. The Schlesinger edition of opus 111 was so defective that Beethoven considered himself forced to collaborate with Diabelli in bringing out an unauthorized but corrected edition (see MM 419). The complex and in large measure unsolvable problems involved in seeking a definitive text for any Beethoven composition are discussed at length in Unverricht: *Die Eigenschriften und die Originalausgaben von Werken Beethoven* (Bärenreiter, Kassel, etc., 1960). See also Note 168.

[44] In the first (1851) edition of the Breitkopf & Härtel *Thematisches Verzeichnis*, the octet opus 103 is described as being 'nach dem Quintett Op. 4, arr. vom Componisten.', but by the time the more familiar second (Nottebohm) edition appeared in 1868, all who had given the matter consideration recognized that the octet must have come first. KHV dates the octet '1792' and the quintet '1795–96'.

[45] It has been generally accepted that the *Sonate Pathétique* and the Eight

Variations on Süssmayr's *Tändeln und scherzen*, WoO 76, were first published by Eder (the Simrock edition of the latter work, referred to by Schindler at the end of his catalogue, was certainly a reprint). By an acute process of musical detective work, Hill (*Notes* XV [1958] 396) and, working independently, Tyson (MT CIV [1963] 333) have shown conclusively that the first publication of these two works was by F. A. Hoffmeister, who apparently sold his plates to Eder after skimming the cream off the musical market.

⁴⁶ On this point, KHV (34) says: 'The first performance cannot be identified with certainty, but it was probably in 1798 in a concert that Beethoven gave in the *Konviktssaal* in Prague', though it is possible, as stated by Hanslick (p. 127) that Beethoven played a preliminary version of this concerto at one of the concerts that he gave in Vienna in 1795 (see KHV 45). At the concert of 2 April 1800 in the Burgtheater (not the Kärntnerthortheater), Beethoven played a concerto that may have been either opus 15 or opus 19 (see TK I 266; TF 255).

⁴⁷ In addition to the reviews cited here (AmZ I [1799] 366, 607, 570), there was also a brief review (col. 541) of opus 11, quoted in TK I 306 and TF 277 though by typical editorial carelessness identified by TK as referring to opus 6.

⁴⁸ The 'arrangement by Mozart' that the critics referred to was indeed published as such in the B. & H. collection (1798), but is now generally conceded to be spurious. See Köchel, Anh. C 26.02, p. 895.

⁴⁹ It is interesting, in the twentieth century, to note that this review of the three violin sonatas gives not the slightest indication that another instrument than the piano was involved. That is in accordance with the thinking of the day: opp. 12, 23, and 24 were published as sonatas 'for piano with a violin': opus 30 was 'three sonatas for the pianoforte with the accompaniment of a violin'. Opus 47 appeared as 'sonata for piano and obbligato violin', and only in opus 96 do we find today's recognition of the equality of the two instruments in the simple description: 'sonata for pianoforte and violin'. As an indication that the subordination of the other instruments to the piano did not disappear with Beethoven's day, it will be noted in the present volume (p. 212), written by Schindler in the late 1850's, that opp. 44 and 66 are listed as 'variations for piano with accompaniment'.

⁵⁰ This review of opus 10 was in AmZ II (1799) 25; the review of opus 13 was in II (1800) 373. For completeness it might be mentioned that the second volume of AmZ also contained a brief and non-committal review of the variations *Tändeln und scherzen*, WoO 76 (AmZ II [1800] 425; see also BusZ II 129). No works by Beethoven were reviewed in the third volume of the journal.

⁵¹ The phrase in question is usually transcribed *Leipziger O——* with the conjecture that the abbreviated word was *Ochsen* (oxen). Some scholars read the initial as 'R', and conjecture that it stood for *Rindfleische* (cattle). There is nothing in the letter to indicate more than transitory impatience with the reviewers, and accordingly nothing to support the assumed epithets, 'oxen' or 'cattle'. Unger (DM XV [1923] Heft 5, p. 338) makes the less argumentative

assumption that Beethoven meant *Rezensenten* (critics); and Anderson (Letter 44) and Forbes (TF 269) agree.

[52] And., p. 48n, speaking of the entire passage quoted here, says, 'This sentence about the Leipzig reviewers, which is included at this point in all the German editions and in TDR II, 211, does not appear in the facsimile' of the letter formerly in the possession of the president of C. F. Peters Co.

SECOND PERIOD

1801 to the End of 1814

Don't speak to me of rest!

BEETHOVEN to WEGELER

Before resuming the thread of our story, let us consider the circle of friends surrounding the great master at the beginning of this period. We should also make note of the duration of the friendships within this group and the changes that it underwent so that we may later answer Beethoven's enemies on this point.

From the first period we already know Prince Lichnowsky, the father-friend and patron of the young master, as well as his brother, Count Moritz Lichnowsky. A third member of the group was the Imperial Court Secretary, Nikolaus von Zmeskall.[53] The circle was enlarged early in the second period by the inclusion of Count Franz von Brunsvik, Baron Joseph von Gleichenstein, and Baron Pasqualati.[54] Furthermore, in the spring of 1800 Stephan von Breuning had come to Vienna from Bonn for the purpose of entering the Austrian civil service.*

The only professional musicians in this close circle of friends were Ignaz Schuppanzigh, whom we met earlier, and the well-known and much admired poet, composer, and critic F. A. Kanne. Ferdinand Ries must also be considered a member. He came to Vienna in the autumn of 1800 at the age of seventeen to take piano lessons with his fellow-townsman Beethoven. During the second half of this period, two new members joined the group, Oliva and Karl Bernard, the former a philologist, the latter a poet and writer. All of these men, with the exception of the Prince and Ferdinand Ries, were about Beethoven's age. The only change that occurred in this circle of friends during the course of the second period was the departure of Ries in 1805. He stopped in Vienna on his return from Russia in 1808, but only for a few months. Beyond this inner circle, there swarmed a whole galaxy of admirers and

---

* A very close friend of Beethoven's was Amenda, a Courlander, who left Vienna in 1799 to become a pastor in his native land. He was a good musician and a composer of quartets. The last known correspondence between Beethoven and this friend is dated from Talsen, 20 March 1815.[55]

satellites of the bright new star, intent upon winning his intimacy by offering all kinds of advice and affection. This kind of public demonstration seems to be the lot of all brilliant prodigies, especially in music.

It may occur to the reader to ask whether the members of the nobility included among Beethoven's friends were musical. We already know that Prince Lichnowsky and his brother had been pupils of Mozart. Their proficiency at the piano was that of an artist. Count Brunsvik, the Hungarian grandee, and Zmeskall were both 'cellists, Brunsvik being one of the foremost in chamber music. We shall often have cause to speak of this remarkable man in his relationship with Beethoven and with music in general. The two barons had less of a musical background (Gleichenstein had extensive holdings in the grand duchy of Baden, while Pasqualati was a wholesale merchant in Vienna) but they, too, were undeniably artistic in taste and inclination.

We know from Beethoven's dedications of the high regard that he wished to express to these estimable men: to his friend and patron, the Prince, opus 1 (the three trios), the *Sonate Pathétique*, the sonata opus 26, and the second symphony;[56] to Count Lichnowsky, the fifteen variations opus 35 and the sonata opus 90; to Count Brunsvik, the sonata in F minor opus 57 and the *Fantasy* opus 77; to Baron Gleichenstein, the cello sonata opus 69; to Baron Johann von Pasqualati, the *Elegy* opus 118; to Stephan von Breuning the violin concerto opus 61; and to Zmeskall the quartet in F minor opus 95.

Prince Lichnowsky died in 1814, but all the rest of the men in the group survived Beethoven, and were my close friends or at least my acquaintances. I was always in communication with Count Lichnowsky; I spent the winters of 1828 and 1829 with Count Brunsvik in Pesth; our common musical interests, particularly our interest in Beethoven, brought me in close touch with Kanne and Schuppanzigh. These men, and especially Stephan von Breuning, are the live sources for much of my information about the years before I was personally acquainted with Beethoven.

A circle of cultivated men such as these, filled as they were with love for and loyalty to Beethoven, and bound to him by ties of mutual respect, would hardly be likely, despite occasional differences of opinion, to create discord or trouble the harmonious atmosphere in which the composer could best work. Even those acquaintances outside the inner circle could only be harmful in so far as too many heads and too many minds seldom achieve good results. What was it, then, that had the power to penetrate the strong bulwark that surrounded our master, ruin his peace of mind, and drag him into the depths of despair? What was it that was able to overcome the good, selfless influence of these devoted friends and eventually drive all of them away? It was a pair of brothers bound to Beethoven by ties of blood. These brothers possessed such hypocrisy, such cunning and malice, that they were able by evil and persistent methods to negate the kindly ministrations of Beethoven's friends and often estrange them, though not always without bitter conflict.[57]

Surely Nature played a curiously malevolent trick when she gave Beethoven, who was highly moral and singularly gifted but also in certain respects weak, a pair of brothers capable of nothing above the mentality of a shopkeeper. These brothers were the two persons under the composer's supervision who were mentioned in the first period. The elder of the two was Karl, born in 1774. He followed Beethoven to Vienna, where the composer was able to secure a position for him in the National Bank. The youngest brother was Johann, born in 1776. He, too, made his way to Vienna after having learned the trade of apothecary in Bonn.

In a word, the disposition of these two younger brothers towards Beethoven's friends was fundamentally evil. Let us first hear what Ferdinand Ries has to say about the situation on page 97 of his *Notizen*:

His brothers took great pains to keep all of his intimate friends away, but, no matter what they did to him, as long as he was wholly convinced he would, upon their first pretence of remorse, dismiss the whole thing, saying, 'They are, after all, my brothers', and his friends would receive only bitter reproaches in return for their kindness and candour. The brothers were so successful in achieving their end that many of Beethoven's friends withdrew from him, particularly after his deafness had made all conversation very difficult.

A letter written by Karl will only reinforce any statement made here about the relationship that existed between Beethoven and these dependants. This letter is in answer to one from the music firm of Johann André in Offenbach to the composer, asking for new manuscripts that they might publish. The original of Karl's letter is in Frankfurt-am-Main in the collection belonging to Frau Belli-Gontard, who was kind enough to make me an exact copy in her own hand. The letter reads:

Vienna, 23 November 1802

Dear Sir:

We have received your letter asking for some of my brother's pieces, for which we thank you very much.

At the moment we have nothing but a symphony and a grand piano concerto, each priced at 300 florins. If you should want three piano sonatas I shall have to have 900 florins for them, all in Viennese currency, and these you cannot have immediately, but one every five or six weeks, as my brother doesn't bother much any more with such trifles, but writes only oratorios, operas, etc.

We would expect eight copies of any piece you might print. In any case, whether you care for the pieces or not, please answer, because otherwise I would be delayed in selling them to somebody else.

We also have two adagios for violin with complete instrumental accompaniment which would cost 135 florins, and two little easy sonatas of two movements each which are yours for 280 florins. Please give my best wishes to our friend Koch.

Your most humble

K. v. Beethoven

R. k. Treasury Official

Does not this letter call for the strangest kind of commentary? What a disappointment to see the sublime composer bound to such a common scoundrel! The nonsense about 'such trifles', 'only oratorios, operas, etc.', though too damaging to be merely laughable, is nothing compared to the rest of the letter. Operas had hardly entered Beethoven's mind in 1802; as for oratorios, it is true that he may have been working on the cantata *Christus am Oelberge* at that time. Who knows how many similar letters may have been in circulation, calling attention to the Beethoven brothers and their trade in music manuscripts?

It is now clear that a great wall arising out of this fundamental evil was gradually being built around the master. This barrier alone makes the biographer's task difficult. The present writer feels compelled to treat these circumstances and relationships somewhat like ballast, preferring to emphasize the brighter aspects of the composer's life and work, for these will be of more benefit to the musical world and of greater interest to Beethoven lovers.

But we cannot dismiss the matter before asking what Beethoven's attitude was in respect to this handling of his finances. He was like one who turns his back on such things, being totally devoid of all business sense. It was without difficulty that a swindler could exploit this shortcoming at every opportunity. We have already encountered this weakness in the master's nature in the first period, so that to dwell on it here would be superfluous. This state of affairs, however, did not remain forever static. At the end of the third period we find, perhaps to our surprise, that Beethoven had learned a lesson in business from his brothers. We shall see what, with the help of a clever accountant, he attempted and what he was able to accomplish.

[I]

— 1801 —

The beginning of the second period is marked by an event of great significance in Beethoven's life and art, the composition and perform-

91

ance of the ballet, *Die Geschöpfe des Prometheus*. I was in error when, in the first edition of this book, I dated the first performance as two years earlier. My mistake arose from the disagreement among the various reports, none of which was reliable. Then, as chance would have it, a play-bill from the year 1801 turned up, giving not only the date the ballet was first performed, but proving also that the music was Beethoven's, a fact about which there had been doubts raised. This is just one more instance of how a historical event, even a recorded one, can be lost, so that only a few years later its very existence can be debated. We are indebted to Dr. Leopold Sonnleithner for the discovery of this incontestable evidence as well as for his many helpful observations about the history and tenor of the times. Dr. Sonnleithner is the court magistrate of the Benedictine monastery Zu den Schotten in Vienna.

According to Dr. Sonnleithner and his theatre bill, the first performance took place on 28 March 1801 in the Hofburgtheater. The ballet was repeated many times that year and in the year following. Then it disappeared for many years and was not again seen until 18 November 1843, when it was performed under its former title with music by Beethoven, Mozart, and Haydn, 'in two acts and six scenes'. Only the most interesting sections of Beethoven's score were used. This version was maintained for several years. The notice of this latter performance states that on 22 May 1843 a ballet of the same name had been produced by Salvatore Viganò at the Scala in Milan, but differing considerably in treatment and execution from the Viennese production. The Milan performance had used Beethoven's music, but with the incorporation of several numbers by Haydn and other composers.

Beethoven composed this ballet score for Salvatore Viganò, then ballet master at the Court Theatre, immediately after completing the first symphony. We know that after the ballet was laid aside in 1802, the *Prometheus* music was never heard again during the composer's lifetime. The overture, however, was very popular and, like the Mozart overtures that were easy to play, was performed over and over again that year by Viennese orchestras. I relate this seemingly trivial circumstance only to show what an adverse effect a single chord (in this case, the opening chord of the overture) can produce. It is indeed a matter to be noted when one chord is able to arouse irreconcilable enmity within the ranks of the musically learned.

Beethoven used to say that any members of the corps of old Viennese music teachers who did not already consider themselves his enemies were sufficiently antagonized by this one chord to join the rest. Not only that, but some of these old masters (especially Preindl (1756–1823), Kapellmeister at St. Stephan's and author of a textbook on composition),* feeling that Beethoven, like a foolhardy knight, had insolently thrown a gauntlet in their faces, declared themselves henceforth his sworn foes. Moreover, they kept their oath: grammarians are known for their enmities. They continue beyond the grave to persecute the object of their wrath. In close ranks with Joseph Preindl in his fight against such unheard-of innovations stood his colleagues Dyonis Weber, later director of the Prague conservatory, and Abbé Maximilian Stadler, once a friend of Mozart's. These last two adhered longer than any others to their open battle against the subversive deviations introduced by Beethoven. We shall have the opportunity of alluding to the Abbé again, for later he played a significant role in getting Beethoven's music accepted by an important circle of musicians of the Haydn and Mozart era. Suffice it to say here that he survived the master by six years. Dyonis Weber (born in 1756) lived much longer, and died in his late seventies.[58]

—• 1802 •—

The year 1802 did not bring forth any important new compositions, perhaps because the master had been satisfied during the preceding months to write 'trifles', awaiting the termination of his brotherly duties and obligations before producing any deeply poetical works. The compositions published during this year include the sonatas for violin, opp. 23 and 24, in A minor and F major respectively, the sonata in A flat major, opus 26, with the Funeral March, and the two sonatas *quasi fantasia* in E flat major and C sharp minor, opus 27, which had been composed a year or two earlier. It is interesting to note the reaction of the Leipzig critics to these works. We quote here a few sentences from the review of the sonata in A flat major and the two opus 27 sonatas because of the indications for correct performance it contains.

We read in AmZ IV (1802) 651:

These are the three piano compositions with which Herr v. B. recently enriched a selected few cultivated musicians and accomplished pianists. I say enriched, because they are truly an enrichment and belong among those few works of art of the present day that will scarcely ever grow old; certainly number three can never grow old.

---

* This textbook teaches the old guild regulation that every piece of music must begin with a tonic triad. Until Beethoven, no one had broken this rule. The *Prometheus* overture opens with a dissonant chord: hence the hue and cry against the malefactor. In Preindl's book, which is a handbook of all that the Viennese composer needed to set himself up in business, the science of composition is reduced to a few simple rules (Ignaz von Seyfried recently brought out a new two-volume edition entitled *Wiener Tonschule*). Too much learning makes the head spin. How many whiplashings Beethoven administered to this 'textbook for old *Reich* composers' to avenge himself on the pedantic old fogies![57a] We shall often need to refer to the Viennese music theorists again.

Was this prediction not a bitter pill for the music teachers to swallow?
Further on in the review we find:

Number one may be in places contrived and artificial, but this accusation
cannot be made of the truly great, solemn, and magnificent chordal section that
the composer has inscribed 'Marcia Funebre sulla morte d'un Eroe' to indicate
to the pianist the proper tone of the piece, for in this section all the weight and
wealth of the music must be fully expressed. Anyone who complains that this
march, sections of number two, or almost any part of number three is too
difficult to understand or to play is like those folksy philosophers who would
like to translate a very serious discussion into facile tea conversation.

We must, however, quote almost all the review of the *sonata quasi una
fantasia* in C sharp minor:

This fantasy is from beginning to end one pure whole, rising out of the
deepest emotions of the soul, carved from a solid block of marble. There cannot
be a single person in any way sensitive to music who can fail to be seized by
the first Adagio, led up and up and finally, deeply moved, sublimely uplifted
in the Presto agitato, affected as one can be affected only by free-form piano
music. The two movements, Quasi una fantasia and Presto agitato, are entirely
appropriate to the awesome key of C sharp minor. The composer indicates
everywhere, in so far as such things can be expressed in conventional symbols,
how the music is to be performed, how the piano is to be played in order to
bring out the best qualities of the instrument. One can see from these execution
marks and even more strikingly from the whole presentation of his ideas how
perfectly Beethoven understands his instrument, as perhaps no other composer
besides Philipp Emmanuel Bach has understood it. But some of these movements—the whole first movement of number three, for instance—require a
very good piano if the playing of them is to be a pleasure.

In the musical portion of this book, we shall return to the subject of
these valuable aids to the performance of Beethoven's piano music. I
should like to mention in passing that the composer's direction that the
whole first movement of the *sonata quasi una fantasia* should be played
without the use of the damper pedal (*senza sordini*) is no longer valid
because of the fuller tone of our present-day instruments.

One more 'trifle' was produced in 1802, the highly significant sonata
in D major opus 28. The Leipzig critic seems hard put to it to know
what to say about this work. He extricates himself from his embarrass-
ment thus:

Beethoven remains true to his character and style; and truly, an artist like B.
can do no better than remain true to himself. . . . What is there that one can
say for or against this or that component of a work of art? For a work of art is
no more the sum of its parts than a cliff is a heap of stones. The parts can be
very pleasant and constitute an interesting whole but still not a perfect work

with a pervading unity and intelligence that will be comprehended by those for whom the music has meaning.

Having seen the critics' reaction to our master, let us examine his relationship to his publishers. The reader will not be surprised to learn that the genius in Germany has always, even to the present day, been a prey to exploitation. Beethoven was no exception. The products of his genius were snatched away, and one can imagine how bitter it made him to submit all his life to this unimpeded plundering without ever being able to protect himself effectively. He had reason to complain, 'The publishers are getting rich on my money while I, poor devil, often go hungry!'

Let us hear his first protest against such exploitation. In the fourth announcement supplement of the AmZ, Vol. VI (November 1802) the following notice appears:

I believe that it is my duty to the public and to myself to proclaim that the two quintets in C and E flat major, one taken from a symphony of mine and published by Herr Mollo in Vienna, the other taken from my septet opus 20 and published by Herr Hoffmeister in Leipzig, are not original works of mine but mere arrangements made by the publishers.* A composer has no recourse nowadays against arrangements being made of his works (and ours is an age in which arrangements abound), but one has the right at least to expect the publishers to acknowledge the arrangement on the title-page so that the composer's honesty may not be brought into question or the public deceived. This is in order to avoid such misrepresentation in the future. I also wish to announce that Breitkopf & Härtel of Leipzig will very soon publish a new and original quintet by me in C major opus 29.

Ludwig van Beethoven

The master ridicules his age in which arrangements abounded, but this abundance was only beginning. What would he say to the almost countless arrangements, though they are clearly designated as such, that we have of his works today? No composer's works have been so variously abused, transcribed, rearranged, dismembered, as his. Truly the master would have become wealthy if a law had granted him a modest royalty on each arrangement made of his music. But it is only since his death that the arrangements of his symphonies, quartets, and trios have assumed the proportions of a deluge! When kings sow. . . .†[60]

A second, more emphatic protest published by the master in November the following year attests to the failure of the first. It appeared in

* The arrangement of the septet as a quintet was thus not Beethoven's own, as Ries claims it was.[59]

† A. B. Marx is in error in assuming in volume I of his excellent book, *Beethoven, Leben und Schaffen*, that the nine arrangements dating from this period that he lists on pp. 158–9 are all of the master's own doing. Not more than three or four of all the existing arrangements of his works were made by the composer himself. The creative artist, constantly driven to new accomplishments, was not interested in rewriting his old pieces.

the third announcement section of the AmZ under the heading, 'Warning', and read as follows:

Herr Carl Zulehner, an engraver in Mainz, has announced an edition of my collected works for piano and stringed instruments. I consider it my duty to make it clear to all music-lovers that I have nothing whatsoever to do with this edition. I would never allow publication of my collected works, which I find in itself a premature undertaking, without first conferring with the original publishers of the various compositions and ensuring the correctness that was in some cases lacking in the first editions. Furthermore, I must say that this illegal edition of my works can never be complete, since various new works are shortly to appear in Paris and Herr Zulehner, as a French citizen, cannot reproduce them. I shall on another occasion explain my own intentions concerning a collection of my works that will be issued under my own supervision and only after they have been thoroughly revised.

Ludwig van Beethoven

But even this vigorous warning was of little avail; the master's works were becoming more and more widely known, and the publishers' greed grew in proportion. There occurred during the course of this period incidents involving other engravers that forced the composer to give utterance to even more resentful reprimands. At times the affair took on the aspect of a comedy over which he could laugh. In short, every newly published work seemed to be free for the use of everyone, and it was Beethoven's lot to sigh all through his life about the situation of which he was the victim. Even though all of Beethoven's music is now the legal property of every publisher, his 'Warning' of 1803 has not lost its meaning, for it states clearly how carefully Beethoven would have corrected all his works if he had not been deprived of that privilege. We ought to be all the more conscientious in our publication of his works today.

If the year 1802 had been freer of disturbances for our composer, his output of works would surely have been even more considerable. To be specific, he became seriously ill,[61] and was attended by the highly renowned physician, Dr. Schmidt. In gratitude for his kindly care, Beethoven dedicated to the doctor the trio that he himself had arranged from his septet. For his convalescence, he chose a spa named Heiligenstadt, a good hour's distance from the capital. It was here that in the years following he wrote many of his greatest works.

In Heiligenstadt he composed the following will—or perhaps we should say letter of farewell—for his brothers. It is an unforgettable document that bespeaks not only the deep dejection caused by his deafness but also the complex and noble nature of the man.* Every reader

---

* The original manuscript used to be in the collection of Franz Gräffer, but is now better placed with the violin virtuoso, Ernst.[62]

will surely agree with Friedrich Rochlitz, who wrote of the will: '. . . And surely this document will have a single effect upon all (unless they be totally insensitive) who become acquainted with it. I do not know what more favourable, more convincing thing can be added here to honour the deceased, not as an artist but as a man.' (See the Introduction.)

The Heiligenstadt Will reads as follows:

For my brothers Carl and . . . Beethoven:

O ye men who consider or declare me to be hostile, stubborn, or misanthropic, how unjust you are to me! You do not know the secret cause of what seems so to you. From childhood my heart and mind were filled with the tender feelings of good will; I was ever ready to perform great things. But consider that for six years I have been afflicted with an incurable complaint, made worse by incompetent physicians, deceived year after year by the hope of an improvement, forced at last to accept the prospect of a lasting infirmity, whose cure may take years or indeed be impossible.

Born with an ardent, active temperament, ever inclined to the diversions of society, I was forced at an early age to seclude myself, to live in loneliness. If at times I tried to ignore all this, how harshly was I driven back by the doubly sad experience of my poor hearing, yet I could not say to people, 'Speak louder, shout, for I am deaf!' Alas, how was it possible for me to admit to an infirmity in the one sense that in me should be more perfect than in others, a sense that I once possessed in the greatest perfection, a perfection, indeed, such as few in my profession enjoy or ever have enjoyed—oh, I cannot do it.

Forgive me, then, if you see me draw back from your company which I would so gladly share. My misfortune is doubly hard to bear, since because of it I am certain to be misunderstood. For me there can be no recreation in the company of others, no pleasures of conversation, no mutual exchange of thoughts. Only just as much as the most pressing needs demand may I venture into society; I am compelled to live like an outcast. If I venture into company I am overcome by a burning terror, for I fear that I may be in danger of letting my condition become known.

Thus has it been during the last half year, which I have spent in the country. Ordered by my wise physician to spare my hearing as much as possible, he almost encouraged my present instinctive mood, although, often moved by the urge for companionship, I have let myself be tempted into it. But how humiliating it was when those standing near me heard a flute in the distance that I could not hear, or someone heard the shepherd singing and again I heard nothing.[63]

Such experiences brought me to the depths of despair—a little more, and I would have put an end to my life. Art alone stayed my hand; ah, it seemed impossible for me to quit the world until I had brought forth all that I felt under an obligation to produce. And so I endured this wretched existence—wretched indeed, with so sensitive a body that a progressing change can transport me from the best condition to the worst. Patience, I am told, I must choose as my guide. This I have done; my determination, I hope, will remain firm until it shall please the inexorable Fates to break the thread. Perhaps my condition will improve, perhaps not—I am content. To be forced at the early age of twenty-eight to become a philosopher is not easy, less easy for the artist than for any other.[64]

O Divine One, thou lookest down into my innermost soul, thou seest into my heart and knowest that love of mankind and a desire to do good dwell therein. O Men, when some day ye shall read these words, reflect that ye wronged me, and let the child of misfortune be comforted that he has found one like himself who, despite all the obstacles that Nature has thrown in his way, yet did all that lay within his power to be received into the ranks of worthy artists and men.

You, my brothers Carl and . . . , as soon as I am dead, if Professor Schmidt be still living, request him in my name to describe my malady, and to this document that you now read attach the account of my ailment so that, at least as far as possible, the world may be reconciled with me after my death. At the same time, I declare you two to be the heirs of my small fortune (if so it can be called). Divide it fairly; bear with and help each other. What you have done to harm me, that you know was long since forgiven.

To you, brother Carl, I give special thanks for the affection you have shown me of late. It is my hope that your life may be better, more free from care, than mine. To your children, recommend virtue, for that alone, not money, can give happiness. I speak from experience: it was virtue that sustained me even in my affliction; to it, next to my art, I must give thanks that I did not end my life by suicide. Farewell, and love one another.

I thank all my friends, particularly Prince Lichnowsky and Professor Schmidt. It is my wish that the instruments from Prince L.[65] be preserved by one of you, but let no quarrel arise between you because of them. If they can serve a better purpose for you, just sell them—how happy I shall be if, even in my grave, I can be of help to you.

So let it be. Joyfully I hasten to meet death. If it comes before I shall have had the opportunity to develop all my artistic capabilities, then, in spite of my hard fate it will still come too soon, and I shall probably wish that it had been delayed. Even so, I should be content, for will it not release me from a state of endless suffering? Come when thou wilt: I shall meet thee bravely.

Farewell, and do not wholly forget me in death. This much I deserve from you, for in life I have often given thought how to make you happy. Be ye so.

Ludwig van Beethoven

(seal)

Heiglnstadt [sic]*
6 October 1802
For my brothers Carl and . . . to read and to execute after my death [at side].*
Heiglnstadt [sic]*, 10 October 1802. Thus I take leave of you, and indeed sadly. Yes, the fond hope that I brought hither with me, that at least to a certain degree I might be cured, this hope I must abandon entirely. As the autumn leaves fall withered to the ground, so is my hope blighted. I leave here almost as I came;

---

* The three bracketed additions are the editor's.

even that buoyant courage that often animated me in the beautiful days of summer has left me. O Providence! grant me but one day of pure joy! It has been so long that true joy has been a stranger to me. When, oh when, Divine Power, can I once more feel it in the temple of Nature and of men? Never? No, that would be too hard.

It is surprising to see the name of the younger brother omitted and replaced by dots in this document. The reason for this is hard to determine. Can it be because of the lesser affection that Beethoven already felt for this brother?[66] It is only conjecture. This much is however certain, that as the years went by, the rift between the composer and his 'pseudo-brother', as he commonly referred to him, grew wider as the brother's arrogant behaviour in public and his many outrageous schemes to line his pockets made him more and more unworthy to bear the already acclaimed name of Beethoven. In any case, this Johann v. Beethoven is by far the most garish portrait in the whole Beethoven gallery.

•—• 1803 •—•

It has already been noted that our master was hindered by illness from producing a richer harvest of works. However, the first performance of his cantata, *Christus am Oelberge*, on 8 April 1803 showed that his illness had only temporarily curbed the flight of his genius and that he would soon be able to dedicate himself as before to strenuous work. Even so, this cantata had been sketched as early as 1801 in the nearby town of Hetzendorf where Beethoven had spent the summer.[67] He himself showed me in 1823 the secluded spot in the garden of the Schönbrunn palace where he had done this preliminary work. It was an oak tree which branched into two strong trunks about two feet above the ground, forming a comfortable place to sit.

In the twenty-ninth issue of the AmZ (fifth volume) this first performance is accorded only a few lines: 'A conviction I have long held is now confirmed: Beethoven will one day bring about as significant a revolution in music as Mozart did. He is quickly advancing towards that goal.' This critic calls the work an oratorio and speaks of the 'extraordinary applause' it received at this first performance. Later critics refer to it as a cantata, which is undoubtedly the more accurate title. It is unfortunate that it was not called a cantata from the start. A similar error in titles, misrepresenting the content of a work, occurred in a later instance. This time it was a concertino, which appeared in print under the name of 'concerto' and remained so against the will of the composer. We shall remember it in its correct chronological context.

It is true that the experts differed widely in their opinions as to the extent to which the composer had attained the lofty goal that he sought in this cantata, but none could characterize the work as an impeccable composition or a consistent entity. A Viennese critic writing for the forty-fourth issue of the AmZ was eager to correct his predecessor. He wrote: 'In the interests of truth I feel compelled to contradict a report published earlier in this journal: Beethoven's cantata was not well received.' Beethoven admitted in part the truth of this verdict, for in his later years he declared that it had been a 'mistake' to have handled the part of Christ in a modern operatic style. The fact that the work was laid aside after its first performance, as well as the lapse of an unusually long interval before its publication (about 1810), indicate that Beethoven himself was not particularly pleased with it and probably made extensive changes.[68]

During this year the hard-working master published the following piano works: three sonatas for violin and piano, opus 30, three piano sonatas, opus 31, *Fifteen Variations and Fugue*, opus 35. The first of the sonatas for violin and piano, in A major, was severely criticized in the AmZ, which even said that it was unworthy of Beethoven. On the other hand, the *Fifteen Variations* were highly praised, but only as 'a significant little work'. Every player should familiarize himself with this review because it includes detailed directions for the execution of each variation. (Would it not be a most worthy undertaking for a music firm to make available to the public a collection of the reviews of Beethoven's works that appeared in the AmZ? Many of the articles elucidate the work they deal with, thus fulfilling the first obligation of good criticism. Bound in a single volume, they would be easily available to all, but scattered through some twenty-five volumes of the journal they are to all intents and purposes lost to the world. Even the few excerpts quoted here are an indication of the lasting value of these critical articles, apart from the fact that, as I mentioned on page 74, they constitute a part of the master's life and cannot easily be separated from it.)[69]

We now come to an incident the dating of which has caused the writer great difficulty. The writing of history would be a pleasant task were one not always constrained to ask exactly when each event took place. But events and their chronology are so tightly interwoven that the time must be determined in each case. In this instance, the incident itself is not the difficult thing to establish, nor is it very hard to come to the heart of the matter. The real problem has been finding out beyond the shadow of a doubt in what year, on what day, the incident occurred. The political historian is usually able with the help of state documents to determine the various dates with accuracy, so that it is relatively easy for him to progress chronologically from one fact to the next. But the writer of art biography dealing with events of half a century ago, dependent on the memories of a few surviving contemporaries, often finds himself in a labyrinth of contradictions from which he can extricate himself only by boldly cutting his way through or by waiting for a happy coincidence to free him from his predicament.[70]

As for this particular circumstance, I had great difficulty in placing it in its proper sequence among all the important events of Beethoven's life. Of all those I asked for help, no one was able to solve my problem, for in every case memory proved false. It was not until I went to Paris and met Cherubini that I was able to trace accurately the date that had eluded me in Vienna. Soon after their arrival in Vienna in 1805, Cherubini and his wife had learned about this event as having taken place two years previously. They were able to tell me definitely that its effect on Beethoven's morale had already been dispelled. (More later of the close relationship that existed between the two composers.) Having followed this clue further, I am now able to declare almost positively that the event that in the earlier edition I had dated 1806 actually took place in the year 1803.

When we heard the composer mention in a letter to Wegeler an 'enchanting girl' who had granted him 'moments of bliss', we said that this enchantress, who had brought about beneficial 'changes' in Beethoven's disconsolate state, was the same who soon afterward caused him great suffering. We must now take time to look into this matter of the heart. Since the first edition of this book, German and French pens have been at work on the affair, making it the lucrative object of romantic magazine stories. The writers of these fantasies have been fortunate in that their love story has been made even more poignant by its connection with one of the best-known of the piano sonatas, that in C sharp minor, opus 27, dedicated 'Alla Damigella Contessa Giulietta Guicciardi'. This was the full name of the enchantress. The reader should not, however, expect to find more information on the subject in this edition than in the first, for it is a matter of some delicacy, and out of deference for those still living can be only lightly touched upon. It cannot be said for certain whether it was a question of faithlessness on the part of the woman alone, as has been claimed, or whether intrigues from another side severed the alliance and prompted the young lady quite suddenly to become the wife of the famous composer, Count von Gallenberg.

Yet there is more to say about the effects of this rupture on the spirits of the master who had been so happily in love. In his despair he sought consolation with his esteemed and trusted friend, Countess Marie Erdödy, whose name appears in the dedications of the two trios, opus 70, and the two sonatas for piano and cello, opus 102. While spending a few days at her estate 'Jedlersee' in the Marchfeld he disappeared, and the Countess thought he had returned to Vienna. But on

1 Diary note written by Beethoven in Baden in 1817 or 1818 (see page 104, and Note 113)

the third day her music-master, Brauchle, found him in a remote corner of the palace garden. This incident remained for a long time a close secret, and only after several years did those familiar with it confide it to Beethoven's nearest friends, long after the love affair had been forgotten. One can only deduce that the unhappy man had intended to starve himself to death. Observant friends have said that they noticed that after that time Beethoven was unusually attentive to the music-master. (In 1850 the readers of the *Revue des deux mondes* found mention of the Jedlersee incident in an article by Scudo entitled 'Une Sonate'. I communicated with Scudo while he was writing the article, for I felt that I could perhaps furnish him with unknown material on the C sharp minor sonata. On that occasion I told him of the incident. He chose, however, to twist the facts a little in order to enhance their romantic quality.)

Apparently this experience did not make Beethoven renounce the idea of conjugal happiness. A handwritten note dating from 1817 or 1818 reads: 'Love—yes, love alone can make your life happy! O God, let me find someone who can strengthen my virtue, let me possess someone whose love I am allowed. Baden, 27 July, when M. passed by and, I think, looked at me.'*

I am well acquainted with the object of this autumnal love, and I still have in the correspondence left me by Beethoven two letters written to him in 1825 and 1826 by Marie L. P . . . r, who was later married and lived in Graz. She was a lady as beautiful as she was talented. Beethoven was for many years attracted to her, as she well knew. She and she alone was able to affirm the confession that Beethoven made in September 1816 to Giannatasio del Rio, the head of a boys' school. The confession was published by Giannatasio's daughter, together with twenty-eight letters from Beethoven to her father, in the second quarterly volume of the *Grenzboten* for 1857, and reads:

. . . that he is unhappy in love. For five years he has known a certain person, and he would consider it the greatest happiness in the world to be more closely bound to her. It is out of the question, impossible almost, a chimera, and yet the love is as strong as on the first day. He has not yet found this harmony. There has, however, been no explanation. He cannot bring himself to make one.

In the third period we shall again speak of Fräulein Giannatasio's article. The family was very well known to me.

What I have already said of the affair with Giulietta Guicciardi was substantiated by things the master let drop in my presence. To quote his words here seems all the more important because they are written out in his own hand. Count Gallenberg lived for several years with his wife

* Editor's note. The facsimile of this note that appeared in the 1860 edition, is included in the present edition as Facsimile I on pp. 102–3.

and family in Italy, where he composed mainly ballet music for the stage. When the famous impresario Barbaja leased the Kärntnerthor theatre in 1821 and brought the Italian opera to Vienna, he also engaged Count Gallenberg to supervise the theatre library. In 1823 Beethoven needed to see the score of his *Fidelio*, which was in that library, and so I went to see the Count. Gallenberg took the liberty on this occasion of making some abusive remarks about Beethoven, and I felt it my duty to communicate some of these remarks to the master. This gave him the opportunity of reminiscing about the events of 1803, mostly in writing, for we were in a public place and he was afraid of speaking too loudly. Here are a few of the sentences he confided in me:

I was, through the agency of others, his anonymous benefactor. . . . J'étois bien aimé d'elle et plus que jamais son époux. Il étoit pourtant plutôt son amant que moi, mais par elle j'apprenois de son misère et je trouvois un homme de bien, qui me donnoit la somme de 500 florin pour le soulager. Il étoit toujours mon ennemi, c'étoit justement la raison, que je fusse tout le bien que possible. . . . Elle est née Guicciardi. Elle étoit l'épouse de lui avant son voyage en Italie. . . . Arrivée à Vienne elle cherchoit moi pleurant, mais je la meprisois. . . .[71] And if I had wanted to spend my strength and my life in this way, what would have been left over for the nobler, the better part.

(The master can hardly be complimented for the way in which he expressed himself in the French language. The entire passage would have to be rewritten to be good French. The phrase, *que je fusse*, should read, *que je lui faisais*, and the germanism, *elle cherchoit moi*, should be changed to read, *elle m'a fait une visite*.)

This elucidation is sufficient to explain the nature of the affair and also to illustrate Beethoven's attitude in matters of the heart, surely only to his credit. It will also serve to controvert what Seyfried and Ries have written about the composer's capacity to love—he who felt so sensitively, so deeply! But three letters that I have in Beethoven's own hand, written to his beloved Giulietta from a spa in Hungary,[72] should now be quoted, for their contents seem appropriate as a seal with which to stamp this affair. I cannot give their exact date. After Beethoven's death Stephan von Breuning found them among several other letters of importance in the secret drawer of a cabinet. Might they have been returned to him after the rupture in 1803? Who can say? Because their existence has been doubted, the second letter, dated 'Monday evening 6 July', is reproduced in facsimile at the end of this book.*

---

* Editor's note. It is reproduced in the present edition as Facsimile II on pp. 107–9.

SECOND PERIOD

1.

6 July, in the morning

My angel, my all, my very self:

Only a few words today, and these in pencil (in *your* pencil). Not until tomorrow will my lodgings be definitely engaged. What a useless waste of time such matters are! Why this profound sorrow when necessity speaks? Can our love exist except through sacrifices, through not demanding everything? Can you change it that you are not wholly mine, that I am not wholly yours? O God, gaze upon nature in all its beauties and let your soul be calm at what must be. Love demands all, and rightly so—thus it is for me with you, for you with me, but you forget so easily that I must live for myself and for you. Were we wholly united, you would feel this painful necessity as little as I.

My journey was terrible. I did not arrive here until four o'clock yesterday morning. For lack of horses, the post-coach chose another route, but what a terrible road it was! At the last stage but one I was warned against travelling at night. They cautioned me about a forest, but that only spurred me on. I was wrong: the coach broke down because of the terrible road, unmetalled, a mere country road. Without such postilions as I had, I should have been left stranded. Esterházy, travelling hither by the usual road, met the same fate with eight horses as I with four. Even so, I found some satisfaction in it as I always do when I successfully surmount difficulties.

Now a quick change to things internal from things external. We shall soon see each other again, I am sure, and today I cannot tell you the thoughts about my own life that I have had during these few days. If our hearts were always close together I would surely have no such thoughts. My heart is filled with many things to tell you—ah, there are moments when I find that speech is futile indeed.

Be of good spirits; remain my true, my only treasure, my all as I am yours. The rest the gods must send us, that which must and shall be for us.

Your faithful
Ludwig

2.

Monday evening, 6 July

You are suffering, my most precious one. I have just learned that letters must be posted very early. Mondays and Thursdays are the only days on which the post goes from here to K. You are suffering—ah! wherever I am, there also you are with me. . . . Arrange affairs so that I may live with you. What a life!! Thus!! Without you! Pursued hither and yonder by the kindness of people that I believe I wish I deserved as little as I really do deserve it. This humility of man towards man: it pains me. And when I consider myself in relation to the universe, what I am and what it is that man calls the greatest—and yet, herein lies the divinity in man.

I weep to think that probably only on Saturday will you receive the first news of me. However much you love me, I love you more, but never hide yourself from me.

Facsimile No. 2 zu Beethovens Biographie von Anton Schindler.
(Vergl. Seite 98.)

Abends Montags am 6ten Juli —
Du leidest du mein theuerstes
Wesen — eben jezt nehme ich wahr
daß die Briefe in aller frühe
aufgegeben werden müßen.
Montags — Donnerstags —
die einzigen Täge wo
die Post von hier nach K.
geht — du leidest — Ach wo
ich bin, bist du mit mir, mit
mir und dir rede ich mache
daß ich mit dir leben kann,
welches Leben!! !! so !!!!
ohne dich — Verfolgt von
der Güte der Menschen hier
und da, die ich meine — eben so
wenig verdienen zu wollen, als
sie zu verdienen — Demuth
des Menschen gegen den
Menschen — sie schmerzt
mich — und wenn ich mich

II   Letter in Beethoven's hand dated 'Monday evening, 6 July', and supposed by Schindler to have been written to Countess Giulietta Guicciardi in 1803. It was in fact probably written in 1812 to another person whose identity has not yet been established (see p. 106, and Notes 70, 72 and 113)

SECOND PERIOD

Good night! Since I am taking the baths, I must go to bed. Ah, God! so near! so far! Is our love not truly a heavenly edifice, yet firm as the vault of heaven?

3.

Good morning on 7 July

While still in bed my thoughts hurry to you, my immortal beloved, here and there joyfully, then sadly again, waiting to know whether Fate will hear us. I can live only wholly with you or wholly apart from you. I have decided to wander far away until I can fly to your arms and say that with you I have found my true home, can send my soul enwrapped in you into the realm of spirits.

Yes, it unfortunately must be so. You will be the more resolved since you know my fidelity to you. No other can ever possess my heart—never—never. O God! why must one be separated from one so beloved? And yet my life in Vienna is a miserable one. Your love makes me at once the happiest and the unhappiest of men. At my age I need a uniformity and a regularity of life. Can this exist with our relationship?

My angel, I have just learned that the post leaves every day. Accordingly I must close at once, so that you may receive my letter the sooner.

Be calm, for only by calm consideration of our lives can we attain our objective of living together. Be calm, love me. Today, yesterday, what tearful longings for you—for you—for you, my life, my all.

Farewell! Continue to love me; never misjudge the most faithful heart of

Your beloved

Ever yours
Ever mine
Ever ours

> *There is no better, no more blessed state*
> *Than when the wife and husband in accord*
> *Order their household lovingly. Then those*
> *Repine who hate them, those who wish them well*
> *Rejoice, and they themselves the most of all.*
> *Odyssey VI*, 230–34

∼ 1804 ∼

In July 1804 the symphony No. 2 in D major and the piano concerto in C minor were first performed in the concert series at the Augarten.[73] An interval of fully four years had elapsed between the first performance of the C major symphony and this new one, enough time for the creative and ambitious artist to free himself entirely from Mozart's style and to evolve his own. This new work is proof of Beethoven's vigorous independence, yet this emancipation had already exhibited itself in Beethoven's previous works of chamber music. A pronounced personal style in melody and phrase structure is apparent as early as the opus 2 sonata in F minor or the E major Adagio in the third sonata of the same group, or in the sonata in E flat major opus 7, or even more distinctively in the movements with unifying characteristics in the C minor and D major sonatas opus 10, not to mention the *Pathétique* and the six quartets opus 18 which, entirely free from any stylistic influence, already bear the mark of the truly individual Beethoven style, as if they were the products of later years.

The tone of the AmZ's critical review of this new symphony is curious, truly strange, even in the light of its absolute dedication to the Mozart style. The Viennese critic writing here is content to call it 'a work full of new, original ideas, of great strength, sensitive in orchestration and intellectual in concept, but one that would surely benefit from the abbreviation of some passages and the total deletion of others, for the modulations are entirely too eccentric.' The new piano concerto, on the other hand, was acclaimed one of Beethoven's most beautiful works and its 'very sustained, expressive performance' by Ferdinand Ries highly praised. We should note that this concerto is reviewed from the standpoint of the performer in the seventh volume of the AmZ. This review is highly recommended for pianists who wish to gain a deeper insight into the work, for it is less a critique than an instructive treatise.

This year is one of the poorest in new publications, and no major new work appeared in print.[74] Artaria issued an arrangement of the *Prometheus* ballet music for string quartet. In connection with the numbering of this composition, it should be noted that the opus number 24 assigned to the transcription for piano solo published earlier by Cappi & Co. is undoubtedly correct, considering when the work was composed. Later catalogues that designate it as opus 43 are obviously in error.

[II]

Continuing our history of events and their ramifications in as orderly a sequence as possible, we encounter now for the first time a new and unexpected interest, one that has to do not with music but with political science. We must, however, come to expect to find our composer concerned with this area of human activity, for though it seems far removed from his essential domain, yet one side of his nature inclined irresistibly in a political direction. We shall, therefore, often find him concerned with matters of politics.

The ambassador of the French Republic to the Austrian court was at that time General Bernadotte, who later became King of Sweden.[75] His salon was frequented by distinguished persons of all ranks among whom was Beethoven, who had already expressed great admiration for the

First Consul of the Republic. The suggestion was made by the General that Beethoven should honour the greatest hero of the age in a musical composition. The idea soon became a reality which the master, having battled with his political scruples, gave to the world under the title of *Sinfonia Eroica.**

Beethoven's admiration for Napoleon was not based so much on that general's countless military victories as on his success in bringing, within a few years' space, political order out of the chaos of a bloody revolution. And the fact that this new order was founded on republican principles, even if they were not dictated by the First Consul himself, could only raise Bonaparte and the new régime in Beethoven's estimation. For Beethoven already held strong republican sympathies, personally inclined as he was towards unimpeded freedom and independence. His belief in democratic constitutions probably arose, too, from his assiduous study of the writings of Plutarch and Plato, which surely nourished republican political thought, though the republics they described resembled the order that became established in France in nothing but name.

Goethe says: 'The doers want to make the world secure; the thinkers want to make it logical.' The latter applies to Beethoven. He demanded logic for each political system according to the standards he had learned from Plato. Above all he hoped for a logical order of things in France, expecting Napoleon to apply, perhaps with some modifications, the main principles of the Platonic republic, thus laying the foundation—as he saw it—of general, world-wide happiness. May Beethoven not have had a second, more basic political objective: one which, for an intellectual like himself, was within the realms of possibility? May he not have wished to bring about a general political change in the world, including the world of art, such that the whole structure of social standards and relationships would be raised to a higher plane? We have only to remember the status of the artist in the society of that day.

The first edition of this book was rather severely criticized for its treatment of this point. The critic felt that I had not documented my theory sufficiently, but perhaps he was forgetting the fundamentals of Plato's philosophy of the state. Beethoven's interest in Plato was again contested recently by the reviewer of Oulibicheff's book, *Beethoven, seine Kritiker und seine Ausleger*. The review appeared in the supplement to the *Allgemeine Zeitung* in July, 1857, and reads:

That Beethoven should favour above all Plato's form of republic, which is based on the community of goods and wives, and which banished artists, seems more

---

* The writer knows that it was General Bernadotte's idea that Beethoven should undertake this work, because the composer said as much himself when, in 1823, he wrote a letter to the King of Sweden.[76] The circumstance will be elaborated on in the appropriate place.

difficult to believe than that he was in his heart a republican. That besides the writers of antiquity he read Shakespeare, Goethe, Schiller, and all the good German poets, that he was a daily reader of the *Allgemeine Zeitung*—how are we to reconcile all this with the Platonic republic?

Even this critic, though otherwise very cautious, seems not to have remembered accurately the essential teachings of Plato, for he appears to have echoed the Brockhaus *Encyclopedia*, where this somewhat distorted interpretation is given. It therefore seems necessary for us to review some parts of Plato's *Republic* before proceeding with the *Eroica* symphony in order to clear up some of these confused issues. The *Republic*, an interesting enough work in itself, becomes even more worthy of our attention when we realize that it corresponds well with Beethoven's political beliefs. I have before me the translation by F. Schleiermacher, the version that Beethoven also used.[77]

The first thing to notice is that all of the political theories are set forth in the form of conversations between Socrates, Glaucon, Thrasymachus, and others. Plato, far from wishing to banish the arts from his state, merely intended their purification by submitting them to controls or censorship. When at the beginning of the third book he speaks of the gods (p. 166), 'what from childhood on the young ought and what they ought not to hear', he adds: 'We must also exercise some control over the story-tellers. . . . We must ask Homer and the other poets not to be angry when we strike out certain passages, not because these passages are unpoetic or unpleasant for the people to hear, but precisely because the more poetic they are the less they should be heard by boys and girls whose spirits should be free and who should fear servitude more than death.' Plato then quotes several passages from Homer and other poets as he did at the beginning of the second book, to show which parts should be deleted because they are morally dangerous.

Continuing his treatment of the arts, Plato enters on a very engaging and, for music-lovers, very informative chapter on vocal music and its accompaniment. He states his preference among the fifteen modes for four,[78] the Ionian* and Lydian,† which he calls the soft modes, then the Dorian,‡ which he describes in the following interesting manner: 'Give me a mode whose notes and metre are appropriate to one who exhibits valour in war and strength in all conflict and who, when things go against him, when he is wounded or overtaken by death or any other misfortune, meets his fate with courage and endurance'; and the Phrygian§ to which he ascribes this characteristic:

* Our C.
† Our F, but without a flattened B.
‡ Our D without a sharpened F and C.
§ Our E without a sharpened F and, whether as ending or descending the scale, with minor sixth and minor seventh.

And then there is the mode for the man who leads a peaceful life, not of violence but of quiet pursuits, whether because he has prevailed upon and convinced another—either God by supplication or man by precept and admonition—or, on the contrary, because he has quietly submitted to the requests, teachings, and persuasions of another, showing no conceit but behaving in a cheerful and temperate manner, and is finally satisfied with the outcome of his docile bearing. Give me, then, these two modes, one violent, the other peaceful, which most beautifully imitate the tones of the happy and the unhappy, the discreet and the valorous.

(We shall remember these assigned characteristics of the various Greek modes in the section entitled 'Personal Characteristics', for there we shall speak of Beethoven's agreement with the new aestheticians who, partially inspired by these Greek principles, ascribe different personalities to our keys.)

Plato is next concerned with the musical instruments and the rhythms that he will need for his state. For the first, he rejects the harp and the dulcimer because of their many strings; the flute, too, is outlawed, and only the lyre and the kithera are retained 'for the city'. For the shepherd on the hill he recommends 'some sort of pipe'.

When he comes to metre and its function, Plato seems unsure. He says on page 188:

For there are three kinds of metre from which all the rhythms can be composed, just as of all modes there are four. I have looked into the matter and can affirm it to be so. But I am unable to say what kind of life each metre typifies. . . . Let us therefore ask Damon which rhythms inspire vulgarity, mischief, violence, and other bad behaviour, and which rhythms we ought to keep because of their good influence.

On page 190:

Should we then control only the poets, constraining them either to write so as to inspire only the highest morality or to cease their writing altogether? Or should all work be overseen so that no one would be allowed to create anything evil or undisciplined, either as a portrayal of life or in architecture or in any other work. And if there be one who cannot abide by our rules, he shall no longer be allowed to work here. . . . We must seek out talented artists and exhort them to emulate the nature of beauty and goodness in all things so that our youths will ever benefit, as if living in a healthful place, where every mild breeze brings something of beauty either for the eye or for the ear, and so from childhood on, without realizing it, they would be similarly led to friendship and agreement with beautiful discourse. . . . Is not music, then, the most important part of education? For rhythm and euphony penetrate the soul with righteousness, making the hearer righteous if he has been correctly educated, but having the opposite effect if he has not.[10]

The conversation about music closes with the sentence: 'The objective of music should therefore be love of beauty.' Later on we encounter this sentence: 'After music, our children should be educated in gymnastics,' etc.

The fifth book deals with the common possession of wives. On page 264: 'The nature of the community must be explained, for there are many possibilities.' When Glaucon asks to be enlightened on this score, Socrates asks:

Do you ask that in order to give me courage?—Yes.—The effect is, however, the opposite, for if I were absolutely certain of what I am speaking about, this conversation would be a pleasure. For reasonable and kindly men can express the truth about those things that they hold most dear without danger, but to try and express something of which one is only vaguely certain, as I am trying to do, is a delicate matter.

This is proof that Plato himself was not sure of this aspect of his political theory; moreover, he speaks in such a way that even the highly moral Beethoven could take no offence if, as a student of history, he placed himself within the mentality of pagan antiquity.* Fräulein Giannatasio refers in her notes to a conversation she had with him on this topic:

He was an extraordinary person, and his ideas and opinions on this subject were extraordinary, too. Any form of binding relationship between people, he said, was intolerable to him. He meant, as I understood it, that a person's freedom must not be restrained: he finds it far more interesting when a woman gives him her love and her all without being obliged to do so.

Does not this contradict the words we quoted earlier: 'O God! let me find someone who can strengthen my virtue; let me possess someone whose love I am allowed'? These words date from the same time as the master's frequent visits to her father's house when she had the opportunity of talking with him. This should be enough to convince the reader that there is nothing insidious in a cultured person admiring these Platonic theories. Furthermore, Beethoven's respect for these theories is in no wise incompatible with his respect for Shakespeare, Goethe, Schiller, and the *Allgemeine Zeitung*. We shall, however, see how Beethoven's republican sentiments changed in the third period as a consequence of his acquaintance with the British constitution.

After this necessary preface on Greek philosophy, let us resume the thread of our history and our discussion of the *Sinfonia Eroica*.

The fair copy of the score, with the dedication to the First Consul of the French Republic inscribed simply 'Napoleon Bonaparte' on the title-page, was ready to be given to General Bernadotte, who was to send

---

* We cannot be sure that Beethoven himself had made up his mind concerning the ecclesiastical and civil laws regarding marriage.

it to Paris, when the news reached Vienna that Napoleon had allowed himself to be proclaimed Emperor of the French. It was Count Lichnowsky and Ferdinand Ries who brought the news to Beethoven. No sooner had the composer heard it than he seized the score, tore out the title-page and, cursing the 'new tyrant', flung it on the floor.

When one considers the distance between the capitals of Austria and France, it is understandable that Napoleon's ascent to the throne should come as such a surprise, for the Viennese could have had no knowledge of the preceding plebiscite or of the fact that, according to the most recent guarantees, every act of the state had to be put into effect immediately, just as happened forty-eight years later.

It was a long time before the friends of the democracy-loving composer were able to calm his righteous anger, but finally his passions gave way to quieter reflections on what had occurred. In the end he consented to the publication of the work under the title *Sinfonia Eroica* with the sub-title 'Per festeggiare il sovvenire d'un grand Uomo.'* Yet fully two years passed before the actual publication of the symphony.

The admiration that Beethoven had felt for Napoleon was, however, no more; it had changed into hatred, and not until the emperor met his tragic end on St. Helena was the composer able to forgive him. Can we not recognize in Beethoven's obstinacy a trait inherited from his Dutch ancestors? But he was able to joke sarcastically about this earthshaking event and his change of heart. He pointed out, for example, that he had already composed the music appropriate to such a catastrophe, namely the Funeral March in the *Eroica*. He went even further in describing the symbolism of this movement, for the theme of the middle section in C major was supposed to represent a new star of hope in Napoleon's reversed fortunes (his return to the political stage in 1815), and finally the great hero's powerful decision to withstand fate until, at the moment of surrender, he sinks to the ground and allows himself to be buried like any other mortal.

When I quote his symbolic explanations, however, I do not wish to imply any literal interpretation such as that of the modern Beethoven interpreters. In fact, the master always decried with great energy all such treatment of his, or any, music as I have already mentioned and must reiterate here. He frequently drew analogies, sometimes casual ones, sometimes deeply penetrating ones, both to his close friends and to the world at large. In this particular instance, though, we must realize his political temperament at the time when he pretended to find in his Funeral March a specific association with the passing of a greatly admired person. Witty, trenchant minds like our composer's may often let fall a remark that aptly characterizes its object. Yet such a remark

* 'To honour the memory of a great man.'

116

taken out of context and broadly published can be very misleading and can result in very embarrassing consequences. We must, therefore, consider Beethoven's remarks in their true context.

⚊ 1805 ⚊

The year 1805 was one of the most productive in terms of creative output as well as a year rich in experience. In January the *Eroica* had its first performance, following the appearance of the C major symphony.[79] The AmZ (IX (1807) 321) had this to say about the new work which, because of the story of its dedication, had been awaited with great anticipation:

This long, most difficult composition is an extremely drawn-out, bold, and wild fantasy. There is no lack of striking and beautiful passages that bespeak the energetic and gifted spirit of their creator. Very often, though, the work seems to lose itself in musical anarchy. . . . This critic is surely one of Beethoven's most devoted admirers, but in the case of this symphony he must admit that he finds too many garish and bizarre elements, making an overall view most difficult and obliterating all sense of unity.[80]

There follows in contrast a eulogy of a new symphony by Eberl.* Our master was thus given to understand that he would do better to write in a similar style.

A second performance of the *Eroica*, conducted by Beethoven himself, followed closely upon the first. The same critic expressed himself thus (AmZ IX 500):

At any rate, this new work of Beethoven's has large, bold ideas and, as one would expect from a man of such genius, was powerfully executed. But the symphony would gain greatly (it lasts a full hour) if Beethoven could bring himself to cut it and to introduce more light, clarity, and unity. . . . There is, for instance, instead of the usual Andante, a Funeral March in C minor, which is then treated fugally. A fugal movement is pleasing when order can be perceived within the apparent complexity; when, as now, coherence escapes the most attentive, unprejudiced, and practised listener, even after several hearings, he is left confused. It is not, therefore, surprising that the work has not been generally well-liked.

From this review it may clearly be seen how difficult a battle this symphony had to fight in Vienna; and the battle was repeated in every city in which the work was performed. We need no witness to tell us

---

* Anton Eberl (1765–1807), who was born and died in Vienna, was one of the most renowned pianists and composers. He lived for many years in St. Petersburg, and conducted the first performance in that city of Haydn's *Creation*. In 1800 he returned to Vienna where he immediately became one of Beethoven's most dangerous rivals as a composer for piano and orchestra. None of his works have survived.

what deadly assaults it received from the old music teachers. The tremendous anger on the part of Dyonis Weber, among others, afforded our master great amusement in later years, after all these battles had been decided in favour of the symphony. At the Prague Conservatory the *Eroica* was banned as Beethoven's most 'morally corrupting' work. It was not until the early 1840's that the work was first performed at that institution: it was not until the director, old and mellowed to Beethoven's dissonances, was nearing his own final resolution that he had been 'preparing' for seventy years. All the battles over this work, in which the composer exhibits his own personality to the fullest, were finally won in a similar way.

However, there is more to be said on the subject. In addition to the unaccustomed length* of some of the movements, the dissonances that were too harsh for the aural sensitivities of the time, and the fugal section of the Funeral March, one aspect of the work that particularly incensed its scores of enemies was the melody in the fourth movement:

Ex. 2  etc.

which was still familiar from its occurrence in the finale of the *Prometheus* ballet music. Those who condemned the symphony asked how one melody could be a dance in one place and the commemoration of a hero in another. This melody had been used much earlier in a collection of quadrilles, and somewhat later we find it again as the theme of the opus 35 variations. This repeated use of a single theme presented in an unaltered form but for different purposes is the only example of its kind in the Beethoven literature. Another earlier instance of the repetition of a theme, the minuet in E flat of the septet opus 20, which we also find in G in the little sonata in G major opus 49, is hardly comparable, as it is in both cases a minuet even though it is developed differently in the final movement of the sonata. This sonata, however, is one of Beethoven's earliest compositions even though it was not published until 1805, and the minuet melody was probably first written as the sonata finale.

Only two works of major importance made their appearance in 1805: the violin sonata in A minor opus 47 and the great sonata in C major opus 53. In the former we find the first extension of the piano keyboard from five octaves to include the third G above the staff, while the latter

---

* The composer himself recognized the unusual length of the symphony. For this reason he requested in an accompanying note that it should be performed at the beginning of the programme so that the audience would be fresh and receptive to the special impact that the composer had intended. This precaution no longer seems necessary, as the work has been generally acknowledged and understood.

sonata reaches A.[81] The violin sonata was originally written for Bridge-tower, an American sea-captain with whom Beethoven was very intimate and who had spent many years in Vienna where he had become an accomplished violinist;[82] but with the appearance in Vienna of Rodolphe Kreutzer, the co-founder of the rightly named 'great French violin school', Beethoven changed his mind and dedicated the work to the French master. (Beethoven frequently changed his dedications.)

The review of the sonata opus 47 that appeared in the seventh volume of the AmZ is undoubtedly one of the most intensive criticisms of Beethoven's music. It reads in part:

To discover the inner being of this music, and to express its character in words, is impossible for me, and *erit mihi magnus Apollo* anyone who could undertake such a task successfully. I have tried, with the attention due to this composer and even to this work, to approximate an understanding of the ideas here. Having filled a whole page on the first Presto alone, though, I shall spare the readers of the AmZ the trouble of going through it.

What kind of effect must such an article have had on Beethoven? It is not conceivable that he was then so hardened as to be impervious to such obscure attacks, especially when they provided the host of his enemies with a battle cry.

During the second half of July 1805 Cherubini arrived in Vienna with his wife for the purpose of writing a new opera, *Faniska*, for the Theater an der Wien.* The issue of the AmZ for 5 August reported that the renowned composer had already conducted a performance of his older opera, *Der Wasserträger*, which was enthusiastically received by the public, and that he had made several changes in tempo, such as taking the Allegro of the overture more slowly, 'whereby this difficult piece of music gained in clarity'.

I have already said that during my sojourn in Paris in 1841 and 1842 I had the pleasure of making the acquaintance of Cherubini and his wife. As might be expected, we talked a great deal about Vienna and also about Beethoven. Mme Cherubini still had her Vienna journal, which made frequent mention of our master and their experiences with him. With almost youthful earnestness she would defend Beethoven's conduct, though it was not always praiseworthy, in the face of her husband's sharp criticism, and she would not hesitate to express her sympathy, though it was still half-hearted, for the 'brusque' Beethoven, as Cherubini characterized him. It seemed that Cherubini wished to describe the whole man and everything about him with the one word 'brusque' (moody, impetuous, irritable), for he would conclude every remark about him, every objection to him, with the refrain, 'Mais il

---

* This opera was first performed on 6 February 1806.

était toujours brusque'. His delicate mouth twisted into a sardonic smile one day when his wife asked me for a specimen of Beethoven's handwriting. One would know how Cherubini felt about the muse of his German contemporaries simply from his reaction, after his return, to *Fidelio*, even if he had not already taken every opportunity to express openly his poor opinion of the opera.

In the autumn of 1841 John Cramer came from London on an extended visit to Paris. I had the honour of making his acquaintance through Jacob Rosenhain. Cramer had spent the whole winter of 1799 to 1800 in the Austrian capital and had been very close to Beethoven. He was a frequent guest in the Cherubini household, and I met him there on several occasions when the talk was about Vienna and especially about Beethoven. The opportunity of hearing two such excellent musicians exchange reminiscences and opinions of Beethoven, one of them having but little admiration for him, the other bearing in his heart great love and respect for the master, was of great importance to me, for they spoke of a time long past and of circumstances that others had forgotten or remembered inaccurately, so that many points were unclear. I am the most indebted to Cramer for his warm sympathy towards the composer.

From these conversations I tried to learn two things in particular: the nature of Beethoven's piano playing at that time, and his social behaviour. I left the rest to chance, and was rewarded by learning all I wanted to know.*

The two musicians agreed about Beethoven's piano playing, and we shall quote them in the musical section of this volume. In their conversations about Beethoven's social behaviour, Cramer took the side of Mme Cherubini, which lent heightened interest to the discussions. But they all agreed that in unfamiliar company our composer was reserved, stiff, and seemingly haughty, whereas among friends he would be comical, lively, and sometimes even loquacious. He was fond on such occasions of giving full play to his wit and sarcasm, though he was sometimes indiscreet, especially in expressing his outspoken political and social views. Cramer and Cherubini could also remember many occasions on which he had handled objects such as glasses and coffee cups clumsily, at which point Cherubini would add his refrain, 'toujours brusque'.

All that I had learned from Beethoven's older friends was confirmed in these conversations. At the time of our stay in Paris, Cramer had already read Ferdinand Ries's astonishing observations on the subject.

---

* It is necessary to add that one of the supplements to the first edition of this book, which deals with my conversations with Cherubini and his wife, was published in 1841, just before my second journey to Paris, and therefore does not include my meetings with Cramer at Cherubini's house.

He rejected them emphatically, thinking them, as I did, the expression of an immature youth as yet incapable of understanding so unusual a man. Ries had formulated a superficial picture of his teacher, based on things that Beethoven had said in impatience, anger, and irritation. Otherwise it is inconceivable that he could have portrayed Beethoven so harshly. These passages in his *Notizen* are like smears on a clean background and should receive no further special notice.

One more bit of information I learned during my Paris sojourn seems worth repeating, for it concerns a different aspect of Beethoven's social deportment—one which women will be more competent to judge. Mme Cherubini saw the salons of Viennese high society, especially those frequented by women, through the eyes of a cultivated Parisienne dedicated to republican ideals of equality. Needless to say, she drew comparisons between her ideals and the attitudes prevailing in Germany, for we have quite recently seen evidence of how difficult it is for women of noble rank to relinquish so much as the smallest portion of their traditional prejudices, and even in the house of God put themselves on a level with other classes. How much more class-conscious in their hearts and minds must have been the Austrian princesses and countesses of the first decade of our century! We need only mention the observations of a perceptive Frenchwoman on the subject of Beethoven's reaction against this section of society. Mme Cherubini describes his outward bearing thus in her memoirs: 'He simply ridiculed their high and mighty prejudices, and showed no more deference to a princess than to a bourgeoise; he generally contented himself with a single formal phrase.' We shall speak elsewhere of his inward feelings.

'This humility of man towards man: it pains me', as Beethoven wrote to his beloved Giulietta. These few words are the key to Beethoven's whole social philosophy. Mme Cherubini had many opportunities during her nine months' stay in Vienna to notice that Beethoven's bearing with the princesses was indistinguishable from his bearing with women of any other rank. She also noticed that his exacting standards for the intelligence and sensitivity of women made such acquaintanceships very difficult for him, and social relations were always tentative and could be effaced by the slightest contrary wind, especially his relations with the very beautiful but (because they were the most prejudiced of all) obstinate women of society. Mme Cherubini told him quite candidly that his ideals were too high in this regard, and that this was the reason that he had found so little satisfaction in his relations with women, but he passed it off with a scornful or ironic rejoinder.

This aspect of Beethoven's behaviour seems to result from the nature of his character and attitudes and also from the fact of his being an artist. An artist whose works so far surpass his contemporaries' ability to comprehend them as did Beethoven's cannot judge his fellows too severely without incurring their bitter resentment. The memoirs of the honoured lady, who, as I write this, is still alive, lead us to conclude once more that many of the rebuffs in the life of our master were caused by his lack of indulgence for human frailty and social imperfection; many, too, were inherent in his manner of demanding in people more general culture than most individuals are capable of acquiring. We noted the same difficulty in his relations with the Viennese musicians.

Having recorded these candid and interesting observations made by Beethoven's friends in Paris, I turn to a presentation of the circumstances attending one particular work of our master's, a work that occupies one of the highest rungs on the ladder of his creations, a work that was his *enfant de prédilection* not because he considered it outstanding as a work of art but because its genesis and birth caused him more pain and heartbreak, though at the same time more happiness, than any other of his compositions, despite its many undeserved reverses and misfortunes. It is the opera *Fidelio* that will concern us now.

There are several sources available that will be of help in this undertaking. Friedrich Treitschke, who was for many years a close friend of Beethoven's and who collaborated with him intimately in the evolution of this passionate musical drama, wrote a brief history of the creation of the opera and of its first performances which at the same time served as a memorial dedicated to our master. Treitschke was at that time the stage manager and theatre poet for the two court theatres, and later became the manager of the imperial Burgtheater in Vienna. His article entitled 'Fidelio' was published in *Orpheus: Musikalisches Taschenbuch für das Jahr 1841*, edited by August Schmidt in Vienna. We shall concern ourselves only with the essential contents of the article in order not to be guilty of violating our guiding principle: utmost brevity in the presentation of all material. The eye and ear-witness writes:

Towards the end of 1804 Baron von Braun, the new owner of the Theater an der Wien, requested the still youthful Ludwig van Beethoven to write an opera for his theatre. The oratorio *Christus am Oelberge* had convinced him that the composer had a great deal to offer in the medium of dramatic as well as instrumental music. He was offered a fee and an apartment in the theatre building. Joseph Sonnleithner was assigned the libretto, and chose the French book *L'Amour conjugal*, although it had already been the basis for two operas, one with music by Gaveaux, the other in Italian set by Paer as *Leonore*, both of which had been translated into German. Beethoven was not intimidated by his predecessors and went to work with a will, completing the opera, as he thought, about the middle of 1805.

There arose, however, considerable difficulties of performance. The female parts could be sung satisfactorily by Fräulein Milder and Fräulein Müller, but there were no men capable of handling the male roles.* The libretto presented several apparently insoluble problems. Moreover, distant rumblings of an attack against Vienna made audiences uneasy and incapable of enjoying a work of art. The greatest efforts were put forth in order to sell the unwanted tickets. *Fidelio* had to do the best it could, and opened under no lucky star on 20 November.†

We learned to our sorrow that the work was too advanced for its time; it was misunderstood by Beethoven's friends and enemies alike. It was performed on three consecutive days, and then was not repeated until 29 March 1806. ‡ A few minor changes, such as dividing the opera into two rather than three acts, did nothing to alleviate its unfavourable reception.§ The opera was repeated once more on 10 April before it was relegated to the dust of the theatre library. A few performances at the same time in the provinces enjoyed no greater success.

I must add a few comments, for the estimable Treitschke's memory was on some points inaccurate. When he speaks of 'a few minor changes', the telescoping of three acts into two seems in itself no mean undertaking. Among other changes made for the later performances was this one: a new aria had to be written for Pizarro and the chorus because the singer refused unequivocally to sing the original one in B flat major. Furthermore, a duet in C major for Leonore and Marzelline with violin obbligato and cello accompaniment was deleted, as well as a comic trio in E flat major for Rocco, Marzelline, and Jacquino. When Treitschke says that these two songs were cut out in 1814 when he and the composer revised the book and the staging, he is in error. He was never connected with the Theater an der Wien in an official capacity, and he could not have had any part in the backstage workings of *Fidelio*.[83]

It is interesting to note that the Florestan of 1806, Herr Röckel, is still alive and well. He recently spent some time in Wiesbaden and Würzburg, and now again lives in Bath, England. As a member of the opera he must have been aware of the changes recommended by Prince Lichnowsky, and he still has in his possession the manuscript of his part, written in Beethoven's own hand. I myself was well acquainted with these events, for Count Lichnowsky frequently spoke of them in our circle of acquaintances, yet I was very grateful for Röckel's comments.

* The tenor, Demmer, had already lost his voice, and the *basso*, Meyer, had a crude voice and equally crude dramatic ability.

† The nobility had left the capital, and the populace was afraid of the enemy. The public, therefore, avoided the theatre, and the performances of *Fidelio* were attended principally by the French military.

‡ Treitschke forgot to mention here that the performances of the revised opera took place under the new name of *Leonore*.

§ This new version was mentioned in the AmZ of 1806 (col. 460): 'The opera has been improved and has made a better impression. D. V.'

On page 104 of the *Notizen* Ries speaks, on Röckel's authority, of the meeting at Prince Lichnowsky's. What he says supplements the point in question and should settle all arguments on the matter. Ries writes:

Those present at the meeting included the Prince, the Princess (who played the piano and was assuredly an excellent pianist), Hofrat von Collin, Stephan von Breuning (these two had already discussed the abridgements to be made), the principal *basso* Herr Meyer, Herr Röckel, and Beethoven. At first Beethoven defended every measure, but when everyone else agreed that whole sections must be left out, and Herr Meyer protested that no singer could perform Pizarro's aria effectively,* the composer became sullen and said no more. In the end he promised to compose a new aria for Pizarro (it became No. 7 in the *Fidelio* score),[84] and the Prince suggested that these sections should be omitted on a tentative basis for the first performance; they could always be included again or used in some other way, but to leave the opera as it stood would be to rob it of its effectiveness. After much discussion, Beethoven gave in, and the deleted passages were never again performed. The meeting lasted from 7 o'clock in the evening until 2, when the matter was closed with a congenial supper.[85]

The statement by Ries, on Röckel's authority, regarding the initial form of Florestan's aria at the beginning of the second act—that originally there was no Allegro section, but that it closed with the Adagio in $\frac{3}{4}$ time—is not correct.

Friedrich Treitschke wrote:

Eight years later (1814) the principal members of the Imperial and Royal Court Opera, Saal, Vogel, and Weinmüller, were given the opportunity to produce, for their own profit, any work of their choosing. They had, of course, to find an opera that would involve no financial outlay. The choice was a difficult one: there were no suitable new German operas, and old ones would not be attractively profitable. The recent French operas were neither good not popular, and the producers, as singers, lacked the courage to undertake an Italian work. (This was attempted a few years later, with suicidal results.) Amid all these deliberations, *Fidelio* came to mind, and the producers approached Beethoven for the loan of the score. He agreed most unselfishly, but upon the condition that many changes were made. He suggested to me that I might use my humble talents in this undertaking. I had for some time had the privilege of his close friendship, and my double duties as opera poet and stage manager made his wish a pious obligation for me.

It would be of no interest to the reader to go through the changes that Treitschke now lists in detail: how, for instance, the placement of certain passages was changed, how the properties were to be used, how

---

* We shall soon learn the reason for Meyer's objection to this aria. It is an amusing episode in the history of *Fidelio*, the only bit of comedy in an unhappy situation that caused Beethoven great depression over the first performances.

the guards were to march, how the minister was to approach, how the prisoners were to bow down before Don Fernando, etc. Friedrich Treitschke continues:

The second act presented serious difficulties right from the start. Beethoven wished to introduce the unfortunate Florestan with an aria, but I felt that a man nearly dead of hunger should hardly be expected to sing in a bravura style.*

We tried this and that; at last Beethoven felt that I had hit the nail on the head. I wrote words that described the last flickerings of life before its final extinction:

> *And do I not hear soft, gentle, whispering breezes?*
> *Does not a glow illumine this tomb?*
> *I see at my side, to comfort me,*
> *An angel in a roseate cloud.*
> *An angel so like my Leonore, my wife,*
> *To lead me to freedom in the realm of heaven!*

What I am now about to recount will always remain a vivid memory. Beethoven came to me about seven o'clock in the evening. After we had spoken of other things, he asked me how the aria was coming along. I had just finished it, and handed it to him. He read it, pacing up and down the room, murmuring, growling, as he generally did instead of singing, and threw open the piano. My wife had often begged him in vain to play for us. This day he set the aria text on the music rack and began to improvise wonderfully. What a pity there was no magical means of preserving those notes! From them he seemed to be conjuring the theme of the aria. Hours passed, but Beethoven continued to improvise. The supper that he had been invited to share with us was served but he would not be disturbed. Finally, when it was quite late, he embraced me and, refusing any food, hurried home. The next day the wonderful aria was finished.

Soon, towards the end of March, the libretto was complete, and I sent Beethoven a copy. A couple of days later he wrote me this note of acknowledgement:

'My dear T! I have read with great satisfaction your improvements to the opera. I am now determined to rebuild the desolate ruins of an old castle.

Your friend

Beethoven'

---

* Allow me to insert a strong rebuttal here. Would Beethoven introduce Florestan with a bravura aria, with runs, trills, and other like ornamentation?! Such an assumption is at complete variance with the existing autograph of this aria as it was sung in 1805 and 1806, and it would be too damaging to Beethoven for me to allow such a charge to go undenied. This aria is found in the oldest piano score of the opera (Breitkopf & Härtel) in its original form. It consists of a recitative ('Gott! welch' Dunkel hier!'), followed by the Adagio in A flat major, 3/4 time ('In des Lebens Frühlingstagen') and a third section *andante un poco agitato* ('Ach! es waren schöne Tage'). The aria remains unaltered in Otto Jahn's new vocal score based on Beethoven's autograph (with all its variations) of the original *Fidelio* (Breitkopf & Härtel). Who can say in a work of so many parts that such and such is original and so and so is an alteration, especially when, as in this opera, so much has been changed and on two different occasions? Perhaps even the composer could not say for sure. Friedrich Treitschke had absolutely no musical training, which explains how he was able to make such a statement.

The principals were pressing for completion of the opera so that they might benefit from the best season, but Beethoven was making slow progress. When I, too, wrote to him, he answered, 'This opera is the most troublesome thing in the world. I am dissatisfied with most of it—there is hardly a number which, here and there, does not need to be patched up to my satisfaction. There is a great difference between this reworking and allowing oneself to be inspired.'*

Rehearsals started in mid-April although the score was far from ready. The performance was announced for 23 May. On the 22nd the dress rehearsal took place, but the promised new overture was still in its creator's pen. The orchestra was summoned to rehearse on the morning of the opening. Beethoven did not come. After waiting for some time, I went to get him. I found him in bed, fast asleep. Beside the bed were a cup of wine and some biscuits. The sheets of the overture were scattered over the bed and the floor. A burned-out candle showed that he had worked far into the night. Obviously the overture could not be completed, and for this performance the overture to *Prometheus* was used with the announcement that 'due to unforeseen circumstances the overture must be omitted'. The large audience had no difficulty in guessing the real reasons.

You already know the rest. The opera had been thoroughly rehearsed: Beethoven conducted, but his enthusiasm often made him miss the beat,† and it was the Kapellmeister Umlauf who stood behind his back and succeeded by look and gesture in keeping everyone together. The applause was loud and grew louder with each performance. In lieu of a fee, Beethoven was to receive all the profits from the seventh performance on 18 July. To make this performance more attractive, he inserted two new pieces, a song for Rocco and a longer aria for Leonore, but since the latter impeded the pace, it was later left out. This performance, too, was very well received.

As for the 'two new pieces' supposedly composed expressly for this performance, we read in column 550 of the AmZ that one was Rocco's song, 'Gold ist eine schöne Sache', and the other Leonore's long aria in E major with obbligato for three horns. The former may indeed have been a new composition, for it does not appear in the older piano score, but once inserted it has never been taken out.[86] The aria, however, belongs to the original score, though a different version of it, which has been used ever since, was sung on 18 August 1814. We may take the word of the AmZ critic for it against that of Treitschke.

Treitschke should not have failed to mention the contribution the singers made to the success of these performances. Beethoven himself acknowledged that they had saved his opera. To give truth her due, never has a group of such excellently trained singers worked in such

---

* The last sentence was written in a hurry and its meaning is clouded. What Beethoven meant is: He would far rather write a whole new work than to have to think how to correct one written several years ago.

† This must be denied. The truth is that, despite his poor hearing, Beethoven frequently conducted large orchestral and choral groups in 1813 and 1814, and with complete competence. If he had been unable to do so, he would have put another on the podium.

complete harmony as for those 1804 presentations of *Fidelio*, either on the Viennese court stage or anywhere else. The powerful voice of Milder-Hauptmann (Leonore), then at the zenith of her career, is well known to music-lovers throughout Germany. Outside Vienna, however, the names of Michael Vogel (Pizarro) and Weinmüller (Rocco) are not known though, both as singers and as actors, they can only be described as perfect artists. Even the Italian, Radicchi (engaged for the German opera though his German was atrocious) sang the part of Florestan as if his voice, manner, and bearing were made for it. The inclusion of *Fidelio* in the present-day opera repertoires of Germany and Italy is due not merely to the lack of a work suitable for a benefit performance, nor merely to the changes made by Treitschke, but primarily to the four artists named above and to the intrinsic worth of the opera itself. Without the initiative of the three singers who requested the work, however, *Fidelio* would be unknown today.

The composer of this immortal opera was not allowed to rejoice for long over its resurrection. Hardly had he tasted the satisfaction of seeing this work that had caused him such pain finally appreciated, when the singer Milder-Hauptmann signed a lifetime contract with the Royal Opera in Berlin and bade Vienna forever adieu. Another such Leonore was never to be found. The opera was set aside, and it was eight years before it could be staged again. In the third period we shall speak of its revival. We should note here, though, an entry in one of Beethoven's journals: 'The opera *Fidelio*, March to 15 May 1814, rewritten and improved'. Let us all take note that the master considered this revision an improvement.

Let us now turn to the four overtures written for *Fidelio*. Four overtures for a single opera! *Fidelio* is the only instance of such an occurrence in the whole history of opera. 'Why did the already overburdened composer write such a quantity?' I hope that I can satisfactorily answer this question that is so often asked by the musical public; I hope that I will be able to explain once and for all the four overtures, the order of their composition, and the difference between them.

The very first overture to *Fidelio* begins:

Ex. 3

As soon as he had finished it, the composer himself was dissatisfied with his work, and his friends were of the same opinion. The piece was played by a small orchestra at Prince Lichnowsky's, and was pronounced inadequate as an introduction to the opera. The Areopagites sitting in judgement on the overture found it wanting in ideas, style, and character. It was therefore laid aside. Steiner & Company, the publishers, immediately secured the publishing rights.[87] It was not printed, however, until the 1830's, and is listed in the catalogues as the master's last work.

The next overture, also in C major, was the one that was actually performed with the opera in 1805. It opens with an Allegro:

Ex. 4

A considerable portion of this version was always spoiled by the woodwinds. The cello theme, which is introduced by the violins:

Ex. 5

alternated with this:

Ex. 6

both then pass to the winds, which play the two themes antiphonally while the first violins (doubled by the violas an octave lower) repeat the rising figure heard at the beginning of the overture:

Ex. 7

(see pp. 52–57 of the score).

Rather than simply cutting out this obstacle to good performance (31 measures), Beethoven (since he was already rewriting other parts of the opera) decided to revise the whole overture. He retained the themes of the Introduction and the Allegro and, to give the latter a richer tone, made the cellos and the first violins play it together. Using the material of the second overture, he constructed a new one with the addition of several new ideas. With this altered overture, the revised version of the opera opened in March 1806.*

---

* Cherubini, who attended the first performances of *Fidelio* in 1805 and 1806, told the Paris musicians that this overture was so full of modulations that he could no longer tell what the fundamental key was. This bit of undeserved criticism was never forgiven him.

The overture in its new form had gained so much new material that it was considered by those competent to judge to be too long for an opera overture. We can surmise from various indications that Beethoven agreed with them. Most listeners preferred the earlier version because it stated the same main ideas more briefly and was more consistent with the traditional opera overture, whereas the revised version was called a 'concert overture'. Moreover, the strings as well as the woodwind were unable to perform the running passage at the end of the overture (in the revised version it was even marked *presto*) to the satisfaction of the composer. For all these reasons, when the opera was revived in 1814, Beethoven composed for it a fourth overture in E major that would present the orchestra with no particular problems:

Ex. 8

This overture is, however, the least suited of the four for use as an opera introduction; it is far more typical of the concert overture in style. The master is indeed an enigma. The second version of the C major overture was published as early as 1810 by Breitkopf & Härtel. It has since become the decided favourite of all orchestras because it offers them the opportunity of exhibiting their great facility and sometimes, alas!, their virtuosity.

Shortly before his death Beethoven entrusted to me the score of the original *Fidelio* overture (actually the second of the four) along with all the opera parts he had, with the specific injunction that I should keep the whole bundle in a safe place.* This request is significant, for he had not shown concern about the preservation of any of his other manuscripts. Close examination of this score revealed several cuts and alterations: the Introduction had a different ending and the recurring trumpet fanfare in the Allegro and the running figure for the strings in the Finale were both crossed out.[88] It is clear that these cuts had been made by the master himself, though there is no apparent reason for his having made them. At any rate, one had the feeling that the overture had been mutilated. In 1852 Professor Otto Jahn, in the course of some research work in Vienna, happened to come across a fair copy of the complete score of this overture in the Artaria publishing house. It was immediately printed by Breitkopf & Härtel. A comparison of this original overture with the revised version will afford the musician as

* It has resided since 1845 in the Royal Library in Berlin.

much pleasure as comparing the woodwind octet with its child, the string quintet in E flat major opus 4. A study of both revisions is heartily to be recommended.

If the sensitive A. B. Marx declares his preference for the first *Fidelio* overture, let me for my part adopt the second. On page 356 of the first volume of his *Beethoven, Leben und Schaffen*, Marx writes: 'Beethoven was inspired; he was in love with his Leonore when he composed the first overture.' As for his being in love, it cannot be denied; the intensity of the music betrays it, though the characters are drawn only in vague outline. Of inspiration, however, true Beethovenian inspiration, there is very little. What a powerful, what a perfectly integrated portrait, on the other hand, we have in the second overture, a portrait with sublime features (none of them overdrawn as in the case of the revised version) which the master unified into a single penetrating expression, just as he was to do later in the *Coriolanus* and *Egmont* overtures!

But we should see how the composer himself evaluated each of these two overtures. In respect to the first we would do well to remember the sentence from Beethoven's letter to Matthisson that is quoted at the end of the first period: 'The more progress an artist makes, the less satisfied he is with his earlier works.' It is true that our master frequently went to excesses in the matter of dissatisfaction with his work, so that, as in the case of the quintet for piano and winds, opus 16, his self-doubt would sometimes drive him to do violence to an earlier composition. We may ascribe to this severity the fact that he forgot all about the first *Leonore* overture until the year 1823. We shall have more to say about that occasion when we come to it. Remember, though, that it was the second overture that, along with a bundle containing the rest of the opera, he entrusted to me for safe-keeping.

When Marx goes on to attribute the rejection of the first overture to the influence of Beethoven's friends who convinced him that 'only the greatest, the mightiest, the most extraordinary music was expected of him', and when he adds to this that 'the second and third overtures are no longer prologues to an opera but symphonic works inspired by the ideas in the opera', he is making bold conjectures such as frequently flow from the pen of the musicologist. Only when Beethoven's own intention or inclination in regard to an act was in agreement with his friends' wishes or, better yet, only when he had openly declared his intentions or inclinations, as in the case of the first overture, could anyone else induce him to sit down at his desk. Otherwise he never exhibited the least accommodation or compliance; certainly coercion would have no effect whatsoever on him. If only Marx could have spent a week in Beethoven's company and heard him talk!

I promised in a footnote a few pages earlier to give the real reason for the rejection of the first aria written for Pizarro and chorus. This amusing anecdote involving the *basso* Meyer* and his aria is a fitting conclusion to this rather extensive section on *Fidelio*, for it is typical of a kind of experience that occurred several times in Beethoven's life.

We have already heard Treitschke's observation that when the various roles were assigned, the male singers left much to be desired. Meyer, however, had an exalted opinion of his own ability, perhaps because he had been good as Sarastro and perhaps, too, because he was related by marriage to Mozart. He made much of this relationship, and felt himself capable of anything. Beethoven resolved to cure this man of his overbearing conceit. How did he go about such a thing? By a simple but strange and drastically effective means.

There occurred in the aria the following passage:

Ex. 9

As one can see from this example, the voice moves over a series of scales played by all the strings in such a way that accompanying each new note in his part the singer must hear the orchestra's appoggiatura of a minor second. A singer who is firmly in the saddle will not be thrown by a frisky colt such as this. Our Pizarro of 1805, however, could not, despite all kinds of contortions and gestures, make his way safely through the dangerous passage, especially when some of the players were mischievous enough to accent the offending minor second. The outraged Pizarro was thus at the mercy of the bows of the fiddlers

---

* Friedrich Sebastian Meyer (1773–1835). [Editor's note. Schindler uses the spelling 'Meier' throughout.]

throughout the whole passage. This caused laughter; the singer, humiliated at having been forced to demonstrate his incompetence, emitted a bellow and let fly insults at the whole gathering including the composer: 'My brother-in-law would never have written such damned nonsense!'*

This single comic incident in the otherwise dreary proceedings having to do with the 1805 production of *Fidelio* continued to amuse our master years afterwards, particularly when he would chance to meet his old Pizarro on the street. Does not this remind one of the youthful prank played on the singer Heller in Bonn that was recorded in the first period? In any case, the practical joke of which Meyer was victim had a happy outcome, for the aria that replaced the insignificant one in B flat major is as fine a piece of music as any in the opera.

Having recorded the most important events in the genesis of an opera which in our day is one of the most esteemed, it remains only to make a few comments on Beethoven as a composer of songs, for the subject is relevant.

The opening sentences of Treitschke's article on *Fidelio* suggest that Beethoven's *Christus am Oelberge* recommended him as an operatic composer; that is, he not only had exhibited his talent for dramatic music, but had shown that he knew how to write for the voice. What techniques he had not already completely mastered would surely be learned in the composing of a large work. It is generally agreed, and with justification, that the ability to write good vocal music has seldom been the lot of the instrumental composer, especially when he himself is a pianist. All observations seem to indicate that vocal music is the most difficult of all to write. That one must become completely familiar with the physiology of the voice and the rules of song-writing imposes limitations on the art of vocal composition that are as inexorable as a primary law of nature, and no vocal score should ever reach the light of day if it does not satisfy this minimal prerequisite. Otherwise we get results such as those we find abounding in our time: almost all German composers from Carl Maria von Weber on have treated the voice to a greater or lesser degree as though it were an instrument.

In respect to Beethoven, there can be no doubt that the restrictions imposed by the composition of vocal music must have been most burdensome, both because of the natural bent of his genius for instrumental music as the medium allowing his fantasy the broadest freedom, and because he was so deeply imbued with piano music. Accustomed as he was to yielding to the impulses of his fantasy, restrained only by the rules of harmony and rhythm and the idiom of the instrument, and being

---

* Meyer's wife was the eldest sister of Frau Mozart. It was for her that the role of Queen of the Night was written.

moreover unable himself to sing a single true note, he must have had to do continual battle with himself in order to produce *Fidelio*.

On hearing *Fidelio*, Cherubini concluded that the composer was insufficiently schooled in the art of vocal writing. He did not lay the blame on Salieri, Beethoven's teacher of vocal composition, for Cherubini had already heard from him how matters stood with this pupil. The French master, who was at least ten years Beethoven's senior, accordingly took the liberty of recommending that he undertake further study of writing for the voice. To this end, he ordered a copy of the textbook used at the Paris Conservatoire and presented it to the Viennese composer.* The authors of the text are Méhul, Adam, Jadin, Gossec, Catel, Cobert, Eler, and Cherubini.

If one examines the vocal compositions that preceded *Fidelio* (Cherubini was not acquainted with them): *Adelaide, Christus am Oelberge*, and the six songs by Gellert, it is immediately apparent that in all cases the voices are handled with thorough understanding of their specific characteristics. How well, for instance, the vowels *e* and *i* are differentiated when they are used in the soprano and tenor parts, a detail that C. M. von Weber and later composers largely ignored. It is true that this was less rigidly observed in *Fidelio*, but it was never violated without reason. What was it, then, that caused the singers to complain and argue over almost every section? The real stumbling block was Beethoven's obstinate insistence that everything he had written was good and singable, and neither humble suggestions nor diplomatic entreaties could induce him to change a note.†

The author heard the singers' viewpoint from Frau Milder-Hauptmann, who told him of these proceedings when they met in Aachen in 1836. She recalled that even she had had to struggle with the master, mainly because of the ugly, unsingable passages that strained her voice in the *adagio* section of the E major aria. Her remonstrances were, however, of no avail until in 1814 she flatly refused to walk on to the stage unless the aria were rewritten. That ultimatum brought the desired result. A comparison between the present aria and the original prompts one to be as thankful to this singer as to the *basso* Meyer for his similar victory. The contents of the note to Treitschke: 'This opera is the most troublesome thing in the world', now need no further explanation, for the cause of the composer's despondency is clear. For all this, the experience gained through these struggles was of great benefit to the tenacious master, although sometimes against his will, and had he

---

* This book remained in the master's small personal library until his last days. Beside it stood the six sections of the German translation of the same textbook, published by Breitkopf & Härtel.[89]

† This observation refers, of course, to the first version of *Fidelio*, not to the one that is sung today.

had occasion to write a second opera, he would certainly have profited from the lessons of the first.

As for the pecuniary benefits accruing to the composer after all these difficulties, they were lamentably small. Perhaps this was the first instance in Austria of the composer of an opera stipulating to a theatre management a fee of a certain percentage of the proceeds from each performance. As we have seen, however, the upper classes had left Vienna because of the enemy invasion, so that the theatre audiences were depleted. Add to this the poor reception on the part of the public who filled the house only for the first performance of each series, three in November 1805 and about the same number in March 1806, and the reader will not be surprised to learn that Beethoven's percentage did not amount to two hundred gulden.

The period of five years just described in which the artist and the man had to withstand so many severe trials may be characterized by a passage copied out in Beethoven's own hand from Christian Sturm's work of teaching and edification. It is a passage that reveals much about the composer's religious feelings:

I must acknowledge Thy goodness, for Thou hast tried every means of bringing me unto Thee. Sometimes Thou madest me to feel the heavy hand of Thy anger; Thou hast, by various chastisements, humbled my proud heart. Sickness and other misfortunes hast Thou inflicted upon me so that I might realize my transgressions. . . . I have but one prayer, O God: do not cease to work to make me better. Let me be fruitful only in the good works that Thou wouldst have me do. (Sturm: *Betrachtungen über die Werke Gottes* (9th ed., 1827) I 197).

Perhaps in the following years we shall see a change for the better in Beethoven's circumstances and his relations with other people.

[III]

━ 1806 ━

It was necessary to treat all the circumstances having to do with the opera *Fidelio* as a unit. It was therefore impossible to keep this narrative within a strictly chronological framework. The first portion of that chapter dealt, as we have seen, with the years 1805 and 1806. At that point we had to skip several years in the tone-poet's life. If the composition of the opera wearied him so that he needed rest, it took very little time, as we shall see, for him to recover. Indeed, the master's creativity appears from this point on to be as rich as if not a drop had been drawn from this deep well. It might have been surprising if several years had elapsed between the composition of *Fidelio* and the many new works, but in actual fact barely a few months intervened.

The first work to follow the exertions over *Fidelio* was the sonata in F minor opus 57.[90] It is a work that has won much admiration, for in unity of character it has very few equals among the piano sonatas. The master wrote it at a single stroke while taking a short holiday at the estate of his friend, Count Brunsvik,* to whom the sonata is dedicated. It is worth mentioning that in this work the piano reaches to the second C above the staff. Piano manufacturers did not extend the keyboard beyond this note for over ten years.[91] (According to F. Ries, the piano concerto in G major, designated as opus 58, was written in 1804 immediately before *Leonore-Fidelio*. It has not been possible to ascertain the exact date of its composition.[92])

The first war with France had a detrimental effect on the social life of the Austrian capital and therefore on the artistic life as well. Even the beloved morning concerts in the Augarten were discontinued, for the nobility and a large section of the music-loving public had remained in the country even after the French army had withdrawn. Private concerts were out of the question because of the expense, since no musician would appear before an audience without an adequate orchestra. It was characteristic of the period that the various musical genres were strictly separated. It was therefore not as simple for an artist to give a concert as it is today. The present-day anomaly of programming a song or a piano piece next to a symphony, turning the orchestra into an involuntary audience, was unknown at that time, and it bespeaks the truly cultivated taste of that era that such nonsense would not have been tolerated.

As winter approached, Viennese society began to gather once more. Franz Clement,† leader of the orchestra at the Theater an der Wien and one of the most gifted musicians of his day, was the first to give a large orchestral concert. For this occasion Beethoven gave him the violin concerto in D major that he had just completed: this is famous for its artistic peculiarities (use of short bow strokes, following the old Italian school of Tartini and Nardini, and predominant use of the highest

* On page 99 of his *Notizen*, Ries says that he heard Beethoven himself play the finale of this sonata, but does not tell us the date on which this occurred. We may deduce that the sonata was already worked out in the composer's mind before it was put on paper at the Count's estate in Hungary. The master had been occupied for the whole preceding year with his opera.

† Franz Clement (also written Klement) was born in Vienna in 1780 and died there in 1842. Both in Austria and abroad, he was probably the most admired child prodigy since Mozart. His most amazing facility was his memory which surpassed any other in the history of music. Seyfried says of him in Schilling's *Encyclopedia*: 'He was endowed with a memory of such powers that in a few rehearsals he memorized complete scores down to the last detail of orchestration.' A famous incident involving Cherubini illustrates this point. The French master wanted to put this well-known talent of Clement's to the test. After the third rehearsal of his opera *Faniska* he asked the conductor to play from memory some piece from the opera on the piano. Clement complied by playing not merely one piece but half the opera. And that was not all. The next day Clement brought Cherubini one of the most difficult numbers in the opera written out in full score. Cherubini told me of this incident, noting that he had never encountered anyone who could even approach such powers of memory.

positions). The concerto enjoyed no great success. When it was repeated the following year it was more favourably received, but Beethoven decided to rewrite it as a piano concerto. As such, however, it was totally ignored: violinists and pianists alike rejected the work as unrewarding (a fate it has shared with almost all of Beethoven's piano works until the present time). The violinists even complained that it was unplayable, for they shrank from the frequent use of the upper positions. This marvellous work has only recently come into its own in its original form.

The only other major work that was published during this year was the sonata in F major opus 54.[93] The fact that the keyboard used in this work does not exceed five octaves may be an indication that the sonata was composed several years earlier and should be numbered before opus 47. How the Leipzig critic would kick himself if he could today reread the severe words he wrote about this sonata! After the man says that the two movements of which it consists 'are again filled with amazing vagaries', he goes on:

Others have written often in these pages of Beethoven's idiosyncrasies, praising some and decrying others, and even the most dedicated admirers of his truly great genius have complained of them elsewhere. Yet he continues to flaunt his disdain of all criticism. There is nothing to add here except to remark that this new work offers much of the same kind of material as that which inspired the criticisms of its predecessors (AmZ VIII (1806) 639).

▬ 1807 ▬

We now come to the extremely productive year 1807, in which we shall have much to speak of.

The violin concerto was immediately followed by the composition of the fourth symphony in B flat major.* Next came the completion of the three quartets in F major, E minor, and C major, opus 59. This set of quartets had been 'started on 26 May 1806', as it says on the first page of the manuscript, but the work was laid aside for several months. Then followed the *Coriolanus* overture. All these works were composed during the winter of 1806–7.

In February[95] the new symphony was performed at a benefit concert for the composer, for which, contrary to present-day usage, subscriptions had been solicited. The rest of the programme consisted of Beethoven's other three symphonies, in C, D and E flat, a programme that surely made great demands on its hearers and would seem daring in our time even though all of these works are now familiar to concert goers.†

---

* The composition of this symphony was wrongly dated in the first edition of this book, which placed it immediately after *Fidelio* in the year 1806.[94]

† We shall soon learn of another and far greater demand made on an audience.

That audiences of that time did not shrink from such a programme seems to indicate clearly the favourable reaction of the general public to Beethoven's orchestral music, as even the critics conceded. It also bears witness to the appreciation already accorded to the master's compositions in general and no less to the level of culture that prevailed at the time. The composer had the pleasure of seeing the immediate success of his new symphony. Its impact was stronger than any of the others, stronger even than that of the first symphony in C major, which had made its début eight years earlier. The Viennese critics hailed the new work without reserve or qualification, an honour that had been granted to almost no other instrumental composition by Beethoven. Another work created in the year 1807 was the mass in C major, written for Prince Esterházy. Later on we shall have the opportunity of demonstrating how very high Beethoven had climbed in the esteem of the public from the beginning of the first period to this point in his life.

We still have the original manuscript of a contract between Beethoven and Muzio Clementi, the famous pianist, composer, and founder of a large music publishing house in London. The contract is dated at Vienna, 20 April 1807, and is signed by the two contracting parties with Baron Gleichenstein as witness. According to this contract, Clementi was to pay the sum of £200 sterling for the right to publish the following works in England: the three quartets opus 59, the fourth symphony, the *Coriolanus* overture, the fourth piano concerto in G major, the violin concerto in D major, and the arrangement of the violin concerto as a piano concerto. By this contract Clementi further agreed to pay the sum of £60 for three sonatas still to be composed.

Our master was the recipient of many valuable gifts, all of which, however, soon disappeared. The friends closest to him used to say that the 'evil genius' was capable not only of driving kindly disposed persons from Beethoven's presence but also of putting a distance between him and his treasures. When asked what had become of this ring or that watch, Beethoven would generally reply after a moment's reflection, 'I do not know.' He knew very well where they had gone but was reluctant to accuse his brothers openly.

Towards autumn of this year we find the Viennese society that had been dispersed as a consequence of the war gathering again in the capital, and with a renewed vigour that resulted in the formation of an association for large concerts. The banker, Hering, who was known to all music-lovers as an accomplished violinist, became the conductor of a large orchestra made up almost entirely of amateurs, many of them members of the aristocracy. The orchestra met in the Mehlgrube Hall (now the Hotel Muntsch). Soon, however, this meeting place became too small, and the newly formed orchestra had to leave this acoustically excellent room for the University auditorium, whose acoustics were very poor. After only a few weeks Hering gave up his place because of various misunderstandings, and was replaced by Franz Clement, the experienced leader of large orchestras. The change was one for the better.

Beethoven, too, became associated with this society of devoted music-lovers. At a December meeting of the group he himself conducted the *Eroica* symphony and the première of the *Coriolanus* overture. At a later gathering he conducted his B flat major symphony, which was greeted this time with far louder applause than when it was first performed.

In 1807 the *Eroica* symphony, opus 55, the great sonata in F minor, opus 57, and the *Thirty-two Variations in C minor* were published.[96] How it happened that the last of these works was never given an opus number, but instead appears in the catalogues as No. 36, cannot be determined. This oversight can be explained only by the disorder that already characterized the numbering of Beethoven's works in respect to both their dates of composition and their dates of publication. The venomous attacks made on the first two of the above-named works in the AmZ are again of the strangest kind. Even considering the artistic taste of the time, it is most difficult to believe in the impartiality of a critic who writes as this one does of so richly original a work as the first movement of the F minor sonata. The following excerpts may amuse the reader.

Everyone knows Beethoven's method of composing a major sonata; and in all of them, in his most multitudinous ways of presenting bizarre material, Beethoven generally adheres to the same method. In the first movement of this sonata he has once again released many evil spirits similar to those already familiar through their appearance in other major sonatas. But truly, this time it is worth the trouble of fighting to overcome not only the extreme difficulties of the piece but also the repugnance that one frequently feels over forced waywardness and eccentricity! We have already spoken so often of these vagaries of the master's fantasy that we have nothing new to add here.

On the other hand, the second movement, Andante con moto, and the third, Allegro ma non troppo, find favour with the rigorous critic; he even expresses pleasure at hearing them. In this third movement the critic finds 'none of that choppiness and artificiality that are characteristic of several of Beethoven's other strong and vigorous finales' (!?) (AmZ IX (1807) 433).

The review of the *Eroica* deserves to be quoted in part:

Just as surely as some of Beethoven's smaller works may justly be reproached for being over-contrived, weird, and unnecessarily difficult to perform, or because they have practically nothing to say or perhaps nothing that could not be said as well or better if it were expressed more simply, more naturally, more lightly; just as surely, I say, he will ignore all such reproaches when it comes to writing a piece like this one, filled with insurmountable difficulties even for the thoughtful hearer and the practised musician. A conversation about everyday things should not be obscure, difficult, or long; he, though, who demands that the expression of lofty, abstract material be exhaustive and at the same time as easy, pleasant, and brief as such a conversation, that man demands the impossible, and usually does not know himself what it is that he wants. This is not to say that the work is not superlative throughout, nor that Beethoven's genius does not exhibit its character even in this work, for his particular idiosyncrasy consists in writing music that, where mechanical and technical aspects are concerned, is impossible to perform adequately, either for the instruments or for the hands. As for the artistic and aesthetic aspects, the genius himself is even here not limited by tradition but only by the unalterable laws of man's aesthetic capacities; and when he, the genius, characteristically demands more than is consistent with these laws, this characteristic itself must be remembered, so that the genius makes himself a law in order that his works shall not be chaos. However, as soon as this composition becomes known, it is sure to give rise to a whole multitude of excerpts and arrangements.

(AmZ IX (1807) 321.)[97]

What must have been Beethoven's reaction to this evaluation of his stylistic traits, an evaluation that in all probability had been turned out at the editor's desk? As to the 'multitude of excerpts and arrangements', however, the critic guessed right: the catalogue lists no less than fifteen of them.

Another article containing reviews of both the *Eroica* and the B flat major symphonies appears in a Supplement in this book.[98] Written by Carl Maria von Weber, it is very different in both form and content from the one in the AmZ.

⟶ 1808 ⟵

For the attentive observer of a great genius, it is an interesting undertaking to trace his development from stage to stage and to observe his approach to perfection until he reaches such heights that no further ascent is possible. Such an observer is like a mountain climber who hour by hour sees himself nearing heights that appear to be unsurpassed when suddenly in his progress he is confronted by gigantic peaks which he knows, even without mathematical calculations, must be the highest pinnacles for many miles around. It seems to the author as though we have reached the point in the unfolding of Beethoven's genius that would in the material world be called the summit. We have watched his rapid progress from one work to the next, usually achieving greater altitudes with each flight, until he seems to have exhausted every expression of tone and harmony. We stop at the completion of the fourth symphony to take a look at the limited view we have, and yet these heights that so inspire us are only the foothills.

There can be no doubt that the year 1808 represents the midsummer of Beethoven's career, the climax of his creative power, the point of perfection. It is moving to read the following excerpt from Christian Sturm's *Lehr- und Erbauungsbuch* copied out in one of the composer's journals:

> Soon I shall reach the autumn of my life. I should like to be like one of those fruit-bearing trees that drop ripe fruits into our laps. But in the winter of my life when I shall be grey and tired of living, I should like my repose to be as honourable and as beneficial as Nature's repose in winter.*

Does it not appear that Beethoven himself recognized his own midsummer period when he singled out this passage from Sturm's book? Yet it must be remembered that the duration of his greatest creative power was not limited to the year 1808 but maintained itself at a uniform height for several years. Let us tarry a while beneath the tree that bears the name of our master and see what fruits he brought forth during this year.

The summer concerts in the Augarten included the first performance of the *Concertino* for piano, violin, and cello. It was accorded a very poor reception because the performers took the piece too casually. It was not heard again until 1830, when it was performed with great success at the *Concerts spirituels* by the artists Bocklet, Mayseder, and Merk. The work was composed for Archduke Rudolph and the musicians Seidler (violin) and Kraft (cello).

It was not until 22 December that the public was given proof of the extraordinary productiveness of this year. On this day the master conducted a concert in the Theater an der Wien at which the following works were first performed. The AmZ records the exact wording of the programme:[99]

I.

1. *Pastoral* symphony (No. 5). Not so much a painting as the expression of feelings.
2. Aria.
3. Hymn with Latin text, written in church style with chorus and solos.
4. Piano concerto played by himself.

* From the chapter: 'Nature's Winter Repose' (I 49).

II.

1. Symphony in C minor (No. 6).
2. 'Holy' (Heilig), with Latin text, written in church style with chorus and solos.*
3. Improvisation for piano alone.
4. Improvisation for piano with gradual entrance of the orchestra and finally a choral section and finale. (The reader will recognize this last work as the so-called *Choral Fantasy*, opus 80.)

On glancing over this programme, the reader will be surprised to see the *Pastoral* symphony called No. 5 and the C minor No. 6, for it is the other way round on the title-pages as published. Undoubtedly there was a reason for the above numbering. Since Beethoven was not infrequently involved in the simultaneous composition of two or even three works, sometimes all of different types, we may assume that he worked on both symphonies at the same time. It is probable, however, that the C minor symphony was the first to reach completion and was therefore, upon publication, placed before the *Pastoral*.†

The reaction of the audience to all these works was hardly the applause that had been hoped for, yet the composer himself might well have expected no greater success. For the power to comprehend so much and such extraordinary music simply was not there; moreover, faulty performance kept the audience from giving the music its undivided attention. In fact, the *Choral Fantasy* fell completely to pieces. A particular circumstance that obtained at that time (and still does) explains why Beethoven had to offer so much new music in a single concert. One must realize that the composer of long works whose performance calls for large groups of instruments or voices had at his disposal only two opportunities a year: the first two days of the week before Easter and the last two days before Christmas. On these days the Viennese theatres were available for concerts. The demand, however, was great, and several influential organizations, including an old corporation of artists, contended for these opportune days. It was therefore almost impossible to secure a theatre for more than one day a year. Our master's difficulties in taking advantage of these so-called *Norma-*

---

* This was the Sanctus and Benedictus from the mass in C major that had been composed the year before. At that time the strange rules of the Viennese censor forbade the use of Latin words from the liturgy on theatre posters, but allowed settings of the Latin texts to be sung in theatres. In 1824, however, we find censorship far more rigid, a fact that we may take as an indirect indication that during the intervening sixteen years the Austrian people had taken a step backwards culturally rather than progressing. Why else would we find censorship?

† Again in 1813 the C minor symphony was performed in Vienna and recorded in the Viennese notices of the AmZ (XV (1813) 416) as No. 6, although both works had been published in 1809, with the *Pastoral* designated as No. 6 and the C minor as No. 5.

Tage were compounded by the fact that the orchestra and chorus put at his disposal generally had to be augmented to perform his music. And then there were the inevitably huge expenses! Some bills dating from 1814 will give the reader an idea of the expenses that Beethoven incurred for a concert.

These difficulties in presenting a concert seem sufficiently discouraging, yet we have not yet mentioned the one that plagued the master most of all, for it was a decisive factor in the life or death of any musical work performed. All German orchestras right up to the present day have this sin in common: they are insufficiently and poorly rehearsed. Even if Beethoven, who had no official jurisdiction over the orchestra, had been willing to sacrifice all financial benefit to achieve the best possible performance of his music, he would not have been able to wring it out of the musicians. If the composer was able to get them to play the correct notes in one, or at the most two, rehearsals, he had to be satisfied with the results. As for any notion whatsoever of deeper nuances, Viennese orchestras lacked both the capacity and the interest. This chapter in the personal experiences of the great master was one of the most painful, and could not have failed to leave scars that he bore till the end of his days.

The AmZ's critic had this to say about the unhappy première of the *Choral Fantasy* at this concert:

The wind instruments varied the theme that Beethoven had introduced on the piano. Then it was the oboes' turn. The clarinets counted wrong and came in too soon. A curious mixture of notes resulted. Beethoven jumped up and tried to make the clarinets stop playing. He could not get their attention until he shouted unnecessarily loudly at the whole orchestra: 'Quiet, quiet! It won't do! From the beginning, from the beginning!' And the orchestra had nothing to do but start the unfortunate fantasy all over again.*

This account by an eye-witness should be compared with the version that Ries gives in his *Notizen* (p. 83):

Beethoven gave a grand concert in the Theater an der Wien, at which were performed for the first time his C minor and *Pastoral* symphonies and his *Fantasy* for piano with orchestra and chorus. During the last of these, the clarinettist made a mistake at the point at which the last beguiling theme is varied, and repeated eight measures. Since only a few instruments were playing, the error was all the more conspicuous. Beethoven sprang up in a rage, cursing the musicians in the crudest terms in a voice loud enough to be heard by the whole audience. At last he shouted, 'From the beginning!' The theme was recommenced, everything went well, and the success was brilliant.[100]

* J. F. Reichardt, who was in Vienna at this time, gives a similar account of this incident in his *Intimate Letters from Vienna*. He gives the whole programme for this 22 December concert, including the aria, 'Ah perfido!' sung by Fräulein Killitschky (Schuppanzigh's niece), who later went to the Royal Opera in Berlin and under the name of Frau Schultz was for many years a shining light of this artistic institution.

This comparison demonstrates with lamentable clarity the gaudy colours that Ries chose in which to paint his biographical portrait. Would not one suppose that he wrote in anger and, here at least, on hearsay? Yet Ries was present at the concert of 22 December 1808. Would it not have been more seemly of Beethoven's pupil and friend to relate this incident honourably, to say something of the new compositions which noticeably impressed the musicians, or at least those among them who were kindly disposed towards the composer? But no, only this dry note, couched in terms that an enemy of Beethoven would have used. And to crown it all, that last remark! Truly, it gives one cause to wonder.

Up to this point we have had occasion to become familiar with those characteristics of the composer that to a greater or lesser extent affected his intellect and his intellectual achievements. We have considered his religious and political views and have seen that they rested on foundations of firm principle. We have observed his social behaviour which, though quite different from that of other artists, can only be considered estimable, since it had an ethical basis and was consistent with his total character. Now we must look at yet another trait, one that influenced no less his temperament, his creativeness, and his music itself. It is of Beethoven as a nature-lover that we shall now speak.

Once more we may call as our witness that much-quoted book of sermons by Christian Sturm. In the essay entitled 'Nature as a School for the Heart' (II, p. 493) we find the following excerpt underlined:

One may truthfully call nature a school for the heart, for she teaches us in a very enlightened manner the obligations to God, to ourselves, and to our fellow man that it is our duty to fulfil. . . . From now on I wish to be a pupil of this school, to bring for instruction there a hearty thirst for knowledge. Here shall I learn wisdom without cynicism. Here shall I learn to know God and in this knowledge of Him to find a foretaste of heaven.

It would be a grave error to suppose that Beethoven's love of the out-of-doors was merely the result of a predilection for beautiful scenery or of a need for physical exercise. Even if we had no testimony but the way in which he studied the many and various natural phenomena discussed in the above-quoted textbook, we could be sure that he mastered at an early age the art of reading the great book of nature and understanding all its manifestations.* The present author, who had the great pleasure of accompanying Beethoven on countless walks through the open country over hills and dales, is moreover in a position to state that the master was frequently his nature guide and this instruction was generally more enthusiastic and lengthy than his musical teaching.

* Besides the Reutlinger edition of Sturm's book (1811), Beethoven had another, older edition. The dog-eared condition of the book showed how much Beethoven occupied himself with it.

Let us put it more clearly by saying that in Beethoven we have a man in whom nature was fully personified. It was not so much the laws of nature that fascinated him as its elemental power, while the only aspect of his total pleasure in nature that preoccupied him was his own emotional response. In this way he became totally sensitive to the power of nature, and thus able to compose a work that has no peer in the whole of musical literature, a tone-painting in which the listener is made to see both scenes from life in society with his fellows and scenes from nature: the *Pastoral* symphony.

To write of this work of artistic philosophy is for me a great joy, for the composer himself instructed me concerning its composition and particular features. I have even walked by his side over the ground where he found the inspiration to write the symphony. It would be utterly superfluous to enter upon an explanation of the work, for it is self-explanatory throughout and has long been familiar to music-lovers. However, it will not be superfluous to make a few comments designed to clarify the composer's intentions regarding two sections, especially as they have never been made elsewhere.

The *Pastoral* symphony, like the C minor, was written in Heiligenstadt, a place whose name the reader will recognize from the events of 1802. This village, which is situated on the right bank of the Danube, was at that time the master's habitual summer retreat, and it was not until several years later that he chose the resorts to the south of the capital, Hetzendorf, Mödling, and Baden, the latter two being recommended for their baths by his doctors.[101]

One day in the latter half of April 1823, a time of many troubles and reverses, Beethoven decided to take a respite by returning north to Heiligenstadt and its lovely surroundings. It was a place where he had put many musical works on paper and where, too, he had conducted his studies of nature; but he had not been there for ten years. The sun shone warmly and the landscape was already arrayed in its most beautiful spring finery. After we had seen the Heiligenstadt spa with its striking gardens and other pleasant sights, and had reminisced about the works composed there, we turned our steps towards the Kahlenberg in the direction of Grinzing. Between Heiligenstadt and Grinzing there lies the pleasant, grassy valley of a gently murmuring brook that rushes down from a nearby mountain-side.[102] While crossing this valley, overhung here and there by tall elm trees, Beethoven would frequently pause and let his enraptured gaze wander over the spectacular scene before him. Once he sat down on the grass and, leaning against an elm, asked me if there was a yellow-hammer singing in the topmost branches of the trees. But all was quiet. Then he said, 'It was here that I composed the 'Scene at the Brook', and the yellow-hammers up there, the quails, the nightingales, and the cuckoos composed along with me.' When I asked him why he had not put the yellow-hammers into the scene, he seized his sketchbook and wrote:

Ex. 10

'It is the little lady up there who composed that,' he said, 'and does she not have a more important role to play than the others? Those other songs are merely meant for a joke.' And truly, the entrance of this theme in G major lends the tone-painting new charm. Continuing on the subject of the whole symphony and its parts, Beethoven said that the song of this species of yellow-hammer was very close to the scale that he had written down in *andante* tempo and the same pitch. He explained that he had not labelled the yellow-hammer's passage because such a thing would only have added to the great number of malicious interpretations that had already hampered the reception and reputation of the work in Vienna and elsewhere. All too frequently the symphony has been denounced as a burlesque because of the second movement. In some cities it shared the fate of the *Eroica*, and in Leipzig the name 'Fantasies of a Composer' was applied rather than 'symphony' in the belief that the work would be better received (AmZ XI (1809) 437).

The other indication I was given of the composer's intentions concerns the third movement: 'Merrymaking among the Country Folk'. Viennese music-lovers of the time must have guessed the composer's intentions regarding this movement without his explaining them. They apparently recognized in the phrasing of the first part in $\frac{3}{4}$ time an imitation of Austrian peasant dances, if not a parody of them such as a man like Beethoven would have been capable of writing. At that time there still existed in Austria a typical folk music whose rhythms, harmony, and performance could not have failed to charm even the most highly educated musician. The peasants of the mountainous regions of Lower Austria and Styria had for centuries maintained a musical tradition that has now been lost along with folk poetry, though verses in peasant dialect are still written. In these regions as everywhere else the intrinsic character of the folk music was destroyed first by the barrel-organ and then by the methodical industrialization processes of civilization with its men's singing societies that made an end of all honest ethnic culture. Once folk art has disappeared, practically nothing can be done to revive it, especially in the realm of music, which finds its sources in the thought and feelings of the people.

There are circumstances that indicate the particular interest that Austrian dance music aroused in Beethoven. Until his arrival in Vienna in 1792, he claimed to know nothing of folk music except for the songs of Berg* with their strange rhythms. How much attention he subsequently gave to dance music can be seen in the catalogue of his works. He even tried his hand at writing Austrian dance music, but the musicians were unwilling to confer Austrian citizenship on these attempts.[103] The last attempt dates from 1819, a time, strangely enough, when Beethoven was engrossed in the *Missa Solemnis*. Further details of this composition will, fortunately enough, bring us back to the *Pastoral* symphony.

At the inn of 'The Three Ravens' on a marshy meadow near Mödling there had for many years been a band consisting of seven instrumentalists. It was from this group that the young musician newly arrived from the Rhineland first heard the genuine national music of his new homeland. They became acquainted, and Beethoven immediately composed some sets of Ländler and other dances. In 1819 he once more agreed to a request from this group for new music. I was with him when he handed the new score to the leader of the Mödling band.[104] The master remarked gaily that he had written these dances in such a way that the musicians could take turns laying down their instruments to rest or take a nap. When the visitor had left us, full of joy over the famous composer's gift, Beethoven asked me if I had noticed how village musicians would often fall asleep while playing, sometimes let the instrument sink and not play for a while, then wake up with a start, make a few hearty blasts or bowings at random, yet usually in the right key, and then go back to sleep again. In the *Pastoral* symphony he had tried to 'copy these poor people'.

Now, dear reader, take the score in hand and see for yourself the 'devices' on pages 106–9.[105] Notice the stereotyped accompaniment in both violins on pages 105 ff; notice further the drowsy second bassoon with its repeated two notes while the contrabass, cello, and viola are not heard at all. The viola does not wake up until page 108, then it seems to awaken its neighbour the cello. The second horn emits three blasts, then falls silent again. At last the contrabass and both bassoons rouse themselves with renewed vigour, and the clarinet is allowed to take a break. The Allegro on page 110, in $\frac{2}{4}$ time, is inspired too, in form and character, by Austrian dance music of the time. There were dances in which the $\frac{3}{4}$ measure suddenly gave way to a $\frac{2}{4}$ bar. In the 1820's I still used to hear such dances in villages within a few hours' distance of the capital,

---

* The duchy of Berg and Cleves in the Lower Rhine. Even there the folksong has disappeared from the life of the people and can only be found in collections. These are rare treasures.

such as Laab, Kaltenleutgeben, Gaden, and others. Finally, in the first movement we hear this figure of Austrian folk music:*

Ex. 11

The *Pastoral* symphony! Just as a painter makes his whole landscape harmonious while completing each section, so, too, Beethoven painted his tone picture. The foreground is quiet; the detailed sections blend smoothly. After the fears and apprehensions aroused by the thunderstorm, the background is quiet once more, and when in the very last measures we hear the distant notes of the horn, we feel we have been in the great concert-hall of Nature. Praises be thine, exalted master!

In the crown of the master's symphonic creations, the C minor symphony stands next to the *Pastoral*. Indeed, as free poetry which, though independent of all outer influences, still owes its existence to external forces, it surpasses the *Pastoral* and represents the greatest triumph in instrumental music up to that time. Among the hundreds of compositions written by many masters, no work bears out more fully than Beethoven's C minor symphony the maxim that every true work of art is a realization of the divine, whose purpose it is to confer the loftiest blessing on man by the enlightenment of the earthy and the spiritualization of the sensual as well as by the sensualization of the spirit. What a marvellous union of pathos, majesty, mystery, and grandeur is contained in those four movements! What a life of poetry this work unfolds before our senses, allowing us to see into its depths! The composer himself provided the key to those depths when one day, in this author's presence, he pointed to the beginning of the first movement and expressed in these words the fundamental idea of his work: 'Thus Fate knocks at the door!' Critics and aestheticians have long sought to dissect and analyse this symphony. The best analysis, the one that penetrates deepest into the essence of the poetry without excessive wordiness, is to be found a few pages further on. It would be presumptuous to attempt a better.

Major works published in the course of this year include:

(a) Concerto No. 4 in G major for piano and orchestra, opus 58.
(b) Symphony No. 4 in B flat major, opus 60.
(c) Concerto for violin and orchestra in D major, opus 61. The arrangement as a piano concerto appeared at the same time.[106]

---

* An omission in the score must be pointed out. In the first movement, page 35, the three-measure rest in the first violins should be occupied by the triplet figure of the third measure. This figure should be heard for four measures, then passed to the violas and played for four more measures.

SECOND PERIOD

In 1808 there occurred an incident that stirred up much interest at the time. It is an episode characteristic of Beethoven's life, and all the more worthy of our attention because its reverberations continued to affect the master's life years later and became an indirect impetus for the composition of one of his most important piano works. The AmZ (XI (1809) No. 3) saw to it that every detail of this incident was recorded. The present author will quote only such excerpts from the article as contribute to our purposes. The journal vouches for the truth of the matter while treating it critically. We read:

One of the first ladies of Vienna had the idea of conducting a composition contest for amateurs (of both sexes) and for most of the popular German and Italian composers. She chose for this contest a pretty little Italian love poem well suited as a song text. When the entries had been submitted, she gathered them into a collection and had it printed privately in order that she might make gifts of the copies to each of the contestants and to many other music-lovers. This collection remained only in private circulation and was never published generally.

This is the text of the song:

> *O let me rest in peace*
> *In the darkest night of death!*
> *Thou should'st have felt this sadness*
> *While yet I drew life's breath.*
>
> *Vanish and let my shadow*
> *Sleep th' eternal sleep.*
> *My ashes draw no warmth from*
> *The hot tears thou dost weep!*[107]

Of the entries using the lyrical grace of the Italian verse, some had the flaw of being artificial and contrived, others were heavily overladen, and some were in a pompous bravura style. The simple nobility of the Old German declamation gave rise in most instances to a conventional operatic aria form. In either case, most of the versions were dramatic in style.

Among the composers were ladies of high rank and princes, dukes, barons, and other amateur musicians. Some composers submitted several settings of the text; for instance, Zingarelli, who entered ten versions in the newest styles of the canzonet, arietta, and operatic aria; Salieri, who entered two versions; Sterkel (three), and Paer (two). Some of the amateurs, too, made more than one setting of the text. Other notables in the list of composers were A. Eberl, A. Förster, V. Righini, C. Zelter, W. Tomaschek, C. Czerny, F. Weigl, and finally Beethoven, whose composition was No. 63, the last in the collection.

So far so good—but the supplement!

It was a blatant parody of the work, its tragic content, and the emotions it aroused. It consisted of a large engraving showing a ludicrously formal Dutch or French garden. In a funereal arbour cut out of box-trees there stands an elaborate monument with a cinerary urn and the most vulgar little cherubs. A grieving woman dressed in a very wide hoop-skirt, plumes, and all the portentous appurtenances of the *ancienne cour* kneels sedately, her handkerchief pressed against her forehead, apparently to keep her rouge from running—and so forth. But here, too, there is music provided: Jakob Heckel had composed for the caricature a stiff, clumsy, heavy-footed minuet in B minor.

This parody enraged many Viennese composers, for they felt it represented an insulting and vulgar satire on their work. It was unanimously decided to lodge a public protest. Salieri, Beethoven, and Weigl were chosen as spokesmen. After the customary consultation, however, they decided against publicizing the affair. The work in question was not familiar to the public; moreover, a public protest would incur the risk of becoming itself the object of further satire. Experience had taught them that even the most exalted work of art is not immune to parody and ridicule. They therefore decided to content themselves with writing a letter of protest to the lady who had prompted the collection. This incident and its subsequent effects on our master will be remembered when we come to the third period (1823).

[IV]

— 1809 —

Continuing with our narrative of the most important events of Beethoven's life, we encounter at the very beginning of 1809 just such an occurrence.

The course of the master's life up to this time has shown that his social position had remained one of dependence upon his own efforts for his income. This was not because he had never aspired to an occupation away from his own writing-table that would have taken him more out into the world and that would have assured him a means of self-support, but for reasons that were partly external and partly within himself. The conditions under which Prince Lichnowsky had assured him in 1800 of a yearly allowance of 600 gulden indicates that he had expected years before to find such an occupation; for, as the written promise states, the subsidy would be continued only so long as Beethoven was without a 'suitable position'. Yet we see our tone-poet still obliged in 1809 (his thirty-ninth year) to live on nothing but this allowance and the income from his compositions.

Faced with such a situation, one may ask what a 'suitable position' for Beethoven might be. Nothing less than the conductorship of a large orchestra. Then the question arises whether Beethoven, with his increasing deafness, would be able to consider a post as conductor. And then, in view of the heights he had already attained as a creative artist, there is a third question: could anything less than a major court be thought of as a suitable appointment? But then think of the man's political principles, his all-consuming desire for unlimited freedom and independence: with these characteristics could he possibly be part of an imperial or royal court—Beethoven, the diametric opposite of a courtier, Beethoven, the man who in his heart despised the 'boot-licking servant of the court who creates nothing but more court air'? Yet at the time of which we are now speaking his deafness was not yet so advanced; the defect was apparent only from time to time. Moreover, Beethoven himself recognized less than anyone else the doubtfulness of his ability to perform practical functions, so that, despite all these inner obstacles, Beethoven had never abandoned his intention of finding a situation that would provide him with a secure livelihood.

We said, however, that there were also external reasons for Beethoven's dependence on a private patron. To determine these, let us take a closer look at the circumstances surrounding him. The reader may be surprised to learn that the large number of extraordinary works with which Beethoven's genius had enriched the world of art up to that time had favourably impressed neither the composer's declared opponents in Vienna nor the secret ones, many of whom were professional musicians. The latter group in particular found even in the C minor symphony a new opportunity for attacks and charges of heresy; for the old school boys who had learned the catechism of Haydn and Mozart were able to ferret out of this symphony much that, because it had never been heard before or because it violated the school rules, they could criticize or even ridicule. This last was the lot especially of the trio of the Scherzo.*

When we remember, however, the description already given of the intellectual level attained by the Viennese musicians of that day, we may readily understand by how much each of Beethoven's major works exceeded the horizons of all but a very few of his contemporaries, lacking as they were in any true understanding of the nature or the intrinsic morality of art, or of its place in the life of men. One who seeks in music only amusement, stimulation, or excitement set in the framework of a traditional formalism will, when confronted with Beethoven's music, deny the fundamental principles of criticism. He will examine the technical aspects, rhythm and harmony of the music to see if it contains any departures from or attacks on traditional rules. He will then apply

---

* The account in the AmZ (XI (1809) 269) of the first performance on 22 December 1808 closes with this sentence: 'Furthermore, it is generally known that Vienna, more than almost any other city, exemplifies the biblical saying about a prophet in his own country.'

his accustomed ruler to various passages, and will indeed find that they are longer than comparable passages in Mozart or Haydn. He will thus busy himself purely with the outward aspects of the work of art, for he has not sufficient artistic cultivation to penetrate its inner being. For this reason he will not be able to admit that a genius of such power as Beethoven's constitutes a rule unto itself, and may therefore demand that its products be measured and judged according to its own yardstick.

Of all this the musicians of Beethoven's time had no comprehension, and unfortunately this dimness of insight persists in most heads right up to the present day. Most of the AmZ articles on Beethoven's music in every medium represent this mentality, though we can assume that the authors of these articles were circumspect enough not to express all that they felt. We shall have to quote many such specimens of short-sightedness, prejudice, and an almost fossilized adherence to tradition, and perhaps some of them will even cause us to lose our patience and our indulgence for the taste prevailing at that time.

Yet the Austrian capital itself was notorious for having become the seat of the empirical school of music. The empirical point of view, while recognizing its own shallowness and weaknesses, has always treated the scientific approach to all the arts as its avowed enemy. As for Beethoven, this powerful and massive force refused to recognize him as anything but a revolutionary in art, one who as a prisoner of his own darkness is driven by an unrestrained passion to make himself talked about. It can only be surmised how Beethoven's genius was affected by these demonstrations of envy, jealousy, or complete neglect. This opposition would have been expressed all the more openly if Beethoven had appeared to be seeking a position in the imperial court. The fact that Archduke Rudolph had the year before entrusted to Beethoven's hands the continuation of his musical education had already made the enemies fear that 'the newcomer', 'the republican', might one day gain access to the court.*

* We must here record an almost unbelievable event whose truth is substantiated by the AmZ. It is a dramatic illustration both of the power of tradition and of Beethoven's slight impact on the Viennese musicians. When the composer conducted performances of the *Eroica* symphony in 1805 and 1806, the programme always indicated the key, quite properly, as E flat major. The term 'E flat' for a piece of music written in three flats was however then unknown in Vienna, and perhaps elsewhere as well. This key was known, as in the time of Jubal, as D sharp. When the musicians received their printed parts of the work, they made haste to ignore Beethoven's 'innovation' and for all subsequent performances to use the term D sharp—this was the indication used by Haydn and Mozart. The notices from Vienna printed in the AmZ frequently made much of this curious procedure; for instance (X (1808) 540): 'During Holy Week of 1808 a great concert took place in the Theater an der Wien with Mozart's *Davidde Penitente* and Beethoven's *Sinfonia Eroica*, the latter (designated on the programme as being in the key of D sharp). . . .' This concert was conducted by the Kapellmeister Ignaz Ritter von Seyfried and the orchestra leader was Franz Clement. Even in the 1820's the designation D sharp was still used for the key of E flat. The Viennese school of music was in any case a potpourri of incredible oddities that would cause one both to laugh and to cry.

Beethoven was well aware of the dilemma in which this unfortunate state of affairs embroiled both his outer and his inner life, and he was just as keenly aware of the difficulty of solving it. He therefore decided on a protracted voyage to Italy to remove himself for some time from the presence of his enemies and also to give himself a rest, for the years of intensive work and the intrigues of the various factions had taken their toll on his body and spirit. Upon his return from Italy he would consider moving to another German city.

Then suddenly in the midst of all these perplexing problems there appeared a *deus ex machina* to give a different direction to Beethoven's affairs. He was summoned by Count Truchsess-Waldburg, the Lord Chamberlain of the King of Westphalia, to accept the post of Kapell-meister to the King. 'Wonderful irony of fate!' the reader will say, remembering the events of 1804 and the *Eroica* symphony and the righteous anger of the composer who is now offered the position of Kapellmeister by the brother of the French Emperor. More wonderful yet when one recognizes this as an invitation to the royal court of Cassel. Yet this summons was an event that could not fail to cause a great to-do in all circles of Viennese society. As always, the public did not comprehend the greatness of a resident artist until it was threatened with his removal to another abode. His patrons were particularly dis-quieted, for they were convinced that Beethoven, whom each of them claimed with justifiable pride as his own, should remain in Vienna, the capital of German music, and continue without foreign influence to journey on his own self-made road.

After deliberating on this circumstance, Archduke Rudolph, Prince Joseph von Lobkowitz (Duke of Raudnitz), and Prince Ferdinand Kinsky met together to do alone what the honour of the capital demanded. On 1 March they signed the following document:

The proof that Herr Ludwig van Beethoven gives each day of his extra-ordinary talent and genius as tone-poet and composer awakens the desire that he may surpass the greatest expectations that his achievements up to this time have justified.

It is, however, clear that only a person who is as free from worries as pos-sible can devote himself exclusively to his profession, and that such single-minded application, without the intrusion of any other concern, is alone able to produce great and sublime works honouring the name of art.

The undersigned have accordingly resolved to place Herr Ludwig van Beethoven in such a position that he will not be embarrassed by the necessities of life and that his powerful genius will have no other distractions. They there-fore pledge themselves to pay him an annuity of 4,000 (four thousand) gulden according to the following schedule:

His Royal Highness the Archduke Rudolph . . Fl. 1,500
His Majesty Prince Lobkowitz 700
His Majesty Prince Ferdinand Kinsky . . . 1,800
Total . . . . Fl. 4,000

which Herr Ludwig van Beethoven may draw, against receipt, at half-yearly intervals from each of the contributors according to the terms of this agreement.

The undersigned, moreover, are willing to continue this annuity until Herr Ludwig van Beethoven shall accept an appointment that will assure him the equivalent of the above-named sum. Should such an appointment never be available or should Herr L. van Beethoven be prevented by any misfortune or age from practising his art, the contributors shall continue this annuity as long as he shall live.

Herr L. van Beethoven shall, for his part, oblige himself to reside in Vienna, the residence of the undersigned, or in another city within His Majesty the Austrian Emperor's patrimonial dominions that may be agreed upon, and shall leave his city of residence only for such periods as may be necessary for errands of business or art, regarding which the high contributors shall be consulted and shall give their consent.

Beethoven was thus bound by honour to Vienna and to his patrons with ties that could be wrought only in mutual respect and esteem. We need not dwell upon the defeat that this frank recognition of his importance as an artist inflicted upon the army of his enemies. Most of them were not so much malicious as deluded and set in their obsolete musical prejudices; these were able to accommodate themselves to the altered state of affairs. From that time Beethoven was for a period spared any further persecution at the hands of the Viennese musicians for, now that they could no longer harm him financially, they found it more practical to remain aloof. Perhaps they would not even have objected to his being placed at the imperial court where he would have exercised considerable influence on art and artists. Such a post, however, was not easy to come by. We shall have occasion in the third period to see what insurmountable obstacles stood between Beethoven and admission to the imperial palace.

The author must point out, though, that Beethoven was able to enjoy the full amount of his annual stipend for only a very short time, for in 1811 there occurred in Austria an event that shook the whole economy and worked great hardship upon our tone-poet. Through this, also, Beethoven's patrons, who had made certain stipulations in order to free the composer from financial cares, encountered difficulties of which we shall speak further on. We shall see how the bonds wrought of mutual respect and esteem subsequently became one of the causes of a discord so bitter that it could not fail to have an adverse effect on the master's work.

The amazing productivity of the next few years, however, shows what a powerful impetus Beethoven's vigorous genius derived from this promised annuity, as the reader will soon have occasion to see for himself. It almost fulfilled the master's dearest wish that we spoke of earlier; that when he reached the autumn of his life he might resemble a tree that would shower down its ripe fruits into our laps. Truly, when one considers the number and the quality of the works composed between 1809 and 1815, one is impressed with the simile and is even tempted to think that before 1809 the fruit that the tree had brought forth had been but meagre.

It is necessary, therefore, to warn the reader that from this time until the close of the second period, Beethoven's life was marked by very few noteworthy events. We must accustom ourselves to find him chained to his work-table almost constantly for the next years, although his seriously impaired health should have required frequent periods of repose. Because of this preoccupation with composing, the biographer has no choice but to treat the next few years in the manner of a chronicle.

During 1809 there occurred an incident that is hardly worthy of mention, but that Ferdinand Ries considered important enough to include in his *Notizen*. We shall be brief in our report of it. On page 121 of Ries we read: 'During the short period in 1809 when the French were firing on Vienna, Beethoven was so uneasy that he spent most of the time in the cellar of his brother Caspar's house, his head covered with cushions to keep out the sound of the cannon.'

This remark by the pupil (who had left Vienna for London before the approach of the French army)[108] accuses the teacher too blatantly of fear if not of downright cowardice. Ries should have taken his information from better authority before claiming to compile from 'original sources' an authentic Beethoven biography. Despite his youth at the time of his intimate acquaintance with the master, he ought to have been a better judge of the composer's personal courage and fearlessness if he aspired to make an unbiased evaluation of his character. If Beethoven had feared the possible danger in staying in the besieged city, he could have escaped the danger by leaving as many others did. He chose, however, to remain just as he had done during the French occupation in 1805 when he had been busy with the production of *Fidelio*. If it is true that during the bombardment of the city he took refuge in the cellar, he did only what any rational person would do at such a time.

Even Wegeler, who generally accepted everything that Ries said as gospel truth, was not able to gloss over this particular passage, and poses this question: 'Is it not possible that the noise of the cannon was painful to his ailing ears?' I cannot refrain from adding that there has hardly been a great man whose character has been the subject of much public concern, who has been portrayed so irresponsibly, so condescendingly, so foolishly, as Beethoven is portrayed in Ries's *Biographische Notizen*. I refer the reader to the foreword of this volume.

The goddess of war had spent her wrath, and the peaceful heavens once more spread themselves over beautiful Austria and all Germany, inviting the scattered people to return to their cities and their beloved task of cultivating the arts. Meanwhile, however, the publishing house of Breitkopf & Härtel in Leipzig was busy printing works that were eagerly anticipated by the whole world of German music-lovers. Soon after the enemy armies had withdrawn, the *Pastoral* and C minor symphonies were distributed to the music dealers. One can imagine how eagerly the orchestras pounced on these new compositions. The accounts in the AmZ for this year and the next of the performances everywhere of these works indicate (sometimes in very strange language indeed) with what anticipation the symphonies were received. In addition to these symphonic giants there also appeared in the same year the marvellous sonata for cello in A major, opus 69.

With the publication of the two symphonies, the Leipzig critics did a *volte-face* in favour of almost every Beethoven composition. Not that the symphonies had, as they appeared, been unkindly received by that art tribunal, as we have already seen from excerpts reprinted in this book, but the piano music, which is the true messenger of the deepest secrets hidden within the genius of Beethoven, had until this time been misunderstood and consequently grievously underestimated. From this time on, the piano music was only rarely so abused. Up to now, however, the critics had also failed to penetrate the poetic depths of the symphonies; it was almost always the pettifoggery of the grammarians that had called the tune in musical criticism.

In this respect, too, things took a turn for the better. The reviews of the *Pastoral* and C minor symphonies in the twelfth volume contained the first indications that the old, tradition-bound school rules were beginning to lose their foothold in Leipzig. Beethoven learned that these reviews were written by Amadeus Wendt,[109] one of the first Leipzig critics who not only tolerated the many innovations of the 'new school' in Vienna but, as we shall soon see, embraced them heartily.

From the critical articles this excellent man wrote about the two symphonies in question, we shall quote a few sentences that the reader will find instructive. On the *Pastoral*, designated as No. 6 though it preceded the other:

The work presents in symphonic form a painting of rustic life. 'A painting? Is music supposed to paint? Are we not long past the heyday of musical painting?' At any rate, we have sufficiently recovered from it that the representation of external objects in music is considered as tasteless as the aesthetic values of anyone who uses such cheap devices for effect. This observation does not in the least pertain to the work we are examining, for the music is not a representation of specific rural objects, but rather of the feelings and emotions aroused in one by the sight of such objects. Anyone who has thought about music and about the nature of the emotions that it is supposed to express will readily understand that a painting such as this is far from being in poor taste, and in no way violates the function of music.

The following is an excerpt from the introduction to the article on the C minor symphony, No. 5, an article that occupied no less than twenty columns:

Beethoven's music inspires in its listeners awe, fear, horror, pain, and that exquisite nostalgia that is the soul of romanticism. . . . Beethoven carries deep within his spirit the romanticism of music and expresses it in his works with the utmost skill and discrimination. This reviewer never felt this romanticism so keenly as when listening to this symphony, which right up to the climactic finish develops Beethoven's sense of the romantic, expressing it more urgently than any of his other works, until the hearer is irresistibly compelled into the awesome spirit-realm of the eternal.

We shall again call upon Amadeus Wendt at the close of this period to give his perception of the spirit of Beethoven's music, for his is the most reliable testimony. It behoves the biographer to make known these first well-founded and generally accurate revelations of the deep resources within our master, in order that we may thereby preclude all contention; for though these articles by Wendt have great cultural and historical interest, they lie buried in library dust. Indeed, all subsequent explanations (up to the most recent outlandish confusion in the interpretation of Beethoven's compositions by the conductors of 'music of the future') are based on Wendt's writings and are to them what variations are to the theme—a fact that makes Wendt all the more noteworthy.

⸺ 1810 ⸺

In the year 1810 the following fruits were 'shaken down' from the tree named Beethoven into the laps of his countless admirers:[110]

(a) Two great trios (D major and E flat major) for piano, violin, and cello, opus 70.*

(b) Sextet in E flat for 2 clarinets, 2 horns, and 2 bassoons, opus 71. Beethoven had composed this work several years earlier. It was first performed in April 1805 at a quartet concert given for the benefit of Schuppanzigh. This opus number is, therefore, incorrect.

(c) Quartet in E flat for 2 violins, viola, and cello (No. 10), opus 74.

* A penetrating and learned criticism of this work appeared in AmZ XV (1813) 141; see also *Beilage* facing column 144.

In later years some simpleton dubbed this the 'Harp Quartet'. No one has been able to give a reasonable explanation for the nickname.

(d) Six songs by Goethe for solo voice, opus 75.

(e) Variations in D major for piano, opus 76.

(f) Fantasy in G minor for piano, opus 77.

(g) Sonata in F sharp major for piano, opus 78.

(h) Sonatina in G major for piano, opus 79.

(i) *Fidelio* (*Leonore*), first and second versions (dating from 1805 and 1806): complete vocal score, opus 72.

(j) Overture to *Fidelio*, second version (1806), for orchestra.

(k) Sextet in E flat major for 2 violins, viola, cello, and 2 obbligato horns, opus 81b.

(l) Concertino in C major for piano, violin, and cello, opus 56.

During the course of this year one incident occurred to interrupt the master's quiet, secluded industry. It is an incident that has long constituted a lively preoccupation for the reading public: it received comment even in the first edition of this work because it was so untrue to the essence of Beethoven's character. The incident concerns Beethoven's acquaintance with Bettina Brentano (Frau von Arnim) and its many consequences. We need only touch upon the great interest the literary world took in these consequences, how they were discussed and analysed in Goethe's *Correspondence with a Child*, and finally how the publication in the 1830's of three letters from Beethoven to Bettina became the subject of a personally offensive, dissonant argument. While the literary world was debating the authenticity of these three letters, I for my part contented myself with questioning the statements attributed to the Viennese composer in them. My efforts enjoyed no better results than today's criticism does that falls on the deaf ears of virtuosi, singers, and actors. Yet this is not the end of the matter; the subject must be treated again here, for my personal opinion on the question of truth or fraud regarding these letters has changed in the meanwhile, and I must be more specific than in the first edition.[111]

A son will recognize with certainty whether or not a saying attributed to his father is really his, because the son is completely familiar with the father's thoughts and his manner of expressing them, both orally and in writing. The same may be expected of the friend to whom, through years of companionship, every corner of Beethoven's heart was revealed, while every verbal expression became so familiar that even his written words assumed the sound of his voice in the friend's ear. Both son and friend will thus be able, if necessary, to determine easily whether or not a given piece of writing corresponds to the father's or friend's sentiments and manner of speech, and will be able to tell if the example is totally false, or at least questionable. It was thus with the utmost confidence that I was able to write on page 80 of the first edition:

Anyone reading in Goethe's *Briefwechsel* (vol. II, p. 190) what in her letter of 28 May 1810 the apparently over-excited Bettina reports Beethoven to have said, will be unable to refrain from thinking what a wit, what a monstrous swaggerer he must have been. The impression will be entirely false. Beethoven's manner of expressing himself, both in speech and in writing, was always of the utmost simplicity, brevity, and conciseness, as the many letters we have in his hand show. He disliked hearing affected speech or reading an affected style of writing, for in everything he demanded natural straightforwardness without a trace of ostentation. Beethoven did indeed frequently speak and think of his genius as Bettina says, recognizing in it a higher revelation and placing it above any philosophy, yet he always minimized his own worthiness.* . . . How amazed Beethoven would be to read the words put into his mouth by the prattling Bettina! . . . He would no doubt have exclaimed, 'My dear chatterbox of a Bettina! It was you who must have had a *raptus* when you wrote such things to Goethe!'

For Bettina says, among other things in her letter of 28 May 1810 to the patriarch of Weimar, that she wrote down all the things Beethoven had told her about art and so forth while they were taking a walk together, and the next day showed him what she had written, whereupon he asked in amazement, 'Did I say all that? I must have had a *raptus*.'

With these words of Beethoven's we may dismiss the well-meaning outpourings of Bettina's pen. The letters themselves, however, cannot be disregarded, for though what they are supposed to say is questionable, their existence is not.

During my fairly long stay in Berlin in 1843, I had the honour of making the acquaintance of Frau von Arnim. She told me many interesting things about her literary efforts, about what she had achieved and what she had failed to achieve. About her relationship with Beethoven, however, I could not induce her to say a single word, though she knew of my book about him and knew that she was personally mentioned in the book. Without asking directly if I might examine the famous letters, I hinted that it was extremely important for me to see the originals. The esteemed lady would at such times wrap herself in a deep cloak of silence, pretending to hear nothing I had said.

It is the third letter, dated 'Teplitz, August 1812', that I particularly suspect and shall continue to suspect until the whole letter is produced, at least in facsimile. My suspicion is aroused because of what Beethoven writes there about his behaviour towards the Emperor's family when

* Beethoven never exhibited the least sign of conceit such as abounds in Bettina's quotations.

he was with Goethe. The question that comes to mind is this: how could Beethoven on this unusual occasion have shown such disrespect for the noble companion who accompanied him on these walks, as well as for the whole imperial family, as Bettina would have us believe? For Archduke Rudolph, who was also present, had always been his highly respected pupil and patron. Only the year before, as we have seen, he had demonstrated so eloquently his admiration for Beethoven, and he was at this time still a frequent and intimate companion of the master. If indeed Beethoven was guilty of such boorishness it is quite understandable why Goethe should have struck his reminiscences of the composer out of his memoirs, and the imperial family would have had good reason to treat such crudity on the part of an artist with painful indifference. And if from this time on the imperial family did in fact snub the composer, the reasons were quite different from those one might deduce from the wording of this letter. Frau von Arnim would be serving the interests of the master and of her own credibility if she were to lose no more time in publishing a facsimile of the letter of August 1812, thereby preventing any further mistaken notions about the matter.* Otherwise, one will be obliged to recognize in these letters 'the uninhibited flights of her imagination', so that the letters will henceforth be devoid of all scholarly interest or importance: they can no longer be accepted as 'self-revelatory witnesses to Beethoven's nature'.†

⚊ 1811 ⚊

The year 1811 was one of financial disaster for the Austrian people, for it saw the devaluation of the florin to one-fifth of its former purchasing power. We can understand how seriously this affected our composer when we realize that all contractual obligations expressed in paper money were reduced to only a fifth of the value of the sum promised, so that Beethoven's annuity of 4,000 gulden in bank notes had shrunk to 800 gulden in [new] paper money.[114]

In the midst of this calamity that upset the whole economy, Archduke Rudolph made haste to send his afflicted teacher a new document,

---

* While this section was in the press, the esteemed lady of letters passed away. Let us hope that her heirs will make her literary *Nachlass* available or will allow the letters in question to be published in facsimile.

† Recently someone at Teplitz claimed to have read a sonnet that Beethoven was supposed to have written on the occasion of Bettina von Arnim's marriage. This fable appears in *Unterhaltungen am häuslichen Heerd*, IV (1858), No. 7. Beethoven, though a master of rhythm, was not schooled in the rules of metre, and never in his life wrote a real piece of verse. If such a sonnet written in his hand actually does exist, he merely copied it. I still have in my possession copies that he made of poems by both famous and unknown poets.[112] The duration of his infatuation with Bettina can be seen from the facsimile No. 2 reproduced at the end of this volume. We have referred to it already, answering once and for all any questions concerning the length of Beethoven's attachment to Bettina.[113]

according to which the promised sum of 1,500 gulden in bank notes was assured as fully payable in notes of redemption. This was truly a noble gift, and could not fail to inspire the genius with new vigour as it raised him for a time above material worries. A few years later this arrangement was modified so that Beethoven was given a pension of 600 gulden in silver for life with no conditions attached. At Beethoven's request, Prince Lobkowitz also consented to having his portion (700 gulden) paid in redemption bonds. Only Prince Kinsky's 1,800 gulden remained for a while an unknown quantity.[115]

If the economic depression robbed the empire of much material wealth, Beethoven gave to the world such cultural riches as:

(a) Concerto No. 5 in E flat major for piano and orchestra, opus 73.

(b) Fantasy in C minor for piano, chorus, and orchestra, opus 80.

(c) Sonata in E flat major for piano (*Les Adieux, l'Absence, et le Retour*), opus 81a.

(d) Four ariettas and a duet (in Italian and German) with piano accompaniment, opus 82.

(e) Three songs by Goethe for solo voice with piano accompaniment, opus 83.

(f) Overture to Goethe's *Egmont* (full score), opus 84.[116]

(g) The oratorio *Christus am Oelberge* (orchestral and vocal score), opus 85.

In respect to the E flat major piano concerto, the summit of all concerto music ever written for this instrument both as regards its spiritual content and the technical difficulties it presents, it must be mentioned that of all Beethoven's concertos and concerted chamber music, it is the only one that had not been heard prior to its publication. This work was first performed on 12 February 1812 at a private concert in the opera house (together with an exhibition of paintings) in honour of the Emperor's birthday.[117] The pianist was Carl Czerny who, as a result of Beethoven's coaching, brought out the very best in the music.

The poster announced the dedication of the work: 'To His Imperial Majesty, Archduke Rudolph'. Such a public statement of dedication was not customary, and it may be taken as an indication of Beethoven's desire to proclaim to all his deep gratitude to the most illustrious of his patrons. A glance at subsequent dedications gives one reason to believe that throughout the next few years Beethoven composed almost exclusively for the Archduke.[118] The Archduke, for his part, endeavoured by assiduous study of music and also by emerging as a skilful composer in his own right to give joy to his teacher and mentor. If only I could add that the atmosphere of mutual esteem between master and pupil remained unchanged! The pupil did indeed remain constant in his devotion, but the teacher's vile temper and stormy moods were unleashed in later years even against his noble pupil and foremost patron. All this we shall report in due time.

The very brief review of the E flat concerto by the critic of the AmZ will be sufficient to give the reader an idea of the public reception of the work. Here is his review in its entirety: 'The immense length of the composition robs it of the impact that this product of a gigantic intellect would otherwise practise upon its hearers.' Who would today find this concerto excessively long? This critical remark shows us once more that it was then, as later, the external form of Beethoven's works that gave the most offence. For even today there are learned persons who busy themselves by counting the measures in a movement, comparing Beethoven's works with Mozart's on the basis of mere volume. Since the epoch knew no musicians who departed from classical forms other than Mozart and Haydn, we can understand the reasons for the continuing opposition to Beethoven's formal innovations. If Johann Sebastian Bach's music had been known, appreciation of the individual characteristics of Beethoven's might have come sooner. One would have realized that other forms were possible besides those used by Haydn and Mozart—that other forms in fact existed.

We must add, in connection with this masterpiece of piano music, that during the lifetime of the composer it was played only once more, again by Carl Czerny, at a private concert given by the great horn-player Hradetzsky on 12 April 1818. Moreover, the virtuosi of the time approached the Beethoven concertos with unconcealed reluctance, while the public showed no liking, or very little, for them. The C minor concerto and the *Choral Fantasy* were each performed perhaps twice in fifteen years, and the violin concerto was performed (as we have mentioned) by Franz Clement in 1806 with no success at all. A second attempt the next year was better received but not nearly well enough to overcome the prejudices that the work had already aroused. A third bold attempt was made by an amateur violinist at a Gesellschafts-Concert in the Great Redoutensaal on 3 March 1816, and though the soloist was to play only the first movement, he made a complete failure of it, confirming the prevalent opinion that the work was impossible to perform. Thus this magnificent work remained unknown from 1807 down to our own day. The piano concerto in G major suffered a similar fate. It lay untouched for twenty years after its first performance, while the *Triple Concerto* was neglected for an even longer time.

The principal cause of this neglect was a change in the style of piano playing introduced by Hummel, Moscheles, Czerny, and others. This new style was totally foreign to Beethoven's music, both in form and in material. Its salient characteristics—elegance, polish, and technical display—were inappropriate to Beethoven's piano compositions and failed to convey to audiences the profound spiritual nature of the concertos. Yet recent times have expiated the sins of the past by retrieving these works from library dust and restoring them to their rightful place: technique has assumed its proper relationship to genius, so that Beethoven's works now rightfully stand above all others.

Of all the reviews of Beethoven's works published by the high court of criticism in Leipzig, that weather-vane to which Beethoven's adversaries looked for confirmation of their prejudices, one of the most curious was the article on the new sonata (*Les Adieux*). Its tone gives us one more concrete demonstration of the frivolous attitude that Beethoven's contemporaries assumed in respect to works by him that our own time cannot cease to admire. This curious piece of criticism reads as follows:

An occasional piece [sic!] but one such as only a master of genius could write! The leave-taking begins with an Adagio whose simple theme seems to say 'Farewell', then a more vehement and amplified Allegro bespeaks the pain of parting. The emotions of absence are indicated by a rather heavy principal theme, Andante espressivo, accompanied by an undercurrent of nervous restlessness. (It seems as if it would go on for a long time but is soon and unexpectedly interrupted—one can easily see why.) [!?] And finally we are surprised with a lively, joyful, expansive Allegro signifying the reunion.

That was all the critic had to say about this work.

Since we are on the subject of this sonata, I should like to ask parenthetically why in some catalogues, including the Breitkopf & Härtel *Thematic Index*, it is designated by the term 'characteristic'. Are we to suppose that all the other Beethoven sonatas are not characteristic simply because they bear no title by which the emotions of the hearer are led in a certain direction? One day this author heard the master lament that he had ever added the designation *pathétique* to the opus 13 sonata. 'The whole world,' he complained, 'seizes upon a single sonata because it has a name that the pianists can exploit.' Music dealers say that while piano music in general is now in greater demand, the *Sonate pathétique* sells more copies than any other piece. No wonder a German publisher once told the composer that he would pay ten thousand gulden for a new *Sonate pathétique*! Such is the strength of a foreign word whose meaning remains unknown to the majority of the piano-playing public! How often Beethoven would have had to append the designation *pathétique* to every kind of composition if he had wanted to be consistent! When we look at the general meaning of this word: 'That which is truly pathetic expresses a strong emotion earnestly and with dignity', we realize that it is a word that summarizes the fundamental character of all of Beethoven's music, and if we were to add another supplementary word to describe the piano works alone, it would be the word 'rhetorical'. This, however, is a term that applies only to speech-making.

⌐ 1812 ⌐

The year 1812 is notable for being the only year in the second period of the master's life that is not marked in the catalogue by a single new work, an occurrence that we shall encounter repeatedly in the third period.[119] Yet it was a year that saw the genesis of several new works that were to enhance their creator's fame greatly: the symphonies in F major and A major, the music for *The Ruins of Athens*, and the overture to the Hungarian national play, *King Stephan, Hungary's Greatest Benefactor*. The poetry for the festival play, *The Ruins of Athens*, was written by August von Kotzebue, to be performed with Beethoven's music and in conjunction with the above-mentioned national play for the opening of the new municipal theatre in Budapest in the early autumn.

In the first edition of this book, I was in error regarding the sequence of these works, particularly the two symphonies. My error was corrected by Count Brunsvik, who was much with the master at the time in question. According to the information he gave me in 1843, *The Ruins of Athens* music was composed in the early months of 1812. At the same time, Beethoven was sketching out both symphonies, and it was while visiting his brother Johann in Linz in the spring that he completed the F major symphony (No. 8). From there he went to the baths at Teplitz, where he wrote the overture to *King Stephan*. After his return to Vienna the master, now rested, started work on the A major symphony (No. 7). The numbers of these two symphonies were thus reversed, just as in the case of the *Pastoral* and C minor symphonies.[120] Count Brunsvik had no satisfactory explanation for this phenomenon. For my part, I find a reason in the fact that the same key, F major, was used for the *Pastoral* and the symphony that immediately followed it, later designated as No. 8.

We have already learned from Beethoven's correspondence with Bettina Brentano of Beethoven's stay in Teplitz in 1812. It was during his journey there from Linz that the following incident occurred. In order to stabilize his economic situation Beethoven presented himself in person to Prince Kinsky, then living in Prague, to request that he should do as the two other noble parties to the Annuity Contract of 1 March 1809 had done, namely specify his portion as payable in redemption bonds. The Prince granted his request, and gave the composer sixty ducats as payment on account, directing him to go to his treasurer upon returning to Vienna with an order for the remainder of the sum due. But while Beethoven was in Teplitz the Prince was fatally injured by being thrown from a horse, before his order had been delivered to his treasurer in Vienna.[121] The trustees of his estate would not honour the promise made to Beethoven by the deceased, and wanted to keep to the provisions of the devaluation act—reduction of the specified sum to one-fifth. Beethoven felt himself compelled to bring the suit before the Bohemian civil authorities. The decision of the superior court, issued on 18 January 1815, ordered the trustees of the princely estate to pay an annuity of 1,200 gulden in redemption bonds instead of 1,800 gulden in bank notes, starting from 3 November 1812. A few years later this sum was changed to 300 gulden in silver. It remained fixed at that amount.[122]

⚊ 1813 ⚊

The long years of continuous and strenuous work at his desk without respite or relaxation could not have failed to exert an adverse effect on the health of our master, and particularly on his intestinal condition that had always given him trouble. What benefits he derived from his convalescence at Teplitz were nullified within the next few months. Throughout the year 1813 Beethoven's health suffered more acutely than ever before. According to information communicated to the author by Andreas Streicher and his wife, who were especially close friends of the master at this time, Beethoven's state of mind was at the lowest ebb it had been since the difficult year of 1803.

He planned, therefore, on the recommendation of his doctor, to try a cure at nearby Baden. From the contents of the following letter from his imperial pupil, Archduke Rudolph, this appears to have been Beethoven's first treatment at this spa.[123] The Archduke wrote :*

Dear Beethoven!

It was with great pleasure that I read in your letter of the 27th of last month, which I did not receive until the night before last, of your arrival in my beloved Baden. I hope to see you here tomorrow morning if you have the time, for the few days of my stay here have been so beneficial to my health that, without fearing any ill effects, I may again listen to and even play some music. If your stay in this healthful and beautiful place has the same good effect on your condition, my intentions in taking care of your lodgings will be completely fulfilled.

Your friend,

Baden, 7 July 1813. Rudolph

These lines written by the Archduke are a clear testimony of the warm friendship between pupil and teacher. The imperial prince had in loving consideration for his sick teacher taken it upon himself to find

* The original of this letter was found in the Franz Gräffer collection of autographs in Vienna.

him suitable lodgings in his 'beloved Baden'. This relationship is so reminiscent of Leopold Schefer's novel, *Master and Pupil*, that I cannot refrain from quoting one of the most appropriate passages from that book:

As students of art, we enter into an indescribable relationship with our master. He leads us into a great and eternal realm, one that exists in the world and yet above all worlds. He introduces us to men who have long been dead and who nevertheless through their works are with us, illuminating, moving, and even governing us. Through his spirit, his knowledge, and his ability, he gives us the spirit of art. He opens his soul to us and enables us to understand the greatness, the beauty, the sweetness of the whole world until, revealed to us by the master, comprehended and recreated by the powers of reason that he has taught us, the world at last becomes ours. Or to express it more truly: we first achieve through him the mastery of our own capacities, then enrich through him the treasures of our heart and mind. A relationship between master and pupil lasts a whole lifetime, and only a good-for-nothing will ever renounce his respect for his teacher, even if he should surpass him tenfold. A grateful pupil will rejoice in his master's creations, efforts, and achievements in every realm as only a man and an artist can rejoice.

The imperial prince was until the end of his life an example of such a pupil.

According to the information communicated by Frau Streicher, who also spent the summer of 1813 in Baden, our composer's general physical condition was in a state of neglect. He lacked good clothing, especially linen. It cannot be said whether this neglect was caused by his total absorption in his work or by brother Karl, for whom he felt a constant responsibility. Perhaps both are to blame.* On her return to Vienna, the kindly lady, with the help of her husband, saw to it that Beethoven had the things he needed. When his sojourn in Baden came to an end, our rejuvenated master took up residence once more in the apartment that had been reserved for him in the house of his friend, Baron Pasqualati, on the Mölker Bastei. It was here that the author of this book had the honour of first making the composer's acquaintance towards the end of March 1814. A servant was engaged who was also a tailor and who used the composer's front room as his shop. He and his wife, who, however, did not live in the house, tended the master with care and consideration until 1816. This systematic mode of life suited the composer very well. If only it could have lasted a few more years!

Prince Lichnowsky responded to this situation with signs of such love

---

* The master's entry in his diary for 15 May 1813 contains the following: 'It would be a great deed to stop altogether. O how different that would be from the slothful life I so often appear to be leading. O dreadful circumstances that do not impair my desire to be frugal but my ability to practise frugality. O God, O God, look down on unhappy B. and do not let it continue thus any more.' This outcry serves as a commentary on the situation.

and veneration that they are worth closer study. The Prince was in the habit of frequently visiting his protégé in his study. By mutual agreement, no notice of his presence was to be taken so that the master might not be disturbed. The Prince would greet him, leaf through some piece of music, watch the composer a while as he worked, then with a friendly 'Adieu' leave the room. Even so, Beethoven did feel disturbed by these visits and would sometimes lock the door. Cheerfully the Prince would go back down the three flights of stairs. But when the tailor-servant was in the front room, His Serene Highness would stay and chat with him until the door was opened so that he could pay his friendly respects to the prince of music. What was needed was thus accomplished. This anecdote forms a pleasant companion piece to the sentiments we have just heard expressed by Archduke Rudolph. It was not, however, possible for the venerated patron of art to enjoy for much longer his favourite protégé, for on 15 April of the following year he departed this life.

The year 1813 saw the appearance of only one new work, the first mass in C major, opus 86. This work had been composed in 1807, as we noted at the time. It was written for Prince Esterházy and performed at Eisenstadt under the composer's direction in the summer of 1808.[124] We know from the life story of Joseph Haydn of this art patron's predilection for church music, though he wanted it not so much for his spiritual uplifting as for his entertainment. This circumstance accounts for the frequently secular tone of Haydn's masses in which the Kapellmeister endeavoured to satisfy the Prince's taste, probably often against his own better instincts. But the practice spoiled the Prince so that he measured all other compositions against Haydn's yardstick. At this time the great master was already dead, and it was Johann Nepomuk Hummel who held the position of Kapellmeister at Eisenstadt.

The performance of this mass at the Prince's palace occasioned the following incident. It was the custom at this court that after the religious service the musical *élite*, both residents and foreigners, would gather in the Prince's chambers to discuss with him the works just performed. When Beethoven entered, the Prince turned to him and asked, 'But, my dear Beethoven, what have you gone and done now?' The effect on our composer of this strange question, which was probably followed by several critical comments, became all the more painful when he saw that the Kapellmeister, who was standing beside the Prince, was laughing. His sensitivity was such that nothing could induce him to stay on at a place where his work was not appreciated, particularly when he thought he had detected a certain malicious joy on the part of his fellow musician. He left Eisenstadt before the day was out.[125]

Beethoven's estrangement from Hummel dates from this event, though they had never been intimate friends. Unfortunately the two never came to an understanding that would have made it possible to explain that the fateful laugh may not have been at Beethoven's expense but at the curious manner in which Prince Esterházy criticized the music they had just heard (a manner that we, in turn, might criticize at length).

But there were other very different factors, that fed Beethoven's animosity. One concerned a girl to whom both he and Hummel were attracted. Another had to do with the new direction in piano playing and composition for that instrument, a direction of which Hummel had been one of the first proponents, as we mentioned earlier. It was not until Beethoven had his last illness and Hummel appeared at his bedside that the clouds that had gathered darkly between the two artists were suddenly dispersed. More on this matter will be said in the chapter on Beethoven's characteristics.

On the subject of the C major mass it remains to be said that its publication was delayed so long because it was in Prince Esterházy's possession. It was not heard in Vienna until 1816, when it was performed by Gebauer in the Augustine Court Church.

[V]

We now stand at the threshold of one of the most important times in the master's life when, with the exception of a few professional musicians, all the voices that up to this moment had been at odds finally united in unanimous acclaim. The event was the performance on 8 and 12 December 1813 in the University auditorium of the A major symphony and the symphony entitled *Wellington's Victory, or the Battle of Vittoria*, at a concert sponsored by the royal and imperial court mechanic Maelzel for the benefit of the Austrian and Bavarian soldiers wounded in the battle of Hanau.

We have a copy in Beethoven's own hand of his letter of thanks, written for publication and addressed to the artists who contributed to this performance. Before giving this letter it might be well to quote certain passages from the article on this concert that appeared in the AmZ (XVI (1814) No. 4), for the article may be looked upon as reflecting the public opinion prevailing in the capital at the time.

Long honoured here and abroad as one of the greatest orchestral composers, Herr van Beethoven in these performances celebrated his triumph. A large orchestra made up of the foremost instrumentalists of the country joined without remuneration to express their patriotic fervour and gratitude for the blessed success of the united efforts of Germany in the present war, and by their precision under the direction of the composer afforded pleasure that amounted to overwhelming enthusiasm. The new symphony in particular fully deserved the loud applause and the exceptionally warm reception that greeted it. One must hear this newest work of Beethoven's genius as ably performed as it was here to appreciate fully its beauty and to enjoy it to the utmost. . . . The Andante* had to be repeated, and delighted musicians and amateurs alike. As for the *Battle*, if one were to attempt to describe it in musical notes, one would have to do it just as it is done here. Once one accepts the idea, one is pleasurably surprised at the result, and especially at the ingenious and artistic way it is achieved. The effect, even the illusion, is quite extraordinary, and leads one to conclude without hesitation that there is no work equal to it in the whole realm of tone-painting.

It took a work like the *Battle* symphony to unify the conflicting opinions and thus stop the mouths of the opponents of every type. It succeeded, but whether or not the success was permanent we shall see in the third period.

This is the text of Beethoven's letter of thanks:

I consider it my duty to thank all the esteemed participants in the concerts of 8 and 12 December, given for the benefit of the imperial Austrian and royal Bavarian soldiers wounded in the battle of Hanau, for the zeal that they showed in so worthy a cause.

It was a rare assembly of outstanding artists, in which each one, inspired by the sole thought of contributing by his art something for the benefit of the Fatherland, worked together without thought of rank and in subordinate positions to bring about an outstanding performance.

Not only did Hr. Schuppanzigh as leader of the first violins carry the orchestra with him by his fiery and expressive playing, but Hr. Chief-Kapellmeister Salieri did not disdain to give the beat to the drums and the cannonades. Hr. Spohr and Hr. Mayseder, each by his artistry worthy of the highest leadership, played their parts at the second and third desks, and Hr. Siboni and Giuliani likewise occupied subordinate places.

The leadership of the whole assemblage fell to me only because the music was of my composition. Had it been by someone else, I should have been as willing as Hr. Hummel to take my place at the great drum, since we were all filled solely with the purest feeling of love for the Fatherland and with the joy of giving of our powers for those who had given so greatly for us.

But our greatest thanks are due to Hr. Maelzel, since it was he who first conceived the idea of this concert, and to him fell the most burdensome part of the enterprise, the necessary preliminary work, care, and management. Beyond this I must express my particular thanks to him since by this concert that he brought about and by the compositions written specifically for this worthy purpose and delivered to him without fee, he brought to fulfilment my long-

* The original designation of the second movement of this symphony as 'Andante' is worthy of notice. When the instrumental parts were printed, 'Allegretto' was substituted, making for misunderstandings and misinterpretations of the character of the movement. In later years the master recommended that the first designation be restored.

II Beethoven. Engraving by Blasius Höfel after the drawing by Louis
Letronne (1814)

cherished ardent wish to lay one of my great works upon the altar of the Fatherland under the present conditions.

Since, however, a notice will soon be published of all those who collaborated on this occasion and the part that they played, the public can then see for themselves with what noble self-denial a number of the finest artists worked together for one fine objective. It was through my encouragement that the leading masters [?] were assembled.[126]

Ludwig van Beethoven

It is to be noted that the
original idea for the work on
Wellington was mine.

▬ 1814 ▬

And so we have come to 1814, the final year of the second period. It is indisputably the most brilliant year of Beethoven's life, for here we see the composer at the very peak of his glory. I might add that from a material point of view it is also the most rewarding. If we learned above that there were periods of several years when he could not afford to invite music-lovers to a concert, he was able in the course of this single year to gather a large audience no fewer than four times. This was made possible by the extraordinary success of the A major symphony and the *Battle of Vittoria*, by the revisions he had made in the opera *Fidelio*, and finally by important historical events.

As early as January the A major symphony and the *Battle of Vittoria* were repeated, this time in the Great Redoutensaal. This hall afforded an opportunity to put into execution for the first time the many subtleties written into the *Battle* symphony. From the long corridors and opposed rooms one could hear the enemy armies advance towards each other, creating a stunning illusion of the battle. The author of this book was present and can testify that the enthusiasm of the audience, heightened by patriotic emotions because of the victory just won, reached overwhelming proportions. An appropriate addition to the programme was the solemn March with Chorus and the bass aria of the High Priest, 'Mit reger Freude', that follows it, from the festival play, *Die Ruinen von Athen*.

On 27 February the master returned to the same rooms to conduct the same two great works with the addition of the symphony No. 8 in F major, which was given its first performance on this occasion. The order of the programme was as follows: (a) symphony in A major; (b) new trio for soprano, tenor, and bass, *Tremate, empi*, sung by Frau Milder-Hauptmann and the mastersingers Siboni and Weinmüller; (c) the new symphony in F major; and (d) the *Battle of Vittoria*. This programme demonstrates once more how many and how varied were the works that the master offered to his audiences.

Anyone who can picture to himself a gathering of five thousand listeners in a highly emotional state due to recent world-shattering events on the battlefields of Leipzig and Hanau, but due also to their extreme enjoyment of the superlative artistic offering before them, can begin to imagine the elation shared by this assemblage of music-lovers. The joyous outbursts during the A major symphony and the *Battle of Vittoria*, in which, thanks to repeated performances, all the parts meshed in perfect precision, surpassed anything ever yet experienced in a concert hall.

Before continuing with our enumeration of the outstanding events that characterized this glorious year, let me recount how the humorous Allegretto in the eighth symphony came to be written, for it is of particular interest in the Beethoven literature.

In the spring of 1812 Beethoven, the mechanic Maelzel, Count von Brunsvik, Stephan von Breuning, and others were gathered together for a farewell dinner to celebrate first of all Beethoven's journey to see his brother Johann in Linz where he was to work on his eighth symphony before going on to the baths of Bohemia,[127] and secondly Maelzel's projected trip to England where he was to have presented his famous mechanical trumpeter. The latter project had to be given up and postponed for an indefinite length of time. The metronome, which had been invented by this mechanic, had at that time enjoyed so much success that Salieri, Beethoven, Weigl, and other prominent musicians had given a public testimonial of its usefulness.* Beethoven, who in the company of his intimate friends was, as usual, cheerful, witty, satirical— 'unbuttoned', as he called it—improvised at this farewell dinner the following canon, which the guests present joined in singing:

Ex. 12†.[128]

* The AmZ (XV (1813) 785) mentioned this testimonial and also the journey that Maelzel planned to make to London.
† The misinterpretation, or rather the hurrying, of the Allegretto of the eighth symphony by even the most distinguished conductors prompted me to publish this canon along with the anecdote about its composition in the *Niederrheinische Musik-Zeitung*, 1854, No. 49. But I doubt that my comments have made any difference.

From this canon the Allegretto emerged: the first voice presents note for note the theme of this movement, the words indicate its humorous character, and the metronome marking shows the proper tempo for the *allegretto* movement. 'Ta, ta, ta, ta' are the pendulum strokes of the metronome. I am indebted to Beethoven himself for having this canon in my possession, since in 1818 he allowed me to copy it.

Now, more of the events of 1814. On 11 April we find our master once again taking part personally in a concert for charity sponsored by Schuppanzigh in the hall of the tavern 'Zum römischen Kaiser'. It was on this occasion that the great trio in B flat major, opus 97, for piano, violin, and cello was heard for the first time. Beethoven played the piano, Schuppanzigh the violin, and Linke the cello. In May the trio was repeated at a quartet matinée given by Schuppanzigh in the Prater. This performance in the Prater, which I attended as I had the one on 11 April, was Beethoven's last public appearance as a pianist. At this matinée the new quartet in F minor, opus 95, was also given its first performance, though it had been composed in 1811.

On 23 May the opera *Fidelio*, extensively revised, was brought back and given at the Imperial Opera House. I spoke of this performance, as well as of the one on 18 July given for the composer's benefit, in my account of the years 1805 and 1806, and would call the reader's attention to that section of this narrative.

Yet all the honours accruing to the master in the course of this year, and perhaps even throughout his whole lifetime, were surpassed by the proceedings of 29 November of this year. The great political events that had brought almost all the European monarchs together in Vienna collaborated to make of 29 November a day of the greatest glory and acclaim an artist like Beethoven can experience.

Beethoven, having been invited by highly placed art lovers to perform the new works during the Congress, decided to commemorate the historical moment with a musical setting of Dr. Aloys Weissenbach's cantata *Der glorreiche Augenblick* and to present it together with the A major symphony and the *Battle of Vittoria* at an evening concert. The cantata deals with the homage paid by the city of Vindobona [Vienna] to the foreign monarchs. With praiseworthy generosity the imperial chamberlain put at the composer's disposal both imperial Redoutensäle for two evenings, giving this musical event all the solemn honour of a court celebration. Beethoven personally invited the monarchs, all of whom attended the festivities. (The author was in the second violin section of the orchestra.) The emotions shared by the audience of almost six thousand and the members of the very large orchestra and chorus were beyond description. In a unanimous gesture of respect, the audience reverently withheld its applause, giving the whole occasion the character of a religious service. Each person seemed to feel that such a moment would never recur in his lifetime. Only one thing was lacking: Wellington himself was not present, though he had certainly been invited. The victorious general did not arrive in Vienna until the celebration was over.* On 2 December the performance was repeated, and though the audience was smaller, its enthusiasm was even greater. The solos in the cantata were sung by Frau Milder-Hauptmann and Fräulein Bondra, Herr Wild and Herr Forti.

With reference to the cantata we must note that Beethoven's decision to adapt this text to music was a courageous one, since the poetry defies musical setting. With the poet's help, he tried to revise and polish it, but Weissenbach merely made it worse. The poem was then given to Karl Bernard for complete rewriting, all of which entailed a great loss of time. These circumstances explain why in this work the genius of the composer does not attain its usual heights. Moreover, he had only a few days to write out the music. The chorus, made up of amateurs, had to be handled very gently, for in those days of general excitement there was neither time nor will for adequate rehearsing. The only outstanding number is the soprano aria with violin obbligato. The publisher Haslinger in Vienna did well, therefore, to discard the whole Weissenbach-Bernard text, written as it was for a single moment in history, and substitute for it the poem by F. Rochlitz, *Preis der Tonkunst*, a noteworthy poem that Rochlitz had given Beethoven when he was in Vienna in 1822.[129]

Remembering that eight years before this time our master's hearing was already weak, one might well ask how he managed to conduct such a large orchestra and chorus. This question seems all the more puzzling when we recall Friedrich Treitschke's words regarding the revival of *Fidelio* in 1814: 'Beethoven conducted, but his enthusiasm often made him miss the beat.' What sort of conductor was that whose enthusiasm often made him miss the beat and who had to have another standing behind or next to him to restore order? The performances that Beethoven conducted on 8 and 12 December 1813 in the auditorium of the University, and the performances in January, February, November, and December 1814 in the Great Redoutensaal, where the podium was pushed forward for him and no helper stood at his side, are proof enough that he was well able to hear masses of instruments and voices as well as soloists and small ensembles. Anyone acquainted with the difficulties of rehearsing and directing the *Battle* symphony could perhaps wonder

---

* A poster for this special concert is before me. It says among other things: 'Third, a great work for full orchestra written to commemorate Wellington's victory in the battle of Vittoria.'

about the precise entrances of instruments that were at times in separate parts of the auditorium. As one of the performers I can affirm that in the matter of precision nothing was lacking, and truly, the difficulties of conducting *Fidelio* are nothing compared to the *Battle* symphony. In the two performances of the B flat major trio in April and May of this same year, Beethoven's hearing was apparently entirely adequate; not so, though, the agility of his fingers.

Such great exertions concentrated in a short time span could not, however, but have an injurious effect on his weakened hearing. It was at this time that the general deterioration of his right ear set in. As for Beethoven's ability as an orchestral conductor in general, anyone with musical training would readily admit that he was not a faultless director. Even for one who is endowed by nature with all the talents of a conductor, such excellence is developed only through years and years of continuous experience with an orchestra, preferably in the theatre. We have already learned how seldom the great composer had an opportunity to work with an orchestra or a chorus. The career of a music director requires above all unremitting practice.

Later on we shall have reason to speak once more of Beethoven's deafness. Let us now return to the matters at hand. When we listed the obstacles that attended the performances of the *Pastoral* and C minor symphonies, we mentioned as one of them the 'enormous cost', and promised to reproduce some of Beethoven's accounts dating from 1814 in order to give the reader an idea of these expenses. We still have these documents with the composer's notations in the margin.

The 27 February concert included, as we have said, the symphonies in A major and F major, the *Battle* symphony, and the trio *Tremate, empi*. The cost of copying the A major and *Battle* symphonies alone had exceeded the proceeds from the concerts of 8 and 12 December 1813, so that Beethoven had to pay out of his own pocket for copying the trio and the eighth symphony. The itemized bill reads: 452 pages at 12 kreutzers a page, a total of 90 gulden 24 kreutzers. The itemized account for the paying of the orchestra for this concert shows 344 gulden. Yet among the first violinists there were only seven and among the second violinists only six paid musicians mentioned by name, each receiving five or in some cases seven gulden, for in each of the two sections there were twice as many amateurs as professionals.

The itemized account for copying the cantata *Der glorreiche Augenblick* for the 29 November performance shows 1,468 ½ pages at 15 kreutzers a page, equalling 367 gulden 7 kreutzers. The total cost of performing the *Pastoral* and C minor symphonies, the *Fantasy with Chorus*, and portions of the first Mass in C major on 22 December 1808 in the Theater an der Wien apparently amounted to 1,300 gulden.

A glance at these figures makes it easy to guess what sort of a gross profit such a concert would have to return if our master were to clear a few hundred gulden for himself. It was above all the copying costs that absorbed so large a part of the receipts. What a difference the introduction of lithography has made in this item of expense! For this reason the pecuniary aspect could be favourable only for concerts given in the Great Redoutensaal, provided no chorus was needed. But until 1814 we never saw the master in these rooms. His good fortune in being able to realize a profit from the 1814 concerts was due most of all to the political considerations that had caused the rulers of Europe to gather in Vienna, each with his royal household. The extraordinary effect on the public of the *Battle* symphony was a second reason for the financial success of the concerts. The gifts that most of the monarchs gave him made it possible for Beethoven to consider setting aside a little capital in the form of Austrian bank shares.

APPENDICES TO THE SECOND PERIOD

APPENDIX 1

The Catalogue

Before enumerating the works composed in the first period, we spoke of the disorder in the cataloguing of Beethoven's works and said that such confusion had seldom if ever occurred in the listing of any other writer's compositions.

Before proceeding with the index of works composed in the second period, it is imperative that we examine this confusion more closely, for by this time it had reached gigantic proportions. A letter from the publisher Domenico Artaria to Beethoven will be the best witness to this lamentable state of affairs. Artaria writes:

Vienna, 24 July 1819

Dear Sir:

Enclosed are the proofs, which I believe are free of errors.* In the catalogue of your works the following numbers are missing, and though I have made every effort, I have not been able to find them: Opp. 46, 48, 51, 65, 66, 71, 72, 87, 88, 89, 103.[130]

On the other hand, the following works are not numbered at all:

Fidelio [opus 72][131]
The overture to *Leonore* (Artaria undoubtedly meant No. 3, which had been published in 1810.)
Finale from the Singspiel *Die Ehrenpforten* [WoO 97]
Polonaise for piano, published by Mechetti [opus 87]
Finale from the Singspiel *Die gute Nachricht* [WoO 94]
Rondo in C ⎱
Rondo in G ⎰ published Artaria [opus 51]
Six Songs by Gellert, Artaria [opus 48]
Adelaide by Matthisson, Artaria [opus 46]
Variations for 4 hands in C [WoO 67]
Great Trio for 2 oboes and English horn, Artaria [opus 87]
Great Quintet for 2 violins, 2 violas, and cello, E flat major, Artaria [opus 4]
Prelude for piano in F minor, Riedel [WoO 55]

* These were the proofs of the great sonata in B flat major, opus 106.

12 *Deutsche* for the Redoutensaal ⎫ Artaria ⎫ [WoO 8]
12 Minuets for the Redoutensaal ⎭ ⎭ [WoO 7]

Quintet in C for 2 violins, 2 violas, and cello, Mollo
[probably the arrangement of the first symphony published
without opus number by Mollo about 1810 or 1811]

Scene and Aria, 'Ah, perfido', Peters [opus 65]

Variations on a March by Dressler, Steiner [WoO 63]

Variations for piano on the air, *La vie est un voyage*, Paris, Janet [opus 66
—see KHV, page 157]

Sextet for 2 clarinets, 2 horns, and 2 bassoons, Breitkopf [opus 71]

Songs by Goethe and Matthisson, Riedel [WoO 136, 137, opus 75 Nos. 1
and 2]

Italian and German songs, 4 folios, Peters [opus 32, WoO 124, and six
songs from opus 52, published 1806–12, by the Bureau de Musique—see
KHV, pp. 82, 123, 587]

and other unnumbered works described in the catalogue on the back.

We therefore request, dear sir, that you consider and let us know to which
works we may assign the missing numbers.

We also respectfully ask that you return the enclosed proofs as soon as
possible.

In anticipation of a prompt answer, we remain most respectfully, etc.

Beethoven, who at that time was in Mödling working on his D major
mass, answered immediately:[132] he had no time then to devote to this
matter and was at any rate incapable of straightening it out; the publishers had brought about the confusion and they could do what they
might to get themselves out of it. Finally, he referred Artaria to his
colleagues Steiner & Co. who might be able to help him untangle the
knot. This publishing house, however, declined to co-operate, as it was
already on not too friendly terms with Beethoven. Just recently it had
seen fit to put out two songs by Beethoven, giving each one a separate
opus number, without first asking the master. They were the little
songs, *Der Mann von Wort* and *Merkenstein*, designated as opus 99 and
opus 100 respectively, each consisting of no more than two pages. Beethoven's protests against such arbitrary and whimsical numbering were
disregarded. Such was the continuing indifference of publishers to the
authors' desires and interests, as we have already shown at the beginning of the second period.

Carl Czerny's remark, in the second chapter (p. 60) of his piano
textbook, about the confusion in Beethoven's catalogue deserves our
notice. He says: 'Besides, there appears in the listing of his compositions a vast disorder, as a result of which the existence of a great number
of interesting works is entirely unknown.' The situation becomes
almost hopeless when one realizes that some numbers appear three or
even four times.

Wherever possible, the reader should refer to this letter from Artaria in reviewing the list of works belonging to both the second and third periods. Perhaps in the future the catalogue can be better organized; even an establishment of the chronological order would be very desirable. However, until the arrangements are separated from the original works and placed in a distinct category, there can be no progress in this direction. Naturally, the arrangements should bear the same opus numbers as their original versions. To weed them out would leave gaps in the sequence of numbers, but this would not be as confusing as the existing hotchpotch. It would hardly be advisable to change the numbers of the originals, since the public has long been familiar with the present opus numbers.

APPENDIX 2

List of Works

The list of works belonging to the second period is not arranged in chronological order as was possible for the first period but, because of the difficulties of cataloguing just mentioned, in groups according to medium, thus facilitating a quick review of the period. For the sake of completeness some works have been included with first performance in the earlier period or publication in the following period, as we can see, for example, with the symphonies.

SYMPHONIES

No. 1, Symphony in C major, opus 21, first performed 1800, published 1801, by Peters, Leipzig [Hoffmeister].[133]

No. 2, Symphony in D major, opus 36, first performed 1804 [1803], published 1804 by the Industrie-Comptoir.

No. 3, *Sinfonia Eroica*, E flat major, opus 55, first performed 1805, published 1807 [1806] by the Industrie-Comptoir.

No. 4, Symphony in B flat major, opus 60, first performed 1807, published 1808 by the Industrie-Comptoir.

No. 5, Symphony in C minor, opus 67, first performed 1808, published 1809 by Breitkopf & Härtel, Leipzig.

No. 6, *Pastoral Symphony* in F major, opus 68, first performed 1808, published 1809 by Breitkopf & Härtel.

No. 7, Symphony in A major, opus 92, first performed 1813, published 1816 by Steiner & Co., Vienna.

No. 8, Symphony in F major, opus 93, first performed 1814, published 1817 by Steiner & Co.

Wellington's Victory, or the Battle of Vittoria, opus 91, first performed 1813, published 1816 by Steiner & Co.

CONCERTOS FOR PIANO AND ORCHESTRA AND THE CHORAL FANTASY

No. 2, Concerto in B flat major, opus 19, first performed 1800 [perhaps 1795, perhaps 1798], published 1801 by Hoffmeister & Kühnel, Leipzig.

No. 3, Concerto in C minor, opus 37, first performed 1804 [1803], published 1805 [1804] by the Industrie-Comptoir.

No. 4, Concerto in G major, opus 58, first performed? [1807], published 1808 by the Industrie-Comptoir.

No. 5, Concerto in E flat major, opus 73, first performed 1812 [1811], published 1811 by Breitkopf & Härtel [1810, Clementi].

Choral Fantasy in C minor, opus 80, first performed 1808, published 1811 by Breitkopf & Härtel [1810, Clementi].

VIOLIN CONCERTO IN D MAJOR, OPUS 61

First performed 1806, published 1808 (simultaneously with the arrangement as a piano concerto) by the Industrie-Comptoir.

CONCERTINO IN C MAJOR FOR PIANO, VIOLIN, AND CELLO, OPUS 56

First performed 1808, published 1810 [1807] by the Industrie-Comptoir.

VOCAL WORKS WITH ORCHESTRA

A. *Christus am Oelberge*, cantata, opus 85, first performed 1803, published 1811 by Breitkopf & Härtel.

B. *Fidelio*, opera, opus 72, first performed 1805, different sections published in different years by Breitkopf & Härtel, Artaria, and Simrock.

C. *Mass in C major*, opus 86, first performed 1808 [1807], published 1813 [1812] by Breitkopf & Härtel.

D. *Die Ruinen von Athen*, opp. 113 and 114, first performed 1812, different sections published in different years, first publisher Artaria.

E. *Der glorreiche Augenblick*, occasional cantata, opus 136, first performed 1814, published about 1836 by Haslinger.

APPENDIX 2. LIST OF WORKS

OVERTURES FOR ORCHESTRA

A. Overture to the ballet *Prometheus*, opus 43, first performed 1801. The complete *Prometheus* music appeared in various arrangements in 1802 [1801] and 1805. First published by Hoffmeister [Artaria].

B. Overture to *Coriolanus*, C minor, opus 62, first performed 1807, published [1808] by the Industrie-Comptoir.

C. Overture to *Egmont*, F minor, opus 84, first performed 1808 [1810], published 1811 [1810] by Breitkopf & Härtel.

D. Overtures to *Fidelio*, opus 72. No. 1, C major, published about 1838 [1836] by Haslinger; No. 2, C major, first performed with the opera in 1805, published about 1842 by Breitkopf & Härtel; No. 3, C major, first performed with the opera in 1806, published 1810 by Breitkopf & Härtel; No. 4, E major, first performed with the opera in 1814, published [1822] by Breitkopf & Härtel.

E. Overture to *König Stephan*, E flat major, opus 117, first performed 1812, published 1823 [1826] by Haslinger.

SEPTET IN E FLAT MAJOR, OPUS 20

First performed 1800, published 1801 [1802] by Hoffmeister & Kühnel.

SEXTET IN E FLAT MAJOR, OPUS 81B

Published 1810 by Simrock in Bonn.

QUINTETS

Opus 16, E flat major, for piano, oboe, clarinet, horn, and bassoon, published 1801 by Mollo.

Opus 29, C major, for 2 violins, 2 violas, and cello, published 1803 [1802] by Breitkopf & Härtel.

QUARTETS

Opus 18, F major, G major, D major, C minor, A major, B flat major,* published 1802 [1801] by Mollo.

Opus 59, F major, E minor, C major, published 1807 [1808] by the Industrie-Comptoir.

Opus 74, E flat major, published 1810 by Breitkopf & Härtel [Clementi].

* The first three of these quartets were published in 1801 by Mollo. Thus they were composed in the last years of the first period. The other three (C minor, A major, B flat major) are referred to in Beethoven's letter of 1801 to his friend in Courland, Karl Amenda, who had left Vienna in 1799 as we saw at the beginning of this period. The reference to the quartets reads: 'Do not show your quartet to anyone else, for I have changed it considerably. I am just now really learning how to write quartets, as you will see when you receive these.' But what did Beethoven have in mind when he had six quartets published under a single opus number, at a time when he could still impose his own will? Such abundance is a blatant contradiction to the practice that prevailed later, when he was no longer able to control such things, of honouring trivial pieces with separate opus numbers, as we saw in the case of opp. 99 and 100—two tiny little songs.

SECOND PERIOD

TRIOS FOR PIANO, VIOLIN, AND CELLO

Opus 70, D major and E flat major, published 1810 [1809] by Breitkopf & Härtel.

Opus 97 in B flat major, first performed 1814, published 1816 by Steiner & Co.

SONATAS FOR PIANO AND VIOLIN

Opus 23, A minor, published 1801 by Mollo.

Opus 24, F major, published 1801 by Mollo.

Opus 30, A major, C minor, G major, published 1803 by the Industrie-Comptoir.

Opus 47, A major, published 1805 by Simrock.

Opus 96, G major, published 1814 [1816] by Steiner & Co.

SONATA FOR PIANO AND CELLO

Opus 69, A major, published 1809 by Breitkopf & Härtel.

SONATA FOR PIANO AND HORN

Opus 17, F major, published 1801 by Hoffmeister & Kühnel [Mollo].

SONATAS FOR PIANO SOLO (INCLUDING 1 SONATINA AND 1 FANTASY)

Opus 22, B flat major, published 1801 by [Hoffmeister &] Kühnel.

Opus 26, A flat major with Funeral March, published 1802 by Johann Cappi in Vienna.

Opus 27, E flat major, C sharp minor, published 1802 by Johann Cappi.

Opus 28, D major, published 1802 by the Industrie-Comptoir.

Opus 31, G major, D minor, E flat major, published 1803 [1803–4] by Nägeli and Simrock.

Opus 49, G minor, G major, published by the Industrie-Comptoir.

Opus 53, C major, published 1805 by the Industrie-Comptoir.

Opus 54, F major, published 1806 by the Industrie-Comptoir.

Opus 57, F minor, published 1807 by the Industrie-Comptoir.

Opus 77, Fantasy, G minor, published 1810 by Breitkopf & Härtel [Clementi].

Opus 78, F sharp major, published 1810 by Breitkopf & Härtel [Clementi].

Opus 79, Sonatina, G major, published 1810 by Breitkopf & Härtel [Clementi].

Opus 81a, *Les Adieux*, E flat major, published 1811 by Breitkopf & Härtel [Clementi].

VARIATIONS FOR PIANO SOLO, AND ALSO WITH ACCOMPANIMENT

Opus 34, Six Variations on an original theme, F major, published 1803 by Breitkopf & Härtel.

Opus 35, Fifteen Variations and Fugue, E flat major, published 1803 by Breitkopf & Härtel.

Opus 76, D major, published 1810 by Breitkopf & Härtel [also Clementi].

Opus 44, Fourteen Variations, E flat major, for piano, violin, and cello, published 1804 by Peters [Hoffmeister & Kühnel].

Opus 66, Twelve Variations, F major, for piano and cello, published 1799 [1798] by Artaria [Traeg].

(The letter from Artaria that was quoted above bears on these last two works. It is particularly difficult to see why the 'Twelve Variations' came to be called opus 66, for it is one of the master's earliest compositions, and was critically reviewed in AmZ I (1799) 366. The Trio for 2 oboes and English horn, designated as opus 87, also dates without question back to the first period.)

ROMANCES FOR VIOLIN ACCOMPANIED BY A SMALL ORCHESTRA

Opus 40, G major, published 1803 by Hoffmeister & Kühnel.

Opus 50, F major, published 1805, first publisher unknown [Industrie-Comptoir].

Opus 25, Serenade in D major for flute, violin, and viola, published 1802 by Simrock [Cappi].

Most of the songs and *Lieder* belonging to this period have already been mentioned in the text.

APPENDIX 3

Beethoven's Musical Character

Who can fail to be amazed at this list, at the unequalled productivity exhibited by Beethoven's genius in all the media of musical composition, and at the unremitting toil that in a period of fourteen short years brought forth all these works? If no others had followed, these would have been enough to assure the master of a place among the foremost men in the history of art, for the peoples of Europe had already recognized and honoured him as one of the foremost representatives of their culture and their glory in the realm of music. How little art criticism contributed to this recognition has already been sufficiently shown in the foregoing excerpts.

One man, however, deserves to be elevated above his fellows, a single voice that was the first to separate itself from the chorus, shattering the old prejudices that favoured only the traditional and the familiar in music. This writer endeavoured to approach the spirit of Beethoven's compositions and to reveal their special qualities both in overall expression and specific application, thus raising the torch so that the public might see and comprehend. We have already met him in his review of the C minor symphony written for the AmZ: Amadeus Wendt.[134] We must now present to Beethoven's admirers more of the writings of this enlightened harbinger and so render to him the thanks that each one of us owes him. For it was his glorious mission to make known to his contemporaries the nature of the composer who had until then been misunderstood and hated, and thus to bring about a memorable act of reconciliation.

In its seventeenth year of publication (1815), the AmZ carried in six issues an article entitled, 'Thoughts about the New Art of Composition and about van Beethoven's music, especially his *Fidelio*', by Professor Amadeus Wendt. From this comprehensive essay I should like to reproduce here a small portion that applies to Beethoven's music in general.

After an introduction dealing with the nature of opera, in which he accords Mozart his deserved place of honour, Wendt goes on to his main theme, which he entitles 'Beethoven's Musical Character':

The above reflections were occasioned by the work of a master whose colossal genius, sparked by Mozart and Haydn, has built of romantic instrumental music a cathedral that rises up into the clouds. It is unlikely that another living composer will surpass him in his wealth of great and serious musical ideas, which seem to stem not from reading or hearing the compositions of others but from his own explorations of a sublime region never before discovered. No one else is likely to display his boldness of imagination, the flights of which carry us (as in the *Sinfonia Eroica*) on to the field of battle where the golden hopes and glorious heroic era of one nation are defeated while another nation celebrates its day of resurrection, or again into the gay embrace of nature to join the jovial peasants, as in the *Pastoral* symphony.

We do not by any means intend an apology for descriptive music or for 'musical painting', for which Beethoven, like his teacher Haydn, seems to have a propensity; no, except for a few instances of playfulness, Beethoven remains what a musician can and must be : a painter of passions. And just as passion is not necessarily without thought, so the moods of a fantasy that the composer of genius captures in musical tones may become the object of visual images. He sees the scenes whose atmosphere he is portraying, and the clarity with which he sees his tone pictures as they are inspired and developed may easily become so distinct that he feels he has portrayed something visible, something even with a geographical location.

Actually, though, Beethoven's music is so far from being a description of reality or of concrete objects that it imparts to emotion an indescribable and extraordinary degree of depth and intimacy. Indeed, a scholar conducting research on the soul of Beethoven's music might become more fully aware of the breadth and variety of passions of which the human heart is capable. In fact, if Beethoven were to be measured solely by this criterion, it alone might well be enough to place him ahead of all his musical contemporaries. His range of passions is beyond measure; his tones express ever anew a bliss never before experienced or enjoyed; he captures in the sounds of this world both the heavenly and the infernal, making of these sounds something new and infinite.

One will note at once that in his musical images, the grand and the spacious predominate. Could we then call him the Shakespeare of music? For he is as capable of portraying and expressing in tones the innermost depths of the struggling heart as the sweet magic of innocent love; the bitterest, deepest pain as delight rejoicing aloud to the skies; the most grandiose as the most graceful;* yet his spirit inclines most devotedly towards statements of deep solemnity, fiery ecstasy, and lofty grandeur, and sets the highest emotions in harmonious accord. We may best understand this breadth of expression by remembering that Beethoven's genius was first applied to music at a time when, through Haydn and Mozart, instrumental music was in its glory. To further glorify it with his original spirit is the primary task of his life. He has studied with depth and perception the hidden soul of each instrument, and while a number of his contemporaries are able to write with understanding for some one instrument, exploiting its special character, we know of no living composer except Beethoven and perhaps Cherubini who knows every instrument according to its particular qualities and can compose with such originality and variety, using the instruments in such wonderful combinations.

To one who has achieved this power over the soul of music, there must necessarily come a compelling desire to exercise his mastery. This can best be done through the medium of orchestral music, which is not suited to the trivial but can be used to portray only the incisive and mighty forces of human passions. When one makes use of the whole power and vastness of orchestral music, sounds hitherto unheard are possible, and the hearer is aware of a superhuman strength which at moments makes him feel that he is of a higher world. All the instruments must unite, not in plaintive lament, not in weak sensitivity or to give the semblance of power where there is none, not to do little with much (though this would seem to be the motto of some composers of today when they set the whole orchestra bowing and blasting for a simple little flute concerto), but to combine the various musical forces into a single intense, climactic expression, to fulfil the promises that Mozart so eloquently made us on behalf of the romantic spirit of music.

* What a difference between the wonderfully sweet, sensitive melody of the Goethe song, *Ich denke dein*, or the melancholy *Adelaide* and the titanic struggles in the *Eroica* symphony, a struggle far deeper and more acute than any experienced in *Faust!* A. W.

And in all this the master himself has the same power and control over the orchestra that the virtuoso has over his instrument. In truth, instrumental music seems to have reached its zenith with composers like Beethoven, for whom all the instruments for which he writes, all the instruments of the whole orchestra, must play together as if they formed collectively a single instrument in the hands of a virtuoso. No one may play for himself alone; all combine in an everlasting flux, blending and recombining in a living tonal universe.*

These remarks have served, we feel, to characterize Beethoven's greatest orchestral compositions. As for reproaches against the master, they could be made only by a layman or by a musician who failed to understand the power and meaning of his own art. And as difficulty is in any case a relative matter— otherwise instead of continuing to play Mozart, Haydn, and Cherubini one would stop at Hiller, Benda, Vanhall, and their confrères—the law of art is: with little do much. And degree of difficulty is not the most important criterion of music; otherwise the lighter media, such as songs with piano accompaniment, would be the highest art form, and Italian music universally preferred to all others. No, every art has its form which each medium must exploit to its fullest limits and through which it must express its all-encompassing unity.

APPENDIX 4

Criticisms of Difficulty and Incomprehensibility

[Editor's note. This is a continuation of the article by Wendt.]

When we think of music as difficult, we must realize that many of us remember a time when few orchestras had clarinets and none had trombones, when pieces that today any little orchestra can play easily almost at sight had to be laboriously studied, and other works that are now played everywhere simply for the pleasure of playing them were rejected as impossible of performance. Indeed, we clearly remember that Mozart's music was at first reluctantly put aside by many orchestras, while those orchestras that prefer Italian music still distrust it. Even worthy men such as Hiller, upon hearing Mozart's *Così Fan Tutte*, would from their limited point of view say that the composer showed promise but that he worked too hard and was too pretentious.

We must not forget that there are minds that fly on the wings of genius and arrive before their time; not until years later, sometimes not until they have long departed this world, can they expect the fullest and deepest comprehen-

* If only this excellent member of the Leipzig art tribunal had been able to hear the ninth symphony as well! A. S.

sion of their works. In philosophy we have the example of Kant; in poetry Klopstock, Schiller, and Goethe, whose first appearance in print made so unfavourable an impression that the commonest critics of the time considered them as no more than equals and treated them as such. Even Mozart's *Don Giovanni*, which today affords its audiences a musical and dramatic festival every time it is performed, was at first avoided because of its sinister ghosts.

Beethoven is one of these precocious minds, as many of his orchestral compositions (besides those mentioned, the great C minor symphony) testify. And his *Fidelio*, we embolden ourselves to prophesy, will also one day stand as proof of his greatness: as it becomes performed with the mastery that it both demands and deserves, it will give pleasure and gain respect from many quarters. For the true sign of great works is that they are repeatedly and increasingly enjoyed, and that, through the unfolding of the infinite beauty that encompasses the whole, they afford an ever richer pleasure, just as the observant eye looking into an enclouded sky finds and discovers worlds beyond worlds.

We now know how accurately this prophecy made in 1815 by an art scholar from Leipzig has been fulfilled. In respect to *Fidelio*, Amadeus Wendt undertook a careful analysis and comparison between the opera in its original version and the two-act revision, then made a statement deserving of our attention:

Apart from the overture, it was not essential to alter the numbers retained, except to accommodate the rearrangement of the stage settings. And since this rearrangement did little to improve the dramatic tension of the opera, and in fact confused the relation of the acts to one another, we would like to recommend that this opera be performed in its original version. We are sure that with the pleasure of repeated performances by experienced and gifted singers and orchestras, true music-lovers will come to acknowledge the opera, and that its name will one day be gratefully engraved in the national sanctuary along with the divine operas of Mozart.

Yet it can hardly be assumed that the insight of this scholarly writer was completely unbiased in this article, or that Wendt was not in many respects a product of his time, sharing the common prejudices of his generation. His essay, 'Beethoven's Mannerisms', contains clear cases of erroneous preconceptions that today would be generally recognized as false. One example, though in another connection, will serve to illustrate this point. Wendt says:

Many of Beethoven's works, e.g., several of his symphonies and sonatas, can only be regarded and classed as musical fantasies. In them even the attentive listener loses the main idea; he finds himself in a splendid labyrinth where his eye is attracted to lush vegetation and rare flowers on every side, yet he cannot regain the thread that will lead him back to the peace of his own home. The artist's fantasy flows irresistibly on with hardly a respite, and one impression is frequently nullified by what follows it; the main idea is completely lost, or shimmers only vaguely in the dark distance from the flow of the changing harmonies.

In a conversation that took place long after the appearance of this essay, Beethoven was asked about it. The master answered: 'There is much wisdom in what he said, but much of the mentality of a school boy, too. They ought to re-read it now, and then read it again after a few more years.' That was all he had to say on the subject.

What was the true meaning of this oracular remark? Is the first ('wisdom') supposed to mean the eternal, immutable truth, even in relation to his words, while the second ('school-boy mentality') indicates something that will be modified, revised at a later time? Perhaps! Herder says:

Where the form is created once and for all, as in sculpture and painting, it is the appreciation of it that must be sharpened, refined, expanded. But it seems to be another story with those arts that reverberate in the air, music and speech. Who can contain in a single view the swelling sea, or impose a form where every wave disappears with the moment? It is for this reason that different nations, times, and men judge music and poetry so differently! And again, it is for this reason that music and poetry vary so widely between nations, times, and men! Thus it seems that the basis of agreement lies both in the artistic means employed and in the nature of the human sensations that respond to these means. The rules of harmony are the same for all people; the responses of our organs of sense can be systematically trained so that their reactions can be anticipated and allowed for. In this way a general standard, a basis of agreement, is possible.

EDITOR'S NOTES (53–134)

Second Period

⁵³ In Hungarian orthography, the family name of Beethoven's good friend was *domanoveczi és lestinei Zmeskál Miklos*, which in English would read 'Nicholas Zmeskal of Domanovecz and Lestine', and in MM the present editor adopted the spelling Zmeskal (not Zmeskall). This was probably an excess of zeal, in view of the fact that all evidence points to the spelling *Zmeskall* as the one used by the Count during the forty years or so that he lived in Vienna. In the present volume, therefore, the customary spelling will be retained.

⁵⁴ It was Baron Johann Baptist von Pasqualati who was Beethoven's landlord, adviser, and friend from 1804 until the composer's death, but his younger

brother Baron Joseph Andreas was active on Beethoven's behalf in 1815 and 1816 in connection with payments from the Kinsky estate.

[55] And. 541 is a letter from Beethoven to Amenda dated 12 April 1815. In the spring of 1816 Dr. Karl von Bursy came to Beethoven with a letter of introduction from Amenda (Leitzmann I 72). KHV (691) suggests that Col. von Düsterlohe of Courland, who visited Beethoven in January 1825, may have been the bearer of greetings from Amenda.

[56] Beethoven's first dedication to Prince Lichnowsky was one of his earliest publications in Vienna, the variations on *Quant'è più bello*, WoO 69, published in December 1795.

[57] The judicious reader should take at less than face value Schindler's invectives against the brothers and against other individuals—Karl Holz and Nephew Karl are two outstanding examples—with whom he was compelled to share his hero. Undoubtedly Brother Karl was presumptuous in his position as confidant of the great musician; equally certainly, Brother Johann was slightly ridiculous as a man of unexpectedly acquired wealth. Both were for these reasons liabilities to the composer in his relationships with his associates, but Schindler's charges of 'hypocrisy, cunning, and malice', brought to bear on Beethoven's friends by 'evil and persistent methods', cannot be supported. One of Thayer's many fundamental contributions to Beethoven scholarship is his discussion of this subject in *Ein kritischer Beitrag zu Beethoven-Literatur* (1877), esp. pp. 16 ff.

[57a] Nottebohm, *Beethoveniana*, 183n, points out that Preindl's *Wiener Tonschule*, in an edition by Seyfried, was first published only in 1827 after Beethoven's death.

[58] Schindler gives '1771' as the year of Weber's birth. He died in 1842 in his seventy-seventh year. Schindler also gives '1758–1826' as the dates for Preindl.

[59] On page 93 of the *Notizen*, Ries lists an arrangement of the septet for string quintet as one made by Beethoven. The present announcement (which also appeared in the *Wiener Zeitung* for 30 October 1802) shows that this is not so. As for Beethoven's strictures against publishers who issue arrangements, note that in his letter of 22 April 1801 to F. A. Hoffmeister (And. 47), Beethoven asked the publisher to prepare and issue an arrangement of the septet as a quintet for flute and strings. As Beethoven complained, the title-page of the septet arrangement (KHV 50), and presumably that of the symphony, gave no indication that the work was not originally written for quintet.

[60] Dr. Hans Halm kindly pointed out that Schindler's '*Wenn Könige säen . . .*' is a misquotation of the epigram from Schiller's *Kant und seine Ausleger*:

Wie doch ein einziger Reicher so viele Bettler in Nahrung setzt! Wenn Könige baun, haben die Kärrner zu tun.

(To how many beggars a single rich man gives food! When kings erect magnificent edifices, the labourers have much to do.)

[61] There seems to be no other record of a serious illness in 1802 (TK I 348; TF 300), though there was such an illness, with slow convalescence, in the spring of 1804 (TK II 27; TF 352). Presumably Schindler confused the two years.

[62] A discussion of the Heiligenstadt Will published by Kinsky in the *Schweizerische Musikzeitung* LXXIV (1934) 519 may be summarized as follows:

The history of this document after Beethoven's death as given by Thayer (TK I 351) is not accurate. Upon Beethoven's death his papers were taken by Schindler and Stephan von Breuning for use by Rochlitz (at Beethoven's request) in the preparation of an official biography. In September 1827 Schindler sent a transcript of the will to Rochlitz, who published it on 17 October 1827 in the AmZ (XXIX [1827] 705).

Presumably Artaria withdrew the document, because of its intimate character, at the time Beethoven's papers were being appraised before the public sale of 5 November, and on 21 November gave it to Jakob Hotschevar, guardian of Nephew Karl, who (according to the endorsement) gave it to Brother Johann. There is no convincing evidence that the document passed to Gräffer or to Fuchs, as stated by Schindler and Thayer respectively, but in 1840 Liszt offered it for sale in London for fifty guineas, presumably on behalf of Amalie Waldmann-Stölzle, the illegitimate daughter of brother Johann's wife. [Editor's note. Amalie died on 10 March 1831, leaving a four-month-old son.] In 1843 the will was acquired by the violinist Ernst, who presented it in 1855 to Jenny Lind and her husband Otto Goldschmidt. In 1890 Goldschmidt donated the will to the library of his native city of Hamburg.

[63] Ries (TK I 352 and TF 304, quoted from *Notizen*, p. 97) gives an account of the incident of the unheard flute.

[64] Until 1810 (see MM 72) Beethoven believed that he had been born in 1772.

[65] The instruments that Beethoven refers to—two violins, a viola, and a cello, now in the museum of the Beethovenhaus—are discussed in MQ XLVI (1960) 41. Only in 1964, however, did it become known that the viola of this set was probably an instrument made in the late eighteenth century by the German *luthier* Johann Anton Gedler (*Verein Beethoven-Haus 1889-1964*, p. 46).

[66] Actually, in the two places in the will in which Brother Johann's name should have appeared, a blank space was left, but dots were not used. Mueller von Asow (*Ludwig van Beethovens Heiligenstädter Testament*, p. 6), gives the possible explanation that Beethoven was uncertain whether to use the name Nikolaus, by which his brother had been known within the family, or Johann, which he had adopted after his arrival in Vienna.

[67] KHV (234) questions Schindler's statement, though concurred with by Ries (*Notizen*, p. 75), that *Christus* was sketched during the summer of 1801. Several letters from Beethoven are cited as proof that the work was written very hastily during a few weeks in March 1803. The oak tree may have been the spot at which Beethoven worked on opp. 27, 28, or 29, any one (or all three) of which may have been under way during the summer of 1801, or Beethoven may have been thinking of the work on *Leonore* that he did in Hetzendorf in the summer of 1805.

[68] Schindler is correct in his conjecture that Beethoven made 'extensive changes' before releasing the work for publication: the engraver's copy consisted of '44 sheets in Beethoven's hand and 118 from a copyist, but with so

many corrections, annotations, changes, and new passages inserted by the composer that it must be considered a reworking of the composition' (KHV 235). Publication was in October 1811.

[69] An index to the reviews (more than 75) that appeared in the AmZ is given at the end of the book.

[70] Schindler's narrative in the next few pages, in which he sets forth his contention that the Immortal Beloved letters were written to Giulietta Guicciardi in July 1803, is of great importance in the history of Beethoven scholarship, since for years his conclusions were accepted almost without question. As the flaws in his facts and his reasoning became more evident, other scholars proposed other female friends and other times. The weight of evidence now seems to point to 1812 as the year in which the letters were written, but the identity of the inamorata is, and probably will remain, a matter of conjecture. The subject has fascinated writers of the most diverse merits as biographical analysts. Of the many books, pamphlets, and journal articles upon the famous letters and the problems that they raise, three in particular may be recommended for their scholarship and dispassionate reasoning: TK I, ch. XXI; Sonneck, *The Riddle of the Immortal Beloved* (New York, 1927); and Unger, *Auf Spuren von Beethovens 'Unsterblicher Geliebten'* (Langensalza, 1910). Mention may also be made of a recent and highly controversial book by Kaznelson, *Beethovens Ferne und Unsterbliche Geliebte* (Zürich, 1954). A useful summary of the many conjectures regarding these letters may be found in TF 1088 ff. Some of the statements made by Schindler merit more detailed discussion here.

I. Schindler's Paris diary, as published by Becker (*Anton Schindler, der Freund Beethovens* [Frankfurt-am-Main, n.d. (1939)], p. 41), shows that he first met Cherubini on 3 February 1841, when the old composer was in his eighty-first year. The detailed account of this visit in the diary makes no mention of any discussion of an *affaire de cœur* of Beethoven. Two days later Schindler spent a few minutes with Cherubini who was too ill and weak to talk much. What was presumably his third and last visit took place on 7 March 1842, only eight days before Cherubini's death (Becker, p. 83). In the diary there is no indication that at any time except the first visit was there any conversation bearing upon Beethoven. If, as Schindler says, the question of Beethoven's great love had been settled by Cherubini, after years of vain searching by Schindler, it is most improbable that the diary entry of 500 to 600 words for 3 February 1841 would have included not even a hint that the subject had been touched upon, let alone settled. It is the conclusion of the present editor that, nearly twenty years after the Paris sojourn, Schindler's memory played him false in calling upon Cherubini as the key witness in determining a date for Beethoven's famous letters.

II. The story that Schindler solemnly presents of Beethoven's attempt at suicide by starvation is laughed off the stage in TK I 324.

III. There is no reason to doubt that when in 1817 Beethoven met Marie Pachler-Koschak, who was at that time twenty-three years old and a bride, he was charmed by her as a musician and as a woman. A brochure published in 1865 by her son, *Beethoven und Marie Pachler-Koschak*, and the testimony of facts brought out by later biographers dispose of Schindler's conclusion that she was the object of Beethoven's 'autumnal love'.

[71] The evidential value of the passage that Schindler has quoted here from a Conversation Book is reduced to zero by his addition of a few words, indicated as a part of Beethoven's remarks, that Beethoven never uttered and that completely change the sense of a crucial passage (see MQ XLVI [1960] 45).

[72] It is probable that Giulietta Guicciardi was the 'enchanting girl' to whom Beethoven referred in his letter of 16 November 1801 to Wegeler, but it may be stated with virtual certainty that she was not the addressee of the famous letters.

[73] Actually, the first performance of these two works took place at the concert of 5 April 1803 at which *Christus am Oelberge* also was first heard.

[74] This statement overlooks the publication of the *Prometheus* overture by Hoffmeister & Kühnel in January 1804, the second symphony by the Bureau des Arts et d'Industrie in March, the third of the opus 31 piano sonatas by Nägeli in May or June, and the C minor concerto by the Bureau during the summer. The arrangement of the *Prometheus* ballet for string quartet was published by Artaria in the summer of 1803; the piano transcription of the ballet, which Czerny attributed to Beethoven himself, had appeared as opus 24 from Artaria in June 1801 (KHV 102).

[75] Bernadotte was in Vienna only from 5 February to mid-April 1798.

[76] Schindler's statement is not borne out by the facts. The only known letter from Beethoven to King Karl XIV Johann of Sweden, whom Beethoven had known while he was in Vienna as General Bernadotte (And. 1150 of 1 March 1823), makes no reference to Napoleon or to the *Eroica* symphony. Note also that more than five years elapsed between Bernadotte's sojourn in Vienna and the composition of the symphony.

[77] Schindler's too frequent disregard of chronology, and the undependability of his factual statements except as regards events in which he was a participant, are illustrated here: Schleiermacher's translation of the *Republic* was first published only in 1828 (Brit 24–331). No works of Plato were included in the inventory of Beethoven's library that was prepared after his death (Leitzmann, *Ludwig van Beethoven* [1921] II 379–83), and except for these statements by Schindler, there seems to be no evidence that at any period of his life Plato was one of the classical writers with whose works Beethoven was familiar. Apart from these considerations, 'how could anyone believe that the much-employed Beethoven, at the age of twenty-seven, he who had refused two years before, even despite Wegeler's urging, to listen to a single private lecture on Kant, had become in so short a time a Platonic philosopher?' (TK I 214).

[78] Schindler is not the only writer whom the modes have led up the garden path to a labyrinth well strewn with pitfalls. The descriptions that he gives are of the medieval modes with a sixteenth-century addition, not of the Greek modes of the same names (see Grove 5–798). Instead of trying to correct Schindler's identification of the various scales, the editor will content himself with repeating the quotation with which Reese (*Music in the Middle Ages* [1940], p. 20) introduces his discussion of Greek musical theory:

'The only professor of Greek I have ever known who was also a musician always refused on principle to give me any help with a stiff passage from a Greek author on music. His reply was always the same: "Put that stuff away. Nobody has ever made head or tail of Greek music, and nobody ever will. That way madness lies." '

[79] The C major symphony had received its first performance in April 1800 and had been published in December 1801. During the winter of 1804–5 a series of concerts under the leadership of Clement was given. 'New performances of Beethoven's first two symphonies and the concerto in C minor—pianoforte part by Ries—prepare the way for the production of "an entirely new symphony". . . . It was the *Sinfonia Eroica*—its first semi-public performance. Its first really public performance was in the Theater an der Wien on Sunday evening 7 April [1805]' with Beethoven as conductor (TK II 42).

[80] A more extensive excerpt from this review is given in TDR III 22.

[81] In the piano sonatas up to opus 31, Beethoven seems to limit himself to the five octaves from the F below cello C, but in the C minor concerto, which assumed its final form not later than the spring of 1803, the upward compass was extended to the second C above the treble clef. The Erard piano that was presented to Beethoven in the summer of 1803 had a compass corresponding to these requirements (BStud II 223). The violin sonata opus 47 remains within the five-octave range from F to F: the piano sonata opus 53 extends upwards to A above high C. A discussion of the pianos available in Vienna in 1795, together with rather detailed specifications of the piano that Mozart used in the 1780's, may be found in Hanslick, pp. 129–30.

[82] Schindler crammed much misinformation into this one sentence. Bridgetower (1779 or 1780–1860) was not American and not a sea-captain. Beethoven was associated with him only in April and May 1803. Bridgetower was in Vienna only during these two months, except for a visit in 1845. He had come to London as a *Wunderkind* from his native Poland in his tenth year, and it was in that city that he developed his artistry. It might also be added that there is no record of Kreutzer's presence in Vienna for half a dozen years prior to the dedication of opus 47.

[83] The changes that Schindler mentions are: (1) the portion of the first act finale from Pizarro's entrance, further discussed on page 129 of the present volume; (2) the duet *Um in der Ehe froh zu leben*; and (3) the trio *Ein Mann ist bald genommen*. Each of these numbers was retained, with only slight changes, in the 1806 version of the opera, and deleted only in the 1814 version, so that Treitschke's statement on this point was correct. In connection with these three numbers, see Schindler's letter of 1 December 1841 to Breitkopf & Härtel (*Der Bär*, 1927, p. 113). The text and the music of the three versions of *Fidelio* are discussed in great detail in Hess: *Beethovens Oper Fidelio und ihre drei Fassungen* (Zürich, 1953); vocal scores of the 1805 and 1806 versions were prepared by Erich Prieger (Breitkopf & Härtel, 1905) and Otto Jahn (Breitkopf & Härtel, Pl. No. 8404, 1851) respectively.

Schindler's statement that Treitschke was never connected with the Theater an der Wien in an official capacity is directly contradicted by the *Oesterreichische*

National-Enzyklopädie of 1836 as quoted in BHdb II 332: 'During the French invasion he was made vice-director of the Theater an der Wien for the first time and, upon the separation from the k. k. Hoftheater in 1811, for the second time', remaining at the Theater an der Wien as stage manager and theatre poet until he returned to the Hoftheater in 1814.

84 No. 8 (not No. 7) in the 1806 version is indeed an aria for Pizarro (*Ha! welch' ein Augenblick!*), but this was carried over almost unchanged from the 1805 version. The 'new aria' was the passage for Pizarro and chorus in the first act finale that was referred to in Note 83 above.

85 Joseph August Röckel (1783–1870) is the source of three separate accounts of the meeting at Prince Lichnowsky's in December 1805:

(1) The one given here.

(2) In a letter to Thayer of 25 or 26 February 1861 (TK II 53; TF 388; SBSK–Br 367).

(3) In an article in *Gartenlaube* 1868, p. 601 (Sonneck Impr., p. 60).

These three accounts are in general the same, though differing in many details, notably as to the list of persons present. The substitution of Röckel for Demmer was the only change in the cast for the performance of the second version of the opera from that of the first.

86 This point has been discussed by Hess (SchwMZ LXXIV [1934] 743), whose conclusions may be summarized as follows: Only one number appearing in both the 1805 and the 1814 versions of *Fidelio* was omitted from the 1806 version as actually performed: Rocco's 'Gold' aria (No. 4 in the final version). Though not performed, a revised version of this number appears in the draft score of the 1806 revision of the opera, the aria in this form differing somewhat in text and in music from both the 1805 and the 1814 versions.

87 The history of the *Leonore* overture No. 1, opus 138, is obscure, but it is most improbable that it was acquired by Steiner in 1805, since there is no valid evidence that Beethoven had established any contact with Steiner before 1814 (KHV 413). The overture was published by Tobias Haslinger, Steiner's successor, in the spring of 1838. The history of this overture is discussed in KHV 188.

88 These changes are indicated in the Prieger vocal score of 1905.

89 The textbook that Schindler had in mind was probably the *Méthode de chant du Conservatoire de musique*, but neither it nor its German translation is listed among the books owned by Beethoven at the time of his death (Leitzmann, LvB II 379–83; BStud II 185–97). However, Part III of the B. & H. edition, with translations of various Italian words in Beethoven's hand, is in the archives of the Beethovenhaus (KatH, Item 97). M. Bardet, librarian of the Conservatoire, has kindly pointed out that this text was edited by a committee of ten members of the faculty, only three of whom (Cherubini, Gossec, Méhul) were among those named by Schindler. He further stated that the German edition (B. & H.), like the original, was in three parts, not six.

90 Opus 57 was published only in February 1807, but sketchbook evidence shows that it was composed simultaneously with *Fidelio* in 1804–5 (KHV 134). On 26 August 1804 (And. 96) Beethoven offered B. & H. three new piano

sonatas (presumably opp. 53, 54, and 57). This may be taken as an indication that at that time opus 57 was at the least fairly well advanced. Ries's statement that he heard Beethoven struggling with the finale of the sonata while at Döbling substantiates this dating, since Beethoven spent part of the summer of 1804 at this resort. Schindler's statement that the sonata was written 'at a single stroke' at Count Brunsvik's estate accordingly does not bear scrutiny. Regarding the extended compass of the piano keyboard, see also Note 81. The upward range of opus 57 does not exceed that of opus 37, composed in 1803.

[91] Schindler's statement that the compass of the piano keyboard was not extended above c ′ ′ ′ ′ until the second decade of the century is disproved by Beethoven's transcription of opus 61 as a piano concerto (1807), in which he writes to e ′ ′ ′ ′ in the body of the concerto and to f ′ ′ ′ ′ (a fifth below the present highest string) in the cadenza. That this extended range was an innovation is shown by the description of the transcription in Beethoven's contract of 20 April 1807 with Clementi (And. 1419): 'The concerto [for the violin] arranged for piano with additional notes.' It should be noted, however, that as early as 1803 pianos were being built with a compass of six octaves (*Der Bär* [1927] 63).

[92] KHV 136 assigns the G major concerto to 1805–6, so that it was in general simultaneous with the work on the first two versions of *Fidelio*.

[93] The *Eroica* symphony was published in October 1806 (KHV 129), not in 1807 as Schindler says a few pages later. Opus 57 was not published until February 1807 (KHV 135).

[94] Schindler was right the first time: the autograph is dated '1806' in Beethoven's hand (KHV 144), thus placing it probably just before the violin concerto instead of just after it.

[95] TDR III 8 indicates that the reference is to two subscription concerts 'for the benefit of the composer' at the palace of 'Prince L' (probably Lobkowitz) in March 1807. The programmes included the first four symphonies, the *Coriolanus* overture, the G major concerto, and some arias from *Fidelio*, opp. 58, 60, and 62 being presented for the first time. Only Schindler seems to be the authority for the statement, which on the face of it seems most improbable, that the division of these works between the two programmes threw all four symphonies into a single concert. TK II 100 and TF 416 quote the AmZ to the effect that the concerts 'contributed a very considerable sum for the benefit of the composer'.

[96] As mentioned in Note 93, the *Eroica* was published in October 1806. In addition to opus 57 (February 1807) and the *Thirty-two Variations* WoO 80 (April), the *Triple Concerto* opus 56 was published in June 1807.

[97] Further extensive excerpts from this review are given in TDR III 22 ff.

[98] See Supplement F, p. 479 *infra*.

[99] In his tabulation, Schindler omits Nos. 2, 3, and 4 of the first part of the concert. The 'aria' was *Ah perfido!* (opus 65), sung by Josephine Killitschky; the 'hymn' was the Gloria of the C major mass; the 'piano concerto' was probably that in G major. See MM 58.

[100] Moscheles, who was also present at this performance, gives his recollections of the incident in Vol. I, p. 115n, of his English version of the 1840

Schindler *Biographie* (see Note 1). According to Moscheles, the breakdown came at the passage on p. 15 of GA 9/71 some ten measures before the change of key, but since this entire passage is for strings and solo piano, Moscheles's testimony conflicts with the stories that attribute the confusion to the unhappy clarinet player. The account in AmZ, as well as Ries's, would seem to point to the area around pp. 7 and 8 of the GA score. See also TK II 130 and TF 448.

101 And. 32 to Amenda, undated but certainly written during the summer of 1799, includes the statement: 'Today I received an invitation to Mödling in the country. I have accepted it and am going off there this very evening for a few days.' In the summer of 1801, Beethoven took lodgings in Hetzendorf, a village 4 to 5 miles south-west of Vienna (TK I 288; TF 280). 'At the beginning of the warm season [in 1803] Beethoven, as was his annual custom, appears to have passed some weeks in Baden . . . before retiring to the summer lodging whose position he describes in a note to Ries [And. 80] as in Oberdöbling' (TK II 13; TF 335). See also p. 164 and n. 23 *infra supra*.

102 'Schindler here is mistaken. The "walk towards the Kahlenberg" took them northerly into the valley between Heiligenstadt and Nussdorf, where an excessively idealized bust of the composer now marks the "Scene by the Brook". After thirty years of absence from Vienna, Schindler's memory had lost the exact topography of these scenes; and a friend to whom he wrote for information upon it mistook the Grinzing brook and valley for the true ones. This explanation of his error was made by Schindler to the present writer very soon after the third edition of his (Schindler's) book appeared.' (TK II 120n; TF 437n.)

103 As pointed out in TK I 211 (see also TF 200), this statement is refuted by the 'very considerable number of [Beethoven's] waltzes, Ländler, minuets, écossaises, allemandes, and contradances which have been preserved', as well as by the fact that the minuets (WoO 7) and Deutsche Tänze (WoO 8) that Beethoven wrote for the Redoutensaal in November 1795 were repeated at the ball given two years later (TK I 202).

104 These eleven waltzes and Ländler disappeared before Beethoven's death, and were recovered only in 1905 by Hugo Riemann. They are discussed in KHV as WoO 17.

105 GA 1/6, pp. 47–50.

106 To this list should be added the three quartets opus 59 and the *Coriolanus* overture opus 62.

107 English version by Constance Jolly. The original read:

In questa tomba oscura
lasciami riposar.
Quando vivo era, ingrata,
dovevi a me pensar.
Lascia che l'ombre ignude
godansi pace almen,
e non bagnar mi ceneri
d'inutile velén.

108 Ries had returned to Vienna from Paris and Russia in August 1808, and

was certainly in the city as late as five days before the bombardment on 11 May 1809, as shown by his letter of 6 May from Vienna to Simrock (SimJb II [1929] 36). Grove 7–165 indicates that Ries did not leave Vienna on the journey that four years later would end in London until after the city had been occupied.

[109] According to Kroll (NBJ III [1927] 127), the review of the *Pastoral* symphony was written not by Wendt but by M. G. Fischer of Erfurt, and that of the C minor symphony by E. T. A. Hoffmann.

[110] In the light of modern knowledge, this tabulation should be somewhat modified (see KHV 753):

The trios opus 70 were published in June and August 1809 (KHV 167). The review of these trios that Schindler refers to, though unsigned, is generally accepted as having been written by E. T. A. Hoffmann.

The vocal score of *Fidelio* published by B. & H. in August 1810 was an incomplete version of the 1806 revision. As stated in Note 83, a complete vocal score of the 1806 revision was published only in 1851 as a result of the researches of Otto Jahn; a vocal score of the 1805 version was first published only in 1905 (Erich Prieger).

The *Triple Concerto* opus 56 had been published in 1807 (see Note 96).

The songs opus 75, Nos. 5 and 6 were first published in July 1810.

The *Choral Fantasy* opus 80 was published in England in October 1810, though in Germany only in July 1811.

The piano concerto No. 5 in E flat major, opus 73, was published in England in November 1810, though in Germany only in February 1811. (Regarding these last two works, see MMR XC [1960] 228, and Alan Tyson, *The Authentic English Editions of Beethoven* [1963].

The orchestral parts of the overture to *Egmont*, opus 84, were published in December 1810.

The following works without opus numbers were published during 1810: WoO 134, 136, 137, 138, 139, and perhaps 27.

[111] The authenticity of the 'Bettina' letters and the validity of Mme Arnim's various accounts of her relationship with Beethoven are discussed in detail in MR XIX (1958) 14 ff. The letters in question are given in Supplement I, p. 490, *infra*.

[112] Regarding the sonnet '*In tiefster Demut will ich gratulieren . . .*' attributed to Beethoven on the occasion of Bettina's marriage to Ludwig Joachim von Arnim in March 1811, see MM 90. Unger, in *Auf Spuren von Beethovens 'Unsterblicher Geliebter'* (1910), p. 62, says, 'The authenticity of this poem cannot be questioned'. After further consideration, however, he declared this sonnet as well as the first and third 'Bettina' letters to be spurious, saying, 'They are doubtless compositions of Bettina, who wished to make herself "interesting"' (ZfM CIII [1936] 1069).

[113] The editor can hazard no guess as to what Schindler meant by these last two sentences. Facsimile II shows the second of the Immortal Beloved letters, which Schindler refers to on his p. 98 (p. 106 of the present volume). Facsimile I, referred to on Schindler's p. 95, is the diary jotting written in Baden in 1817 or 1818 'when M. passed by and, I think, looked at me' (p. 102).

There would seem to be no conceivable connection between the coquettish Bettina in 1810 and the Immortal Beloved, whoever she might have been, in 1803 (Schindler's dating) or someone with the initial 'M' in 1817 or 1818. Beethoven met Bettina in May 1810; there can be no doubt but that she charmed him greatly, or that she was greatly impressed by him, but it can be stated with confidence that their association was no more than a meteoric and transitory flirtation.

[114] Schindler's statement is not correct. By the terms of the *Finanz-Patent* of 20 February 1811, a contract made in March 1809 (the date of the Annuity Contract) that did not specifically call for payment in specie would be satisfied by payment at the rate of 1 florin (in the new paper currency) for each 2.48 florins called for by the contract. Beethoven's annuity was thus reduced from 4,000 florins to 1,611 florins, a painful shrinkage but far better than Schindler's figure of 800 florins. The *Finanz-Patent* receives illuminating discussion in TK II 211–13 and TF 522–23.

[115] In September 1811 the affairs of Prince Lobkowitz were put into the hands of administrators, and payments to Beethoven were suspended (TK II 213n). 'According to the judgement of the Court, entered on 19 April 1815, the future annual payments were fixed at 700 florins (the equivalent of 280 fl. convention coin, silver), and the 2,508 fl. arrears were ordered to be paid in notes of redemption within two months.' About this same time a similar settlement was arrived at with the Kinsky estate, whereby Beethoven was to receive 1,200 florins annually with a payment of 2,497 florins for arrears. 'Payments were made accordingly, and . . . from 1811 up to his death, Beethoven received on the annuity contract the following sums every year:

From Archduke Rudolph	1,500 fl.
From Prince Kinsky	1,200
From Prince Lobkowitz	700
Total	3,400 fl.'

(TK II 306; TF 611)

See also Note 144.

[116] The orchestral parts of the *Egmont* overture opus 84 appeared in December 1810 (see Note 110). The score of the overture was first published only in 1831 (KHV 231).

[117] This was the first performance in Vienna. The concerto had, however, been performed in Leipzig on 28 November 1811 by Friedrich Schneider (KHV 195).

[118] In all, the following works were dedicated to Archduke Rudolph:

Piano concerto No. 4 in G major opus 58 (1808)
Piano concerto No. 5 in E flat major opus 73 (1811)
Piano sonata in E flat major (*Les Adieux*) opus 81a (1811)
Fidelio opus 72 (vocal score) (1814)
Violin sonata in G major opus 96 (1816)
Trio in B flat opus 97 (1816)
Piano sonata in B flat major opus 106 (1819)

Missa Solemnis opus 123 (autograph dated 1823)
Grosse Fuge opus 133 (autograph dated 1825)
Grosse Fuge (transcription for piano 4 hands) opus 134
(autograph dated 1826)

[119] Schindler's statement is not quite correct, since the following works were first published in 1812:

Egmont: complete incidental music (orchestral parts and piano transcription)
Mass in C major opus 86 (score)

[120] The documentary evidence that is available does not bear out the statements of Schindler and Breuning. The music to *Die Ruinen von Athen* opus 113 (overture and 8 numbers) and to *König Stephan* opus 117 (overture and 9 numbers) was composed in August and September 1811 for the projected dedication of the new theatre in Pesth, originally set for early October 1811, though later postponed until 9 February 1812. Sketching of both symphonies began in the autumn of 1811; the autograph score of opus 92 is dated 13 May 1812 and that of opus 93, 'Linz im Monath october 1812'. (KHV.) There seems to be no evidence that Beethoven was in Linz during the spring of 1812. He went to Teplitz by way of Prague from Vienna, not from Linz.

[121] Beethoven met with Prince Kinsky in Prague in the first days of July 1812 'and received 60 ducats on account. Unfortunately, he delayed the definitive settlement of the annuity matter; had he attended to it at once he would have been spared the negotiations which followed the sudden death of the Prince' on 3 November 1812 (TK II 222; see also TF 533).

[122] The record of payments made by the Kinsky estate, given in detail in MM 72–73, shows that the payments continued at the rate of 1,200 florins per year up to the time of Beethoven's death. See also Note 115.

[123] Beethoven had made the *acquaintance* of Baden long before 1813. Ries tells of a brief visit to Baden by Beethoven in 1802 (TK I 350), and in the early summer of 1803 the composer spent some weeks there (TK II 13; TF 335). Letters are known that were written from Baden in July 1804, June and July 1807, September 1809, and August to October 1810 (And. *passim*).

[124] Actually on 13 September 1807.

[125] In Viktor Papp's *Beethoven és a magyarok* (Beethoven and the Hungarians), p. 51, a quite different account of this incident is given. After remarking that the Prince, diplomat and lover of the arts, would hardly have spoken so sneeringly to his guest of honour, Papp presents newly discovered facts to explain Beethoven's dissatisfaction with the treatment he had received. Instead of being assigned a room in the castle for his stay in Kismarton like any other social equal, Beethoven was quartered with the Court Secretary of Music, Joseph Baranyai, whose principal residence was in Vienna and who had at Kismarton only a furnished apartment (probably no more than two rooms in a building not designed as living quarters) that two years later was refused by a tenor singer of the court because it was too damp. A facsimile is given of Baranyai's receipt for twenty florins as compensation for quartering Beethoven for the period 10 to 16 September. The dates given in this receipt should dispose of Schindler's story that Beethoven left Kismarton in a huff on 13

September, the day of the performance. A transcription of the Baranyai receipt is given in BHdb II 481. Regarding Beethoven's relations with Hummel, see TK II 109 and TF 424.

[126] This closing paragraph and the postscript are found in the autograph of this Notice (facsimile in DM XI₂ [1912] No. 7) but were omitted by Schindler. The autograph is headed, 'For the "Public Notices" section of the *Wiener Zeitung*, to be published only once in roman type-face'. However, the Notice was never published, presumably because of the disagreement between Beethoven and Maelzel that a few months later developed into a bitter quarrel (see TK II 271; TF 579, 1094).

[127] Actually, Beethoven remained in Vienna until about 1 July 1812, when he went to the Bohemian resorts (Teplitz, Karlsbad, Franzenbrunn) via Prague. He left Bohemia about the end of September, and probably went direct to Linz, where he remained from about 5 October until about 10 November (TK II 222, 230, 232; TF 532, 540, 542). TK II 234 and TF 544 give reasons for the conjecture that the 'farewell dinner' took place in February 1813, when Beethoven and Maelzel planned to leave for England (TK II 251; TF 560).

[128] Schindler gives the first voice of the entire canon WoO 162. TK II 233–35 and TF 543–44 discuss the history of Maelzel's invention, and comment on the dependability of Schindler's account of the genesis of the canon. See also Note 141.

[129] KHV 416 says categorically that Rochlitz did not give *Preis der Tonkunst* to Beethoven in 1822, pointing out that the publisher's introduction to the score of the cantata, issued in 1837, indicates strongly that the poem had been written only a short time before, presumably at Haslinger's request. Schindler probably confused this poem with *Der erste Ton*, which Rochlitz submitted to Beethoven through Haslinger in September 1822 (TDR IV 287), but of which Beethoven made no use.

[130] In the catalogue of Beethoven's works that Artaria published as a part of the second printing of opus 106 at the end of October 1819, all the unused numbers listed in this latter except 103 were assigned to specific compositions. In most cases the numberings were those that are used today, but the following deviations may be noted (see KHV *passim*):

51 Artaria used this number for the sextet opus 71, and used the number 71 for WoO 55. The two rondos received the number 51 in the *Thematisches Verzeichnis* issued by Hofmeister in 1819.

71 See comment on number 51 above. In the 1832 edition of the Artaria catalogue the sextet was listed twice: as opus 51 and as opus 71.

72 In his first (1819) catalogue, Artaria used this number for WoO 97 and in his second (1832) catalogue for WoO 136. The opus number 72 for *Fidelio* was suggested by Härtel in his letter of 24 September 1810 to Beethoven (ZfMw IX [1927] 335) together with the numberings 73 to 86 that were in fact used, but the present editor knows of no use of the opus number '72' for the opera earlier than the B. & H. *Thematisches Verzeichnis* of 1851. Jahn's vocal score of the 1806 version, published that same year, gives no opus number.

87 Artaria assigned this opus number to the Waldstein Variations WoO 67; Hofmeister in his 1819 catalogue assigned it to the wind trio.

103 In both editions of his catalogue, Artaria left this number unassigned. Presumably it was first used for the wind octet in the B. & H. catalogue of 1851.

[131] The opus numbers or KHV *Werk ohne Opuszahl* numbers now assigned to these works are shown in square brackets.

[132] This letter to Artaria is apparently lost.

[133] Corrections to Schindler's data are given in square brackets. The documentation of the statement that Clementi in London published opp. 73, 74, 77, 78, 79, 80, and 81a before B. & H. in Leipzig may be found in MMR XC (1960) 228 (see also Tyson, *The Authentic English Editions of Beethoven* [1963], *passim*). No attempt has been made to add to Schindler's list various other works that were composed during the second period. For such information the reader is referred to KHV 745 ff.

[134] See Note 109.

THIRD PERIOD

1815 to Beethoven's Death

*And fate weighs more and
more heavily upon him.*

In the preface to *Dichtung und Wahrheit* Goethe gives the biographer this directive:

The primary obligation of biography seems to be to represent the man in his temporal context and to show to what extent he is hindered and to what extent aided by his environment, how he builds from these cross-currents attitudes towards the world and man, and to what extent, if he is an artist, poet, or writer, he reflects the influences of his time.

This author feels that he has understood Goethe's directive and followed it truly in the periods he has treated. The various situations in which we met our hero, the conflicts, sometimes in affairs of the heart, sometimes with publishers, sometimes with his brothers, friends, or society in general were all of such a nature that they could not be considered extraordinary. With the single exception of the circumstance that our musician was also at heart a man of politics, as we shall see him again, his life had much in common with the lives of other men. The list of works from the second period is ample proof of the firm purpose with which the master followed his own self-made path without allowing himself to be misled by the acclaim, sparse enough at times, of his contemporaries. The many contradictions of our master, moreover, in word and deed, were not so extreme that they could be considered extraordinary or surprising, even if they were not usual. However, *tempora mutantur, et nos mutamur in illis*. This and the chapter heading from Goethe must be frequently recalled as we enter upon this third period.

In the course of this period we shall find Beethoven in quite different circumstances. Lawsuits of a most offensive nature and the resulting conflicts in the courts; outrages committed by a friend against his compositions; family troubles; base ingratitude and other irritations, all with a debilitating effect on his morale—such were the fateful occurrences that followed one another in almost uninterrupted succession, and many of them gave rise to long periods of depression. Because of these complex situations, the biographer has had to resort to a different method in recounting the events of these years, for the circumstances are so entangling that a simple chronological treatment is not possible.

From this introduction we can see what an unpleasant and difficult task awaits us. Indeed, it would be quite impossible to accomplish it had the author not had the good fortune to observe these things from very close range and had he not had the opportunity, as a result of his friendship with the composer, to be personally involved in most of these situations. How this friendship came about and how it fared through several years should receive a fuller explanation than was given in the first edition of this work, for it is of interest in the accomplishment of the tasks that the third period assigns us.

Before resuming the thread of our narrative, it might be advisable to take a look at Beethoven's circle of close friends in order to see which of those members named at the beginning of the second period still remained in association with him, which ones had by this time left him and who had replaced them, and in general which men constituted the circle at the beginning of the period and how the circle fared in the course of the remaining years. Beethoven's enemies have made much of this matter and just recently Alexandre Oulibicheff wrote in his book, *Beethoven, ses critiques et ses glossateurs*: 'Schindler gave himself to Beethoven as one gives oneself to the Devil: body and soul. He stayed; others were less faithful, and gradually the great artist found himself alone. He was eventually abandoned by his best and oldest friends, and only a few of them gathered at his deathbed.' The truth of this allegation may be seen in the following paragraphs.

When speaking of the events of the year 1813 we had occasion to mention Prince Lichnowsky and his unaltered affection for our master. Other intimate friends still surrounded him with the old love and understanding: Count Moritz Lichnowsky, Baron Pasqualati, Stephan von Breuning, von Zmeskall, Streicher, Schuppanzigh, and the newcomers: Maelzel, Oliva, and Karl Bernard. Only Count Brunsvik and Baron Gleichenstein had left the circle by the beginning of this period, the former to take up residence in Budapest and the latter to return to his homeland, the Grand Duchy of Baden. Our master continued to see Brunsvik frequently in Vienna, but he saw Gleichenstein only once again when the Baron visited the capital in 1824. Ferdinand Ries had left Vienna in 1805. Upon his return from Russia in the late autumn of 1808 he remained in the city only through the first winter months.

Everything here on earth is subject to change; how could it have been otherwise than that this intimate circle of friends, too, should change? As early as 1814, as we have seen, Prince Lichnowsky, the senior member of the group, departed after he had had the joy of seeing his favourite protégé at the peak of his glory. In 1816 Schuppanzigh left Vienna to take over the conductorship of a court orchestra in Russia. He did not return until 1823. In 1817 Oliva left the imperial capital for good and became a professor of German literature in St. Petersburg.[135] In 1817 there was a quarrel between Beethoven and his old friend Breuning. This, and Schuppanzigh's departure, constituted the composer's most painful losses. If Schuppanzigh was the frequent stimulus (sometimes even the coercer, and in his own interests) to Beethoven's composing or conducting, Breuning was the constant, thoughtful, selfless guide and helper in moments of trouble. He and Beethoven did not meet again until 1826, after both men had aged by nine years.[136]

The composer's relations with his other friends changed little by little, and gradually there seemed to be less and less occasion for seeing one another. He lost Zmeskall's companionship, for the latter was for many years confined to his bed with arthritis. For reasons of his own, Kanne withdrew in later years from society. He remained, none the less, a critic, and would occasionally allow Beethoven to invite him to dinner. This unequalled eccentric and our composer finally lost their desire to engage in the obstinate discussions that had so often entertained and instructed those privileged to listen. The one had always liked to look into the future, the other had looked to the past, and their views on the theory of art or aesthetic principles were seldom in agreement. (For more details see Section 1 of 'Personality, Individual Characteristics, Anecdotes, etc.') Some of these vacancies were filled before long, one by the lawyer, Dr. Johann Baptist Bach, another by the author of this book, and lastly another at the end of the period, in 1825, by Karl Holz.

It is now time to recount briefly how it happened that the author was brought into close association with Beethoven. From the account of the events and circumstances surrounding the master it will incidentally emerge how I gradually won his sympathy, confidence, and affection.

In the winter of 1813–14, a well-to-do music-lover by the name of Pettenkofer used to assemble every Saturday in his home a considerable group of young people to play orchestral music. I was a member of this group, along with several of my university friends, including Dr. Leopold Sonnleithner, whom the reader met at the beginning of the second period. At such a gathering towards the end of March 1814 one of the musicians next to me asked me to deliver to Beethoven the following morning a note from Schuppanzigh, who was his teacher, for he himself was unable to do so. The note concerned a rehearsal that had been proposed, and Beethoven, who was to take part in it, had to answer simply Yes or No. I accepted the commission joyfully. And so it was that my desire to stand for even a moment in the presence of the man whose works had for many years inspired in me the greatest respect for their author (I was then eighteen years old) was unexpectedly, extraordinarily, fulfilled. The next morning, with pounding heart, the messenger climbed the four flights of stairs of the Pasqualati house and was immediately admitted by the tailor-servant who led him to the master busy at his desk. When Beethoven had read the note, he turned to me and said, 'Yes'; a few hurried questions and the audience was over. But at the door I permitted myself to pause a moment to observe closely the man who was already back at his writing.

Soon after this incident, which up to that time was almost the most important thing that had ever happened in the life of this poor student, he made the acquaintance of Schuppanzigh. He honoured me with a ticket to the concert he had organized for 11 April, when Beethoven himself took part in the first performance of his great trio in B flat major, opus 97. On this occasion I presented myself with somewhat more confidence to the great master and greeted him respectfully. He responded in a friendly manner and showed that he remembered the messenger who had brought him the note. Schuppanzigh invited me to take part in the great concerts of 29 November and 2 December. Thus I had several opportunities of seeing the creator of the A major symphony at very close range. This was the unlooked-for beginning of a close relationship. It probably would have gone no further but for a misfortune that soon after befell me.

In our narrative we have come to the time when the Carbonari had begun to agitate in Italy, as a result of which anyone who moved from one place to another aroused the suspicions of the police. These suspicions were augmented by the sympathies somewhat too loudly expressed by the Austrian people for Napoleon when they learned of his escape from Elba. Young people were particularly vocal in these expressions, and the author was no exception. It was surely only a coincidence that at the same time there occurred a riot among a small fraction of the Viennese students, a riot which in itself was insignificant but which nevertheless drew the attention of the officials, so that one of the most venerated professors was removed from his post.

Towards the end of February 1815 I accepted a teaching assignment in Brünn. Hardly had I arrived there when I received a summons from the police. I was asked what connection I had with the rioters at the university in Vienna, and was requested to give information about certain Italians in Vienna in whose company I had often been observed. To cap it all, my papers were not in order, and the document listing the lectures where I had been in attendance was missing (through no fault of my own), with the result that I was imprisoned despite the offer of a

highly placed official to give bond for me. After a few weeks of correspondence back and forth, it was established that I was not a propagandist, and I was released. But a whole year had been lost in my
academic pursuits.

Once back in Vienna I received through a close acquaintance of
Beethoven's an invitation to present myself at a certain place where the
master wanted to hear from my own lips the events that had taken place
in Brünn. As I talked, Beethoven revealed such warm sympathy and
concern over my unfortunate experience that I could not keep back my
tears. He invited me to come often at four o'clock in the afternoon to the
same place where he was in the habit of coming almost every day to
read the newspapers. His handshake said even more. We had met in a
remote room of the tavern 'Zum Blumenstock' in the Ballgässchen. I
became a regular visitor to the place, and before long I realized that it
was a sort of cell of a small number of Josephinists of the truest dye.[137]
Our composer was not in the least out of place in this company, for his
republican views had suffered a serious blow as a result of his becoming
acquainted at this time with the British constitution. A captain in the
Emperor's bodyguards and Herr Pinterics, a man generally known in
Viennese musical circles and one who played an important part in
Franz Schubert's artistic life, were the master's closest associates in
this society and, in the exchange of political opinions, his seconds who
would both stimulate him and agree with him.

Soon I began to leave the tavern with the composer to accompany
him on his walks. By 1816 he was already involved in affairs that demanded considerable writing. Dr. Bach, in whose office I worked a few
hours each day, suggested to Beethoven that he entrust all this writing
to me. And so it was that I became Beethoven's private secretary—
without pay. Other tasks were soon added to the arrangement. From
that time until his death I counted it my duty to be of service to him to
the best of my ability. Our association was interrupted only once,
briefly, towards the end of his life, for reasons that will be explained in
the proper place. It is this devotion that Oulibicheff, a man thoroughly
imbued with hostile feelings for the great composer, termed, 'Giving
himself body and soul to the Devil'.

[I]

◦ 1815 to 1820 ◦

At the end of the second period we saw the composer at a height of fame
never before achieved by a musician who was still in the midst of his
artistic activity. Let us not forget, however, that this fame was the fruit
of twenty years' unremitting toil. This moment of glory, coinciding as

it did with a moment of profound historical significance, was one of the most brilliant events in the whole history of music. One will forgive the apparent extravagance of this statement when one remembers that nearly all of the European rulers gathered at the Congress of Vienna concurred in affirming our master's greatness.

It was at this time that the Russian ambassador, Count Rasumovsky, was raised to the rank of prince by his Tsar, who was in Vienna for the Congress.[138] This promotion occasioned, in addition to the customary elaborate parties, the most extraordinary celebrations in the palace of this Maecenas on the Danube Canal, and of course our Beethoven was always in attendance. At these times the master was an object of general curiosity to all the foreign visitors, for it is the lot of genius, particularly when that genius is accompanied by an element of the heroic, to attract the attention of the nobility. May we indeed not term it heroic when we recall that the composer had to struggle against prejudice of every kind, against the traditions of his art, against the jealousy, the conceit, the ill-will of the vast majority of the other musicians, and moreover against the one sense so indispensable on many counts to the practice of his art, namely his sense of hearing; and again when we recall that despite all adversity he reached such an exalted position? No wonder everyone sought to pay him homage! Prince Rasumovsky presented him to the assembled monarchs, and they acknowledged their regard for him in the most flattering terms. The Tsarina of Russia in particular was lavish in her compliments. The presentation took place in the apartments of Archduke Rudolph, where Beethoven was greeted by other dignitaries as well. Apparently the Archduke wished to have a part in the triumph of his exalted teacher when he had invited the foreign nobles to his own rooms to meet Beethoven. In later years the great master would recall not without emotion those days in the imperial castle and the palace of the Russian prince and would say with a tinge of pride that he had allowed himself to be courted by the highest rulers of Europe and had comported himself admirably.

It would be a pleasure to dwell at length on this situation so rare in the life of an artist, but other circumstances compel us forward. We must already bid adieu to this moment of glory and follow the dictates of affairs and events. These events occurred in such a way that we must relate not a gradual succession of small changes but a sudden and violent alteration in the composer's situation. Oh, how brief the unmolested joy in the fragrance of those hard-won laurels! What bitter fate for an artist steeped in the purest poetry to find himself suddenly embroiled in a vulgar, mundane fight that could not but ruin his peace of mind and lead to still more serious consequences!

As we embark upon the narration of the torments suffered by our master, it is necessary to think back to the glorious days of 8 and 12 December 1813, when the A major symphony and the *Battle of Vittoria* were performed for the first time. Furthermore we must remember the letter of thanks that Beethoven prepared on this occasion, and how at the end of the letter he said explicitly that the court mechanic, Maelzel, had given these concerts, that Beethoven had written the *Battle* symphony solely for this purpose, and that he had presented it free of charge to the mechanic. The letter also mentions this man's intention of travelling to England.

In order to clarify what happened between these two friends, it is necessary to explain a previous incident. In 1812 Maelzel had promised the composer that he would make him devices that would enable him to hear better. Hoping to spur him on, Beethoven composed a piece called *Battle* symphony for the panharmonicon that Maelzel had just invented. The effect of this piece was so unexpected that the mechanic urged Beethoven to orchestrate it. The composer, who had long entertained the idea of writing a long 'battle symphony', took his friend's advice and went to work immediately. Eventually four hearing devices were produced, but only one of them, the smallest and simplest, was found to be useful.[139]

The first clash between the two friends came about in 1813 when Maelzel, who made all the arrangements for the 8 December concert by himself, took the liberty of printing on the notice posters that the *Battle* symphony was his own property, a gift to him from Beethoven. The latter lost no time in protesting against such an act of usurpation. Maelzel countered by stating publicly that he claimed the work in question in exchange for the hearing devices together with a considerable sum of money. This disagreeable argument formed the prelude to the forthcoming artistic celebration. The court mechanic's conduct towards his friend was certainly beneath the dignity of a cultivated man, and remained for a long time the object of general disapprobation.

Immediately after the first performance on 8 December, Beethoven was warned that Maelzel was trying to get possession of the score. When this attempt failed, he managed to procure some of the instrumental parts, which had been carelessly guarded. He put them together to reconstruct the score; the missing voices were filled in by some hireling. In April of 1814 Beethoven received word from Munich that the *Battle* symphony had been performed there by Maelzel,* who had proclaimed that with this work he must clear 400 ducats to meet Beethoven's demand for payment.

It was now time to seek the protection of the law in guarding his own property. In the deposition drawn up for his attorney (this document is

---

* AmZ XVI (1814) 291 contains a report from Munich on this performance.

still in existence and is reproduced word for word in the supplementary material at the end of this book)[140] Beethoven explains:

We agreed to give this work and several others I had written in a concert for the benefit of the veterans. At this time I was beset by severe financial embarrassments.* I was alone here in Vienna, abandoned by the whole world, awaiting a change for the better, and Maelzel offered me fifty gold ducats. I took them and told him that I would repay him here or, if I did not go with him to London, I would give him the work to take along and would direct an English publisher to pay him the fifty ducats.

Two other documents must be noted, one an explanation drawn up by Baron Pasqualati and the court lawyer, Dr. von Adelsburg, and the other an announcement addressed by Beethoven to the musicians in London. The first document still exists in the original; dated 20 October 1814, it states that Beethoven had in no way relinquished his claims to the work in question. In his letter to the London musicians, Beethoven tells what happened in Munich and declares: 'The performance of these works (the *Victory* symphony and *The Battle of Vittoria*) by Herr Maelzel is a deception on the public and an injury to me, for he procured them in an unlawful way'; he concludes by warning the musicians against these 'mutilated' works.†

As a result of the letter, Maelzel did not dare to attempt a performance of these works in London. The lawsuit in Vienna was inconclusive, for the defendant was far away and his representative managed to postpone the trial for an indefinite time, causing the plaintiff considerable expense and perpetual vexation. Our master decided not to prosecute further, for in the meantime the affair had become well-enough known to deter the bad friend from making any new attempts. The legal expenses were equally divided. Maelzel never returned to Vienna[141] but later resumed his correspondence with his former friend in the hope of gaining Beethoven's endorsement of the metronome. We have here his letter written from Paris on 19 April 1818. In it he claims to be working on a hearing device that Beethoven could use when conducting (!), and even suggests that they go to England together. The master informed the mechanic of his satisfaction with the metronome, but he heard nothing more about the hearing device.[142]

This incident constituted in the life of our master an introductory lesson in a subject about which he was yet to learn a great deal more, a subject of which everyone would prefer to remain ignorant. At the same time it gives us a foretaste of other events soon to follow. The immediate result of this experience was that Beethoven began to distrust everyone around him. Moreover, from this time on he had almost all

---

* We have already depicted the melancholy situation that obtained in 1813.
† This document is given in the supplementary material.

his works copied in his own apartment. When it was not possible for him to keep an eye on the copyist himself, he would put him under the surveillance of another, yet it sometimes happened that even such a guardian, tempted past endurance by publishers, sold the manuscripts. A note he wrote me from Hetzendorf on 1 June 1823 shows Beethoven's constant fear lest the publishers play him false with his manuscripts. The note reads:

Have the Variations [opus 120] been sent off to London yet? As far as I recall, there is no mention in the invitation to Prince Esterházy of the fact that the Mass will be distributed only in manuscript. What mischief may be caused by this omission! I imagine that Herr A . . . offered to give the Prince the Mass free of charge, so that Hr. A . . . could a third time steal one of my works. Wocher* must be made aware of this.

This suspicious remark is not in the body of the letter but on the outside of the envelope, and the name of the music publisher associated with the Prince is written out in full.[143]

Another lawsuit followed immediately upon the one already discussed, constituting a second lesson in this primer of disturbing, depressing experiences.

Prince Lobkowitz, the great Maecenas of art, the connoisseur in particular of vocal music, had in his love of art strayed too far from the line that the cautious accountant never fails to make between debit and credit. He brought to his palace every virtuoso singer of Italy for the pleasure of his musical friends. It was through him that music-lovers had the joy of hearing Crescentini, Brizzi, the two Sessi's, and many other famous Italian artists. In 1816 these occasions came to an end with the death of the Prince. But for our master of sound, this death had a further significance: the Prince's entire estate was sequestrated and the 700 florins contribution that the deceased prince had contracted to pay the master according to the annuity contract of 1 March 1809 became the subject of dispute. Accordingly, Beethoven instituted an action in law against the curators. In this case the outcome was the exact opposite of that resulting from the dispute with Prince Kinsky's executors. Beethoven was the defeated party; he won nothing. For the first time in his life he had a chance to see how legal points, clearly drawn up, can be interpreted by one judge as white and by another as black, how apparently insignificant details can lead to a verdict, causing a long-standing legal right to be suddenly turned into a violation—in short, he had seen the dirty nose of the law.[144]

These legal dealings, first with Prince Kinsky's executors, then against the court mechanic Maelzel, and then the sequestration of

* Prince Esterházy's secretary.

Prince Lobkowitz's estate, had gone so far in acquainting our master with the mysteries of Themis that one would think he would have gone to any lengths in consideration of his career as an artist and of his physical well-being to avoid all further contact with the law in order not to make his situation any more difficult than it already was. Such, however, was not the case. Fate had yet harder trials in store for him and led him against his better judgement along even more tortuous paths.

Before we accompany the master on his way into the innermost chambers of these mysteries, we should take a look at the products of his muse for the time just preceding, and also take note of the attendant circumstances. It will be interesting to learn what music was put on paper after the eventful year of 1814, particularly after that restless, frenetic historical moment.

First there came the sonata in two movements in E minor, opus 90.* When we consider the medium and nature of the compositions directly preceding this sonata (the seventh and eighth symphonies, the *Battle* symphony (opus 136), the cantata *Der glorreiche Augenblick*), we are seized with amazement at the deep tenderness and intimacy of this newest composition in contrast to its predecessors' energy and power. Such intimacy as we hear developed in the second movement would be hard to find in any work preceding it. Our amazement is even greater when we hear the sustained mood of the next work, the A major sonata, opus 101, which Marx called 'the Sensitive'. It is worth noting that of all Beethoven's sonatas, this is the only one that was publicly performed during the life of the composer. The concert was arranged by Schuppanzigh in February 1816, and the composer was present. He had entrusted the performance to an artistic and cultivated amateur, Stainer von Felsburg, having first initiated him in the poetic elements of the work and the extraordinarily difficult first and third movements.[145] The master named these two movements 'Impressions and Reveries'; they are to be played in a free tempo.

This sonata is dedicated to the Baroness Dorothea von Ertmann, a name to which we must turn our attention for a moment, for this lady was considered to be one of the foremost pianists in the musical world of Vienna of that day. Frau von Ertmann, *née* Graumann, came from Frankfurt-am-Main; she was the wife of the colonel of the royal and imperial infantry regiment of the 'Hoch- und Deutschmeister'. A through-and-through soldier and at the same time a through-and-through musician, this man earned the gratitude of the Viennese for the many years of pleasure afforded them by his excellently trained military band.†

* This work should undoubtedly bear the opus number 100.
† This regiment had Vienna as its recruiting district.

Since this lady, an artist in the truest sense of the word, excelled particularly in the expression of the graceful, the tender, and the naïve in music, as well as the deep and sentimental emotions, her repertoire included all the works of Prince Louis Ferdinand of Prussia and some of Beethoven's. Her playing of this music was unequalled. She grasped intuitively even the most hidden subtleties of Beethoven's works with as much sureness as if they had been written out before her eyes. This sensitive musician used the same insight with respect to nuances of tempo in a way that cannot be described in words. She knew how to give each phrase the motion of its particular spirit, how to move artistically from one phrase to the next, so that the whole seemed a motivated unity. Thus she was often able to make our master greatly admired. She seemed to have an inborn instinct for playing free tempo correctly. The colouring, too, she would treat according to her own feelings, which were sometimes contrary to the printed indications: as an artist she exercised her right of poetic licence. In certain movements that other pianists had quite misunderstood she brought out effects that had hardly been suspected; every passage became a picture. If the listener forgot to breathe during the mysterious Largo in the trio in D major, opus 70, she would have him sighing for love in the second movement of the sonata in E minor, opus 90.* She would play the recurring main theme of this movement differently each time, sometimes flatteringly and caressingly, sometimes in a melancholy vein. By such wiles this artist was able to play with her audience.

But these demonstrations of her gifts were not solely the result of her own sensitivity; they were based largely on Beethoven's own style of playing his works and had much to do with the instruction inherent within his compositions, which no one had at that time assimilated better than this lady. For many years, until Colonel von Ertmann was made a general and transferred to Milan in 1818, she gathered around herself a circle of true music-lovers who would meet either in her apartment or in other places, including Carl Czerny's home. This salon made a great contribution to the maintaining and advancing of the purest taste among the *élite* of society. She was a conservatoire all by herself. Had it not been for Frau von Ertmann, Beethoven's piano music would have disappeared even sooner from the repertoire in Vienna, but this lady of beauty, high birth, and sensitive nature was

* The sensitivity of Count Lichnowsky, to whom this sonata was dedicated, made it possible for him to know the work and grasp its particular significance. When he asked the composer about it, Beethoven replied that he had set the Count's love-story to music, and if he wished to have names for the movements, the first could be, 'Conflict Between Head and Heart', and the second, 'Conversation with the Beloved'. After the death of his first wife, Count Lichnowsky had fallen in love with a highly esteemed opera singer, but his family opposed their marrying. He was not able to overcome all obstacles to the marriage until 1816, after several years of conflict.

motivated by the most noble impulses towards a sense of better things that pitted her against the emerging new directions in composition and piano playing introduced by Hummel and his disciples. Beethoven therefore had a double reason for revering her as a priestess of musical art and calling her his 'Dorothea-Cecilia'.

Another key to Frau von Ertmann's ability to enrich so greatly the artistic wealth of the music she played was her characteristic refusal to play any piece of music that did not suit her individual style. She never played, for instance, such works as the violin sonata in A minor, opus 47, or the trio in B flat, opus 97, for audiences in large rooms, for she felt that her physical strength was not sufficient. Out of respect for such works she kept to the maxim: Not everything is appropriate for everyone. Virtuosi of both sexes today are unfortunately ignorant of this maxim, but flounder about in all musical genres and all musical periods. In the musical portion of this work we shall remember this artistic wife of a military man in connection with another priestess of art from the same epoch.

The importance of this musician in Beethoven's life is seen not only in the sonata he wrote for her and her particular qualities of performance, but also in the letter he wrote to her on 23 February 1817 to accompany the printed score of this work. The original of the letter is in the autograph collection of her nephew, Alfred Ritter von Frank in Vienna. The master writes:

My dear, treasured Dorothea-Cecilia:

You must often have misjudged me, when I must have seemed opposed to you. Much was due to the circumstances, especially in earlier days, when my style was less understood than now. You know the teachings of the unbidden apostles, who help themselves along with means far different from the Gospel. I did not wish to be counted among them.

Receive now what was often intended for you, and what may be taken as a proof of my admiration for your artistic talent and for yourself as well. That I was not able to hear you play at Czerny's recently must be charged to my illness, which at last seems to be about to yield to my healthy constitution.

I hope soon to hear from you how matters at St. Pölten are going with the [Muses],* and whether you still hold in esteem your

Admirer and friend,

L. van Beethoven

All good things to your worthy husband and consort.†

The first portion of this letter is interesting for its reference to certain phases of the master's life story. We read here his own confession that

---

* Editor's addition.

† Herr and Frau von Ertmann were at that time in St. Pölten, six or seven hours away from Vienna. Herr v. Ertmann was colonel of the infantry regiment of which a part was garrisoned there.

he was then suffering an emotional depression such as he had experienced before. We learn that this depression had been the cause of continuous ill-humour, and we may conclude from his words that his behaviour had been less understood in the past than at that time and that he was in this respect not entirely unhappy with the present.* By the 'teachings of the unbidden apostles' the master meant the harbingers of the new school of piano playing to which the masses flocked, musical apprentices and amateurs alike, as breathlessly and as thoughtlessly as a few years later they threw themselves under the spell of Italian opera. Let us hear what Homer says in the first book of his *Odyssey*:

All men most applaud
The song that has the newest theme.

These are words whose deeper meaning was not lost upon our master, for he had underlined them in his copy and had also written them out. What would he have said about the gospel of the 'music of the future' with which its apostles seek today to advance themselves?

Directly following the A major sonata came the [cello] sonatas in C and D major, opus 102. The master dedicated these musical poems to his esteemed friend, Countess Marie Erdödy, *née* Countess Niczky, whom he had already honoured with the dedication of the two great trios, opus 70. What this lady had for many years been to Beethoven may be summed up in his name for her: he called her his 'Father confessor'. To her nobility of birth she joined a nobility of spirit not always to be found to the same degree in her peers. Countess Erdödy never wavered in her friendly affection nor in the openly acknowledged reverence she felt for the master. The same cannot be said for many others of her class, almost all of whom deserted Beethoven when a new constellation rose in the Italian sky. In 1820 she changed her permanent residence to Munich; I have not been able to ascertain the year of her death.

These works were attended by experiences and events of such an unusual nature that they must be recounted. First of all we need to know that the Bonn music publisher, Simrock, who is still alive, had the manuscript from the composer's own hand in Vienna in 1816. Beethoven had noted in his journal that the work had been composed in 1815. Simrock published it in 1817.

Up to this time the grammarians and their followers had subscribed to a maxim that had the authority of dogma: 'Beethoven is incapable of writing a fugue'. And there was no evidence to disprove or even to cast doubt upon this assertion. Neither *Christus am Oelberge* nor the C major Mass had anything like a fugue, even where one would have been

---

* Compare this to what is said on pp. 237 ff.

appropriate. Indeed, the Mass should have had a fugue for two reasons: first, because Prince Esterházy, for whom the work was composed, was known to be especially fond of this art form, and secondly, because the musical world was awaiting in the Mass itself a piece of evidence to disprove the maxim quoted above. Passages that seem to anticipate a fugue merely gave weight to the belief in his inability. The fugue in the C major quartet, opus 59, could not be presented as adequate evidence; the fugal passages in the Funeral March of the *Eroica*, in the Andante of the A major symphony, and in various other works, only supported the opponents' argument.

Then there appeared opus 102, and as the final movement of the sonata in D an Allegro fugato. The fat was in the fire. Immediately nearly the whole army of Philistines started flailing this movement with both fists; nor did they spare the other movements of the sonata, not even the Adagio, which is among the richest and most deeply sensitive inspirations of Beethoven's muse. If any person had made so bold as to defend the work, he would have been stoned by the embittered enemies. It really seemed that the hatred directed against the great master, whose works had already obscured so many composers living in Vienna, had only been dozing, awaiting the opportunity to assert itself openly.

Never was violent enmity less justified than this. The objection made to this Fugato was its want of clearness, its 'confusion' as Beethoven's enemies maintained, yet the passage that provoked these attacks is a mere twenty measures ending with a cadence on the major triad of F sharp. Less colourful modulations would not have so affected the clearness, since the theme is always present, though sometimes in retrograde motion. The difficulty of mastering the task of playing the work had to serve as a pretext for calling the whole thing bad music and rejecting it. Right up to the present day musicians are prejudiced against both these marvellous works, so worthy of their author's name. It is high time to set the score straight. A well-phrased performance on both instruments will undoubtedly bring these works the recognition they deserve.

From one passage in the Leipzig journal's criticism of these works as a whole we may see to how great an extent that high court in its evaluation of opus 102 supported the enemies' allegations. It reads:

These two sonatas are surely among the most extraordinary, the strangest piano works in any form to be written in many years. Everything here is different, very different from anything ever heard before, even from the composer himself. We hope he will not take it amiss when we add that it does not appear an unimportant work, and as it seems to be well-ordered, well-divided, well-formed, its effect is all the more bizarre (AmZ XX (1818) 792).

The enemies endeavoured to make the expressions in this criticism even stronger, and were outspoken in their ridicule. They spread a rumour that the publisher had demanded reparations from the composer and that he had settled the obligation by giving him without fee his *Ten Themes with Variations*, opus 107. An edition of these sonatas published by Artaria in 1818, which appeared without the consent of the publishing house in Bonn, was considered by the enemies as proof of the rumour they had invented, and was used to propagate other harmful lies. Certain Viennese publishers whose offers Beethoven had repeatedly declined were only too willing to help spread the rumour.

The immediate effect on our master of these intrigues was one that the musical world cannot lament, for they led him to apply himself to an art form he had previously neglected, namely the fugue. *Ab hoste discimus*. It was characteristic of the epoch to revere the fugue as such and to cultivate the form assiduously. The community of musicians would therefore regard as good enough to be worthy of their respect only that composer who could acquit himself skilfully in this realm. From this time on we therefore find in many of Beethoven's works carefully worked-out fugues. Indeed, the next great sonata, that in B flat major, opus 106, has an impressive three-part fugue, whose like is to be found in no other piano work. If the master indicates that it is to be played with 'certain liberties' [*con alcune licenze*], he merely wishes to show that he is quite familiar with the rules he has ignored. Although this great work incurred—and still incurs—the pedants' cavilling, it is a composition worthy of a Beethoven and, when played with perfect mastery, a clear and comprehensible piece of music that requires of its performers a high degree of virtuosity and knowledge of this art form. It is a bunch of grapes that hangs very high. Later on, in the sonata in A flat major, opus 110, we find a three-part fugue that contains neither 'shocking passages' nor 'certain liberties', that is not difficult to play but is full of charm and beauty. Then come the powerful fugues in the Gloria and the Credo of the *Missa Solemnis*, and finally the great fugal overture, opus 124. With these the master stopped the mouths of his enemies for all time, except they should be inflexible devotees of Bach or Mozart.

The following works also date from the year 1815: *Meeresstille und glückliche Fahrt* (Goethe) for chorus and orchestra, and the C major overture, opus 115. These two works, together with the cantata *Christus am Oelberge*, were first performed at a benefit concert given for the Citizens' Hospital Fund on Christmas Day of the same year in the great Redoutensaal under the direction of the composer himself. The programme listed no sub-title for the overture, but the catalogues list it sometimes as the 'Name-Day Overture' (*zur Namensfeier*) and sometimes as the 'Hunting Overture'. On 10 May 1818 this overture (already the property of the publishing firm of Steiner & Co.) was performed a second time at a concert given by Messrs. Mayseder, Moscheles, and Giuliani under the sub-title *à la Chasse*. Beethoven inquired why it had been so named and who had taken this liberty. He could secure no answer, for each party blamed the other. The Breitkopf & Härtel catalogue lists it as the *Namensfeier* overture, perhaps because it was first performed on Christmas Day.[146]

As a direct result of this 25 December concert, the Municipal Council of Vienna resolved to confer on our master the title of honorary citizen.[147] The official record in the newspaper announces this recognition in the following words:

> The Municipal Council of the Royal and Imperial Capital and Residence-City of Vienna, in recognition of the generosity with which he has repeatedly dedicated his compositions to benevolent causes, has conferred on Herr Ludwig van Beethoven . . . the certificate of honorary citizenship.

Only for services rendered to benevolent causes! Not a word of recognition or honour to him as an artist! Not the merest hint of a sentiment that might have read: 'We are proud to be able to claim you as our fellow citizen.' This document serves as a witness for all time to the way in which the authorities of old Vienna regarded the city's art and artists. Did Beethoven value his status as honorary citizen of the city of Vienna? The answer to this question may be ascertained from events and circumstances that will be discussed later.

At about this time (1815 or 1816), our master began to occupy himself with arrangements (harmonization and accompaniment) of Scottish songs. We know from the correspondence between Beethoven and the collector of these songs, George Thomson of Edinburgh, that Beethoven arranged well over a hundred of them. A considerable number, probably never published, several of them for three voices and none of them with text, constitute some of the pages of manuscript found in the composer's *Nachlass*. These papers are now in the Royal Library in Berlin. The thematic index of the works printed in England does not show whether the songs now in Berlin were ever published. In 1841 I had the opportunity of addressing inquiries regarding these direct to Thomson himself in Edinburgh. Instead of giving me the information I sought, however, he referred to his advanced age and announced his intention of selling the whole collection. The group of twenty-five songs for solo voice with piano, violin, and cello accompaniment, published as opus 108 by Schlesinger in Berlin, is only an excerpt from the complete collection, which was published in England. In any case, it seems that this light, relaxing work came at a good time for our master, for it was during a long period of emotional tension when he was not up to strenuous creative efforts.[148] The list of works composed in 1816, 1817, and 1818 is an indication of the master's state of mind during those years.*[149]

It may be the appropriate place here to record an episode that bore only indirectly on Beethoven but that is of interest to the historian of art: the dismissal in 1816 of the Rasumovsky Quartet. There were two principal reasons for this dismissal: the advanced age of the Prince and, more important, the destruction by fire of his palace, which had been filled with treasures from all the realms of art and science. Nothing could be saved: all the things that had made the Prince's life pleasant were wiped out at a single stroke, and even his beloved music had no power to soften his grief. His commitments, however, regarding the lifelong pensions to be paid to the artists were fulfilled to the letter, in contrast to what Beethoven experienced, as we have seen. Schuppanzigh immediately assumed a post as conductor of an orchestra in Russia (as we said at the beginning of this period) and Sina moved to Paris. The other two members of the quartet remained in Vienna.

It lay within the character of the times that such art events were suspended for several years, for their popularity began to decline from day to day. Since the days of the Congress the physiognomy of the Imperial City had assumed throughout all echelons of its society an outlook that contrasted sharply with its former expression. The public that had filled the concert halls and theatres lost both the composure necessary to an enjoyment of the arts and the decorum of their external behaviour. Even the character so pleasantly expressed by the phrase 'Gemütliches Wien' had disappeared. These long-cherished qualities were replaced by the legacies of the Congress, crudeness and depravity of every kind. Later on we shall have the opportunity of unveiling this new physiognomy entirely. Meanwhile a few sentences from the AmZ about the changed situation in Vienna will serve to support what has just been stated. In the report for May 1817 the critic harangues the Viennese public in the following words:

For some time now the unbiased observer has been forced to recognize that our public is attempting to imitate the public of Paris and London. The highly admired Austrian genteel easy-going disposition, the tolerant and liberal attitude, seems to have vanished, at least from the theatre. In its place there have appeared rudeness, openly expressed hostility, whistles, scornful laughter, uninhibited pounding with the feet, and other such ill-mannered expressions, leading us to fear future scenes which, even if not quite so violent as those in *Germanicus*, would yet be bad enough to make any peace-loving citizen wish with

* The author gave to Professor Otto Jahn a stout notebook containing about forty of these songs, neatly copied and corrected in Beethoven's own hand. On the first page is inscribed plainly in the master's writing the year '1810'.

all his heart that a higher authority would restore order before it is too late (AmZ XIX (1817) 427).

The authorities, however, ignored all such warnings; in fact, they aggravated the trouble no end by levelling only the loosest censorship at the Viennese local farces, while the severity with which they judged good, serious plays knew no bounds. There were other well-known factors that undeniably brought about a general, systematically exploited demoralization: religious indifference and lack of faith had for many years been more prevalent in Vienna than in any other large European city, and no other capital in Europe lent itself so easily to a childish aping of foreign manners as Vienna. The events of 1848 showed the culmination of this demoralization. The seeds of this harvest had been sown decades before. How these things impinged upon the hero of this book, to what extent they affected him, will emerge from what follows.

We have now reached the entrance to a long, narrow, twisting gorge that is not to be circumvented. I therefore invite the reader to follow me with patience and with consideration for our master. We must first explore the causes of an exhausting lawsuit in which our master was entangled through four long years, and then the consequences it entailed for his whole artistic life. My exposition of these facts is facilitated by one circumstance, the publication of a correspondence that bears on these events and that has let down all barriers to their communication. This correspondence consists of twenty-eight letters from Beethoven to Giannatasio Del Rio (1816–18), which were published along with the latter's memoirs about Beethoven at that time. These were mentioned in the second period.

In November 1815 Beethoven's elder brother Karl, an official of the Austrian national bank, died. With the death of this man there begins in the life of our master an episode of particular importance, an episode poor in artistic impulse but rich in exalted moments that, more than anything up to this point, show the composer as a man of uncommon moral honour and strength. Through this new conflict of persons and personal relationships our master entered for the first time into close contact with the life of the ordinary citizen. The course of events will show us how he withstood the test.

In the fifth clause of his will of 14 November 1815, Karl van Beethoven asked his brother to assume the guardianship of his son Karl, then nine or ten years old. The wording of this clause is as follows:

I designate as guardian my brother, Ludwig van Beethoven. Since this my most dearly beloved brother has often sustained me with true brotherly love in the most generous and most noble manner, I have the utmost confidence in his noble heart, and trust that the love and friendship he so often showed me he will also show to my son Karl, and that he will do everything in his power to ensure the spiritual education and further welfare of my son. I know that he will not refuse me this request.

In the sixth clause the testator names the attorney Dr. Schönauer as the executor 'for the carrying out of the will and also all other matters pertaining to my son Karl, with the added stipulation that he be consulted on all matters having to do with my son's property'. (We still have the legally recorded copy of this will.)

In a letter to Ferdinand Ries dated 22 November of the same year, Beethoven speaks of his brother's death and goes on to say: 'I estimate that I gave him 10,000 florins in Viennese currency in order to make his life easier.' Elsewhere in the same letter Beethoven says: 'He had a bad wife.'

Beethoven felt that his first duty in carrying out his dead brother's injunction to the fullest extent was to remove his nephew from the bad influence of his mother; indeed, in his concern for the boy's welfare he went far beyond the literal wording of the brother's will, for he decided to adopt the nephew. This decision was in glaring contrast to his whole mode of living and to his artistic needs as well. His friends on all sides tried to dissuade him, but he was determined; his reply was that he felt obliged to rear his nephew as a good man and a good citizen.

In order to execute this plan without delay, however, and also to stand a better chance of success with the legal authorities, Beethoven's first step was to give up his bachelor life and establish a regular household; in other words, to bury with his own hand the very foundation of his personal and artistic freedom and independence and, in creating a home for his nephew, to destroy what was the home of his genius, the only home in which he could operate creatively.

We have a small sample of the method the master used in establishing his household, in the form of an original document, no doubt obtained from an experienced housekeeper, in the form of a legal questionnaire, with questions on the left and answers on the right. Beethoven asks:

1. What does one give to two servants to eat at dinner and supper, both as to quality and as to quantity?
2. How often does one give them meat? Should it be both at noon and at night?
3. The food for the servants: is it the same as the master's or do they make themselves a separate meal; i.e., do they prepare themselves different food from what the master has?
4. How much meat does one reckon on for three persons? Etc.[150]

What must the composer have felt, accustomed as he was to dwelling in another realm altogether, as he read the detailed answers concerning the operation of a kitchen? Might not one expect that the idea of dealing with the various kinds of cabbage, carrots and turnips, *Sauerkraut* and dumplings, herring and potatoes, would make him recoil from such an undertaking? Love and a sense of duty, however, overcame any prospect of difficulty with servants in case there was no housekeeper to oversee them.

As early as February 1816 Beethoven took the boy from his sister-in-law and, for the time being, turned him over to the school of the above-named Giannatasio Del Rio. It was an extra-legal act, and the sister-in-law filed a complaint immediately. The suit was entered in the superior court, 'the Lower Austrian civil authority' (das niederösterreichische Landrecht), for it was this tribunal that dealt with cases involving members of the nobility and the clergy. (Up to that time Beethoven had been taken for a nobleman because of the prefix *van* before his name.) The defendant had first to prove that his sister-in-law was an immoral woman and therefore unfit to have any part in the upbringing of her son, surely a painful task for a man who had always borne the faults of his family with patience.

As so often happens in the course of a litigation, the counsel only aggravated the hostility between the disputing parties. As factual evidence came to light, the lawyer Dr. Adlersburg, a coarse individual, seemed to forget the respect that he, as Beethoven's representative, owed his client. The opposing attorney Dr. Schönauer, a notorious schemer, took the opposite course, and took it much further. The duelling by the advocates led to wrangles (at the expense of the contesting parties, naturally) such as at that time and place were commonplaces of the profession. Vulgar insults and tricks of every kind, both written in the record and spoken in the presence of the judge, belonged to the prerogatives of a lawyer. But they did not fail to make bad blood. Yet our master emerged from this hearing victorious, as the authorities accepted his extra-legal act and left the nephew in his care pending the final outcome of the suit.[151]

Among the already mentioned notes of Frl. Giannatasio Del Rio (*Grenzboten* XVI, Part I, Vol. II (1857) 29) is the following:

The woman Beethoven used to call the 'Queen of the Night', his nephew's mother, finally disputed his nobility and his title of *van* Beethoven, and the case was referred to the *Magistrat*.[152] This turn of events injured him deeply, for the first court treated him with more deference. Thus it was eventually settled that he lost his right of guardianship, and his nephew was returned to the mother. What a painful blow to him!

This noteworthy statement, as important to the situation as a legal document because in it we hear a non-partisan voice,[153] leads us to further investigation of the matter. For the circumstances that caused the suit to be referred by a high court to a lower court offer us a characteristic moment among all the wearisome and vulgar proceedings.

After the trial had already dragged on for over a year, the attention of the high court was called by the opposing lawyer's denunciation (it is said) to the fact that in Dutch family names the predicate *van* did not denote nobility, and that Beethoven was therefore not of noble descent, so that the high court was not the appropriate authority to judge the present case. It was accordingly decreed that Beethoven should prove his nobility. On the appointed day he appeared in person before the tribunal and declared that 'his nobility was *here* and *here*', pointing to his head and his heart.*[154] For such nobility, however, there was not in Austria, nor in any other state, nor has there ever been, a special legal authority. The high court of Lower Austria could do nothing else but refer this litigation to the *Magistrat* for further trial. This lower court was very favourable for the plans and schemes of the opposing lawyer. Beethoven's only hope of success here lay in dismissing his counsel and pitting a new personality against his opponent. His choice fell upon Dr. Johann Baptist Bach who had just entered the ranks of the court lawyers, a man feared as an opponent by his colleagues and a man of broad cultural background, a music-lover and himself a performer, a chamber-music 'cellist with more than an amateur's talent. The high respect that he enjoyed is indicated by his having been appointed for three terms dean of the faculty of law at the University of Vienna.

The relegation of the lawsuit to a police court was a bitter blow to Beethoven. It would be hard to say whether or not he attached any importance to the general belief that he was of noble blood, for his origin and his family connections were generally known, the latter especially because of the middle-class occupations of his brothers. It is certain however that it was of great importance to him to have his case judged by the special superior court, partly because he was accorded a greater respect there (as Frl. Giannatasio so truly noted) and partly because the unfavourable reputation of the lower court inspired in him little hope of success. It may be stated with no less certainty that, had the nobles not believed him to be one of them, neither his genius nor his works of art would have won for him the favoured position he had enjoyed in aristocratic circles up to that time. There were many illustrations of this truth as soon as the incident in the superior court became public knowledge. It was in the upper class, not the middle class, that

---

* The master should have quoted the well-known words of Napoleon Bonaparte: 'I wish to trace my nobility from myself alone'.

the little word 'van' had exercised a magic power. At any rate, it is a fact that from the time of his encounter with the civil code of Lower Austria, Vienna and its environs became too confining for our aggrieved master, and, if the duties he had assumed under his brother's will had not bound him there, he would have carried out his often proposed trip to England. He might even have stayed there, for he admired the political institutions of that country above all others.

To emphasize the effect on Beethoven of this event, here is a word-for-word excerpt from a conversation between him and his friend Peters. The exchange is recorded in a diary dating from that time, and, as the two men were in a public place, their whole conversation had to be carried on in writing because of Beethoven's deafness. The very first words of the master show what social status he had claimed as his own. Only his confirmed enemies would interpret them falsely.

Peters: You are as discontented today as I.

Beethoven: The middle-class burgher ought to be excluded from the society of higher men, and here I am one of them.*

Peters: In three weeks you will have nothing more to do with either burgher or magistrate. People will ask to testify on your behalf and will deliver the most sympathetic testimony for you.

Beethoven: If that should happen, I would not want to remain any longer in such a country. I would go where there were neither guardians nor uncles like me. Memorandum![155]

At the time Dr. Bach took over the conduct of the suit the situation was already in turmoil. Beethoven's right of guardianship had been suspended (ostensibly because of his deafness) and an interim guardian appointed in the person of an official of the *Magistrat*, the city sequestrator, Nussböck. Moreover, the *Magistrat* in its much-touted wisdom recognized the rights claimed by the plaintiff regarding the rearing of her son, and, ignoring entirely the judgement of the superior court, had decreed that the boy should be returned to her. In the meantime the boy, surely a pitiable object of all this wrangling, had for two full years (from February 1816 to February 1818) enjoyed a good education, financed by his uncle, at the Giannatasio school. After that he was for some time tutored in his uncle's apartment and then was once more entrusted to a school, the Blöchlinger Institute. And now the decision of a police court was going to remove the intelligent boy, with whom his teachers were well pleased, from this excellent and expensive school without any regard for the boy's future. Frl. Giannatasio had reason for exclaiming: 'What a painful blow for Beethoven!' Truly, after making

---

* This sentence would deny Beethoven's sympathy for the common man and betray him as an out-and-out aristocrat if one did not realize that he was speaking exclusively of the Viennese middle class and its cultural level at that time.

so many sacrifices and suffering so much humiliation, this was the last straw. In vain Beethoven protested again and again his sole right of guardianship. The final, vigorous protest, with the date of presentation marked 30 October 1819, is among the legal papers which, along with Dr. Bach's other papers and documents, were put at my disposal. The *Magistrat's* decree of 4 November of the same year refers to former decrees and repeats its dismissal of the case.

The case was now taken for the first time to the Court of Appeals. The first presentation was made on 7 January 1820; this text is also among the legal documents. The second item reads as follows:

My nephew is now approaching the age when his higher education must be attended to. Neither his mother nor his present guardian is suited to the task of leading the boy in the paths of learning. The former is unsuited because she is a woman and, as I have documented, her conduct is such that, without saying more about it, no witness has come forward to testify to her character.* It is for this reason that the superior civil court excluded her entirely from the custody of the child. How the honourable *Magistrat* could reinstate her is past understanding.

Still another particularly characteristic passage from the petition should be quoted:

The sole objects of all my efforts and desires are the best possible education for the boy, for his abilities justify the highest hopes, and the fulfilment of the expectations that his father placed in my brotherly love. The stalk is yet flexible, but if any more time is wasted, it will grow awry from under the hand of the gardener who cultivates it, and his rectitude, knowledge, and character will be lost for ever. I know no duty more sacred than supervising the education and rearing of a child. The only obligation of the Probate Court is to honour the good qualities and to provide the practical ones. Only then does it devote its most zealous attention to the welfare of its ward. But by obstructing the good qualities it will neglect its obligation.

Obviously these are the words of Beethoven, written down by himself and sent to his lawyer. Thus in his letter to me of 9 June 1839 Dr. Bach was able to call my particular attention to this passage and remark: 'No aspect of this great soul must be forgotten, for he is proof that to an inexhaustible intellect there may also be bound a noble spirit.'

Two more excerpts from this petition deserve to be quoted to help us gain a more accurate picture of the situation and also to help us to a fuller understanding of the consequences that this lawsuit held for our master:

* Perhaps the biographer should say more about the conduct of this woman in order to justify Beethoven's claim: even while the lawsuit was still in progress she gave birth to a child, and this is just one instance of her depraved nature.

Truly, with the best interests of the boy at heart, I have no objection to the mother's having some form of joint guardianship, an arrangement by which she might visit the boy and have knowledge of all the provisions made for his education. But to give her sole custody and not provide a virtuous guardian to share the responsibility would be to abandon the boy to inevitable ruin.

The other section reads:

I have made formal declaration to the honourable *Magistrat* that I have paid the expenses for his present schooling out of my own earnings, and that I would like to furnish the funds necessary to employ several tutors. As I am rather hard of hearing, and conversation is difficult for me, I have requested a joint guardian (I have proposed the name of Herr Peters, councillor to Prince Lobkowitz), so that a man of the highest calibre will be in charge of my nephew's education and development, a man who is universally respected for his knowledge and his morality, a man whose co-operation will give assurance to me and to all concerned with the boy's welfare that the boy may and will receive education and training commensurate with his abilities.

This appeal had favourable results for the master, for all of his suggestions were adopted and all his wishes were fulfilled to the letter. The Court of Appeals accepted the superior court's interpretation. Accordingly, the widow van Beethoven was excluded from any participation in her son's upbringing and was not permitted any direct influence on him; our master was granted full powers of custody.

So ended a lawsuit in which all of musical Vienna had taken the liveliest interest. Despite all these changes in his rearing and education, the nephew's progress in his studies and in music showed that he had genuine talent. And so it seemed that the noble master, after so many years of wrangling and insult, of unparalleled love, concern, and sacrifice, had at last reaped the gratitude he deserved and would from then on experience nothing but joy in his nephew. Whether the outcome was a fulfilment of this promise, whether his hopes were realized, we shall learn in due time.

Let us close this most disagreeable courtroom episode with an anecdote that may supplement this introduction to the Viennese lower courts of that day.

Beethoven, now bereft of his claim to nobility, figured in the documents of this lawsuit simply as a composer. When Dr. Bach took over Beethoven's case, he stipulated that from then on his client must bear the title of Kapellmeister, for the worthy magistrates were mostly boors, and a composer meant nothing to them. In Austria one had to have some sort of official title if he were to gain anything like respect from the lower courts, and a night watchman was more highly thought of than a composer or a poet. On the other hand, if a spurious title of nobility should be casually used, a certain official dignity on the part of the client would, in the eyes of the court, lend that much more weight to his case. In vain Beethoven resisted assuming the title of Kapellmeister, for he was afraid that, as in the matter of furnishing proof of his nobility, the court might require him to prove by producing a contract that he was entitled to use even this title. But the lawyer, well versed in the ways of the country and the people, disregarded this scruple and without more ado promoted the insignificant 'Composer' to the position of Kapellmeister—'in partibus infidelium', as the master sarcastically termed his promotion. On all documents signed by Dr. Bach, Beethoven was designated 'Kapellmeister and Composer'. After the successful completion of the suit, Bach claimed jokingly that it had been won only by the effect of the title.[156]

From the master himself we learn of his financial condition during the second year of the lawsuit. On 1 November 1817 he wrote to Giannatasio:

Changed circumstances may well require that I leave Karl with you no longer than the end of the present quarter, and accordingly I am compelled to give you notice for the next quarter. Difficult as this decision is to me, my straitened circumstances do not permit me to withhold this from you. Otherwise I would with the greatest pleasure hand you the payment for an entire quarter, as a slight token of my gratitude, at the time I take Karl from you. . . . If I should ever be restored to full health, so that again I may earn more, I shall still further demonstrate my gratitude to you. . . . I say in all truth that I am forced to admit to you my impoverished situation at this time.

But if his financial situation was already bad in 1817, it became steadily worse until 1820. We have only to mention that during this period, no short length of time considering Beethoven's wealth of creativity, the only works composed and sold were the sonatas opp. 102 and 106, the *Ten Themes with Variations*, opus 107, and the Scottish songs. We shall soon hear of the methods by which our master provided for the needs of himself and his nephew, which grew day by day. One wonders whether he is more to be blamed or pitied in this instance, for we know that from the concerts given in 1814 he had cleared a considerable sum, which he had invested in bank shares.

At any rate, he wrote, instead of the usual quantity of musical notes, a great number of letters that deal partly with the establishment of his household, partly with the suit, and partly with the education of his nephew. These are among the most depressing, the most pitiful statements of his inner turmoil and of the relentless way these matters worked on his mind.* Those of his friends and close acquaintances who allowed

---

* In this connection let us observe a similarity between Rubens and Beethoven. The life story of the great painter reveals that in his many existing letters there is not one reference to his art, a most regrettable circumstance. So, too, in the countless existing letters of Beethoven only a very few contain any mention of music.

themselves to become involved in these three concerns were deluged with letters and requests, so that they all blessed the hour in which the suit was concluded. Most of these letters might well be destroyed, for, apart from their value as autographs of a great man, many are likely to present their writer in a very poor light, unless one is willing to excuse a temporary bad humour and to understand its causes, or perhaps, as Ferdinand Ries does, adhere to the very questionable maxim that great men may with impunity say anything they please. In order to prevent a derogatory interpretation of this statement, which in my opinion is one of the most deplorable ever made, I should like to make public here and now the text of Beethoven's letter that gave rise to this commentary. On 5 March 1818 Beethoven wrote to Ries, saying in part:

. . . I hope and wish for your sake that your happy circumstances may improve daily. Unfortunately, I cannot say that of myself: by my unfortunate connection with this Archduke I have been brought almost to beggary. I cannot see anyone in want—I must give. You can imagine how my sufferings are increased by my present situation. . . . If it is in any way possible, I shall get away from here even sooner, to avoid my complete ruin; then I shall arrive in London in the winter at the latest. I know that you will stand by an unfortunate friend. . . .

Certainly the generous Archduke Rudolph would not have taken amiss this unfounded attack on his name. He would surely have attributed the affront to the master's pressing tensions, which could be alleviated only by carrying out his plan to go to London where he had received brilliant offers from the Philharmonic Society. The Archduke would have been the last to oppose such a journey, especially since his appointment to the archbishopric of Olmütz, and his consequent departure from Vienna, had been made known about the middle of 1818. What other reason had the composer for abandoning his travelling plans than his immeasurable love for his nephew? At any rate, our master's lament over his financial state and about his friend is not to be taken seriously, for poverty was his *idée fixe* and he all too frequently used his friend as a scapegoat to explain difficulties of his own making. In all honesty we must not gloss over the many striking contradictions between word and deed, of which many more examples will still be cited.

The importance to our master of this journey, both in furthering his artistic interests and in improving his economic situation, may be seen in the notes he wrote, some of them in the form of words of admonition to himself, in his diaries of the preceding years. In his journal for 1814 we find the following passage:

Perfect the hearing machines if possible, and then travel. . . . This you owe to yourself, to mankind, and to Him, the Almighty. Only thus may you be able to develop all that remains shut within you . . . and a little court, a little chapel . . . the song of praise, written in it by me, to be performed to the glory of the Almighty, the Eternal, the Infinite. . . . Thus may my last days pass . . . for future humanity. In my room, portraits of Handel, Bach, Gluck, Mozart, Haydn. . . . They can help me to deserve indulgence.

In the journal for 1816 there are two passages that show emphatically how eagerly he hoped to travel:

Something must happen, either a journey and the writing of the works that would be necessary for it, or an opera. If you should remain here during the coming summer, the opera would be preferable in case the conditions were only of small account. If you are going to spend the summer holidays here you must soon decide: how? where? Help me, O God! Thou seest me deserted by all mankind, but I will not do what is not right. Hear my prayer only to be with my Karl in the future, for nothing now seems to indicate a possibility of that. O harsh fate, O cruel destiny—no, no, my unhappy condition will never end.

There is no other way to save yourself but from here. Only by so doing can you once again soar to the heights of your art, while here you sink into mediocrity. Only a single symphony, and then onward, onward, meanwhile receiving the payment that comes each year. Throughout the summer, work for the journey. Only thus can you complete the great work for your nephew. Later, wander through Italy and Sicily with a few artists. Make plans and be hopeful for L. . . .[157]

It is now time to have a look at the master's domestic situation in order that we may determine whether his difficulties would have been alleviated by leaving most of the necessities of his advancing age to the care of an inn, or whether his life was more comfortable, more amenable to his artistic needs, when living in his own home with servants. The latter consideration was a decisive factor in his establishing a household. Beethoven's praiseworthy habit of writing notes about himself, his thoughts and feelings, included recording his household affairs. For this purpose he generally used empty pages of a calendar that served as a sort of domestic journal. Such journals have been found for the complete years of 1819, 1820, and 1823. The first (1819) contains only the following notations:

January 31: gave the housekeeper notice.
February 15: kitchen maid installed.
March 8: gave the kitchen maid fourteen days' notice.
March 22: new housekeeper installed.
May 12: arrived in Mödling.
Miser et pauper sum.
May 14: engaged a maid at six florins a month.
July 20: gave the housekeeper notice.

The year 1820 is richer in household notations. For instance:

April 17: kitchen maid installed.
April 19: bad day (i.e., the master had nothing fit to eat because he had stayed so long at his desk that the food was overcooked or entirely ruined).
May 16: gave kitchen maid notice.
May 19: kitchen maid left.
May 30: woman installed.
July 1: kitchen maid installed.
July 28: kitchen maid ran away in the evening.
July 30: the woman from Unter-Döbling was installed. For four bad days, August 10, 11, 12, 13, ate in Lerchenfeld [a suburb outside the walls of Vienna].[158]
August 28: the woman's month is up.
September 6: maid installed.
October 22: maid left.
December 12: kitchen maid installed.
December 18: kitchen maid dismissed.
December 27: new housemaid installed.

If this is a discouraging picture of the household affairs of a man who worked with his mind, the events of the years just enumerated were to those of 1823 as a miniature is to a fresco. Throughout that whole year there was not a single month that was not marked by one or two changes of servants, often accompanied by violent scenes. From the notes of Frl. Giannatasio we learn of a scuffle between the master and his valet in 1816 at Baden when Hr. Giannatasio was visiting there with his daughters. The renowned master greeted his guests with scratches on his face, saying, 'You see how he has used me'. This rowdy servant was dismissed and another not much better engaged, then dismissed on 17 May 1817, according to the journal. From that time no more male servants were hired. Close to this notation in the journal is the following entry: 'Living alone is like poison for you in this condition of deafness; you have no choice but to live in constant suspicion of an inferior person about you.'

No doubt it occurs to the reader to ask who was more to blame for this domestic disorder, the master or the servants. Both shared the blame, but not equally: only the lesser portion of it falls to Beethoven. Excessive irritability nourished by both a congenitally uneven temper and the moodiness of an artist, suspicion particularly of the serving class, partly due to his own experience and partly from hearsay, and finally the impossibility of oral communication with the servants: these three obstacles occurring in varying combinations inevitably made a smooth home life difficult, nay impossible. If only the servants had possessed a measure of training, a degree of that quality of good breeding that is frequently found among the serving classes of northern and western Germany, often accompanied by a fine moral sense, they would surely have exercised a beneficial effect on our master by keeping everything around him in good order. He could not help comparing his present domestic situation with the memories he had brought from his homeland. But he was in Vienna, the gathering place of the most vulgar, crude, and base elements of the serving class from all the races of the empire, without education, without religion, without morals. It is sometimes said of large cities that they are in certain respects schools for every kind of vice. If this is true, the Austrian capital was the foremost among them! Only a very few households were fortunate enough not to see their domestic peace ruined by the wantonness of their servants. Perhaps the situation has improved. So much for the reasons for such chaos in Beethoven's domestic life at that time. Further on we shall have to examine more closely the underlying causes of this situation in relation to his whole character.

As we have said, the appointment of Archduke Rudolph as Archbishop of Olmütz had become public knowledge by the middle of 1818. The date of his installation was accordingly set for 9 March 1820, the day of commemoration celebrated every year for the patron saints of Moravia, Cyrillus and Methodius.[159]

Without a suggestion from anyone, Beethoven decided to write a Mass for this solemn occasion, and so he applied himself once more after many years to that facet of his art which, as he often said, was with the symphony his favourite medium. This decision would clearly prove that the above-quoted invective against 'this Archduke' was nothing more than a passing mood, even if we did not know that the master never missed an opportunity to demonstrate the utmost affection for his most illustrious pupil.

In the late autumn of 1818 I saw him start work on this score, just after he had completed the gigantic sonata in B flat, opus 106. Our master returned to Mödling to spend the summer of 1819. I frequently visited him there and saw the Mass take shape. I also heard him express doubts as to whether it would be finished in time, for as he worked on each section it became much longer than he had originally anticipated. Presumably another reason for the slow progress of the work was his continuing legal preoccupation with the Vienna *Magistrat*. When at the end of October 1819 he returned to Vienna, he brought the completed Credo, and when the Archduke started on his journey to Olmütz for the installation ceremony, the master had got as far as the Agnus Dei. If, however, the reader should wonder how Beethoven felt about the completion of every one of his works, how much time he spent perfecting each in respect to content and form, it may be said that up to the day of the installation no part of the Mass was finished to the satisfaction of the composer. It was not until 1822 that he put the finishing touches on this work.

When I think of the events of the year 1819, particularly during the time the composer in the Hafner house in Mödling was busy with the Credo, I remember his mental excitement, and I must admit that never before and never since that time have I seen him in a similar state of complete removal from the world. Perhaps I may recount one incident. Towards the end of August I arrived at the master's rooms in Mödling accompanied by the musician Johann Horzalka, who is still alive in Vienna.[160] It was four o'clock in the afternoon. As soon as we entered we were told that both Beethoven's maids had left that morning and that there had occurred after midnight an uproar that had disturbed everyone in the house because, having waited so long, both maids had gone to sleep and the meal they had prepared was inedible. From behind the closed door of one of the parlours we could hear the master working on the fugue of the Credo, singing, yelling, stamping his feet. When we had heard enough of this almost frightening performance and were about to depart, the door opened and Beethoven stood before us, his features distorted to the point of inspiring terror. He looked as though he had just engaged in a life and death struggle with the whole army of contrapuntists, his everlasting enemies. His first words were confused, as if he felt embarrassed at having been overheard. Soon he began to speak of the day's events and said, with noticeable self-control, 'What a mess! Everyone has run away and I haven't had anything to eat since yesterday noon.' I tried to calm him and helped him to make his toilet. My companion hurried to the bathhouse restaurant to order something for the famished master. While he ate, he complained to us about the state of his household. But, because of the circumstances I have already described, there was no solution. Never has such a great work of art been created under such adverse living conditions as this *Missa Solemnis*!

This is a colossal work, in which the composer concentrated his entire musical wealth, but for which he was paid only a relatively small sum. It still does not return to the performing musicians a profit commensurate with its worth and, moreover, gives rise to the most contradictory evaluations. All these are circumstances that we shall not discuss at length here. The whole history of the *Missa Solemnis* will be treated when we come to speak of its first performance, which the author himself organized in 1824.

THIRD PERIOD

CONCLUSION

The year 1820 shows us Beethoven at the consummation of his wishes, so long striven after and now at last fulfilled. 'To be able to be with his Karl', as we heard him exclaim, was now a reality. The effect on his spirits of the successful outcome of the trial was all the more overwhelming because he had always despaired of it. Due to his great joy and satisfaction over the victory he had won against evil and intrigue, and also over the salvation (as he believed) of his talented nephew from bodily and spiritual danger, he wrote little or no music that summer, though perhaps this only seems to be true because the pages of the sketchbooks were almost empty. All the wounds he had suffered through four years seemed to have healed and been forgotten. Even the more far-reaching consequences of that bad period, which for the moment we shall not go into, did not worry him, for trusting in God and his own creative genius, he hoped to overcome them shortly and to see the path of his future freed of all obstacles.

The biographer, too, close as he was to the events of those days, sharing the joys and sorrows of his dear friend and teacher, finds himself at this moment full of happiness that this tempestuous time is past and that he may resume his way along the broad stream of the life and work of this extraordinary man. From now on he may pursue, with only occasional backward glances, a chronologically ordered sequence in his historical account.

[End of volume I of 1860 German edition]

[II]

REVIVED ENERGY; RENEWED STRENGTH

⊷ 1821 ⊷

It is customary for men to watch the mountains in order to predict from their clear or clouded summits the coming weather. They do the same with the summits in art and in science: some watch out of idle curiosity, while others are genuinely interested in the enrichment of art or in the scientific knowledge upon which a new invention is based.

So it was with Beethoven. Earlier he had over-indulged his audiences, publishing work after work, keeping the curious occupied, while those who had already acknowledged his genius were continually thrilled and surprised afresh. Then, for reasons that had already been developing, five years of apparent idleness intervened when, except for a few piano works (opp. 101, 102, and 106), nothing significant seemed to have been composed.[161] Of these one at least, as we saw above, was widely discussed in Viennese musical circles, but the last was made known only to a very small company by Carl Czerny. The public had been quick to forget the sad events surrounding the lawsuit for his nephew's guardianship, and since no one could say positively whether Beethoven was working on a major composition (he always admonished those close to him not to give out any information concerning his current work until it had been completed), an easy reason for this silence was soon discovered: 'Beethoven has exhausted his talent; he has nothing more to write.' His reputation as a woman-hater grew, another effect of the same lawsuit, in which large numbers of the female general public had been vocal in their sympathy with the sister-in-law.[162]

One incident in particular was widely cited as evidence of Beethoven's supposed 'exhaustion'. On 17 January 1819 he had agreed to conduct his symphony in A major at a large benefit concert for the widows and orphans of deceased professors of law. The performance took place in the auditorium of the University which, as we saw earlier, was acoustically so poor that vocal and orchestral ensembles sounded deafening even to a healthy ear. How, then, could the sound have been anything but distorted to an ear whose deterioration was already far advanced! It was only too obvious that the master was no longer capable of conducting his own works.*[163] And when the AmZ (XXIII (1821) 539), and subsequently the Viennese newspapers, published a notice saying, 'Beethoven now busies himself, as Papa Haydn once did, with arrangements of Scottish songs. He is apparently quite incapable of greater accomplishments', the popular rumour that Beethoven had written himself out was fully corroborated.[164]

These rumours concerning his intellectual exhaustion seemed only to amuse Beethoven, but in reality they incited him to renewed activity. He would retort with comments such as, 'Just wait; you'll soon change your tune!' In late autumn, when he returned from Mödling where, as usual, he had spent the summer gathering and storing up ideas, he sat down and composed the three piano sonatas opp. 109, 110, and 111 'at a single stroke', as he expressed it in a letter written to Count Brunsvik to reassure him concerning his mental state.[165] Those who are familiar with these three sonatas will understand what Beethoven meant by 'at a single stroke'. The first of the three sonatas, about which we had already heard the previous winter, was published by Schlesinger in 1822,[166] the other two not until early the following year.[167] The main reason for this delay was the lengthy procedure of determining a date for the simultaneous appearance in Berlin, Paris, and Vienna, besides the proof-

* In 1822, as we shall see, he was able to conduct a more successful performance, despite his increasing deafness.

reading, which Beethoven himself undertook. The Paris edition had to be returned to Vienna twice, and since the second copy still contained a great many mistakes, the composer demanded a third reading, which the publisher refused. Beethoven was almost beside himself with exasperation and despair.[168]

The task of returning the corrected copy to the publishers was entrusted to me. Concerned with the unpleasant business of the sonata opus 111, I ventured in my innocence to ask Beethoven why he had not written a third movement appropriate to the character of the first. He replied casually that he had not had time to write a third movement, and had therefore simply expanded the second. Since at that time I had heard only fragments of the sonata as the composer was working on it, I was satisfied with this explanation. But later, when I had listened to the sonata, I began to wonder about the reason he had given me for not writing a third movement, and I must confess frankly that I still deplore it. I could not then and still cannot understand how two movements of such sharply differing character could possibly produce an integrated and satisfying whole. Here we find almost unrestrained passion broken only by a few lovely melodic passages, followed by a musical figure tenaciously, even gloomily, held practically throughout, a completely new phenomenon in all Beethoven's work up to that time. It is as if in this movement he were vying with himself to develop a multiplicity of devices and to contrive a mathematical labyrinth from the simple material of the Arietta (the theme of the variations)—a tendency that we repeatedly encounter in subsequent works. The Leipzig reviewer remarked of this movement in part:

The devices that the composer has seen fit to employ for the development of his beautiful material are so artificial that we find them quite unworthy of his great genius. In his use of this musical technique he is like a painter who uses a miniature brush and a single colour to execute a whole altar-piece (AmZ XXVI (1824) 213*).

At the beginning of this article, which thoroughly explores the nature of the last three sonatas, the author employs a sensitive metaphor in describing Beethoven's music in general. It seems fitting to reproduce

* This movement inspired in the principal critic of the *Berliner AmZ* a most extraordinary vision. He entitled his interpretation, 'The death of a great man'—namely, Beethoven—and this is how it went:
Do not the harmonies of the theme swell like the music of a distant funeral procession echoing through the night? And in the second part we hear the sounds of the grave. Then the first pall-bearers in long veils and the friends weeping quietly come nearer and nearer; the ruddy glow of the torches approaches, while the digging of the grave is heard throughout. Memory takes us back to the deathbed and once more I hear through the pealing bells the last heavy breathing of the dying man . . . [and so forth].[169]
I can testify that this and similar misinterpretations of his music greatly disturbed the composer, who was still enjoying good health. More and more interpretations of Beethoven's music are being published, and may soon become as popular as interpretations of the Bible.

the passage here, for it will be particularly useful in discussing subsequent works.

One might compare a life rich in art such as this one to a beautiful park with wonderful paths winding through woods, across meadows, into valleys, and down rocky gorges. Such parks present occasional sweeping vistas which one often comes across unexpectedly and which can often only be fully enjoyed by the use of field glasses. So, too, in a glorious musical landscape such as the one Beethoven has given us, there emerge certain entrancing scenes. Here, too, the paths wind from time to time, often leading us to the most enchanting resting places and then so suddenly in the opposite direction that the hearer feels, at least for a moment, that he has lost the way that still promised so much artistic pleasure, and wonders how he will bear its loss. Yet in both cases the wanderer willingly allows himself to be led by the creator of the masterpiece, for who could be a better leader? And one learns with joy that not every turning point is a point of culmination.

1822

The first thrust of renewed artistic vigour was closely followed by a second. It brought the master once again before the public after several years of withdrawal.

Carl Friedrich Hensler, the popular writer of comedies who was loved throughout Germany for his plays, *Der Alte überall und nirgends*, *Das Donauweibchen*, *Rinaldo Rinaldini*, *Der Teufelsmüller*, *Feige von Bomsen*, and others, had for some years been director of the combined theatres of Pressburg and Baden (near Vienna). Since our Beethoven had paid frequent visits to the latter town, he had made Hensler's acquaintance; indeed, the poet of music and the poet of the people were quick to show in many ways their mutual respect and consideration.

In 1821 Hensler had bought the licence of the Josephstadt Theater in Vienna. This differed from the suburban theatres in that its repertoire included all kinds of theatrical performances; in this respect it was similar to the imperial theatres. Hensler decided to build a completely new theatre, and he set the opening for the eve of the Emperor's name-day, 3 October of the following year. As an appropriate piece with which to dedicate the new theatre, *Die Ruinen von Athen* was chosen, the same work that in 1812 had opened the theatre in Budapest. The folk poet Carl Meisl was to alter Kotzebue's text to make it appropriate for the new institution. On the command of Zeus, Minerva is awakened from two thousand years' sleep and led by Mercury to the newly erected commercial town on the Hungarian shores of the Danube. There she is to establish a dwelling place for the Muses, for their old home has fallen into the hands of the barbarians, and in fact exists no more. Now in the Emperor's city, in the very place where art has for so long fallen into a state of decadence to the moral disgrace of the people, a safe home is to be erected for the Muses.

Beethoven was asked to contribute to the occasion by making certain alterations in his music and adding new numbers. While spending the summer of 1822 in Baden, where the author was also staying, Beethoven put the finishing touches to the *Missa Solemnis*[170] and in July went to work on his new task, but the season was warm and his progress was slower than everyone wished. One of the numbers was to be a chorus interspersed with solo and group dances, and the new director envisioned a complete ballet troupe with soloists. There was great pressure on Beethoven to finish the music for this number, but the work did not progress because the composer and the librettist could not agree. The ballet master was especially persistent for, as a newcomer to his position, he was eager to rehearse his troupe. At last the number was finished, but lo! the composer absolutely refused to give it up. All the director's pleas and suggestions were of no avail. The master responded that until he could revise the entire work and fit the parts into the whole, he would not release a single note. While these difficulties prevailed, so similar to the circumstances surrounding the revision of *Fidelio* in 1814, the theatre poet, the ballet master, and others having to do with the production were all free with their imprecations. We have in the composer's handwriting an epigram on Meisl's name: 'He is a fine chisel (Meissel), but is he a sculptor?'

Time was passing, and it was September. It was time to see about writing a new overture, for the master had long felt with justification that the overture to the *Ruinen von Athen* was not appropriate to the forthcoming dedication ceremony. One day while walking with his nephew and me in the lovely Helenental near Baden, Beethoven told us to go ahead and wait for him at a certain spot. He soon caught up with us and remarked that he had jotted down two themes for the overture. He explained that he planned to develop one of them freely and the other in the formal style of Handel. He sang them both as well as his voice would allow and asked which one we liked better. His discovery put him for the moment in a gay mood, as if he had found two precious stones for which he had long been searching. The nephew liked both themes, while I said I should like to see the fugue subject developed in a strict Handelian style. At any rate, Beethoven did not write the overture *Zur Weihe des Hauses* just to please me, but rather because he had long entertained the idea of writing an overture specifically in the style of Handel. This is not the place to say whether or not he succeeded. Many loud voices have condemned the work. Undoubtedly these critics went too far, however, when they maintained of our master that in this overture he had denied his own individuality. Certainly he had never intended to produce an imitation of Handel; he merely wished to invoke the style of his great predecessor. We shall later come to speak of the other theme of the overture.

As had so often been the case with other works, the overture was not ready on the appointed day. The events of 1814 regarding the *Fidelio* overture in E major were almost repeated: as we saw then, the overture was not completed in time for the first performance, so that the overture to *Prometheus* had to be used. The newly constituted orchestra of the Josephstadt Theater received the music on the afternoon of the day of the opening, with countless copying mistakes in every part. All that a rehearsal in front of an auditorium that was already filling up could accomplish was to correct the most noticeable of these errors.

Beethoven had stipulated that he should conduct at the ceremonial opening of the theatre. Accordingly he took his place at the piano in a position in which he was facing most of the orchestra and where his left ear, which was still of some service to him, was turned towards the stage. The Kapellmeister Franz Gläser (now Court Kapellmeister in Copenhagen) placed himself on Beethoven's right where he could oversee the whole performance, while I led the orchestra from my place at the head of the first violins. I was no longer simply an amateur musician; I had recently given up the law, a change brought about in considerable part through the influence of our composer.

It cannot be said that the musical success of this festal performance was particularly brilliant, despite the zeal with which all the participants co-operated, stirred by the encouraging words of the master. The principal conductor's straining to hear and his dragging of the tempo, sometimes in absolute contradiction of his two subordinates, resulted in frequent lapses both on the stage and in the orchestra, causing the greatest tension. Beethoven was not aware that he was mainly to blame. His warnings about 'hurrying too much' were futile, for hurrying was not the problem. Nevertheless, the performance came to an end without noticeable mishap, and the great master was repeatedly called back to the stage by the highly enthusiastic audience. He appeared holding the hand of the worthy director, Hensler.

At the dress rehearsal for this ceremonial performance, something had occurred that had pleasantly surprised the many people present. During a duet between soprano and tenor the young soprano, through nervousness, had dragged considerably. Beethoven noticed the trouble at once and called the singer to him, showed her the places where she should pick up the tempo, spoke to her encouragingly, and recommended that she listen closely to the tenor, who was competent and sure of the music. Then he had them do the duet again and when it was finished expressed his satisfaction in these words: 'This time it was very good,

Fräulein Heckermann!' The tenor in this duet was the present director of the City Theatre in Aachen, Michael Greiner, a man whose acquaintance our master had already made in the Baden theatre.* As for Beethoven's ability to hear on this occasion, I should point out that here he had only to judge the performance of two voices, not of the whole ensemble. All those who watched the master through the rest of the rehearsal and the performance had to admit with the greatest sorrow that he was no longer capable under any conditions of conducting large groups.

The overall success of the Josephstadt Theater's opening ceremony prompted the managers of the court opera to invite the master to conduct the next performance to be held in that venerated hall of art, promising him even greater honours. The work was to be *Fidelio*, now performed for the first time in eight years, with Wilhelmine Schroeder as Leonore and others capable of handling the demands of the difficult work. The performance was to take place in November for the benefit of Fräulein Schroeder.

Beethoven asked around among his friends whether he should dare undertake the direction of the opera with the help of his highly esteemed friend, the Kapellmeister Umlauf. We all advised against it, in fact we pleaded with him to resist his own desires and to remember the difficulties that had attended the concert in the University auditorium as long ago as 1819, and again at the Josephstadt Theater performance. After several days of indecision, he finally declared his readiness to conduct the work, a deplorable decision on many counts. At his request I accompanied him to the dress rehearsal. The E major overture went perfectly, for despite several hesitations on the part of their leader, the bold army of the orchestra moved in their customary disciplined ranks. But in the very first number, the duet between Marzelline and Jacquino, it was apparent that Beethoven could hear nothing of what was happening on the stage. He seemed to be fighting to hold back. The orchestra stayed with him but the singers pressed on, and at the point where knocking is heard at the prison door, everything fell apart. Umlauf told the musicians to stop without telling the master the reason. After a few minutes' discussion with the singers, the order was given: *da capo*. The duet began again and as before the disunity was noticeable, and again

---

* We may demonstrate the degree to which the left ear was functioning by relating a frequently recurring incident that Herr Greiner often witnessed. At the restaurant next to the Josephstadt Theater there was one of those musical clocks so popular at that time, which used to play overtures, single numbers from good operas, and the like. Beethoven always used to sit near it so that he could hear his favourite piece, the overture to *Medea* by Cherubini. He did not like to hear the trio in F major from his *Fidelio* because the tempo was too slow. He could recognize each piece from the first measure and would follow it, commenting to us on the music as it went along. But if he turned his right ear to the clock, the whole would become to him a chaotic din.

at the knocking there was general confusion. Again the musicians were stopped.

The impossibility of continuing under the direction of the creator of the work was obvious. But who was to tell him, and how? Neither the manager, Duport, nor Umlauf wanted to have to say, 'It cannot be done. Go away, you unhappy man!' Beethoven, now growing apprehensive, turned from one side to another, searching the faces to see what was interrupting the rehearsal. All were silent. Then he called me to him. I stepped to his side in the orchestra and he handed me his notebook, motioning for me to write down what was wrong. I wrote as fast as I could something like: 'Please don't go on. I'll explain at home.' He jumped down on to the floor and said only: 'Let's get out of here.' Without stopping he hastened to his apartment in Pfarrgasse in the suburb of Laimgrube. Once there he threw himself on the sofa, covered his face with both hands, and remained so until we went to dinner. During the meal he did not say a word; his whole demeanour bespoke depression and defeat. After dinner, when I wished to go, he asked me not to leave him until theatre time. When I left him, he asked me to go with him the next day to see Dr. Smetana, his physician at that time, a man who had gained a reputation in ailments of the ear.

In the long years of my association with the mighty composer, there was never any experience to equal that day in November. Whatever difficulties, unpleasantnesses, or disturbances to mind and spirit might have occurred as a result of unhappy personal relations or other circumstances, I had always seen the master only momentarily out of sorts or occasionally depressed. Very soon he would regain his composure, carry his head erect, stride ahead with his customary purpose and vigour, once more master in the workshop of his genius as though nothing had happened. But he never wholly recovered from the effect of this blow. Two passages that he used to quote from the *Odyssey* seem relevant to the situation:

> *For in my bosom dwells a mind*
> *Patient of suffering; much have I endured,*
> *And much survived; . . .*   (*Odyssey* V, 267–69)

> *The deathless gods respect the prayer of him*
> *Who looks to them for help. . . .* (*Odyssey* V, 535–36)

Dr. Smetana prescribed medication to be taken internally. This seemed to be an indication that he wished to occupy his patient with something, but that he entertained no hope whatsoever that an improvement in the impaired hearing could actually result. Yet the doctor knew from experience how this impetuous, distraught patient regarded medical prescriptions. The dosage read: 'One teaspoonful to be taken every hour.' Bah! what good was a mere teaspoonful? The patient went about correcting the order as if it were a copyist's error in one of his musical scores. It ought to say a tablespoonful—that is the way to take medicine. If he remembers to take his medicine at all, the bottle is empty in a few hours, and the prescription must be refilled. So it goes for days, with no indication to the doctor as to the patient's progress unless the doctor himself makes inquiries. Generally the progress is poor, and the patient feels much worse than before starting the treatment for he is forced to drink quantities of water, thereby precluding the slightest chance of any benefits from the medicine.

Such a patient was our Beethoven, when indeed he bothered to go to a doctor at all. It was not without its dangers to the doctor involved, for his cavalier attitude towards prescribed dosages frequently produced detrimental effects for which the physician was held responsible. At the beginning of his hearing difficulties, the master was treated by his Rhenish compatriot, the Emperor's staff-surgeon, Dr. von Vering. Accustomed to his patients' strict observance of his instructions and exercising a certain authority over the musician, Vering expected Beethoven to follow his orders precisely. But this patient disregarded the orders and did whatever he wished, and was just as intransigent about having his freedom restricted in the matter of medication as in his personal life. Absolute freedom in the commission or omission of any deed, limited only by the laws of morality: such was the guiding principle of this unique character.

Hardly had the treatment under Dr. Smetana begun when the master remembered Father Weiss at St. Stephan's, the capable ear-doctor whom the reader met when we first spoke of Beethoven's hearing difficulties. He was consulted again. I accompanied the master on this visit. The priest was moved by what his renowned visitor told him, and though he made no promises, he so encouraged Beethoven by his sympathy that the composer had hopes that his condition would improve. He vowed he would follow all the doctor's orders to the letter and would be regular and persistent in his visits.

The first phase of Father Weiss's treatment was simply an oil injection which the patient accepted docilely. According to medical law, the cleric was allowed to see patients only in his apartment. Our master was thus instructed to visit his kindly doctor every day. Yet after a few days he stopped going. Father Weiss wrote him a note warning him not to interrupt the treatment, for he hoped for success at least with the left ear. But the 'obstinate donkey' who in the Bonn days had balked at going to his pupils now found it just as difficult to take himself to the rectory near St. Stephan's. Admittedly there was now a compelling reason for the composer's impatience with a prolonged course of medical treatment, namely the pressing work at home on his desk, the nature of which we shall soon discover. This alone, however, would not have prevented Beethoven from continuing the treatment if a more personal, far more potent element of his personality had not intervened and silently made him give up all attempts: his impatience and lack of respect for any medical treatment that did not achieve the hoped-for results within twenty-four hours.

I have now described in full the condition of Beethoven's deafness. The reader now knows what the sufferer did, and what he failed to do, to relieve the great misfortune that with almost no surcease permeated his whole life. This chapter may then be closed by adding that the conflict that followed the incident at the opera was the last of its kind. From then on no such attempts were undertaken. Following the example of so many wise men of ages past, the master submitted to his hard fate without uttering another word of complaint.

[III]

━ 1823 ━

We are already well acquainted with the unhappy state of Beethoven's finances. We know that the main cause was the four years of litigation over his nephew. Furthermore, we have seen how the adoption of the boy increased Beethoven's expenses, and we know how few works were composed between 1815 and 1822. As a result, the total income during these seven lean years, including the annuity of 900 florins CM, fell far short of defraying his expenses, especially as the piano works brought in very little in comparison with other musical forms. Thirty or forty ducats was the highest sum paid for a single sonata that took on an average three months to compose. The last three sonatas, however, brought in almost twice as much because they were published simultaneously in Germany, England, and France. Until then, piano compositions were completely without profit in France, while in England only a few were successful.*

Such a long-lasting drain upon his coffers made it necessary for Beethoven to seek help elsewhere. One step of the hard-pressed master can hardly be condoned: instead of selling some of his bank shares, which were then at a high price, he went into debt. It was especially deplorable that two of his creditors were among his publishers, one in Vienna and the other in Leipzig.[171] These people are notorious for their ruthlessness towards those who seek help in this way. Our master had already had ample experience with these men since the days when his fame had

---

* Thalberg told me that for each of his Fantasies he had received an average of 5,000 francs.

begun to ascend and his creations had begun to be remunerative. He should never have surrendered to one of this company, for to place himself at the mercy of a creditor was truly like imprisonment for an artist who suffocates unless he is free and independent.

The dire consequences of this surrender caught up with the composer in 1822 when Beethoven had the temerity to give his last three sonatas to other, better-paying publishers, Schlesinger and Diabelli,[172] whereupon the Viennese creditor claimed sole rights to the works.[173] Yet before we proceed with this game of blind-man's-buff between our renowned master and his Viennese creditor, let us see what method was devised to raise a large sum of money in a short time so that the composer might once more become master of his situation. He himself felt all too keenly the indignity and ambivalence of the position that forced him to resort to subterfuge. It offended his sense of honour and uprightness towards those publishers who had always dealt fairly with him (all the foreign publishers were in this category) and who did not regard him cynically as their fatted calf.

Beethoven's plan, which had been evolving for a long time, was to offer the manuscript of the new Mass to all the courts, both large and small, and to set a price of fifty ducats for each copy.[174] He left in my hands the management of the whole affair, which involved many formalities and details. The German text of the announcement described the work as his most successful, whereas the subscription invitation sent to the French court called it 'l'œuvre le plus accompli', the most perfect work. They both stated that the Mass could also be used as an oratorio, meaning that it was suitable for performance in the concert hall.

The result of this subscription venture was that a total of seven copies were ordered, a gross intake of 350 ducats.[175] When one figures that it cost sixty gulden to have each one copied, the remainder is a negligible sum, certainly nothing to justify the trouble of correcting the copies, a task in which the author was busied for nine full months. The subscribers included the highest courts of Russia, Prussia, France, Saxony, and Hesse-Darmstadt, and also Prince Anton Radzivil, the governor of Posen, and Schelble, the president of the Cäcilia Society in Frankfurt, who ordered a copy for his organization. In 1823 the master sent an eighth copy to Prince Nicolai Borissovitch Galitsin in St. Petersburg. We shall later have occasion to speak again of this copy and what came of it. All we need to know now is that the total gross sum raised by the subscription was 400 ducats.

The Austrian court was not approached. An invitation was sent (at the specific request of the publisher, D. Artaria) to Prince Paul Esterházy, but he declined to enter a subscription. Soon after the announcement had been sent to this princely patron of the arts, Beethoven wrote to me from Hetzendorf: 'You might ask about the reception it received. I doubt that it was favourable, since I don't think he has a very high opinion of me, at least if our last encounter was any indication. I rather think that only through women can one attain much success with him.' Was not Beethoven recalling the Prince's criticism of his first Mass when it was performed in Eisenstadt in 1807?

The first order for a subscription copy came from the Prussian court, conveyed by the royal ambassador to Vienna, Prince Hatzfeld. The following revealing incident occurred at that time. The King's acceptance was delivered to the master by the chancellor of the embassy, Hofrat Wernhard. There is no way of knowing whether Prince Hatzfeldt brought the following commission from Berlin or if he spoke with his own authority; in any case, Wernhard asked Beethoven on behalf of the Prince if he would not prefer a royal decoration to the fifty ducats. Beethoven answered without hesitation, 'Fifty ducats!' The impoverished, hard-pressed master was in need of cash, and here they were offering him a ribbon to wear on his coat! I was a witness of the scene. As soon as the chancellor had left the room, the outraged composer gave vent to a series of sarcastic remarks about various contemporaries and their greed for royal orders, which in his opinion were usually won at the sacrifice of art. When, on the other hand, we find him writing to Wegeler three years later (7 December 1826) that a decoration 'at this time would not be unacceptable', we must remember that the change had been brought about only through the persuasion of Karl Holz and Dr. Spiker of Berlin, who was then in Vienna. As the Conversation Books testify, both these men knew how to bring around the opinions of even the most obstinate.

Beethoven sent a letter to Goethe at the same time that he sent the subscription invitation to the Grand-Ducal court of Weimar, to ask the poet's aid in advancing the composer's interests, but neither the court nor its minister honoured the hopeful composer with a reply. A similar letter asking for help in the court of France was sent to Cherubini. Here again the famous fellow artist declined to answer.[176] The Parisian master told me in 1841, however, how deeply he regretted that he had not kept the letter. The invitation to the Swedish court was accompanied by a very carefully worded letter from Beethoven to King Karl XIV Johann in which in moving words he recalled the earlier days. Yet no answer was forthcoming. It is interesting to note the master's memories of his personal association with the Nordic king who, as General Bernadotte, the representative of the French Republic in Vienna, had first put into words the idea of commemorating the greatest soldier of the time, the first consul of the French Republic, in a musical piece. This was the genesis of the *Sinfonia Eroica*.

Beethoven even turned to Zelter, the director of the Royal Singing Academy in Berlin, for help in this subscription effort, a circumstance that proves how sorely he was pressed. For our 'progressive' considered Zelter one of the 'old German imperial composers' whose favour he despised. In his reply to Beethoven's request of 22 February 1823, Zelter stated that in his institute only *a cappella* music (without instrumental accompaniment) was performed, and asked that a special edition be prepared for the academy, since Beethoven had once mentioned that the *Missa* could almost be performed by the vocal parts alone. On 25 March the Viennese wrote again to the Berliner:

I have given careful thought to your suggestion concerning the Singing Academy. If the work should ever appear in an engraved edition, I shall send you a copy and accept nothing in return. The work could certainly be sung almost entirely *a cappella*, but the whole thing would have to be rewritten, and perhaps you have the patience to do that. Anyway, one complete number is already *a cappella*, and I would like to call this style the only true church music.

Beethoven was referring to the Kyrie.[177] Here we find the master expressing criticism of his own work in a way that commands our attention. It would be extremely interesting to see this entire correspondence published.

In the midst of the worries over the outcome of this project, there came from the royal court in Paris a winged messenger to bring the distressed master the reply to his invitation to Louis XVIII. The first chancellor to the King, the Duc d'Achâts, announced in the most flattering terms that it had pleased his majesty to honour the artist with a gold medal showing the King's head, in lieu of a monetary subscription to the *Missa*. This honorary gift had the weight of twenty-one louis d'or, and inscribed on the back were the words: 'Donné par le Roi à Monsieur Beethoven.'[178] It was the greatest distinction conferred upon the master during his lifetime. One may surmise that it could not fail to awaken in the artist a consciousness of his greatness and to raise his spirits to new heights.

On the other hand, such recognition is inevitable cause for comparison of the attitudes towards the master of the courts of Paris and of Vienna, a comparison in which the imperial court and administration are found lamentably backward in their almost total disregard of art and science. For in those days, and for a long time thereafter, the Austrian state was in part a mere legal institution and in part a great barracks. The leaders had no notion of what a state should be: they did not know that its function is to further the spiritual, material, and in particular, the legitimate aspirations of its people. Even less were they aware that art and science are among the most noble flowers of the national spirit and require careful cultivation by those in authority.

Thus we have arrived at the important chapter concerning Beethoven's politics. We must deal with it now so that we may have done with it. Beethoven's political opinions were described both during his lifetime and after his death by various writers in such various ways that for this reason alone we are obliged to present a frank and detailed explanation. The necessity is all the more pressing as our explanation will provide a firm basis for many of the events yet to come. Such an explanation was included in the manuscript for the first edition of this book, but Dr. Bach struck it out, in his own interests no less than in mine. This deletion left a most obvious blank in the whole picture, one which could not benefit our composer, for *de mortuis nil nisi* [*sic*].

Fortunately, however, Austria today is entirely different from the Austria of Beethoven's time, and it is no longer inadvisable to set forth openly the things that are a part of history in general and that bore a special relationship to Beethoven's life. If Dr. Bach had realized that the hour of Austria's political reform was not far away, indeed if he had known that his own nephew was to be summoned to play a prominent part in the changes about to take place,[179] he would not have felt that his social position made caution imperative, and would have withheld his red pencil. But, like thousands of middle-class subjects of the Emperor, he had long since despaired of any improvement in the political structure. The inexorable Fates cut his life's thread in 1847, almost on the eve of the Austrian people's long-awaited new day.

Every historical figure should be extracted out of his time and presented as a unique entity, and unless we are to do him an injustice, we may not presume to judge what he would have done under quite different circumstances, or what position he would have taken *vis à vis* the higher and highest authorities. If this generalization has any practical truth, it applies to our account of the master's political opinions regarding the Austrian state.

Most of the published criticisms of Beethoven as a political figure start from the premise that he was one of the many so-called harmless 'tavern politicians', whose ire could be aroused by a single catch-word. Most of these critics were foreigners very little acquainted with the situation prevailing in Austria and totally ignorant of the attainments and culture of the people, especially in the large cities. They were equally ignorant of this aspect of Beethoven's character, and they drew their conclusions from what they had heard him say during one or two casual encounters. But our master was wise enough to know better than to expose his most secret thoughts before strangers; at any rate, they would not have been comprehensible to one without a special knowledge of the circumstances. Still, hardly anyone could fail to realize that there was method in his reasoning. How could it have been otherwise with a man who had so thoroughly studied the history of states and peoples, particularly the ancients?

Out of the great quantity of such criticisms, let us examine just three, for they come from the pens of well-known and highly respected men. Dr. W. C. Müller, founder of the society concerts in Bremen, inventor of the harmonicon, author of the interesting book, *Aesthetisch-historische Einleitungen in die Wissenschaft der Tonkunst*, and other books, visited our master in Mödling in 1820 on his way to Italy. In his article entitled 'Something about Ludwig van Beethoven' (AmZ XXIX (1827) 345), he says:

This sense of freedom as a citizen of the world plus his feeling for others (which had affected his financial state) may well have been the reason that in restaurants he would talk continuously, expressing himself openly and without reserve, critically or satirically, on everything; the government, the police, the morals of the nobility. The police knew it, but they left him alone, either because they considered him a crackpot or out of deference for his genius as an artist. Therefore he believed and maintained that nowhere was one more free to speak his mind than in Vienna. Yet his idea of a constitution was that of England.

Friedrich Rochlitz saw Beethoven three times in the summer of 1822. I was present at two of these meetings. From his articles on our master, published in the form of a number of letters as the Foreword to the AmZ of 1828, and also in his book, *Für Freunde der Tonkunst*, we may excerpt the following:

His whole conversation and activity formed a chain of peculiarities, some of them most strange. Yet all of them reflected a truly childlike good nature, geniality, and trust in all who approached him. Even his fierce tirades, such as those against the Viennese of his day, were only outbursts of fantasy and momentary passion. They were poured out without conceit, without bitterness or hatred—with a light heart, a kindly nature, and a sense of humour; and there is an end to them.

What a complete misunderstanding of the character and the person is here! And Rochlitz was to have been Beethoven's biographer?!

Let us compare the opinions of these two foreigners with the opinions of a Viennese. Seyfried expressed himself on the question of Beethoven's politics in *Beethovens Studien*:

Within the circle of his intimate friends his favourite topic of conversation was politics, on which he would speak with an enlightened power of observation, correct interpretation, and clear vision such as one would never expect even from a votary of the diplomatic corps living solely for the exercise of his art.

It should be noted that this observation dates from a much earlier time, since all communication between Beethoven and Seyfried ceased in 1806.[180] (More on this subject in the supplementary essay, 'Studies in Thoroughbass, Counterpoint, and Composition'.)

It would be superfluous to dwell at any more length on this matter; it will therefore be dealt with summarily according to the best of my ability and conscience without resorting to the art of dialectics.

The principal causes of Beethoven's consistent opposition to Austrian politics, the government, and the imperial court may be enumerated under the following points:

A. The legal system, particularly in the lower courts. His own case furnished him with ample material for observation and unhappy associations. Whim and bribery were sanctioned by centuries of common practice, especially in the rural probate courts where justice was often administered by civil servants with no education in the law, and where bribery reached Turkish proportions. The monstrous confusion that called itself 'legal procedure' gave the judges a free hand to abuse their authority, and allowed the lawyers on both sides to practise every kind of harassment to humiliate the parties to the case.

B. The police and their excessive overstepping of their already extensive powers. They were not mere keepers of the peace in the usual sense as in other countries; they had also been given the administration of what elsewhere are the duties of a justice of the peace. The result of this system was that the police officers in the large cities became powerful in the extreme, and even petty officials were given broad areas in which they could exercise every kind of caprice and satisfy their personal desires. No one judged them, for no one dared challenge them. It was not rare for the highest legal authority to have to rein in the police.

C. The bureaucracy that pervaded all branches of the state, generally in very crude forms. Its influence was everywhere all the more demoralizing because the officials all lacked any notion of the humanity or citizenship of the people, but regarded them merely as subjects who should obey them. So it was that any act decreed by the government was given out as an act of compassion, though it often meant heavy taxation.

D. The decadence of the aristocracy. Because its members, who poured forth much money upon the populace, occupied the chief offices in the court and the civil administration, and because of their great influence and, more significantly, great power in many areas, they felt free to indulge in the crudest excesses. It may truly be said that after the Congress of Vienna virtue and morality had disappeared from the highest strata of the capital's society.* We cannot make a study of the

---

* In 1817 the Viennese critic for the AmZ spoke of the prevalent immorality in that city, as we saw on page 216.

reasons for the disequilibrium which at this time characterized the highest echelons of nobility's learning and breeding, its inner and outer culture, in comparison with fifteen years earlier and at the end of the first period.

Yet to exonerate to some extent the German-Austrian nobility, the observation should be made that most of the degeneracy among this class was introduced by the rich, boorish aristocrats of the eastern provinces whose manners and morals were almost oriental. The idle life of these 'cavaliers', conditioned by the spirit of the age and by a false sense of the meaning of aristocracy and favoured, moreover, by the loose morals in all levels of society, could not but have a detrimental effect on German nobility when the two came into close contact, in spite of the excellent example of virtue that the Emperor's household had always held up to the world. These highly placed offenders against public morality could not be reached by police ordinances,* for *dat veniam corvis*. From the time of the Congress of Vienna the practice of keeping mistresses flourished, and almost no one could gain a position at the court or in the government who scorned paving his way to the excellencies and highnesses with a long series of despotic courtesans. One may imagine how Beethoven, who had always been as upright as Cato in the matter of morality, felt in the presence of such a distasteful situation.

E. The Emperor's public audiences. Beethoven called them 'public deceptions'. Every Wednesday through the winter, two or three hundred petitioners from all classes enjoyed the privilege of placing their requests directly in the hands of the Emperor. With such a number of petitioners, there could obviously be no adequate consideration of their individual requests. They were generally referred to the appropriate department to be studied and reported on, a system that greatly taxed the functionaries. As one may suppose, it was only very seldom that the petitioner—occasionally coming from the provinces, Tyrol, Bohemia, or even Transylvania—received any kind of satisfaction.

These public audiences, which were held in the presence of numerous guards, dated from the patriarchal time of Austria. Perhaps then, when the law was still in the process of formation and when political consciousness among the people was unknown, they may have had a beneficial effect on the whole population. But in Beethoven's time no democrat dared question the divine right of the Emperor, and no prince ever took his divine right more personally than Emperor Franz. For this reason alone democratic tendencies, if known to the police, were interpreted as political disobedience, and those exhibiting them were not

---

* Only one was singled out of the many and taken to court: Prince Kaunitz-Rietburg. He was forever exiled from the Austrian states.

allowed to approach the All-Highest. They were accorded no audiences; only beggars and those seeking the most insignificant things enjoyed the privilege. Beethoven would become enraged at the thought of having to figure in such an audience as a suppliant, for the Emperor was notorious for his low opinion of artistic genius and his esteem only for 'the useful man'.

F. The stinginess of the imperial court in support of the arts and sciences, and its complete lack of interest in anything outside the palace. Whatever activities connected with music there had been in earlier years, though solely for the entertainment of the court, vanished at the death of Emperor Franz's second wife, whom we met as a singer in the first period. The year of her death (1807) marked the end of an almost uninterrupted series of musical events that for two centuries had been conducted in the grand style, a practice in which the crowned heads themselves had participated seriously.[181] After that time, Polyhymnia came to court only as a beggar when concerts were given. With the exception of Archduke Rudolph, the members of the imperial household turned their backs on the sublime muse, and it meant nothing that some of them would buy a small number of concert tickets and sometimes even attend the concerts. The Emperor himself cultivated quartet music and had a love for and sensitivity to church music; all interest in the other forms, however, was gone.

The teachers of the Emperor's children were Anton Teyber, who became court composer, and then Joseph Eybler, who succeeded Salieri as court Kapellmeister. Each one guarded the palace doors like an Argus lest any other musician gain access to his imperial pupils; each one prided himself that he was safe from evil influences. These two court musicians arrayed themselves in the forefront of Beethoven's enemies, and Teyber did not fail to take advantage of his opportunities to discredit the great master at court. An emperor's composer enjoyed far more prestige than a Beethoven, and could with high good humour ridicule and revile him. If anyone at court had taken the slightest notice of our master, his obstinacy would perhaps have softened enough to make a reconciliation possible through Archduke Rudolph's mediation. In earlier years his friends had wanted him to accept a title, such as 'Imperial Court Virtuoso', for which he would not receive a penny as subsidy, but his artistic pride would not allow even that.

This summary does not exhaust the subject of Beethoven's rigid stand against the authorities of the city and the nation. A more important point remains to be discussed: the religious education of the people. It may seem surprising, indeed almost incredible, to learn of a musician who was deeply concerned about matters far removed from his own field, since musicians are especially notorious for their lack of interest in anything not connected in some way with notes. The reader has already been given so many evidences of Beethoven's exceptional nature, however, that he should not find it altogether strange if the composer exhibited a profound interest in the hearts and minds of the people. An eager spirit like Beethoven's, with its broad powers of knowledge and understanding, could not encounter a single significant field of inquiry without interest and critical comment. His frequent association with country folk at a time when spoken conversation was still possible for him, and his many experiences with his servants and those in the homes of his friends had sufficiently acquainted him with the almost unheard-of indifference of the lower classes to religious matters.

The amazing part of it is, however, that such a busy musician should take the time and the trouble to agitate for the religious education of the people in order to elevate them to a better knowledge of God and His creation. This Beethoven did, and in a most direct way. Once again we must think of the two-volume work by Christoph Christian Sturm: *Betrachtungen über die Werke Gottes im Reiche der Natur und der Vorsehung auf alle Tage des Jahres*. The contents of this work seemed to the master of music to be a clear summary of everything the people needed to know. When he came into contact with priests during his stays in the country, he never failed to call their attention to this book of teaching and personal growth, and even recommended that it be read from the pulpit. But his words fell on deaf ears, and when the pastor in Mödling, in answer to his recommendation, responded that 'our people do not need to know any more about the revelations of the firmament than that the sun, moon, and stars rise and set', the zeal of the propagandist soon began to diminish. In his later years he never uttered another word about the religious culture of the people unless it was to voice a piece of bitter sarcasm.

This was not the case when it came to other aspects of his life. An avid follower of world affairs, a man with none of the 'weak intellect of the common subject', our composer found ample material in his daily reading of the *Allgemeine Zeitung* to broaden his knowledge of politics. Dr. Müller was quite right in saying that Beethoven's idea of a perfect constitution was that of England. In order to be able to read the parliamentary debates at his leisure, he had the *Allgemeine Zeitung* delivered to his home. He was frequently enthusiastic over Lord Brougham's speeches, which often drove the troubled clouds from his mind.

As I relate these particulars, it comforts me to think that there is at least one still alive to whom I saw the master open his heart on all these matters, a fellow-sufferer who could contribute to the subject from his own bitter experience. I am speaking of the poet of the banned work, *Oestreich, du Capua der Geister*, Franz Grillparzer. An accurate picture of these oppressive circumstances is given in Count Auersperg's *Spaziergänge eines Wiener Poeten* (Hamburg, 1831). How bitter that our master could not live to read this public indictment!

It was Beethoven's friend Count Moritz Lichnowsky who chiefly took it upon himself to work out some way to bring the master to the imperial court in the hope that, once the first step had been accomplished with some success, further agreement and a full reconciliation might be reached. The director of the imperial court musical organization, usually called 'Music Count to the Court', was at that time Count Moritz von Dietrichstein, who was at the same time tutor to the young Duke of Reichstadt, a close friend of Count Lichnowsky's. It was to him that the faithful Lichnowsky had already turned earlier, hoping to work out a suitable means of effecting his plan, but such means were neither simple nor immediately available. Then in November 1822 the afore-mentioned court composer, Anton Teyber, died. This gave the Count his opportunity. He urged Beethoven to write directly to Count Dietrichstein about the vacant position and ask his advice on the best way to approach the Emperor. As we shall see, the master followed his friend's suggestion. The two counts proposed to Beethoven that he compose a Mass for the Emperor for, as we mentioned before, the Emperor's love of sacred music had remained keen. The 'Music Count to the Court', who was familiar with both art and his highest lordship's tastes, thought it best to make a few suggestions that would help the master to compose something that would accomplish his ends. We have a letter to this purpose addressed by him to Count Lichnowsky on 23 February 1823. It reads:

Dear friend:

It was my duty long ago to answer the good Beethoven who put his confidence in me. But after I spoke with you, I decided to remain silent until I had acquired more exact information about our known objective. Now, however, I can tell you confidently that the place of the deceased Teyber (who was composer to the court, not to the household) is not going to be filled.*[181a]

I would rather not write this information to Beethoven, for I do not want to adversely affect a man whom I honour so sincerely. I am therefore asking you to break this news to him at an opportune time. Then please write to me and tell me when and where I can talk with him again, for I have forgotten his address.

I am sending you the score of a Mass by Reutter† that Beethoven wanted to see. It is a fact that His Majesty the Emperor likes this style, but Beethoven,

---

* The 'composer to the household' (*Kammer-Compositeur*) was at that time Franz Krommer. After his death in 1831 this post, too, remained unfilled. These two cases are ample proof that at the imperial court, interest in music in general was dead.

† Georg von Reutter (1708–72) was imperial court and cathedral Kapellmeister. After Predieri's death he became the principal court Kapellmeister.[182]

if he writes a Mass, does not need to imitate it. He should be guided only by his great genius, and should remember merely that the Mass ought not to be too long nor too difficult to perform. It should be a Mass for chorus with only short solos for soprano and alto (I have two good boys for these parts) but no solos for tenor, bass, or organ, especially not for tenor, for then Barth would have to sing. As for instruments, a violin, oboe, or clarinet solo could be included if he wished.

His Majesty is very fond of fugues, so long as they are clear and appropriate and not too long. The Sanctus and Osanna should be as short as possible so as not to delay the Transubstantiation, and (if I may add a comment of my own) the Dona nobis pacem should follow the Agnus Dei without a complete break. This pattern achieves a particularly beautiful effect in two masses by Handel (made up of his anthems), and also in two by Naumann and one by Abbé Stadler.

These would in short be the considerations my experience would lead me to take into account if I were to write such a piece, and I would consider myself, the court, and art itself most fortunate if our great Beethoven would soon lay his hand to this task. Please have the goodness to send me a short notice that you have received the score from the music archives of the court. I shall take the first free moment to tell you in person of my old and constant friendship for you.

Your devoted friend,
Moritz Dietrichstein

We also have a letter from Count Dietrichstein to Beethoven dated 10 March 1823. He sent the master three texts for graduals and three for offertories, all having to do with the composition for the Emperor's chapel music. Dietrichstein wrote in the accompanying note: 'I regret very much having missed seeing you when you were kind enough to call on me with Count Lichnowsky. I shall make every effort to meet you as soon as possible. Please accept this assurance of my highest regards.'

Our master had hardly expected such cordial and friendly greetings from a man so highly placed and so influential in the Emperor's court, and his surprise was all the more pleasant. Remembering that it was a matter of composing music specifically for the Emperor's chapel, the province of the 'Music Count' who would thus extend to the composer and his compositions the direct patronage of the highest court in the land, we should expect Beethoven to give up everything else so that he might proceed immediately with the work that conformed so closely to his own wishes. Unfortunately, this was not the case. As usual, he discussed the matter at great length and considered it from a succession of quickly changing viewpoints; at last, after months had gone by, he declared his final intention: the compositions for the Emperor must be put off until a later date. This was the solution of this declared democrat to the paradox in which he found himself ensnared. He remained what he had always been. His guiding principle, 'Liberty ennobles the soul and exalts the spirit', had wavered for a time, but was again firm and resolute. But what now? His hesitation and inconsistency had been exposed.

The two kind counts received letters thanking them for their trouble and giving as reasons for the decision: (a) the subscription copies of the *Missa Solemnis* had to be corrected; (b) the Gesellschaft der Musikfreunde des östreichischen Kaiserstaates was exerting pressure on him to finish the oratorio he had promised to write for them years before; and (c) he had just accepted an engagement to compose a piano work for the publisher Diabelli by an appointed date. All these reasons were true. But the two counts could not believe that these other obligations were as pressing as Beethoven claimed, and Lichnowsky, who had already frequently accused our master of 'old Dutch pigheadedness', was blunt in his remarks. When he complained to Archduke Rudolph of Beethoven's behaviour, he too reproached the master who finally extended his apologies. According to the Archduke's secretary, Baumeister, who was better acquainted than anyone else with the intimate relations between the teacher and the pupil, Beethoven's explanations were found among the Archduke's private letters that came into the possession of the GdMf after his death.

To the three reasons stated above, a fourth was soon added: an invitation came from Prince Nicolai Borissovitch Galitsin in St. Petersburg to compose some quartets for him. Actually, however, there was only one governing reason for postponing the composition of the Emperor's mass, and it was not *ad Kalendas graecas*: Beethoven was in dire need of ready cash to rid himself of a persistent creditor and in general to wipe out old debts. But even these considerations could have been waived if Beethoven had been able to put aside his deeply rooted aversion to the imperial court. The kind of *rapprochement* with the court that had been proposed did nothing to hamper his independence. The notebooks for that time include sketches marked specifically, 'for the C♯ minor mass'. Whether these were meant for the Emperor's mass or not remains a secret. At any rate, the plan that had aroused such interest and controversy was never again mentioned.

We must however take a closer look at these reasons of Beethoven's, except for item A. But first a warning: some of the points to be touched on are so sad, and also so complex, that they are not unlike an epitasis in the life-drama we are to depict. The reason that we designated as 'governing' is clearly specified in an entry in the master's hand in a Conversation Book from 1823. He had at that time received an invitation to compose 'for any price' an oratorio for the Philharmonic Society of Boston in North America.[183] To an inquiry from his friend Bihler regarding this oratorio, Beethoven answered: 'I do not write only the things I would most like to write; my choice is governed by money, which I need. It cannot be said, however, that I write only for money. Once this period is over, I hope to write the thing closest to my heart, the most sublime work of art: *Faust*.'* This candid confession provides the key to the situation. We shall soon show its specific application.

The publishing house of Diabelli & Co. had in the winter of 1822–83 proposed to a large number of composers the idea of compiling a collection of variations for piano.[184] The theme, a waltz, had been made up by Diabelli himself. Each composer was to contribute one variation. Beethoven, too, received an invitation. The plan immediately recalled to his mind the collection of songs on the text *In questa tomba oscura*, assembled in 1808, which we discussed in the second period. Immediately the master felt again the bitterness that had been occasioned by that work and the ridicule it had suffered. He declared that he had vowed never again to have anything to do with a collective work: if at that time someone had dared to make fun of the profound seriousness of the poem, in this instance the theme itself would leave the contributors open to ridicule. Moreover, he did not care for the theme with its 'cobbler's patches' (rosalias†), and so forth. For this reason, the invitation was declined.

Ex. 13

Artists commonly call these little passages 'cobbler's patches': patch after patch.

Not long after this categorical refusal, Beethoven asked me to find out from Diabelli if it would be all right for him to work out a set of variations on the theme by himself, and if he were to do so, how much Diabelli would pay for them. The publisher was happily surprised and immediately proposed eighty ducats.[185] He wrote a brief note to the master confirming his decision and asking only for six or seven variations. For his part, Beethoven was no less happily surprised by the unusually high price offered for a set of variations, and replied immediately with a written acceptance, remarking to me at the time, 'There! Now he shall have his variations on his cobbler's patch!'

Early in May the master occupied a villa in Hetzendorf belonging to

---

* Friedrich Rochlitz had suggested the idea of composing music for Goethe's *Faust*. Later on we shall hear what Rochlitz himself had to say about it.

† The musically uninitiated reader will need to understand that in composition studies 'rosalias' are short passages consisting of phrases that succeed one another in stepwise progression, generally at equal intervals, like beads on a rosary.

Baron von Pronay. The house was surrounded by a lovely park and commanded a charming view. The first composition he undertook there was the variations on Diabelli's waltz which had taken his fancy in a curious way. In no time at all there were ten, then ten more, then twenty-five variations on paper, and he kept saying, 'That is not all.' The publisher, concerned lest the work should get too long and the publishing costs too high, wanted him to bring the work to a close. But the eager composer, who wanted to demonstrate what could be done with an ordinary waltz, and even with a 'rosalia',* told him to be patient yet a little longer.

And so we have the *Thirty-Three Variations on a Waltz*, opus 120, which clearly reflect the cheerful mood in which they were written. The master's enemies remained in ignorance of this work and the unusual high spirits that inspired it. They would have been able to see in it—if they had wanted to—how cheerful, almost playful, Beethoven occasionally was, even in his later years, and not 'always dark and brooding', as they liked to picture him. The extraordinary variety in the use of the theme—it even adapted itself to a transformation into Mozart's 'Notte e giorno faticar', then to the structure of a fughetta, and finally to a fugue in regular form—gives ample evidence of the pleasure and even self-gratification out of which this work, which can be played only by virtuosi of the first order, was created. Indeed, if the ridicule occasioned by the collection of 1808 in any way influenced or prompted the composition of this work, we may be grateful for it, and we must regard the episode as something more than a mere incident in Beethoven's life story.

Let us return to the matter of Beethoven's debts, which in 1823 concerned our master most seriously. It must be regarded as unforgivable lack of completeness and thoroughness on the part of the biographers of Demosthenes, Cicero, Dante, Shakespeare, and other great men of the past that they would not reveal to future generations the monetary debts of their respective subjects or the names of the creditors, though the biographers must have had access to such information. There can be virtually no doubt that the knowledge of these particulars would have contributed much to the understanding of the innermost spirit of these men and at least some of their works. Moreover, the number of their commentators and conjectural critics would have been considerably reduced if these could have applied to their difficult task a more exact knowledge of their heroes' financial affairs. Especially in the case of Shakespeare, the meaning of each word would not have remained

* We are reminded of an entry in the master's hand in his journal for 1815: 'The Scottish Songs snow what the most ordinary melody is capable of when it is well harmonized.' Then there is this remark: 'I must show the English what riches there are in *God Save the King*.'[186]

subject to question for the past century if his interpreters had from the beginning been better acquainted with his situation with regard to his creditors. It appears, however, that in his time there was a principle which stated that any portrait of an important man painted for future generations should be all of a piece, distinct from parallel issues so long as these were not part and parcel of the man's character but merely circumstances forced upon the individual by unfavourable external pressures, for the parallel issues with no basis in the subject's essential character were not supposed to hold any interest for readers of a later time whose sole concern is with the artist's surviving works.

In writing the earlier editions of this book, I allowed myself to be guided substantially by these same principles, particularly in discussing Beethoven's debts, and I failed to exhaust this important subject with the proverbial 'German thoroughness'. How greatly a straightforward account of the situation would have helped in gaining a sure foothold on the poetic content of the ninth symphony which, as we have already shown in part, was composed amidst financial stress as well as the most extraordinary confusion in the master's household! And what an impenetrable chaos of mystical darkness the second part of *Faust* would be still, had not certain particulars in the life of the poet (the turnip and other material trifles) given the conjecturers the key to its revelation! Such striking results should prompt me to do likewise. Perhaps an exposition of this topic, candid but concise as possible, will succeed in contributing materially to the definition of what the modern art philosophers and Beethoven pedants call the 'second and third styles' in the master's work. In the first place, the composer himself has given us a master key to his varieties of style in his reply to Bihler's question. I would consider myself truly happy if I could satisfy in my discussion of this matter those Beethoven lovers who once exhorted me rather tartly: 'Say everything about everything, not just half about everything!' Well then!

Several years earlier, in 1816, just at the beginning of the long series of embarrassments and calamities of every kind, the Leipzig publishing house of Hofmeister* suggested to our tone-poet a plan for the publication of his complete piano works under conditions that were not very different from those that would have been acceptable to the composer. Beethoven consulted Antonio Diabelli, who at that time had not yet entered the publishing business. Diabelli's critical comments and his reaction to Hofmeister's plan are contained in a detailed letter to Beethoven dated 22 August 1816. The following excerpts will suffice to inform the reader:

---

* Editor's note. Not Hoffmeister as in original text.

I rather think you had better stick to your original demands, namely: for the public authorization to publish your piano works and for editing them, 3,000 florins CM: for the new sonatas, of which there will be one for each volume, an average of forty ducats apiece.

The stumbling block in the plan was basically payment by the page. Diabelli remarked on this:

Nothing is gained by charging a stated number of ducats per page, and I strongly advise you against such an arrangement. We can be sure that the publisher counts on a clear profit of 4,000 florins, though perhaps after ten or more years. . . . I hope with confidence that the publisher will concur in your demands if you make them known to him as your last and final conditions.

The negotiations with Hofmeister were not carried out with diplomatic secrecy, and unfortunately they came to the ears of the devoted friends in the Paternostergässchen in Vienna, whose love and self-sacrifice for the great master's interests remained constant. Speculators like Steiner & Co. (i.e., Steiner and Haslinger) could not fail to realize that if the Leipzig plan were to go into effect, they would be at a disadvantage with their Beethoven publications, while in the future no new works at all would be forthcoming for them. They accordingly drew up a similar plan of their own, requesting that the master grant them just two or three years to begin the project. With mathematical computations they showed him the greater advantages, both in the matter of composer's fee and the general preferability of being able himself to supervise all the work, proof-reading, and the like. These chimerical promises were enough to make the master drop the Hofmeister plan then and there.

Some time later this Viennese publisher presented the master with a list of all the musical forms, starting with the symphony and oratorio and going right down to the song. For each form a corresponding price was named. We still have this list, written out in Tobias Haslinger's hand.[187] A symphony, for example, is listed as worth 60–80 ducats, a 'major' oratorio is 300, a 'minor' one is 200, a requiem 120, a grand opera 300, a sonata for piano solo 30, a grand sonata for piano solo 40. The whole plan was much more detailed than any ever suggested to the master before. We can well imagine his favourable reaction. The following comments, written in his hand on the list, give evidence of his pleasure:

One could reserve the right to change the price on occasion or to make other conditions. Considering that these prices pertain only to Austria and possibly France, and that I can still count on England besides, I feel it is acceptable. In the case of several of the forms, one could reserve the right to set one's own price. As for an edition of the complete works, perhaps England and France might be reserved for the author. The publisher would pay a fee of 10,000 florins CM. Since they also are interested in an edition of the complete works, I should think such a contract would be for the best. Perhaps we should reserve rights for London and Paris, and ought therefore to write to Schlesinger.

This plan, so logically and reasonably thought out, contained the stipulation that Beethoven should bind himself to give everything he should write in the future to this Viennese publisher exclusively, a stipulation that Beethoven was willing to accept. But this plan suffered the same fate as Hofmeister's: it was betrayed. Immediately a hue and cry broke out among the ranks of the other Viennese publishers. Like the Sultan of Turkey having his ears filled with the outcries of his pashas because of some proposed government ordinance, our master was assailed by the Artarias, the Mollos, the Cappis because of the Steiner monopoly system. And Vienna's sultan of music allowed himself to be convinced that the charges made by these rivals were infallible, that the Steiner plan would work to his disadvantage. Like the Leipzig proposal, this, too, was set aside, so that the little ship and its helmsman, though he continued to watch for every wind, remained grounded, high and dry, despite his own warning written in his journal for 1816. But his freedom and independence remained intact, though surely the independence was of a very dubious sort. It was Domenico Artaria who enjoyed the first fruits of this freedom: the great sonata in B flat major, opus 106.

Having armed ourselves with these facts, we feel ready to attack the events of 1823 and to resume the historical course of our narrative.

The reader will remember that Beethoven, in order to cover his necessities, took the deplorable step of borrowing, and that two of his creditors were his publishers, one in Vienna and one in Leipzig. The reader will remember further that he needed money in order to rid himself of a persistent creditor. This latter was the publishing house of which we have already heard so much, Steiner & Co., and the debt was 800 florins WW.* So it was these very same men, whose manipulations concerning the interests of our master we have just seen from the foregoing events, who for a considerable number of years had been associated with him in matters of business, who more than anyone else knew how to flatter him and use him for their own purposes, whom for years and years he had suspected with concealed animosity, but from whom, however, he could not free himself until in 1823 the break came about in an almost violent manner. And all the while they pressed him more and more closely, for they could clearly see one new work after another being given to other publishers.

---

* On page 131 of the first edition it says '800 florins CM'. Dr. Bach subsequently corrected this error, which he had overlooked in the manuscript.

The dependence of the master on these gentlemen had already gone on too long, for it had begun as early as the sorrowful year of 1813.[188] The reasons are almost obvious. I should hesitate to speak so positively of these circumstances if another close observer of the situation were not still alive to support me: the publisher P. J. Simrock in Bonn.[189] When Simrock visited Beethoven in Vienna in 1816, the master's state of dependence on the publishing house named above could not escape his attention. In fact the composer himself initiated him into the mysteries of this relationship when he handed him the manuscript for the two sonatas opus 102 and 'prayed him not to let Messrs. Steiner and Haslinger know that he had given someone else his compositions to publish'. In this abject dependence we must recognize one aspect of a character so strong in other respects! His friends were comforted to be assured that no kind of promise, either spoken or much less written, had ever been given by Beethoven to bind his art to the service of this publishing firm.

In the first months of 1823 this quarrel had advanced so far that the people in the Paternostergässchen were threatening legal action. When the composer's brother Johann definitely refused to cover even so insignificant a debt until the expected payments for the subscription copies of the *Missa* had been received, Beethoven no longer delayed putting the matter into the hands of Dr. Bach to be settled. However, the master and his lawyer thought it necessary first to lodge a counter-claim against his blustering creditor. For years this music-dealer had been in possession of various manuscripts: the first *Leonore* overture, which in 1805 had been tried and put aside, as we saw in the second period;[190] the cantata *Der glorreiche Augenblick*, performed in 1814; the five-part fugue in D major for two violins, two violas, and cello, written in 1817; the Italian trio *Tremate, empi, tremate*; the overture to *König Stephan*; and finally the overture in C major, opus 115.

The master demanded immediate publication of these works, claiming that it was contrary to the intellectual and material interests of the composer to hide his creations for years under lock and key. His opponent's reply was short and to the point: 'We bought and paid for those manuscripts; they are our property and we may do as we please with them.' Such was the situation of artistic works and artists' rights in Germany at that time: the former were commodities and the latter simply did not exist. Dr. Bach realized that positive action on behalf of his client would result in nothing but an emotional tension that would actually stifle his artistic activity. He therefore advised the prompt payment of the debt, to be made possible by the sale of a bank share, a step our master resisted for a long time. The truth of this account will be fully confirmed by the exact wording of a note from Beethoven to the author of this book; the note serves also to give a clear picture of him at that moment. He writes:

Dear Schindler:

Don't forget about the bank share. It is highly necessary. I should not like to be sued for nothing at all. My brother's behaviour in this matter is altogether typical of him. The tailor has been ordered for today, but I hope to be able to put him off for now with kind words.[191]

These things had to be in order to free the master at last from the net of the 'friends' who had so long held him in captivity. It is important for a clear understanding of the catalogue numbers to know that in the last ten years of the master's life no new works were given to this publisher. The last opus numbers in the catalogue belong to works from an earlier time published by Steiner.[192] There can be little doubt that the speculation depended upon Beethoven's decease, which might then coincide with the publication of a whole series of new works. And so as the last opus number we have opus 138, the first overture to *Leonore-Fidelio*.*

The Leipzig creditor who had advanced Beethoven the other sum behaved in exactly the opposite way. This was the publishing firm of C. F. Peters. Although the manuscripts contemplated by the advance were delivered as agreed upon by both parties (actually, there was only one manuscript, and we shall later see what it was) the worthy publisher had to wait patiently for his reimbursement until the master's financial situation was somewhat easier. The following receipt, which we have in the original, will make the matter clear:

I hereby request Herr L. van Beethoven in Vienna to return to me now the three hundred and sixty florins CM that he received from me in August 1822. Since we have had no dealings, it is requested that this sum be paid over to Messrs. Steiner & Co., music dealers, in Vienna, and that this document be accepted in return as my receipt.

C. F. Peters

Leipzig, 30 November 1825   Music publisher

The confirmation of the receipt of the 360 florins CM, or 900 florins WW, appears on the same document, dated 7 December 1825, signed S. A. Steiner & Co.

The manuscript that was sent to Peters in the autumn of 1822 was

---

* One item must be included here: soon after the auction of Beethoven's musical *Nachlass* in November 1827, the newspapers spread the report:

Tobias Haslinger took this opportunity to pick up for a song a packet of dances and marches in which he found the full score and instrumental parts of a completely unknown overture of major importance which the master, as Schuppanzigh remembers, had rehearsed a few years ago, and which shows corrections in red pencil in the master's own hand (see AmZ XXX (1828) 111).

An entry in Beethoven's own hand on his calendar for the month of February 1823, which is before us, will serve to dissipate totally this widespread fabrication. The note reads: 'Steiner has everything from 1814 and 1816.'

one of those little pieces one might call 'intellectual sedatives' if such a designation existed in musical literature. There are a considerable number of such 'sedatives' written by the master, some quite clever and instructive. Most of them were written at the time that a major work was in progress. He called them 'bagatelles' and put them on paper as a kind of mental relaxation during the highly concentrated period when he was working on the *Missa Solemnis*. The publisher in Leipzig returned them immediately with the comment that he did not consider them worth the price (I think it was ten ducats) and that Beethoven should think it beneath his dignity to waste his time on such trifles, which anyone could write. This audacious but appropriate remark irritated the master greatly. Contrary to his custom, he marked the day he received the note, 19 March, on the calendar that I still have. It really seemed that he enjoyed this type of intellectual relaxation and hoped to shake some more of these bagatelles out of his cape. Later on the publishing firm of Schott in Mainz bought the pieces and accorded them the honour of publishing them as opus 126.*[193]

It is with some reluctance that I touch upon a third instance of borrowing, one of a more intimate nature and also involving a more considerable sum than the two already described. The beginnings of the matter take us back to 1813, the year in which fate seemed to have knotted itself around our hero's head so tightly that he was never able to completely free himself. It was from the master himself that I learned of this debt but I was ignorant of its origins, and like so many other incidents of that unhappy year whose roots lay deep within his complex nature, they did not become clear to me until my protracted stay in Frankfurt.

In that city there still lives one of the master's oldest friends, a lady whose acquaintance he had made at the home of her father, von B . . ., when he first arrived in Vienna in 1792.[194] In 1798 she married and moved to Frankfurt. The distance did nothing to lessen the mutual sentiments of true friendship and admiration. In a letter to me, the master called this family in Frankfurt 'his best friends in the world'. In his journal for 1814, of which we still have copies, we find the following entry in his hand: 'I owe F. A. B—t—o 2300 florins, that is 1100 fr. and 60♯ (ducats)'. These excellent people never reminded the master of his debt; on the contrary, they tried to induce him to forget it until better days should come. 'The nobility of these friends must not be put

* This instance will demonstrate to the inventors of anecdotes and little stories concerning Beethoven how hard it was for him, even at the height of his fame, to get ten ducats, much less 100. Lately the journals have taken up the story, in the manner of the novelette periodicals, about the master finding himself in financial straits while on holiday in the country. His landlord was directed to take some 'pages covered with notes' to a publisher in Vienna and in the composer's name demand 100 ducats for them. According to the inventor of the tale, the sum was indeed paid to the messenger. Probably it was the publishing firm in the Paternostergässchen, who always had such a high price in readiness for any Beethoven manuscript.

to the test any longer,' as he expressed it in a letter to me. This determined him to sell a second bank share, and once more I helped him negotiate the transaction. All this occurred immediately after the conflict with Steiner in March 1823, as we can see in his calendar notations.

A fourth debt concerns a situation characteristic of Beethoven and, though quite insignificant in itself, is closely associated with the interests of another person. It would be better to leave the discussion of the matter to a more appropriate place. The kindly censor in Vienna deleted it in the first edition, though the matter is recorded in the minutes of a certain organization and is therefore no secret.[195] Its inclusion is now imperative, as we shall see.

When we read in Seyfried's description of Beethoven's traits of character: 'He did not know the true value of money, which he considered only a means for the acquisition of the absolute necessities', we may well ask in the light of what we have just learned from what distant time Ritter von Seyfried is speaking. One would think that situations such as have been discussed would teach one the value of money. Our master did indeed learn something from this experience, and knew the theories by heart, but in practice he did as so many others have done; he was often niggardly in matters of dire necessity, but when it came to things he really liked or that conflicted with some peculiarity of his, then theory and practice went their respective ways. We shall speak of such cases. Let us, however, leave for a time this unhappy theme in the life of our master and return to the realm of his artistic genius.

In the winter months of 1822–3 there spread throughout musical circles in Vienna a rumour whose accuracy was so certain that all music-lovers were filled with joy. The revival of *Fidelio* in November 1822, after an interval of eight years, had been like the radiant rise of Phoebus over the musical horizon. Its several performances had been so successful* that the management of the Imperial Opera had had the courage to commission our master to write a new opera for this theatre. Beethoven accepted the commission and asked for texts to be given to him immediately so that he might choose one. A considerable number were delivered at once, but none of them would do.†

---

* The artists who participated in these performances were Wilhelmine Schröder (Fidelio), Haizinger (Florestan), Forti (Pizarro), Zeltner (Rocco), Nestroy (Don Fernando), Rauscher (Jacquino), and Thekla Demmer (Marzelline).

† A. B. Marx, in his *Beethoven* [5th ed. (1901) I 397], says that Beethoven had been commissioned to write a three-act opera on a text adapted by Biedenfeld from Schiller's *Bürgschaft*, and states further that Beethoven did not refuse but requested to have the second act (the wedding feast) composed by Weigl, for 'such lighthearted stuff did not appeal to him'. All this is invention, though hardly of Marx's making.[195a] Beethoven respected his old friend Weigl too much to have been capable of such a remark. On the contrary, he took every opportunity to express publicly his regard for the great opera director. He considered him the only living perpetuator of the Mozart tradition in music. 'Weigl said it? Then you must believe it.'

He had at first stipulated that the theme should be from Greek or Roman antiquity, but was told that the classics had already been overdone. The choice now became very difficult, for the master could not decide what kind of subject would be appropriate. Then Franz Grillparzer was bold enough to send, not without hesitation, the opera book *Melusina* that he had just completed. This highly romantic creation, which contained many effective scenes and whose cast of characters included a comic figure (a servant almost of the Leporello type), pleased Beethoven immensely and reversed his earlier preference for a classical theme. The poet and the composer held numerous conferences, at which I was always present. Beethoven felt that the scenario needed to be changed, shortened, and knit together more tightly, to all of which the poet agreed readily. This collaboration brought the two noble singers together for the first time and afforded them the opportunity to open their hearts to each other in melancholy laments on the political and social situation of their common fatherland.[196]

At almost the same time as the commission from the administration of the opera house, a similar invitation came from the manager of the Royal Theatre in Berlin, Count Brühl, who asked the master to name his own price. Without a word to anyone, Beethoven sent him Grillparzer's *Melusina* to look over, adding his own laudatory comments on the text, as we may surmise from the manager's reply, which Beethoven forgot to hide. Count Brühl was no less warm in his praise of the poem, but remarked that the ballet *Undine* was being given at the Royal Opera, and that its subject matter was somewhat similar to that of *Melusina*.[197]

This insignificant coincidence, added to Beethoven's unpleasant memories of the trials connected with his *Fidelio*, was enough to make him suddenly abandon his intention of writing a German opera, though not before he had said many bitter words about German opera singers. He seemed to remember only the events of 1805 in the Theater an der Wien and unfortunately to have forgotten the much-applauded cast at the Court Opera and their excellent performances in 1814 that undoubtedly had had a great deal to do with the success of *Fidelio*. The performances of his opera in the late autumn of 1822 were also received favourably on all sides. Yet this could do nothing to change his opinion of German singers in general. His frequent association in earlier years with Italian singers had not favourably disposed the thoroughly German composer and thoroughly German man towards German singers. He missed in them the reverence for art and the zeal for study that had always characterized Italians, and he deplored in German singers their contentment with mediocre training.*

---

* If the severe master was so critical then, what would he say to the kind of training generally received today by singers, German and Italian alike?

The presence in Vienna at that time of the foremost singers of Italy afforded daily opportunity for a comparison by which the German singers suffered. There were Lablache, Rubini, Donzelli, Ambrogi, Davide, and others, and among the women there were Fodor-Mainvielle, Meric-Lalande, Dardanelli, Eckerlin, and others, who with each performance were able to raise their audiences to the highest pitch of enthusiasm. Indeed, our master who, having first looked at the score, saw this company of distinguished Italian artists perform Rossini's *Barbiere*, was so enchanted with them that he was easily persuaded by the talented Caroline Unger (now Frau Ungher-Sabatier),[198] to write an opera especially for them. With no further prompting he promised these artists that he would begin work the next year.[199] We shall soon learn why this delightful project, too, came to naught.

The spring of this year was marked by an event well worthy of mention, for it is typical of the composer's character. The year before the master received from the Royal Swedish Academy of Arts and Sciences[200] a diploma that in the most flattering words named him an honorary member. The necessary written application was made to the government of Lower Austria for permission to accept the honour. After a long delay the permission was granted, at a time when Beethoven was already occupied at Hetzendorf with the variations on Diabelli's waltz theme. To announce this nordic distinction in the two newspapers, *Oesterreichischer Beobachter* and *Wiener Zeitschrift*, he had me send the editors, von Pilat and K. Bernard respectively, two humorous letters that sounded as though the sentences had been thrown together at random. A third, which I have in my possession, is in the same tenor. It reads:

Most excellent rascal of Epirus and no less of Brundisium:
    Give the letter to the *Beobachter*. But you must put his name on it. . . . I have written 'as honorary member', but I do not know whether that is the correct term or whether it should be merely 'as foreign member', since I am ignorant of such things and have paid no attention. . . . Inquire of both these philosophical journalists whether this appointment is an honorary or a dishonorary one. . . .*

These letters and other similar outbursts are eloquent proof of the happy hours the master spent on his variations on the waltz 'with the cobbler's patch'. But the content of the other two letters expresses the most biting sarcasm, especially in reference to the editorial profession, the government, and the great difficulty it had in granting him per-

---

* The latter term should not be criticized too harshly. The Royal Swedish Academy had by 1823 given hardly any indication of its presence, especially in the field of music, and even today these things seem to be in a primitive state. The opera is an obvious exception.

mission to accept the Swedish honour, a process that took no less than seven or eight months.

In June the variations were finished and given immediately to the publisher Diabelli without the usual time-consuming delay and pains-taking revision. And now Beethoven plunged into the ninth symphony, for which he had already made some sketches. Suddenly the humour which had made him so compliant and affable with everyone disap-peared. He received no callers, and even wished to see me less fre-quently, though before this time I could not visit him often enough. He wrote to me:

Samothracian!*

Don't bother to come here until perchance a hatti-sherif appears. Meanwhile you have not been deserving of the golden cord. My swiftly sailing frigate, the genteelly and nobly born Frau Schnaps, will usually inquire after your health every two or three days. Farewell—and don't bring anyone—farewell.

The chaos of his domestic life, somewhat improved in the previous weeks, began all over again. He would walk over hill and dale, sketch-book in hand, never thinking of regular mealtimes. Over and over again he would return without his hat, something that had never happened before, even at the height of creative impulse. By the middle of August there were thick notebooks full of sketches for the new work. He was suddenly seized by the compulsion to leave Baron Pronay's beautiful villa and move to Baden, because 'every time the Baron met him he would make a deep bow'. We are reminded here of his words to the beloved Giulietta: 'This humility of man towards man: it pains me', etc.

Efforts to dissuade him from this aversion as well as from his intent to move were of no avail. One morning his fast-sailing frigate, the good old housekeeper, appeared at my door (I must explain that since Sep-tember 1822 Beethoven had shared with me his apartment in the Pfarr-gasse, in the suburb of Laimgrube[201]) with a message. The master felt it impossible to work any longer in Hetzendorf and must leave imme-diately. He expected me the next morning at five o'clock to help him find an apartment in Baden. The following lines in his handwriting will bear me out:

Samothracian rascal! Make haste; the weather is just right. It is better to be too early than too late. *Presto prestissimo* we will leave from here.

The journey from Hetzendorf to Baden and the negotiations there are

---

* By the word 'Samothracian' Beethoven is here referring, as in many other letters to me, to the Samothracian mysteries (of the mythical heroic age, 2000 B.C.), which were based partly on music. He designated me thus as a sharer in the Beethoven mysteries.

among my most comical experiences with the great eccentric. He immediately mustered his memories of all the apartments he had occupied there, with all their unpleasant and uncomfortable features. Out of the whole list there was only one that would satisfy his present requirements. 'But the people told me last year that they would not take me again.' Such ultimatums had been given in several other houses as well. Once in Baden, he asked me to go as his spokesman to the house he wanted and in his name to promise more orderly conduct and more consideration for the other tenants (a chief source of complaint). The promise was rejected, however, and I was sent away. My waiting friend was very disappointed. The spokesman was sent back to the landlord with new assurances of good behaviour. This time his words fell on more willing ears. Yet there was another unconditional requirement; Beethoven must have shutters put on the windows overlooking the street as he had had the year before. In vain we tried to guess the reason for this strange request. When the landlord explained that the shutters were needed to spare the composer's suffering eyes from the harsh sunlight, Beethoven complied immediately. Within a few days the move was completed.

But what was the real reason for the shutters, and why were they a condition of Beethoven's tenancy? The reason was simple: Beethoven, already frequently driven by a demon whose closer acquaintance we shall make later on, would, during his stay at the same house the year before, stand at one or another of the unpainted window-shutters and, as was his custom, make long calculations—for example, how many florins were 50, 100, or 200 ducats? Then there were some musical ideas, and in short a whole stream of consciousness written out in pencil so that these thin boards formed a kind of diary. In the summer of 1822 a family from North Germany lived across the street. They used to watch him at this occupation, and when he moved away they paid the landlord a piece of gold for one of these shutters, apparently as a kind of souvenir. Once he realized the value of his window-shutters and their inscriptions, the landlord had no trouble in selling all four pieces to other guests of the baths. When the apothecary T. in Baden told Beethoven of this strange commerce, the master is said to have exploded in Homeric laughter.

If the author feels justified in giving space to an insignificant humorous incident like this, it is because he wishes to demonstrate that the occurrence, the prospering, in short the possibility of many good and perhaps even great deeds needs the simultaneous collaboration of quite trivial secondary circumstances. This is something one learns from experience. Beethoven's impatience with the Baron and his deep bows in Hetzendorf was the reason that his inventiveness would not flow as

III   Autograph sketch of 1823 for beginning of last movement of ninth symphony (see p. 494)

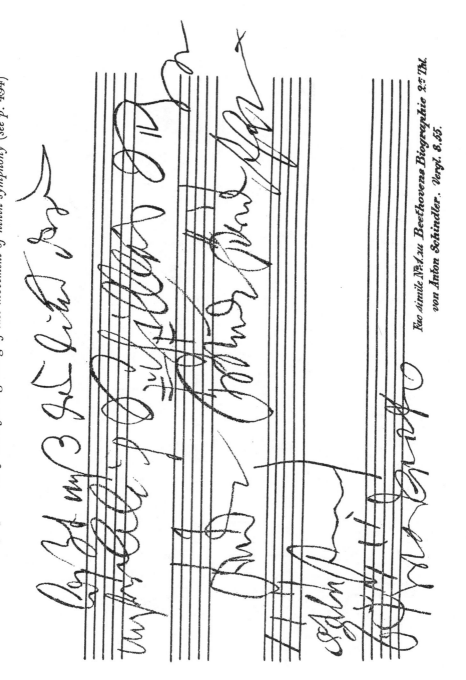

Fac simile Nº 1 zu Beethovens Biographie 2.ᵗᵉʳ Thl.
von Anton Schindler. Vergl. S. 55.

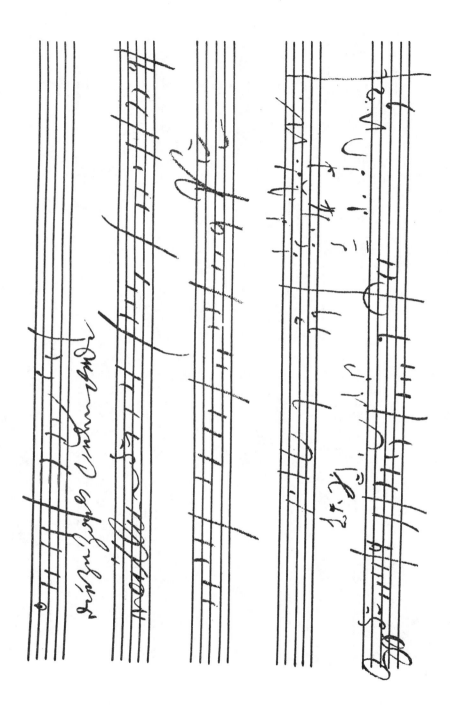

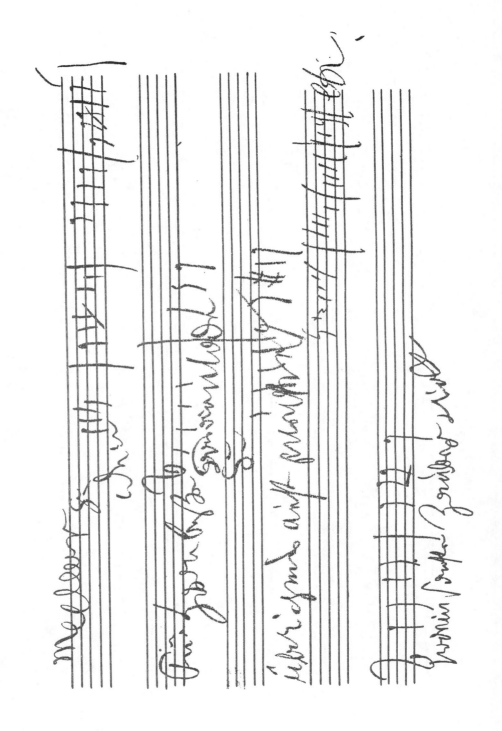

freely as he wished. Hence his desire to get away and to go to a part of the countryside in which, as in Mödling and Heiligenstadt, his genius had exhibited its richest fruition. It does not seem too far-fetched to say that perhaps we have the enterprising landlord in Baden to thank for the existence of the ninth symphony: if Beethoven had not gained access by means of the window-shutters to the house he found so comfortable, it is very doubtful whether the restless master who was so disturbing to the other guests would have found a quiet place to live and work. And to postpone any piece of exacting work to another day was a dangerous matter with him, especially in the last years of his life. We shall soon speak further of this.

In the meantime, let us hear what Friedrich Rochlitz had to say in a letter from Baden dated 9 July 1822, for it touches on this point. Rochlitz had conveyed to the master on behalf of Härtel in Leipzig the idea of writing music for Goethe's *Faust*, somewhat as he had done with *Egmont*. Rochlitz quoted to Härtel Beethoven's own words, including these:

For some time I have been occupied with three other major works. Much of the music has already hatched, at least in my head. I must first get them off my neck: two important symphonies, each one different from my others, and an oratorio. It will take a long time, you see, since for some time now I have not been able to bring myself to work easily. I sit and think and think; I have had it for a long time, but I can't get it down on paper. These big works are always hard to get started. Once I'm into them, they go well.

The master did not return to Vienna until the last migratory birds had left for the winter; it was already the end of October. This time he occupied an apartment in the Ungergasse (in the suburb of Landstrasse) near the city gates. The new symphony was finished up to the fourth movement; that is, he had it all in his head and the main ideas were fixed in the sketchbooks. Contrary to his usual method of working, he frequently put the music aside, especially the fourth movement, for he could not decide which verses to choose from Schiller's ode, *An die Freude*. Yet he was extraordinarily painstaking in writing out the score of the first movement; indeed, among all his scores this one may serve as a model of neatness and clarity, and it is notable for its small number of corrections. The working out of the fourth movement, however, began a struggle seldom encountered before. The problem was to find a suitable introduction to Schiller's ode. One day he burst into the room and shouted at me: 'I have it! I have it!' He held his sketch-book out to me so that I could read: 'Let us sing the song of the immortal Schiller'; then a solo voice began the Hymn to Joy (see the facsimile*). Yet this introduction must later have given place to another, undeniably more appropriate one: 'O friends, not these strains! Let us sing still more beautifully, still more joyfully!'† This alteration completely changed the beginning of this movement from the original plan, as the discarded pages showed. How unfortunate that we lacked the wisdom to keep them! They would be as useful to us now as the various versions of some of the numbers in *Fidelio*.

While composing music for the pianoforte, the master would often go to the instrument and try certain passages, especially those that might present difficulties in performance. At such times he was totally oblivious of anyone present. To this circumstance I owe my acquaintance with the complete sonatas opp. 106, 109, and 110, and parts of the last sonata opus 111. While working on a score, however, he played no instrument, and because it annoyed him to see anyone go through a work that was still incomplete, even those living in the same house heard nothing of a new symphonic work until it was rehearsed. From the discarded pages and the assembled volumes of the score it is apparent that the recitative for the double basses was added later. As for the melody for the first stanza, four versions appear in the sketchbooks, over one of which is written the usual *meilleur*, as may be seen in the facsimile.

In February of the following year, 1824, this colossal creation was finished down to the last detail, and the master began once more to be in a good mood and even to allow himself a few hours of relaxation. He could again be seen strolling through the streets, using his black-ribboned lorgnette to examine attractive window displays, and greeting many acquaintances or friends after his long seclusion. Since his visit from Carl Maria von Weber in November of the previous year (after the performance of Weber's opera *Euryanthe*) we had not had the pleasure of hearing the master set off one of his fireworks of crackling, sparkling wit and sarcasm.

No one was more delighted with the new state of affairs than the poet Karl Bernard and the president of the GdMf, for now there really seemed reason to hope that our master would start work on the oratorio for the Society, *Der Sieg des Kreuzes*. Perfectly satisfied with the poem,[202]

---

* Editor's note. This is reproduced in the present edition as Facsimile III on p. 264.

† Some of the many attacks on this fourth movement made by Oulibicheff in his biography of Mozart are worth noting here. Having said that Beethoven treated the sublime excerpts from Schiller's ode like scraps of an Italian opera libretto, he continues:

And this was supposed to have been composed when the great unhappy one, as Beethoven called himself, was in the deepest abyss of physical and moral decay. Was he capable of the task, old, sickly, suffering, and misanthropic as he was?

Beethoven was then fifty-two years old and his health at that time was quite good. As for misanthropy, which fortunately was never a part of Beethoven's character, even though he liked solitude, one can hardly imagine what kind of a musical work it would have produced! These few words demonstrate what lack of reason and what prejudice this antagonist of Beethoven brought to his evaluation of the composer's works.

Beethoven, too, was looking forward to the undertaking. For the twentieth time he gave his word both to the poet and to the chairman of the Society that he was absolutely serious about the oratorio and that he would certainly start it within the next few months. Yet *accidit in puncto, quod non speratur in annis*. An unexpected occurrence intervened to change all of Beethoven's plans. The wonderful projects he had in mind for composing great new works were postponed one by one *ad Kalendas graecas*, and other works were taken up 'just temporarily'. Let us see what the occurrence was, what its causes and what its effects.

The Italian opera company under the joint direction of Domenico Barbaja and his representative and partner Louis Duport had started performances on 13 April 1822 with Rossini's newest opera *Zelmira*, written specifically for the Vienna season. We have already given the names of the artists who made up the company. It remains to be added that Rossini himself was present and that his wife, Colbran, was *prima donna* in this first season. Although she did not entirely satisfy the expectations of the public, the other artists were so exceptional that an audience as easily excited and as receptive to everything foreign as the Viennese could well be forgiven for their enthusiasm over the company's performance. A less hedonistic audience would undoubtedly have assumed a more moderate attitude after the first surprise, and the works they heard would have contributed to a deeper culture, a broadening of musical horizons. But in Vienna this was not the case. The uninhibited enthusiasm grew from performance to performance until it degenerated into a general intoxication of the senses whose sole inspiration was the virtuosity of the singers. The quality or lack of quality of the operas performed was not even considered. In July the season closed with Rossini's *Corradino*. The critic for the AmZ described the events of this farewell performance in these words:

It was really enough, more than enough. The entire performance was like an idolatrous orgy; everyone there acted as if he had been bitten by a tarantula; the shouting, crying, yelling of 'viva' and 'fora' went on and on.

The management of the imperial theatre, consisting of Hofrat von Füljod,* the court secretary Ignaz von Mosel and, as third in command, the Kapellmeister Joseph Weigl, had paid no attention whatsoever to the requirements of the day or to the wishes of the public. In 1816 Viennese audiences had had a foretaste of Rossini's opera music and the virtuosity of Italian singing in a few performances by outstanding Italian artists (among others, the contralto Signora Borgondio, the first Tancredi in

---

* Nicknamed in Vienna, 'Vieljüd' ['Yid'].

Germany, and the excellent tenor Tacchinardi). These performances were repeated two years later on the same stage. Then Count Ferdinand Palffy of the Theater an der Wien presented a well-attended, soundly applauded series consisting of all the Rossini operas written up to that time, with German singers. Despite the success of these performances, the above-mentioned triumvirate refused almost mulishly to produce a Rossini opera, even though theirs was an extremely able company of artists, far superior in every respect to that of the neighbouring theatre. Egotism and a desire to be different, both on the part of the managers themselves and on the part of the French whose operas they performed, as well as a fear of being supplanted, prompted this perversity. The grievous outcome was several years of enormous deficits hardly calculated to reverse the Emperor's long-standing indifference to the opera. Long before the appearance of Barbaja there had been rumours to the effect that the Emperor wished to lease the excessively costly Kärntnerthor Theater.

A public whose aesthetic sensitivity had fallen as low as Vienna's had at that time could hardly be expected to exhibit an appreciative attitude towards German music and musicians after the departure of the Italian company in July 1822. The whole city went into deep mourning; their only relief from the desolation at the loss of the pleasure in which they had just revelled consisted in ridiculing the German singers. Vocal style was cramped to try to accommodate current taste, and since the German opera singers could not adapt themselves to it, they fell from the high esteem in which they had once been held. Of all the operas only Weber's *Freischütz*, with its visual appeal, remained in favour. It was not until several months had passed that a more sober portion of the public (not the nobility) was cured of its over-extravagant enthusiasm, so that by November, as we have already reported, another production of *Fidelio* could be dared.

But in 1823 the frenzy caused by the Italian opera became thoroughgoing fanaticism. What was left of appreciation of German vocal music disappeared entirely. From this year dates the deplorable state of all music, for the decadence that had spread throughout the Austrian capital had by now infected all the cities of the kingdom. Two years later the Viennese reporter for the AmZ described the beginning of this blight in the following words: 'For years now hardly a single piece of significant serious music has been published. We have nothing but piano arrangements of Rossini's operas. All is barren. What next?'

⤚ 1824 ⤙

The depressing character of this period in history had to be set forth in order to provide the background to understand what is now to follow.

Obviously our great master was sorely hurt by the existing state of affairs. The *Missa Solemnis* had been completed for two years and the ninth symphony was finished down to the last detail. But considering the widespread decadence, how were these two works to be performed with any success at all, either artistic or financial, especially in view of the expense of producing them? Beethoven entered into correspondence with Count Brühl to ask whether under his auspices the two works might be performed in Berlin. Count Brühl encouraged the master in this idea and promised a happy outcome. When this plan became known in Vienna, however, a small band of artists and music-lovers who had retained their sobriety and reason united to avert the disgrace that threatened the imperial capital. This select group drafted a letter to the master, and a delegation of its members delivered it. The following is an exact transcription of the letter.

To Herr Ludwig van Beethoven:

Out of the wide circle of those who in reverent admiration surround your genius in this your second native city, there approach you today a small number of disciples and lovers of art to express long-felt wishes, humbly to present long-suppressed requests.

But since the number of the spokesmen bears but a small proportion to the multitude who joyfully acknowledge your worth and what you have come to be for the present and for the future, in like manner the wishes and requests are in no wise limited to the number of those who speak for others who feel as they do. They assert in the name of all to whom art and the realization of their ideal is more than a means and object of pastime that what they request is echoed aloud or silently by all those in whose breasts there lives a sense of the divine in music.

It is the wishes of those of our countrymen who reverence art that we present here, for although the name and the creations of Beethoven belong to all the world and to those lands where art finds a welcoming spirit, yet it is Austria that may claim him as its own. There still lives in its people the appreciation of the great and immortal works that Mozart and Haydn created within its bosom for all time, and with happy pride they know that the sacred triad, in which their names and yours shine as symbols of the highest in the spiritual realm of tones, sprang from the earth of the Fatherland.

It must cause you all the more sorrow that a foreign power has invaded this royal citadel of what is finest, that over the graves of those who have passed and around the dwelling of the one of that band that still remains with us, spectres are leading a course that can have no kinship with the princely spirits of this royal house; that shallowness is sullying the name and the insignia of art; that in unworthy dalliance with sacred things the feeling for the pure and ever-beautiful is being beclouded and dissipated.

For this reason they feel more strongly and actively than ever before that the great need of the present moment is a new impulse led by a powerful hand, a new appearance of the ruler in his domain. It is this need that leads them to you now, and these are the pleas that they present to you on behalf of all who hold these wishes dear and in the name of the art of the Fatherland.

Do not withhold longer from popular enjoyment, do not withhold longer from the oppressed appreciation of what is great and perfect a performance of the most recent masterworks of your hand. We know that a great sacred composition has been added to that first one in which you made immortal the emotions of a soul permeated and transfigured by the power of faith and by divine light. We know that a new flower glows in the garland of your noble and still unequalled symphonies. For years, ever since the thunder of the 'Victory of Vittoria' died away, we have waited and hoped to see you once again distribute new gifts within the circle of your friends from the fulness of your riches. Disappoint no longer the hopes of all! Enhance the effectiveness of your newest creations by the joy of first making them known by you yourself. Do not allow these your youngest children to be introduced as foreigners in the city of their birth, perhaps by those to whom you and your spirit are strange. Appear soon among your friends, among those who admire and honour you! This is our nearest and first plea.

But still other claims upon your genius have been made public. The wishes and offers extended to you more than a year ago by the directorate of our Court Opera and then by the Society of Austrian Friends of Music have too long been the unspoken wish of all admirers of art and of your name. They had stimulated hope and expectation too much not to have attained the swiftest public knowledge near and far, not to have awakened the most widespread interest. Poetry has done her utmost to support such fair hopes and desires. Worthy material from the hand of an estimable poet awaits your imagination to charm it into life. Do not allow these intimate summonses to so noble an objective to be in vain. Delay no longer in leading us back to those departed days in which the song of Polyhymnia powerfully seized and delighted the initiates of art and the hearts of the multitude alike!

Need we tell you with what deep regret your withdrawal from public life has long filled us? Need we tell you that as all glances turned hopefully to you, all perceived with sorrow that the one man whom we are compelled to name as the foremost of all living men in his field looked on in silence as foreign art invaded German soil, the place of honour of the German muse, while German works gave pleasure only as they echoed the favourite tunes of foreigners, and where the mightiest had lived and worked a second childhood of taste threatened to follow the golden age of art?

You alone are able to assure a decisive victory for the best among us. From you the native Art Society and the German opera await new blossoms, renewed life, and a new supremacy of the true and the beautiful over the dominion to which the spirit of the day would subject even the eternal laws of art. Give us hope that the wishes of all to whom the sound of your harmonies has come will soon see this fulfilled. This is our most urgent second plea.

May the year that has now begun not come to an end without rejoicing us with the fruits of our pleas, and may the coming spring, if it brings the unfolding of one of the gifts that we seek, become for us and the world of art a time of twofold flowering.

Vienna, February 1824.

Signers

Fürst C. Lichnowsky	Ferdinand Graf v. Palffy	Moritz Graf v. Dietrichstein
Artaria und Company	Eduard Frh. v. Schweiger	Ig. Edler von Mosel
		k. k. Hofrath
von Hauschka	Graf Czernin	Carl Czerny
M. J. Leidesdorf	Moritz Graf v. Fries	Moritz Graf Lichnowsky
J. E. von Wayna	I. F. Castelli	Zmeskall
Andreas Streicher	Deinhardtstein	Hofrath Kiesewetter
Anton Halm	C. Kuffner	Leopold Sonnleithner Dr.
Abbé Stadler	Fr. Nehammer	S. A. Steiner & Comp.
	Ständ Secretär	
von Felsburg	Stainer von Felsburg	Anton Diabelli
Hofsecretär	Bank-liquidator	
Ferdinand Graf		Lederer [?]
Stockhammer		J. N. Bihler[203]

The two messengers, the court secretary von Felsburg and J. N. Bihler, had expected Beethoven to read the letter in their presence, which would give them the opportunity of touching on various other matters and of hearing his definite acceptance. They had therefore chosen the time just after the noon meal to bring their document, for at that hour the master was not indisposed to long conversation. But they had miscalculated. Beethoven did not want to read until he was alone. One may well imagine his great surprise at the arrival of this deputation, especially since his confidence in the public's feeling for him had been brutally shaken. As for the ranks of the musicians, Beethoven had told Hofrat Rochlitz in 1822 that his trust in them had disappeared altogether, a fact that we learn from the much-quoted letter that the critic wrote from Baden.

The reader can guess my eagerness to see what first impression the letter would make. I hastened to the master as soon as he had received it, and found him with the letter in his hand. When he had told me what had happened, he handed me the sheet of paper so quietly that I knew he was deeply moved by its contents. While I read the message whose purport was already familiar to me, he went to the window and watched the clouds move across the sky. Silently I laid the letter aside, waiting for him to say something. He remained, however, in the same position for a long time. Finally he turned to me and spoke in a lower voice than usual: 'That was very nice of them. It pleases me very much!' I used the same words to tell him—alas, in writing—of my own joy. He read what I had written, and then said hastily, 'Let's go out!' Outside he was unusually uncommunicative, an unmistakable sign that his soul was greatly moved.

After asking the opinions of various persons concerning the request that had been addressed to the master, and after the Theater an der Wien had been selected as the largest and best-suited for a purely musical celebration, Beethoven entrusted to me the arrangements for the event. The first step was to submit a proposal to the director of this theatre, Count Ferdinand Palffy, whose name we see among the signatures to the above letter. Count Palffy immediately expressed his readiness to comply with Beethoven's wishes, and with almost no hesitation named the sum of 1,200 florins WW for lease of the house, this to include the use of the entire orchestra and opera company. No one was more surprised than Beethoven at the scope of the lease, for it made him the master of the house, and by raising the price of the tickets he would be assured of gross receipts of at least 3,500 florins. It seemed clear that no major obstacle would keep the enterprise from taking place at a propitious time of the year, and the situation seemed all the more assured as Beethoven could have the opera company and the orchestra rehearse as many times as he felt necessary.

There was no way of foreseeing, though such things had happened before, that Beethoven would raise objections to a business proposition that promised him so much, that he would sacrifice his favour with many patrons, in short that the whole plan would come utterly to naught. This is how it came about. Beethoven demanded no less than the withdrawal of the two music directors of the theatre, Ignaz von Seyfried and Franz Clement, whom he wished to replace with Kapellmeister Umlauf of the Court Opera House and Ignaz Schuppanzigh. Count Palffy was not unwilling to let his Kapellmeister go, for he knew of Seyfried's antagonism towards Beethoven; but he had no intention of withdrawing his orchestra leader, whose reputation as a fine artist we remember from the second period when we also learned of his services to the master, both as soloist and in connection with their joint conducting of such of Beethoven's works as the Pastoral and the C minor symphonies in the same theatre in 1808. But Schuppanzigh found this an excellent opportunity to make himself known as an orchestral leader upon his return from Russia, for he had his eye on the position of first conductor at the Kärntnerthor Theater which was soon to be vacant.* Accordingly he made Beethoven promise to get him the place of orchestra conductor for the coming celebration, even though the place was

---

* Schuppanzigh fulfilled his ambition when in 1828 Count Gallenberg took over the administration at the Kärntnerthor, but at Easter 1830 his conductorship was abruptly and painfully terminated.

already occupied. Beethoven felt a deep obligation to Schuppanzigh, but unfortunately no consideration for Clement.

Everything possible was done to dissolve the intrigues that beset Beethoven so that he might remain aloof from the selfish demands of those around him, but the counter-current was too strong. Count Palffy held fast to his pronouncement that he would not allow such pettiness to hurt his talented orchestra conductor. Moreover, he raised his material demands, perhaps with the intention of putting a quick end to the undertaking that would extend over many weeks and that would undoubtedly end in financial failure. With so much against him, Beethoven still persisted in his demands, while the best season for major productions was slipping by. In the meantime he had placed himself at the centre of an unbelievable web of scheming and shameless exploitation of his name.

Yet before negotiations with Count Palffy were completely broken off, I explored the situation at the Kärntnerthor Theater to see if Beethoven's demands regarding Schuppanzigh would present an obstacle there. Contrary to my expectations, they did not pose a problem and there remained only the financial arrangements to be settled. When negotiations were undertaken in earnest to transfer the concert to that theatre, it became at once apparent that the theatre management was selfish in its demands and sought to profit from Beethoven's position. Beethoven soon recognized the dilemma in which he had by his own actions placed himself, but in all Vienna there was not a third door at which to knock. In his anxiety he kept changing his mind even more than usual about the most minute details of the arrangements. One day, for instance, he would oppose selling by subscription the tickets for the boxes and orchestra stalls, the next day he would approve the sale; one day he wanted the baritone Forti (the only one capable of singing the bass part in the fourth movement of the symphony as it was written), and the next day he preferred the deep bass, Preisinger, though his range did not extend beyond D above the staff and he could not reach the E and F sharp written into the part, and so on. On the other hand, the manager had capricious demands not only concerning the financial arrangements but also in keeping the number of rehearsals to a minimum. Think of a theatre chorus that for two years had sung nothing but Rossini operas, now confronted with the enormous difficulties of the *Missa Solemnis*! Duport, who had once been a famous dancer, thought the job could be sufficiently mastered in five or six rehearsals. As for the orchestral rehearsals, he planned from the beginning to have only two, and so it remained.

In order to help our vacillating master stick to a decision, I devised a little scheme. I asked Count Lichnowsky and Schuppanzigh to meet me and Beethoven as if by coincidence so that he would not guess our design. The master would be asked to express his current decision on the questions that were troubling him; one of us would write down what he had said and half jokingly, half seriously, give it to him to sign. The plan succeeded, but what happened then? When he guessed what we were really doing, he did what he had done so often before: he suspected treachery and falseness. The very same day he addressed to us the following sultan-like decrees:

To Count Moritz Lichnowsky:
I despise treacheries. Visit me no more. The concert will not take place.

Beethoven

To Hr. Schuppanzigh:
He shall visit me no more.[204] I shall not give the concert.

B——n

To Hr. Schindler:
I instruct you not to come until I send for you.
The concert will not take place.[205]

B——n

But the irate master had not sent the silken cord with these *hatti-sherifs,* and he did nothing further to us. The following day we gave him the pleasure of expending his anger on one of us, and meanwhile he had had time to reflect on his over-hasty suspicion of falseness and treachery. But throughout the month of April when negotiations with Duport were taking place, he was in an exceptionally bad temper, the effects of which were not lost upon those who were making the arrangements. Suspicion on both sides had already reached such proportions that even if there had been a legal contract witnessed by a public notary, both sides would have deviated from it. The confusion was further increased when the censor objected to the title *Missa* and the Latin text. Given the narrow-mindedness of the times and the even greater narrowmindedness of the religious authorities, to whom the singing of a church text in a theatre was blasphemy, this obstacle constituted the final prohibition of the performance of the *Missa.** At the last minute, Count Lichnowsky presented a hasty petition to the Chief of Police, Count Sedlnitzky, who granted permission for the work to be performed.

The situation may best be described by quoting an excerpt from a letter Beethoven wrote to me:

After six months of talks hither and yon, I feel already cooked, stewed and roasted. What will finally come of this much-discussed concert if the price of

---

* We learned from the discussion of a similar situation in 1808 that at that time there was no objection to the performance of church music with Latin text in a theatre. Only Latin titles on the concert announcements were forbidden.

tickets cannot be increased? What will be left for me after all these expenses, since the copying alone has already cost so much?

and so forth.[206] We see here what the real problem was. If Beethoven hoped to take in even just what he had already spent, he had to comply with Duport's requirements, which had been set forth thus: 'The tickets for the concert must be sold at the usual price and the management must charge Beethoven the sum of one thousand florins WW for the lease of the theatre with chorus and orchestra.' This stipulation decreed from the start the financial outcome of the enterprise.

The performance was to take place on 7 May. We still have an announcement of the concert. It reads:

GREAT MUSICAL CONCERT BY HERR L. VAN BEETHOVEN[207]

The musical pieces to be performed are the newest works of Herr Ludwig van Beethoven.

First: Great Overture [It was the overture *Zur Weihe des Hauses*, opus 124, from the year 1822.]

Second: Three Great Hymns with solo voices and chorus. [Kyrie, Credo, Agnus Dei, and Dona nobis from the *Missa Solemnis*. Because of the length of the whole work, Beethoven had from the first intended to omit the Gloria. Later he was forced much against his inclination to give up the Sanctus and Benedictus as well, though they had already been rehearsed.]

Third: Great Symphony, with chorus and solo participation in the Finale on the text of Schiller's song, *Ode to Joy*.

The solo parts will be sung by Mlles Sontag and Unger and Messrs. Haizinger and Seipelt. Herr Schuppanzigh will lead the orchestra, Herr Kapellmeister Umlauf will direct the whole ensemble, and the GdMf has kindly served to reinforce the chorus and orchestra.

Herr Ludwig van Beethoven himself will take part in conducting the ensemble. [He stood at Umlauf's right and set the tempo at the beginning of each movement.]

Tickets are available at regular prices.

All the seats in the house were filled. Only one box remained empty: the Emperor's, although the master and I had gone in person to present an invitation to all the members of the imperial family, and some had promised to come. The Emperor and Empress were not in residence, and Archduke Rudolph was still at Olmütz.

The gross receipts were 2,220 florins WW. The expenses were as follows: 1,000 florins to the theatre management and 800 florins for copying the parts, so that there remained for Beethoven a sum of 420 florins, some of which had still to be paid out for minor expenses. No one but the poor mathematician Beethoven could be surprised at this result, considering the conditions that had been imposed in advance. When he learned the outcome of the concert, he was utterly dejected.

The government official Joseph Hüttenbrenner, who still lives in Vienna, helped me bring home the exhausted master. I then handed Beethoven the box-office report. When he saw it, he collapsed. We picked him up and laid him on the sofa. We stayed at his side until late that night; he refused both food and drink, then said no more. Finally, when we noticed that Morpheus had gently closed his eyes, we withdrew. The next morning his servants found him sleeping as we had left him, still dressed in the suit he had worn in the concert-hall.

As for the musical success of this memorable evening, it could be favourably compared to any event ever presented in that venerable theatre. Alas! the man to whom all this honour was addressed could hear none of it, for when at the end of the performance the audience broke into enthusiastic applause, he remained standing with his back to them. Then it was that Caroline Unger had the presence of mind to turn the master towards the proscenium and show him the cheering crowd throwing their hats into the air and waving their handkerchiefs. He acknowledged his gratitude with a bow. This set off an almost unprecedented volley of jubilant applause that went on and on as the joyful listeners sought to express their thanks for the pleasure they had just been granted.

To make known more effectively the artistic success of that May evening, let me quote a few sentences from the Viennese report in the AmZ XXVI (1824) 437:

Where can I find the words to tell my readers of these masterpieces whose greatness transcended a performance that left much to be desired, notably in the vocal section, as three rehearsals* were inadequate for a work that offers such extraordinary difficulties, while to convey the imposing overall power, the balance of light and shadow, a perfect sureness of intonation, and subtle shades of colouring was quite out of the question. Nevertheless, the impact was indescribably marvellous and strong; it was acclaimed with enthusiastic shouts raised to the master from overflowing hearts, for his inexhaustible genius had opened up a new world to us, and unveiled never-heard, never-suspected magical secrets of divine music!

Let us hear, too, what this voice of Vienna said about the Finale of the symphony. Despite all the things that have since been said about the movement, this first reaction retains its interest. The critic wrote:

The Finale in D minor opens like a crash of thunder with the diminished ninth cutting shrilly through the dominant. Like a potpourri, all the principal themes already heard are repeated in quick succession as if reflected in a mirror; then they are again paraded in brilliant array. The contrabasses growl out a recitative that seems to ask, 'What is going to happen next?', after which they

* As we have said, there were actually only two rehearsals of the entire ensemble, since the orchestra had music for a ballet to prepare.

answer themselves with a gentle motif in the major, in which they are gradually joined by all the other instruments in extraordinarily beautiful combinations, with nothing of Rossini's bass tremolos and parallel thirds, rising step by step in an overwhelming crescendo. At last, after a summons by the bass soloist, the full chorus intones in majestic splendour the song in praise of joy. Then the joyful heart stretches wide to encompass the heavenly sensations of blissful pleasure, and a thousand throats join in praise: 'Hail! Hail! Hail, divine music! Glory, praise, and thanks be to thy most worthy high priest!'

The critic now sits at his desk, his composure regained, yet he can never forget the emotion of that moment. Art and truth here celebrate their most glorious triumph, and with full justice one might say: *ne plus ultra!* Who can ever surpass these nameless heights? It therefore lies in the realm of the impossible for the remainder of the poem, set partly as choruses, partly as vocal solos, with different tempi, changing keys and time signatures, to achieve a comparable effect, no matter how perfectly the individual sections are handled. Indeed, the composer's most ardent admirers are firmly convinced that this truly singular Finale would be all the more imposing if it were drawn together into a more concentrated unity. The composer himself would share this opinion, had not cruel fate robbed him of the faculty of hearing his own creations.

This brilliant success and the public's loud clamour prompted the money-loving manager to propose a repetition of the musical celebration. The master was guaranteed 500 florins CM (1,200 florins WW); Duport wished to delete all of the *Missa* and substitute for it other vocal compositions by Beethoven with the addition of two solos by other composers to be sung by Italian singers. The management of the theatre would pay all costs and receive all profits. Beethoven was reluctant to have a repetition because of the first evening's miserable intake, but at last circumstances forced him to accept the proposed programme with only a few modifications.

The concert took place at noon on 23 May in the Great Redoutensaal. Of the *Missa* only the Kyrie was performed. The rest of the programme consisted of the great overture with the double fugue, opus 124; the trio *Tremate, empi* (not heard since 1814), sung by the stars of the Italian opera, Sgra. Dardanelli and the singers Donzelli and Botticelli; and the ninth symphony with the same soloists as at the first performance. Henriette Sontag also sang brilliantly one of her favourite bravura arias by Mercadante. A special drawing card was to be a performance of the cavatina from Rossini's *Tancredi*, 'Di tanti palpiti', written for contralto but sung on this occasion by the idolized tenor of the Italian opera, Davide, who transposed the piece several notes higher and sang it almost throughout in a falsetto. Fortunately our master did not hear this parody on the solemn occasion. And what was the financial success of the 23 May concert compared to that of the 7th, which we already know? The hall was not even half full, for the bright sun had lured the music-lovers out of doors. The theatre registered a deficit of 800 florins WW, and even the applause was weak in relation to the number of people in the audience.* Deeply pained at this unexpected rebuff, Beethoven at first refused the 500 florins he had been guaranteed, and consented to accept them only after the most urgent entreaties.

The author is by no means insensitive to the demands he has had to make on the reader's patience in this prolonged account of the events having to do with the performances of 7 and 23 May. He is therefore almost hesitant to add further to the matter, but what follows is related directly to the works that were performed and is therefore worthy of our attention; moreover, it serves as a not uninteresting supplementary episode. Remembering that descriptions of battles that have been fought generally deal in minute detail with the positions of the troops, the forward, backward, and lateral movements, the strategy and tactics of the commanders, the success or failure of each attack, comment on every mistake that was made, and even the ultimate consequences of the success or failure of the action, for it all educates and enlightens the student in the art of warfare—remembering this, then, the author feels that these supplementary episodes should not be omitted, especially as in one way or another they serve to fill in the picture of our glorious general on the battlefield of music.

Our account should open with an incident connected with Karl Bernard that took place a few days before the first concert.

Beethoven had entrusted to this friend the task of writing the notices for the public papers. Bernard was at that time on the staff of the old and esteemed *Wiener Zeitschrift*. He was of the opinion that, lacking any title or order, even the degree of doctor of philosophy or of political science, the master's interests would be advanced by an enumeration of the honorary distinctions he had been awarded. His announcement accordingly read: 'Ludwig van Beethoven, honorary member of the Royal Academies of Arts and Sciences at Stockholm and Amsterdam and also honorary citizen of the Royal and Imperial Capital and Residence City of Vienna, will . . .' etc. No sooner had the master read these words than he addressed to Bernard a decree in the despotic language of a sultan. Bernard was commanded to avoid in the future 'such childish display that could lead only to ridicule'. To make sure that the announcement contained nothing of the kind, Beethoven had a copy sent to him for his approval before publication.

---

* Ever since the second decade of the nineteenth century, when the Viennese had lost their unfettered love of pleasure, no German city could claim an audience as undependable in respect to its demonstrations of approbation as Vienna, for art cannot gamble and remain effective. Every standard of measurement for appropriate and just show of applause had been lost. That is why Beethoven used to call Vienna's music-lovers 'music-haters' (Kunstfreunde—Kunstfeinde).

Another typical incident occurred during the rehearsals of the solo parts in the *Missa* and the fourth movement of the symphony, and involved Beethoven and the female soloists. First of all we need to mention that both women were young, and as most of their training had been in Italian music, they failed to grasp the greatness and difficulty of the work they now faced. Both felt that any notes their voices could not comfortably reach could be changed.

The preliminary rehearsals took place in Beethoven's lodgings, and Beethoven himself played the voice parts on the piano. Henriette Sontag's desire to be allowed to sing *mezza voce* at first was granted, although this made the contralto's task more difficult and was a strain on Beethoven's weak hearing. But when the really serious study of the work began, when the master asked to hear the full chest tones, when the broad rhythm of the Christe in the Kyrie section of the *Missa* was to be delivered in a round, resonant tone, both 'pretty witches' weakened and began to argue with the master about speeding up the tempo of the movement. They were refused, of course, but in a good-natured manner. When the symphonic movement was rehearsed in earnest and the master would make none of the revisions they asked, storm clouds gathered and Caroline Unger was bold enough to tell the master to his face that he was a tyrant over all vocal cords. Beethoven replied, smiling, that both singers had been spoiled by Italian music which accounted for their present difficulties. 'But these high notes here,' rejoined Frl. Sontag, pointing to the words *Küsse gab sie uns und Reben*, 'couldn't they be changed?' 'And how about this place?' chimed in Frl. Unger, 'It is too high for my contralto voice. Couldn't you change it?' No! no! and no again! 'Oh, all right! Let's struggle on with it for God's sake,' said Frl. Sontag, and that was an end to it.

Similar complaints were loudly voiced during the rehearsals of the theatre's chorus. The chorus director pleaded for certain simplifications, especially in the soprano part. No. Finally he contented himself with requesting a change in the four B flats above the staff that the sopranos had to sing in the fugue subject of the Credo, protesting that none of his sopranos could reach high B flat.[208] Kapellmeister Umlauf also came to his aid. Their pleas were in vain; the master would countenance no alteration of the score.

The result of this obstinacy was that the soloists and members of the chorus made their own simplifications: when they could not reach the high notes as written, the sopranos simply did not sing. Anyway, the composer, though he was standing in the midst of the ensemble, could hear nothing of what went on! No one could remember that he had ever been so obdurate in the past. Ignaz von Seyfried says in the chapter of anecdotes and personality traits in *Beethovens Studien*: 'Our Beethoven was not at any rate one of those self-centred composers whom no orchestra can satisfy', etc. What then of the events of 1824 and the voice parts? When a composer, contrary to his own best interests and judgement, treats the human voice like an instrument, the only thing he can do is to wage a peevish war in defence of his caprice. Preisinger procured the one single alteration that was made. It occurs in the bass recitative of the fourth movement, and is reproduced here to inspire the gratitude of every genuine *basso* who ever undertakes this part. The passage originally read:

Ex. 14

The revision goes like this:

Ex. 15

This change was not enough to protect Preisinger's voice from strain. After repeated rehearsals, his voice gave way, and Seipelt, the *basso* of the Theater an der Wien, though his voice was excessively nasal, was kind enough to sing the bass solos at the performance after only one rehearsal.

And now for the *Missa Solemnis*. When the story of the composition of this colossal work was first mentioned, we noted that the composer here brought all his wealth of art and knowledge to its fullest fruition, though he received relatively little for it. The publisher's fee for the work will be stated later. But as yet the *Missa* has brought to the whole world of art very little specific gain. The lamentable truth is that the work has given rise to widely divergent reactions. These two latter points are worthy of closer analysis, and this seems the appropriate place.

If one wishes to make an unbiased evaluation of this work, one must confess that in disregarding canonical principles Beethoven surpassed Cherubini's second mass in D, though the latter is a considerably longer work.[209] A critical examination may be severe without being unjust, for a sentence from Beethoven's letter to Zelter gives us his own criterion: 'Anyway, one complete number is already *a cappella*, and I would like to call this style the only true church music.' First of all, the Agnus and Dona nobis sections of the *Missa* can hardly settle the argument, for it is apparent from the composer's own words that he placed himself in a position in which no one with pious inclinations could easily follow him. The indication at the beginning of the Dona nobis, 'Plea for inward and outward peace', could have done nothing to induce the composer to withdraw this section entirely from the realm of church music, for he included in it trumpet fanfares, recitatives, and even a whole symphonic movement in *tempo presto*. Thus the conception of what is appropriate to church music (in our time, at any rate) was not only stretched to the furthest point, it was so completely disregarded that even the artistic wealth of the work could not redeem it. Moreover, the composer's statement that the *Missa* could also be performed as an oratorio could not reconcile the differences, for even a concert-hall audience would demand appropriate interpretation and treatment of a religious text. We should not be misled by the composer's words in his subscription invitation, where he calls this work his most successful and most perfect. It would be more accurate to recognize in these words an out-and-out contradiction of the self-criticism he expressed in the above-quoted sentence addressed to Zelter.

The argument that is revived with every new performance of the *Missa* would be settled, and the whole work would be improved if, as in the dramatic works of the greatest composers and even in Handel's oratorios, the dramatic section of the Dona that many justifiably find so offensive were omitted. If there is no feasible way to cross over the wide, though divided, stream, the crossing must be effected at the expense of a few beautiful moments. One could well skip from the second measure on page 252 of the score to the first measure on page 289 where the full chorus and orchestra enter with a marvellous D major section and carry the movement to its conclusion.[210] This advice is not intended for the fanatical Beethovenians: they would never admit a mistake by the great composer, nor the need to omit anything.

The reporter for the AmZ (XXVI (1824) 439) spoke for all in Vienna who, having heard this movement several times in 1824, were competent to pass judgement on it:

The character of the Agnus Dei in B minor is anxious melancholy and deep sorrow; the extraordinary use of four horns produces a remarkable effect here. The Dona opens with a pleasant Allegretto in D major, $\frac{6}{8}$ time, which is developed with charming variations until suddenly the movement modulates to B flat major, the timpani begins to rumble on the dominant like distant thunder, the alto soloist intones a recitative without any unifying rhythm, once more on the words *Agnus Dei qui tollis peccata mundi*. This outcry is answered by a flourish of trumpets in B flat until at last the full chorus breaks into a fearful shout: *Miserere nobis*. What the composer meant by this section is as hard to fathom* as his reason for the orchestral fugal passage in $\frac{3}{4}$ time that follows, during which no voices are heard until they return with a recapitulation of the Dona that serves as a sort of keystone to the whole movement. If only it were all more compact, less chopped up!

Another no less weighty bone of contention was the handling of the voices, in respect both to the overreaching of their natural range and to their musical treatment. This consideration is the prime reason why the work cannot be as beneficial to the world of music as one would wish, for a performance requires power, quite apart from excellent training in choral singing, such as one finds only in very few places. Thus after thirty years the *Missa* has remained a stranger to many large cities. It is worth while to explore briefly the reasons for this surprising phenomenon. All the choral compositions before the *Missa* prove that Beethoven was a master in the proper use of the voice. The books in his personal library that deal with the voice all show signs of having been used a great deal. Moreover the critics have generally had nothing but praise for Beethoven's handling of voices. Allow me just to quote the last words of a review of the vocal work *An die entfernte Geliebte*,[211] written only a few years before the *Missa* in 1816 and published in 1817 (AmZ XIX (1817) 73):

We are once again reminded that the master has here given perfect proof that when he wants to he not only can write songs as well as anyone else, which no one can doubt, but that he writes for singers; for, with the exception of only a very few places, it is impossible to write more flowingly or to compose a line more perfectly suited to the human voice.

If we cannot find in an ignorance of the rules setting forth the capability of the vocal organs the reasons for such unsingable handling of the voices in the *Missa*, where can we look? Some have claimed that when Beethoven was still able to hear, the orchestral pitch had been a half-tone lower than it is now, so that his whole being was conditioned to the lower pitch.[212] But think of the various circumstances surrounding the 1824 rehearsals, when undoubtedly the Viennese orchestral pitch was

---

* The audience was not told about the directions written over the Dona: 'Plea for inward and outward peace', nor is this explanation given to audiences today.

not even a quarter-tone higher than twenty years before, and think of all the well-founded complaints made then.* Even if we imagine the orchestral pitch half a tone lower than it now stands, will we find it so simple to do what is demanded of the voices in the Credo? And, aside from unheard-of difficulties in regard to high notes and the vocal line, how can we justify the countless *sforzando* notes for the voices and almost all the instruments, which make demands that violate all the rules of vocal composition and which are simply impossible for a chorus to perform? Then there are the wide leaps in all the voices: how is such an obstacle to smooth performance to be explained on the part of a composer familiar with the art of vocal writing? The unconditional admirers of Beethoven overlook these problems, many or most of which are imperceptible in the total performance, but they fail to take into account the excessive strain placed on the vocal organs and its serious results, especially with the enormous size of present-day orchestras.

But if the critic takes unbiased cognizance of these actual flaws, he will not be unfair in viewing them as the outcome of pure and simple caprice. When it comes to the master's later products, however, such an explanation would hardly be adequate; the reasons must be sought elsewhere. His deafness (to which practically everyone attributes them) has nothing to do with these reasons, for the master no more needed to hear with his ears what he had written down than another person needs to read aloud a letter he has just written. The god who had reigned as the creator within the artist sometimes abandoned him in his last years, and the man, weak and broken, remained behind. And how was the man to avoid being affected by his afflictions? To close one's eyes to them can only lead to dangerous and mistaken notions that would be harmful to art.

Yet there is more to add on this *opus summum viri summi*.

When the composer sent the fair copy of the score to the publisher, he had forgotten to indicate the tempo for the Benedictus. The master made haste to send the missing direction in a letter, but it was too late and the printing had already advanced too far for any additions to be made. Moreover, the publisher forgot to publish the correction later. For years all the performances of the Benedictus completely negated the character of the movement, for the conductors thought the *tempo sostenuto* that characterizes the prelude applied to the Benedictus as well. Then in 1853 Otto Jahn published Beethoven's letters to the publisher and it was learned that he had intended this movement to be *andante*

---

* In the third year (1855) of the *Niederrheinische Musik-Zeitung*, Nos. 8 and 9, this author had an article on the history of the changes in orchestral pitch in Vienna that were initiated in 1816 and continued thereafter.

molto cantabile e non troppo mosso. The present author lost no time in announcing this discovery by means of an article in the *Niederrheinische Musik-Zeitung*, and feels that it should also be included in this book.

On the occasion of a congress of German scientists and physicians at Bonn in September 1857, the city presented a musical celebration under the title, 'Beethoven Concert'. The programme included the Kyrie, Sanctus, and Benedictus from the *Missa*. In his review of this concert the editor of the *Niederrheinische Musik-Zeitung*, Ludwig Bischoff, posed the question:

Did Beethoven really write the two numbers Pleni sunt coeli and Osanna for four solo voices to sing against such frightful orchestral tumult? It seems to us that we read somewhere that he had intended it as a chorus. Perhaps A. Schindler would be kind enough to instruct us on this point. For our part, we would not regard it as a crime to have these numbers sung by the chorus. (Issue No. 39.)

The forty-first issue of the same periodical contains my reply, the principal import of which reads:

The information I am able to give on this point is very brief compared to traditional music analyses. . . . While Beethoven and I were occupied with correcting the scores to be sent to the subscribers, we had the following conversation concerning these movements: I remarked that it seemed to me that the two movements would be more effective if sung by full chorus than if sung by four solo voices. I also objected to the small use made of the chorus in the Sanctus and Benedictus, for I felt it was unfortunate that they should sit through these movements as passive listeners. Beethoven replied at length, but the substance was that 'Solo voices it must be'.

Beethoven, who would frequently go into panegyrics on the past, especially in matters of music, liked to compose for the great singers of his time. When he was writing these two movements—in fact, when he was writing the entire *Missa*—he had in mind singers like Tomeoni, Buchwieser, and even Milder (his Leonore in the 1814 *Fidelio*) or Campi, Anna Wranitzky, and others of a comparable quality. The calibre of these singers justifies his intention (an expression indicating the highest degree of inspiration), especially if the orchestra were the small ensemble generally used in churches. But since our time has not produced such great singers, and since the orchestras today are so tremendously massive, some adjustment must be made, for it is inconceivable to oppose a weak voice with a huge orchestra in a concert hall. Even a small chorus would be lost, for each of the four voices is accompanied or rather pulled along by a number of instruments playing *forte* or *fortissimo*. This constitutes an inner contradiction. I regard the tempo marking for the Pleni as an outward contradiction. The colouring of all the voices obviously calls for a lightly moving rhythm, yet the movement is marked *allegro pesante*, which imposes a leaden weight on the motion. What is the reason for the word *pesante* (heavy, weighty) here, a term hardly known in the ordinary lists of tempo designations? No wonder, when the conductors are misled by an erroneous direction, the four voices have such a hard time performing the movement! An Allegro moderato in the tradition of the classicists would in any case be the correct indication for the tempo of this movement.

If it should ever happen that this gigantic work were sung with German text as in the case of the Mass in C major, the person setting the text (and he must be an expert) will have little difficulty in correcting these errors. At that time the orchestral passage within the Dona will be given the true basis for its existence, for in a piece of church music, as the Latin mass must always be considered, it has no apparent validity.

Let us therefore hesitate no longer; let the movements Pleni and Osanna, at least in the concert hall, always be performed by full chorus. The effect on the spirit of the whole work will then be extraordinary.

To enumerate all the requests for explanations, either of the whole work or of sections, that over the years have been addressed to this author would take too long. Yet they are not without interest, for almost all of them bespeak an unconcealed fear of battling with the work. A statistical summary of the complete performances in Germany between the publication of the work in 1827 and the present time should be included here because of its historical interest.[213]

The first performance was on the occasion of the unveiling of Beethoven's statue in Bonn in 1845 under the direction of Ludwig Spohr. This performance broke the ice in musical circles of the Lower Rhine and far beyond. It is principally to the royal music director in Cologne, Franz Weber, that we owe thanks for his faith that a performance of the *Missa* was not only possible but (and this is of far greater significance) that its performance could be perfect in every respect. With unflagging zeal he spent months rehearsing all the participating choral societies of the Rhine Province in their respective towns, thereby achieving a sureness and unity that was a source of wonder to the thousands of listeners who came from all parts of Europe.

The second complete performance took place a full ten years later. It was a benefit concert for those affected by the flooding of the lower Rhine, and took place on Palm Sunday 1855 under the direction of Ferdinand Hiller. The participants were the Concert Society of Cologne and all other musical associations of that city.

In the latter part of 1855 the music director Rühl in Frankfurt had the courage to have his newly organized choral group perform the work with the theatre orchestra. This was the third in the list of performances.

The fourth was in May 1856 in Berlin by the Stern choral society, and the fifth was on 1 November of the same year in the Odeon Theatre in Munich under the direction of Franz Lachner.

Repeat performances in Cologne, Frankfurt, Berlin, and Munich followed one another in close succession. The reviews we have of these concerts describe the reception on the part of most hearers as marked appreciation.

Another complete performance must be mentioned. It took place on 4 August 1857 in the Freiburg cathedral in Baden on the occasion of the University's centennial. In the series of performances this was the sixth, but as a performance for High Mass it was the first.

Research in the musical periodicals does not reveal any more complete performances. The NZfM XI (1839) 36 mentions a performance in 1830 in Warnsdorf near Rumburg in Bohemia, but it does not say whether this was a performance of the complete *Missa* or only of sections.[214] Portions of the work (the Kyrie, Gloria, and Credo) were performed at High Mass in the Cologne Cathedral in 1838; the other movements were taken from the Mass in C major.[215] Also in Breslau and by the Cäcilien-Verein in Frankfurt,[216] sections were sung from time to time. The latter choral group has not even yet attempted the Credo. About 1840 there was a performance at the music festival in Lusatia, but it is not certain whether the complete work was presented or only portions of it.

As for the highly musical imperial states of Austria, with their five or six existing conservatories, the work has not been attempted to my knowledge, with the exception of the one performance in Bohemia that was mentioned.

This statistical enumeration demonstrates that in thirty years the *Missa Solemnis* has brought the musical world very little in the way of monetary profit. Let us hope that in the next thirty years the results will be more favourable.

These critical observations, which may be worthy of notice at some later date, even if not at present, brought about a break in our discussion of the events surrounding the memorable days of 7 and 23 May 1824. Let us hasten to close our account of these events with a final incident that introduced the first jarring note into my eight years' association with the master, and that struck a harsh dissonance in the small circle of true friends and admirers.

Beethoven felt under obligations to Umlauf, Schuppanzigh, and me for the trouble we had taken. To express his thanks, he proposed a dinner at the tavern 'Zum wilden Mann' in the Prater a few days after the second concert.[216a] He appeared with stormy countenance, accompanied by his nephew. He was the reverse of cordial; everything he said was biting and critical. We all expected some sort of outburst. As soon as we had sat down he launched into a discourse on the financial outcome of the first concert, accusing the manager, Duport, and me pointblank of conspiring to cheat him. Umlauf and Schuppanzigh attempted to prove to him the impossibility of any fraud, reminding him that every coin had passed through the hands of both theatre cashiers, that the reports agreed exactly, and that his nephew had, at the insistence of the apothecary-brother and contrary to all custom, stayed with the cashiers as a sort of inspector. Beethoven, however, stuck to his accusations, adding that he had been informed of the fraud by reliable sources. I waited to hear no more. As quickly as possible Umlauf and I departed, and Schuppanzigh, after having received a few volleys on his ample person, soon followed. We repaired to the tavern 'Zum goldenen Lamm' in Leopoldstadt to resume in peace our interrupted meal. The furious master was left to vent his spleen on the waiters and the ceiling beams and to eat the elaborate meal alone in the company of his nephew.

This incident may serve to typify Beethoven's behaviour towards his friends, so that we shall not need to speak of it again. Ferdinand Ries gives witness to its first manifestations at the beginning of the second period of the composer's life. But as external hardships and internal depressions piled up in the course of the third period, his most faithful friends, including the Archduke, as we have seen, suffered greater and greater discourtesies at his hands. It was always insults that drove his friends away. Gullible, inexperienced, suspicious as he was, jealous plotters had no difficulty in blackening the name of every one of his friends; and in addition to his brothers there were always plenty of such creatures about. It was to them he owed a considerable number of bitter experiences. On his deathbed he made to Breuning and me a general confession of all these sins, along with an account of some specific incidents. Yet he would often bring about a reconciliation, and in such a candid, generous manner, openly acknowledging his fault, that one immediately forgot one's hurt pride. It was in this mood that he approached me in November of that year after his return from Baden, and everything that had happened was consigned to oblivion. Where there is much light there is also much shadow, and Goethe's words, 'Whether one is great or little, one must always suffer for one's humanity', apply in more than one respect to Beethoven.

Before continuing with our historical narrative, we should mention in passing another plan to go to London. Just at the time of the troubles in connection with the choral concerts, Beethoven received from Charles Neate, the London composer who several years before had spent some time in Vienna, an invitation to visit England. He immediately decided to go the following autumn, accompanied by the author of this book. His ever-lively imagination helped in elaborating his travelling plans, as he thought of stopping to see old friends in his native land, Wegeler in Coblenz, father Ries and the music publisher Simrock in

Bonn, who for a long time had been concerned about him. But the events that occurred just after the concert caused him to forget all his travel projects. The last days of this year brought another invitation from Neate, dated 20 December and written at the direct command of the Philharmonic Society. We still have this letter, a part of which reads as follows:

The Philharmonic Society has proposed to give you the sum of 300 guineas for your visit and expects that in return you will conduct the performances of your works, at least one of which will be included in each concert. The Society also expects that you will write one symphony and one concerto to be performed during your stay with us, but which will then be your property. . . . You would be able to give a concert at which you would make at least £500. In short, there are many ways to use your talent and your fame. If you bring along your quartets, there would be another £100,[217] so that you may be assured a large sum of money to take home with you. I see no reason why you should not take enough to make your future life much more comfortable.

I hope you will reply without delay, and say that you accept the proposal. I shall take advantage of this opportunity to tell you that I am your true friend and that you will find yourself surrounded by many who will seize this occasion to show their respect and admiration for the great Beethoven, whose fame now shines in this land more brilliantly than ever before.

Why did Beethoven not accept these generous proposals with their promise of·a better life and a greater fame, quite apart from his desire to visit the land of the golden guinea? Degenerate behaviour on the part of his nephew, the adopted son whom he still loved beyond measure, had already attracted considerable attention, and was the reason Beethoven put aside all thought of going abroad.[218] The numerous deeply disturbing incidents involving this boy will occupy our close attention later on.

Now, with the troubles in connection with the performance of the *Missa* and the ninth symphony behind him, and the unhappy consequences duly recorded; now, once Beethoven was back in his beloved Baden, the question naturally arose as to which of the long-projected works he should turn to next, the tenth symphony or the oratorio *Der Sieg des Kreuzes* for the GdMf. For we heard him say in 1822 to Rochlitz's suggestion that he write music for Goethe's *Faust*, that he must first get two great symphonies, each one different from his others, and an oratorio 'off his chest'. One of the symphonies was now behind him. We would expect, therefore, that both inner pressure and the promises made so often would prompt him to turn to the oratorio, thereby doing the honourable thing by the poet who had spent so much time adapting his text to the composer's requirements.[219] Everyone knows that this oratorio does not exist in the Beethoven literature any more than a tenth symphony does. We could give positive reasons for this negative fact or we might simply pass over it without comment. It is because of my friendly censor that I kept silence on the matter in the first edition. Dr. Bach gave reasons for omitting this apparent mystery, and his reasons seemed convincing at the time.

But now rumours have emanated from Vienna to the effect that Beethoven died owing the GdMf a considerable sum of money, and it is my duty to discuss the matter. Here, then, let me resort to my 'German thoroughness'. I already wrote (and see p. 270) that the question had been formally recorded in the journal of the society concerned. The president of the Society lost no time after the concerts were over in using various means to remind the master of his frequent promises that his very next composition would be the oratorio. These solicitations called forth written answers, of which we still have accurate copies. It is my hope that the inclusion here of excerpts from the Society's minutes will be sufficient to settle the question to the satisfaction of all parties.

Excerpts from the minutes of the Society of Music-Lovers of the Austrian Imperial Capital City of Vienna concerning the composition of an oratorio by Herr Ludwig van Beethoven.

(1) See entry No. 112 for the year 1815. Herr von Zmeskall was asked to use his influence with Beethoven to fulfil the Society's desires. After a long delay, Beethoven wrote to Zmeskall that he was ready to undertake this honourable commission and asked that the Society grant him a fee of 400 gold ducats.

(2) Accordingly, in 1818, under entry No. 191, the Society charged Herr Vincenz Hauschka to negotiate with Beethoven on the following terms: that for a payment of 200 ducats in gold Beethoven should write an oratorio of a heroic nature for the exclusive use of the Society for the year after its first performance.

(3) Beethoven answered by a letter from Mödling dated 15 June 1819, entered in the minutes under No. 254, that he was in full agreement, acknowledging the receipt of 400 florins WW as an advance against the oratorio to be composed.

(4) In 1820, under minute No. 303, a letter dated 21 December 1820 was sent by the Society to the poet Bernard asking when he could deliver the text of this oratorio for Beethoven.

(5) Bernard replied (minute No. 384 for the year 1823) that two years before he had given Beethoven the first section of the text with a detailed outline of the whole poem, and that at the date of writing (22 October 1823) Beethoven was in possession of the complete text.

(6) Minute No. 393 for 15 February 1825 states that the Society had instructed Hr. Hauschka to pay Hr. Bernard the remainder of the fee for the oratorio.

Two letters from Beethoven to the member of the Music Society charged with following the project, the finance councillor Hr. Vincenz Hauschka, should be given in this context.

1.

Dear, valued friend:

Since I am writing to you to say that as soon as I have returned to the city I will write the Bernard oratorio, I request that you release the honorarium to Hr. Bernard. Beyond that, we will discuss in the city what in addition we need and require, since I hail you as the most puissant Intendant of all singing and humming societies, as the Imperial and Royal Violoncello-in-Chief, as the I. R. Inspector of all I. R. hunts, as the deacon of my most gracious master without domicile, without house or home, and (like myself) without a stipend, the most faithful servant of my most gracious lord—I wish you this and that, of which you may select the best.* So that there may be no mistake, we assure you that absolutely without fail we will set Bernard's oratorio *Der Sieg des Kreuzes* to music, and will finish it very soon, as attested herewith by our hand and seal.

L. van Beethoven

Baden, 23 September 1824

2.

Best Chief Member of the Society and Great Cross of the Order of the Violoncello!

I have only a sacred subject, but you want a heroic one! That suits me too, but I think that for such a mass of people it would be quite in order to mix in a little of the sacred. Hr. Bernard would be quite satisfactory to me, but it is up to you to pay him—I say nothing about myself. Since after all you call yourselves Friends of Music, it is to be expected that you stand ready to act generously in this regard. . . .

As for myself, I wander about here in the mountains, ravines, and valleys with a piece of music paper, and scrawl much for the sake of bread and money, for in this all-powerful, disgraceful Land of the Phaeacians[220] I have attained such heights that to gain for myself some time to write a great work, I must first do a vast amount of scribbling† to secure money to maintain myself for the great work.

Aside from that, my health is greatly improved, and if time is pressing I can accommodate you. . . .

In haste, your friend Beethoven

The second letter is not dated, but seems without question to have been written in 1818 as the answer to Hauschka's request that Beethoven compose a heroic oratorio for the Society. The words, 'wander about here in the mountains, ravines, and valleys', quite clearly indicate

---

* Sarcastic reference to the functionary of the imperial and royal court, the ever-faithful Vincenz Hauschka.

† By 'scribbling' Beethoven may have had in mind the composition of the *Six Varied Themes* opus 105 and the *Ten Varied Themes* opus 107, and perhaps the Scottish songs opus 108, all of which were written about this time.

this year (of which we have already discussed various occurrences), when the master spent the summer in Mödling. Abbé Stadler's heroic oratorio, *Die Befreiung von Jerusalem*, which had just been performed several times by the Society with extraordinary success, was probably the inspiration for the request from the Society that Beethoven should write a similar work.

Of special interest to us in these two letters are the remarks having to do with the master himself, for they give us quite a clear picture of his unhappy financial situation. As for his invectives against Austria, we need take no note of them. His frequent attacks on this 'Land of the Phaeacians', in direct allusion to his means of subsistence, were without foundation. This may be proved in a number of ways. An additional piece of evidence is contained in the commission from the Music Society. With a fee of two hundred ducats from this society and three hundred ducats (for a major oratorio) from Steiner & Co., or from any other publisher, in prospect, the master might have had five hundred ducats in his pocket at the end of the year.

Moreover, 1818 was the year he had planned to go to London. In 1823 there was the invitation from the Emperor to write a mass and some smaller church pieces. There were the simultaneous invitations from Vienna and Berlin to compose an opera. Another prospect of that year was an edition of his complete works under conditions that were certainly very favourable. Then in 1824 there was Diabelli's offer of eighty ducats for a sonata for four hands, which he accepted. And finally there came in the same year the advantageous invitation from the Philharmonic Society of London. All these opportunities prove that our master was offered many ways and means of materially improving his mode of life, not to mention the opportunity these commissions offered to fulfil his own desires, for he often protested that he wished he could write only major works and not have to 'scribble', that he desired above all to be of greater service to the art he so devoutly adored. This desire he was soon to fulfil with a series of chamber works.

The master's state of affairs brings to mind the reproach often levelled at the whole German fatherland: that it leaves its great men to live in want or die of hunger. This complaint was trumpeted abroad throughout the world after Beethoven's death and recently has been revived, again in the most exaggerated terms, with the deaths of Lortzing and Konradin Kreutzer. Those who shout the loudest generally choose to ignore the bad temper, the capriciousness, and the mistakes (usually consciously made) on the part of artists, poets, and scholars to the detriment of their own material interests, and heap the blame for their misfortunes upon Germany alone. As we have just conclusively illustrated, Beethoven himself bore sole responsibility for his poverty.

I could show the same in the case of Kreutzer, partly by means of letters he wrote to me, partly by means of what his wife has written, partly through what I observed from personal experience. I could prove that his bad temper, especially his conceit, his scheming nature at a time of great and undeserved good fortune (1823 to 1830), and an exaggerated self-esteem so overbearing that he made a show of belittling Beethoven, brought him to the state of wretchedness in which his life ended, far from his homeland. He knew how to be the forger of his good fortune, but he did not know the art of maintaining himself at the peak of fate's cycle.

To return to the course of our history, we must next take a look at Beethoven's further relations with the Viennese musical society and with his patient, obliging friend, the poet Bernard. He did not answer the Society's letter of October 1824, which repeated the request for a heroic oratorio, just as he had ignored in silence so many other promised projects. As for Bernard's poem, Beethoven seemed from now on to find nothing good to say about it. His promises to the Society, written, signed, and sealed, were nothing to him. His many assurances of complete satisfaction with Bernard's poem were forgotten, and even the dissolution of an old friendship and the poet's withdrawal from his circle seemed to trouble him very little. The president of the Society let the situation rest, though it must have been most painful to him, and never took steps to recover the 400 florins he had advanced to Beethoven in 1819.

For this biographer, who was a close observer of all these events, reporting them is by no means a pleasant task, but in the interests of truth they may not be kept secret. Since the whole affair is recorded in the minutes and letters of the GdMf, that organization deserves nothing but praise for its open and honest treatment, while Beethoven is truly to be blamed. Let me add in his defence only that throughout the course of his whole life he never a second time exhibited a similar character trait. Yet this deviation from the principles he had always upheld in regard to his dealings with others constitutes a surprising psychological phenomenon deserving of our consideration.

What reasons can be given for such a departure from the master's principles? Two positive ones may be offered: Beethoven's excess of love for his nephew, and a commission from the Russian prince, Nicko-lai Borissovitch Galitsin, for the composition of a group of quartets. The first reason became from this time on a greater and greater factor in the master's course of action. A third reason may well have been Beethoven's artistic individuality, which could not easily tolerate any limitations placed on his work other than those imposed by musical laws. And the composition of the oratorio would have involved such limitations. The many grievances voiced by the singers and singing teachers over the excesses in the *Missa* and the ninth symphony could not have failed to have an effect on him, even though he showed none. In composing instrumental music, his poetic subjectivity was bound by no rules other than the rules of harmony that had long since been absorbed into his very being. Here the flow of his rich fantasy was impeded by no difficult verse, no questions of syntax, nor any of the other countless considerations of vocal music. It was in instrumental music alone that Beethoven found himself in his own true element, and it is this tenacity to his inborn preference that accounts for his profound, immortal creations.

In order to conform to the chronology of events, however, let us leave the story of the quartets to the next chapter, of which it will form a considerable portion. The dispute that took place in 1852 and 1853 between Prince Galitsin and the author on the subject of the quartets aroused lively interest in the reading public, most of whom sided with the Prince, at least until the counter-arguments were published. To avoid excessive verbiage, the dispute will be only touched upon in its chronological place, but in Beethoven's interests it is more fully elaborated upon in the supplement.[221] I owe to this dispute the opportunity to correct a few unimportant errors, and also the satisfaction of being able to substantiate all the significant things I said on this subject in the first edition of this book.

I do not hesitate to confess that the chapter now to be entered upon discusses many points that are most painful to me. Many of these unpleasant incidents were omitted in the first edition. It is now, however, imperative that I describe certain events, most of which took place before my eyes and which are furthermore substantiated by documentary evidence. These events show an almost unbelievable reversal of our master's maxims and principles, but the roots of this transformation could be explained only by a psychologist.[222] The spiritual life of the individual was apparently split into two distinct and different halves, which nevertheless touched at a certain point and under certain conditions supplemented each other.

After the ninth symphony, the highest triumph of orchestral music perhaps of all time, the spontaneity of its creator seemed to wane. Moreover, reflection occupied an ever-increasing area of the master's being; indeed, it became a governing characteristic of the artist who had up to this time always composed freely and spontaneously. On the other hand, arithmetic preoccupied the master to such an extraordinary extent that any time left free from artistic reflection was filled by commercial speculation. For a third intellectual pursuit there was almost nothing left, unless it be newspaper reading and interest in politics.

This turning point in his essential being became obvious in 1824, although indications of it had been apparent in the two previous years and in his artistic productions, as witness the second movement of the sonata opus 111. Concrete proof of this is the story of the window-shutters and their inscriptions from the guest house in Baden, as well as calculations scribbled in the margins of his manuscript papers. Every halfway-suitable surface was covered with long columns of figures. Only a family misfortune in 1826 had the power of calling an imperative halt to the speculations into which the master had sunk. He heeded this call and raised himself once more in word and deed to his native artistic mentality. Alas! this reawakening came only after many opportunities had been lost!

[IV]

A CHAPTER OF CONTRADICTIONS
AND CONTROVERSIES

— 1824 and 1825 —

The period of commercial speculation, when poetry was subordinate to business, begins in the first months of 1824, right in the midst of the preparations for the performance of the *Missa Solemnis* and the ninth symphony, under the exclusive instigation of the 'pseudo-brother', Johann van Beethoven, that cunning and experienced master of this particular craft.[223]

In contrast to his usual practice of discussing every plan he made with his closest friends, Beethoven did not say a word about what he had in mind. But as always, he left his letters and Conversation Books lying about, and it was an easy matter for one who saw him every day to read them. The immediate goal of his speculation was to find a publisher who would buy the *Missa* and the ninth symphony as a single lot, together with the C major overture, opus 124, a string quartet that was still to be written, and some small pieces. To this end he wrote to Diabelli in Vienna, Probst in Leipzig,[224] Schott in Mainz, Schlesinger in Berlin, and perhaps others as well. We have three letters of reply from Probst, the first dated 22 March 1824. There are five from Schott (all addressed to 'Herr Hof-Kapellmeister Beethoven'), the first of which is dated 24 March 1824. Nothing has been found from Schlesinger,[225] and Diabelli said he wanted to buy only the *Missa*.

The Leipzig publisher asked for the overture, three songs, and six bagatelles, but declined the *Missa* and the ninth symphony. We may appropriately quote here a few amusing lines from his third letter, written on 16 August of that year, in answer to one written from Vienna on 28 July:

I should have liked to publish your ninth symphony, but I hope to retain the assurance of your confidence and friendship. Unfortunately the piratical reprinting of first editions everywhere, and especially in Austria, often prevents the German publisher from paying the appropriate price for a work. Already I see the Vienna thieves lurking about on the look-out for works you are about to compose, in order to rob me under protection of the law. One could not publish anything that was any good and still be safe from them, and I would not be any kind of a music publisher if I gave the world something bad.

This excerpt shows that free plundering flourished among German publishers in the year 1824—to the disgrace of all governments and to the detriment of all writers—just as it had at the beginning of the century. Was there not one which did not permit itself to take liberties with the property of a colleague?

The publishing firm of Schott in Mainz asked in its first letter only for the projected quartet, for which it would immediately deposit fifty ducats in Vienna as an advance against the delivery of the manuscript. With regard to the *Missa* and the symphony, they proposed to pay the required price in four half-yearly instalments, explaining: 'Under this arrangement we would dare to undertake the publication of these two very great and very important compositions, and we would be proud to engrave them as beautifully as possible and to engrave the parts as well as the score so that the works might be performed without delay.' In a later letter of 27 April 1824, from the same publisher, we read: 'We should appreciate an answer to our letters of 24 March and 10 April.' This letter also expresses the wish that Beethoven should name his own terms of payment.

A letter from Schott, dated 19 July 1824, announced the consummation of the transaction in the following words: 'In reply to your valued letter of the 3rd inst., we wish to proceed with no more loss of time, for we have agreed with the firm of Fries & Co. that they draw against our account in accordance with the terms you named and that they put at your disposal the stipulated sum. You will accordingly have the goodness to deliver to Fries & Co. the two manuscripts, namely the great Mass and the new great symphony.' The agreement between the artist and this publishing house was for 1,000 florins CM (128 Napoleons d'or) for the *Missa* and 600 florins CM for the symphony.[226]

In the first edition of this book, we said that Prince Nicolai Borissovitch Galitsin still owed Beethoven 125 florins for the three quartets he had commissioned the composer to write for him.[227] In 1852 the Prince brought the matter into the open in an 'Explanation directed to Herr Brendel, editor of the *Neue Zeitschrift für Musik*'. The announcement was published in the issue of 6 August (No. 6) for that year. But as early as 1832 Seyfried had written, on page 12 of the section called 'Character

Traits and Anecdotes' in his book *Beethovens Studien,* of the 'sum of 125 ducats that Beethoven had not received for compositions delivered to a foreign prince'. We learn from Galitsin's 'Explanation' that Beethoven had set a price of fifty ducats for each quartet and that the Prince had sent the money for the first one in 1822; that is, he had deposited it with the banking house of Henickstein & Co. for Beethoven to withdraw upon delivery of the manuscript. In the same 'Explanation' we read this extremely surprising sentence: 'I am sorry to have to tell you that during my association with Beethoven it became clear to me that his delicacy was not equal to his genius.'

The Prince later explains this slanderous invective against the master by saying that the publishing firm of Schott in Mainz had received the first quartet much earlier than he himself, that he had been 'shoved aside', as he expressed it, and had not received the work until March 1825. He adds: 'With the best will in the world one could not regard such action as being of a nature that one could term delicate behaviour' (NZfM, 1853, No. 2).

It is a simple matter to answer this charge. The quartet in question, E flat major opus 127, was completed in the first weeks of the year 1825 and performed publicly by Schuppanzigh in March of that year (AmZ XXVII (1825) 246). It was not until after this performance that the manuscript was sent to Mainz. Thus the Prince's accusation is unfounded.[228]

To give a clearer picture of the composer's speculative period, let us go back for a moment to the year 1822 in order to expose a situation so bizarre on all counts that it would be difficult to believe if we did not have the proof before us. This situation can undoubtedly be viewed as a consequence of Prince Galitsin's quartet commission.[229] Our proof is contained in a letter from Charles Neate to Beethoven, written in French and dated, 'Londres, le 2 septembre 1822'.[230] This letter is a reply to a request from the master that Neate sell the manuscripts of three new quartets in London.* He had been led to believe that the works were already finished. Since, however, we are told by Friedrich Rochlitz that in the summer of 1822 Beethoven announced his intention of writing two new symphonies and an oratorio, we are almost forced to conclude from the steps taken in London that these three quartets were to be composed before the three proposed major works. For it would be the purest folly to put garden vegetables up for sale two or three years before they had even been planted.

* The reader may be surprised that in such a delicate situation Beethoven turned to a stranger rather than to refer the transaction to Ferdinand Ries, who up to that time had attended to the master's commercial affairs in London. The master had for some time entertained a grudge against his friend and pupil,[231] and was too preoccupied with his own advancement to speak openly. If he had done so, many stumbling blocks between them might have been removed and perhaps the tension could have been relieved entirely. These matters may be more appropriately discussed in the musical portion of this book.

Let us see the essential part of Neate's letter:

It is a very unpleasant duty that I must discharge in making you the following announcement. It was my intention to ask a number of musical friends to join me in purchasing the manuscript of your three quartets, as I am not rich enough myself to buy them alone, though I am ready to subscribe my portion. I foresaw no obstacle to such an arrangement, but I am sorry to say that I have encountered more difficulties than I had expected. Some say they must be absolutely certain of the arrival of the manuscript; others claim that they do not wish to deprive the public of them, etc. However, I think I can finally manage to get you the sum of 100 pounds sterling; but I am sorry to add that it cannot be paid until the manuscript has arrived here, because I shall have to collect the funds and I am quite sure that the friends to whom I addressed myself will fulfil their obligations as soon as the manuscript is here. There is one more difficulty: some fear that the quartets will have been copied in Vienna. I am confident that you will take care to prevent such a thing.

This last sentence implies more clearly than all the rest that this transaction was intended not for a publisher but for an individual or a group of individuals to undertake in private, and that these quartets would be reserved for the exclusive use of this person or these persons for a certain period, perhaps for the space of one year, as in the case of the art-lover in St. Petersburg. For my part, I can only see the mind of the 'pseudo-brother' behind this incredibly strange London scheme, for his head alone was capable of hatching a plan that could dishonour the composer to such an extent. How distressing to Beethoven the distrust of his word so openly expressed in this letter from London![232]

While speaking of the subscription copies of the *Missa Solemnis*, we noted in passing that Beethoven sent a copy to Prince Galitsin and received for it the fifty ducats that had been deposited in Vienna for the first of the quartets ordered. There is no reason for assuming that this happened without the foreknowledge and consent of the Prince.[233] From the controversy between the Prince and the author certain facts emerged clearly: the sending of the copy, the receipt of the fifty ducats, and the replacement of this withdrawn sum by an equal deposit from St. Petersburg. We have the translation of a letter from the Prince to Beethoven concerning his receipt of the *Missa*. The letter is dated 29 November 1823, and begins:

It was with inexpressible joy, dear sir, that I received the Mass that you recently composed, and though until now I have been able to judge it only from the score, I have found the same grandeur in it that distinguishes all your compositions and makes your works impossible of imitation. I am trying to get this work performed in a manner worthy of its creator and of those who help to bring about the festival for the purpose of hearing it.

THIRD PERIOD

In another existing letter of 11 March 1824, the Prince speaks of the promised quartets. Here he writes explicitly:

I pray you, let me know about when I may hope for the quartets I am awaiting so impatiently. If you want money, withdraw the amount you need from Messrs. Stieglitz & Co. in St. Petersburg; they will pay you any amount you wish.

This note bears the unmistakable mark of a princely character, and it must have strengthened and encouraged the composer, not to mention the 'pseudo-brother', to have such a generous music-lover as a patron.

In a third letter that we have, written on 8 April 1824, the Prince expresses enthusiastic praise for the *Missa*, which had been performed by a large orchestra and chorus in St. Petersburg the day before.[234] The Prince writes:

One might say that your genius is centuries before its time and that perhaps there is no listener sufficiently enlightened to appreciate the full beauty of this music. But future generations will honour you and bless your memory more than your contemporaries are able.

The writer of the letter closes with this sentence: 'Forgive me for occupying so much of your time with my letters, but this is the honest tribute of one of your most ardent admirers.'

These excerpts are enough to give us a picture of the Russian prince as a noble-spirited patron of the arts, a character who could not fail to make a deep impression on our master, for this Russian took his place among the Germans and Poles we remember—Lichnowsky, Lobkowitz, Kinsky, Schwarzenberg—not to forget his compatriot Rasumovsky, and others who in better days stood in the forefront of art patrons in the Austrian capital. If only this Russian nobleman had remained constant in the role he had begun so promisingly, it would have behoved the biographer to write with nothing but praise of the encouragement to creation that he afforded our master and his behaviour towards the composer in the matter of works that he had commissioned. Alas, it was not so! The Prince went back on his word, and after Beethoven's death it became the duty first of the guardian of the nephew, then much later of this biographer, to lodge a vigorous complaint against him.

Let us leave for now the subject of the quartets and resume it later at the appropriate moment. Let us turn, too, from Beethoven's financial preoccupations, after mentioning that at the time of preparation and rehearsals for the performance of the first of these quartets our master made the acquaintance of a new friend such as one would have hardly expected, one he needed in his existing state of mind, a friend capable even of supplanting the scheming brother. His name was Karl Holz.[235]

302

Beethoven's association with this young man, born in 1798, a clerk in one of the government offices and second violinist in the Schuppanzigh Quartet, was the last of a great number of contradictions in word and deed. It placed the composer in a situation that his older friends deplored, and as many as could avoided him altogether. Karl Holz was a man of good breeding who had had a classical education and good musical instruction as well, as is proved by his acceptance into that noteworthy chamber group. On the other hand, he was every inch a Viennese 'Phaeacian' of the first water, one of a class against which Beethoven had always shown a deep-rooted antipathy,* and he could hardly have overlooked his new friend's allegiance. But this young man was an exceptional calculator, and it was this quality alone that in Beethoven's eyes made both the 'Phaeacian' and the musician acceptable. For in the duality of his spirit he was as sorely in need of this capability as Wallenstein was in need of the astrologer Seni. More and more our master was obsessed with the acquisition of money in order to make his beloved nephew a wealthy man. As early as 1823 he had begun to demand imperiously that his brother bequeath everything to the nephew.[236] To fulfil this ambition he needed the aid of a calculator whom he could call upon every day, for the composer had never mastered the art of addition. He was reluctant to lay his plans before his old friends and ask their advice, for he was sure they would not listen to him. Moreover, none of them was the kind of mathematician Beethoven needed, with the exception of Andreas Streicher, who in 1824 drew up a plan of which we still have the original, for publishing an edition of the complete works, a project he assured Beethoven would bring him 10,000 florins CM. Many musical means had been presented, as we have already seen, for putting the master in possession of large sums of money, but he refused all of them and dreamed of fulfilling his ambitions by means of arithmetical calculations. Who could call such behaviour anything but an almost senseless wandering from the natural path?

The association with Karl Holz probably would not have had such dire consequences for our master, would not have forced him to remorseful confessions at the edge of his grave, would not have caused ugly gossip after the composer's death, if this young man had been able to measure the greatness of the artist, if he had not possessed such power over him, and if instead of pushing him further and further he had held

---

* In the fifth book of the *Odyssey*, the 'magnificent sufferer' is shipwrecked in a storm and thrown upon a strange shore. It is the land of the Phaeacians, whom Homer describes in the seventh book, beginning with the lines:

> The Phaeacian princes here
> Were seated; here they ate and drank, and held
> Perpetual banquet.   (*Odyssey* VII, 118–20)

This explains Beethoven's reference to Viennese life in his letter to Hauschka (p. 294).

him back in his almost passionate aspirations. If Fétis in his biographical article calls Beethoven a skinflint and a miser, if Dr. Wawruch, the master's last physician, describes him as a drunkard brought by liquor to his final illness,[237] the only justification for such claims, even though they contradict one another, is this friendship. When Oulibicheff in his book, *Beethoven, ses Critiques et ses Glossateurs*, speaks of the master's last days, when Beethoven was deserted by his few remaining friends, his only mistake is in saying that the author of this book was the only one to stay. Even I had avoided my friend and teacher who was now sunk in mathematical speculations, and seldom talked with him between March 1825 and August of the following year.

I kept informed, however, of his principal activities, and the papers he left behind put me in full knowledge of everything that happened during that interval. These papers contain not only pieces of buffoonery written in Holz's hand, not only insults to highly placed persons and others but, more important, they show explicitly the high pitch of inner excitement in which the master was constantly sustained. That he had abandoned old, deep-rooted principles became apparent when Beethoven would follow his young friend into strange gatherings in beer and wine taverns and into the shops of the music-dealers he patronized. All this could not fail to attract public attention. Holz seemed to want to prove that he could do anything with the master who had once been so retiring, and truly he had worked an incredible transformation. What stronger proof than this: amid all the speculative frenzy in which he was at that time involved, Beethoven became the godfather of his new friend's first-born son?![238]

The master's nature had undergone a metamorphosis that was absolutely astounding. It is the lamentable truth that under this new direction Beethoven sometimes brought offerings—before the eyes of strangers—to the wine-god, a tendency that increased the concern of his true friends and admirers. Dr. Wawruch's incriminating words, *sedebat et bibebat*, can refer only to this association.* Thankfully, the duration of these excesses was only the months between autumn 1825 and summer 1826. What works were composed during this period? We shall soon see.

With these unhappy circumstances behind us, let us turn to the last works of the great master, the last five quartets which, as we know, were inspired by Prince Galitsin. In the entire Beethoven literature no other compositions have given rise to more argument and controversy, and we can hardly hope for agreement or a satisfactory explanation, at least not in the sense that other, earlier works have been explained. It is a fact that the contemporary critics, out of deference to the earlier works,

* See Supplement B: **Beethoven** and his Last Physician, Dr. Wawruch.

were generally cautious and reserved in their evaluation of these quartets. But even then there were unbiased art connoisseurs who, after spending years studying this legacy, came to the conviction that in some parts (not all, as the attackers maintain) the combination of notes seemed to be carried to the furthest extreme of intellectual reflection, a circumstance that inevitably endangered the logic necessary to the relating of ideas. Everyone except the unconditional believer will have to concede that this situation will remain a permanent obstacle to a sure understanding of the music's poetic intentions, that all one can do is make random guesses and specious explanations. This author could relate incidents he personally witnessed during the composition of these works, but they would not materially alter the situation.

One of the most enlightened connoisseurs of Beethoven's music was his friend Count Franz von Brunsvik in Budapest, who could truly call himself Beethoven's pupil. We spent two whole winters together studying thèse quartets with the help of his excellent fellow-students. Our study revealed the harmonic and technical beauties of the music, but, as for recognizing a logical sequence of ideas, our efforts here and elsewhere remained fruitless. From time to time Count Brunsvik thought that with his sharp telescope he had found what he was looking for, but then he would lose it in the fog, and he would call himself a 'feeble-minded idiot'. Years later he told me that the darkness had in many places remained as obscure as at our separation in the spring of 1829.

Beethoven began the planning of the first of these quartets in the summer of 1824 in Baden, and upon his return in October he set himself to writing it down. For the first time in many years he took an apartment in the city so that his nephew, who from this time on lived with him and who planned to attend lectures in philosophy the following term, could be near the University. The revision of the score had not been completed when the master fell ill of a sickness that lasted for several weeks. The cause of his illness was the trouble in his intestines that had bothered him almost constantly. Since his falling out with Dr. Malfatti in 1815, his physician had been the equally renowned Dr. Staudenheim. As this practitioner had always insisted on the strictest observation of his prescriptions and would allow himself to speak sternly to his disobedient patient, Beethoven now called upon Professor Dr. Braunhofer. But he was no more lenient than his predecessor in handling his stubborn patient; in fact, he brought to his task a degree of Viennese bluntness that impressed the patient and contributed to his recovery. Still, it was not until his next summer's vacation in Baden that Beethoven's illness disappeared entirely.

The first performance of the first of these quartets, in E flat major, by Schuppanzigh and his companions took place, as we said, in March

1825. It was an almost total failure, and the audience that had come with high expectations left the concert hall in a state of bewilderment. People asked one another what it was they had just heard. The critic for the AmZ (XXVII (1825) 246) wrote that the work had been understood and completely comprehended by only a very few, and confessed: 'We were not one of them.' Schuppanzigh was blamed for the failure, for he was no longer considered capable of playing correctly or understanding fully the difficult task he had undertaken. Bitter altercations arose between him and the composer. Beethoven was unwilling to let matters rest as they were and sought an honourable vindication of his work. He accordingly asked Joseph Böhm, professor at the Conservatory, to take Schuppanzigh's place in a repeat performance. Böhm, more a concert violinist than a quartet player and therefore more of a virtuoso able to overcome the technical difficulties of the music, was somewhat more successful; but even so, the deep obscurity of some movements was made no clearer. Unfortunately, the composer was told that the performance was a complete success, as though everyone had comprehended it as clearly as the earlier quartets.

The original copy of the note that the master wrote to the musicians before the first performance of this quartet reads:

Most excellent Fellows!
With this note each of you receives his part, and each is pledged and bound upon his word of honour to do his best, to distinguish himself, and to vie in excellence with his companions.
Each who is to take part in the said matter must sign this paper.

Beethoven
Schindler, secretarius

Schuppanzigh, m. p.

Weiss, m. p.

Linke, m. p.
The accursed violoncello of the great master

Holz, m. p.
The last, but only in signing

The second quartet, in A minor, was first performed in November 1825. The reception was far more favourable than in the case of the first, since Schuppanzigh and his group practised it with great care. Here the only obscure section was the variations on the *Heiliger Dankgesang eines Genesenen an die Gottheit, in der lydischen Tonart*. This title (Hymn of Thanks in the Lydian Mode Offered to the Deity by a Convalescent) clearly refers to the composer's recent illness and recovery. In August of that year[239] Beethoven had already had this newest work privately performed before a small group of listeners at the request of the publisher Maurice Schlesinger. Karl Holz had been first violinist at this performance, while the master sat beside the musicians. Schlesinger immediately obtained publication rights for France and Germany, and took the manuscript with him to Paris.

⊸ 1826 ⊸

The next quartet to be composed was that in B flat major with six movements, rightly called the monster of all quartets. Its first performance in March 1826 was at the final concert in the chamber-music series for that year. Every lover of quartets in Vienna was present to witness the first playing of this newest creation about which many strange things had already been said. Let us hear what the critic for the AmZ (XXVIII (1826) 310) had to say about the success of this concert:

The first, third, and fifth movements are serious, dark, and mysterious, and sometimes bizarre, abrupt, and capricious. The second and fourth are full of mischief, playfulness, and roguery. Here the composer who, especially in his most recent works, has seldom been able to find balance or goal, has expressed himself briefly and concisely. With tumultuous applause the audience demanded encores of both movements. But the meaning of the fugal finale was lost upon this critic—was for him incomprehensible, a sort of Chinese puzzle. When the instruments of the north and south polar regions have to battle against enormous difficulties, when each of them ornaments the theme differently and they cut across one another in irregular progressions and in innumerable dissonances, when the musicians, distrustful of themselves, fail to play with absolute precision, then, indeed, the confusion of Babel is complete; then we have a concert that only the Moroccans might enjoy. Perhaps so much would not have been written into the piece if the master could hear his own works. Yet we must not denounce the work prematurely; perhaps there will come a time when what at first glance seems to us so turbid and confused will be perceived as clear and perfectly balanced.

The reader may picture to himself from the words of this generally accurate reporter of public opinion the mood of the departing audience, for never has an instrumental work opposed such sharp contrasts to one another as this quartet: the listener, after the most delighted enjoyment of clear skies above, is suddenly either shrouded in mysterious darkness or confronted with the utmost solemnity, as if the composer intended to make a game of his emotions. Then, to crown everything, the finale in the form of a fugue! This composition seems to be an anachronism. It should belong to that grey future when the relationship of notes will be determined by mathematical computation. Unquestionably such combinations must be regarded as the extreme limit of the speculative intellect, and its effect will always remain one of Babelic confusion. We cannot speak here of darkness in contrast to light.

The composer of this much-discussed and still very elusive quartet was more correctly informed of its success than he had been in the case of the first quartet. This time it was the publisher Matthias Artaria who, as purchaser of the manuscript, took the initiative. He offered to buy the fugue as a separate work if Beethoven would compose another finale in free style to put in its place. The master complied with this condition and wrote the movement that appears in the published version of the work. This was his very last composition, and was written in November 1826. Those diligent folk who pride themselves on their ability to distinguish Beethoven's various styles would surely come to grief over this movement if the time and the conditions of its composition were not known, for is not this finale similar in style and clarity to many of the quartet movements of an earlier period? The same is true of the fourth and sixth movements of the C sharp minor quartet, and no less true of the second, fourth, and fifth movements of the A minor quartet. Who can deny that one meets in these last works the deepest depths of obscurity right next to the brightest light of clarity? A sustained style can be found only in the four movements of the quartet in F major, opus 135.

On 22 April 1827, when the composer was no longer among us, Schuppanzigh performed for the second time the quartet in B flat major, this time with the new finale. The audience was happy to be persuaded that now the whole work was more comprehensible and that the obscurity was now confined to the first and third movements. It is strange indeed that quartet players today are no more confident in their approach to this fearsome work than in 1827, and that all the quartet groups, even the Paris quartet of Maurin and Chevillard, have always been most reluctant to attack this monster.[240]

Let me note in passing that the fourth movement, Alla danza tedesca, now in G major, was first written in A major, and we still have the original manuscript. It appears to have been composed as an integral part of another quartet, not improbably the A minor, the immediate predecessor of the B flat major.

The genesis of the fourth quartet, in C sharp minor, also with six movements,[241] falls in the first half, mostly in the summer months, of the year 1826. Schuppanzigh never performed it because he had been by no means encouraged by the outcome of the previous three. On the other hand, in March 1828 he attempted the fifth, in F major, which had already been published.[242] The performance was a success, since the work offered no stylistic, harmonic, or technical peculiarities.

If Beethoven's enemies find in his last works, especially in these five quartets, nothing but confusion and contradiction, they must be reminded that even confusion is honourable if it is based on great and noble intentions and is carried out by pure means. And it cannot be proved that our master's intentions and means were otherwise. This fact may one day vindicate the works and should encourage the student not to grow weary in his research.

The master's repeated attempts to work out the motif of the fourth movement of the C sharp minor quartet, as they appear in the sketch-books and are discussed in the Supplement (page 494 *infra*), demonstrate how fastidiously he elaborated his themes until he was satisfied that they were just right and could be correctly performed. Before his quartet themes could be employed, they had to pass as rigid requirements as the subject for a fugue. This motif in the C sharp minor quartet even had to be adaptable to different time signatures. In the sketchbook it is first noted in $\frac{6}{8}$ time, then in $\frac{4}{4}$, then twice again in $\frac{6}{8}$ (the second time marked *Meilleur*), then in $\frac{2}{4}$, the sixth version in $\frac{4}{4}$, and finally the last time in $\frac{4}{4}$ with variations. The published version also had the theme in different rhythms.

The explanation for the words, 'The difficult decision', that appear in the fourth movement of the last quartet, in F, is found in the list of works belonging to this period.

Let me add an important word concerning an error in the assigning of opus numbers to these quartets. The opus numbers ought to conform to the sequence in which the quartets were composed. Once more we have an instance where the three publishers who shared this work proceeded without consulting one another. The numbers should be as follows:

Quartet in E flat major	opus 127
Quartet in A minor	opus 130 instead of 132
Quartet in B flat major	opus 131 instead of 130
Quartet in C sharp minor	opus 132 instead of 131
Quartet in F major	opus 133 instead of 135

The fugue in B flat major, which the composer released as a separate work, should, in the proper order, follow the five quartets and have the opus number 134. The piano arrangement no more needs a number all its own than any other arrangement. This particular arrangement was not even made by the composer, as the catalogue claims, but by Anton Halm, though the master did revise it.[243] Throughout the time Beethoven was composing these five quartets, he did nothing else. Yet the catalogue inserts two little pieces from a much earlier time with opus numbers: the arietta *Der Kuss* is given opus number 128, and the *Rondo a Capriccio* for piano is opus 129.

I must also object to the words, 'From the *Nachlass*', that appear on the title-pages of the quartets in A minor and F major. We know that M. Schlesinger received the former from the master's hands as early as

August 1825. The other was sent to him in the autumn of 1826. Even these two insignificant examples illustrate how the publishers took every liberty with Beethoven's works. At any rate, if it is true that the body of our master's works, in each of its categories, has enjoyed a greater audience among all the cultured nations than the works of any other classical composer, it is no less true that no other composer's works have suffered the dismemberment, the violations, that have befallen this literature, though surely (as the publishers and dismemberers protest) only in the public interest. The *Thematic Index* of Breitkopf & Härtel is evidence of all I have said.

[V]

[1825 to 1827]

Having covered, I hope not unsatisfactorily, the story of the last compositions, we must occupy ourselves exclusively with the course of the master's life and the effect of his family circumstances upon it and upon his state of mind. Let us see first of all what these were. A passage from the *Odyssey* that the master especially liked will serve as an introduction and will concentrate the reader's attention on this point:

> *Few sons are like*
> *Their fathers: most are worse, a very few*
> *Excel their parents.* (*Odyssey* II, 348–50)

We learned a short time ago that Beethoven's nephew started at the University in the autumn of 1824 and took up residence with his adopted father.[244] He planned to study philology, but it is well known that at that time, and even much later, the Austrian University offered nothing in this department, for the state needed merely good functionaries. If the young Beethoven, talented in this area as he was and already well prepared, had been taken to some good foreign university, very probably his natural inclination and his good secondary education would have combined to make him an outstanding scholar, worthy of his famous name. But with the Austrian university system, whose slack mechanism discouraged the concentration of the mental faculties and in fact distracted and dispersed them, even the most diligent student acquired nothing except perhaps a degree of bureaucratic mentality. The members of the university faculty themselves were no exception.

Our student took his prescribed terminal examinations at Easter of 1825 with dubious success, and the famous name 'Beethoven'—that is, his uncle's renown—had to exert its influence to enable him to enter the second term.[245] During the master's summer stay in Baden, the student was sent to board with a reliable man who, however, was not able to control the youth's activities. A gross misuse of free time, a penchant for gambling, and frequent visits to his unhappy mother whose moral degradation had reached the furthest extreme, conspired to prevent the nephew from even taking his examinations at the end of the second term. The life of a scholar was given up once and for all. Our master's heartbreak over his painful situation may best be expressed in the lament from the *Odyssey* that he had underlined:

> *But I am like whomever thou mayst know*
> *Among mankind, inured to suffering;*
> *To them shouldst thou compare me.*   (*Odyssey* VII, 252-54)

We have documentary proof that Beethoven did not fail to warn his nephew in serious and fatherly words at the very beginning of the boy's wayward life. These words display the composer's nobility of heart and mind. As such, they are of historic interest. They are contained in twenty-nine letters which the master wrote from his summer retreat at Baden in 1825, but which came back into his possession after the catastrophe that befell the young man in August 1826, the details of which we shall presently hear. Beethoven felt that the letters contained the best vindication of his treatment of his adopted son. To this end he entrusted them shortly before his death to Stephan von Breuning and this author. I am carrying out the will of our friend in quoting excerpts from these letters.[246] The letters themselves are preserved in the Royal Library in Berlin.

1.

I am delighted, my dear son, that you are happy in the career that you have chosen and, since this is the case, that you are zealously doing all that is required for it. I did not recognize your writing. I am asking now, to be sure, only about the sense and the meaning, since now you must also attain a fine external appearance.

If you find it much too difficult to come here, do not bother, but if in any way you can come, I shall be happy to have a human heart here with me in my exile. . . . I embrace you with all my heart.

Your faithful father

2.

18 May

. . . It is indeed becoming for a youth hardly nineteen years old to combine the duties for his education and advancement with those that he owes to his benefactor and supporter. This I did indeed with my poor parents. I was happy to be able to help them. How different your attitude towards me!

Frivolous one, farewell

THIRD PERIOD

3.

22 May

Thus far only suppositions, though I have been assured by someone that once again there have been secret meetings between you and your mother. Must I once more suffer the most horrible ingratitude?! If the tie is to be broken, so be it, but you will be despised by all impartial people who hear of this ingratitude. The remark of my worthy brother . . . and your remark yesterday regarding Dr. S . . . r, who, of course, must feel offended with me, since the law court decided the opposite of what he requested*—should I once again involve myself in these squalid matters? No, never again. Is the pact burdensome to you, in Heaven's name? I leave you to divine providence: I have done my duty, and thus can appear before the supreme Judge of all judges. . . .

4.

Baden, 31 May 1825

. . . And that's an end to that. Spoiled as you are, it would do you no harm at last to cultivate simplicity and truth, for my heart has suffered too much from your deceitful behaviour towards me, and it is difficult for me to forget. And even if I were willing to drag the whole burden without murmuring, like a yoke-ox, still your behaviour, if it is directed in this way against others, can never attract to you people who will love you. God is my witness that I dream only of getting completely away from you and that wretched brother and this miserable family of mine. May God grant my wish, for I can no longer trust you.

Your father, or better: not your father

5.

(Regarding the accounting for money that he has received)

Baden, 28 June

. . . Do not let me hark back still further. This would be easy, but only painful for me. At the end all that would be said would be, 'After all, you are a very good guardian', etc. If only you had some depth of character, you would for the most part have acted altogether differently. . . .

6.

18 July

Dear son! . . . Be sure and observe moderation. Fortune has crowned my efforts; do not let your misfortune be founded on wrong opinions of yourself. Be truthful and accurate in the listing of your expenses; for the time being, let the theatre go. Follow your guide and father; follow him whose thoughts and endeavours are at all times for your moral well-being and who is not wholly useless for your everyday existence. . . . Be my beloved son! What an unheard-of dissonance it would be if you should be false to me, as people already contend you are.

* This passage has to do with the lawsuit against the sister-in-law in the superior court.

7.

. . . I am steadily getting thinner; each day I feel worse rather than better, and have no doctor, no sympathetic person. Come if in any way possible, though I don't want to keep you from doing anything. If only I could be sure that Sunday would be well spent away from me. I must learn to give up everything. If only the boon might be granted me that my sacrifices, great as they are, would bear worthy fruit.

Where have I not been wounded, stabbed to the heart? Do not permit yourself to enter into secret relations with my worthy brother—above all, into secrecy against me, against your most faithful father. If indeed you see me in anger, attribute it to my great solicitude for you, since you are readily threatened with dangers. Do not give me cause for anxiety; give thought to my sorrows. For this reason I must have no apprehension over the course of the law—what indeed have I lived through?!

8.

Come soon!
Come soon!
Come soon!
All right! . . . Yesterday my worthy brother with his brother-in-law. What a miserable fellow! . . . If Cato, on seeing Caesar, shouted: 'He and we: what can one do against such a person?' . . . As always, your loving and solicitous father.

9.

· . . I don't want you to come to me on 17 September. It is better that you finish these studies. God has never forsaken me; no doubt someone can be found who will close my eyes. On the whole, it seems to me that there is some collusive plan in what has gone on, in which my worthy (pseudo-) brother has a hand. I know that later on you will not want to live with me; of course, in my household things are carried on in a somewhat too upright manner. . . . You need not come on Sunday either, for there can never be true harmony and concord with your behaviour. Why this hypocrisy? Only then will you become a better man. You need not dissemble, need not lie, and this will in the end be better for your moral character. Thus, you see, you are reflected in me. What good do the most loving reprimands do? Besides, they make you angry. However, don't worry: I shall always continue to take care of you as I am doing now. Think what scenes you bring me to create! . . .

Farewell. He who admittedly did not beget you, but has certainly provided for you and, more important than anything else, has cared for the cultivation of your mind like a father—yes, more than that—begs you most earnestly to follow the one true path of all that is good and right.

Your faithful, kind father

10.

Stop, no further! Just return to my arms; you will hear no harsh word! O

God! do not abandon yourself to misery! You will be received here as affectionately as always. We will lovingly discuss what is to be considered, what is to be done for the future. No reproaches, on my word of honour, for in any case they would no longer do any good. You may expect only the most loving help and care. But come! come to the faithful heart of your father

Beethoven

11.

5 October

I have just received your letter. Already filled with anxiety, I had already decided to hasten to Vienna today. Thank God, it is not necessary! If only you follow me, love, like happiness of the soul united with human happiness, will be our lot, and to your outward happiness you will unite an intensive spiritual existence, though it would be better if the latter took precedence over the former. . . . I embrace and kiss you a thousand times, not as my son who is lost but as my son who is newly born. . . . Your loving father will always care for you who have been found again.

12.

14 October

I write you in greatest haste to say that I shall certainly come home tomorrow morning, even if it rains, so be sure that I find you there. I shall be happy to see you again, and even if you see lowering clouds, do not attribute them to deliberate bad temper. They will be completely dispelled by the better effort you have promised me for your true and pure happiness founded on hard work. . . . Who would not rejoice if the erring one returns again to the right path? This I hope indeed to experience. . . .

As we have learned, the degenerate youth did not take his examinations at the end of the second term, so that promotion into the second year of studies under the philosophy faculty was impossible. Now what was to become of him? The upshot of these talks was simply that the young man should find his own way. He chose to undertake business studies for which he had no inclination whatsoever. Courses at the Polytechnic Institute were to prepare him for this work.

This turn of events caused our master to shorten his stay in Baden and hurry back to Vienna. He took a spacious apartment on the second floor of the so-called Schwarzspanierhaus, situated on the 'glacis' of suburban Währing. This was his last earthly abode. Because the apartment was at some distance from the Polytechnic Institute, the nephew was left with the same reliable man who lived very near it. Soon these distressing events seemed to have been forgotten, and the master was again free to pursue in peace his studies and speculations. He felt reassured when the vice-director of the Institute, Reisser, accepted his request to assume co-guardianship of the nephew, and the master be-

314

lieved that with this man's help he had recovered his 'newly born' son. Alas! this proved to be only a dream! In spite of all his uncle's love and care and his co-guardian's watchfulness, the youth resumed all too soon the rakish way of life he had so recently abandoned; and went so far that, when he failed to take any of the second term's examinations, he chose suicide as an escape.

The attempt failed and, according to the law, he came into the hands of the police, for it was assumed that since he was neither insane nor emotionally disturbed, such a deed could be committed only from lack of religious feeling. The nephew of the man we once saw so actively interested in the religious education of the common people was accordingly taken into safe custody so that his religious training could be seen to. What misery the great artist suffered at the hands of the nephew he had nurtured for so many years and at such expense, and who had promised so much in his earlier years! Once more a favourite line from the *Odyssey* sums up the situation:

For quickly doth misfortune make men old.   (*Odyssey* XIX, 441)

One could see in the master's stooped posture his deep grief over the public infamy that had once more befallen his name. The once sturdy, vigorous body now stood before us like an old man of nearly seventy, broken in will, docile, bending to the lightest breeze.

His agony was increased when many blamed the guardian for the ward's crime, feeling that he had driven the boy to this catastrophe. This was certainly an exaggeration.[247] Yet the master could not be acquitted of a certain portion of the guilt. One could not consider a man as possessing the qualities best suited for educating the young (even if he were in perfect physical condition) if he were obsessed with an excess of love, as well as an excess of hatred and distrust. Let us review the circumstances that led our composer to assume this task; let us remember moreover the obstacles that prevailed and their sources. We see reason upon reason for the master's unmitigated hatred of the nephew's mother, for his outspoken reviling of her, all too often expressed in the presence of her son. Beethoven was, moreover, shortsighted in putting his complete confidence in the boy even though he often caught him in the grossest lies, inventions, and hypocrisies, and in worse offences, such as unfounded accusations, even of his teachers. These traits of character developed as time went on into a propensity for slandering his uncle's truest friends. The circumstances were on many counts so exceptional that many thoughtful, peace-loving teachers or guardians in Beethoven's place would have made the same mistake, except for his excessive love for his ward. For if one attempting to correct a person filled with obvious ill will and evil intent sees his efforts constantly frustrated by intrigue, his patience will be tried to the point at which his equanimity can be maintained only with the greatest difficulty.

In the cheerless situation into which our master had fallen, he remembered one of his closest childhood friends, a man who had for many years observed at first hand his ever-growing fame, whose experience, wisdom, and good advice had helped him out of many an embarrassing situation, but who nine years earlier had become estranged from him as the result of an insult, a man now active in the imperial government as director of a large department in the war ministry and in a position to be of service to the unhappy composer. He was Stephan von Breuning, a man of gentle temperament and rare firmness of character, who remained faithful to the muse of poetry right into old age, despite the work and preoccupations of government business. We can truly call it an unpardonable mistake on the part of the hot-blooded musician that he had not years before taken the first step towards reconciliation.* In this situation, and in another similar one that we shall recount, the words copied out from the *Odyssey* were of no help:

> *If any word*
> *That hath been uttered gave offence, may storms*
> *Sweep it away forever.*　　　(*Odyssey* VIII, 495–97)

The following letter to this friend, surely from these days of 1826 though the letter bears no date,[248] shows us Beethoven's first step towards reconciliation with his faithful Steffen:

Behind this painting, my good, dear Steffen, let there be forever hidden what passed between us. I realize that I have broken your heart. The emotion within me, which you must certainly have observed, has punished me sufficiently for having done so. It was not malice that rose within me against you—no, for then I should no longer have been worthy of your friendship. It was passion on your part and on mine, but distrust of you arose within me. People came between us who are not worthy of you or of me.

My portrait† has long been intended for you—you knew, of course, that I always intended to give it to someone. To whom, indeed could I give it with a warmer heart than to you, true, good, noble Steffen! Forgive me if I caused you pain: I myself suffered no less.

When for so long a time I saw you no longer with me, only then did I fully realize how dear to my heart you were and always will be. Surely you will once more fly to my arms, as in former days.

Soon after his reunion with Breuning, the master sent this author, too, a request to take his former place in the master's circle of friends.

---

* Breuning had energetically tried to dissuade Beethoven from adopting his nephew, thus touching the master's most vulnerable spot.

† It was the lithograph of the portrait by Stieler, of which the master had somewhat earlier sent a copy to Dr. Wegeler.[249]

I complied immediately. In Breuning's company our friend seemed to recover, and gradually the atmosphere of his house became purified of its months of contamination by Phaeacian selfishness. In the supplement we shall see how boldly the master's dazed condition following his first blow was exploited. But soon we were overjoyed to see our friend recover his characteristic strength of spirit and will, as he once more proved how powerfully he could recover mastery over his fate. He comforted and exalted his soul by thinking about the experiences of great men of antiquity and about their relevance to his situation. Our Stoic and Peripatetic would even lecture on this or that thesis of these philosophical systems. At such moments his whole being was a demonstration of true classical majesty.

Meanwhile the time had come, about the end of October, when the nephew's religious exercises under the surveillance of the state were to be terminated. During this period the young man had decided to dedicate himself to the army, in which there were no semester examinations. The vice-director of the Polytechnic Institute had resigned his post as co-guardian, and Breuning took his place. The prisoner was released to his two guardians by the police authorities with explicit orders that he should not remain in Vienna longer than one day. But since there were important and time-consuming conditions to be fulfilled before the youth could be taken into the army, Johann van Beethoven offered Master Ludwig and the prospective warrior his house at Gneixendorf, on the left bank of the Danube not far from the town of Krems, as a temporary domicile until Hofrat von Breuning could find the colonel of a regiment who not only would agree to accept the ward as a cadet in his regiment but would place him under a captain with more than the usual officer's training, one who would take special care of his charge. Lieutenant Field-Marshal Baron von Stutterheim accepted the young man into his infantry regiment out of deference for his two guardians, and chose the company commander Captain von Montluisant as the new cadet's commanding officer. In his gratitude, Beethoven dedicated to this general the C sharp minor quartet. This decision was not, however, communicated to the publisher Schott in Mainz until 10 March 1827, though the manuscript was sent in October 1826, as we can determine from the existing notification of receipt dated from Mainz on 28 November 1826.

Notes concerning the master's stay in the company of his family in Gneixendorf (consisting of the brother, his wife, her illegitimate grown-up daughter, and the nephew) were found in the journals and in other papers written in the brother's hand. They show so much controversy, so much that is offensive, that it does not seem advisable to go into detail. Let us be brief in our treatment of the matter. There was an unbelievable lack of consideration for the master's physical needs as to both lodging and food; the nephew became intimate with his aunt who was apparently equal to his mother in immorality; the long-suffering adopted father was completely neglected. What is more, he was confined to his room because of the cold, rainy November weather.[250] Under these conditions Beethoven composed his final work, the last movement of the quartet in B flat major, opus 130, full of grave mirth and humour. Although Breuning's solicitations had not yet achieved the desired end, our master felt that for the reasons just mentioned he must leave Gneixendorf and return with his nephew to Vienna, though they would incur the risk of coming into conflict with the police. In addition to all his other inconsiderateness, the 'pseudo-brother' refused to lend them his closed carriage for their journey to nearby Krems, and they were forced to travel in an open calash. The result of this trip was an intestinal chill that was serious from the first day.

On 2 December Beethoven arrived in Vienna with his good-for-nothing nephew. It was not until several days had passed that I learned of his return and his physical condition. I hurried to him immediately and learned, among other things, the distressing news that he had called repeatedly for his old doctors, Braunhofer and Staudenheim, but in vain. The former would not come because it was too far, while the latter had promised to come but never did.[251] Someone had sent him a doctor, but he did not know who or how, and this doctor knew nothing of Beethoven or his temperament. It was Dr. Wawruch, professor at the hospital. I later learned from the doctor himself the strange circumstances that had brought him to Beethoven's bedside. A servant (*marqueur*) from a coffee-house in the city had been brought to the hospital, and had confided in him that Beethoven's nephew had been playing billiards at the coffee-house a few days before and had asked him to get a doctor for his sick uncle. The servant had himself been unwell and could only now execute his commission to get a doctor to go to Beethoven. When the physician arrived at the composer's bedside, he learned that the patient had had no medical attention.[252]

I leave it to the reader's compassion to judge this situation and all the injuries and insults the master suffered at the hands of his family. This summary contains the obvious explanation of the true reasons for his early death.[253] To have to tell in detail the facts that spring from ignoble, ruined, or simply evil hearts spoils any pleasure the biographer might otherwise take in his work. It becomes truly painful for an author who with his own eyes saw most of these things happen and had to watch their blighting effects. How different the work of the biographer who experienced nothing personally of the things he puts on paper, who uses only existing materials, many of which have biased or self-interested sources, while others may date from a time when events and circumstances have lost their significance, perhaps because their results have already been forgotten or have come to be thought of as of little importance, and which with very few exceptions merely add details of secondary importance to the already overfilled store.

In such a situation the biographer is left a great deal of freedom in interpreting facts according to his own subjective temperament, and may pick and choose as he wishes among a great many conflicting opinions, for with the passage of time the conditions and circumstances of the hero's life assume a much-changed appearance. Histories on every subject are ample demonstrations of this fact. Let us take an example from our hero's history. When Beethoven had been dead thirty years someone in Vienna published faulty information concerning his body measurements. After another thirty years perhaps his artistic deeds will also be relegated to the realm of myth. These mistakes we owe to the writers of novels and short stories who unscrupulously twist historical facts of every kind to suit their purposes, completely negating the being of the person about whom they write. And as we know, the masses much prefer this type of writing to historical works.

Having made these side comments necessitated by the circumstances and conditions of the situation, let us return to the ever-darkening path of events. Our drama has now reached its turning point.

In the second half of December, the nephew was finally able to leave for his regiment in the Moravian town of Iglau.* Neither Breuning nor this author was present at his leave-taking from his benefactor. We know, however, that Beethoven took the separation with a light heart, because when we next saw him he was in an unusually good humour. It was as if he had been delivered from a wicked enemy. This humour was not a transitory one; in fact, it lasted for some time. His good cheer was due to his complete faith that he would soon be cured. He made various plans, and spoke of the music he would write—in short, he felt once more as free in mind and spirit, as 'unbuttoned', as in former times. The Stoic now had the time and the will to expound to his heart's content on his philosophical system. All this would have made our association with him very pleasant if we had been able to rid our thoughts of a troubling apprehension that catastrophe was imminent.

In this respect Breuning's eleven-year-old son[254] was happier than we, a cheerful and intelligent boy who, because of his candour and his unawareness of our friend's condition, was better able than we to entertain

* This character thus exits from our stage. It is fitting that we outline briefly the remainder of his life. Karl van Beethoven, first philologist, then merchant-to-be, shortly thereafter soldier, abandoned this profession, too, and took a position as a private secretary. His good qualities, salvaged from his earlier conflicts with life, later made him a respectable family man sensitive to the weight of his famous name. He died on 13 April 1858.

him. Gerhard von Breuning, the favourite companion and excellent attendant of the sick Beethoven, now a practising physician in Vienna, earned the master's heartfelt thanks, and perhaps thinks back even now, not without emotion, to those days so important even for a childish comprehension. Except for us three the patient wished to see no one, not even his brother, for his memories of the recent events in Gneixendorf were most bitter.[255]

The illness from which Beethoven was suffering was an inflammation of the lungs, a complication that developed from his intestinal chill. This condition was diagnosed much too late by Dr. Wawruch and, by the time the correct diagnosis was made, the phase of dropsy was already far advanced. We shall learn in the Supplement B how the doctor rationalized this mistaken diagnosis. The symptoms of the disease became so obvious within a few days that on 18 December the first puncture had to be made. The second took place on 8 January and the third on 28 January.[256]

The events of these days destroyed our faint hopes. The decline in his physical and mental powers filled even the soul of our sick friend with dire apprehensions. His faith in his doctor, diminishing over the last weeks as the quantities of medicine he took completely paralysed his already weak digestion, was altogether gone, so that the sight of the man filled him with dread. In this understandably frightening situation, Beethoven remembered his old friend, the now famous physician Dr. Malfatti, with whom twelve years earlier he had quarrelled and to whom he had not spoken since. In this man he now placed all his hopes of recovery. But when I went on the master's behalf and asked Malfatti to come, he would not listen, and turned me coldly away. I dared a second and even a third attempt at arousing his compassion for the suffering composer.

At last I prevailed upon him to give the patient at least the pleasure of a professional visit as if he were going to the bedside of a complete stranger. He expressed the wish that this visit should take place in the presence of the physician who was in charge of the case. Beethoven was opposed to such an arrangement, for he wished to be alone with his former friend whom he hoped to reconcile. He pretended, however, to accept Malfatti's condition. Malfatti appeared and found that his colleague was not there but only the open arms of his remorseful friend asking his forgiveness. All that had happened was forgotten. From that day Malfatti came almost every day along with Wawruch. The latter's treatment was immediately stopped, and only a frozen punch in rather large quantities was prescribed. Under this regimen the patient felt refreshed, and was sometimes so strengthened that he thought he would be able to compose again, and even that he would recover entirely.

The doctors prohibited any writing but suggested some light reading. The novels of Sir Walter Scott were just then in vogue, and the patient was easily persuaded to make the acquaintance of the 'Great Unknown'. But when he was still on the first volume of *Kenilworth*, he grew angry and threw the book on the floor, exclaiming: 'The fellow is just writing for money!' He replaced Scott with his oldest friends and teachers from antiquity: Plutarch, Homer, Plato, Aristotle, and other such guests. And since he knew only a few of the compositions of Franz Schubert, whose talent the adoring public had already made suspect, I took the opportunity of laying before him some of the greater songs calculated to give the master much pleasure, such as *Die junge Nonne*, *Die Bürgschaft*, *Der Tauscher*, *Elysium*, and the *Ossianische Gesänge*. He expressed his opinion of the songs in these words: 'Truly there is a divine spark in this Schubert'. At that time only a few of Schubert's works had been published.

Throughout most of the time that we stayed at the master's sickbed, he was oppressed by anxious thoughts concerning his further means of subsistence. His fears were aggravated when the doctor said that his illness would be of long duration, and that intellectual work would be out of the question during this time. The anxiety that tormented him was: if the doctor's prognosis was correct, where was he to get the means to support himself and his nephew? It was a natural question, one that would frighten any artist or writer in a similar situation. At first the master could take comfort from his daily expectation of the money that Prince Galitsin owed him: 125 ducats for the second and third quartets that had been written for him and for the dedication of the great overture in C major, opus 124. These three compositions had been sent during the winter of 1825-6.

After waiting in vain for some time, Beethoven turned to the banking firm of Stieglitz & Co. in St. Petersburg which, according to the above-quoted letter of 11 March 1824 from the Prince, was to pay Beethoven whatever he requested. The bank replied, however, that Prince Galitsin had gone to Persia with the army and that he had not issued any order of payment to Beethoven. When early in December Beethoven became sick again, he wrote to the Austrian ambassador in St. Petersburg, asking him to mediate in this situation. Lo and behold! about the middle of the same month there came a letter from the Prince sent from Charkoff[257] and dated 10/22 November 1826, containing in French the following message:

My dear and esteemed M. van Beethoven:
You must think me quite capricious and inconsiderate to have neglected to answer your letter for such a long time, especially after I received from you two new masterpieces from your immortal and inexhaustible genius. But there

have been misfortunes! . . . I now live at the other end of Russia, and before many days I shall leave for Persia to take part in a war. Before leaving I shall surely send Messrs. Stieglitz & Co. the sum of 125 ducats, and all I can do is offer you my thanks for your masterpieces and my excuses for not having written to you for so long a time. . . .*

The arrival of this letter dissipated the patient's oppressive and frightening thoughts and the promised sum was looked for daily, for the necessity of establishing the nephew in his future career and the increased expenditures for medication had made serious inroads in Beethoven's finances. But week after week passed, and the letter we so eagerly anticipated from St. Petersburg did not arrive. February came, but still nothing from Stieglitz & Co.

Then the patient remembered the offer years before from the Philharmonic Society in London to give a concert for his benefit.[258] He considered this proposal at length and consulted with Breuning and me whether this course should be taken. We did not conceal our fears that such a step was bound to become public knowledge sooner or later and would create a bad impression. We made so bold as to remind our sick friend of the government bonds he still had in his possession, and recommended that he postpone for some time asking aid from a foreign quarter. But we were informed that he no longer regarded these bonds as his property but as the inheritance of his nephew. We could not overcome this arrangement, and it was we two in whose hands was placed the task of communicating with London.

Beethoven chose Sir George Smart and the harp-manufacturer Stumpff, and at my suggestion Herr Ignaz Moscheles, for my particular association with the latter made it possible for me to explain the special circumstances to him.† When the master concurred in this plan, I wrote each of these three gentlemen a letter which Beethoven signed. The essential content of all three may be seen from the letter to Moscheles, dated from Vienna on 22 February 1827:

My dear Moscheles:

I am sure you will not take it amiss that I trouble you with a request, and Sir G. Smart as well, to whom I enclose a letter. The matter in short is this: some years ago the Philharmonic Society in London made me a handsome offer to arrange a concert for my benefit. At that time, thank God, I was not in a situation in which I needed to avail myself of this noble offer. But the situation

---

* The existence of this acknowledgement of indebtedness was known to all Beethoven's friends, and I begged it in vain from Prince Galitsin on the occasion of his visit to Vienna in 1852. I owe my possession of it to the famous music scholar Herr B. Damcke, who lived at that time in St. Petersburg and who now resides in Brussels. His two letters to me from St. Petersburg, written on 7 January and 13 February 1853, are given in Supplement C. They shed the clearest light on the dispute with the Prince, and vindicate Beethoven absolutely on several points.

† Beethoven himself was never in the least acquainted with Moscheles.[259]

now is altogether different, since for nearly three months I have been confined to my bed with an exhausting illness. It is dropsy; Schindler will tell you more about it in the letter that he is enclosing.

You have for a long time known the manner of my life, and have known how and by what means I live. For a long time to come, composing will be out of the question, and for this reason I may find myself in the position of lacking the necessities of life.

You have not only a broad circle of acquaintances in London, but also significant influence in the Philharmonic Society. For this reason I ask you to use this influence to the utmost so that the Society may once more adopt this resolution and without delay put it into execution. The enclosed letter to Sir Smart is to the same effect, as is one that I have already sent to Herr Stumpff.* Please be so good as to hand the letter to Sir Smart and to join with him and all my friends in London in carrying out this objective. . . .

Your friend
Beethoven, m. p.

On 14 March Beethoven dictated to me a letter to Moscheles that contained the following passage:

On 27 February I was operated on for the fourth time, and now indications are already evident that I must soon expect a fifth operation. What will be the end of it, and what will become of me if this continues? Truly, my lot is a very hard one. However, I submit to the will of Fate, and pray to God only that in His divine wisdom He may decree that as long as I must endure this living death, I may be protected from want. This will give me the strength to bear my lot, however hard and terrible it may be, with submission to the will of the Almighty. . . . Hummel is here. . . .†

Hardly had this letter been mailed when a letter from Moscheles and Stumpff arrived from London, dated 1 March. It showed what a deep impression our letter of 22 February had made there. Moscheles and Stumpff wrote in particular:

The Society has resolved to demonstrate to you its good will and heartfelt sympathy by asking you to accept one hundred pounds sterling (1,000 florins CM) so that you may procure those things that you need and anything that will make you comfortable during your illness. Herr Rau of the firm of Eskeles will give you part of the money or, if you prefer, the total sum, and will take your receipt.

* A. A. Stumpff, a German from Thuringia, who had been living for more than forty years in London where he had made a considerable fortune. He was an esteemed friend of Goethe's, and had come to Vienna in September 1824 to make Beethoven's personal acquaintance. In 1826 he presented the complete works of Handel in forty volumes to our master. Beethoven was only sorry that he did not know English well enough to be able to compare the text and the music. Nevertheless, his joy in this very valuable gift was great. At the auction of the musical works in Beethoven's *Nachlass*, Tobias Haslinger purchased the entire set for 100 florins CM, though in England it had cost almost seventy pounds sterling. From this example the reader may guess for what small price items of lesser value went at that auction.

† A noteworthy incident that occurred during Hummel's first visit to our master will be recorded in the section on Beethoven's character, traits and peculiarities.

Moscheles moreover assured the sick master that the Philharmonic Society would be glad to be of further service and that Beethoven should simply write if he had further need.

The day after he had received the hundred pounds sterling (on 18 March) Beethoven dictated to me the following letter to Moscheles:

> I cannot describe in words the emotion with which I read your letter of 1 March. The generosity of the Philharmonic Society with which they almost anticipated my request has touched me to the innermost depths of my soul. Therefore I ask you, my dear Moscheles, to be the organ through which I express my most heartfelt thanks to the Philharmonic Society for their special sympathy and aid.[260]
>
> I found myself obliged to draw the entire sum of 1,000 gulden CM at once, since at that time I was in the unpleasant situation of having to raise money. . . .
>
> May Heaven soon restore my health to me, and I will show the generous Englishmen how greatly I appreciate their sympathy in my sad fate. Your noble behaviour I shall never forget, and I shall soon express my thanks in particular to Sir Smart and Herr Stumpff. Please hand the metronomized ninth symphony to the Philharmonic Society. The markings are enclosed.
>
> Your friend who esteems you highly,
>
> Beethoven, m. p.

Let me also quote a few lines from the letter I wrote to Moscheles and sent with the above in order to prepare the London friends for the master's imminent death.*

> The letter to you of the 18th inst. was dictated by him word for word; it is probably his last letter. [It was indeed![261]] Today he whispered to me, 'Write to Smart and Stumpff.' If he is still able to sign these letters, he will do so to-morrow morning. [This was not possible, and so I complied with his wish and communicated to both worthy men Beethoven's gratitude immediately after his death.] He feels that his end is near, for yesterday he said to Breuning and me: 'Plaudite, amici, comoedia finita est.'[262]
>
> The last days have been extraordinary; he anticipates his death with true Socratic wisdom and great serenity of spirit. Yesterday we were even fortunate enough to put his will in order. Three days after receiving your letter he became extremely agitated and wanted his sketches for the tenth symphony, concerning the plan of which he told me a great deal. He firmly intends it for the Philharmonic Society. The form this work now takes in his sick fantasy would make it a musical leviathan. . . .[263]

It was also on 18 March that Beethoven asked me to take care of the dedication of his last quartet in F major, and wanted me to choose one of his most worthy friends. Since I knew how highly he regarded the Viennese merchant Johann Wolfmayer, and how much this man had

---

* I decided to delay sending Beethoven's letter of 18 March for a few days so that I might observe the course of events.

done for him (he was one of the quietest but most helpful of the master's patrons), I communicated this name to the publisher.[264] Wolfmayer found himself in possession of a considerable number of manuscripts of Beethoven's major works. This fact first became known in 1850 when these manuscripts, which at that time had already been passed on to his nephew, were auctioned in Vienna at a very low price.

On the morning of 24 March the master asked for the last sacrament, which he took in a spirit of true devotion. At about one o'clock in the afternoon he showed the first signs of his approaching death. A frightful struggle between death and life began, probably as a result of his extraordinarily strong nervous system, and continued without respite until a quarter to six on the evening of 26 March, when during a heavy hailstorm the great composer gave up his spirit.[265] He was 56 years, 3 months, and 9 days old.

The fortunate one who was able to close our friend's eyes in the hour of death was the esteemed composer and music-lover Anselm Hüttenbrenner, who had hurried to Vienna from Graz so that he might see Beethoven again. Breuning and this author had gone that afternoon to the village graveyard at Währing to seek out a suitable last resting-place. The storm prevented our quick return. When we entered the sick-room someone called out to us, 'It is finished'.*

Stephan von Breuning and this author made the arrangements for the funeral ceremony, though it was the publisher Tobias Haslinger who saw to the music. The burial took place on the afternoon of 29 March. The bier was followed first by Johann van Beethoven with his brother-in-law, a Viennese baker, then came the Imperial Counsellor von Breuning with his son, now a physician, and the author of this book, as 'mourners'. The pall-bearers on the right were the Kapellmeisters Eybler, Hummel, Seyfried, and Kreutzer, and on the left Weigl, Gyrowetz, Gänsbacher, and Würfel.[267] Nearly twenty thousand persons accompanied the procession from the apartment of the great deceased to the parish church in Alster where the service took place. The grave in the cemetery in Währing is marked by a pyramidal stone on which is written simply:

* In A. B. Marx's *Beethoven* we read in volume II, page 329, surely based upon something Anselm Hüttenbrenner said somewhere, that he and Dr. Wawruch had begged Beethoven to take the last sacrament, and that after this had been done, Beethoven had said to Hüttenbrenner and the other friends present: 'Plaudite, amici, comoedia finita est! Didn't I always say it would be like this?'
We must say in reply to this account that Herr A. Hüttenbrenner was a complete stranger to Beethoven,[266] and that unknown persons were not admitted during the last two weeks, as Dr. von Breuning can testify. Let Herr Hüttenbrenner content himself with what actually took place, as here recorded, between him and the dying composer. In the house of the dying man at the time of Hüttenbrenner's arrival in Vienna we already considered our friend among the dead, so that strangers were permitted entrance.

BEETHOVEN

A great man's deeds continue to work
Upon other men's lives through the ages,
For the good a virtuous man can do
Cannot be done within the span of one man's lifetime.
So lives he on beyond his death
And works as truly as in life;
The virtuous deed, the well-spoken word
Fight on, immortal, as he, a mortal, fought.
So liv'st thou, too, through measureless time.
Rejoice in thy eternity![268]

APPENDICES TO THE THIRD PERIOD

APPENDIX 1

From the Autopsy Report

On 27 March, Dr. Johann Wagner performed an autopsy on Beethoven's body and published his report. He wrote the following on his findings with respect to the auditory organs and the skull structure:

The auditory nerves were shrunken and indistinguishable; the auditory arteries that paralleled them were thickened and cartilaginous as though stretched over a raven's quill. The left, much thinner, auditory nerve originated in three very thin grey fibrils and the right nerve in a single thicker pure white strand, both arising from the substance of the fourth ventricle, which in this area was of a firmer consistency and more vascular. The convolutions of the brain, ordinarily much softer and more oedematous, here appeared twice as deep and more numerous (more spacious) than usual. The cranial vault was of a great thickness throughout and approximately one-half inch thick.[269]

APPENDIX 2

Wills and Financial Situation

Our master drew up two wills during his last days, but neither of them bears a date. The date of the second must be 20 or 21 March. It was written in the presence of Breuning and myself, because the executor and the co-guardian would not agree to the wording of the first will, which had been written on the 15th or 16th of March.[270] Since this situation reveals an interesting aspect of Beethoven's character, it should be recorded here in detail. The first will, drawn up in letter form and addressed 'To Herr Dr. Bach', reads:

Esteemed friend!

Before my death I designate Karl van Beethoven, my beloved nephew, as the sole heir to all my property, including chiefly seven bank shares and whatever cash may be in hand. Should the law prescribe any modifications in this, I ask you so far as possible to turn them to his advantage. I appoint you his trustee and ask that with Hofrat Breuning, his guardian, you act in the capacity of a father to him. May God be with you. A thousand thanks for the love and friendship you have displayed towards me.

Ludwig van Beethoven, m. p.

(L. S.)

Because this will contained no limitations or precautionary measures in regard to the sole heir, and because he would come into the total inheritance as soon as the property settlement was completed, the guardian and the executor objected with good reason to the conditions of the will. They found it unacceptable, particularly in view of the heir's extreme irresponsibility, as well as from the standpoint of the young man's own interests. They accordingly recommended to the master that he should change the will in such a way that the inheritance would be held in trust, with the nephew to draw the interest and the principal to pass to the nephew's legitimate offspring after his death.

At first Beethoven saw the logic of such a revision, and accepted it. But then he found such a restriction on the nephew he still loved dearly too harsh and remonstrated against the arrangement. He even went so far as to reproach Breuning, calling him the inventor of such a severe regulation. We have a note in Breuning's hand written to Beethoven that defends in reasonable words the stipulation he felt so necessary.

The tone of the letter seemed to impress the master, and he promised to comply. At his request Breuning laid before him the new proposal contained in three lines, and the master began to copy it immediately, a deed that went hard with him. When he was done, he exclaimed: 'There! I won't write another word.' We were astonished to see that on Beethoven's paper the words 'legitimate offspring' had been changed to 'natural heirs'. Breuning explained the controversies that might arise from such a wording, but Beethoven rejoined: 'One is the same as the other. Leave it that way.' This was his very last argument. After some discussion between the executor and the guardian as to which of the two wills was the less bad, they decided on the first one, which was then presented for probate.[271] It was sent to me by Dr. Bach, unfortunately after the first edition of this book had been published, along with the record of presentation and entry by the *Magistrat*, dated 27 March 1827. It has been kept along with the other court documents.

The handling of the estate belongs in the same chapter as the situation regarding the will.

III Beethoven on his deathbed. Drawing by Joseph Danhauser done on 28 March 1827 (see p. 332)

APPENDIX 3. LETTER FROM VON BREUNING

According to the executor's report, the total assets, consisting of cash, the proceeds from the sale of furniture and music, and the seven bank shares, amounted to 10,232 florins CM. From this were deducted liabilities in the form of medical and funeral expenses and other legal debts, amounting to 1,213 florins CM, leaving a net estate of 9,019 florins CM.[272]

Dr. Bach accompanied this report with the following remarks:

It is indeed true that this monetary legacy is small in proportion to the great master's worth, and would put his contemporaries in a bad light if its causes were not to be found in his manner of thinking and doing business. He was merely a master; he knew only art. He left the profits of his genius to others.

We ought also to note that the 'net estate' includes the gift of 1,000 florins CM from London. It was found still untouched at Beethoven's death. According to the wording of Moscheles's letter of 1 March, sent on behalf of the Philharmonic Society, the Society had a right to ask that the sum should be returned. It actually took steps to recover the money because it did not want the master's unworthy relatives to get it. But when the inventory was taken after the master's death, this sum too was taken into legal custody, and later the executor opposed its return. Since the Society in London did not wish to take the matter to court, the sum was left intact, to the advantage of the sole heir.[273]

APPENDIX 3

A Letter from Stephan von Breuning
The Death-Mask by Danhauser

Beethoven expressed explicitly his desire to have Breuning and myself attend to all matters not pertaining to the guardianship of the nephew. Part of this desire had to do with his biography. As I have explained in the Introduction, in August of the previous year he had allowed himself to be seduced into an agreement that he now felt too weak to undo.[274] We shall hear more details of this affair in the supplementary chapter, 'Beethoven and Karl Holz'. Similar precipitous acts may have been concealed in other ways, to come to light only at some future time. There were other matters, arrangements with publishers and the like, about which Breuning, who for nine whole years had been estranged from Beethoven, had to consult with me since I was acquainted with everything. A difference of opinion with a worthy character like Breuning

Fac simile No. 2. zu Beethovens Biographie 2.r Thl.
von Anton Schindler. Vergl. S. 150.

Die Ankündigung der Stunde der
Leichenfeyer unseres verschiedenen
Freundes geschieht morgen oder doch
gewiß übermorgen im Beobachter,
u. vielleicht auch in der Wiener Zeitung,
statt jeder andern Karte. Ich habe
darüber an H. v. Bernard geschrieben u.
zusagende Antwort erhalten.
Morgen früh wünscht ein gewisser
Buchhändler einen [illegible] Abdruck von

IV   Letter from Stephan von Breuning to Schindler dated 27 March 1827 (see p. 332) was hardly thinkable. But providence ordained it otherwise. Two months after Beethoven's death Breuning, too, departed this life. The noble man died of a broken heart as a result of repeated bitter mortifications on the part of his superior, Prince Hohenzollern-Hechingen, at that time president of the imperial war ministry and a man who ruled over his high office in a medieval spirit. Breuning was barely fifty years old.

Dr. Bach now turned to the relatives of the nephew's mother for his choice of a guardian, a most deplorable step.[275] This was sufficient reason for my having nothing more to do with the whole matter. Some things, though by no means all, could have been very different if Breuning had lived just a few more years. Many important, purely musical matters might have been taken care of with the help of Count Moritz Lichnowsky and Carl Czerny. Let us speak only of the first event after the departure of our friend, for it was implied in Beethoven's wish mentioned above. The day after the catastrophe Breuning sent me the following lines:

The announcement of the hour of our departed friend's funeral will appear tomorrow, or at the very latest day after tomorrow, in the *Beobachter* and perhaps in the *Wiener Zeitung*, but nowhere else. I have written to Herr v. Rau about it and received his consent.

Tomorrow morning a certain Danhauser wishes to take a plaster cast of the body. He says it will take five minutes, or at the most eight. Write and tell me whether I should agree. Such casts are often permitted in the case of famous men, and not to permit it might later be regarded as an insult to the public.

Vienna, 27 March 1827   Breuning

This plaster cast (taken by Danhauser, who later became renowned as a sculptor) still exists. The facsimile of this letter from Breuning is given at the end of this volume.* It proves the authenticity of the death-mask, and is an example of the handwriting of the friend who for so many years remained true and constant to the great composer.

APPENDIX 4

Catalogue of Works Composed in the Period

Although some of the works included in this catalogue appeared in the list of works pertaining to the second period, they had to be repeated here because their publication date falls in the third period.

---

* Editor's note. It is reproduced in the present edition as Facsimile IV on p. 330. A drawing Danhauser did of Beethoven on his deathbed on 28 March is reproduced as Plate III, facing p. 328.

APPENDIX 4. CATALOGUE OF WORKS

A. *Vocal Music*

Missa Solemnis, opus 123, first performed 1824, published 1827 by Schott.*

Die Ruinen von Athen, opp. 113, 114, poem by August von Kotzebue, a festival piece and postlude with chorus and solos, first performed for the opening of the great theatre in Budapest in 1812, and, as may be deduced from the unusual use of two opus numbers, published in sections at two separate times by Artaria [Steiner].[276]

Meeresstille und glückliche Fahrt, opus 112, poem by Goethe, for four voices with orchestral accompaniment, first performed 1815, published in 1822 by Steiner & Co.

Empi, tremate, [sic] opus 116, trio, for soprano, tenor and bass, written and performed 1814, published 1826 by Haslinger [Steiner].

Elegischer Gesang, opus 118, for four voices accompanied by two violins, viola, and cello, or by piano, published 1827 [1826] by Haslinger.

Twenty-five Scottish Songs with German and English text, opus 108, for solo voice [in most cases] accompanied by piano with violin and cello obbligato, published [1818 by George Thomson, Edinburgh] 1825 [1822] by Schlesinger.

Opferlied, opus 121b, poem by Matthisson, for solo voice with chorus and orchestra, published 1826 [1825] by Schott.

Bundeslied, opus 122, poem by Goethe, for two solo voices and three choral parts accompanied by two clarinets, two horns, and two bassoons, published 1826 [1825] by Schott.

(The latter two songs were written in 1822 for the tenor Ehlers to sing at his benefit concert in Pressburg.[277])

Der glorreiche Augenblick, opus 136, poem by Weissenbach, cantata for four [solo] voices, [chorus] and orchestra, performed 1814, published about 1836 [1837] by Haslinger.

(Because Weissenbach's text was written for the festivities in honour of the monarchs assembled in Vienna for the Congress of 1814, the publisher deemed it advisable in the interests of future performances to set this text aside and replace it with Friedrich Rochlitz's poem, *Preis der Tonkunst*. Rochlitz himself had given our Beethoven this poem as a text for musical setting in 1822.[278])

An die ferne Geliebte [sic], opus 98, poem by Alois Jeitteles, a song cycle for solo voice with piano accompaniment, published 1816 by Steiner & Co.

---

* The talented and learned Ferdinand Kessler of Frankfurt (d. 1856) did the proof-reading of both the *Missa* and the ninth symphony. His contribution in regard to these two works merits true recognition. Beethoven himself wrote Kessler a letter praising him for his careful proof-reading of the symphony.

THIRD PERIOD

B. *Instrumental Music*

SYMPHONIES

No. 7, Symphony in A major, opus 92, first performed 1813, published 1816 by Steiner & Co.

No. 8, Symphony in F major, opus 93, first performed 1814, published 1817 by Steiner & Co.

No. 9, Symphony in D minor, with Schiller's *Ode to Joy*, opus 125, first performed 1824, published 1826 by Schott.

OVERTURES

Opus 115, C major, written and performed with no further title, 1815. In 1818 the musicians Mayseder, Moscheles, and Giuliani received this overture from the publishing firm of Steiner & Co., who were already in possession of the manuscript, to play at their concert on 10 May.[279] On this occasion the work appeared on the programme under the title *à la chasse*, although the composer protested about it. The title *Namensfeier* Overture that designates this work in the most recent catalogues is no more authentic.[280] Published about 1830 [1825] by Haslinger [Steiner].

Overture to the Hungarian folk-play *König Stephan, Ungarn's erster Wohlthäter*, E flat major, opus 117, performed for the opening of the Budapest theatre in 1812, published 1828 [1826] by Haslinger [Steiner].

Zur Weihe des Hauses, C major, opus 124, with double fugue, performed for the opening of the new Josephstädter Theater in Vienna in 1822, published 1826 [1825] by Schott.

Overture to *Fidelio*, C major, opus 138, written in 1805, then set aside, first performed at Bernhard Romberg's concert in Vienna in February 1828, published about 1830 [1838] by Haslinger.

CHAMBER MUSIC

Grand Trio in B flat major, opus 97, for piano, violin, and cello, first performed 1814, published 1816 by Steiner & Co.

Two Sonatas for piano and cello, opus 102, in C major and D major, published 1817 by Simrock.

QUARTETS FOR TWO VIOLINS, VIOLA, AND CELLO

Opus 95, F minor, published 1815 [1816] by Steiner & Co.

Opus 127, E flat major, published 1826 by Schott.

Opus 130, B flat major, published 1827 by Matthias Artaria.

Opus 131, C sharp minor, published 1827 by Schott.

Opus 132, A minor, published 1827 by Schlesinger.

APPENDIX 4. CATALOGUE OF WORKS

Opus 133, *Great Fugue* (originally intended as the final movement of the quartet opus 130) published about 1830 [1827] by M. Artaria.

Opus 135, F major, published 1827 by Schlesinger.

Opus 137, Fugue in D major, written in 1816 [1817] for two violins, two violas, and cello, published about 1827 by Haslinger.

SONATAS FOR PIANO SOLO

Opus 90, E minor, published 1815 by Steiner & Co.

Opus 101, A major, published 1816 [1817] by Steiner & Co.

Opus 106, B flat major, published 1819 by Artaria.

Opus 109, E major, published 1822 [1821] by Schlesinger.

Opus 110, A flat major, published 1823 [1822] by Schlesinger and by Diabelli.[281]

Opus 111, C minor, published 1823 [1822] by Schlesinger and by Diabelli.[282]

Opus 120, *Thirty-three Variations on a Waltz by Diabelli*, for piano, published 1823 by Diabelli.

Opus 119, Twelve New Bagatelles for piano, published 1823 by Diabelli.[283]

Opus 126, Six Bagatelles for piano, published 1826 [1825] by Schott.

Besides the works listed with opus numbers in the three catalogues, there are many small compositions with no number at all. Most of these consist of essays in the various classes of composition and date from the first period. Several, including the most significant ones, were found and published after the death of the great master. They ought, therefore, to appear in this catalogue.

For orchestra:

    (a) Allegretto in E flat major [WoO 3], published by Artaria.

    (b) Triumphal March from the tragedy *Tarpeja*, in C major [WoO 2a], composed during the second period [1813], published by Steiner & Co.[284]

For stringed instruments:

    Andante Favori in F major [WoO 57], originally composed for piano in the second period [1803–4], published about 1805 by the Industrie-Comptoir.[285]

For wind instruments:

    (a) Rondino in E flat major for two oboes, two clarinets, two bassoons, and two horns [WoO 25], published by Diabelli [1830].

    (b) Three Duets in C major, F major, and B flat major for clarinet and bassoon [WoO 27], published by André.[286]

(For piano and orchestra:)

Rondo in B flat major, [WoO 6], published by Diabelli.[287]

Three Quartets in E flat major, D major, and C major for piano, violin, viola, and cello [WoO 36], published by Artaria.

Trio in E flat major for piano, violin, and cello [WoO 38], published by Dunst.

Little Trio in one movement, in B flat major [WoO 39], dedicated in 1812 to his little friend M. B. (Maximiliane Brentano), published by Dunst.

Rondo in G major for piano and violin or cello [WoO 41], published by Simrock.[288]

Three Sonatas for piano solo in E flat major, F minor, and D major [WoO 47], dedicated to Elector Max Friedrich, composed 1781 [1782–83], published by Rath [Bossler] in Speyer.

Easy Sonata in C major for piano [WoO 51], dedicated to Eleonore von Breuning in Bonn, published by Dunst.

Prelude in F minor for piano [WoO 55], written in the second period, published about 1805 by the Industrie-Comptoir.

Besides these works, the catalogues list a number of variations for piano and dances of every type for orchestra and piano, most of which were written in the first period. On the other hand, almost all of the many songs date from the second and third periods. The following are the most noteworthy for their exceptional handling of the text:

a. *Sechs deutsche Gedichte* from Reissig's *Blümchen der Einsamkeit* [WoO 146, 143, 138, opus 75, Nos. 5 and 6, WoO 139], composed about 1813 or 1814 [between 1809 and 1816], published by Artaria.[289]

b. Three Songs: *An die Geliebte, Das Geheimnis, So oder So* [WoO 140, 145, 148], written for the *Wiener Zeitschrift*,[290] published by Simrock.

c. *Lied aus der Ferne; Als mir noch die Träne der Sehnsucht nicht floss* [WoO 137], published by Breitkopf & Härtel.

d. *Andenken* (by Matthisson): *Ich denke dein* [WoO 136], published by Breitkopf & Härtel.

e. *Empfindungen bei Lydiens Untreue* [WoO 132], published by Simrock.

f. Two Songs: *Resignation, Abendlied* [WoO 149, 150], published by Kistner and Diabelli.

(Both these songs were written in the third period for the *Wiener Zeitschrift*. The first, *Resignation*, though one of the shortest, is one of the rarest pearls in the master's entire collection of songs. He himself recognized its exceptional value and spoke of it in a letter to the editor of the *Zeitschrift*, Schick, asking him to communicate to the poet, Count Haugwitz, his gratitude for giving him such a 'happy inspiration'. He had honoured only a few poets in this way before: Matthisson for *Adelaide*, Tiedge for *An die Hoffnung*, and Jeitteles for his song cycle. The little song, *Resignation*, contains a great piece of musical wisdom.)

APPENDIX 5

'The Difficult Decision'

This is the heading for the fourth movement of the last quartet, in F major, opus 135, as well as the questioning motif of the Grave, 'Must it be?' and the answering motif of the Allegro, 'It must be!'

Two explanations of these headings are possible, but we cannot know with certainty which of them actually prompted the master's serious joke, or joking seriousness.

1. In Beethoven's household the housekeeper was given money each week. It was often difficult for her to get it at the right time, for the master was not to be disturbed at his work. Old 'Frau Schnapps' used to stand at his desk, all dressed to go to market, and wait until a chance (or perhaps an angry) look would fall on her basket. Then would come the question in various tones, sometimes even sung: 'Must it be?' to which the old woman would nod her head or stamp her foot and answer: 'It must be!' This joke was repeated almost every Saturday, and when the housekeeper had to prove with a calendar that it was payday, the master was always amused in a way that only the sly but faithful old servant could amuse him.[291]

2. In Vienna there was in the house of the court agent, von Dembscher, for many years a quartet with Mayseder as first violin. When that music-lover heard of the completion of the quartet in E flat major opus 127, he asked for the honour of having it played for the first time in his house. However, it had been written as the main attraction for a concert that was to be given for Schuppanzigh's benefit. Despite this arrangement, Dembscher made so bold as to request of the composer the favour of a first performance. Beethoven consented on condition that Dembscher immediately pay Schuppanzigh fifty florins as compensation for any loss he might sustain at his benefit concert. The quartet-

lover then asked the master if he were serious. The answer was, 'It must be!' This peremptory reply left the court agent no choice but to pay Schuppanzigh the required sum. The new quartet was thus played for the first time in Dembscher's house.[292]

Of the two versions, the first is certainly well-founded, for almost every necessary expenditure of money entailed a difficult decision on the part of the master. It was no less true that the court agent did have to pay Schuppanzigh fifty florins. In either case, the French translation of this title, *un effort d'inspiration*, misses the point and goes much too deep.

EDITOR'S NOTES (135–292)
Third Period

[135] Schindler's date is in error. Oliva was apparently away from Vienna for five years or more from the summer of 1813 (see And. 427), but Conversation Books Nos. 2–16 as transcribed by Schünemann indicate that during the period spring 1819 to autumn 1820 he was back in Vienna and was by a wide margin Beethoven's most frequent associate. In the late summer of 1820 he referred several times to plans for going to Russia (SchKH II 210, 249, 263); a notice published in the *Wiener Zeitung* of 8 May 1822 (TDR III 131) indicates that he had put this plan into execution in December 1820.

[136] The period covered by the estrangement with Breuning cannot be stated with certainty. The break may have occurred as early as 1809 (TF 464) or 1815 (TK II 322), or 1817 may be the correct date (TK III 24; TF 746). The friendship was resumed no later than autumn 1825, when Beethoven moved into the Schwarzspanierhaus near Breuning's residence (TK III 213; TF 967); Schlösser said that he saw Beethoven in the company of Breuning and Schindler after a performance of *Fidelio* on 4 November 1822 (TK III 85; TF 848).

[137] The Josephinists were partisans against the rigid, 'police-state' rule imposed by Metternich after the Congress of Vienna. The movement took its name from the idealistic policies that Emperor Joseph II had tried in vain to establish during his reign (1780–90).

[138] According to TK II 301 and TF 601, Rasumovsky was not elevated to the rank of Prince until 3 June 1815. It may be stated with confidence that no 'extraordinary celebrations' accompanied this event: the work of the Congress was virtually completed (the Final Act, embodying all the separate treaties, was signed on 9 June), the return of Napoleon had once more turned Europe into a battlefield (Napoleon had entered Paris on 20 March, and by 3 June the Battle of Waterloo was barely two weeks away), and the Rasumovsky palace had been destroyed by fire more than five months before (TK II 301; TF 601).

[139] These are probably the ear trumpets shown by Ley in *Beethovens Leben in Bildern*, p. 77, and by Bory, p. 161.

[140] See Supplement H, p. 486 *infra*.

[141] Schindler's memory again plays him false: his own words in a Conversation Book (TK II 235; TF 545) state that he and Maelzel took part together in an impromptu performance of the *Ta, ta* canon at a Viennese tavern in 1817 when the friendship between Beethoven and Maelzel was restored.

[142] The quarrel with Maelzel is discussed impartially and at length in TK II 274n and TF 1097 ff.

[143] 'Herr A . . .' was Artaria, whose pirating of the quintet opus 29 in 1802 has already been mentioned.

[144] It seems to be generally accepted that Beethoven received no payments from the Lobkowitz estate after the death of the Prince. Leeder, whose discussions of the recipients of dedications from Beethoven seem for the most part to be very accurate, says of Lobkowitz: 'His *Nachlass* was disposed of in bankruptcy. Beethoven renewed his petition, but this time was unsuccessful, and thus entirely lost the Lobkowitz payments' (DM IV$_4$ [1905] 186; see also ibid., p. 178).

This statement, however, is contradicted by much evidence to the effect that the agreed payments were continued until the end of Beethoven's life. Various passages in the Conversation Books indicate that payments were received from the Lobkowitz estate as they are known to have been from Archduke Rudolph and from the Kinsky estate:

Oliva: 'It seems to me that it would be best for me to go this afternoon to Lobkowitz's cashier. He might give me the money at that time, and then we would have time to think about something else.' (SchKH I 105—early December 1819)

Bernard: 'At the end of June you will receive the interest on your bonds and the dividends on your bonds and your payment from Lobkowitz.' (SchKH II 129—mid-May 1820)

Oliva: 'Now you can get the money from Lobkowitz.' (SchKH II 194—late July or early August 1820)

Oliva: 'Regarding the money from Lobkowitz, you should see about it when he comes from Berlin.' (SchKH II 203—late July or early August 1820)

Beethoven: 'Regarding the Lobkowitz cashier—Oliva.' (SchKH II 248—about 1 September 1820)

The inventory of Beethoven's *Nachlass* (BStud II 177) includes an item of 66 florins 53 kreutzer CM receivable from the Lobkowitz cashier. This corresponds to 87 days' accrual against the annual subsidy of 280 florins CM (corresponding to 700 florins paper currency). It would indicate that a payment had been made for the period ending 30 December 1826 (31 December 1826 was a Sunday), and would further indicate that all payments up to that time had been made.

This evidence goes far to substantiate the statement in a letter from Köchel to Thayer that the agreed payments were made by Lobkowitz, as well as by the other two noble signers of the contract of 1 March 1809, throughout the eighteen years that elapsed until Beethoven's death (TDR III 491; see also TK II 306, TF 611, and Note 115).

[145] All accounts agree that in February 1816 Stainer von Felsburg gave a public performance of one of Beethoven's piano sonatas, which Schindler refers to as the only such instance during Beethoven's lifetime. The occasion for the performance and the identity of the sonata that was heard are however open to question. Nohl III 82 and TDR III 586 agree that the concert-giver was Linke, which would place the date of the performance as 18 February (TK II 338; TF 641). Schindler, on the other hand, says that it was Schuppanzigh (11 February).

A review of the concert quoted in Nohl III 827 refers to a 'new sonata'. Schindler says specifically that it was opus 101, and Nohl III 82 and TK II 338, but not TF 641, repeat this statement. This is impossible, since that work was composed only during the summer of 1816 (KHV 279). TDR III 480 makes the alternative conjecture that the sonata was opus 90, which had been published in June 1815 (KHV 249), and which therefore could legitimately be described as a 'new sonata'. Schindler's reference to the soloist's playing of the first and third movements might seem to throw doubt on this identification, since opus 90 has only two movements. The fact that he was writing more than forty years after the event may safely allow this identification to be disregarded.

All facts considered, it may be assumed with confidence that at Linke's farewell concert on 18 February 1816, Stainer von Felsburg played opus 90. Commenting on Schindler's statement that this was the only public performance of a Beethoven piano sonata during the composer's lifetime, Hanslick (p. 278) says: 'Beethoven's piano sonatas failed to appear on concert programmes, not because they were by Beethoven but because they were piano sonatas', and goes on to explain that at that time piano sonatas were considered suitable only for performance in the home, not in public.

[146] See Note 280.

[147] The date of the diploma of honorary citizenship, transcribed in full in TDR III 524, is 16 November 1815; Thayer says that the diploma was formally delivered to Beethoven about 1 December. A facsimile of the diploma is given by Bory, p. 183. In the light of these dates it is obvious that the honorary citizenship was not a 'direct result' of the concert of 25 December.

[148] The correspondence between Beethoven and George Thomson (1757–1851) extended over a period of nearly seventeen years: from July 1803, when Thomson approached Beethoven to compose some sonatas on Scottish airs, until June 1820. Beethoven sent his first batch of song settings, 53 in number, in July 1810. A total of 132 settings that Beethoven made appear in Series 24 of the *Gesamtausgabe*, and 23 more are listed by KHV as WoO 158; starting in 1814, Thomson published 125 of these, of which only 25 (opus 108) were published in Germany during Beethoven's lifetime. More than fifty letters passed between Beethoven and Thomson; these are summarized in M. & L. XXXVII (1956) 27. A detailed bibliographical study of the settings published by Thomson is given in *Edinburgh Bibliographical Society Transactions* II

(1939–40) 1, and III (1954) 121. The Variations opp. 105 and 107, an offshoot of this work on national airs, are discussed in MR XII (1951) 45.

149 The years 1816–18 were indeed unproductive: the only compositions of any substance from this period are the song cycle *An die ferne Geliebte*, opus 98, and the A major piano sonata, opus 101, both completed in 1816.

150 Further excerpts from this questionnaire are given in TK II 387 and TF 689. Walter Nohl (*Beethoven und die Frauen*, p. 151; see also KBr III 50) says that these questions were addressed to Nannette Streicher; he gives the complete list of questions, together with her very detailed answers. For example, her reply to the first question was: 'On week days the two servants are given two plates of soup, the same quantity of vegetables, and a pound of meat. At night they get soup and vegetables. If some of their meat is left over from the noon meal, so much the better for them; if not, they cannot demand it.' See also Sterba, *Beethoven and his Nephew*, p. 124.

151 Schindler's narrative differs in various details from the account of this episode, based to some extent on court records, as given in TK II 331 and TF 634. The week after Brother Karl's death, his widow Johanna was named guardian of her son, with the composer as associate guardian. Beethoven promptly petitioned that the guardianship be transferred to him, and after several hearings he was formally appointed to this post on 19 January 1816. Except as mentioned by Schindler, there is no record of Adlersburg having taken part in this action, but it is not improbable that he did so, since in 1814 he had represented Beethoven in the Maelzel case and in the wrangle with the Kinsky heirs. Adlersburg may have been a 'coarse individual', but from 1820 he was a member of the faculty of law at the University of Vienna, and in 1834 he was named Rector of the University. As Schindler says, Nephew Karl was placed in Giannatasio's school in February 1816, but in doing so Beethoven was acting entirely within his powers as the court-appointed guardian.

152 'To translate the word *Magistrat* by the English word 'magistrate', as is done in several generally used works of reference, is as naïve and as misleading as to translate the German word *also* by the English word spelt the same way. The *Magistrat* was the aggregation of bureaux and departments through which the affairs of the city were administered. Staffed by appointed, salaried civil servants, the *Magistrat* enforced the ordinances and executed the policies laid down by the *Magistrats-Rat*, an elective body corresponding to our Board of Aldermen, City Council, or the like.

'Beethoven's principal contact with the *Magistrat* was with the department that supervised the guardianship of minors and incompetents: the *Obervormundschaft*. He also had occasion to turn to what in American municipal organization would be known as the police courts or the magistrates' courts: the *Polizeibehörde*. In general, however, whatever group he was dealing with was to him the *Magistrat*' (MM 157).

153 Fanny Giannatasio was far from being 'a non-partisan voice': the title that Nohl gave to his publication of her diary—*Eine stille Liebe* (A Secret Love) —fairly represents her feeling towards the composer.

154 Here Schindler diverges widely from the facts (see TK II 403 ff;

TF 708 ff). The trial had not 'dragged on for over a year'; the petition that Beethoven laid before the court in November 1815 had been decided in January 1816 and the matter closed. In December 1818, after Nephew Karl had been withdrawn from Giannatasio's school, Johanna filed a new petition asking that she should be allowed to send him to the Imperial *Konvikt* for schooling. At a hearing on this petition, Johanna stated (TK II 408; TF 711) that she believed her husband was of noble birth and that documentary proof of nobility was in the possession of the composer. Beethoven, however, trapped himself into the statement that ' "Van" was a Dutch predicate which was not exclusively applied to the nobility; he had neither a diploma nor any other proof of his nobility'. In a conversation with Karl Bernard a year or so later, Beethoven confirmed his understanding of the significance of the predicate; ' "Van" designates a noble and a patrician only when it stands between two proper names, as "Bentink van Dieperheim", "Hooft van Vreeland", and the like' (SchKH I 160). Schindler's reference to a statement by Beethoven before the court that his nobility lay in his head and his heart is wholly unsupported by the official transcript of the hearing. TK II 409 justly refers to it as a 'pretty romance'.

155 The first three of these entries are found in SchKH I 247, and probably date from about 8 February 1820, a few days after the *Magistrat* had recommended to the Court of Appeals (to which Beethoven had turned) that its appointment of Johanna as co-guardian with the court functionary Nussböck should be confirmed. The last entry by Beethoven that Schindler quotes is not given in SchKH. At the request of the editor, Dr. Karl-Heinz Köhler, Chief of the Music Division of the Deutsche Staatsbibliothek (where the extant Conversation Books are preserved) checked the original of this passage. Dr. Köhler reported: 'Schünemann's transcription of the questioned passage is altogether correct. The last remark by Beethoven is apparently an addition by Schindler.' The 'Memorandum' to which Schindler caused Beethoven to refer was a long communication that Beethoven addressed to the Court of Appeals on 18 February in justification of his acts as guardian. This Memorandum is given in MM 285.

156 TK II 377 cites a document (apparently unpublished) issued by the upper court on 29 November 1815 in which Beethoven was referred to as 'Royal Imperial Kapellmeister and Music Composer', so that the use of this designation had in a way been sanctioned by the court. Thayer's use of this passage (see TDR IV 51) to document Schindler's undependability regarding details does not seem to be well founded, since Schindler does not claim that Dr. Bach *introduced* the use of the title, but merely that he required that it should be used.

157 Ley (abridged edition of Schindler *Biographie* [1949], p. 503) conjectures that 'L' may have been a slip of the pen (or a misreading) for 'K' (= Karl).

158 In the first (1840) edition of the biography, p. 119, Schindler comments on this entry: 'When, therefore, we heard that the . . . "four bad days" were so described for the reason that, quite without ready cash, he was obliged to make his dinner of a glass of beer and a few biscuits, as I have heard from his

own lips, I for my part was inclined to see there the beginnings of his subsequent parsimony, which was one day to enrich an unworthy, laughing heir'.

[159] Various scholars have given various dates for Rudolph's installation as Archbishop of Olmütz. The correctness of the date given by Schindler has been verified by the editor through correspondence with the Vatican Secretariat of State.

[160] TK III 15n and TF 735 give reason to believe that Schindler's companion on this visit was not Horzalka.

[161] Except for the composition and publication of the song cycle *An die ferne Geliebte*, opus 98, during 1816, Schindler's statement regarding the non-productiveness of the years 1816–20 is fully confirmed in KHV 750–52, though work on the Diabelli Variations, opus 120, and the *Missa Solemnis*, opus 123, was under way from 1819.

[162] This passage is the only one known to the editor in the Beethoven literature of the nineteenth century—indeed, the only one that he knows earlier than the comments of the Sterbas in their iconoclastic *Beethoven and his Nephew* of 1954—that admits that anyone could have had anything good to say about Johanna.

'In attempting at this late date to appraise Johanna's character and habits, due weight must be given to the fact that virtually the only information on this score that we have about her, or ever can expect to have, is from Beethoven, whose animus against her approached the degree of an obsession, or from members of his closest circle of intimates, who must be considered quite the reverse of impartial witnesses. . . . We must never lose sight of the fact that Fate, not Justice, has withheld from us any single word that would favour Johanna' (MM 329).

[163] The review of this concert quoted in TDR IV 157 gives no indication that Beethoven showed himself unfitted for further appearances as a conductor.

[164] The writer in the AmZ was several years behind time: see Note 148.

[165] The letter to Count Brunsvik that Schindler refers to, which may have been written about the time of opus 57 (see pp. 135, 231), is not otherwise known. The 'single stroke' seems in fact to have been spread over nearly two years: opus 109 was composed in the late summer of 1820; the fair copy of opus 110 is dated '25 December 1821', and the last movement was revised during the following spring; the copy of opus 111 for the publisher was ready in the spring of 1822 (KHV *passim*).

[166] Actually, November 1821 in Berlin (KHV 312).

[167] Opus 110, engraved in Paris, was published almost simultaneously in Paris, Berlin, and Vienna in August 1822 (KHV 315). See Tyson, *Acta Musicologica* XXXV (1963).

[168] For discussions of the devious course the many editions of opus 111 followed, see Unverricht, *Eigenschriften und originalausgaben Beethovens* (1960), Lowens, *Library of Congress Quarterly Journal of Current Acquisitions* XX (1962)1, and Tyson, *Acta Musicologica, op. cit.*

[169] The review by Marx (*Berliner AmZ* I [1824] 95), of which Schindler

gives only a brief excerpt, is given *in extenso* in Lenz, *Beethoven: eine Kunststudie* (1860) V 104.

170 'The completion [of the *Missa*] was prolonged to the end of 1822 (Rochlitz [AmZ XXIV (1822) 676] mentions the beginning of October). During the next months various further tasks were carried out: preparation of the organ part, addition of parts for trombones, etc., so that the final version was ready only about the middle of 1823' (KHV 361).

171 The publishers referred to were Steiner in Vienna and C. F. Peters in Leipzig. The former was for several years from 1815 Beethoven's sole outlet for compositions of any significance, publishing opp. 90–101 and other works. The debtor-creditor relationship between Beethoven and Steiner is discussed by Schindler in detail and with much warmth and partisanship.

C. F. Peters, successor to Hoffmeister & Kühnel as proprietor of the Bureau de Musique in Leipzig, published nothing by Beethoven in an original edition during the composer's lifetime. In the summer of 1822 he advanced 300 (or 360) florins to Beethoven against compositions to be received. Beethoven apparently sent only a single package of music (songs, bagatelles, WoO 20), which Peters found unsatisfactory. For some years thereafter there was correspondence regarding a quartet that Peters might accept to offset the payment, but no decision was reached, and Beethoven repaid the advance in December 1825. Thus Schindler speaks loosely when he refers to Peters as one of the composer's publishers to whom he went in debt. His inclusion of Peters among those 'notorious for their ruthlessness' is a wholly unwarranted distortion of the facts.

172 In 1821–23 Beethoven sold the sonatas opp. 109–11 to Schlesinger. The only original work that Diabelli received was the variations opus 120 that he had commissioned, though Beethoven collaborated with him in 1823 in preparing a corrected reprint of opus 111.

173 Except for this statement, the editor knows of no claim by Steiner to rights in opp. 109–11. Undoubtedly he felt aggrieved that the works had gone to his German rival, and he may well have expressed his feeling of ill-treatment in unmistakable terms, but this is quite different from claiming proprietorship as a matter of right.

174 The first mention of this plan in documents that are still extant seems to have been in Brother Johann's letter of 22 or 27 December 1822 to Pacini (NBJ VI [1935] 112; ZfM CIII [1936] 415) and in Beethoven's letter of 7 January 1823 to Griesinger (And. 1122). Letters as late as autumn 1822 (e.g., And. 1097–99, 1101, 1103) mentions the Mass only in connection with its sale to some one of various publishers. Shortly before 23 January 1823 (And. 1125) Beethoven asked Schindler to make up a list of the foreign legations in Vienna. TK III 93 ff, and TF 822ff give the names of more than a dozen courts to which invitations were sent (see also SchKH II 360). A typical letter is given in facsimile, transcription, and translation in Sonneck, *Beethoven Letters*, p. 121 (see also MM 355).

175 The subscription list as sent by Beethoven to Schott on 25 November 1825 (And. 1452) and as published in the engraved edition of opp. 123–25

(see Bory, p. 193) includes the names of two other monarchs: the King of Denmark (Frederik VI) and the Grand Duke of Tuscany (Ferdinand III, Archduke of Austria). Kalischer (*Anton Schindler's Beethoven-Biographie* [1909], p. 341n) quotes a letter from Wilhelm Behrend of Copenhagen on the matter of a subscription to the *Missa* from Denmark: 'As I stated in my great illustrated History of Music, I have made a search of the national archives of that period. It is unfortunately not possible to determine whether the King of Denmark was actually one of the subscribers, since no correspondence on the matter was to be found. The Royal Archivist doubted it since the King was not interested in music.'

[176] In the diary of his stay in Paris during the first months of 1841 (Becker: *Anton Schindler* [1939], p. 42) Schindler tells of his visit to Cherubini on 3 February. When Schindler asked about the letter from Beethoven (see Supplement F), the old composer assured him that he had never received the letter, which Beethoven may have forwarded to Maurice Schlesinger for delivery (see SchKH III 199), and urged Schindler to make this fact publicly known. This Schindler did in his book, *Beethoven in Paris* (1841), p. 97; it was probably only through inadvertence that no mention was made in the present biography. The statement here that Cherubini 'regretted that he had not kept the letter' is contradicted by Schindler's diary entry: 'Mais mon Dieu je n'ai pas reçu cette lettre'.

[177] Whether *a cappella* was used in its customary sense of a composition for unaccompanied voices or its obsolete sense of a composition in which instruments are used but only to reinforce the voices by doubling in unison or at the interval of an octave, an *a cappella* performance of any section of the *Missa Solemnis* is unthinkable. A conjecture by Krehbiel (TK III 117n) is the only attempt known to the present editor to explain Beethoven's remarkable statement. 'On 10 March [1823] Dietrichstein sent Beethoven three texts for Graduals and a like number for Offertories from which to choose words to be used in the Mass to be composed for the Emperor.' A setting of the 'Tantum ergo' was also apparently being considered. 'Possibly after abandonment of that project they were associated with the Mass in D', one or more of these additional pieces to be set *a cappella*. If Beethoven had even half-way decided to do this, it would be in keeping with his general practice to speak and write as though the work of composition had already been completed.

[178] This medal is illustrated in Ley: *Beethovens Leben in Bildern*, p. 112. It weighs 143.5 grams (4.6 troy ounces).

'The biographer is certainly in error when he intimates that the medal was given in payment of the subscription price. . . . Beethoven's needs and the reply which he gave the messenger from Prussia when he offered a decoration instead of the 50 ducats, indicate plainly enough how he felt as to the remuneration. . . . Evidently King Louis XVIII paid the money in the regular way and sent the medal as a special mark of distinction' (TK III 101; TF 829).

[179] The reference is presumably to Baron Alexander von Bach (1813–93), Minister of Justice and then Minister of the Interior under Emperor Franz

Joseph, who from 1851 to 1860, after the failure of the Hungarian War of Independence in 1849, administered Austria-Hungary as a single unified state in which Hungary had lost its historical identity. The strong nationalistic spirit of the Hungarians, as well as of the minority peoples within Hungary (Croats, Serbs, Slovaks, and others) doomed this system to a failure that was resolved by the Compromise of 1867, which restored Hungary to the status of a free nation under the suzerainty of the Emperor of Austria.

[180] On the matter of the duration of Beethoven's association with Seyfried, Schindler's memory failed him badly. And. 302 of 11 April 1811 is a letter of thanks to Seyfried for his many kindnesses; in And. 391 to Haslinger (probably 1815) Beethoven sent regards to 'His Seyfriedelity'; And. 1109 (autumn 1822) is a cordial letter of thanks to 'my dear and beloved brother in Apollo', probably for Seyfried's performance of opus 124 at a charity concert.

[181] For generations the royal family of Austria had been active in music. Franz's great-great-grandfather Leopold I (1640-1658-1705) was a composer and a performer on several instruments. Compositions by Leopold I and by his father Ferdinand III (1608-1637-1657) and his son Joseph I (1678-1705-1711) were published in 1892-93 under the editorship of Guido Adler. Franz's great-grandfather Emperor Karl VI (1685-1711-1740) composed masses that were sung long after his death. His uncle Emperor Joseph II (1741-1765-1790) was a singer, pianist, 'cellist, and skilled score reader. Another uncle, Maximilian Franz, Elector of Cologne (1756-1801), a viola player, built up the orchestra and opera company in Bonn with which Beethoven was associated in his youth; an aunt, Marie Antoinette, was active in the support of Gluck against Piccini in Paris (DM IV$_4$ [1905] 179). According to Novotny (*Wiener Geschichtsblätter* XVI [LXXVI] [1961] 344), Emperor Franz 'was not a bad violinist, and enjoyed the string quartets of Haydn'.

As noted by Schindler, the Empress Marie Theresia of Naples (1772-1790-1807) was a great music-lover and a trained singer who took part in performances of opera at the court (DM III$_2$ [1904] 425). In 1799 Haydn wrote his *Maria Theresia Mass* for her; it was to her that Beethoven dedicated the septet opus 20, and she was instrumental in securing the permission of the censor for the performance of *Leonore* in 1805.

[181a] On 30 January 1823 brother Johann had told Beethoven: 'It's a shame for you to write a mass specifically for the Court, since Teyber's post will not be filled. Recently I have been with Count Dietrichstein twice, and the second time he told me that he now knew for sure that this post would not be filled. He told me that the last time I was with him' (SchKH II 345).

[182] Schindler erroneously gives 1705 as the year of Johann Adam Karl Georg von Reutter's birth, and names Gassmann, not Luc' Antonio Predieri (1688-1767), as his predecessor. In fact, Florian Gassmann (1729-74) founder of the *Tonkünstler-Societät*, succeeded Reutter as Court Kapellmeister. Reutter had filled the post of Principal Court Kapellmeister since Predieri's retirement in 1751, but received the title only in 1767. In 1735 he had succeeded his father Georg (1656-1738) as Kapellmeister at the Stephanskirche, a post that the father had held for forty-nine years.

[183] The invitation was from the Handel and Haydn Society of Boston (see TK III 87; TF 834).

[184] It can be stated with confidence that Diabelli's project was initiated much earlier than 1822–23. The first contribution (from Carl Czerny) was dated 7 May 1819 (KHV 348), and sketches by Beethoven for several of the variations antedate work on the *Missa Solemnis* that must have been done early in 1819 (NBJ VII [1937] 167).

[185] Note, however, the statement in a letter from Beethoven (And. 1105) that Unger (SBSK–Br 114) assigns to early November 1822: 'The fee for the variations would be 40 ducats at most, provided they are worked out on as large a scale as suggested. But if this should *not materialize*, then I would quote a *smaller* fee.'

[186] It was probably about this time that Beethoven made for Thomson the setting of *God Save the King* (WoO 157 No. 1) for soloist and unison chorus with accompaniment of violin, cello, and piano.

[187] This list, with prices assigned to 42 different categories of musical works, is given in the 1840 edition of the biography, p. 246n.

[188] Nohl III 88 says that Beethoven became indebted to Steiner as early as 1813 through advances against unpublished works, and BHdb I 74 refers to an initial loan of 1,500 florins from Steiner, saying that it was probably needed to assist Brother Karl, who in 1813–14 was in dire need of money. Both of these statements are probably based on the passage in the biography under discussion. In And. 533 of 10 March 1815, Beethoven told Breitkopf & Härtel that he had been forced by the need of raising money to have dealings with a publisher in Vienna. This was undoubtedly Steiner, and is the first reference in extant documents to the borrower-lender relationship between the two men. If Schindler's statement is accepted it would mean that Beethoven had borrowed substantial sums from Steiner nearly two years before his first known letter to the publisher that can be definitely dated (And. 527 of 1 February 1815).

[189] At this point Schindler inadvertently named N. Simrock instead of his son Peter Joseph (1792–1868). Nikolaus Simrock, founder of the publishing house in Bonn, had died in 1833; it was Peter Joseph who went to Vienna in 1816 to settle the negotiations for the cello sonatas opus 102.

[190] See Note 87.

[191] This note probably dates from late January 1823. Two postscripts to it that Schindler did not include are given in And. 1127. An entry by Beethoven in a Conversation Book of that time (SchKH II 313) indicates that he owed his tailor 300 florins. From And. 1128, to the attorney Joseph Uibel, we may conclude that the 'kind words' were not accepted as payment of the tailor's bill.

[192] Between 1822 and 1826 Steiner published opp. 112–18 and 121a but, as Schindler states, all of these were composed not later than 1815, though some of them were revised thereafter.

[193] The bagatelles that Beethoven promised to Peters on 22 November 1822 (And. 1106) and sent to him presumably on 8 February 1823 (And. 1137) could only have been those of opus 119, published by Clementi in June 1823

(MQ XLIX [1963] 331), since the bagatelles opus 126, published by Schott in 1825, were not completed until early 1824 (KHV 381).

¹⁹⁴ The reference is to Frau Antonia Josepha von Brentano, *née* von Birkenstock (1780–1869), wife of Franz von Brentano (1765–1844). A letter to Frau Antonia of November 1815 (And. 570) referred to 'your generosity to me'; And. 659 (probably 29 September 1816) spoke of 'the cheque that you and F[ranz] have sent to me'. The relationship between Beethoven and various members of the Brentano family is discussed in MR XIX (1958) 6.

¹⁹⁵ The reference is to the commission given to Beethoven by the Gesellschaft der Musikfreunde for the composition of an oratorio, which is further discussed on pp. 270–1, 294 As is made clear there, the 'kindly censor in Vienna' was Dr. Bach; the 'other person' was Karl Bernard.

¹⁹⁵ᵃ The authenticity of this story is vouched for by Biedenfeld himself (BusZ IV 119; Kerst II 76).

¹⁹⁶ The relationship between Beethoven and Grillparzer is discussed at some length in M. & L. XL (1959) 44.

¹⁹⁷ Schindler has here confused two different negotiations with Count Brühl. Marx (*Beethoven*, 5th ed. [1901] I 396) agrees that in the spring of 1823 the Count requested a new opera for Berlin. That such a request was made is indicated by a conversation (SchKH III 369) with a Herr Deetz from Berlin in early July 1823 (BusZ I 338 suggests that Deetz may have come as a representative of Prince Radzivil), in which the visitor said, 'I hear that we will have the pleasure of a new opera by you.' The statement that at this time Beethoven referred the libretto of *Melusina* to Count Brühl seems without foundation.

A letter of 15 April 1826 from A. M. Schlesinger to Beethoven (BusV 124) said that with his letter of 27 February (lost) Beethoven had sent the libretto of *Melusina*, which Schlesinger had in turn forwarded to Brühl, and that Brühl's reply had been sent by Schlesinger to Beethoven. A letter direct from Brühl to Beethoven, dated 6 April 1826, is given in DM III₂ (1904) 436, confirming these statements and expressing the opinion that *Melusina* would not be suitable because of its similarity to the Fouqué-Hoffmann *Undine* that had been performed with much success in 1816–17. Beethoven's letter of 31 May 1826 to Schlesinger (MM 443) closed the matter.

¹⁹⁸ The Riemann *Lexikon* points out that when Caroline Unger sang in Italy (after 1824) she used the name Carlotta Ungher—Ungher to indicate the correct pronunciation of her last name (in Italian, Unger would be pronounced with a soft 'g').

¹⁹⁹ Kalischer (*Anton Schindler's Beethoven-Biographie* [1909], p. 378n) quotes a letter written by Duport in Barbaja's name, dated 20 April 1824, that gave tentative acceptance to a proposal by Beethoven that he write an opera for Barbaja's theatre.

²⁰⁰ Schindler gives the name of this body: 'königl. schwedischen Akademie der Künste und Wissenschaften'. The diploma, dated 28 December 1822 and bearing the name of the Royal Academy of Music of Sweden (Konigl. Svenska Musicaliska Academien), is shown in Ley: *Beethovens Leben in Bildern*, p. 104. Beethoven introduced another variant in the name of the scholarly body in his

letter of 7 December 1826 to Wegeler (And. 1542) when he referred to his membership in the 'Royal Scientific Society of Sweden' (k. Gesellschaft der Wissenschaften in Schweden).

Through the courtesy of the American Embassy in Stockholm, a letter has been received from Dr. J. Viktor Johannson, Secretary of the Royal Academy of Arts and Sciences (Kungl. Vetenskaps- och Vitterhets-Samhälle) in Göteborg that includes the following sentences: 'I wish to inform you that Beethoven was not a member of the Royal Academy of Arts and Sciences in Göteborg. The statement that he was a member of 'die schwedische Akademie der Künste und Wissenschaften' must be in error. . . . The Royal Academy of Music is not a component part of the Royal Academy of Arts and Sciences.'

[201] This statement must be looked upon with scepticism. About 22 October 1822, after leaving the Magdalenenhof in Baden, Beethoven moved into an apartment at Kothgasse 60, now VI Bezirk, Gumpendorferstrasse 14 (Kobald: *Klassische Musikstätten* [1929], pp. 270 ff.). Presumably the house in question fronted on both Kothgasse and Pfarrgasse. It was to this apartment that Schindler brought Beethoven after the disastrous rehearsal of *Fidelio* on the afternoon of 3 November 1822. The account on p. 237 *supra* does not indicate that this was also Schindler's home. From the invitations to dinner that Beethoven extended to Schindler in the first months of 1823 (And. 1126, 1127, 1148) it is clear that at that time Schindler did not live with Beethoven.

The first paragraph of MM 358 indicates that after Beethoven had gone to Hetzendorf for the summer on 17 May 1823, Schindler had moved into the Kothgasse apartment. Beethoven had apparently taken the apartment only until 25 July, the feast-day of St. James the Apostle (And. 1205). When Beethoven returned to the city in the autumn, he occupied rooms at Landstrasse No. 323. And. 1274 to Schindler, written probably in mid-November 1823, was addressed to him in Beethoven's hand at Kothgasse No. 60, indicating that Schindler had remained at this apartment after the expiration of Beethoven's lease.

Schindler would undoubtedly have been ecstatic at sharing an apartment with his master, but in the absence of independent evidence that he did so, his statement appears to be wishful thinking.

[202] And. 1260, written on 23 January 1824 to the directors of the GdMf, indicates clearly that Beethoven was far from satisfied with the poem. He commented on Bernard's inexperience in writing texts to set to music, even though he had approved of Bernard when the oratorio project was first presented to him in 1818 (And. 903), and concluded this part of the discussion: 'Now, however, several passages—indeed, many passages—in Bernard's oratorio must be changed. . . . Although the story is very well conceived and the poetry has some merit, it cannot remain as it is.' In September 1824 Beethoven instructed the Society to pay Bernard his fee, and concluded his letter: 'So that there may be no mistake, we assure you that absolutely without fail we will set Bernard's oratorio *Der Sieg des Kreuzes* to music, and will finish it very soon, as attested herewith by our hand and seal' (And. 1309), but there is no evidence that Beethoven ever put a note on paper for this oratorio. The entire

project is discussed at length in TK III 173 ff and TF 883 ff; excerpts from the minutes of the GdMf that refer to the oratorio are given on p. 293 of the present book.

203 The names of the signers as given here, differing somewhat from the list in the *Biography*, were transcribed from the facsimile in Bory, p. 190.

204 This is an instance of the regular practice between Beethoven and Schuppanzigh, in correspondence and in Conversation Book entries, of addressing each other in the third person.

205 In quoting these notes, as in so many other passages of his book, Schindler was forced to depend upon his memory, since the pertinent documents had been turned over to the Berlin Staatsbibliothek in January 1846 (MR XXIV [1963] 68). The notes to Schuppanzigh and to Schindler are given in facsimile in Ley's *Beethovens Leben in Bildern*, p. 115; the translation of the note to Schindler given here, differing in several details from the transcription in the *Biography*, is based on this facsimile. The fact that all three notes were included in the Beethoven material in Schindler's possession after the composer's death may be taken as proof that Beethoven never sent them.

206 And. 1281, prepared from the autograph, gives no indication that there was more of this letter than Schindler presents here.

207 A facsimile of the poster announcing this concert, which differs in minor points from the text as given by Schindler, may be found in Ley: *Beethovens Leben in Bildern*, p. 114, and in Bory, p. 191.

208 The passage specifically referred to (GA 19/203, p. 157 at the tempo indication *Grave*) and several others in the *Missa*

'are certainly crimes of the worst malignity, and few choralists can attempt the most severe of them without physical suffering. They are chiefly due to Beethoven's ignorance of one of the fundamental principles of vocal writing (a lack of knowledge shared by not a few modern composers)—that actual compass is a small matter compared with the way in which high registers are treated, that upper notes may be easily reached and maintained for a reasonable time if approach is on certain lines, that remaining on dizzy heights for any long period is exhausting, and that the pronunciation of words in exalted altitudes is the cruellest task that can be set a singer.'

Whittaker, from whose article 'The Choral Writing in the Missa Solemnis' (M. & L. VIII [1927] 296) the above quotation is taken, suggests minor modifications to a number of the most taxing passages that are worthy of consideration by any conductor who proposes to perform the *Missa*.

209 By no stretch of the imagination can the *Missa Solemnis* be considered as falling within the limitations laid down by Pope Pius X in his decree *Motu Proprio* (22 November 1903) that sets forth the characteristics of music permissible for liturgical use. It might be noted that the Cherubini *Requiem* was specifically included in a list of compositions 'clearly opposed to the principles of the *Motu Proprio*' that was issued in 1922 by the Society of St. Gregory of America. See Slonimsky, *Music Since 1900* (1949), pp. 629, 636.

210 If Schindler's references are to the original (1827) edition of the score as published by Schott (which seems to have been the only edition of the score

that had been published at the time that Schindler was preparing this edition of his biography), the cut that he calls for is complete nonsense musically: it can be explained only by the assumption that both page numbers as given in the text involve typographical errors. It would correspond to a cut from p. 216, measure 3, to p. 249, measure 5, in the B.&H. *Gesamtausgabe*.

If Schindler wanted to omit the portions of the Dona nobis with what might be considered warlike overtones (the Allegro assai with the recitatives and the Presto), he might have recommended a cut from GA p. 225, just before the Allegro assai, to p. 248 at the change of key from B flat to D major. This could have been accomplished so that musically it would not have been nonsense; it would merely have been musical vandalism. With a recommendation like this (if Schindler did in fact recommend the cut he seems to have recommended) and with his repeated reference to the quartet in B flat as a 'monster', one might be justified in wondering whether Schindler was musical.

[211] The autograph of the song cycle opus 98 bears the title that Schindler uses here (KHV 274), but the first edition (Steiner, October 1816, not 1817 as Schindler says) was under the title now invariably used: *An die ferne Geliebte*.

[212] According to Grove 6–793, Mozart's piano in 1780 was tuned to $A = 422$ cps. When Sir George Smart visited Vienna in September 1825, he carried with him a fork tuned to $A = 433$ cps, and reported that at several of the theatres of the city and at the private performance of opus 132 for Schlesinger the pitch was 'rather above' his fork (Cox & Cox: *Leaves from the Journals of Sir George Smart* [1907], pp. 99, 100, 110). Grove reports 'Vienna, high pitch (1859)' as $A = 456$ cps. Smart's fork was about 0.4 semitones above Mozart's pitch, and the Vienna high pitch of 1859 was 1.3 semitones above Mozart's pitch. Today's standard of $A = 440$ cps is about a quarter of a semitone above the pitch that Smart found in Vienna in 1825.

[213] The first complete performance of the *Missa* anywhere was in St. Petersburg on 7 April 1824 NS (26 March OS) at the instigation of Prince Galitsin (MQ XLVI [1960] 53, but see *ibid*. XLIX [1963] 143; see also Note 234). Ginsburg (BJ 1959/60, p. 60n) refers to a repetition of this performance the following year. Vetterl (*Musica divina* XVII [1929] 6) says that the score and parts of the *Missa* recently discovered in the library of St. Jacob's Church in Brünn give strong indication that this work received its first liturgical performance in that church during the first half of 1824, Leopold Streit (director of music at the church) leading an orchestra of about forty players and a chorus of more than this number of singers. Müller-Reuter, *Nachtrag*, pp. 73–74, lists the following early performances that escaped Schindler's notice:

> Reichenberg (1832)
> Pressburg (1835) as a part of High Mass
> Dresden (13 May 1839)

[214] This performance on 29 June 1830, under the direction of the local schoolmaster Johann Vincenz Richter, is now accepted as the first performance of the complete work in Austria (KHV 361). Schindler erroneously refers to the town as Wärmsdorf, not Warnsdorf.

215 The Kyrie and Gloria had been performed at Elberfeld under Johann Schornstein on 4 June 1827 as a part of the tenth Niederrheinische Musikfest (KHV 363).

216 This society was one of the ten subscribers to the manuscript edition of the *Missa* (TDR IV 375), and its conductor, Johann Nepomuk Schelble (1789–1837), was a subscriber to the first engraved edition in 1827 (KHV 364). Except as stated here, there seems to be no record of an attempt by the Cäcilien-Verein to perform the *Missa* under Schelble's direction.

216a TDR V 94n and TF 911 say that this incident took place after the first concert, not the second.

217 This mention of an additional £100 if quartets are brought refers to negotiations that had been under way with Neate for the sale of three new quartets in London.

218 The charge of 'degenerate behaviour' (*Ausartungen*) on the part of Nephew Karl is entirely unsupported by any known facts. During the autumn of 1824 he continued his studies at the University without enthusiasm. To Beethoven's great dismay he mentioned his desire to become a soldier, a course that he followed two years later with credit and benefit to himself, but he did not press the matter. He did poorly in his autumn examinations, and at Easter 1825 transferred for commercial studies to the Polytechnic Institute.

219 The course taken by the negotiations regarding this oratorio, as well as a synopsis of Bernard's poem, is given in TK III 172 ff and TF 883 ff (see also Note 202).

220 This contemptuous reference to Vienna and the Viennese alludes to the mythological land of Scheria and its indolent, pleasure-loving inhabitants (*Odyssey* VI–XIII). See also Schindler's note on pp. 216, 272.

221 See Supplement C (p. 459 *infra*) and TDR V 552 ff. For a discussion of the relationship that is more sympathetic to Prince Galitsin, see BJ 1959/60, pp. 59 ff.

222 See TK III 51 and TF 795.

223 Efforts to sell the *Missa* had started long before 1824. Beethoven offered this work to Simrock in his letter of 10 February 1820 (MM 284; see also TK III 44, 53 and TF 758, 784), to Schlesinger on 13 November 1821 (MM 320), to Peters on 5 June 1822 (And. 1079), to Artaria on 22 August 1822 (And. 1093), and to Diabelli no later than the spring of 1823 (TK III 107; TF 854). Reconciliation with Brother Johann, from whom Beethoven had been estranged since Johann's marriage ten years before, came only in the spring of 1822 (see And. 1078, 1086), and then upon Beethoven's initiative (see TK III 68).

As far as recorded information shows, the only way that Brother Johann was concerned in Beethoven's dealings with publishers during these years was in connection with the sale to B. Schott's Söhne of opp. 121b, 122, 124, 126, and 128, compositions that Beethoven had made over to Johann in repayment of a loan (And. 1321; see also And. 1323, 1325).

224 The first known letters from Beethoven to Probst (MM 382 of 25 February 1824) and from Beethoven to Schott (MM 383 of 10 March 1824)

indicate clearly that in each case it was the publisher who had approached the composer, not the other way round.

[225] A letter of 2 July 1822 from A. M. Schlesinger (BusV, p. 94) reads in part: 'We are quite in agreement about the Mass. Please send it and the two songs as soon as possible and draw upon me at 14 days' sight for 650 reichsthalers, which I shall promptly accept and pay.'

The 'two songs' were probably opus 122 and the setting of the *Opferlied* (not opus 121b) upon which GA 25/268 was based.

[226] In *Cäcilia* for April 1825, and in subsequent issues, Schott published an invitation for subscriptions to an engraved edition of opp. 123, 124 and 125 (facsimile in Müller-Reuter: *Nachtrag*, pp. 38–40). A total of 213 (not 210) subscriptions were received (see KHV 363–64). The three works were issued to subscribers as follows: opus 123, March or April 1827; opus 124, December 1825; opus 125, late August 1826.

[227] The dispute over payments due from Galitsin, which was not completely resolved even as late as 1861, is summarized from Thayer's researches in TK III 229n and TF 1100 ff. The résumé by Thayer in *Grove's Dictionary* that Krehbiel refers to appeared in the third (1927) edition and presumably in the earlier editions, but was omitted from the fifth (1954) edition.

The financial aspects of Beethoven's dealings with Galitsin, up to the time of Beethoven's death, may be summarized as follows:

The Prince agreed to pay 50 ducats for each of three quartets (see MM 347; TDR V 553), 50 ducats for the manuscript edition of the *Missa* (TDR V 554), and a 25-ducat gift for Beethoven's dedication of opus 124 (TDR V 567), a total of 225 ducats. This amount was to be net, without charge for banking service or conversion of foreign exchange (see TDR V 564). Beethoven was to send the Prince copies of opp. 116, 124, and 125 without charge, but the Prince was to pay for the copying.

A remittance of 50 ducats was made through Henickstein on 22 October 1823 (MM 372), this being specifically stated as payment for the *Missa*.

A remittance of 50 ducats was sent on 5 December 1824 through the Austrian ambassador to Russia (TDR V 563).

A remittance of 460 florins in silver was referred to in the Prince's letter of 21 June 1825 (TDR V 566). The basis for this remittance is not known (possibly for copying expenses), and it seems probable that the money was never sent.

In his letter of 22 November 1826 (TDR V 569) the Prince specifically acknowledged an unpaid obligation of 125 ducats. This amount was still unpaid at the time of Beethoven's death, as was any additional amount due for copying expenses.

[228] Opus 127 received an unsatisfactory first performance under Schuppanzigh's leadership on 6 March 1825, and was repeated on 23 March with Böhm as first violin (TK III 192; TF 937; see also DM IX_3 [1910] 42, 90 and Mahaim, p. 48). In late March 1825 Beethoven wrote to Schott: 'The quartet is now ready' (And. 1355), and on 7 May he wrote: 'By now you will have received the quartet' (And. 1368).

Thus, if the Prince received the quartet in March 1825, it can be stated with confidence that his copy was forwarded by Beethoven a number of weeks earlier than Schott's copy. More probably, the two copies were sent about the same time, perhaps at the end of March or in the first few days of April: in his letter of 29 April 1825 to Beethoven (TDR V 564) the Prince announced that the quartet had been received and played with delight.

229 Here Schindler's chronology fails him: Galitsin's first letter was dated 9 November 1822 (TDR IV 324), more than two months later than Neate's letter.

230 The possibility must be considered that the date of Neate's letter as given by Schindler is in error, the true date being 1823. Two facts support this conjecture: (1) The request from Galitsin that initiated Beethoven's work on these quartets was made only on 9 November 1822 (TDR IV 324); (2) Neate's letter is apparently in response to a letter from Beethoven dated 25 February 1823 (MM 350) in which Beethoven confirmed the offer of three quartets to be sold in London for 100 guineas. The letter from Ries transmitting Neate's expression of interest, referred to in MM 350, is not known. In two letters written to Neate in the spring of 1825 (And. 1352, 1378) the sale of the quartets in London is again mentioned, but nothing came of it.

231 This statement, while containing a kernel of truth, is very misleading. Beethoven was indeed somewhat vexed at the fact that none of Ries's mature compositions had been dedicated to him (And. 1084, 1135, 1143, 1175; see also MM 328 and pp. 429 ff. infra), but Beethoven's first letter to Neate about the quartets (MM 350) shows that the original approach had been through Ries. Until Ries left London to establish himself at Godesberg in the spring of 1824 (see And. p. 1178n) it was he who served as the link between Beethoven and the Philharmonic Society on all matters concerned with the sponsorship of the ninth symphony and Beethoven's projected visits to London (see MR XXI [1960] 1), as well as with London publishers (And. 1133, 1143, 1167, 1175, 1209). Ries arranged for the production of the ninth symphony and *Christus am Oelberge* at the Aachen festival in May 1823 (MM 401, 403; And. 1358; TDR V 168). All this hardly indicates serious 'stumbling blocks'.

232 Such caution by London music-lovers in negotiating with Beethoven for new works might well be explained by the experience of the Philharmonic Society in 1815, when for seventy-five guineas they received not the three concert overtures written especially for them that they had expected, but instead three overtures (opp. 113, 115, and 117) composed as *pièces d'occasion* for Austrian or Hungarian ceremonial celebrations in 1812 and 1814 (MR XXI [1960] 1). The feeling expressed at that time by the publisher Birchall, 'For God's sake, don't buy anything of Beethoven' (TK II 337; TF 640), was not quickly allayed. Ironically enough, if the proposed transaction in London for the quartets had been consummated, they would indeed have been 'copied in Vienna' and sent to St. Petersburg for the exclusive (?) use of another purchaser, the Russian Prince.

233 Correspondence published or cited in TDR V 555–56 makes clear that the fifty ducats that Beethoven received from the banker Henickstein on 22 October

1825 (MM 372) had been specifically approved by Galitsin as payment for the *Missa*.

234 The Prince said in his letter, 'two days before': 'I hasten, Sir, to give you the news of the performance of your sublime *chef-d'œuvre* that we made known to the public here the day before yesterday' (TDR V 559). Newspaper notices in St. Petersburg show conclusively that the performance was on 7 April NS (26 March OS), so the Prince was guilty of a slip of the pen either in dating his letter (for 8 April read 9 April) or in saying that the concert was 'day before yesterday' (avant hier) rather than 'yesterday' (hier). See MQ XLIX [1963] 143; BJ 1959–60, p. 60).

235 See Supplement E, p. 474 *infra*.

236 As Fate would have it, this wish of Beethoven's came to pass. Brother Johann outlived his wife Therese (d. 20 November 1828) and her daughter Amalie (d. 10 March 1831) (MQ XXXV [1949] 541). Four days before his death on 12 January 1848, Johann signed the following will: 'I name my nephew Carl van Beethoven as my sole heir' (Thayer: *Ein kritischer Beitrag*, p. 36). The estate amounted to 42,123 gulden, enabling nephew Karl to spend his last ten years as a gentleman of leisure.

237 As far as the present editor has been able to find, Dr. Wawruch never made the statement that Schindler attributes to him, or anything like it. The closest approach to it is to be found in Wawruch's account of Beethoven's medical history as given in Kerst II 210 (see also Nettl: *Beethoven Encyclopedia* [1956], p. 40). At the age of thirty, when both deafness and digestive disorders began to manifest themselves, Beethoven 'began to develop a liking for spirituous beverages to stimulate his decreasing appetite, and to aid his stomachic weakness by excessive use of strong punch and iced drinks'. Later in the report, Wawruch mentioned that Beethoven's old friend and former physician Dr. Malfatti was aware of the patient's fondness for 'spirituous' beverages, and for this reason prescribed frozen punch during Beethoven's last weeks, until Beethoven began to abuse the prescription. From all the information that has come down to us, these statements would seem to be completely factual.

238 Schindler must have had in mind a promise by Beethoven that he would assume this intimate office. The exact date of Holz's wedding is not known, but the correspondence (e.g., MM 452; And. 1521, 1524, 1525, 1527, 1536) and the testimony of the Conversation Books (see TDR V 436) indicate that it took place in the last days of 1826 or at the beginning of 1827.

239 Actually, on 9 and 11 September, with Schuppanzigh as Vln I and Holz as Vln II (TK III 206; TF 960).

240 The Maurin-Chevillard Quartet can hardly be accused of avoiding the quartet opus 130. The *Société des Grands Derniers Quatuors de Beethoven* (J. P. Maurin, J. P. Sabatier, Louis Mas, Alexandre Chevillard) presented its first cycle (the last five quartets and the *Grosse Fuge*) in Paris between December 1852 and March 1853. They opened their first tour of the Rhineland on 7 December at Frankfurt with opus 130; during their second tour through Germany in 1856 they performed opus 130 five times, and later in that season they performed it at least once in Paris. Before 1856 there had never been more than five performances of opus 130 in any one year by all the quartets that were active in Europe. Dr. Ivan Mahaim is to be thanked for this detailed information.

241 It is customary today to follow the practice of the *Gesamtausgabe* (6/50) in considering the eleven-measure introduction (Allegro moderato, Adagio) to the variations section as a separate movement, so that opus 131 is considered to be in seven movements, not six.

242 Müller-Reuter, *Nachtrag*, p. 118, contends that in the first performance of opus 135 on 23 March 1828 Böhm, not Schuppanzigh, played first violin, but the weight of evidence seems to favour Schuppanzigh for this distinction (see Mahaim, p. 69).

243 As pointed out in KHV, p. 406, this statement by Schindler is incorrect. Matthias Artaria, who had purchased the quartet opus 130, had asked Beethoven for an arrangement of the *Grosse Fuge* for piano four hands, and Beethoven asked Halm to make this arrangement. Halm's letter to Beethoven saying that his task had been completed was dated 24 April 1826 (TDR V 298). Beethoven passed the arrangement along to Artaria, who on 12 May paid Halm forty florins for it (NB II 365). Upon reconsideration, Beethoven was dissatisfied with Halm's transcription (see TK III 224; TF 976) and prepared one himself, for which Artaria paid him twelve ducats in gold on 5 September 1826 (NB II 365). And. 1529 deals with this transaction. It was Beethoven's arrangement that was published as opus 134. For comments by an eminent pianist and scholar on the relative merits of the two transcriptions, see Sonneck Letters, p. 80; see also NBJ VI (1935) 171.

244 In this statement, Schindler is in error by one year. Nephew Karl left Blöchlinger's school in August 1823 (TK III 132; TF 866), took his examinations for entrance to the University on 28 August (And. 1232), spent the next weeks (probably until late October) with Beethoven in Baden (see TK III 137; TF 872), and in the autumn of 1823 entered the University, living with his uncle (TK III 171; TF 882).

245 Here again Schindler's dating is wrong: the conditional failure was in the autumn of 1824 (TDR V 212). By Easter 1825 Karl had decided to transfer to the Polytechnic Institute, and took no examinations at the University.

246 1. Incomplete (see And. 1393). This letter was probably written not long after 7 May 1825, after Beethoven had gone to Baden for the summer. The choice of a career that is mentioned refers to nephew Karl's transfer the previous month from philological studies at the University to commercial studies at the Polytechnic Institute. In the last sentence, the transcription in TDR V 539 gives *Einöde* (solitude) instead of Schindler's *Exil* (exile).

2. Incomplete (see And. 1374). Nephew Karl was born on 4 September 1806. The last two sentences and the close as given here are taken with minor changes from a letter that Beethoven wrote to his nephew in mid-July 1825 (TDR V 536; And. 1400).

3. Incomplete (see And. 1377). This letter reflects the bitterness of the losing battle that Beethoven fought to keep nephew Karl completely estranged

from his mother, whom Beethoven considered as an evil and immoral influence upon the boy and (not realized by himself) as a rival for Karl's affections.

The person named by Schindler as 'Dr. S . . . r' was probably Dr. Ignaz Sonnleithner, member of a noteworthy Viennese musical family and nephew Karl's teacher of commercial law at the Polytechnic Institute (TDR V 514). Schindler's explanatory footnote only adds to the obscurity of the passage: the lawsuit by which Karl's mother Johanna was excluded from the guardianship had been settled in the spring of 1820, more than five years before this letter (see MM 296), and there is no record that Ignaz Sonnleithner, his brother Joseph, or his son Leopold took any part in this case.

The alternative conjecture in Nohl's *Briefe Beethovens* No. 343 that 'Dr. S . . . r' was Dr. Johann Michael Schönauer, attorney named by brother Karl in his will as curator of his estate and of the material interests of nephew Karl (TK II 320; TF 624), seems equally improbable. Dr. Schönauer was indeed on the losing side of the court case, but he does not seem to have appeared in Beethoven's affairs since 1820.

4. Incomplete (see And. 1379). Schindler's transcription differs somewhat from that given in TDR V 528.

5. Incomplete (see And. 1391). In the first part of the letter, Beethoven insisted that nephew Karl keep a detailed account of his expenditures. The letter ended with a blast at Beethoven's servants.

6. Incomplete (see And. 1402). The last two sentences as given here do not appear in the transcription of this letter in TDR V 537, but are taken from Beethoven's letter of 2 August to nephew Karl (TDR V 540; And. 1406).

7. Incomplete (see And. 1375). Reference to Beethoven's illness indicates that this letter was written about the middle of May 1825. Except for the first sentence, the second paragraph does not appear in the transcription of this letter in TDR V 526 or in any other letter known to the present editor.

8. Incomplete (see And. 1396; TDR V 540). This letter probably dates from the second week in July 1825.

9. Incomplete (see And. 1430). This letter was presumably written during the first week or so of September 1825 (the Sunday that is referred to was probably the 11th, possibly the 18th) while Beethoven was still in Baden and nephew Karl was carrying on his studies at the Polytechnic Institute.

10. And. 1445 gives an extended postscript that was written on the outside of this letter. The letter probably dates from shortly after Beethoven's return from Baden on 17 October 1825, and indicates that nephew Karl had again gone to his mother.

11. Incomplete (see And. 1439).

12. Incomplete (see And. 1443).

[247] For a twentieth-century study of the relationship from this standpoint, see R. and E. Sterba, *Beethoven and his Nephew* (New York, 1954).

[248] It may be stated with confidence that the letter quoted by Schindler did not come from Beethoven's last years. The date that is more generally accepted for this letter is autumn 1804, healing a quarrel that had arisen over the joint occupancy of an apartment by the two young men (see TK II 27; TF 352).

Neither the handwriting of the letter (see facsimile in Ley: *Beethoven als Freund*, p. 153), its literary style, nor the reference to mutual anger as a contributing cause of the break applies to the situation of the 1820's.

The cause of the long estrangement here referred to may have been (as Schindler says) Breuning's advice, perhaps in late 1815 or 1816, against Beethoven's adoption of nephew Karl, or it may have resulted from a breach of confidence on Beethoven's part that could not possibly have taken place later than 1815 (see Note 136). 'They had met occasionally *ad interim*' (see the account in TK III 85 and TF 848 by Louis Schlösser of having seen Beethoven leaving a performance of *Fidelio* on 4 November 1822 in the company of Breuning and Schindler; see also Nohl III 580 and the reference in And. 1380 of May 1825 to a visit to Breuning by nephew Karl), 'but it was not until they became neighbours [i.e., until Beethoven moved into the Schwarzspanierhaus in October 1825] that the intimate friendship which had existed in earlier years was restored' (TK III 213; TF 967).

249 Gerhard von Breuning (*Beethoven als Freund*, p. 152n) says that the portrait referred to was the miniature painted on ivory by Hornemann about 1802 (SBSK–Bi 1). This is much more probable: the letter makes clear that what was being sent was an original, an *unicum* and not a published lithograph. It was probably on 10 December 1826 (see And. 1551) that Beethoven sent Wegeler a copy of Dürck's lithograph of the Stieler portrait, which had been published by Matthias Artaria at some time during the latter half of 1826 (TK III 41; see BStud I 96n, 97). Gerhard von Breuning also says that on his thirteenth birthday (28 August 1826) Beethoven brought a copy of this lithograph to his friend Stephan, Gerhard's father (*Beethoven als Freund*, p. 175). It was probably this gift that Schindler had in mind.

250 The painstaking inquiries conducted by Thayer in Gneixendorf in 1860, corroborated by the evidence that he educed from the Conversation Books, give so completely different a picture of the composer's life with his brother during these two months that no effort can succeed in reconciling the two accounts. Thayer's integrity and the care with which he conducted his researches and formed his judgements are beyond challenge. One can assume only that Schindler allowed his malice towards brother Johann to get the better of his obligations as a biographer. In fairness to the memory of the composer's brother, anyone who reads Schindler's account of the two months' stay in Gneixendorf as set forth in this volume should also read the account by Thayer that appears in TK III 238 ff and 267 ff, and in TF 1005 ff and 1012.

251 In fact, Staudenheim took part in the consultation that preceded the first tapping on 20 December (TK III 276; TF 1023), and he may have joined with Wawruch and Malfatti in a further consultation on 11 January (TK III 284; TF 1030).

252 The actual course of events during Beethoven's first week in Vienna after his stay at Gneixendorf, as reconstructed from the indisputable records of the Conversation Books (TK III 272 ff) is completely different from that stated by Schindler. Within two (or at the most, three) days from the arrival of the sick man at his apartment, Holz had been notified of the situation, and on 5 Decem-

ber Dr. Wawruch, summoned by Holz, had begun daily visits to Beethoven. That the composer's condition during the few days prior to Dr. Wawruch's arrival was apparently not serious is indicated in his note to Holz written about 4 or 5 December (And. 1541), in which he said merely that he was *unpässlich* (indisposed)—and Beethoven was not one to minimize his ailments. Schindler did not appear in the sick-room until more than two weeks had passed.

The narrative given here, with its reference to the summoning of the physician by the billiard-marker, is substantially identical with that in the first (1840) edition of the *Biography* (p. 179), which was written while Schindler was in possession of all the pertinent documents, and first appeared in Schindler's letter of 11 April 1827 to Moscheles (Kerst II 243). It is difficult to see how Schindler can be absolved of the charge of having prepared a cruel fabrication, known by him to be false from beginning to end, for the purpose of vilifying the nephew who had given Beethoven so much pain and so much happiness.

[253] Dr. Waldemar Schweizheimer, who has made exhaustive studies of Beethoven's ailments and their effects on his creativity, concludes that with the advanced stage of the liver cirrhosis disclosed by the autopsy, no degree of skill or lack thereof would have had much effect on the lengthening or shortening of Beethoven's life (*Beethovens Leiden* [1922], p. 201). See also BJ 1959/60, pp. 7 ff.

[254] Actually, thirteen-year-old. Gerhard von Breuning was born on 28 August 1813. His account of Beethoven's last days was published in 1874 under the title, *Aus dem Schwarzspanierhause*, and was reprinted as a part of Ley's volume, *Beethoven als Freund der Familie Wegeler-von Breuning* (1927).

[255] 'On 123 pages of the Conversation Books, covering the months of January and February 1827 (the evidence of which cannot be gainsaid, since the books were long in the hands of Schindler to do with as he willed), there are 48 entries by Johann van Beethoven, 46 by Gerhard von Breuning, and 30 by Breuning the elder. Schindler's entries number 103' (TK III 295). In addition, entries by thirteen other visitors (not including the physicians) appear.

[256] There were in all four tappings—20 December, 8 January, 2 February, 27 February (see TK III 276, 283, 294, 290; TF 1023, 1029, 1033, 1038)—and a spontaneous opening of the puncture on 16 March (TK III 292; TF 1041).

[257] The reference may be to the town of Koslov, some 650 miles south-east of St. Petersburg where, according to the letter sent to Beethoven by Stieglitz & Co. on 18 January 1827 (TDR V 570), the Prince was then staying. The letter from the Prince included the statement that as a result of the 'misfortunes', he had been declared bankrupt (TDR V 569).

[258] This offer was referred to in Beethoven's letter of 18 May 1816 to Neate (And. 636). In the letter Beethoven indicated that he would welcome such a benefit concert.

[259] No explanation can be suggested for this extraordinary statement, or for Schindler's vicious blast at Moscheles that appears on pp. 371 ff. Moscheles first met Beethoven in 1810, when the young pianist was sixteen years

old (TK 11 282; TF 585). During the summer and autumn of 1813, Moscheles frequented the workshop of Maelzel while Beethoven was engaged in the composition of *Wellington's Victory* (Schindler-Moscheles I 153n). In the summer of 1814 Moscheles prepared a vocal score of *Fidelio* under the close supervision of the composer (Schindler-Moscheles I xii). It might be noted that Schindler first met Beethoven only in March 1814, and that his close association with the composer began no earlier than 1819, so that he was not in a position to know, except by hearsay, what contact there might have been between the two men up to that time. After the end of 1819, Moscheles was in Vienna only on a brief visit from mid-October 1823 to the beginning of 1824, at which time, as Schindler tells on p. 372, Beethoven, Moscheles, and Schindler dined together. Aside from the established facts of association in 1814 and earlier years, Beethoven's letters from his sick-room are not such as would have been written to a stranger. The subject of Moscheles's relations with Beethoven is discussed at length by Kalischer in BusZ IV 43–65.

260 At this point Nohl (*Briefe Beethovens* No. 398) gives an extended paragraph which he said was included in the original draft of the letter in the Berlin collection but crossed out before the fair copy of the letter was made for transmission to Moscheles.

261 Unger (DM XXXIV [1942] 153, 294) points out that Beethoven's letter of 21 March 1827 to Stieglitz & Co. (MM 471) was later than this letter of 18 March to Moscheles, and was presumably the last letter, and one of the last four documents, that Beethoven signed.

262 See Note 266.

263 This is a very rough paraphrase of a portion of the letter that Schindler actually sent (dated 24 March), which is transcribed from the original in Ley: *Beethoven als Freund*, p. 235.

264 For a conflicting account of this dedication in which Schindler had no part, see KHV 410.

265 One is tempted to think of the story that the Titan of music died in the midst of a violent storm as being what Slonimsky calls 'musico-biographical folklore', but such is not the case. Records of the Vienna Weather Bureau for 26 March 1827 show that, '*mirabile dictu*, the famous thunderstorm at the time of Beethoven's death, reported by all Beethoven biographers, actually did occur! . . . At three o'clock in the afternoon stormy weather began, and at four o'clock lightning and thunder struck, with strong winds' (MQ XLVI [1960] 21).

266 This statement is flatly contradicted by Hüttenbrenner's reminiscences as given by him to Thayer in 1860. About 1815 or 1816 he met Beethoven through Joseph Eppinger (TK II 355; TF 658) and thereafter saw him often at Steiner's shop (BHdb I 226), though there is no indication that he was more than a casual acquaintance. Hüttenbrenner stated that about a week before Beethoven's death he visited the sick-room in company with Schindler and his intimate friend Schubert (TK III 300; TF 1044), a fact (if it be a fact) that Schindler does not mention.

It should be noted that in his letter of 12 April 1827 to B. Schott's Söhne

(*Cäcilia* VI No. 24 [May 1827] 309; KS II 475) Schindler himself said that the exact words quoted from Hüttenbrenner were uttered by Beethoven immediately after he had received the sacrament on 24 March, though Unger (DM XXXIV [1942] 153) gives evidence that this was not the case. Hüttenbrenner also told Thayer that he had not been present when Beethoven took the last sacrament, so that he could not in reason be named as the source of these disputed words (TK III 306; TF 1049).

[267] Accounts of the funeral ceremonies, not agreeing in every detail, are also given by Thayer (TK III 311; TF 1052 ff), Nohl (III 796), Seyfried (*Beethovens Studien* [2nd ed.] Appendix, p. 39), Cramolini (Kerst II 236; BJ II [1909] 381), and in an account published in the *Dresdener Abendzeitung* (Kerst II 239; Sonneck Impr., p. 226).

[268] This epitaph (*Es wirkt mit Macht der edle Mann . . .*), in iambic four-foot lines of rhyming scheme A B A B C D C D E E, is attributed by Schindler to Goethe. The present editor has been unable to confirm this attribution, and one Goethe specialist has expressed strong doubts as to its authenticity.

[269] This portion of the autopsy report is discussed from the standpoint of present-day knowledge of pathology in BJ 1959/60, pp. 27–28. Accounts by many contemporaries agree that some hearing remained in the left ear after the right ear had become completely deaf. London (*Archives of Internal Medicine* CXIII [1964] 442) gives a detailed case-history of Beethoven's physical ailments and a discussion of the findings, with the summary: 'If Beethoven paid for his deafness with some of the greatest music mankind has ever known, he appears to have paid for his music in turn with frustration, alcohol, pancreatitis, and death from cirrhosis of the liver. Sic transit gloria musicae!'

[270] The autograph of the earlier will is known (see TDR V 439) and bears the date 'Wednesday 3 January 1827' (And. 1547; facsimile in Bory, p. 212). As Schindler says, the wisdom of this unrestricted bequest was questioned by Beethoven's advisers, and for this reason this letter-will was not signed until shortly before Beethoven's death. Unger (DM XXXIV [1942] 158) is of the opinion that this will of 3 January bears Beethoven's last signature.

A facsimile of the second will, with the holograph date 'Wien am 23. März 1827' and the signature 'Luwig van Beethoen' [sic], a pathetic proof of the master's failing strength and consciousness, is given in Ley: *Beethovens Leben in Bildern*, p. 140, and in Bory, p. 213. (Ley indicates that as from 1925 this document was in the archives of the City of Vienna.)

Four years before, however, Beethoven had on 6 March 1823 (And. 1151) written a letter to Dr. Bach that was in effect a will containing substantially the same provisions as the two later documents, and on 1 August 1824 (And. 1302) he had asked Bach to prepare a formal will and send it to him for signature.

[271] Both wills were filed with the *Magistrat*: that of 3 January on 27 March (TDR V 439) and the will of 23 March on 29 March (TDR V 485). See also BStud II 173.

[272] A detailed breakdown of the estate settlement records, showing a net value of 10,125 fl. 13 kr. CM, is given in TDR V 579 and, in even greater detail, in BStud II 171.

273 Excerpts from two letters concerned with this gift, written by Rau in Vienna to Moscheles in London, are given in Schindler-Moscheles II, pp. 322, 326.

274 This reference is to the memorandum of 30 August 1826 (And. 1451) by which Beethoven authorized Karl Holz to write his biography (see TF 1085, and also TF 942). Regarding this, TK III 196–98 says:

Holz had his entire confidence, and when the great catastrophe of 1826 came, Holz was the strongest prop upon which he leaned. . . . There can be no question as to the sincerity of the desire which finds utterance in this declaration. It was made in the midst of a period when Holz was of incalculable service to him, and he had every reason to believe that Holz had both the ability and the disposition to write the truthful, unvarnished account of his life which he wanted the world to have. Holz made no use of the *imprimatur* which he had secured from Beethoven.

Schindler's statement is one of too many examples of his inability to write impartially about those—Johanna, Brother Johann, Nephew Karl, and not the least Karl Holz—towards whom he felt hostility or jealousy.

275 Jakob Hotschevar, the husband of the stepsister of Johanna's mother (TK II 405; TF 707) and a legal draftsman for the court, had in 1818–19 represented Johanna before the *Landrecht* and the *Magistrat*. He was appointed guardian on 26 June 1827 (BStud II 181), but since Nephew Karl was then in the army, in which he remained for nearly five years longer (MQ XXXV [1949] 544), Hotschevar's services could only be those of a trustee of Karl's estate.

276 Corrections or additions to Schindler's data are given in square brackets. Strictly speaking, opus 113 includes all of the *Ruinen von Athen* music. In 1822 this music, except the overture, was adapted to a new text by Meisl, *Die Weihe des Hauses*. Minor modifications were made in the music of opus 113/6, which was published a few years later as opus 114; a new overture, opus 124, and an additional chorus, WoO 98, made up the music specifically composed for the revised work.

277 As pointed out by Herbst in NBJ V (1933) 137, Beethoven made at least four settings of Matthisson's poem. The version used by Ehlers in December 1822 was for *three* solo voices, chorus, and small orchestra. The final version described by Schindler, published as opus 121b, was completed only in the summer of 1824 (KHV 354).

278 Regarding this erroneous statement by Schindler, see Note 129. Haslinger published two versions of the cantata in 1837, one with the original Weissenbach text and one with the Rochlitz poem.

279 The actual date of this concert was 16 April 1818; it was repeated on 23 April (NB I 37; TDR IV 217n, 569). The date '10 May' appearing in TDR III 478 is presumably a repetition of Schindler's error. Nottebohm says that at a concert on 6 December 1818, opus 115 was given under the title of *Jagdouverture*; KHV 332 mentions that at some time after 1830 Maurice Schlesinger in Paris issued a reprint under the title: *La Chasse, grande Ouverture in Ut* . . . .

280 In making this statement, Schindler disregarded (or perhaps was un-

aware of) Beethoven's notation on the autograph: *Abends zum Namensfeier unsers Kaisers.* To avoid confusion, some name is necessary to distinguish this overture in C major from the overture in C major opus 124, *Die Weihe des Hauses.*

[281] There seems no reason to doubt that the Diabelli edition, published in Vienna not more than two months after the Schlesinger edition appeared in Paris and Berlin in July 1822, was unauthorized.

[282] See Note 168.

[283] Five of the eleven bagatelles first appeared in January 1821 in Starke's *Wiener Piano-Forte-Schule.* The first edition of the complete set came from Clementi in London in June 1823 (MQ XLIX [1963] 331).

[284] An arrangement of WoO 2a for piano solo was published in 1813 by the Hoftheater Musik-Verlag. The score was first published in the GA in 1864.

[285] WoO 57 was first published for piano solo about September 1805 by the Bureau des Arts et d'Industrie (Industrie-Comptoir). The arrangement for string quartet was published by Hoffmeister about 1806.

[286] Two of the three duos WoO 27 (or perhaps all three) were first published by Lefort (Paris) about 1810–15 (KHV 466). The André edition (about 1830) was the first publication in Germany and perhaps the first publication anywhere of all three of the duos.

[287] The version of WoO 6 as published by Diabelli in June 1829 and as given in GA 9/72 had been revised (presumably by Czerny) to provide a more brilliant piano part. The first publication of the rondo in its original version was in *Supplemente zur Gesamtausgabe,* Vol. III (B. & H., 1960). See also Note 328.

[288] The list of works by Beethoven that were published by Simrock (SimJb II [1929] 16) shows Pl. No. 581 (probably from early 1808) as 'Rondo, G major, for violin and pianoforte; the same, arranged for flute and pianoforte', with no mention of an arrangement for piano and cello. The first B. & H. *Verzeichniss* (1851, p. 127) lists WoO 41 under works 'for pianoforte and violin (or violoncello)', published by Simrock in Bonn and Dunst in Frankfurt, but gives no further details. The Nottebohm *Verzeichnis* of 1868 (p. 144) lists a transcription for flute but none for cello. KHV (p. 485) shows the Simrock first edition and the Dunst reprint only as for piano and violin.

Altmann's *Kammermusik-Katalog* is of no help, since under works for two instruments it includes only compositions in sonata form. It is altogether probable that someone at some time has made a transcription of WoO 41 for cello, but there is no evidence that such a transcription had been published at the time of Schindler's book.

[289] In 1816 or 1817 Artaria published these six songs as *Sechs deutsche Gedichte aus Reissigs Blümchen der Einsamkeit,* but each had previously been published in other editions (KHV *passim*). The date '1815' for the *Sechs deutsche Gedichte* given in KHV 204 is certainly wrong, since one of the songs in the collection (WoO 146) first appeared only in June 1816 (KHV 616).

[290] WoO 140 was first published in 1814 in the *Wiener Friedensblätter*;

WoO 145 and 148 in the *Wiener Modenzeitung* (1816 and 1817). In 1817 Simrock published the three songs as a collection.

291 In a Conversation Book of June 1823 (SchKH III 346), a person identified by Schindler as 'the old housekeeper' wrote, 'Today is Saturday and I must have some money again. *Es mus* [sic] *sein.*'

292 The account given in TK III 224 and TF 976, in which the quartet in question was opus 130, not opus 127, seems more in accordance with known facts. An interpretation of this catch-phrase from a very different angle, not at all unreasonable, is given in SchwMZ XCIX (1959) 319. The canon based on these words, which has been mauled by many transcribers, is given correctly in MM 446.

PERSONALITY, INDIVIDUAL CHARACTERISTICS, ANECDOTES, ETC.

1.

RELIGION; THOROUGHBASS; AESTHETICS

Beethoven was brought up in the Roman Catholic religion. His entire life is proof that he was truly religious at heart, as many incidents in the biographical section have shown. One of his marked characteristics was that he never discussed religious subjects or the dogmas of the various Christian churches. We can, however, say almost certainly that his religious views were not so much based on church doctrine as on a sort of deism. Though he never elaborated a specific theory, he acknowledged God revealed in the world as well as the world in God. This view was formed in him as he observed all of nature, and under the tutelage of the much-cited book, Christian Sturm's *Betrachtungen der Werke Gottes in der Natur*, as well as through lessons derived from the philosophical systems of the wise men of Greece. No one who had seen how he absorbed the appropriate content of any writing into his inner life could deny what I have just said.

In addition to these eye-witness evidences of our master's religious foundations, we have a further indication that accords well with what I observed. The following three sentences:

I am that which is.

I am everything that is, that was, and that will be. No mortal man has raised my veil.

He is of himself alone, and it is to this aloneness that all things owe their being.

are inscriptions found by Champollion-Figeac in the temple of the goddess Neith at Sais in Lower Egypt. They are set forth in his *Pictures of Egypt*, page 417.[293] It is not unlikely that our master was acquainted with this highly interesting book. By way of introduction to these inscriptions the author says: 'It would be difficult to give a more exalted or a more religious concept of the creative deity.' We also read there this explanation: 'The goddess Neith took part in the creation of the world and presided over the reproduction of the species. She is the all-moving power.'

Beethoven copied out these inscriptions himself, and kept them, framed and mounted under glass, on his work-table. This valuable relic is still in my possession. A facsimile was included in the first edition.[294]

Beethoven observed the same silence with reference to thoroughbass, or rather to the whole field of music theory, as he did to religious topics. He regarded both religion and thoroughbass as closed issues, things not to be argued about. Yet apart from music theory, there is a subject of great importance to the thinking musician: aesthetics. This topic was quite a different matter with our master from the code of harmonic rules and laws. Aesthetics was a favourite subject in his conversations about art, though it was only certain aspects, for instance the character of the different keys, that interested him. He had made a concentrated study of this particular aspect of aesthetics.

One of the books in his very limited personal library was Schubart's *Ideen zu einer Aesthetik der Tonkunst*, published in 1806, at a time when Beethoven had already begun his reading on the aesthetics of the ancient Greeks and Romans. We have already seen what he absorbed from Plato's *Republic* into his own art. This reading did not, of course, satisfy him but merely whetted his thirst for greater knowledge. Pinterics, whom we met in the first volume as his companion and his second in political conversations, also lent him a helping hand as he expanded his acquaintance with this hitherto unexplored subject.* As a philologist, Pinterics was most familiar with the aesthetic concepts of antiquity. He found for Beethoven excerpts from Aristotle,† Lucian, Quintilian, and Boethius.‡ How warmly our lover of the Greeks must have responded to Aristotle when he encountered such sentences as: 'Aside from nature there is nothing in which are mirrored so clearly and faithfully anger, tenderness, courage, temperance and all the virtuous qualities as well as their opposites, as in rhythm and melody. It is quite apparent that in the notes and their combinations there lies an expression of a great many moral qualities.' Furthermore, the lover of Greek antiquity finds Lucian exclaiming: 'There is a divine breath in the modes!' Lucian

* Pinterics was helpful to Franz Schubert in the same way.
† Beethoven was well acquainted with Aristotle's *Politics*; similarly, he knew Horace's *Epistle to the Pisos* [*On the Art of Poetry*] and could recite whole sections from memory.
‡ Boethius was a Roman consul under Theodoric the Great. Falsely accused by his enemies of carrying on a treasonable correspondence with the Greek imperial court, he was banned from Rome, and in A.D. 524 or 526 was executed. Among the many writings he left are five books on the music of the Greeks. According to Hawkins's *History of Music*, the universities of Oxford and Cambridge prohibited the reading of this work to anyone who had not received his degree in music, for the books demand not only familiarity with art in general and knowledge of Latin, but also a thorough grounding in ancient Greek music.

assigns a special character to several of them, and there are similar passages in Athenaeus and Aristides Quintilianus.

Schubart went further in his research into the psyche of the keys, for he had a large amount of material to study. But our master was not at ease with Schubart's views on the philosophy of art, for he felt a decided reluctance to pursue all philosophy of art once it emerged into the realm of metaphysics and ceased to be of practical usefulness. He would, however, applaud loudly the learned Schubart for his observations on the characters of the various keys, even though he was not always in full agreement. He generally agreed about the minor keys (on which the Greeks had already done the basic work), but he disagreed about some of the major keys, or rather in vocal music he limited their psychical significance according to the tempo of the piece of music and the number of voices singing. As for instrumental music, especially quartets and orchestral works, Beethoven generally disregarded Schubart's characterizations of the keys because many of them were ambiguous or impracticable. He did, however, accept them up to a point in his piano music and trios. But above all he would in any given piece of music distinguish between a coherence to the senses and a lack of coherence altogether. In the first instance the music has a character of its own that loses its specific quality if it is transposed into another key. Nevertheless, Beethoven held Schubart's book in such high regard that he recommended its careful study to those already far advanced in their musical training.

It was this branch of music theory that Beethoven most of all enjoyed discussing with cultivated musicians, and he was in awe of what the genius of his great predecessors, Gluck, Haydn, and Mozart, had accomplished in the use of tonal colouring to characterize their works. If one reason for Beethoven's great admiration for Mozart's *Zauberflöte* was its employment of every musical form, from the song to the chorale and the fugue, another reason was Mozart's use here of various keys according to their specific psychical qualities. But as our master would grow warm in his discussion of this interesting subject, giving his hearers the pleasure of witnessing his defence of his theory as if it were an article of religious belief, he would frequently be challenged by sceptics and out-and-out rejecters of his faith. Both sceptics and rejecters of this aspect of aesthetics in the arts used to be more plentiful than at present. What would the *Corpus musicum*, that considered only thoroughbass and counterpoint sacred to music and that regarded any other science as superfluous, have said to Schubart's ideas on aesthetics? Since Mozart was not a reader of books and yet did 'great things', it was established that reading was totally unnecessary for one to become an artisan of music. This belief obtains even today among musicians, and now as then many of them fear the spectre of opposition from the pages of a good book or a good periodical, or from some indication that it is time to search for new ideas such as may be found in Türk, Albrechtsberger, and Marx, and that the whole truth is not revealed only in the notes themselves.

It was therefore a pleasure to our master when he was challenged by some disbeliever to defend the theory of the specific character of keys. One of these disbelievers was his friend, Friedrich August Kanne, a man who was the personification of scepticism. Kanne was, in any case, one of the most remarkable of eccentrics. A man of universal education, he had studied theology and then medicine at Leipzig before he became a composer and writer on musical subjects. He came to Vienna at the beginning of the century, and composed a dozen operas and *Singspiele*, as well as incidental music for pantomimes. The best known of his works were *Orpheus* and *Sappho*, written for the Kärntnerthor Theater. He himself had written the texts for these operas. He shared Beethoven's tenacity in his opinions and theories, so that to hear a dispute between them on subjects on which they disagreed in principle was both amusing and instructive to the listener, for each man strove to let his light shine the brightest. They addressed each other with the familiar *Du*, which made it easier for them to express themselves without reserve.

Kanne based his argument mainly on the alterations that orchestral pitch had undergone and, as a final expedient, on transposition, wherein he was using the same weapon against his opponent as a renowned physicist has in his recent work. Beethoven based his counter-claim on his unfailing ability to recognize each key even if it were pitched a whole tone higher or lower than the ear was accustomed to hearing it, so that the transposition argument was no longer valid. It was in any case irrelevant, for the centre of the tonal system has its place, even though that place is movable. The orchestral pitch had been raised, but the difference was imperceptible, because our feeling for the psyche of each key had risen along with it, for this psyche is implicit within the scale of each key, as the wise men of antiquity had realized. Transposition, on the other hand, is a sudden change to a half-tone, or even several tones, higher or lower, so that the feelings of the listener are likewise suddenly transplanted as the psyche of the original tone combination is violently forced to change.

Beethoven claimed that when he had no difficulty in distinguishing C sharp major from its enharmonic D flat major, the ear was only secondary in making the distinction, and that first of all came the feeling for the subtle difference between hard and soft that are respectively the characteristic features of these two keys. His judicious and appropriate choice of keys will prove the point further.

You have the harlequin dancing in D flat major; I am going to play it in D major. You say it doesn't matter whether a song is in F minor, E minor, or G minor; I call that as nonsensical as saying that two times two are five. When I make Pizarro sing in harsh keys (even in G sharp major) when he makes his heinous accusations of Florestan to the jailer, I do it to convey the nature of this individual, which is fully revealed in his duet with Rocco. These keys give me the best colours with which to express his character.

Such was the tenor of this extraordinary dialectical conversation.

Could Beethoven have chosen any key but F major as the pre-dominating key to convey most perfectly a sense of bucolic peace for his *Pastoral* symphony? Why is solemnity best expressed in E major, while other major keys are less successful and F and G will not do at all? Just try transposing the Chorus of the Priests in *Zauberflöte* from E to D or F major, and you will be convinced. The critic of the AmZ who re-viewed the C sharp minor sonata, opus 27, said of the first and third movements: 'There is good reason for the two main movements to have been written in the awesome key of C sharp minor.' If one transposes these two movements into the neighbouring minor keys of C or D, or into more remote keys, the completely different effect is obvious.

From the foregoing we may infer whether our master would ever condone transposition. If anyone had dared to play even a little song of his in another key in his presence, the malefactor would soon have regretted his mistake. He was incensed when he heard this or that number from a Mozart opera performed in a key other than its original one. This outrage was often committed by a capricious singer, Grünbaum, in the twenties in Vienna.

Beethoven did not hesitate to declare that before setting a text he would deliberate with himself as to the most suitable key. To deny without reason the special character of the different keys was to Beet-hoven like denying the effect of the sun and the moon on the ebb and flow of the tides, a phenomenon recognized by the ancients and indis-putably established through the studies of Laplace. And I very strongly doubt if our master could have been persuaded that his belief in the special character of the keys was an obsolete and mistaken theory, even by the lengthy studies of the professors Vischer and Zamminer, both of whom attacked the idea, the first in the third part of his *Aesthetik*, the second in his book *Die Musik und die musikalischen Instrumente*. On the contrary, he would probably have answered the learned gentlemen with arguments that far surpassed their thermometer of musical feelings. And it is by means of this instrument that one must attempt to establish the character of the keys, not by physical arguments alone.*

* A. B. Marx's statements in his article on 'The Greek Modes', which appears on pp. 344 ff of Schilling's *Encyclopedia*, are interesting in this connection.

2.

CONTEMPORARIES;
THE MASTER AND YOUNG MUSICIANS

We have amply treated Beethoven's relationship to the Viennese musicians in general in each of the periods of the biographical section. If each member of that musical circle had possessed a true artistic sense based on the consciousness of a true artist, the reproach so often levelled at Beethoven, namely that he had set himself against the artistic world, would be well-founded and would condemn him. But we have examined this situation and we know what the mentality of the musicians was. We must, however, take note of the exceptions to this rule, for Beethoven's accusers seem to have always ignored them. Beethoven respected the following musicians highly: Salieri, the three conductors at the Kärntnerthor Theater (Weigl, Gyrowetz, and Umlauf), Diabelli, the two Czernys, Carl and Joseph (they were not related), three men whom we know from their parts in the master's life, Scholl, Friedlowsky, and Clement, and finally the members of the Schuppanzigh Quartet. It must be said of this small number that they were artists in the strictest sense of the word. They never ceased to revere the great master, while for his part he thought highly of them and took every opportunity to help them to realize their ambitions.

The group of older musicians who had grown up with the music of Haydn and Mozart would often exhibit sympathy for or antipathy to Beethoven's music in the third period of his life according to the whim of old Abbé Stadler, who was open in his rejection of Beethoven. This old Nestor never missed a performance by the Schuppanzigh Quartet, but every time would leave before the beginning of the Beethoven work that always followed one by Haydn and one by Mozart. Maximilian Stadler was born in 1748, eight years before the birth of Mozart, and died in 1833. We can see from these dates the reason for his distrust of the new star: he was no longer capable of raising his eyes to see it. The masses of similarly inclined musicians were content to take Stadler, this living reminder of the time of Mozart, and Stadler's cronies as the barometer of their reception of Beethoven's music.

In addition to the above reproach, we are also told that Beethoven behaved towards the younger musicians in an unfriendly manner, as we can see even in the *Biographische Notizen* of Ries. This reproach can be softened through many examples of opposite behaviour and the incidents of unkindness may be excused on internal and external grounds. The internal reasons were Beethoven's excessive irritability and moodiness, both of which were all too often caused by his deafness and the consequent difficulty in conversing with him. Between 1816 and 1818 the master used an ear trumpet; after that all conversation had to be conducted in writing.

The external causes, however, lay mostly with the younger musicians themselves who came into contact with the great man. Their inexperience in all matters that might have aroused the master's interest, and above all their extreme shyness, which even in the presence of a third person would often so overwhelm them that they could not utter a single word: these were the reasons that such acquaintanceships seldom went beyond the first introduction. Generally these young men regained their breath only after they were out of his sight, no matter how kindly the master behaved towards them. One had to become accustomed to Beethoven in order to get over being oppressed by the combination of his imposing personality and his artistic greatness.

What of the compositions sent him by talented young musicians seeking his opinion? He had the reputation of flouting school rules and following only the dictates of his own fantasy. This unfounded reputation saved him from having to waste time needlessly on such compositions. Yet this rule, too, had its exceptions. Once a young baron from Mainz sent Beethoven several compositions to look over. Despite their pedantry, the compositions pleased the master. 'Here is a baron,' he exclaimed, 'who doesn't need to learn another thing. If it was really he who wrote this quartet, he already knows much too much.' This incident shows that our master was clever at taking the measure of composers.

Let us take a look at a few of the young musicians who came to Beethoven with or without compositions.

First of all, Moscheles will remember Beethoven's kindness when the young man gave the master the sonata in E major that he had dedicated to him. Moscheles will also remember the patience and consideration with which Beethoven corrected the vocal score of *Fidelio* that Moscheles was preparing for D. Artaria, and the encouragement Beethoven gave him until he was at last satisfied with this difficult work. Once Moscheles had to make an arrangement of a number from this opera. Hummel had already arranged the piece for Artaria, but Beethoven had torn up the manuscript without knowing who had done the poor work. At the end of his version Moscheles wrote, perhaps fearing that his work would suffer the same fate: '*Finis*, with God's help'. Beethoven wrote underneath: 'Man, help yourself.' This work that had been commissioned by the publisher dates from 1814, when Moscheles was just twenty years old.

What the author must now relate as a parenthetical adjunct to the above is one of the most unpleasant tasks he has ever had to assume.

The edition of Beethoven's sonatas published by Hallberger in Stuttgart contains, in the first volume, a 'Foreword' by Moscheles. It begins:

Having been honoured by the publisher of this collection with the task of editing it, I wish to place my credentials before the public so that they may judge my competence to undertake this work. I look back to 1806 as the first year of my acquaintance with Beethoven's works and to the period of 1808 to 1820 as the time of my sojourn in Vienna. During this period I enjoyed the personal acquaintance of the composer, and it was my privilege to make the first vocal score of *Fidelio* under his supervision. I witnessed the composition of his works and was among the admiring listeners who heard him play them himself. The study of each of these treasures that I undertook along with the whole admiring musical world of Vienna was a rich and valuable source of joy to me.

We learn in this Foreword that between 1808 and 1820 Moscheles enjoyed the personal acquaintance of Beethoven. No one can be more amazed at this information than the author of this book, for I was myself in constant company with Moscheles from 1815 until his departure for England in 1820, and after that time corresponded with him regularly, as I can prove from a thick packet of letters written to me by him. The letters consist mostly of detailed accounts of all his experiences in London and on his journeys, and would be most helpful to anyone writing his biography. For Moscheles to say while I am still alive that he enjoyed Beethoven's acquaintance is the most unheard-of audacity that has ever been uttered.[295]

In the interests of Beethoven's music, I am forced to say frankly that apart from the instance described above, Moscheles was in Beethoven's company only once. In November 1823, during a short visit that he made to Vienna, I took him to see the master and we three dined together. The reason for this meeting was that Moscheles wanted to ask Beethoven in person if he might use his English grand piano for a public concert that was to take place at the Kärntnerthor Theater. I had already made the request on Moscheles's behalf. Strangely enough, the master's reply was that he suspected Moscheles of some kind of financial speculation, since the piano had too short a keyboard to be of use to him. Nevertheless he lent him the piano. Moscheles used it only for an improvisation, as Conrad Graf had furnished him with one of his pianos.[296]

I am also constrained to say that during all his years in Vienna, Herr Moscheles occupied himself exclusively with his own and related compositions, and that I never heard him play a note of Beethoven's music. Indeed, he avoided Beethoven's compositions as consistently as all the other virtuosi of the new school, to whom this and all classical music represented an 'obsolete point of view', just as today all proponents of the 'music of the future' scorn the past. What I say is supported by a biographical passage on Moscheles in Schilling's *Encyclopedia*. Mentioning that he had studied with Albrechtsberger and Salieri, it says: 'His virtuosity became apparent from day to day to the amazement of his listeners, and before long it placed the young man at the centre of Viennese concert life and made him the darling of that music-loving public which had for so long been accustomed to only the best.'

Anyone can see that we are dealing here with the antithesis of Beethoven, whose music would have raised no one in the second decade of the century to the position of 'darling of the public'. But we must mention in this connection another more important obstacle to any familiarity between Moscheles and Beethoven. This was Beethoven's hatred for the children of Israel in the arts,[297] for he saw how they all turned towards the newest innovations, making profit from the most lucrative trends.* If he had written out his prophecies, the 'Freethinker' in the NZfM of 1850 would have had his predecessor in this respect, too.

The present insinuations of Herr Professor Moscheles have a precedent of even greater magnitude and importance.

All the reporters from the London papers present at the Beethoven Festival in Bonn in 1845 invited me to an interview. Among them were Mr. Hogarth of the *Morning Chronicle*, Mr. Grüneisen of the *Britannia*, the veteran art critic Sir George Smart, the famous violinist Mr. Uri, and others, eleven gentlemen in all. They asked me the following questions: (a) 'Was Herr Moscheles associated with Beethoven?' (b) 'Is it true that Herr Moscheles inherited the legacy of the Beethoven tradition directly from the composer himself?' Moscheles had made this last claim at a rehearsal of the Philharmonic Society during the current season. Since the supplement to the second edition of this book, 'Beethoven in Paris', was not known in London, I had only to refer the reporters to that article, for in it I had treated this most important question. The gathering decided to publish in London what I told them. I was urged to report the incident and its circumstances in a German newspaper. On 25 October of the same year I had the opportunity of publishing this information and other similar incidents in the supplement to the *Kölnische Zeitung*. The effects of this article are apparent in the most recent events in Stuttgart.

The reporters in Bonn had told me that Herr Moscheles was prompted to such arrogance and financial greed by the great sensation that followed his publication in England of the two letters from Beethoven written during the last days of the composer's life. The reader

* In recent times, Christians have had no grounds for reproaching Jews for anything in musical matters.

knows from the end of the last period the circumstances under which these two letters were written. I wrote both of them: Beethoven merely signed them. A comparison will show that their style is not Beethoven's. He did, however, dictate the second, dated 18 March—dictate, that is, as a dying man can.

Herr Moscheles's audacity in making the world believe that he was on terms of brotherly intimacy with all the classical composers has been expanded to include Mozart, Haydn, and Clementi. An article in praise of the Stuttgart edition of these classical composers' works, and also in defence of Moscheles's contribution to it, appeared in the supplement to the *Allgemeine Zeitung* of 16 December 1858 (reprinted from the *Neue Münchener Zeitung*). Here we read:

Moscheles spent many musical hours with Clementi, first in Vienna where the middle-aged composer served him as a model, then in London where Clementi, now an old man though possessed of the fire of youth, allowed Moscheles to play his compositions to him.

The following dates may serve as a commentary on this Leipzig fabrication. Moscheles came to Vienna in 1808 at the age of fourteen. Clementi was not there at that time, having been there in 1807 for the sole purpose of concluding a publishing contract with Beethoven.[298] We still have the original of this document, which bears the date 20 April. Clementi, then fifty-nine years old, had already given up his piano playing. In 1820 Moscheles went to London; Clementi was then seventy-eight.[299] Can the reader imagine the 'fire of youth that still possessed the old man'? Can the reader imagine, moreover, Moscheles, the most modern of modern pianists, and one bent at that time on nothing but increasing his reputation, playing the sonatas of Clementi, who was as assiduously avoided as Beethoven by all the modern virtuosi?[300] They were as scornful of Clementi's sonatas as of the whole body of Beethoven's piano music. On this subject Clementi expressed himself all too clearly during his last visit to Vienna in the summer of 1827. It would not surprise this author if he were soon to hear that Herr Moscheles had entered the ranks of the musicians of the future, for among them are the most fame and the most money to be found.

It is fortunate that we have an account of Heinrich Marschner's first meeting with Beethoven, as related in Professor L. Bischoff's biographical sketch of the royal court Kapellmeister in Hanover that appeared in the second, third, and fourth issues of the *Niederrheinische Musik Zeitung* in 1857. This meeting is a clear illustration of Beethoven's reaction to novices in the arts. Bischoff says:

Marschner later described his first meeting with Beethoven with more humour and a deeper sense of appreciation than he had felt at the time. The twenty-one-year-old youth probably expected the high priest of music to examine in greater detail the manuscript he had brought, and longed for the keys to the secrets of art that he thought he could find only here. But Beethoven was not a man of many words. Nevertheless, he received the young Marschner kindly, looked through the manuscript briefly, returned it with a 'Hm!' that expressed more satisfaction than displeasure, and said, 'I haven't much time. Don't come too often, but bring me something else.'

It went badly with Franz Schubert when in 1822 he brought to the master the variations for four hands that he had dedicated to him. The shy young artist, lost for words, found himself in a very uncomfortable situation, despite Diabelli's bringing him, introducing him, and expressing for him his sentiments for the master. The courage that had stayed with him right to the master's house abandoned him at the sight of the monarch of the arts. And when Beethoven expressed his wish that Schubert himself wrote down the answers to his questions, Schubert's hand was paralysed as if held in a vice. Beethoven went through the manuscript that had been brought to him and came upon an error in harmony. He pointed it out to the young man in a kindly manner, adding that it was no deadly sin. But Schubert, perhaps as a consequence of this encouraging remark, lost his composure entirely. Once out in the street again, he was able to pull himself together and scolded himself roundly. But he never regained the courage to present himself to the master again.[301]

The esteemed pianist and composer, Anton Halm, was quite at ease with Beethoven, and the master used to enjoy his vigorous, military nature. Halm had been an officer in the army, but talent and love of music soon made of him a thorough artist. Beethoven entrusted him with the task of making one of the most difficult piano arrangements, the fugue from the great B flat major quartet, opus 133, and was entirely satisfied with Halm's version.[302] When Carl Czerny tried his skill at the same task, the master threw away his work.

In 1824 Andreas Streicher introduced to Beethoven Franz Lachner, who had recently arrived from Munich. His reception was friendly, but later Lachner told how overwhelmed he had felt in the master's presence, despite Streicher's being there, for Lachner was at that time just twenty-one years old. Like Schubert, he never spoke with Beethoven again.

These instances show how it really was with the 'disciples of Beethoven', about whom we heard so much. It can probably be justly said that of all of them none exchanged with Beethoven more than a couple of words. In order to learn something from him, one would have to live and work in his presence; one would also have to catch him in a mood for teaching. Above all, one would have to have attained a mature age and a mature point of view in order to be able to take full advantage of the privilege of his acquaintance. What had the great master to do with boys who had scarcely shaken the dust of school from their shoes?

And yet we may name a small number of young artists who enjoyed the pleasure of the best reception Beethoven could give: Joseph Böhm, Johann Horzalka, Leopoldine Blahetka. We have already spoken of the first of these in connection with the events of 1825 concerning the new quartet, opus 127. He still occupies a post at the Vienna Conservatory as professor of violin.

This author knows of only one occasion on which Beethoven's reception of a young artist could not be called friendly. The incident has to do with Franz Liszt whom, in the company of his father, I introduced to the master. Beethoven's lack of cordiality sprang in part from the exaggerated idolatry accorded the lad, whose talent was indeed remarkable; but mainly from the request addressed to the master for a theme on which the twelve-year-old boy might base a free improvisation at his forthcoming farewell concert. It was a request as thoughtless as it was unreasonable. In any case, the excessive enthusiasm for this boy exceeded the bounds of all reason. It was so extreme that, after Beethoven had refused the request with obvious impatience, Emperor Franz, or at least Archduke Rudolph, was approached for a theme upon which the little virtuoso might improvise. The idolatry displayed over this child prodigy prompted the master, who had been trained in the school of hard experience, to expound at length on the obstacles and limitations placed in the way of a quiet ripening of true talent once that talent has been discovered and seized upon by an adoring public. Biographical sketches of Liszt have claimed that Beethoven was present at the farewell concert in 1823. Schilling's *Encyclopedia* even adds that Beethoven took the hand of little Liszt after the concert and pronounced him worthy of the name 'artist'. Beethoven did not attend this concert or any other private concert after the year 1816.

As for refusing visitors, only one instance is noteworthy. Twice Rossini tried to gain access to Beethoven in the company of the music dealer, D. Artaria, after Artaria had twice before asked if he could come with the *maestro*. Beethoven always made some excuse not to see them. We should not fail to mention that Rossini's desire to pay homage to the German master became acute when he heard all Beethoven's quartets for the first time, played by Mayseder; he was deeply moved by them. Suffice it to say that Beethoven's refusal was the subject of much comment. Those not sufficiently well acquainted with the existing situation in all German music, a situation brought about through the medium of Rossini's music, or those who made light of such a situation, or those who belittled its long-range effects, reproached our master for not wanting to see Rossini. It is particularly interesting that Beethoven would not tolerate any mention of this incident among his friends, and he never spoke of it to anyone. If Artaria had kept silent (he perhaps took the rejection more to heart than Rossini), the matter would not have come before the public.[303]

3.

BEETHOVEN'S MEMORY

As early as the first part of this work we remarked that Beethoven's memory of things past was always very poor. It is interesting to examine this phenomenon more closely and to see that the failing was not only in regard to his personal possessions and experiences, but that it applied to his musical memory as well. Those who did not know him intimately were always amazed how quickly Beethoven would completely forget the details of the composition he had just completed, not only the complex scores of large orchestral works but even works for piano solo. When he was busy with a new composition, his whole being was so absorbed in the work of the moment that even the passages he had just completed were as far behind him as if they had belonged to an earlier period of his life. All too often he was thrown into a rage when a copyist or some other person asked him about specific points in a composition without having the score in hand. It was the same with other composers' works: in order to remember a piece of music, he had to see it. Only Haydn and Mozart were exceptions.

How can we explain the fact, though, that this apparently poor memory was able to retain long passages from the Greek classics? When asked to identify a quotation, he would answer as promptly as if he had been asked to place a passage from one of his own compositions. Perhaps his lack of musical memory can be explained by the fact that at that time any music performed for an audience was played from the score, so that musicians did not memorize their parts and therefore were not forced to develop the mechanical faculties of the memory. This is no longer the case: today the practice of memorization has been cultivated at the expense of intellectual mastery.[304] Formerly not even the composer played his own works from memory. Such an exhibition of mental gymnastics was neither demanded nor desired. But now we are constantly invited to marvel at the dexterity not only of the hands but also of the mind. Not a few virtuosi have stored up in their memories whole reams of music all the way from Scarlatti down to the youngest of the classical composers, Johannes Brahms, and are always ready to produce any piece they wish. They do not have to waste either time or effort pondering the inner qualities of the music and can skip freely from one composition to another.

4.

BEETHOVEN'S PRIVATE LIBRARY[305]

We have already mentioned in passing our master's modest private library. It is, however, worth our trouble to examine it more closely. Towards the end of his life we noted which of the principal Greek writers occupied places of honour there. We should also say that Homer was represented by both his immortal epics.[306] It is interesting that in Beethoven's estimation the *Iliad* was far inferior to the *Odyssey*. The *Iliad*'s descriptions of military life, the tumult of battle, tactics and strategy, types of weapons and fortifications, and the like, could hold no interest for our Amphion. On the other hand, the *Odyssey*, with its pictures of peaceful life in all its aspects, descriptions of places and peoples, its passages of cunning and adventure, all couched in radiantly beautiful language, never ceased to delight him anew. If we could safely compare Beethoven's personal evaluation of these two epics to that of two of his symphonies, perhaps the C minor and the ninth symphony with chorus, we might realize that the reasons for his preference were inherent in his own nature and do not in any way discredit the less preferred work.

He had the complete works of Shakespeare in the Eschenburg translation.[307] Most of the volumes showed unmistakable marks of careful reading, as did the *Odyssey*, the *West-östliche Divan*, and Sturm's *Betrachtungen der Werke Gottes*.[308] He refused to have anything to do with Schlegel's translation of the great Briton: he pronounced it stiff, forced, and at times too far from the original, which he could deduce only by comparing it with Eschenburg's version.[309] As for Goethe, he had, besides the *Divan*, only *Wilhelm Meister*, *Faust*, and the poems; of Schiller's works he had only the poems and some of the plays.[310] He had Tiedge's *Urania* and the poems of Seume, Matthisson, and a few other contemporary poets. We must mention another book that he valued highly and recommended frequently: Nina d'Aubigny von Engelbrunner's *Briefe an Natalie über den Gesang*.

Beethoven's musical library was very meagre.[311] It contained only a very few of his own works. Of the works of the old Italian masters all he knew—all any of his contemporaries knew—was a small collection of short pieces by Palestrina, Nanini, Victoria, and others that Baron von Tuscher had had published by Artaria in 1824. Beethoven owned this collection. He had nothing by Haydn or Cherubini; of Mozart's music he had a part of the score of *Don Giovanni* and many sonatas. Almost all of Clementi's sonatas were at hand. He had the greatest admiration for these sonatas, considering them the most beautiful, the most pianistic of works, both for their lovely, pleasing, original melodies and for the consistent, easily followed form of each movement. Beethoven had but little liking for Mozart's piano music, and the musical education of his beloved nephew was confined for many years almost exclusively to the playing of Clementi sonatas. Carl Czerny, the nephew's teacher, was much less devoted to these sonatas, and for this and other pedagogical reasons a disagreement arose between him and Beethoven, as a result of which lessons with him were discontinued. He was replaced by Joseph Czerny, a much better teacher than Carl, who profited from his name and its good reputation without being a blood relative of Joseph.[312] Under the new teacher's guidance the nephew advanced along the road prescribed by his uncle. This incident is related here only to illustrate Beethoven's special regard for the works of Clementi.

Also in Beethoven's musical library were the two published volumes of études by John Cramer. In our master's opinion, these études contained all the fundamentals of good piano playing. If he had ever realized his intention of compiling a textbook of piano playing, these études would have constituted most of the practical examples, for because of the polyphony used in many of them, he considered them the best preparation for the playing of his own works. His interpretation of them may be seen in the twenty numbers he marked for his nephew's study, indicating the best possible manner of playing them, with subtly differing accentuation but always in compliance with strict rules. These marked copies are among the most precious papers in the whole *Nachlass*.[313]

In Wegeler's *Nachtrag zu den biographischen Notizen*, Dr. Gerhard von Breuning corroborates my statement that our master intended to write a piano method (he first mentioned it in 1818) in order to protect his works from being badly played. On page 23 of the *Nachtrag*, Breuning says:

I had a copy of the Pleyel *Method of Piano Playing*. He (Beethoven) was dissatisfied with this as with all the other methods. He once said to me as I sat by his bed, 'I wanted to write a textbook for piano students myself, but I never had the time. I would have written something very different.' Then he promised my father he would see about a text for me. Some time later he sent me the Clementi sonatas he had ordered for me, which were not available here (in Vienna). The following note accompanied the music:

'Dear friend:

At last I am able to break away from my negligence. I send herewith

Clementi's *School of Piano Playing* for Gerhard. If he uses it in the way that I will show him, it will certainly produce good results. I will see you shortly, and embrace you cordially.

Yours,

Beethoven'

How most people will shake their heads over Beethoven's extravagant opinion of 'old man Clementi's' little text, especially those who think they have found salvation in one of the modern volumes that have been hailed by the newspapers as a panacea for all problems of piano playing! This incident, however, was directly concerned with elementary piano instruction. But to one who witnessed the master's pronounced aversion to all long-winded expounding of theory and the even longer-winded practical application in the form of études which in the end can do nothing but reduce the pupils to automatons; to one who saw him shake his head over Hummel's voluminous but inconsequential *Method for the Piano*; to one who heard him inveigh against the music teachers who seize every imaginable opportunity to assign composition exercises, the music teachers who would not think of allowing a pupil to 'slip through' without spending at least two or three years on thoroughbass alone, thus crushing out every spark of imagination in the pupil, the music teachers who leave nothing to experience or experimentation, the music teachers who teach composition by making the pupils imitate models (for all these deplorable practices had already been initiated in his time): to such a one, I say, it is quite clear that the master would have recommended the study of Clementi's text at any level.

Beethoven's library contained very little by that patriarch of music Johann Sebastian Bach. Apart from a few motets, most of which had been sung at van Swieten's soirées, he had most of the music of Bach known at that time: the *Well-tempered Clavier*, which showed signs of diligent study, three volumes of the *Clavierübung*, fifteen two-part inventions, fifteen three-part inventions, and a toccata in D minor.[314] This total collection in a single volume is in my keeping. An additional page has been pasted into the volume, on which is copied in another hand a passage from J. N. Forkel's *Sebastian Bach's Leben, Kunst und Kunstwerke*:

The contention that music is an art form for all ears cannot be supported in Bach; the mere existence and uniqueness of his works, which seem to have been destined only for the connoisseur, disprove this contention altogether. Thus only the connoisseur of music, who in a work of art can perceive and feel the inner organization, who can penetrate the artist's will that does nothing without a reason, can be judge here. Indeed, there is no better measure of a music-lover's discrimination than his ability to appreciate the works of Bach.

5. WANDERLUST

At either side of this excerpt there stands in Beethoven's writing a thick, black question mark made with the heaviest of his music pens. The two question marks stand in judgement on this claim made by the learned historian and most distinguished of Bach-lovers. No Hogarth could have made a question mark look more severe or depicted dissent more expressively.

5.

WANDERLUST

In the second and third periods we spoke at length of our master's unhappy financial situation and its causes. In the final paragraphs of the third period we said that almost every expenditure, even a necessary one, became the object of an inner struggle and a difficult decision. Obviously there is a paradox here. Let us examine it more closely.

The reader may have been surprised to hear that almost every year, particularly in the third period, Beethoven moved to another abode. This restless wandering from one dwelling place to another, together with his shuttling between the city and the country, is symptomatic of our master's unstable, discontented nature. How could there have been in all Vienna an apartment with which he could remain satisfied for a number of years when there was not one person there whose company he could continue to enjoy without sooner or later arguing until a separation, temporary or final, was inevitable? We have seen many examples. Let us not forget the consistency of his inconsistency. When we hear how Beethoven would in anger utter invectives even against his friend and patron the Archduke; when during his lawsuit against Maelzel he wrote in his deposition to the lawyer: 'Abandoned by everyone here in Vienna'; when he called the B . . . family in Frankfurt his best friends in the world, surely only because their distance would not allow closer contact, then these complaints sound like a case of his not being able to see the wood for the trees. For Beethoven could number as his friends all those who were admirers of his music.

In his fifty-fourth year he could be entirely satisfied only by nature, and nature and his art alone were able to hold him. People and houses seldom pleased him for both had too many faults. We have already said enough about his difficulties with people and about the reasons for these difficulties, most of which came from his imagination and his suspicions. His letter of reconciliation to Breuning says all that need be said on this score. He was dissatisfied with his dwelling places for similar reasons. This one was not sunny enough; in that one the water from the well did not suit him; a third was reached by a staircase that was too dark. For excuses such as these he would quit the apartment or, during the summer months that he spent in the country, use it only to house his music and his little library. Of course it had to be paid for.

His country lodgings cost him a considerable sum. But even there he did not always spend the entire summer in one apartment. We have already learned from the events of 1823 what strange, almost comical incidents would cause him to move. The deep bows of the noble landlord at Hetzendorf impeded the flow of the master's fantasy and drove him away. Perhaps there would never have been a ninth symphony had he remained in that house. And in the following year a similar incident occurred. At Penzing near Schönbrunn he took rooms in an isolated and friendly house on the Vienna River. Very near the house there was a foot-bridge across the river. People would gather on the bridge and, out of curiosity or out of interest, would stare up at Beethoven's windows. He found this sufficient reason for packing up bag and baggage, pots and pans, Broadwood piano and all his belongings and moving to Baden. Perhaps the curious people were impeding the free flow of his imagination as he was occupied with the first of the five quartets. Each of these summer apartments, the one at Penzing and the one at Hetzendorf, cost 400 florins WW. Add to these 800 florins 400 more for the two seasons in Baden, and the total sum comes to the cost of renting a very good apartment in Vienna for two whole years.

This extravagant passion for changing houses started during the second period. Ferdinand Ries's *Notizen*, pp. 112 ff, tell us that in 1805 Beethoven retained four apartments at once: one in the Theater an der Wien, one in the Rothe Haus by the Alsterkaserne, one in Döbling, and finally the one in Pasqualati's house on the Mölkerbastei. In other words, he was living like a great lord or a great eccentric. The last-mentioned place was through almost all of the second period a refuge for the master when he could find no other rooms. Ries remarks: 'He moved out of the Pasqualati apartment several times, but would always return to it, so that, as I learned later, Baron Pasqualati was kind enough, when Beethoven would move out, to say, "The rooms are not for rent; Beethoven will be back soon." ' Here again we see a case of consistency in his inconsistency: our restless wanderer wanted only apartments with a southern exposure, but the Mölkerbastei apartment faced north!

While we are speaking of such caprices, let us take the opportunity to show the extent to which this deeply serious, thoughtful man was still a child who loved his playthings. The heavy blows of fate did much to dampen this playfulness and childish humour, but there were still moments when he would be disposed to buffoonery and practical joking. Later we shall see an example, but first we must say that even this playfulness cost many florins that could have been better used elsewhere. But the great child liked to keep a table covered with knick-knacks that would amuse him for a while, although some served a higher purpose.[315] His writing-table (in his early years he used a very large one) was also covered with trinkets: paperweights in the form of cossacks and Hungarian hussars, lamps of various shapes, bells of all kinds ranging from silver bells to sheep bells, statuettes of ancient Greeks and Romans (of which we now have only the Brutus he admired so much), and writing implements of the most recent invention. Then there were chains of bells, in one room linked on a costly silk rope, while in another room they were strung on hemp, and many more things. The master spent no more on furniture than the poorest labourer. He always bought his furniture second-hand. When walking along the street he would stop and look in the show windows of this or that shop until he fell in love with something and bought it. Many of these purchases were for his nephew. The constant moving, packing, and unpacking made it necessary to discard these trinkets, some of which were valuable. Only a few could be saved.

These circumstances may serve as an answer to the accusations that Vienna left Beethoven to starve, and even that all Germany was responsible for the unfortunate situation of the great composer. The author hopes that in his discussion of the third period he has sufficiently dealt with this question and other such accusations having to do with all Germany.

6.

A JUVENILE TRICK

We promised our readers an example of our master's disposition, despite his misfortunes and frequent ill-humour, towards buffoonery and practical joking. The wife of Halm, the pianist and composer, wanted a lock of Beethoven's hair. The request was made through Karl Holz, who persuaded the master to send his ardent admirer some hairs from the beard of a goat, actually not too different from Beethoven's own coarse grey hair. The lady, delighted with this memento of her musical idol, boasted far and wide of the gift, but before long she learned how she had been duped. Her husband was still deeply sensitive of his honour as a military officer, and in an aggrieved letter to our master related what he had heard. When Beethoven realized that his prank had been taken as an insult, he atoned for it by cutting off a lock of his own hair and sending it to the lady with a note begging for for-giveness. This incident occurred in 1826.

7.

CERTIFICATE OF SURVIVAL

In order to claim his annuity payment each quarter, Beethoven had to present a certificate drawn up by the pastor of the parish in which he lived to testify that he was still alive.[316] When the master was in the country, it was I or some other acquaintance who was asked to prepare this paper and attend to the necessary formalities. Such requests seldom lacked some joke about his existence and his condition. He would even go to extremes of ridicule. Knowing that it would be taken in good part, he once sent in a paper on which was formally written:

> Certificate of Survival
> The fish lives!
> Vidi
> Pastor
> Romualdus

8.

CONTRAST BETWEEN THE BROTHERS

On New Year's Day, 1823, Beethoven, his nephew, and the author were sitting at their noon meal, when the master was handed a New Year's card from his brother who lived close by. The card was signed, 'Johann van Beethoven, Land-owner'. Immediately the master wrote on the back of the card, 'Ludwig van Beethoven, Brain-owner', and returned it to him.

A few days later this brother boasted to the master that he would never be as smart as the former apothecary had been. One can imagine how this boasting amused the 'brain-owner'.

In order to gain an appreciation of this man's wealth, we must take a look at its source. During the war of 1809 Johann van Beethoven, the apothecary of Linz, furnished medical supplies to all the French army hospitals in Upper Austria and in Salzburg. This led Ludwig, who was always upright and honourable, to make serious and well-founded charges against his 'pseudo-brother'. Anyone acquainted with businesses involving the delivery of merchandise can easily guess what I am not permitted to say here.[317]

At this point let me mention yet another peculiarity of Beethoven, having to do with any of the usual occasions for the expression of good wishes. No one could send him a birthday or name-day card unless he wanted to see him fly into a rage against all 'social tomfoolery and two-faced deception'.

9.

THE TWILIGHT HOUR

Beethoven was especially fond of sitting at his piano in the twilight and improvising. Sometimes he would play the violin or viola that he always kept on the piano. We need not say what this playing sounded like, for his external senses were incapable of guiding him; for the other people in the house his playing, especially of the string instruments which he was unable to tune, was agony to the ears. His extemporizing on the piano was seldom intelligible, for it was usually extremely agitated. Generally the lack of clarity was caused by the left hand being spread wide and laid upon the keyboard so heavily that the noise would drown the much softer playing of the right hand.

In his last years, the piano manufacturer Conrad Graf made him a sounding-board which, when set upon the piano, would better conduct the sound of the notes to the player's ears. The device worked well for single notes, but full chords completely overwhelmed the ear, since the airwaves, confined within a very limited space, must have had a deafening effect.

10.

BEETHOVEN'S DAILY ROUTINE

Beethoven rose every morning the year round at dawn and went directly to his desk. There he would work until two or three o'clock, his habitual dinner hour. In the course of the morning he would usually go out of doors once or twice, but would continue to work as he walked. These walks would seldom last more than an hour, and may be compared to a bee's excursions to gather honey. Beethoven would go out in every season, heeding neither cold nor heat. His afternoons were regularly spent in long walks. Late in the afternoon he would go to a favourite tavern to read the papers, unless he had already satisfied this need in a coffee-house. When, however, the British Parliament was in session, he would read the debates in the *Allgemeine Zeitung* at home. As one would expect, he sided with the Opposition, and was a great admirer of Lord Brougham, Hume, and other orators in that party's cause. Beethoven always spent his winter evenings at home reading serious works of literature. Only very rarely did he work with musical scores during the evening, for the strain on his eyes was too great. It may have been otherwise in his youth, but we know that he never composed at night. He would go to bed at ten o'clock at the latest.

<h2 style="text-align:center">11.</h2>

<h2 style="text-align:center">MOMENTS OF DEEP MEDITATION</h2>

Washing and bathing were among the most pressing necessities of Beethoven's life. In this respect he was indeed an Oriental: to his way of thinking Mohammed did not exaggerate a whit in the number of ablutions he prescribed. If he did not dress to go out during the morning working hours, he would stand in great *déshabillé* at his washstand and pour large pitchers of water over his hands, bellowing up and down the scale or sometimes humming loudly to himself. Then he would stride around his room with rolling or staring eyes, jot something down, then resume his pouring of water and loud singing. These were moments of deep meditation, to which no one could have objected but for two unfortunate consequences. First of all, the servants would often burst out laughing. This made the master angry and he would sometimes assault them in language that made him cut an even more ridiculous figure. Or, secondly, he would come into conflict with the landlord, for all too often so much water was spilled that it went right through the floor. This was one of the main reasons for Beethoven's unpopularity as a tenant. The floor of his living-room would have had to be covered with asphalt to prevent all that water from seeping through. And the master was totally unaware of the excess of inspiration under his feet!

<h2 style="text-align:center">12.</h2>

<h2 style="text-align:center">FOOD AND DRINK</h2>

Beethoven's remarkable eating and drinking habits corresponded to his eccentric housekeeping.

For breakfast he drank coffee, which he usually prepared in a glass coffee-maker. Coffee seems to have been the one indispensable item in his diet, and he was as fastidious as an Oriental in its preparation. He estimated sixty beans to the cup and would often count them out, especially if there were guests. One of his favourite dishes was macaroni and cheese. It had to be particularly bad for him to find it so, and it can be presumed that it was more often bad than not due to his irregular eating hours. But he was very severe in his criticism of other meals and would often rail at his housekeeper, though she was seldom at fault. To protect her was to incur Beethoven's anger and disdain. 'This soup is vile' was not to be contradicted. If one disagreed, one was considered devoid of taste and judgement.

He would become more upset when crossed in matters of diet than in far more important matters, and would for days afterwards talk about such an affront or even go so far as to send a note of rebuke. I have such a letter before me: at the end he upbraids me: 'Your opinion of the soup does not interest me in the least. It was bad!' Such pettiness was a trait of Beethoven's generally recognized despotism.

He was very fond of all kinds of fish, and usually invited guests on Fridays so he could serve a heavy meal of *schill* (a Danube fish resembling haddock in flavour) and potatoes. He seldom ate a rich evening meal, preferring a dish of soup and some leftovers from dinner.

His favourite beverage was fresh spring water, which he drank in large quantities in the summertime. Among wines he most often chose one from Budapest. Unfortunately, he especially liked the flavour of fortified wines which were very bad for his weakened stomach. He would heed no warning. This fact alone is proof that Beethoven was not the drunkard his last doctor claimed he was. The composer often enjoyed a good glass of beer in the evening accompanied by his pipe and his paper.

In his later years, Beethoven often visited restaurants and coffee-houses, which he always entered by a back door—where he could sit in a private room. Strangers who wished to see him were sent here, for his habits never changed and he always chose a coffee-house near his home. He would very seldom engage in conversation with strangers who were introduced to him. When he had read the last page of the newspaper, he would hurry out by the back door.

13.

AN EXPRESSION OF THANKS; OF BEETHOVEN AND HUMMEL

In order to secure a clear picture of the facts we are now to disclose, let us go back to their origins, to the last days of Beethoven's life, to a time when, sensing his approaching death, he began to put his earthly affairs in order, both his own concerns and his obligations to others. One of these items had to do with the author of this book. This was still in the days when the master expected to recover fully and was preoccupied with finding a way of showing his gratitude for all my years of service and sacrifice. As early as 1823 he had promised me a small sum of gold to reimburse me for the losses I had sustained in my own affairs while helping him with the subscriptions for the *Missa Solemnis*. It was never paid. I had had to give up all my private lessons that year and the following year as well.

On his deathbed he was deeply troubled by the problem of discharging his debt to me, which was now considerably greater. I had long since refused to accept cash from him, having learned from years of observation that this was his most sensitive nerve. Then, towards the end of January, an unusual and solemn opportunity presented itself for him to demonstrate his gratitude.

According to the contract concluded in 1822 with the management of the Josephstadt Theater, the author, as orchestra director, was guaranteed one-half the profits from one annual concert or opera performance. The heavy expenditures incurred by the new enterprise prompted the director to request me to postpone my claim to this half until the following year, when I could have the total profits from my benefit performance. The second year of the contract was over, and again I was told that there was no possibility of withdrawing the total receipts for one evening during the good season. When I refused to accept a summer performance, as being contrary to the contract, I was put off until the third winter. But when winter came the management protested so many obstacles in the way of discharging their overdue obligation that they suggested a cash payment instead of the benefit performance.

Hardly had this proposal been made when the manager was removed from the institution by sudden death. His heirs, who immediately took over the management of the theatre, refused to recognize my claim under the pretence that my debt had been superannuated. I then left the theatre and entrusted the untangling of my affairs to Dr. Bach. About a year later I had the satisfaction of receiving a magistrate judgement in my favour. According to the terms of the verdict, the Josephstadt Theater, together with everything and everyone in it, was put entirely at my disposal for the evening of 7 April 1827.

Knowing the intense interest Beethoven took in the outcome of this lawsuit, Dr. Bach went to him immediately with the legal decree. The moment the master had read the document he declared his intention of taking part in the 7 April performance at the Josephstadt Theater. When I came into the room a little later, he handed me the decree, congratulated me heartily, and announced that for this occasion he would finish the overture he had had in mind since 1822, which was to replace the overture in C major with double fugue. Moreover, he wished to conduct the new work himself! This was an unexpected opportunity for him to demonstrate his gratitude to me. The preliminary sketches for this overture were immediately sought out.

In the course of the following weeks, however, as he began to realize that he could not hope to recover before 7 April, he tried to think how he could be useful to me in other ways than through a new composition and personal participation in the performance. While he was thus casting about, the newspapers announced that Hummel was soon to arrive in Vienna. When Beethoven read this news, he said: 'If only he would visit me, I would beg him to take my place at the concert on 7 April!'

Hummel arrived in Vienna about the middle of March. The very next day he appeared at Beethoven's bedside in the company of his pupil, Ferdinand Hiller, and Andreas Streicher. The two artists had not seen each other since 1814. Hummel, appalled at the evidence of Beethoven's suffering, broke into tears. The master sought to quieten him by holding out an etching that Diabelli had sent him of Haydn's birthplace in Rohrau, and saying: 'Look here, dear Hummel, this is the house where Haydn was born. I received it today as a gift, and it pleases me very much. Such a poor peasant hut for such a great man to be born in!' But then he brought the conversation around to the concert in the Josephstadt Theater that the court had decreed, and his vain wishes that he might take part in it. He closed with this charge: 'Hummel, I am counting on you. Take my place at this concert, and I shall be grateful to you.' Hummel gave the master his hand, and Beethoven was visibly surprised at this immediate compliance. This moment, in view of the lack of sympathy these two eminent artists had felt for each other, was a solemn one, worthy in itself of mention even if nothing further had come of it.

A few days after this incident, we accompanied the great composer to his final resting place. Hummel was one of the pall-bearers. He remained true to his word concerning the concert on 7 April. At his request, the situation was explained in the programme in the following words:

Herr Hummel, Court Kapellmeister for the Grand Duchy of Saxe-Weimar, will have the honour of playing the piano for the last time before his departure, and it affords him particularly great pleasure to be able to fulfil the wish of his immortal friend, Ludwig van Beethoven, who on his deathbed asked Herr Hummel to represent him by lending his support to the beneficiary of this performance.

The evening was a solemn occasion, and Master Hummel saw himself surrounded by many renowned musicians. The strange coincidence of events drew a large audience to witness this public proof of the reconciliation between Beethoven and Hummel. The newspapers gave the occasion due publicity. Issue No. 30 of the *Berliner Musikzeitung* for 1827 (edited by A. B. Marx) reported:

Hummel gave us a farewell performance at the Josephstadt Theater in a concert which, according to an earlier contract, was given for the benefit of the theatre's former orchestra director, Schindler. Herr Schindler was in every sense of the word the faithful Pylades of our immortal Beethoven. For years he took care of the composer's private affairs, and was in constant attendance until the master drew his dying breath. The deceased master, when still hoping to recover, wanted to show his gratitude by writing a new composition to be performed for the first time on this occasion. But when he began to feel that it had been decreed otherwise in the book of destiny, he laid his obligation in the hands of Hummel, whom in his dying hour he appointed to take his place in discharging his debt of gratitude to the generous friend who had made so many sacrifices in his behalf. Hummel, his heart broken, gave the master his hand and his word, and postponed his departure in order to fulfil his promise. . . .'

This event and its background are recorded in a similar vein in issue No. 22 of the Leipzig AmZ for 1827.

EDITOR'S NOTES (293–317)

Personality, Individual Characteristics, Anecdotes, etc.

293 Schindler's reference is probably to Jean-François Champollion, 'le jeune' (1790–1832), rather than to his older brother Jacques-Joseph Champollion-Figeac (1778–1867). Champollion le jeune first visited Egypt only in 1828. In 1839 Champollion-Figeac published some of his brother's findings under the title: *Egypte Ancienne: l'universe pittoresque, histoire et description*, etc. A translation of this work, under the title *Gemälde von Aegypten*, appeared that same year from the press of Siegmund Schmerber in Frankfurt-am-Main. The inscriptions cited by Schindler appear, as he says, on p. 417, but obviously Beethoven must have secured his quotations from some other source.

A phrase similar to the first of Beethoven's quotations occurs in the present-day ritual of Anglo-Saxon freemasonry, but it is not known whether such a passage was used in early nineteenth-century freemasonry in Austria, nor can it be stated with positiveness that Beethoven was a member of the Masonic order. The second of the quotations bears a marked similarity to a passage in § 9 of Plutarch's essay *Of Isis and Osiris* which Beethoven, as a devoted reader of Plutarch, may have known:

'Moreover, the temple of Minerva which is at Sais (whom they look upon as the same with Isis) had upon it this inscription: I am whatever was, or is, or will be; and my veil no mortal ever took up.' [Translation from Plutarch's *Miscellanies and Essays*, Vol. IV, ed. W. W. Goodwin (Boston, 1898).]

Leitzmann (LvB II 374) suggests that Beethoven took his three phrases from a book by the philosopher K. L. Reinhold ('Brother Decius') *Die hebräischen Mysterien oder die älteste religiöse Freimauerei* (Leipzig, 1788); what is perhaps the most convincing conjecture, however, is found in a quotation from Schiller's *Die Sendung Moses*, given in TK II 168, in which all three of Beethoven's chosen phrases occur.

The present editor is indebted to Dr. William Stevenson Smith of the Boston Museum of Fine Arts and to Dr. John A. Wilson of the Oriental Institute of the University of Chicago for assistance in preparing this note.

[294] Facsimiles of these aphorisms may also be found in Ley: *Beethovens Leben in Bildern*, p. 129, and in Bory, p. 202. Note also the entries in the Fischhof Manuscript (Leitzmann, LvB II 252–54, 257) that indicate Beethoven's interest in the philosophical writings of India. The period of these entries, as well as Beethoven's reference to the Temple of Isis in his letter of 19 October 1815 to Countess Erdödy (And. 563), suggest an approximate date for the autograph that Schindler quotes.

[295] See Note 259.

[296] The reason for borrowing the Broadwood piano was to demonstrate at the concert of 15 December 1823 the differences between the Viennese piano and the instrument of English design. The range of the Broadwood piano was from the C below cello C to the B above soprano high C (BStud II 228); regarding the range of contemporary Viennese pianos, see Notes 81 and 91. The Viennese piano used by Moscheles at this concert was probably furnished by Leschen, not by Graf (BusZ II 55).

[297] While Beethoven and his associates used the word 'Jew' as a term of opprobrium, the present editor knows of no documented basis for a charge of anti-semitism against Beethoven. Kaznelson, pp. 289, 430, gives a substantial list of Jews who were friends or acquaintances of Beethoven's. Schindler's charge probably reflects his own attitude more accurately than that of Beethoven.

[298] During a tour of the European capitals that lasted from 1802 to 1810, Clementi arrived again in Vienna late in 1808 (TK II 131; TF 450), where he may have stayed several months (TDR III 188). After a sojourn in Rome, he returned once more to Vienna in September 1809 (TDR III 163). It was thus quite possible for Moscheles, who in March 1809 had appeared with success in a public concert in Vienna as both pianist and composer (BusZ IV 45), to have made Clementi's acquaintance in Vienna.

[299] In both statements of Clementi's age, Schindler's arithmetic played him false. Clementi, born 23 January 1752, was 55 years old when he was in Vienna in 1807, and 69 years old, with another eleven years to live, when Moscheles first arrived in London in May 1821 (not 1820). 'He retained his characteristic energy and freshness of mind to the last' (Grove); there seems no reason to doubt that Clementi would have welcomed the brilliant young

virtuoso from Vienna who (Schindler to the contrary notwithstanding) had worked closely with his old friend Beethoven, and whom he himself had very possibly met in Vienna in 1808 or 1809.

300 ADB 22–345, published in 1885, describes Moscheles as 'the most significant piano virtuoso of the first half of the nineteenth century, who successfully maintained the supremacy of the older school of music even against a Liszt . . . and a tireless defender of the classics, at first against the Italians and later against the music of the Wagner-Liszt period.'

301 'Heinrich von Kreissle, Schubert's biographer, adduces the testimony of Joseph Hüttenbrenner, a close friend of Schubert's, who had it from the song composer himself that he had gone to Beethoven's house with the variations, but the great man was not at home and the variations were left with the servant. He had neither seen Beethoven nor spoken with him, but learned with delight afterwards that Beethoven had been pleased with the variations and often played them with his nephew Karl' (TK III 79; TF 806).

302 This is exactly the reverse of the actual situation (see Note 243; TK III 224; TF 976; KHV 406; MM 518). The arrangement by Czerny is mentioned in TDR V 300n.

303 TK III 78 and TF 805 say categorically that Schindler's story is not true, basing this statement on accounts given by Rossini to Hiller in 1856 and to Hanslick in 1867. Each time Rossini said that he was introduced by Carpani (not Artaria) and that Beethoven received him, but that the visit lasted only a short time: 'between his deafness and my ignorance of German, conversation was impossible.' Sonneck, Impr, p. 116, gives an account of a conversation between Rossini and Richard Wagner in 1860 in which Rossini told of his visit in great detail, quoting Beethoven's hearty praise of *Il Barbiere*. Accounts of this visit from other sources are given in Kerst I 288 ff.

304 Hanslick, p. 231, quotes the comment of a Viennese reviewer that at his début in 1816 Joseph Böhm 'stood at the front of the stage, free and alone, and not behind a music rack', and continues: 'Böhm was one of the first in Vienna to play from memory, a practice that became general among violinists only after Paganini set the example' in 1828.

305 Beethoven's personal library consisted of perhaps 200 to 300 volumes. The emphasis was strongly on poetical works, both German and translations from other languages, with a considerable number of religious and speculative works. Of these, Schindler preserved 17 volumes that passed with his *Nachlass* to the Royal Library in Berlin; about 175 volumes in 44 lots were sold at the auction of 5 November 1827, bringing a total of 18 fl. 20 kr. CM (BStud II 179); an unknown number, probably including most of his translations of classical authors, were pilfered during the few months after his death when his *Nachlass* was left unguarded. A list of the books that he owned, so far as they are known, is given in Leitzmann LvB II 379 (see also Kerst II 332).

The catholicity of Beethoven's reading interests is indicated by the dozens of notations in the Conversation Books of books on the widest variety of subjects that had been advertised for sale, with listing of author, title, price, and name of publisher or dealer.

[306] Of all the classical authors whom Schindler and others have referred to as among Beethoven's favourites—Homer, Plato, Plutarch, Aristotle, Euripides, Pliny, Ovid, and perhaps Horace, Quintilian, Tacitus, Lucian, and Xenophon—the only volume from his personal library that has come down to us is the *Odyssey*. Nohl, in *Beethovens Brevier* (ed. Sakolowski, 1901), p. 78, describes this as translated and published by Voss in 1781, a leather-bound octavo volume showing by its coffee stains and flecks of candle wax that it had been much used by day and by night. Nohl tabulated more than fifty passages in the *Odyssey* that Beethoven had underlined or otherwise marked as of specific interest to him.

A note written by the poet Theodor Körner to his father on 10 February 1813 said, 'I have been approached to write *Ulysses Wiederkehr* by Beethoven' (TK II 237; TF 531). The poet was killed in battle before this plan could be put into effect.

[307] Among the books from Beethoven's library at Berlin are two double volumes of the Eschenburg prose translation, which include *Othello, Romeo and Juliet, Much Ado About Nothing, All's Well That Ends Well, The Merchant of Venice, The Winter's Tale, As You Like It,* and *Love's Labour's Lost,* all except the last two showing signs of intensive reading (Nohl II 529). *Beethovens Brevier* includes 31 passages from these plays that Beethoven had marked, 20 of these passages being from *The Merchant of Venice*. The Berlin collection also includes an 1825 reprint of Schlegel's metrical translation of *The Tempest*. The list of books to be sold at auction includes 'Shakespeare's Plays', otherwise unidentified. See MT CV (1964) 260.

[308] *Beethovens Brevier* includes 43 marked passages from the *West-östlicher Divan* and 41 from Sturm's *Betrachtungen*.

[309] This statement conflicts with a passage in Beethoven's letter of May 1810 to Therese Malfatti (And. 258): 'Have you read Goethe's *Wilhelm Meister* and Shakespeare in Schlegel's translation? . . . Perhaps you would like to let me send you these works.'

[310] Item 25 in the list of books to be auctioned consists of 'Goethe's Collected Writings, 24 volumes, of which some are duplicates'; Item 26 is 'Schiller's Collected Works, 21 miscellaneous volumes and 3 volumes of engraved plates' (Leitzmann LvB II 382).

Before the discrepancy between the auction list and the statements in the text is taken as further evidence of Schindler's undependability, consideration should be given to the possibility set forth in the discussion of the library and the auction list on p. 504 *infra*. In that discussion, Schindler suggests that books and music never the property of Beethoven had been introduced into the material to be sold (he uses the word 'smuggled') with the thought that, presented as material once owned by the great composer, these items would bring higher prices than otherwise. There were enough irregularities in the handling of the *Nachlass* so that this conjecture may be well founded.

[311] Regarding the discrepancy between this statement and the official inventory, see Note 310.

[312] As nearly as can be determined, Carl Czerny (1791–1857) was nephew

Karl's teacher from spring 1816 to spring 1818, and Joseph Czerny (1785–1842) from early 1820 to midsummer of that year (see MMR LXXXVIII [1958] 124).

313 An edition of the Cramer Études, with Beethoven's comments, was published by Augener (London) in 1893, under the editorship of J. S. Shedlock. This edition has long been out of print. The comments (but not the études themselves) are given in Anna Gertrud Huber: *Beethoven-Studien* (Hug & Co., Zürich, 1961).

314 In *Bach-Jahrbuch* III (1906) 84, Schneider discusses the availability of Bach's music during Beethoven's lifetime. His findings may be summarized as follows:

As late as 1792, the only works of Bach that had been printed were the four parts of the *Clavierübung*, the 2- and 3-part inventions, the *Kunst der Fuge*, the *Musikalisches Opfer*, various chorale preludes for organ, and a few minor works. The two parts of the *Well-Tempered Clavier*, some of the organ music, four clavier concertos, the *St. Luke Passion*, parts of the *Christmas Oratorio*, 25–30 cantatas, and a few miscellaneous works were available in manuscript copies from commercial sources. Even by the year of Beethoven's death, this list had not been sensibly increased except by the *Chromatic Fantasy and Fugue*, the sonatas for violin and clavier, the *Magnificat*, the D major suite for orchestra, and commercial manuscript copies of the sonatas and partitas for violin solo and the suites for cello solo. Beethoven's familiarity with the works of Bach (e.g., the *B Minor Mass* [see And. 281]) must have come largely from privately circulated manuscript copies.

315 Various of the trinkets referred to here are preserved at the Beethoven-haus. They are described by Schmidt & Knickenberg: *Das Beethoven-Haus in Bonn und seine Sammlungen* (1927), p. 42, and some of them are shown in Ley: *Beethovens Leben in Bildern*, pp. 126–28. See also Supplement P (p. 507 *infra*).

316 Regarding this practice, see MM 217, especially Note 4. The attestation that Schindler quotes does not seem to have been preserved.

317 Referring to the contracts with the French army for medical supplies that brother Johann secured in the spring of 1809, thus laying the foundation for his comfortable fortune, MQ XXXV (1949) 540 says:

The belief that the financial success they brought resulted from profiteering and sharp practice, while possibly due merely to envy, finds some substantiation in the fact that in the spring of 1814 an investigation was sought of the charge 'that the medicaments provided by the apothecary van Beethoven (commoner) were not always of standard quality'.

MUSICAL SECTION

*Letters and notes on paper are but
lifeless signs; and playing the notes as
though they by themselves were this
disclosed word is lifeless strumming
unless the spirit that is in them has
become apparent, has been comprehended
by us, and is brought to life—their
spirit and no other, not our own, not
that of convention or of the pedagogue,
but the spirit given to them by Beethoven.*

A. B. MARX

Twenty years have passed since the first version of this book was written, a sufficient length of time to tell whether the literal word has forced the spirit of the music even further into the background than it had at that time. We must acknowledge with joy that large choral societies have espoused the production of oratorios with even greater enthusiasm than ever before, an enthusiasm that will serve as a firm foundation for the maintenance of this art form inherited from the classical composers. But in the case of all other branches of music, the situation has deteriorated. Other art forms, especially instrumental music, have undergone a revolution, as over four decades technical virtuosity has achieved total domination of the piano and the strings. This emphasis on mechanics has annihilated almost every trace of the spiritual element in music.

As early as 1823, Beethoven said to Ferdinand Ries: 'I shall have to look at your *allegro di bravura* movements. To be honest with you, I am no lover of this sort of thing; at least, all the works of this kind that I know seem to favour all too much the mechanical aspects.' The great prophet was predicting even then that matters of mechanics would supplant all spiritual truth in music. Not only the spirit of the music but the form as well have been destroyed by excessive mechanical brilliance. This modern demon is contemptuous of the spirit of emotional performance inherited from the classical era as well as of the means of achieving emotional response from the hearers. It follows no other command than the one that has grown habitual: all subjectivity is to be suppressed. The hundred-tongued voice of criticism, coming largely from men who have been raised on these fallacies and have identified their views with them, supports the musicians in the mad notion that they have always done the right thing. Surely the maxim attributed to rulers of nations, 'divide and rule', is no less applicable to artistic criticism. The divergence that splits critical views asunder has inevitably brought about the chaotic disintegration of all fundamental principles.

The necessary consequence has been that everything, even the obviously bad thing, finds someone to defend it, and exploits that defender to the hilt. Some venal newspapers are willing to sanctify anything. If this course continues, even the few honest papers still dedicated to the true, the upright, and the lawful, will in a few years have no readers left, for the group of discriminating music-lovers to whom these papers largely owe their existence will have lost their faith in art criticism. To the attentive observer of the musical barometer, it is not difficult to predict this outcome with confidence. It is quite clear that musicians as a body feel little or no concern for the general welfare of music, and for this reason they persist in their truly stupid indifference. Want of reverence and enthusiasm, and an unscrupulous self-seeking are the foremost characteristics of most musicians, especially among the musical aristocracy, that new genus in the arts. Unfortunately, this situation seems to have prevailed throughout history.

In the midst of this situation there are a few solitary voices in the wilderness. But those who disagree, and they are legion, only stare at them and ask, 'Why all these warnings? Why all this advice?' The examples included in the first edition of this book of how Beethoven wanted his music played suffered a similar fate. They were regarded as something strange, incomprehensible, the inventions of the author—and were ignored. If that era just past regarded as strange the kind of aesthetic sense that is basic to an understanding and reproduction of an important musical work, how could it be otherwise today? Let one hear the unreasoned, often wildly exaggerated tempi in symphonies, quartets, trios and sonatas—then let one have the boldness to let fall a word of warning or advice!

It would be completely naïve for one to take the time and trouble to warn the present generation of its deviations from the path of the right and the beautiful. Such folly will be avoided by anyone who has finally become convinced of the futility of his years spent in trying, through journal articles, to effect a change. This situation is sufficient cause for a man to feel an overwhelming dejection in his heart, especially if he has had the joy of having learned from a truly sacred source the little bit of knowledge and understanding of the things of which he speaks.

Because of this situation, and because the author sees himself as the last living member of Beethoven's circle of friends, he feels compelled to write these lines which, he believes, form an integral part of the master's life story. I shall endeavour to present as briefly as possible to a later, perhaps spiritually more stable, age the conditions and explanations essential to an expression of the spirit inherent in the greater part of Beethoven's piano music. These explanations may then easily be applied to his compositions in other media. The words the great master himself intended to write concerning the playing of his music were, for reasons beyond his control, never written, and his achievements in the way of personal instruction, so that at least he might leave a living model, were effective for only a short time. At the appropriate time and place we shall speak in detail of this circumstance that he himself so often lamented.*

Since we have nothing, or very little, in the way of directions written out in the master's own hand, these referring only to his method of playing the piano (as we saw on page 379 with regard to his use of the Cramer études), my only source of information is the instruction I received directly from the master,[319] and the whole classical tradition in general. With the aid of these, I must attempt to spell out that which Beethoven never did. Carl Czerny is another important witness in the matter of Beethoven's piano music. He, too, benefited from the master's personal instruction in the preparation of public performances (such as his playing of the E flat concerto in 1812) or of private recitals before groups of friends.[320] He incorporated what Beethoven had taught him into his textbook for piano, published about twenty-five years ago, but since then his experiences have been ignored and now no one takes any notice of them. Still other men of high artistic calibre, most of them unknown today, should be mentioned, for their words set forth how in the past era, known as the 'classical period', good music was in general played artistically.

We may draw the indirect conclusion that as a whole Beethoven's music is governed by the general standards of performance, but that in special instances it deviates from the normal pattern. Carl Czerny has said repeatedly in his piano text that words are inadequate to express

---

* The author has cause to sing the same lament as Beethoven. A similar motive underlay my own efforts to teach a gifted pupil all the singular qualities of Beethoven's deepest poetry.[318] My instruction lasted for six years. Much was given and most of it was correctly understood, so that my pupil would have been able to shine far and wide as an exponent of good performance. Although the young man is an admirable artist, and though undoubtedly he will continue to strive for the best, he failed to fulfil all the conditions of an arduous education. Was it that he lacked the courage to defy the whole army of virtuosi, and even some individuals who posed as models of Beethoven performance, to speak as a witness before the whole world of music despite contradiction and even scorn? I do not know. My hope that I would not have to carry to my grave the great master's spiritual heritage seemed three years ago to be sure of fulfilment. Now that hope has been dashed. This had to be said in order to meet any remark or accusation that I had done nothing of a practical nature to help the situation. This experience, then, merely contributes to the divers fates of Beethoven's music.

directions for piano performance. But A. B. Marx, who has penetrated deep into Beethoven's music, has in specific areas succeeded in overcoming this difficulty and has found accurate expression for his concepts. I cannot refrain from saying that everything in the appendix to his book on Beethoven has my full admiration. Musical Philistines and those art philosophers who tend to lose themselves in dry theorems will undoubtedly turn up their noses at it and proceed to forget everything there. It will, nevertheless, survive, and it will bear the desired fruit one day when the chaos now prevailing in the arts shall have subsided and, God willing, a more enlightened epoch shall have dawned. In the natural course of events, any trend that violates the fundamental precepts of art, giving itself over to extravagance or even to deception and hypocrisy, must eventually bring on its own death.

Moreover, a thorough study of some of Marx's analyses of certain piano pieces will bear good results, for that learned man wisely confined his instructions to brief indications or fingerings, leaving the student's fantasy considerable room for self-expression. Analytical explanations of inspired musical works in all media surely should not in our time be confined solely to books and learned journals but, like classical literature in all institutions of advanced learning, should be presented in living performances. In books and journals, which are usually in the interests of a few individuals, these analytical explanations suffer the same fate as current literature; for the music-lovers, whose interests are broad, do not know what to do with them, while the professional musicians, who play for large audiences and must cater for their tastes, ignore them.

We have yet to say what Beethoven thought of detailed explanations (as opposed to overall discussions) and the use of pictures with his, or for that matter, anyone else's, instrumental music. One incident will cover this point sufficiently.

Under the direction of Dr. Christian Müller, whose acquaintance the reader made in the third period, there was given in Bremen a series of 'Family Concerts' that had been established in 1782. During the first decade of the nineteenth century the repertoire came to include Beethoven's works for piano, which had been discovered by the only daughter of the founder of this institution, herself an inspired musician. Soon there was in this circle a real Beethoven cult such as existed nowhere else in Germany at that time, or even in the second decade of the century. One of the important participants in the group was a young poet by the name of Dr. Carl Iken. He had taken upon himself the task of writing out interpretations of certain works of Beethoven's, sometimes adding pictorial representations. These interpretations would be presented before the performances of the works they were supposed to depict. There is little doubt that this man has the honour of being the first to feel the irresistible urge to express in this manner the poetic feelings that Beethoven's music aroused in him.* Dr. Müller sent several of these programmes to Vienna, but our master's reaction to them was just the opposite of what his admirer in the old Hanseatic city had expected. The writings were filled with clichés and extravagant images that could only exasperate the serious master. I still have in my keeping four of these interpretations that were among my friend's correspondence. Let me quote a single excerpt from the programme of the A major symphony that was sent to our master in the first months of 1819. We may imagine the composer's emotions on learning what had been made of his work. The Bremen interpreter invented the following fantasy:

It seems to me that in the seventh symphony there is an underlying theme. During a popular uprising, a revolutionary sign is given. All is confusion as people run about and shout. Then an innocent person, or a party, is surrounded and, after a struggle, is taken before the tribunal. The innocent person weeps, and the judge pronounces a harsh sentence. There are sympathetic murmurs in which are heard the voices of widows and orphans. In the second section of the first movement the parties have become equal in numbers. The clamour has become so tumultuous that the judge cannot calm the people. The deafening storm is finally suppressed but not defeated. Individuals raise hopeful expectations, until suddenly the general voice of the people decides in harmonious agreement. . . . But now in the final movement the aristocracy and the commoners join in riotous abandon. Yet the aristocracy is shown by the wind instruments as being still aloof. Strange, bacchanalian madness teases the imagination through related chords—sometimes held here, sometimes there, sometimes on a sunny hill-side, other times in a flower-filled meadow, where in the merry month of May all the rejoicing children of Nature compete in raising cries of joy.†

Apparently this last bit of fantasy was too much for the composer to bear, for in the autumn of the same year he dictated to me a reply to Dr. Müller to this effect. It was a friendly but vigorous protest against explanations and the devising of pictures of his music or of anyone's. If explanations are necessary, they could be confined to the character of the musical work in general, a character that accomplished musicians ought to be able to convey with no difficulty.

But when the fantasy of the explainer is rampant, where will it find its limits, even in a mere general delineation of character? Odious examples of excesses in recent times prompted the author early in 1856

* How many others have since imitated the attempts of the poet in Bremen? Who can count them?

† This bit of poetic extravagance reminds us of a similar interpretation of the second movement of the sonata opus 111 as given in the footnote on page 232.

to advertise for Beethoven's protest of 1819 in a notice that appeared in the *Niederrheinische Musikzeitung* (issue No. 2) in Bremen. Herr Senator Herrmann A. Schumacher of that city honoured me on 9 March of the same year with a detailed statement of the disposition of Dr. Christian Müller's literary *Nachlass*. As the second executor for the will of Elise Müller, Müller's daughter, who died in 1849, the worthy senator was able to tell me that his predecessor in this matter, Senator Iken (the brother of the poet, Dr. Carl Iken, who had died in Tübingen), had taken care of the 'rich' correspondence. However, he promised to do some research on the Beethoven letters, which included more than this protest. If only this letter could be found![321] For it is (as I still remember it clearly) a precious document in its own right, and of particular importance to our age, which has so often degenerated into excesses. The letter would erect a high dam against the absurd practices of our day.

1.

In the third period we spoke of Beethoven's intention of preparing a new edition of his piano works at the suggestion of the Leipzig music publisher Hofmeister. The negotiations that took place in 1816 are fully described in a letter we still have, written by Antonio Diabelli, who had been consulted in the matter. Apart from the material benefits accruing from such a project, there was an intellectual and artistic necessity underlying it. Beethoven hoped to convey the inner 'poetic idea'* that had led him to compose each of his various works, and thus make possible a true understanding of them. As for performances that would reveal this inner poetry, there was much more to be done than meets the eye.

The master had first to compile a detailed method for playing the instrument. We know from the letter to Dr. Gerhard von Breuning given on page 379 that he intended to write a piano textbook that would be very different from all its predecessors. Then he would have to present his principles on the treatment of the internal thoughts and feeling of the music both in general and specifically. His ideas regarding performance in general might be formulated as follows:

---

* The term 'poetic idea' belonged to Beethoven's time, and was one that he used as often as any other, such as 'poetic content', to differentiate such compositions from works in which there is heard only a well-ordered harmony and rhythmic play of notes. Aestheticians of our time object to the term 'poetic content'. They do so rightly if they understand the term to mean programme music, but wrongly if they apply their negation to all of Beethoven's music and thus deny its poetic content. If Beethoven's symphonies and sonatas—at least some of them—convey no special underlying idea, if they are nothing but well-ordered and rhythmic plays of notes, then why this passion for pictorial explanations and interpretations of them? What other composer arouses a similar, almost irresistible desire?

The poet writes his monologue or dialogue in a definite, continuous rhythm: but the orator, to insure that his meaning will be comprehended, must make pauses and rests even at points where the poet would give no indication by any kind of punctuation. In music, the performer may use the same devices as the orator, and there are as many ways of playing a single work as there are musicians to perform it.

This idea needs to be illustrated with examples. If Beethoven's sonatas contain passages of pathos or lyricism that rise to heights of rhetoric, then the methods of the orator must rise to express them. A performance will then result which, without the aid of a written or spoken word, will achieve the appearance of artistic truth. Rhetoric in musical writing differs from performance in the same way that rhetoric in verbal expression differs from public speaking. Freedom with regard to the rhythm, together with a deep insight into the inner meaning of specific passages, is the first requisite of good performance in both categories.

Two of the most pregnant examples that belong in this category will undoubtedly give the highly cultivated musician the key to an understanding of this matter. The first is the second theme, in E flat major, of the finale to the C minor sonata, opus 10:

Ex. 16

With the *fortissimo* in the fifth measure, the regular beat is re-established. But in the recapitulation, when the second theme is heard in C major, it should be played with less pathos and without a change in the rhythm, because of the difference in key. In both instances the shading is left to the performer; his artistic understanding will dictate the tempo to him.

The other example is the mystical passage in the first movement of the D minor sonata, opus 31:

Ex. 17

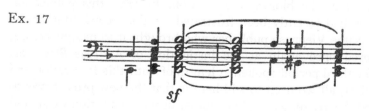

Marx also singled out this marvellous passage and wrote:

. . . Then it [the second theme] angrily swoops down on those powerful chords that can attain their full effect only if they are held back for emphasis. The first time they should be played slowly and powerfully, but when they are repeated an octave higher the idea is softened, and the tempo gradually returns to that of the principal theme until it ends in A minor.

A pianist already familiar with artistic performance may, with these instructions, undertake the study of this, the most difficult passage in the whole sonata, and will, I hope, arrive at the correct interpretation. The tempo is hesitant, restless, somewhat impetuous where the music rises, retarding where it falls, never smooth, passionately agitated throughout. Not until the fifteenth measure is the expression of passion given free rein, and the Allegro comes fully into its own.

Another reason for a new edition of the piano music was the extended keyboard, which fully ten or twelve years earlier had been extended to include four octaves above middle C.[322] Beethoven's piano music up to and including the three sonatas opus 31 (as well as the sonata opus 54 that was published several years after its composition) had been confined to the small space of only five octaves. The obstacles this limited range put in the composer's way, both in expressing his intentions and in conforming to rules, can be seen, for example, in the sonata in C major, opus 2, in the fourth measure of the passage in broken octaves in the first movement.[323] Another instance occurs in the sonata in D major, opus 10, in the broken-octave sequence at the end of the first theme of the exposition, where the composer lacked the third F sharp, G sharp and A above middle C, again in the second section in which the broken chromatic sequence should go up to the third A above middle C, and in other similar passages.[324] The limitations applied to the lower range as well as the upper. Here, too, we find obstacle upon obstacle. We can see that in many works it was not a matter of merely adding a few more notes but of completely rewriting whole sections. This was even more true in the case of works for many instruments, such as concertos and other concerted works, than with sonatas for piano solo.

The intrigues that prevented this intended edition of 1816 have been fully recounted in the biographical section. In 1823 this publication project, which had recently been frustrated for the second time at the hands of the same Viennese publisher who brought it to naught before, was considered once again at the instigation of Andreas Streicher. Having in the third period spoken at length of both this frustration and the new project, all we need to add here is that the new project was to have included the master's complete works. In this connection we should mention the further fact that Beethoven said that he was wondering whether this edition might achieve a greater unity if some of the four-movement sonatas from an earlier time when sonatas with multiple movements were common should be reworked to a three-movement form. He definitely wished to delete the Scherzo allegro from the highly emotional sonata in C minor for violin and piano, opus 30, because of its incompatibility with the character of the work as a whole. He was always unhappy with this movement and wanted to do away with it.

If the proposed edition had ever seen the light of day, there would perhaps have been published a small number of 'eliminated' scherzos, allegros, and minuets. However, this desire on Beethoven's part did not go uncontested, for everyone in our circle had his favourite scherzo or other movement, and would not countenance its being removed from the place it had so long occupied. Then the master would refer to the three-movement sonatas, opus 10 in C minor, opus 13, opus 14, opus 31 Nos. 1 and 2, opus 57, and others. The last sonatas with several movements, such as opp. 106 and 110, are to be thought of in a separate category from their predecessors.

One might object that if Beethoven wished to delete a few scherzos and minuets from the sonatas for the purpose of achieving unity of character, why not the same action in the case of the quartets, quintets, etc.? Such an objection may be answered by considering the emotional states portrayed in many sonatas. The sonatas alone claim the position of true poetry; they alone are portraits of the heart in the truest meaning of the expression, and therefore are confined within a narrower framework than any other musical medium performed in public. With the sonata the lover of musical poetry separates himself from all external influences or intrusions upon his feelings, and finds himself alone with his most intimate friend or beloved. Should the work fall false upon his outer ear, the ear of his heart will hear it otherwise, for his fantasy, awakened by the tones and harmonies, will correct any technical defects. The sonata is best able to inspire reverence in the soul, and often lifts it to prayer.* Its formal requirements are therefore quite different from those of works played for the enjoyment of large groups.

There is no doubt that Beethoven willingly acknowledged the necessity of making improvements in many works, yet he raised many objections to undertaking such a task, the main one being the matter of publishers' copyrights. At any rate, his characteristic indecision affected this situation, and he had almost infantile doubt of its success, especially in view of the virtual disappearance of his piano music from the current repertoire. To this circumstance may be attributed his dissatisfaction with his time and his all-too-frequent suspicion of his contemporaries.

* The unequalled popularity of Beethoven's sonatas that we shall survey at the close of this section appears to indicate an indirect strengthening that has perhaps rendered service to thousands in the manner mentioned here.

When at this juncture his brother came forth with a new plan and whispered in the master's ear a scheme for bringing out his own complete edition at a far greater profit than Streicher's plan would bring, the confusion reached its height.

In a word, the long-talked-of project foundered again, and when our master was once more ready to listen to reason, the complete edition and all the thousands of silver coins it was to bring him had been postponed to another day, for in his mind it had already been replaced by thoughts of the ninth symphony. His friend Streicher gained nothing by bringing it up again in 1824: by then the flattering requests of Prince Galitsin had claimed his attention, and he was already at work on the first of his quartets. It was not until 1826 that he again found time to think of the project and to suggest to the music publisher Schott in Mainz the publication of the complete works. Listen to Schott's answer, written on 28 November of that year (we still have the letter): 'As for the publication of the complete works, we cannot at this time make a decision, for we are now occupied with other obligations.'

We must close this chapter on the publication project that had spun out over ten full years with the knowledge that the great master carried the idea and its execution to his grave. This matter illustrates clearly and depressingly what it was for Beethoven to make a decision and carry it out. His constant calculating and his conferences with his financial advisers, as well as his irresistible impulse to create new things so that any looking backward at old works was extremely difficult for him, probably would have prevented the complete edition from becoming a reality even if he had had another ten years. The only happy consequence for us who observed the many deliberations, plans, and doubts of this Fabius Cunctator was that we were often privileged to hear interesting comments from him about certain works or certain passages. Surely it must be counted a great misfortune that we who survived the master dispersed immediately after his death before we could undertake a joint effort in the interests of his piano music, and a single witness has little if any authority. This one therefore finds himself now obliged to set forth the facts as they were, for otherwise the egg of Columbus would have served as a positive example to all our associates.

2.

By far the most important and most unusual characteristic of our composer was his practice of drawing an idea for a composition from nature or from a poem that had made an impression upon his imagination. He would allow himself to be completely subjugated by this idea, at the same time moulding it into a form that was precise and definite, but having little in common with traditional forms, and this formal structure even differed from composition to composition. Consider the form of the first movement of the first sonata in F minor: how different it is from the form of the first movement of the sonata in E flat major opus 7! And how different again are the first movements of the sonata in C minor opus 10 and of the *Pathétique* opus 13, and so on through the wonderfully inspired sonatas opus 57 (F minor), opus 90 (E minor), opus 101 (A major), right up to the last! Each one different, and yet the master leads us by way of his form along such a sure, clear path that requires little imagination, provided the performance is adapted to the content, to retain the thread of the poetry without losing it for even an instant. Anyone capable of following the form in Beethoven's sonatas, of penetrating it to its foundations, must come to the conclusion that in this respect no other sonatas can compare with Beethoven's. His form is exceptional, and expresses an exceptional musical poetry.

It is said that Beethoven exhausted all formal possibilities. This statement could be justified only in respect to the sonatas. In some movements of his last quartets we see the bounds of this formal perfection violated and overrun. In the piano sonatas named above, and in others as well, we find the musical Shakespeare, to use Amadeus Wendt's comparison—the poet who tells us in music all that can be expressed: the struggles hidden deep within the heart, the sweet magic of love in the most innocent soul, the bitterest, most poignant sorrow, the delights that rejoice to the skies, the depths of sincerity, the fires of ecstasy, the greatest nobility, the utmost grace. It is not overbold to say that a performance of these sonatas, or at least of certain movements, presents problems comparable to those of portraying certain Shakespearian characters if we aim, as we should, at exploring the inner being and at presenting it logically and forthrightly. Just as with Shakespeare most actors grasp only the word and not the spirit behind the word, so also the musicians who play Beethoven sonatas study only the technical aspects of the music, having neither the head nor the heart to penetrate its depths.* Ferdinand Ries, in his *Notizen*, says on page 77, 'When composing, Beethoven often bore a specific object in mind.' These words must be interpreted in the light of what we have just said.

Carl Czerny expresses himself more cogently in Part IV, Chapter 2

* The chapter 'General Comprehension of the Work' in the appendix to Marx's book is particularly to be recommended for musicians and music-lovers whose head and heart are still intact. It also holds up a mirror to the virtuosi who today enjoy such popularity, showing their ignorance and lack of understanding. The comparisons Marx makes in his chapter 'Technical Demands' between sonatas opus 2 and opus 13, opus 7 and opus 28, opus 57 and opus 110, opus 53 and opus 109, etc., show what an extraordinary study of all this eternal poetry he made.

of his *Klavierschule* when he speaks of the character and the correct performance of the sonata in F minor opus 57. He says on page 62:

If Beethoven, who was so fond of portraying scenes from nature, was perhaps thinking of ocean waves on a stormy night when from the distance a cry for help is heard, then such a picture will give the pianist a guide to the correct playing of this great tonal painting. There is no doubt that in many of his most beautiful works Beethoven was inspired by similar visions or pictures from his reading or from his own lively imagination. It is equally certain that if it were always possible to know the idea behind the composition, we would have the key to the music and its performance.

In a footnote, Czerny adds:

He [Beethoven] was reluctant to speak on this subject, except on a few occasions when he was in a confidential mood. He once said, for instance, that the idea for the E major Adagio of the string quartet opus 59 No. 2 came to him when one night he gazed for a long time at the starry sky and thought about the music of the spheres. His seventh symphony in A major was inspired by the events of 1813 and 1814 (as had been the *Battle of Vittoria*). But he knew that the music would not always be felt so freely by its listeners if a specific object were to predetermine their imaginations.

As to the inspiration for the seventh symphony, Czerny is in error, for the work was already almost completed before the great events of 1813 had occurred. Moreover, it does not bear the slightest resemblance to warlike music. The idea for the *Battle of Vittoria*, as well, dates from an earlier time,[325] as we can deduce from Beethoven's deposition in the lawsuit against Maelzel, even though the piece was composed in 1813. He said, 'I had already conceived the idea of a battle piece. . . .'

One day when I was telling the master of the great impression that Carl Czerny's playing of the D minor and F minor sonatas opp. 31 and 57 had made upon the audience, and he was in a cheerful mood, I asked him to give me the key to these sonatas. He replied, 'Just read Shakespeare's *Tempest*.' It is, therefore, to be found in that play. But where? Questioner, it is for you to read, to ponder, and to guess. He was more explicit when I asked him about the Largo in the D major sonata opus 10. He told me that at the time he had written it, audiences were more poetic (sensitive?) than now (1823), and that for this reason it had not been necessary to supply them with the idea. Everyone, he continued, had sensed in the Largo the spiritual condition of a person consumed by melancholy and had felt the many nuances of light and shadow in this portrait of depression, in the same way that everyone had recognized in both opus 14 sonatas the dispute in dialogue form between two principles, without the aid of words written above the score.

(Marx criticizes what I said in the earlier editions of this book about these two sonatas, and his comment is undoubtedly valid. We must, however, remember how little the artistic-aesthetic concept had been formulated at that time, so that all too often a *quid pro quo* approach was adopted. Aesthetics as a science is even now still very young. Thus Beethoven understood a word like 'principle' as meaning not 'predominant voices', as Marx understands the word, but 'opposites'. In this light his other terms, 'dialogue' and 'dialogue form', become understandable and can be justified. Sharply defined opposites (principles) can be seen even more clearly in the C minor sonata opus 10 than in the two sonatas opus 14. This is the reason that opus 10 is one of the most difficult to play, but the opus 14 sonatas serve more readily as examples. It would be necessary to write a whole article if one were to explain the C minor sonata at all adequately. And yet it is considered one of the 'minor' sonatas!)

We shall never know whether Beethoven might eventually have given the public verbal interpretations such as he gave his friends, and the author can only refer to the remarks on page 399. Czerny, who for many years observed the great master, is therefore correct in saying that Beethoven knew very well that music would not always be felt so freely by its listeners if a specific image were to predispose their imaginations. He would certainly have been reluctant to carry out his plan of making explicit the underlying ideas behind his compositions, though it does not seem unlikely that he might have overcome his reluctance in the case of certain works or certain movements. In any case, it is unfortunate that nothing came of his intentions.

The casualness of the classical composers in assigning titles to their works would be surprising if it were not a question of technique. Take, for instance, Clementi's sonata, *Didone abbandonata, Scena tragica*. He had no less confidence than Beethoven in the intelligence of his time, and expected his hearers to guess with certainty what he was saying. In a delightful and at the same time a very instructive manner, Friedrich Rochlitz comprehended these intentions and set them forth in a critical article in AmZ XXIV (1822) 631. The critic is quite correct when in the introduction he says, 'It is indeed a tragic scene, and it is so well constructed, so clearly stated, that one has no difficulty, not only in the principal sections but in the major divisions of each section, in tracing verbally the changing emotions that are developed here.' Then he sets them forth in detail.

Who today would still be able to interpret this musical portrait of the heart, unfortunately written in the traditional rigid sonata form? At best one might, having glanced briefly through it, make the superficial observation, 'The poetic content of this sonata is explained in the title.' This remark was made by a Beethoven scholar. In the year 1827 when I was with Clementi in Baden, he gave me a detailed explanation of the content and correct performance of this composition. Taking advantage in 1856 of a new edition of the work issued by the publisher Johann André in Offenbach, I wrote a foreword for the edition, repeating what the old master had told me. Aside from this musical portrait of a spiritual experience, I know of no other sonata in strict form that can be compared to Beethoven's sonatas for its poetic content.*

I have said enough to show that all of Beethoven's piano music, with a very few exceptions, is based on preconceived ideas never expressed before, and that therefore it must be played differently from any other music. To play this music in the usual way, to fail to differentiate it from ordinary music, is comparable to the singing of Italian music with the use of the German vocal style. Czerny is therefore right when he says on page 34 and elsewhere:

> Beethoven's compositions must be played differently from Mozart's, Clementi's, Hummel's or anyone else's. It is not easy to express this difference in words.

On page 70 he makes the following noteworthy comment:

> Beethoven lived in Vienna and wrote all his works there. It is natural that a sense of comprehension and correct performance should best be conserved, like any tradition, in the composer's own city. Experience has shown this actually to be the case, for how often the tempo and the character of his music have been misconstrued in other cities! The situation becomes all the more critical when we think of the future.

Czerny wrote this in the early 1830's, at least ten years after almost all of Beethoven's piano music had disappeared from the Vienna repertoire, as we have already seen. At best, Schuppanzigh's quartet concerts and the *Concerts spirituels* in the 1820's might perform one or another of the ensemble works, but the sonatas, the vehicles of the deepest poetry, existed no longer. How was it possible for Czerny to find living traces of the Beethoven tradition in musical circles, for his own prodigious output as a composer for many years kept him from the music of Beethoven which, to tell the truth, had become confusing to him? Hector Berlioz, who was well acquainted with all the European capitals, gives us an account of the general understanding of Beethoven's music at that time throughout the world of art in an article published in the *Journal des Débats* of 11 August 1852. He confesses there that among all the virtuosi he has heard, he is hardly able to name

---

* W. H. Riehl, the admirer of Clementi's sonatas, calls the title of the *Didone* sonata a 'pigtail', and yet the 'master of the sonata', as Riehl so rightly terms Clementi, appended this pigtail to his work in the full consciousness of his artistic maturity. Strange! This sonata, which with two others in D minor and A major constitutes opus 50, was published at the beginning of the 1820's almost immediately following the *Gradus ad Parnassum*.

six capable of playing Beethoven's music with true understanding of its spirit. We know from his travel diary how accurately he evaluated matters even in the Austrian capital.

While it is indeed difficult to explain the special qualities of Beethoven's music in words that will bring about a sure understanding and make every aspect self-evident, some means must nevertheless be found of at least approaching this goal. For my part, I think the best guide is to be found in the instructions that Beethoven gave for free performance, for tradition is based first and foremost upon these instructions. The reader will recall what we said on page 209 about Frau von Ertmann's playing. One might answer with reason that a correct understanding of free performance has been lost in the passage of time. We may well doubt, then, whether this manner of performance can be achieved without a previous study of the internal spiritual depths inherent in the music, especially in the sonatas. We remember, furthermore, the complete absence of good models which through sustained efforts would provide practical examples of performance. And so on. There are many obstacles, and yet they must not deter us from doing everything in our power to remedy the situation, if only for reasons of historical accuracy.

In order to understand the attitude of the former (that is, the classical) period towards free performance, let us refer to certain authorities on the subject. But first we must note that the term 'free performance' has falsely been equated with the *tempo rubato* of the Italian singer. The fact alone that the Italian term generally occurs only in *opera buffa* and hardly ever in *opera seria* is an indication that the two terms are not identical. Beethoven protested against the use of the Italian term in regard to his music, albeit in vain, for Italian terminology had come to dominate everything in his epoch, including his own music. Let us have an example.

In his apocryphal work, *Beethovens Studien*, Ignaz von Seyfried says on page 18 of his chapter on 'Character Traits and Anecdotes':

At any rate, Beethoven was not one of those obstinate composers* whom no orchestra in the world could please. In fact, he was at times too indulgent, and would sometimes rehearse a work without going over the places that needed more work. 'Next time it will be all right,' he would say. On the other hand, he demanded great exactitude in the matter of expression, minute nuances, the balance between light and shade, as well as an effective *tempo rubato*,† and would gladly speak to each member of the orchestra individually about these points without showing the least impatience. When he at last felt that the

---

* As for the master's obstinacy, we saw what it was in the various encounters with the Schuppanzigh Quartet. Ries spoke of it (see page 54).

† *Tempo rubato* even in orchestral music!

musicians had grasped his meaning, that they played together with growing enthusiasm, caught up in the magical power of his tonal creation and inspired by it, then his face would become suffused with joy, his features would radiate pleasure and satisfaction, a benevolent smile would play about his lips, and a thundering *Bravi tutti* would reward the musicians' success.

The master then expressed his praise in Italian!

The patriarch of modern piano playing, Philipp Emanuel Bach, says in his *Versuch über die wahre Art das Clavier zu spielen*:

> The correct playing of *tempo rubato* requires a great deal of discrimination and, even more important, a great deal of sensitiveness. For one who has both it is not difficult to achieve a performance perfectly free of constraint and even, if possible and permissible, flexible in all its ideas. Otherwise, however, without sufficient sensitivity no amount of pains can produce proper performance. As soon as one binds the melody line slavishly to the beat, every tempo (phrase?) loses its most elemental essence (its basic character?), for all the voices are forced to conform to the absolute regularity of the beat.

We must note here that the great master had in mind the piano music of his own time, which perhaps allowed for such treatment. How he must have played his *Piano Sonatas and Free Fantasies, together with a few Rondos*, about which Carl Friedrich Cramer spoke so compellingly in his *Magazin der Musik*, as we saw in the *Niederrheinische Musik-Zeitung*, No. 32, for 1858!

Carl Maria von Weber gives us an especially interesting contribution on this subject. Asked by the Leipzig music director Präger in 1824 about the tempos in *Euryanthe*, the composer sent him a list of the tempo marks and also an essay full of important and generally applicable comments, which were published in No. 28 of the *Berliner Musik-Zeitung* for 1827. In this essay, he says in part:

> The beat, the tempo, must not be a controlling tyrant nor a mechanical, driving hammer; it should be to a piece of music what the pulse beat is to the life of a man. There is no slow movement without places that demand a quicker motion in order to avoid a sense of dragging. In the same way, there is no Presto that does not require a contrasting, more tranquil, execution of many passages, for otherwise the expressiveness would be lost in excessive speed. . . . A quickening of the tempo or a holding back must never produce a sense of pushing or forcing. It can occur, then, only in periods or phrases (in the musical and poetic sense of the words) as the emotional content of the performance demands. . . . In music we have no way of indicating all this. It resides only in the feelings of the human heart, and if the feelings are not there, nothing is of any avail, neither the metronome, which serves only to prevent the grossest misunderstandings, nor the expression marks, which are so unsatisfactory but which I might be tempted to use in great abundance if the warning of repeated experience did not remind me that such indications are superfluous,

useless, and generally misinterpreted. When I give any performing indications, it is only because a good friend asks me directly.*

Let us also include some pertinent words by aestheticians. Hand (*Aesthetik der Tonkunst* I 187) says:

Performance should never lack the freedom that beauty always demands. Freedom of rhythm is not lack of rhythm. The person who plays well, therefore, will regard the rhythm not as a prison, but will approach it freely, without ever losing the beat. But this lesson is misunderstood by those musicians who seek by means of arbitrary hesitations or rushes to achieve an individual style of expression, and all too often they destroy the character and meaning of a work.

Schilling (page 367) says:

In every piece of music the particular inner qualities and outer characteristics must be carefully taken into consideration so that in every measure the perfect application of the tempo that is established may be achieved in an imperceptible way for the general motion of the music as well as for the perfect modifications in that tempo.

A. B. Marx, who shares our views and defends them staunchly and with deep insight, makes the following statement in his *Allgemeine Musiklehre*:

We are therefore persuaded that, besides technical skill, a perfect acquaintance with and observance of the written expression marks is indispensable for proper performance. We also hold, however, that in addition to these, sensitivity and insight into those matters that cannot be completely expressed in words are just as necessary. As for the meaning and purpose of the whole work and all its sections, they may be written down and defined or they may be filled out from our personal feelings. At the same time, we must keep in mind that every feature takes its direction from the central idea and purpose of the whole work, and that we too, when we seek to understand, study, and perform a work, must proceed from its central idea. To understand and present a work perfectly, starting with this central idea and following it through all of its parts: this is the objective of artistic performance.

And finally, let us recommend to thinking music-lovers the following statement by an unknown author on objectivity, for it bears directly on this topic:

The new aesthetic requires objectivity in the presentation of the fine arts, for objectivity is basic to style. Subjectivity in a work of art, on the other hand,

---

* The excellent master seems to have had many discouraging experiences in this regard. Probably he was thinking here of the presumptuous conductors who, even in the most routine passages, overlook every word of instruction. He probably was thinking, too, of the large number of pedantic piano teachers to whom the correct playing of the notes is the highest achievement. For each of these categories, everything is indeed superfluous and useless, yet they have the audacity to attack everything that stretches beyond their limited horizons. Celebrities of the virtuoso class suffer the same shortcomings.

is the quality that rests upon personal interpretation and individuality, and consists merely of mannerisms. Objectivity, then, is universal truth, necessity, while subjectivity is only specific truth, the thing that fits the moment. Objectivity alone achieves a true presentation, whereas subjectivity merely achieves a suggestion. The first gives substance, form, and clarity, and is therefore related to the plastic arts; the second is more ephemeral, darker, more akin to the impressions of music. But even music, even lyrical music, should have objectivity. The musician should take a position outside himself. Obviously the law of objectivity cannot be prescribed with equal insistence for all musicians, nor should objectivity suppress subjectivity, for it lends the work interest and warmth.

The present writer cannot state emphatically enough that with very few exceptions everything he heard Beethoven play entirely conforms to this teaching. His playing was free of all constraint in respect to the beat, for the spirit of his music required freedom.

As a general rule we may say of free performance of piano music in the musical period just past that it was usually limited to a modified, more tranquil motion in the *cantabile* sections of *allegro* movements, though the secondary theme and the conclusion were almost always regular throughout. In this regard, Hummel's remarks on the alteration of the rhythm in the Cantilena of his great concerto in A minor are examples that may serve as a model. The fact that these remarks do not appear in the score of the work itself but in his *Klavierschule* that was written later, is one more illustration of the way in which those masters presupposed a knowledge of expressive playing on the part of the virtuosi of their day. Even in Hummel's new method of piano performance there was an effort to do justice to the Cantilena, generally in accordance with the Italian vocal style, whereas in our day the Cantilena is treated as a superfluous secondary work. Hummel's playing of his *La Bella Capricciosa* was charming. The capricious beauty spoke and sang to us out of a sensuous tone-painting that conveyed contrasting moods and feelings.

If Hummel's text fails to devote a chapter to free, declamatory performance, but instead deals almost exclusively with the matter at hand and only fleetingly mentions specific works, we are all the more grateful to Carl Czerny. The chapter 'On Modifications in Rhythm' in the third part of his textbook presents a clear lesson. In the very first paragraph he quite rightly calls this modification 'the most important consideration in performance'. Czerny himself says in the second chapter of the fourth part that everything he says here is still insufficient for playing Beethoven's music. Part of what he says will be of service to us here. First, however, we must consider Beethoven's own manner of playing in order to become acquainted with his personal style, at least in so far as words allow.

The final words of our discussion of Beethoven's first period indicate the general reaction to his playing at a time when, in the opinion of the public, virtuosity had surpassed composition. Let us simply add to this evaluation the term 'heavy-handed', one used to describe not only our master but others of a comparable stature, such as Anton Eberl, Frau Auernhammer, and Joseph Wölffl. Throughout his life the master maintained his vigorous, masculine piano style.* As late as 1822 the critic for the AmZ (XXIV (1822) 310) remarked correctly: 'Our Beethoven seems to have regained his receptivity to music. [He had actually never lost it.] He improvised several times before a group of friends, to their great joy. His playing was masterly, and showed that he still knows how to handle his instrument with power, enthusiasm, and love.' This recital took place at the home of his friend, Baroness von Puthon.

When in the second period we spoke of Cherubini's and Cramer's reports of Beethoven, we promised to discuss later on the opinions these two authorities held of the master's piano playing. We have now reached the proper time and place. The blunt Cherubini characterized the master's playing with one word: rough. The English gentleman, Cramer, on the other hand, did not object so much to the unpolished playing as to the inconsistent performance of a single composition: one day he would play it with great spirit and expression, but the next day it would sound moody and often muddled to the point of unclarity.† For this reason, several friends suggested that Cramer perform in public several works, some of them still unpublished. This suggestion touched Beethoven's sensitive spot. He became jealous and, according to Cramer, a degree of mutual tension ensued.

At any rate, it seems to me that Cherubini, already crowned with fame in Europe and ten years older than Beethoven, must have had a strong influence on our master. There are many indications to bear me out. When we met, Cherubini used to say that he had not been able to resist the temptation of drawing Beethoven's attention to the Clementi text, i.e., to Clementi's style of piano playing, and that Beethoven had always been grateful for these suggestions, with the promise that next time he played for Cherubini he hoped he would be satisfied. Clementi's evaluation of Beethoven's piano playing, which he communicated to this author in Baden in 1827, was confined to a few words. He said, 'His playing was not polished, and was frequently impetuous, like himself, yet it was always full of spirit.' It was in 1807 that Clementi had heard Beethoven play various works in Vienna.

* In the Foreword I spoke of how the master used to chide me during a piano lesson. My faulty playing would prompt him to say, 'So big and husky, and yet you approach the piano in such an unmasculine manner!' His scoldings amused me, but I benefited from them.

† Czerny remarks on this point in paragraph 7, where he says that in respect to purity and clarity, Beethoven's playing was not always exemplary. He had no time for finger exercises.

We must count it as fortunate that the younger master took the advice of the elder. In his note to Stephan von Breuning written during the last days of his life, Beethoven shows his faithful adherence to Clementi's *Method,* as we saw in the third section of the chapter on Beethoven's personality traits. Even though his impaired hearing made it impossible for him to apply Clementi's principles himself, he was still able to recommend Clementi to others eager for instruction. Beethoven learned directly from Clementi how, after searching everywhere for positive rules governing performance, he finally found the key in vocal art. Himself a singer, he attempted to apply the rules of prosody even to certain instrumental passages where stressed and unstressed notes in endless sequence play an important role.* Since we are speaking of Clementi's style of playing, which our master adopted up to the dividing line where his own artistic individuality began, let us remember in passing what Mozart, the German Amphion, thought of the playing of Clementi, the English-Italian master—whose performance he found 'tasteless and devoid of feeling'. This opinion can be explained and supported by an account given by Clementi's pupil, Ludwig Berger.

Berger asked his teacher to tell him about his meeting with Mozart in the presence of the Emperor in 1781. In AmZ XXXI (1829) 467, Berger reports the conversation:

From the tone of Clementi's account, I gathered how very much he was captivated by Mozart's performance. 'I have never heard anyone play with such spirit and charm. I was pleasantly surprised by an Adagio and several of the variations he improvised extemporaneously on a theme of the Emperor's choosing that we, alternately accompanying each other, were to vary.' When I asked him if he had always played in his present manner (this conversation took place in 1806) he said No, that he had formerly preferred a great fluency, a more brilliant flourish, and that he had especially liked double-octave passages, which no one before him had used, as well as extemporaneous performances. It was not until later that he adopted the more singing, more noble style of performance that he had learned from listening carefully to famous singers of the time, and that was made possible by the gradual perfection of the piano,

---

* In the first section of the chapter, 'Personality Traits', we told what Beethoven had abstracted for his art from the Greek and Latin classics. A very interesting article on Clementi from 'Bern in October 1784', reprinted in the *Niederrheinische Musik-Zeitung,* 1858, No. 36, contains the following:

In his composition, especially in his slow movements, he showed me how the middle voice carries the melody. He had learned that from Rameau. From the Latin writers he had learned how to give his composition its own direction. Geometry had taught him the consistency of ideas. His way of leading the individual episodes back to a constant centre is very noticeable, and stems from the maxim of Quintilian: 'Si non datur porta, per murum erumpendum' [If there is no doorway, one must break out through the wall.][326]

Thus we see that Clementi, too, was a disciple of the Romans, just as our Beethoven was, at least in part. The prosodic stressed and unstressed beats to which he referred in the twenty Cramer études (see page 379) are conclusive evidence of his adoption of Clementi's instruction in this regard.

especially by English manufacturers, whereas the earlier, imperfect instruments had made it almost impossible to play with a singing, resonant tone.

I should like to name a few salient traits of our master's playing, and here I am fully supported by the accounts of Cramer and Clementi. His hands and the upper portion of his body were held quiet. His notes were sustained, and his accentuation was always very distinctive. In regard to his sustained style, in which we see the former organist, the master was said in earlier times to have surpassed Hummel, who was, like John Field, considered a model for this style. Here was another reason for Beethoven's argument with the modern trend in piano performance, for, with the exception of Hummel, it abandoned entirely the sustained style. Yet, irony of fate! the creator of so many noble works in all the musical media, with his vigorous opposition to all bodily motion at the piano, had to be content to see a herald of this style take an interest in his piano music and hold off for a few years its total disappearance from the concert repertoire. It was Carl Czerny whose contribution must be proclaimed aloud, even for the very piano style that the great master deplored.

It is no less true that Czerny was the only one among the Viennese virtuosi who took the trouble to hear Beethoven frequently when he was at his best. He deserves our praise up to the point where he began his attempts to improve upon Beethoven's music with the elaborations of the modern virtuosi; from that point on he deserves nothing but censure. These elaborations consist of indiscriminate use of the pedal, the transposition in the *cantilena* sections from the first and second octaves above middle C to the third and fourth (we are already familiar with Czerny's predilection for the highest register from all his compositions), the use of trills and other ornaments, and finally a metronome-like rhythmic regularity. A letter from Beethoven to Czerny written in 1812[327] and published in 1857, after Czerny's death, speaks of the latter's aspirations towards virtuosity, even then. The letter reads:

Dear Czerny!

I cannot see you today, but tomorrow I shall come to you myself to have a talk with you. I burst out yesterday with that remark, but afterwards I was very sorry to have done so. But you must forgive a composer who would rather hear his work just as he had written it, however beautifully you played it otherwise. . . .

The publisher of this and two other letters from Beethoven to Czerny (written in 1816, not 1815) tells us that the performance with which Beethoven found fault included 'alterations, dragging of certain passages, use of higher octaves, etc.' in the quintet in E flat major for woodwind and piano. To think that the twenty-one-year-old pianist allowed himself such liberties in the presence of the composer! What would an accomplished virtuoso have done! What an example this and similar eccentricities held up to his pupils!

Anyone who has seen Herr Franz Liszt play the piano has an accurate picture of the mannerisms he learned from his teacher Czerny: hands always in the air, sometimes even flung above the head, the keys struck from a height of two feet above the keyboard, and so forth. Liszt is merely imitating the didactic model that was held before him for two of his boyhood years. When in 1816 Beethoven wrote to his esteemed friend, Frau von Ertmann (we know the letter from the third period), that illness had prevented him from hearing a recent recital at Czerny's, a more plausible reason may have been his objection to Czerny's annoying mannerisms. By the winter of 1818, however, when Czerny played at his house for a group of admirers, Beethoven had brought himself, for other reasons, to the point of honouring the performer and his guests with his presence. It was fortunate for the sensitive listeners that, accustomed to Czerny's style, their pleasure was not disturbed by it. Even the exacting master's often repeated complaint: 'Czerny never sustains his notes and accentuates badly', was incapable of disturbing the cult, for the group as a whole lacked depth of insight. For this author in particular, Czerny's performances provided excellent instruction, for they afforded the master a unique opportunity to express critical comments and highly interesting and instructive explanations of so many of his works.*

As for Beethoven's particular style of accentuation, the author can speak partly from Beethoven's critical remarks on Czerny's playing and partly from the piano instruction that Beethoven gave to him directly. It was above all the rhythmic accent that he stressed most heavily and that he wanted others to stress. He treated the melodic (or grammatic, as it was generally called) accent, on the other hand, mostly according to the internal requirements. He would emphasize all retardations, especially that of the diminished second in *cantabile* sections, more than other pianists. His playing thus acquired a highly personal character, very different from the even, flat performances that never rise to tonal eloquence. In *cantilena* sections he adopted the methods of cultivated singers, doing neither too much nor too little. Sometimes he recommended putting appropriate words to a perplexing passage and singing it, or listening to a good violinist or wind player play it.

* Czerny gave these recitals, devoted solely to Beethoven's piano music, every Sunday morning from 11 to 1 in his apartment throughout the winters of 1818, 1819, and 1820. Anyone who wanted to come was welcome. None of the limited space was taken up by the crowd-pleasing virtuosi, but all the foreign artists frequented these remarkable gatherings regularly. As worthy collaborators at the piano, Czerny had the high priestess of music, Frau von Ertmann, as well as Herr Pfaller and Herr Stainer von Felsburg, an imperial civil servant. It was the latter who drafted the memorial addressed to Beethoven in 1824 (see page 273).

He set great store by the manner of striking the keys, and its double import: the physical or material, and the psychological, of which Clementi made him aware. By its psychological import, Clementi meant the fullness of tone already conceived in the player's mind before the fingers strike the keys. One who is a stranger to this sense can never play an Adagio with feeling. Our master was a declared opponent of 'miniature painting' in all musical performance, and demanded strength of expression throughout. The performances of the Schuppanzigh Quartet testified to this requirement. In a *forte* the four men gave the impression of a small orchestra, in complete contrast to the flat, sweet tones of the famous quartets of our day.

An even more important aspect of Beethoven's piano oratory was the rhetorical pause and the caesura, both adopted from Clementi. In order not to misunderstand these devices, we must recall what Beethoven taught in regard to declamatory art. The caesura, a sudden break in the flow of speech, is more akin in music to the rhetorical pause than in poetry, in which it must occur in a specific foot of the line; for instance, in a pentameter distich it must always fall on the third foot. The extent of the rhetorical pause, according to Beethoven, was only the lengthening of a written note without an expressly designated rest. These two technical devices are not very different in concept, and both have the effect of heightening the expressiveness of what follows. Of course, they are to be used only in appropriate phrases, and only in order to give them a certain degree of significance. We shall see examples of both.

All the significant features of Beethoven's articulation can be found in detail in his first sonatas; for instance, in the first movement of the first sonata in F minor, in all four movements of the sonata in E flat opus 7, in all three movements of the sonata in C minor opus 10 and in all four movements of the D major sonata of the same opus number, in the *Pathétique*, and in the two opus 14 sonatas. All the characteristic gradations of the naïve, the sentimental, the serious, the gay, and the passionate, are to be expressed in these sonatas. A few examples from the first movement of the C minor and the *Pathétique* sonatas will illustrate the meaning of the rhetorical pause and the caesura. The passages in the latter sonatas are given in the Supplements [M].

The opposition that appears at the very beginning of the C minor sonata between strength and gentleness or, more expressively, between passion and tenderness,* are the rhetorical principles expressed in the first and third movements, which move side by side with appropriate

* Would the terms pathos and ethos be permissible in discussing Beethoven's music, particularly in regard to the sonatas and trios? Surely there is an ethical significance in them, for they do not merely entertain, relax, stimulate, and excite; they also urge one along the path of new, artistic, and consistent forms, and free one from the forms of earlier periods, most of which have already been exhausted.

variations in the tempo. It is one of the most precarious contests between emotion and intellect but, when it succeeds, it is of indescribable
aesthetic and soul-revealing effect.

From the thirteenth to the twenty-first measures we find the rhetorical pause. This is the passage:

Ex. 18

The quarter-note rests in the upper voices are all to be extended to about
double length, and the disconnected phrases violently flung out. The
objective is a heightening of tension. With the twenty-second measure,
the agitated statement is resumed and continues in a regular rhythm
until the measure rest in all voices, measure thirty. How everything
that follows after this point up to the Cantilena in E flat major (second
subject) is to be performed must be omitted 'because', as Czerny says,
'it is not easy to express it in words'. Let us remember, however,
Philipp Emanuel Bach's instructions.

The cadence before the coda of the exposition and the first measures
of the coda itself illustrate the application of Beethoven's instructions
regarding rests where the composer has not specifically marked them.
These pauses also serve to set off the coda more distinctly. The passage
in question is this:

Ex. 19

The passage plunges downward impetuously and stops abruptly on B flat. The coda has a relaxing effect, and so continues calmly in the tempo of the Allegro. Before the F minor Cantabile in the thirteenth measure of the development, the quarter rest in the twelfth measure is to be extended. The caesura in this measure is made evident. The placidity of the Cantabile requires a marked separation from the preceding agitated section.

Czerny remarks on the third movement of this sonata: 'This Finale is already written in that fantastic humour so characteristic of Beethoven'.* Fantastic humour! who can give a comprehensible definition of these words? Certainly this sonata movement does not define them; if it did, every passionate expression in the music would be fantastic. Performance carried to the point of caricature, against which Czerny himself wishes to warn us, would make the passionate, which must always retain form and proportion, subservient to the fantastic, which has neither form nor proportion. In the works of the serious composer there will always be clarity, unity, and originality in well-ordered form. But where are these to be found in the works of the dreamer, the fantast, or the madman? (Just listen to some of the 'music of the future' coming out of Weimar!) Humour in music can accompany the serious or the sentimental as well as the naïve, the gay, or the passionate, but it can never be part of the fantastic, whose principal aim is to violate the laws of

---

* Czerny very frequently uses the words 'humour, humorous, fantastic' to describe the character of certain movements without even so much as hinting how such a character is to be presented. In one place he does say, 'By the successful mastery of all mechanical difficulties'. But if that were all that was required, we would nowadays have hundreds of outstanding Beethoven pianists.

beauty. Nevertheless, Czerny shows by using this term that this movement must be played in a completely exceptional way. This is also true of the first movement.

In the first movement of the *Pathétique* we see two caesuras, one before the entrance of the secondary theme in E flat minor, the other at the end of this theme. If in each place one thinks of a rest held over the bar-line, the caesura will become noticeable and the effect of what follows will be emphasized. In the Supplements [M], further examination of this secondary theme is made, and we shall give there the dynamic indications that are missing in all the published versions. We shall also learn how Beethoven himself played the introductory measure (Grave) before the primary theme of the *Pathétique*.

We encounter both caesuras and rhetorical pauses frequently in Beethoven's sonatas (the latter more frequently than the former), and they are generally there to separate the successive themes from one another.

These remarks about Beethoven's own performing style and about the necessary prerequisites for playing his piano music in general, form only an outline sketch. Everything to do with bringing the inner essence of the music to life can only be achieved orally at the piano with persons having sufficient preparation and receptivity. Nevertheless, the reader can deduce from this much what our master would have said in his projected piano textbook and how it would have differed from others, had his plan ever come to fruition.

It is now the appropriate time to hear what Czerny's *Klavierschule* has to say about certain movements of the Beethoven sonatas. In the main, he underlines everything we have already said here, and in addition gives some helpful guides to performance, though some of these guides are ambiguous and misleading. Regarding the first movement of the first sonata in F minor, Czerny says:

The character is both earnest and passionately agitated, both strong and undecided, yet without those various piano figures and passages that are generally used elsewhere to separate dissimilar ideas from one another. The tempo is a lively yet not too fast *alla breve*. At the fourth measure a small *ritardando* and *crescendo* begin (both unwritten) and increase up to the *fermata* in the eighth measure. Measures 41 to 44 of the exposition are to be played with an increasing *ritardando*, and the tempo does not resume its regularity until the second half of measure 45. In the development, the 22 measures following measure 20 are to be performed with ever-growing strength and vigour, very *legato*, with special expressiveness in the bass.

About the fourth movement of this sonata he says: 'Tempestuous, agitated, almost dramatic, like the description of some important event', and so on. As one can see, there is no small number of comments, truly in the spirit of Beethoven, and yet, without a previous knowledge of all of Beethoven's theses developed above, these comments will hardly help the pianist to produce anything but a distorted version of the sonatas.

Czerny has this to say on the E major Adagio of the third sonata opus 2:

The romantic tendencies that Beethoven later used to create a type of composition in which instrumental music rose to heights of painting and poetry already begin to show themselves in this Adagio. It is no longer merely an expression of feeling that one hears; one actually sees scenes and hears stories told. Yet the music remains music, beautiful and unforced, and these effects are always achieved within the bounds of regular form and consistent writing.

Czerny's remarks concerning the Largo of the D major sonata opus 10 which, as Beethoven himself said, portrays melancholia in all its phases, are particularly to be commended. He gives the following advice:

To perform music of this nature, it is not enough to put oneself in the appropriate frame of mind. The fingers and hands themselves must affect the keyboard with a different, a heavier weight than is necessary for happy or tender compositions, in order to bring out the more resonant tone of each note and to give life to the slow pace of a serious *adagio* movement. The effectiveness of this Largo will be increased by a well-calculated *ritardando* and *accelerando*. Thus, for instance, the second half [only?] of measure 23 should be played somewhat faster, as well as the second half of measure 27 and of measure 28. Measures 71–75 require an augmentation of intensity and power, until in measure 76 the former tranquillity returns.

Beethoven himself said that the pace of this rich movement must be changed fully ten times, though only so as to be perceptible to the most sensitive ear. The principal theme is always to be repeated in the tempo of its first statement; all the rest is subject to variation in the tempo, each phrase according to its own meaning.

As we know, Czerny departed far from the spiritual element in music. We would therefore expect him to take no stand regarding music other than that of the virtuoso. He was indeed a thoroughgoing virtuoso, though not in the present-day shallow sense. It is, then, not surprising that Beethoven's music, too, met the same fate at his hands, even though he had often heard Beethoven himself play and, more importantly, even though he had revelled in the performances of Frau von Ertmann and had had this high priestess of music as his collaborator in his 1818 recitals, as we have already seen.

It is, however, part of the unfortunate nature of the virtuoso that he demeans all these hard-won accomplishments and wishes to substitute technique for spirit. Vanity, the striving after the loud applause of the audience, is still the motivating force behind such extravagances. We have already seen how the young Czerny permitted himself to improve upon Beethoven's works, so that we may be prepared to encounter later even deeper inroads into this music. Yet he probably did most of it with the best intentions, fancying that he was performing a beneficial service.[328] If I were to examine critically his thesis 'on the correct performance of all Beethoven's works for piano solo', it would fill a long article. Let us therefore touch on only a few points of the thesis. For cultivated and unbiased musicians and music-lovers, this will be sufficient.

As we know, Beethoven noted at the beginning of the first movement of his sonata in C sharp minor, opus 27, No. 2, *sempre senza sordini*; that is, the whole movement should be played with raised dampers. This was done with the knee; the pedal was not yet then in existence. The desired sustaining of the notes in this simple melody, which was supposed to sound like a horn, was not solved on the short-toned piano,[329] because all the notes sounded together. Accomplished pianists in the second decade were disturbed by the *senza sordini* instruction, because by that time the pianos could already produce a fuller tone, and the performers had at their disposal the pedal which they could use effectively. Czerny, however, who immediately began to exploit this improvement of the instrument, just as Chopin did later in his mazurkas, said in the 1830's when the piano tone had been considerably increased, that in the first movement of this sonata, 'the pedal indicated is to be used again with each new bass note'.[330] Moreover, Beethoven marked this movement simply as *adagio*. Czerny corrects the composer and writes: 'Since the measure is *alla breve*, the whole piece must be played in a moderate *andante* tempo'. What a distance there is between *adagio* and *andante*!

A closely related instance occurs in the third movement of the sonata in G major opus 31:

Ex. 20   **RONDO**

Allegretto

The virtuoso-pedagogue makes this commentary on the composer: 'Since the Allegretto is *alla breve*, the whole must be played quite fast (*allegro molto*)'. One can hardly believe one's eyes upon seeing this bit of reasoning. Did Beethoven really have such a limited, schoolmaster-like notion of the *alla breve* measure that he would establish it, or any time signature, as the first law in interpreting a piece of music, rather than the particular character of the music itself?* He himself played this rondo, and would have it played, 'at a comfortable pace'. The whole movement has much the character of a quiet narrative.

In this manner Czerny expressed himself on these sacred works, rich in truly deep poetry, the most sumptuous feast for the senses of any truly poetic pianist or listener! But if one compares the metronome marks he sets for each movement with the particular character of the music, one sees at once how he has ignored all classical concepts of *adagio, andante, allegro,* etc. The two movements already discussed are ample illustration. Here can be seen one of the principal springs out of which so much has flowed to spoil Beethoven's piano music, though not so much through the written word as through individual teaching.

Czerny's metronome marking of Beethoven's piano music takes us back to Maelzel's machine, where we must linger a while.

Among the papers left at the death of Ignaz von Mosel of Vienna, there was a letter to him from Beethoven, which is still in the Mosel family. I owe my gratitude to the late Aloys Fuchs for an accurate copy. The letter reads:

Dear Sir:

I heartily rejoice in the same opinion that you share with me regarding the tempo indications that have been handed down from the days of musical barbarism, for what (to take an example) can be more absurd than *allegro,* which means no more nor less than 'merry', and how far removed we often are from this meaning of this tempo designation, so that the music itself is quite the opposite of the designation.†

As for the four chief speeds which are far from having the truth or the accuracy of the four chief winds, we could readily do without them. It is quite another matter with the words that indicate the character of the piece. These we cannot give up, for the tempo is more the body, while these refer to the soul of the piece itself.‡ As for me, I have long thought of giving up these

---

* By making the measure *alla breve,* Beethoven obviously wished to announce the correct pace of this movement. When in an *allegro* tempo one beats four quarter notes rather than a thesis and arsis, the quick succession of the beats produces approximately an *allegro assai.* If in the Kyrie of the *Missa Solemnis,* which moves generally in quarter notes, one marks four beats instead of two, there is no *assai sostenuto,* but rather an *allegro moderato* with an entirely different character. In Haydn's chorus, 'The Heavens are telling the Glory of God', to interpret the *alla breve* as the norm produces a *presto.* Mendelssohn understood it this way at the 1846 Lower Rhine Music Festival in Aachen, and drove the 500-voice chorus in double-quick march to do it—as he so often did. What a fine discrimination, on the other hand, one finds in A. B. Marx's comment regarding tempo! He remarks, quite correctly, in his criticism of Beethoven's sonata in A flat major opus 110 (*Berlin Musik-Zeitung,* 1824) that the first movement should be marked *adagio.* The composer wrote *moderato cantabile,* which might be misunderstood, and generally is, because most pianists adhere only to the traditional concept of *moderato,* which they understand as a moderate *allegro.*

† By 'the opposite' the master means 'seriousness, dignity, sublimity'.

‡ When a work by Beethoven had been performed, his first question was always, 'How were the tempi?' Every other consideration seemed to be of secondary importance to him.

423

senseless designations: *allegro, andante, adagio, presto.* Maelzel's metronome gives us the best opportunity for doing this. I hereby give you my word that I shall never again use them in my compositions.

It is another question as to whether we shall in this way bring the metronome into the necessary general use. I doubt it. I do not doubt that we shall thereby be denounced as tyrants. If the cause were thereby to be served, that would nevertheless be better than to accuse us of feudalism.

For this reason I believe that the best plan, especially for our countries where music has become a national need and every village schoolmaster will be expected to promote the use of the metronome, will be for Maelzel to try to sell a certain number of metronomes by subscription at higher prices, and as soon as this number has covered his expenses he will be in a position to put out the other metronomes for the musical needs of the nation so cheaply that we may without doubt expect the greatest general use and distribution to be attained.

It is obvious that some persons must take the lead in this matter. . . . You may count upon me to do whatever I can, and I look forward with pleasure to the post that you will assign to me in this matter.

The copy of this letter bears the date 1817; this was added by someone else, and is obviously wrong.[331] Our master very seldom showed the year of writing on his letters, a regrettable circumstance in view of the difficulty of dating the letters accurately, as this case shows. Undoubtedly the letter goes back several years before to a time when the master was still enthusiastic about Maelzel's metronome and was also full of patriotism for Austria. AmZ XV (1813) 785 quotes a declaration by Salieri, Beethoven, Weigl, and others on the usefulness of Maelzel's metronome, at that time known by the name 'chronometer'. This leads us to date the above letter 1813. Another reason for this assumption is that he discarded the Italian tempo designations in the sonatas that he composed next, opus 90 and opus 101, in which indications as to the pace and character of each movement are given in German. The four movements of the latter sonata, for instance, bear the following inscriptions: (1) 'Etwas lebhaft, und mit der innigsten Empfindung' (somewhat lively, and with the deepest feeling); (2) 'Lebhaft, marschmässig' (lively, like a march); (3) 'Langsam und sehnsuchtsvoll' (slow and full of longing); (4) 'Geschwind, doch nicht zu sehr und mit Entschlossenheit' (fast, yet not too fast, and with decision). His characterization (among friends) of the first and third movements as 'Impressions and Reveries'* makes explicit the correct concept.

All too soon the English publishers raised objections to these German tempo designations. Moreover, they proved to be no less uncertain and vague than the Italian ones. Beethoven accordingly found it necessary in the two sonatas opus 102 to return to the 'tempo indications handed down from the days of musical barbarism'.

---

* We have already spoken of this characterization.

Regarding the history of the Maelzel metronome, we must recall that there were two separate and quite different machines.[332] The first was a pyramid about twelve inches high with a pendulum suspended from the outside on the front to determine the true horizontal. There is a screw on one of the front feet so that the level may be adjusted. On a metal plate one can read 'Firma Maelzel' and the year, 1815. The pendulum rod has only the numbers 50 to 160.* Because of its high price (three louis d'or) this model did not attract much attention in Germany. The inventor appears not to have shared Beethoven's patriotism. As early as the 1820's Maelzel, who then lived in Paris, had his brother in Vienna manufacture a smaller machine, about eight inches high, for the German trade, to sell at one louis d'or. The pendulum rod had numbers from 40 to 208. The differences between the two types soon gave rise to complaints that any given tempo mark was ambiguous unless it specifically stated which of the two machines was implied.

We should add that Beethoven's metronome marks for all the movements of his symphonies are according to the first machine. This is stated in AmZ XIX (1817) 873. It is obvious what would happen if they were used with the second metronome. For this reason the score of the A major symphony that was published in the 1820's by Steiner & Co. has metronome tempo marks, assigned by the composer, that are quite different. They are for the smaller machine, and indicate a slower tempo throughout. This proves not only that the same number on the pendulum rod of both does not produce the same tempo, but also that the smaller machine gives in general a much quicker beat.

Does not this circumstance answer the question so often asked: Why did Beethoven neglect to use the metronome? Actually, he himself assigned metronome marks to only two of his works: the great sonata opus 106, at the explicit request of Ries for the London edition, and the ninth symphony at the request of the publishing house of Schott in Mainz and the Philharmonic Society of London. In connection with the latter transaction, there occurred an event that illustrates the master's low opinion of the metronome. He asked me to make a copy for London of the metronome notations he had a few days before made for Mainz, but the list had been mislaid and we could not find it. London was waiting and there was no time to lose, so the master had to undertake the unpleasant task all over again. But lo! no sooner had he finished than I found the first version. A comparison between the two showed a difference in all the movements. Then the master, losing patience, exclaimed: 'No more metronome! Anyone who can feel the music right

* The author found a well-preserved example of this first design at the home of the court opera singer Cramolini in Darmstadt.

does not need it, and for anyone who can't, nothing is of any use; he runs away with the whole orchestra anyway!'*[333]

In the earlier edition of this book, the author gave a clear example of the confusion in the matter of interpretations of Beethoven's piano music by comparing some of the metronome marks prepared by Moscheles for the London edition with those made anonymously for the Haslinger edition of the same works. Carl Czerny also has metronome marks for all the Beethoven sonatas in his *Klavierschule* published by Diabelli. This publishing house is on the west side of the Graben in Vienna, while Haslinger is almost directly opposite on the east side. But the difference between east and west is no greater than the difference between the two sets of metronome marks published by the respective houses.

Which of them is correct, which corresponds to the real intentions of the composer? Czerny defends the authenticity of his version by taking refuge in the classical tradition which, as a contemporary of Beethoven, he is certainly justified in doing. Yet his tempo marks, when compared with Haslinger's, frequently show complete eccentricity, and are as far as possible from the dictates of tradition. This is a clear example of how Czerny's memory became confused when his head was filled with eight hundred of his own works.[334] Since these deeds perpetrated by two *coryphaei* of the virtuoso genus, Moscheles and Czerny, great numbers of metronome indications for Beethoven's piano works have been published, both in various editions of the music and in musical journals. The divergence of views we see in them might be compared to the divergencies in orchestra pitch, almost incredible examples of which were given the musical world in February of this year by a commission set up in Paris to establish a standard pitch.[335] Uncontrolled imitation of the Maelzel metronome throughout the world has further increased the unreliability of the machine to a point where it is utterly useless.

These examples are sufficient to show the topography of the musical Babel surrounding Beethoven's piano music, and above all to warn the reader against metronome marks. Let us close this episode by asking if Beethoven's chamber music, with its specific, personal character, is susceptible to metronome markings at all. And does one who sets his hand to such a task not betray a total ignorance of this specific character, indeed, of every higher concept of musical character in general?[336]

Before taking leave entirely of Czerny's influence on Beethoven's music, an influence often coloured by mistakes and misconceptions, in order to go on to the influence exercised by pianists still alive, we must think for a moment of one who was akin to Czerny in thought and deed, who was no less a virtuoso than he, and who was just as much of the

* See Carl Maria von Weber's remarks on the metronome on page 410.

opinion that the music could be improved by changing it. This was none other than Ferdinand Ries, who could boast that in the art of piano playing he had been Beethoven's pupil. The difference between the two virtuosi (in the better sense of the word) was simply that Czerny for many years played under the eyes of the composer in fact, and after the latter's death continued to do so in theory, whereas Ries gave the explanation in London and elsewhere that his alterations of Beethoven's music had been undertaken with the master's consent.

In one aspect, however, the two are similar: to the extent that each of them wished to shine as a composer in his own right, and in order to do so adhered to the new piano style, to the same extent each had to depart from the classical models. Both followed much the same course as the plastic arts in France from the time of Louis XIV until the middle of the eighteenth century: the further they got away from the study of antiquity and the more they strove merely for external effect, the more deeply they degenerated into cheap affectations and theatrical excesses, until Jacques-Louis David finally led them back to antiquity. How is it, even today, with the so-called original compositions by Czerny and Ries? In another ten years what will be left of them? Ries has published close to two hundred such works, representing all forms of musical composition.

In the Foreword we mentioned that for a number of reasons over the course of the years tension and ill will grew up between Beethoven and Ries. It was shown there how Ries nurtured his grudge against Beethoven right up till the latter's death. In the third period the rupture of this friendship was mentioned only in passing because it did not seem the appropriate place to go into the reasons in detail. Because the above picture of Czerny's influence brings us to the subject, and because the disagreement was largely musical in nature, this seems to be an appropriate time to discuss it. This state of affairs is significant not only in musical history, but as a part of the whole cultural history in general if we think of the public's diminishing interest in Beethoven's deepest poetry and remember that by the early 1820's his piano music had been almost entirely forgotten. It is no small matter when two talented, important pianists, both of whom lived in more or less direct contact with the composer, conceive themselves as correctors of his eternal monuments rather than conforming with the most conscientious exactitude to what he had written and, like faithful apostles, witnessing to the world in a practical way what he had taught them. Moreover, the situation that obtained between Beethoven and Ries was so indicative of their characters that a full account of the facts is almost mandatory. First-hand knowledge is necessary, since Ries in his *Notizen* circumvents the most important aspects and since his letters from Beethoven reproduced there could be misleading to one trying to form his own opinion.

MUSICAL SECTION

It is both natural and laudable that Beethoven, concerned about his deafness, should not only train his pupil, Ries, as a strong support in his piano works, but should also maintain him as a model in this field for the time to come. It so happened, however, that the more the pupil (who studied with Beethoven between the ages of 15 and 21) sought to shine as a composer in his own right and to espouse the new direction in piano playing that reflected little work in the spiritual content of the compositions but a great deal of work in achieving a polished, brilliant performance, the more he came to realize that the compositions of his teacher in their true essence were further and further from his own ambitions. When we think how many and how diverse were his productions, we realize that he had no time for the works of others, not even those of his teacher.

Beethoven first learned in 1814 from his friend Salomon how little Ries was doing for his music in London and how, when playing it in public or in private, he would change it or leave out whole movements from sonatas and trios. At the beginning of the third period the London musician Charles Neate, whom we have already met, arrived in Vienna and corroborated what Salomon had said. So did another musician from London, Cipriani Potter, who came to Vienna in 1817. As one might expect, these similar reports enraged Beethoven. This was the first reason for complaints that later grew increasingly bitter against his pupil and friend. Unfortunately, Beethoven said nothing to Ries about what he had heard, though he wrote about it to others in a way that could and did hurt the young man, as I learned from Ries himself.

From these beginnings there evolved further grounds for mutual ill will and tension. Any music teacher who has trained his pupils with similar expectations that they will one day support him in a great undertaking, and has later been disappointed in them, will best be able to judge the validity of these grounds.

Ries also made himself known to Beethoven's German admirers in various places by his treatment of Beethoven's music as well as by critical comments on it. As a result of his critical comments, Ries was sharply attacked in 1830 by Ludwig Berger in Berlin, as this author was informed by Professor Dehn, who took part in the argument. One of the passages Ries found fault with was a place in the sonata *Les Adieux*, opus 81a, near the end of the first *allegro* movement, in which the tonic and dominant harmonies are heard simultaneously, expressing the last farewell between the leave-takers who are already at some distance from one another. This is a place that hardly has its equal in all music for its original character and that in performance requires the utmost delicacy in order for the unusual harmonic combination not to sound unpleasing. This is the passage:

428

Ex. 21

To Ries's ear it sounded no less 'repulsive' than the re-entry of the main theme at the recapitulation in the first movement of the *Eroica* symphony when the horn is heard in the distance. The vigorous dialectician Berger apparently took the critic to task unmercifully. To cite another case, there was the performance of the ninth symphony at the 1825 Lower Rhine Music Festival in Aachen, at which a whole section of the Adagio was omitted, as we can see from the crossings-out in the orchestral score. In general, Ries was made uncomfortable by *adagio* movements: almost all of them were too long and drawn out for his taste. (Carl Maria von Weber made the same complaint about adagios.) Unfortunately, Ries was not capable of depth of feeling, and consequently his playing could not completely master and convey in its proper spirit the nobility of character in Beethoven's music.*

Early in the 1820's another great stumbling block came between teacher and pupil, nourishing the mutual antagonism already there until it could never again be reconciled. In 1816 Beethoven had suggested that Ries 'dedicate something good to his master, to which the master would respond in kind'. In a letter of 6 July 1822 Beethoven remarked, 'I have received no part of your symphony.' (Apparently it had not been published.) In a postscript to the same letter Beethoven said, 'See to it that I receive your dedication so that I may have something to show, which shall be done as soon as I receive it.' In his next letter (which, as Ries remarks, gives no address or date) we read:

Since, as it seems, you wish soon to receive a dedication from me, I shall gladly oblige you, more gladly (between ourselves) than for the greatest of the

---

* The characterization of Ries's compositions in the Schilling *Encyclopedia* confirms what we have said here. The encyclopedia reads:

The rigour of Beethoven's instruction is unmistakably apparent here, but they [the Ries compositions] fall far short of Beethoven's depth, and as for grace and diversity of orchestration, they are not even equal to the compositions of Dussek. Moreover, they make no demands on the brilliance of modern piano style such as Hummel's, Moscheles's, or Kalkbrenner's. Yet they have something to say and have been brought before a large public, with the result that they have been enormously successful throughout the world and especially in England. One might well say that Ries, in his compositions, always has this success uppermost in his mind. He never reaches beyond what the general public likes; what he writes is attractive, easily understood, and enjoyed without any effort of the intellect or sensitivity. To achieve popularity of this sort, little that is new or original can be done; most of the music must be constructed along totally familiar lines.

great men. The devil knows how one can keep from falling into their hands. As for the new symphony (the ninth, with chorus), you will receive it with dedication to you. I hope eventually to receive the one that you dedicate to me.

And again, in Beethoven's letter of 16 July 1823 we read: 'The variations (opus 120) have probably arrived there. I could not myself inscribe the dedication to your wife, since I do not know her name, so write it in yourself in her name and the name of her friend. Surprise her with it, for the fair sex likes this.'

The manuscript copy of these variations that arrived in London actually was inscribed in Beethoven's hand, 'Dédiée à Madame Ries', in accordance with the wish that Ries had expressed earlier that the honour paid him by the master should be shared by his wife. But when Ries took his copy to the publisher Boosey, it appeared that Boosey had already received an edition of these variations, published in Vienna and Paris and dedicated to Beethoven's friend in Frankfurt, Frau Brentano-Birkenstock. On page 124 of his *Notizen*, Ries refers to a later letter (the contents of which Beethoven told me before sending it to London): 'He apologized for the duplicated dedication, and thereupon expressed a most strange request: "I could never consider accepting a gift or a favour in return!" A more astonishing turn of phrase or a more blatant contradiction can hardly be imagined.'

The contradiction would indeed be blatant and a particularly astonishing one in the whole series of contradictions in our master's life were there no explanation for his curious conduct in the matter of this dedication. The contradiction would be explained in part and the puzzle solved to everyone's satisfaction if Ries had published this last letter from Beethoven complete and in its chronological sequence rather than merely quoting excerpts from it. His treatment of the whole affair cannot fail to cast a dark shadow over Beethoven's character. Hirschbach's *Musikalisch-kritisches Repertorium* of 1844 shows the lamentable fruits of this dissimulation. It then behooves the biographer, who has first-hand knowledge of this apparently puzzling matter, to provide the key, for there is no knowing what will be made of it in the future.

In 1823 Beethoven received from a Viennese music dealer some of Ries's newest compositions, including the concerto *Farewell to London*. Beethoven had not seen anything by his pupil and friend for many years because in all Vienna, the music capital of the world, there was not one general music dealer who sold works from other countries, so that foreign music was seldom seen unless it came out in a Viennese reprint. These new compositions convinced Beethoven that Ries had by now wholeheartedly espoused the modern direction in music, and that he was a master of superficiality. This, and the awakened memories of his pupil's disloyalty in past years in regard to his own works, fanned the high priest's righteous indignation into full flame. In the heat of his passion he penned a letter to the editor of the AmZ in which he forbade Ries henceforth to call himself Beethoven's pupil. Fortunately, his friends were able to persuade him not to send the letter, though he did express his wrath in a letter to Ries himself. The rift between them widened still further. Nevertheless, Beethoven still valued his old friend's continuing eagerness to be of service to him.

When judging these things, the reader should put himself in the position and state of mind of the master who had by then been abandoned by all his contemporaries in respect to his piano music. Even Carl Czerny did nothing on its behalf after 1820. How would it have fared had not the Société des Concerts of the Paris Conservatoire kindled an enthusiasm for this portion, too, of the Beethoven literature, with the consequence that all the music of the master who had been so mistreated by his own contemporaries was given new life? For this reason, the history of the introduction of Beethoven's music in Paris deserves a place in this edition, just as it had in the appendix to the second edition.[337]

3.

One hears many complaints these days about the disintegration of the dramatic arts. As proof of this disintegration we are told that although there are any number of actors of the virtuoso school to be seen, the art of representing personages of exalted character, without the frills of virtuosity, has become more and more of a rarity, as well as the ability to grasp the purely spiritual qualities of the great poetical works. This phenomenon undoubtedly has as its fundamental cause the scarcity or indeed the total absence of models worthy of being followed.

In the realm of music, and particularly in the area with which we are to deal next, the deplorable situation in regard to reproduction of the spiritual qualities inherent in musical works stems from the same fundamental cause. Since, as we have just seen, the musical past has bequeathed to the present only errors in the matter of reproducing the inherent spirit of Beethoven's piano music, and since living models from the master's school have done nothing to convey to our contemporaries the depths of his works, how are today's artists to learn to understand and perform these works correctly? Even if music were regarded in the same way today as it was then, still contemporary pianists, though somewhat closer to the master's intentions, would only in individual cases arrive at such understanding, for the achievement is beset with exceptional difficulties and preliminary requirements.

The current era has witnessed the noteworthy virtuosity of Thalberg,

Chopin, and Liszt, of whom the first two were outstanding only within the narrow confines of their own musical individuality, and may therefore be counted among the musical egoists. Although Thalberg's virility of tone could well have been applied to all worthy music, he unfortunately wasted this rare talent on his own insignificant compositions and never in his artist's tours applied his tonal colouring to any masterpiece of music. Chopin's unique talent exhibited itself in his inimitable, highly individual style of playing his Polish national pieces. His manner truly bore a personal stamp, one that defied imitation, even in the playing of his own music. The performance of his pupils, in comparison to his, is like a lithograph set next to a radiantly colourful oil painting. Both of these virtuoso-specialists not only failed to advance the art of piano playing in general; they actually retarded it, though unintentionally, for otherwise many would have made their own ways and perhaps have achieved something admirable, instead of becoming the imitators of the one or the other and as such their imitations could be only of mannerisms and hand positions. The imitators of Thalberg and Chopin were legion.

Liszt emerged from Czerny's instruction an accomplished pianist, if one can say that at the age of twelve anyone's training is complete. What we mean is that the concepts had already been formed, while the recognition of the true, the good, and the beautiful had not only been refined within him but had completely permeated the pupil's way of feeling and thinking, so that the many storms in his artistic career could do nothing to disturb these fundamentals. Can this be possible in a boy of twelve years? When at the age of ten he came to Czerny for lessons, the divine spark that burned within him was already apparent. But it was a great misfortune that he was ever entrusted to Czerny's guidance.[338] In the description we have already given of this virtuoso-teacher enough has been shown to justify such a statement. For the two years that Czerny taught the boy he did nothing but train him in the bravura style. It dominated everything that the pupil was ever to practise or to produce in public. Were these, then, the first steps to Parnassus?

But when, in the vicissitudes of Paris salon life, the teacher's influence began to wane, the disciple became more free to develop his own artistic individuality. Yet this individuality, even in the boy, had taken the form of eccentricity, which became apparent in his so-called free fantasies on given themes. The boy took special pleasure in these impromptu fantasies, and was continually urged to play them. His teacher saw nothing dangerous in this practice. We have since learned, however, to what extremes the great virtuoso went in carrying out this improvisation that was so close in spirit to his own inclinations. Could such an artist be a reliable model of classical music, by whatever name it be called, when his performing style was based on no fundamental system but depended largely on state of mind and mood, or on the desire for applause?

Nevertheless, this virtuoso was not as one-sided as his two above-named rivals. He had indeed mastered Beethoven's music, and some of those pieces that conformed to his particular style made up a considerable portion of his repertoire! This circumstance did the music more harm than good, but not the greatest harm it had to endure, for Liszt's feeling for these works was not devoid of a poetic sense, and there were moments when his playing, though far from Beethoven's, was still in the master's spirit. His performance was never ordinary! He even had occasional times of tranquillity, and even reverence, when he might have completely satisfied the great composer himself—for instance, his performance of the concerto in E flat major at the ceremony in Bonn in 1845 for the unveiling of the Beethoven monument. About ten years ago Liszt exchanged the life of a virtuoso for that of a conductor and composer,[339] so that he need occupy us no further here, and since as a teacher of piano he adheres firmly to the 'old-fashioned principles', it appears that even classical music has little or nothing more to fear from him and his pupils. The Fates be praised!

Next to Liszt, the most ardently admired star in the constellation of the virtuosi is Clara Schumann. For many years this musician has been acclaimed by all German critics as the greatest model of Beethoven performance. This unbounded enthusiasm[340] shows the extent of the confusion that reigns at present in the ranks of these critics. If this were the first instance of totally unreasonable enthusiasm in musical matters, so overwhelming that otherwise thoughtful critics lose their footing completely and flit about like the easily inflamed, easily seduced musical dilettantes (one is reminded of the vogue of Rossini opera in Germany), then one would despair of the sanity of even the wisest among them. It is thus not astonishing to find a critic for the *Monatschrift für Theater und Kunst*,* who last year exclaimed: 'The theory of music is the most fickle, the most changeable science in the world, which constantly adapts itself to the direction of the wind.'

But every vice eventually comes to judgement, and this case is no exception. It was the same journal that shattered the general prepossession in favour of Frau Schumann and avenged the Vienna composer whom for more than twenty years she had sorely maltreated. The *Monatschrift* proved that there were still in Vienna faithful remnants of the Beethoven tradition, along with a general culture in all music, that

* This worthy and truly independent periodical was founded in 1855.[341] Since the beginning of this year it has appeared as a weekly under the name, *Recensionen und Mittheilungen über Theater und Musik.*

for almost thirty years had given no sign of life in the field of criticism. The celebrated, infinitely over-rated artist revisited the imperial capital in 1856 after seventeen or eighteen years, perhaps in hopes of finding another Grillparzer who would sing the praises of her and her playing as he had done on the occasion of her first visit. Instead, she was confronted with this journal of reawakened, independent criticism that had nothing in common with popular opinion and declined to lift its songs to her in pure sonnets. It is one of the long list of misfortunes that befell Beethoven's piano music, starting in the 1820's and culminating with Frau Schumann, that even this periodical gave recognition to the current Viennese opinion. All this taken together proves that the performance of this artist had already prompted competent voices elsewhere to object to her course of action, but without the least effect.

In the issue for February 1856, the performances at the pianist's first concert were reviewed in detail. What was said about Beethoven's sonata in D minor, opus 31, is worth repeating here. Concerning the broken chord that opens the first movement and the recitative passages, the article said:

Frau Schumann simply let these notes fall. She played them without the least effort to give to the thought of the master the correct significance, nor for that matter any significance whatsoever. We must also term her concept of the Adagio as totally false. An *adagio* movement, and especially this one, requires an air of sanctity, solemnity, and majesty that was rendered impossible here by the tempo chosen and by the placid, flat tone that lacked both the appeal of tenderness and the awesomeness of power, so that our impression was simply one of icy frigidity. As for the Finale, it is not a question here of personal dissatisfaction but of the outrageous conduct of an irresponsible artist. Frau Schumann altered the prescribed Allegretto into a Prestissimo that even her amazingly agile fingers were unable to execute. . . . The precipitous rushing-over of the runs, as in that newly-discovered Beethoven Prestissimo and the Rondo from Weber's C major sonata, is simply the deplorable result of an irresistible desire on the part of today's whole musical world to take every tempo faster than the composer and the simplest laws of nature, art, and reason would have them.

In the March issue there appeared the second review of this pianist's performance, which was in full agreement with the first. It discussed her second concert, in which she performed two Beethoven sonatas, opus 106 and opus 81. Let us quote one sentence: 'Her untrammelled love of the fastest tempo, of the so-called chase, was exhibited in Mendelssohn's *Scherzo e Capriccio*, which at this speed lost its clarity.'

These colours suffice to paint an accurate picture of an artist who for many years has been accepted as the prototype for the proper understanding of all classical music. Nevertheless, this author considers it his duty to add a few more touches in order to fill out this picture in the interests of a very important matter, for we have before us a piece of art history from our own day.

In November 1854 Frau Schumann gave two evening recitals in Frankfurt, at which she played the following works: Beethoven's concerto in E flat major and his C major sonata opus 53, the Rondo from Carl Maria von Weber's sonata in C major, the *Variations Sérieuses* by Mendelssohn, *Saltarella* by Stephen Heller, and two movements from Johannes Brahms's sonata in F minor. The impression made by these works, especially the Beethoven and the Weber, upon those who truly understood this music, was most painful, and no one could bring himself to say a word of praise at such inartistic treatment of classical music, save the newspapers, which overflowed with dutiful admiration. Frau Schumann's extraordinary reputation had led us to expect that she understood the art, almost completely lost nowadays, of playing classical music in the classical style, by grasping its very fundamentals and presenting the whole in their light. But we were all wrong; we had to admit reluctantly that she was in this respect just another virtuoso, capable of literally wearing out classical music, but not of truly presenting it. I expressed our feelings in the *Niederrheinische Musik Zeitung* (1854), No. 45. The events of those evenings in Frankfurt had led me to the conclusion that as far as irresponsible treatment of all good music and lack of understanding of all character were concerned, Frau Schumann was no better than the general public, but in respect to her feeling for the psyche of tone and her innocence of the most rudimentary knowledge of musical rhetoric, she had no equal.

In consideration of the situation in art criticism which has raised undeniably great talents to heights of acclaim despite glaring defects, this writer wanted to make of these concerts an important moment in the history of music, and to seize upon this moment in a particular way. Accordingly, he asked two veteran critics of recognized authority living in Frankfurt to answer the following questions, so that the portrait might have a frame:

Granted that subjectivity in the conception and performance of substantial musical works is permissible up to certain limits, within which the character of the composition must always be recognizable even though it may somewhat vary from the intention of the composer, the question emerges: Were the performances of the E flat major concerto and the opus 53 sonata by Beethoven that Frau Clara Schumann played here in Frankfurt kept within bounds so as not to alter basically the essential character of these works, or did the works become almost unrecognizable?

Bearing in mind this pianist's conception of the two works, let us ask:

Did her performance show objectivity and inward reflection or, on the contrary, did it not destroy the character inherent in both works, above all because of the tempi she chose? Did not the sonata in particular, when treated in this manner, exhibit the character of salon music?

Independently of one another, the two veteran critics answered my questions. Their opinions, which have never before been disclosed, were the following:

Though one cannot deny Frau Schumann's great talent as a pianist, I must say in reply to Herr Schindler's questions that she played the Beethoven concerto much too fast. The same is true of her playing of his sonata in C major, and thereby its character was completely lost. Moreover, this pianist often makes improper use of the pedal by using it in the wrong places, so that the notes often become blurred. This is the sincere conviction of the undersigned,

Dr. Aloys Schmitt

In my opinion, Frau Schumann's performance of the Beethoven concerto did not overstep the bounds marking the point where the greatest permissible speed becomes excessive and hides the intention of the composer, but she approached that point. It would have been better not quite so fast. In the sonata opus 53, on the other hand, her playing of the Allegro con brio and the Rondo, Allegro moderato, was much too fast, and the Prestissimo at the end was too slow in proportion to the other movements. Thus her performance of the latter two pieces did impart to Beethoven's work more or less the character of salon music.

Schnyder von Wartensee

The state has the authority to call to account and punish any violation of law and order in the interests of the whole political structure. But who has the authority to call to account the artistic violations of an artist, especially when he is encouraged or protected by a countless number of so-called music-lovers, artists, and art critics, and is rewarded for his crimes against art and indeed against a whole generation of persons laying claim to musical training? The *Monatschrift*'s attack on Frau Schumann, with its reference to the 'outrageous conduct of an irresponsible artist', should have come many years sooner, for long before this attack competent musicians had recognized from her performances that both her training and her limited sensitivity made her playing suitable only for modern music. But Frau Schumann had allowed herself to be misled into taking on all the classical composers in order to modernize —that is, to abuse—all of them.

In regard to Beethoven's music, it was largely Mendelssohn who set the standard: this was a great misfortune for the music. No music will ever recover from the wounds inflicted upon it by this artist, highly esteemed both as a pianist and as a conductor. For the bad seeds he has planted north and south, east and west throughout the musical state have already borne fruit that can never be rooted out, despite the efforts that certain art journals may bend in that direction, for the effects have already poisoned the flesh and blood of a whole generation. Not that there were no conductors before Mendelssohn who, being also virtuoso pianists, saw all music from a virtuoso's point of view and would chase whole orchestras in double quickstep through a piece of music—Conradin Kreutzer is an example—yet their influence was confined to a single place beyond which their authority did not extend. Mendelssohn, on the other hand, even while still a youth, carried his authority as a true aristocrat of music from country to country, from one music festival to another, until it was inevitable that he should be regarded everywhere as the highest model for the performance of every type of music, especially as his productions were supported by eminent qualities of another sort.

When in 1836 this writer had occasion to oppose in the *Kölnische Zeitung* Mendelssohn's treatment of the ninth symphony at the Düsseldorf Music Festival his voice was a solitary one, and was heard with nothing but scorn and derision. At that time it might not have been too late to join forces to erect a dam against the gathering flood or, at least, to make one of the largest streams harmless. But where were they who could dauntlessly have withstood with their better knowledge the musician who had been declared infallible by all the dilettantes and music-lovers of the province? And so there followed one crime in the grand style after another, and with the advent of more piano virtuosi, also hailed as demigods, the character of our time had been established as an accomplished fact, one which will some day give the art historians much to think about.

No doubt Frau Schumann took into careful consideration the thorough criticism of her performances appearing in the *Monatschrift* in 1856 and endeavoured to heed its warning in so far as possible, in order to prove that she, though already possessed of a higher genius, was willing to listen, to advance herself still further in the acknowledgement of the true and the beautiful, and to shine as a good example to the young.

The esteemed aesthetician, Dr. Eduard Hanslick, speaks of this in his review of Frau Schumann's second Vienna concert that appeared in the *Freie Presse* of 11 January 1859. He says at one point:

Since the influence of such an example upon talented young people is very great, I should like to cite one example from the last concert. Who in the audience would have been able to play the first piece of the *Kreisleriana* at that tempo? Schumann marks it *forte* and moreover puts an accent over the first note of each triplet. A *presto* such as Frau Schumann's, however, does not allow the slightest resting of the fingers upon the keys, and even a Dreyschock or a Rubinstein would find it impossible to make a *forte* and accents at this tempo.

These words show that Frau Schumann abused even the music of her late husband. The same critic had already written about Frau Schumann's first Vienna concert: 'Moreover, we found her tendency to rush the tempi much too extreme.'

The *Rezensionen*, issue No. 9 of 2 March 1859, says of Frau Schumann's most recent performances in the imperial capital:

Let us simply hold to the fundamental that this is not a tendency that can be recommended for budding composers and budding pianists to follow. When Frau Schumann plays Mozart or Beethoven, Weber or Chopin, it cannot be denied that one feels oneself in the presence of a master, yet one is forced to admit many shortcomings. Here the tone lacks depth (this is true of women in general), here there is no grace, here no sincerity, here a quality of freshness is wanting, and here there is something lacking in the interpretation.

And with all these flaws, this pianist is proclaimed the greatest example of Beethoven performance!

All this is sufficient to show that Frau Schumann is the same as she was four years ago; indeed, according to Hanslick's findings, she has advanced in her flouting of the true and the beautiful. Thus she exhibits the spirit of modern art aristocracy. Secure in their expectation of applause from the general public who knows no better, and in their expectation of encouragement in their private ambitions from the hundred-tongued voice of faithless criticism, this overwhelmingly large school of musicians closes its ears to any admonitions that issue from the seat of scholarship and gives only its own subjectivity unlimited play. Examples such as these can have no other effect than to force scholarly art criticism far into the background, as we have already seen at the beginning of this section. If they hope to continue to exist for more than just a few years longer, all the art journals must unite to battle this demon.

The *Monatschrift* for April 1857, in its concert review section, surveys the traits characteristic of the virtuosi who go from one concert hall to the next:

One of the most depressing things an ardent concert-goer can experience is to realize again and again how sorely the training of the intellect and of the specifically musical perceptions is neglected in favour of a merely superficial, often actually anti-musical emphasis on technique. The most blatant examples of this are the pianists. Consider, for example, Fräulein X. She has a touch that is quite pleasing, independence of her hands, and exceptionally agile finger technique. Then what is there to say? Physical strength is not given to everyone. A gay, gracious style can be marvellous, but then one must apply oneself heart and soul to it, and exhibit even here spirit and perception as well as technique. Consider what is required in order to perform programmes calling for classical training such as are common today: heroic sonatas by Beethoven, Bach fugues, Mendelssohn rondos, études by Chopin and piano transcriptions by Liszt. Indeed an imposing array of well-sounding names, but there is that initial and all-important question that an artist must ask himself: What can I contribute to this? Frl. X plays the inevitable F minor and C major sonatas. She does not have the full, strong tone to convey their majesty; we search in vain for either a man or a woman who can play an adagio or an andante of one of our classical composers simply, unpretentiously, neither dragging nor with extravagant retards, but with feeling, tone, the correct accentuation, and a beautiful, singing quality.*

Then comes the question of tempo and of the right feeling for tempo that the tempo indication itself, the character of the work, and common sense dictate! But this chasing, this forcing, this hurly-burly, as if there were merit in making a quarter note into an eighth note and an eighth note into a sixteenth note—as if, for instance, Beethoven had made over the last movement of the F minor sonata into a bravura étude for the private edification of today's generation of pianists!

To fill out our picture of an era, let us compare this Viennese comment with one from Leipzig. The *Grenzboten*, No. 19 of 1854, carried a critical article by Otto Jahn on 'The Leipzig Concert Series for the Winter 1853–4'. The following is an excerpt:

A fundamental flaw in all the performances of the orchestra is the exaggerated speed of most of the tempi which, following Mendelssohn's unfortunate example, has become more and more prevalent here. This is all the more deplorable since the orchestra cannot keep up the pace, so that the tempo finally lags perceptibly. It is obvious that such a fast tempo, which no one would confuse with fire and passion, bespeaks a lack of clear feeling, and completely obliterates the character and meaning of the composition, just as it is obvious that the tone and the sound, suffering from this speed, can never come into their own. If this rapidity indicated at least a virtuosity on the part of the orchestra, one would marvel at it, but here it is quite another matter. The orchestra is not capable of playing difficult works at this speed; they make only half a pretence, neglecting all detail, and this style of slipping and sliding, of doing nothing quite correctly, takes over. There is never any more a question of fine nuances and shadings, and for these the gross, vulgar shock-effects are no substitute. This haste and hurry spreads to the whole concept and performance of music, and we can no longer find loving care and perceptive treatment, either in the strict observance of rhythmic divisions or in the distribution between light and shade in polyphonic forms, upon which an understanding of these forms primarily rests. Where recognition of the minor relationships does not exist, it is wishful thinking to expect comprehension and presentation of the deeper content.

(This author had made the same evaluation of the Leipzig orchestra nine years earlier after hearing two Gewandhaus concerts under the direction of Ferdinand Hiller. Mendelssohn at that time had just left for his new post in Berlin.)

* This statement is in full accord with the one we quoted above from Hector Berlioz.

Such is the present situation! Truly, if our classical composers were to come to life and witness this frivolity, they would not recognize most of their own works! If the great musical societies (the mixed choruses) did not hold firmly to the opposite principles and did not represent the true conservatories (institutions for the preservation of the good and the true); if, moreover, a considerable portion of the music-loving public, now grown tired of the behaviour of the virtuosi, had not turned to better things, then the next century would see nothing but ruins on the site of classical music.

It is my hope that this next section will have a more friendly ring than the foregoing, as we near the close of this book. To achieve this end, let us take a backward look at the life of our great composer. A strange destiny awaited his piano music (apart from the concertos), for it was two women who became the most faithful, most deeply dedicated representatives. With the purest and most selfless piety they approached the lofty creations of the master without any of the virtuoso's audacious 'improvements', for they were not virtuosi in the modern sense of the word, and were not subject to the desires and endeavours that characterize that class.

One of these women was Baroness Dorothea von Ertmann in Vienna; the other was the Countess Sidonie von Brunsvik in Pesth. The former, under Beethoven's guidance, was influential in the first and second decades of the century; the latter in the third and fourth. This author spoke at length of Frau von Ertmann in the third period. We said there that this poetess excelled in the expression of the charming and the naïve, and also of the deep and the sentimental; moreover, that she never overstepped the bounds of what she recognized as her limitations when playing for connoisseurs; and finally, that she adhered firmly to the maxim: 'Everything is not appropriate for everyone.' Let us applaud the exceptional courage of this wife of a military man, for she consistently opposed the virtuosi and, despite the public acclaim they aroused, was not in the least impressed by them.*

This was not the case with the great pianist in Pesth. If we may borrow a concept from genre and historical painting, we might compare the intensive and extensive qualities of the two pianists. In contrast to the lady of Vienna, Countess Brunsvik found inspiration for a poetic rendering only in imposing, deeply serious works. Her performances were thus like great murals and the effect was often overwhelming. It was her husband, whose pupil she really was, who introduced her to Beethoven's music.

Nevertheless, the two ladies concurred in two important matters: in

---

* On page 210 we told how much licence Beethoven allowed this artist for subjective expression at the piano, and what conditions or preconceptions he imposed.

faithfully sensing the feelings of the composer, and in recognizing their own strengths and weaknesses. In regard to the former, they never added to or detracted from the character of the works they played, as no truly faithful initiate in any subject would do; as for the latter, they were scrupulously and conscientiously true to their artistic capacities. Countess Sidonie excelled in Beethoven's B flat major trio, in the F minor sonata, in Spohr's quintet in C minor, and in certain works by Onslow. On the other hand, her playing of works that had a different character was too striking, or else the strength of her hands imbued them with a character that was not entirely appropriate. She was highly critical of her own playing, and would play the works for which she felt her style unsuited only for the pleasure of her intimates. Countess Sidonie is still alive but keeps to the company of her friends, and her harp was silenced for ever by the death of her husband in 1847. Both have observed the unhappy changes that have taken place in the realm of concert and chamber music.*

Let us turn now from these dedicated amateurs, worthy examples even for professional musicians, to the leaders of the 'modern direction' of music of that same time: Hummel, Moscheles, Pixis, and their companions, who for several decades held sway over the piano-playing world, not only in Vienna but everywhere. Through their performances they proved that they remained true to their particular style, brilliant bravura playing, and no others have equalled them. Everything they did was done to perfection. They, too, held firmly to the 'old-fashioned principles' just as our 'musicians of the future' do today, for both schools believed that the future was theirs. We should not condemn them too harshly for having ignored Beethoven's works, for these no longer exerted the least appeal on the general concert-going public and were

---

* Count Franz von Brunsvik's house was like a conservatory on a small scale for a select group of musicians and music-lovers with high aspirations. There was a standing quartet of musicians of exemplary training, with Taborsky of the Prague Conservatory at the first violin, the Count himself at the cello, and the Countess at the piano. This musical trio together produced something which at that time in Vienna would have been sought for in vain. We shall see what a teacher and patron of good taste on a large scale Count Brunsvik was. In 1819 he took over the direction of the Municipal Theater in Pesth with the praiseworthy intention of raising it from the deplorable state into which it had sunk. The first year everything went well, and matters improved considerably. In the second year, however, the nobility demanded more Italian operas, while the rest of the audience wanted more Viennese farces. To accede to their wishes would have meant going back to the old situation. The most insistent, the nobility, were not satisfied by the director's concessions, and since Count Brunsvik was obdurate in sticking to his principles, it soon happened that all the boxes remained empty. This did not deter him from getting the best singers and actors and from producing outstanding operatic and dramatic performances with a small number of artists whom he selected himself. When in 1822 Brunsvik gave up the direction of the theatre, an enormous sum of money had been lost, but not honour, nor the satisfaction of having striven for the best and attained it for a small portion of the public. He remained always the wealthy grandee of the kingdom. Some interesting letters from Beethoven to this friend in Pesth date from this time. They encouraged him to continue in his excellent work. Blessed be his memory!

too different from the compositions of the pianists themselves. If the reader wishes to verify this, he may look at the concert programmes of these men, all of which are given in the AmZ. A comparison with the situation of today as it is portrayed in the *Monatschrift* shows that the 'new direction' has long since died away, while the music of our master has been revived, has risen like the Phoenix from the ashes, and has been glorified to an extent that no one could have predicted. Furthermore, the pianists we named above, when their star was setting, occupied themselves by arranging various of the works of the master (such as Hummel's arrangements of the symphonies), and even prepared new editions of these works and (as in the case of Moscheles) set their names to them. These are phenomena that have no parallel in all musical literature. The following survey of the various editions of Beethoven's works is conclusive proof of their unexampled popularity.

The original editions of the piano works are shared by the publishers of Beethoven's own time:

Haslinger in Vienna, who had taken over the entire publishing business of what was once the Industrie-Comptoir;[342]

Spina in Vienna, formerly Diabelli & Co., who had taken over the publishing businesses of Thaddeus Weigl, Matthias Artaria, Pennauer, and Leidesdorf;

Witzendorf in Vienna, who had taken over the publishing businesses of Cappi & Joseph Czerny, Trentsensky & Vieweg, and Eduard Mollo;

Schlesinger in Berlin;

Artaria & Co. in Vienna;

Simrock in Bonn;

Peters in Leipzig;

Breitkopf & Härtel in Leipzig; and

Hoffmeister in Leipzig.[343]

It may be noted that almost all of these firms sold the works that they owned to and through each other, and that there was a great deal of unauthorized reprinting.

Complete editions of the sonatas (with the exception of opp. 106, 109, 110, and 111) were undertaken shortly after Beethoven's death by:

Haslinger in Vienna,

Johann André in Offenbach,

Simrock in Bonn,

Bote & Bock in Berlin, and

Cranz in Hamburg.

Various of the sonatas were published by:

Breitkopf & Härtel in Leipzig,

Nagel in Hanover,

Peters in Leipzig,

Schlesinger in Berlin,
Spina in Vienna,
Spehr in Brunswick,
Böhme in Hamburg,
Witzendorf in Vienna,
Artaria & Co. in Vienna,
Schuberth & Co. in Hamburg,
Weinholtz in Brunswick,
Bachmann in Hannover,
Challier in Berlin,
Schott in Mainz,
Eck & Co. in Cologne,
Löhr in Frankfurt-am-Main
Dunst in Frankfurt-am-Main, and
Nägeli in Zürich.

The last two editions listed above are almost entirely out of print. In addition to the sonatas, the Dunst edition contained all the trios, quartets, quintets, and concertos (most of them in full score) and all the Lieder and songs.

Holle in Wolfenbüttel is publishing a stereotyped edition of the complete works 'under the editorship of Dr. Franz Liszt'. A number of the sonatas and some of the symphonies, arranged for two hands and four hands by F. W. Markell, have already been published.

Hallberger in Stuttgart has begun to publish all the sonatas 'under the editorship of Moscheles'.

Heckel in Mannheim has published all the piano trios and the scores of all the quartets, which have also been issued by the publishers of the original editions.

In Paris there are approximately ten more or less complete editions of the complete piano works. Two publishing houses there have issued the scores of all the symphonies. All the concertos have been published in score by Richault.

In England there are six or eight complete editions of all the piano works; in Belgium and Holland there are five or six; in North America there are between four and six; and finally in Russia there are two or three. The total number of editions of the piano music is more than forty! A thousand copies of each edition is not an exaggerated estimate.

The publishing firm of André has recently undertaken a project in connection with the Beethoven sonatas that is one of the most deplorable and most bizarre phenomena this commercialized epoch has seen in the music-publishing business. We cannot pass over it without mention. This firm has begun to expand the sonatas to four-hand pieces. The *Pathétique*, the sonatas in C sharp minor and D minor have already appeared in this distorted form. The man who has committed this deed announces himself on the title-page as Julius André.

When, about fifteen years ago, the publishing firm of Schott brought out a four-hand version of Johann Sebastian Bach's *Well-Tempered Clavier* arranged by Bertini, all musicians of artistic sensitivity raised a cry of protest against such unheard-of tampering with a sacred work of art. If today we had even a single independent journal of musical criticism in Germany this sacrilege, instead of being praised, would be branded as it deserves to be. In condemning this attempt on the integrity of Beethoven's sonatas I am only doing what I must. To falsify one of these unified works of musical poetry to the extent of rewriting it for four hands is not the same thing as transcribing an orchestral work or a quartet in order to make it accessible to music-lovers to help them gain a better understanding of the music. It is much more like destroying a musical painting, as if a person copying an oil painting were to put yellow or red where the artist had used blue, changing all the colours throughout his copy.

Since the notes of each octave have their own characteristic sound, a melody transposed one or two or even three octaves higher or lower will suffer the loss of the character intended for it by the composer, just as changing the colours of a painting will produce something very different from the original. Can such a violation of a work of art that in its original form is easily within the public's reach, and in which each note has been carefully placed by the composer, claim the least justification for its existence? These sonatas were written to fit within five octaves, and in no place is there any need for expansion. But in André's arrangements we find the most tender melodies doubled and even tripled; we even find the accompanying figures for such melodies doubled for two hands. The violation, actually the massacring, of the third movement of the C sharp minor sonata is without parallel anywhere. And to think that two sons of the scholarly and deservedly respected musician and publisher Anton André would be accomplices to such reprehensible despoiling of Beethoven's poetry! This is one more sign of the impiety and egotistical character of this musical era.

I have often been asked by music-lovers if Beethoven ever expressed the hope that his works might one day receive the recognition they deserve. I can answer with complete confidence that he never did. The general musical situation during the last ten years of his life could not but banish any expectations regarding the future of his works, for he had already witnessed the death of almost every one of his creations except the symphonies and the quartets. Nevertheless, I suspect that he might have hoped for a revival of all his works, even if at a time far in the future. This feeling is based on the following:

Goethe says in the introduction to the chapter entitled 'Towards a Better Understanding' in the *West-östlicher Divan*, which deals with the poetry of the ancient Hebrews, Arabs, and Persians, and with Persian poets:

I sent my first writings out into the world with no introduction, without the least indication of what they were supposed to be about. I did this in the belief that sooner or later they would be of service to the present book. And so it was that some of my work gained immediate recognition, while some of it, being less simple and easily comprehended, has required several years to make any impression. Yet the years have passed, and a second and a third generation have recompensed me double and triple for the injuries I suffered at the hands of my earlier contemporaries.

There is a mark in Beethoven's hand in the margin beside this last sentence in his copy of the Goethe book that I still have. He also copied it out in one of his journals. The reader will remember what was said in the Introduction about Beethoven's manner of reading and the special significance of the excerpts he copied out. May we not take comfort from this sentence for the injuries that our master, too, suffered at the hands of his contemporaries? We have no proof, but conjecture is permissible.

One more thing must be said in this connection. At the time of the Italian musical deluge at the beginning of the 1820's, a group of his friends were discussing this almost hopeless situation, when Beethoven put in emphatically: 'They cannot take away from me my place in the history of music!' This seems to be the only anchor of hope to which Beethoven could bind at least his name, and he seemed satisfied with it. If only he had lived to see at least some of the publications of his complete works! If only he could have had a tiny portion of the revenue from them! But it had been written differently in the book of fate. The words he so often repeated were true throughout his entire life: 'I write notes out of necessity.' [Ich schreibe Noten aus Nöten.]

EDITOR'S NOTES (318-343)
Musical Section

[318] The reference is to Schindler's pupil Franz Wüllner (1832–1902), to whom Schindler devoted his primary attention from 1846 to 1852. As Wüllner matured and as he came to know other musicians, especially Brahms and

Joachim, his dependence on his old teacher became less, to Schindler's bitter disappointment (see MR XXIV [1963] 68; Hüffer, *Anton Felix Schindler* [Münster, 1909], pp. 57 ff).

319 While as a performing musician Schindler was primarily a violinist, the Conversation Books bear witness to the fact that he studied the piano sonatas with Beethoven. 'Schindler had learned to play the piano in Vienna, and during 1818–21 often played before Beethoven, who in turn would play and explain to him the movements that he had struggled with' Hüffer [ibid.], p. 8. In mid-August 1820 he wrote, 'Next time I shall come with the C minor sonata, opus 10. The Largo of the D major sonata is very difficult to perform' (SchKH II 201), and in mid-September 1820 is the entry, 'Sundays and holidays I am always at home busily working on the sonatas. Now I have the *Pathétique* [as well as] opus 26, and two others in hand. . . . When I am able to come again I shall play some of them for you and show you what I have learned, but it is always a struggle with the notes' (SchKH II 261). Finally, in the early spring of 1823 he wrote, 'Now I know all your sonatas by heart' (SchKH III 62; see also *ibid.*, p. 341) (MR XXIV [1963] 52). As one who studied many—or most, or all—of the piano sonatas under Beethoven himself, Schindler must be considered as perhaps the most authentic source of the Beethoven tradition. This fact should be borne in mind in evaluating the comments on interpretation that make up much of this Musical Section.

320 'Czerny shares with Ries and the Archduke Rudolph the distinction of being Beethoven's only real pupils during his Vienna days' (MMR LXXXVIII [1958] 127). On 12 February he gave the first performance in Vienna of the *Emperor* concerto, opus 73 (TDR III 167).

321 The only letter from Beethoven to Dr. Müller that is known (1963) is one written in late October 1820 (And. 1035). The letter that Schindler sought, and any others that Dr. Müller preserved, cannot be written off as irrevocably lost, however, since hardly a year passes without hitherto unknown letters by Beethoven coming to light.

322 See also Notes 81 and 91.

323 The reference is probably to measures 61–64, where in the fourth measure the progression of arpeggios and broken octaves, instead of ascending to the F sharp above high C, steps down a sixth to octaves on A.

324 Schindler does not make clear just which passages he had in mind, but they were probably (1) the ascending scale in octaves that culminates in measure 22, where the octave F sharp was omitted by Beethoven but is supplied in most modern editions; and (2) the broken octaves in measures 198–199, where Beethoven was forced to replace the required high G and F sharp by E.

325 In this statement Schindler is partly right and partly wrong. As discussed in TK II 252 and TF 560,

'the grand engagements of the last fifty years were few indeed which had not been fought over again by orchestras, bands, and all sorts of instruments, not excluding the *Battle of Jena* for two flutes. There can be no doubt, however, that the coincidence of Wellington's great victory on the Peninsula with the plans that Beethoven and Maelzel were making for a journey to London with the panharmonicon was the immediate inspiration for the work that became opus 91. Note that Schindler quoted from the Deposition only as much as served his purpose. The entire sentence reads: "I had already conceived the idea of a battle piece *that would not be adaptable for his panharmonicon*" ' (see p. 486).

[326] Beethoven availed himself of this same maxim in his canon WoO 194, written in September 1825 for Maurice Schlesinger: 'Si non per portas, per muras.'

[327] This letter (And. 610) was first published in Schmidt's *Wiener AmZ* V (1845) 113, 449. Czerny's own account of the incident is given in TK I 316 and TF 610. It seems probable that the concert in question was Schuppanzigh's farewell appearance on 11 February 1816, before his departure for Russia, though (as Schindler says) Czerny himself, writing some thirty years after the event, assigned it to 1812. In 1816 Czerny was twenty-five years old.

[328] The nature and extent of Czerny's elaborations of Beethoven's writing for piano may be seen by comparing the piano part of the Rondo for Piano and Orchestra WoO 6 in its original version as given in *Supplemente zur Gesamtausgabe*, Vol. III (1960), with the version edited by Czerny as it appears in GA 9/72. In the latter, octave doublings and bravura passages abound, and the solo part as edited for 1829 publication far transcends the range of the piano of 1794 for which the Rondo was written.

Before condemning Czerny out of hand for his elaborations, several facts must be considered. (1) In the eighteenth century (when WoO 6 was written) it was the accepted practice, certainly of singers and perhaps of instrumentalists as well, to use the written notes merely as a point of departure for improvised embroidery of the melodic line. (2) As shown by Seyfried's account of the first performance of the C minor piano concerto (TK II 7; TF 329), Beethoven's manuscript of compositions for piano with other instruments was sometimes little more than a skeleton that he would clothe with glowing flesh in performance. (3) Beethoven's improvisation during a performance of the quintet opus 16 in 1804 (TK II 34; TF 350) shows that he himself was not bound even by the printed score.

For these reasons, Czerny may actually have rendered a service to composer and public alike in the editing he did of such early concerted works as WoO 6— it is difficult to believe, for example, that measures 62–69 would have been heard from the concert platform as the bare melodic line that appeared in the autograph. It may safely be assumed, however, that the published version of the piano sonatas represented exactly the notes that Beethoven wished to hear performed, and that the indications of tempo and expression were (within narrow limits) specific commands from the composer. It is to Czerny's innovations in the sonatas that Schindler takes exception, and in these criticisms he is probably on firm ground.

[329] On the Viennese pianos of the turn of the century, with wooden framing and necessarily low string tension, the decay of tone after a note had been struck was sufficiently rapid to make a *senza sordini* passage like this sound like

MUSICAL SECTION

a super-*legato* rather than a smear of notes as on the piano of today. Another example of Beethoven's use of this characteristic of the piano for which he was writing is found in the recitatives that introduce the recapitulation of the first movement of the sonata in D minor, opus 31, No. 2, in which Beethoven's instructions were that the dampers should remain lifted throughout the recitatives (see MM 22).

330 See p. 415 *supra.*

331 Schindler's statement that the date 1817 is 'obviously wrong' is not well founded; in fact, this date is probably correct. In the *Wiener AmZ* of 6 February 1817 (I [1817] 43), a journal of which Mosel was then editor, Beethoven's name is included in a substantial list of composers who presumably had agreed to mark their future compositions with the Maelzel metronome scale. The issue of this journal for 14 February 1818 (II [1818] 58) carried an Announcement signed by Beethoven and Salieri (MM 233) that could not have been more enthusiastic in its recommendation of the metronome if it had been dictated by Maelzel himself.

It seems probable that the letter to Mosel, which Maelzel used as sales promotion material (TDR IV 69), was written between the dates of these two articles. Excerpts from a pamphlet on the metronome that Maelzel published in May 1818 are given by Rothschild in *Musical Performance in the Times of Mozart and Beethoven* (1961), p. 102. Beethoven's use of German instead of Italian to define the tempo and character of the movements of opp. 90 and 101, cited by Schindler, is quite irrelevant to the use of metronome markings.

332 In an article, *Metronomische Bezeichnungen* (NB I 126), Nottebohm contradicts many of the statements that Schindler makes here:

(1) Maelzel's metronome, large or small, or in between, gives the same number of beats for a given setting.

(2) Steiner published only one edition of the score of the A major symphony. This appeared in 1816 and contained no metronome markings. In 1831 Steiner's successor, Haslinger, issued a new edition of the score that did include metronome markings, but these were not assigned by Beethoven.

(3) In 1817 Steiner published two pamphlets giving metronome markings 'assigned by the composer himself' for the first eight symphonies, the septet, and the first eleven quartets (see NB II 519). In addition to these works, NB I 132 lists nine others to which Beethoven assigned metronome markings. While no such markings from Beethoven's hand are known for the *Missa Solemnis* or the last quartets, Beethoven's intention to provide them is shown in various letters to the publisher (And. 1355, 1452, 1466; MM 449).

333 Against this must be considered the statement in a letter that Beethoven wrote to Schott in mid-December 1826 (And. 1545) regarding the first Berlin performance of the ninth symphony on 27 November and the publication of the score: 'The metronome markings will be sent to you very soon. Do wait for them. In our century such indications are certainly necessary. Moreover, I have received letters from Berlin informing me that the first performance of the symphony was received with enthusiastic applause, which I ascribe largely to the metronome markings.'

448

[334] 'His printed compositions amount to nearly 1,000, of which many consist of 50 numbers or even more' (Grove).

[335] In 1858 a French governmental commission was established to look into the lack of uniformity of pitches then in use. The report of the committee, dated 1 February 1859, showed frequencies for A ranging from 434 to 455.5 cps, a spread of about 0.8 semitone (see Note 212).

[336] In writing this, Schindler apparently forgot that Beethoven himself assigned metronome markings to the first eleven quartets and undertook to do so for the last five (see Note 332).

[337] See Note 1.

[338] 'In April 1823 (SchKH III 135; Kerst II 319) Schindler mentions that Czerny is Liszt's teacher, and continues, "It's too bad that the youngster is in Czerny's hands". BStud II 103 comments on this remark: "From other sources we learn that in Beethoven's circle Czerny's playing was already thought extravagant." ' (MMR LXXXVIII [1958] 130).

[339] 'The last concert given by Liszt for his own benefit was at Elisabethgrad towards the end of 1847, after which his artistic activities were exclusively devoted to the benefit of others.' In 1848 he accepted a permanent engagement as conductor of the court theatre at Weimar, where he remained for thirteen years (Grove).

[340] A review of Frau Schumann's Vienna concerts of February 1856 by Eduard Hanslick, most powerful of European critics, illustrates Schindler's point. This review is given in *Vienna's Golden Years of Music* (ed. Pleasants, 1950), pp. 39 ff.

[341] Actually, the *Monatschrift für Theater und Musik* was founded in 1851, and from 1855 to 1865 appeared as *Rezensionen und Mittheilungen für Theater, Musik und bildende Kunst.*

[342] The firm listed by Schindler as the Industrie-Comptoir was known indiscriminately as the Bureau d'Arts (or des Arts) et d'Industrie, the Kunst und Industrie Comptoir, and the Contor delle Arti ed Industria. Between 1802 and 1808 it published thirty-two new works by Beethoven.

[343] The publishing business of Franz Anton Hoffmeister (later Hoffmeister & Kühnel) in Leipzig had in 1814 been taken over by C. F. Peters. Of the firms mentioned by Schindler, no original composition by Beethoven received its first publication from Leidesdorf, Eduard Mollo, Pennauer, Trentsensky & Vieweg, or Weigl. More than twenty publishing firms and at least eight periodicals can claim first publication of one or more of Beethoven's works during the composer's lifetime (see KHV *passim*, noting that there are many errors and omissions in the table of such publications on pp. 773–74). Weinmann's *Wiener Musikverleger . . . von Mozarts Zeit bis gegen 1860* (1956) and Deutsch's *Music Publisher's Numbers* (1946; 2nd ed. (in German), 1962) are useful guides through the tangled jungle of Vienna publishing house proprietorships.

SUPPLEMENTS

A.

BEETHOVEN'S PORTRAITS[344]

If portrait-painting is not to be excluded from the ranks of aesthetic creations, it must reflect the character of the subject, especially in the case of historical persons, for then the portrait may be copied over and over again and become a standard article of merchandise. The physiognomy and expression shown in a portrait, especially in a painting, must do more than merely exhibit a similarity to the subject: it must enable the viewer to experience the spiritual significance of the person. These requirements oblige the publishers of such portraits to reproduce and sell only those portraits that mirror the subject in every respect, and to suppress those that are so opposed to what the eye sees in nature that the viewer can recognize the subject only after reading the inscription on the painting.

Having evaluated the relative worth of the many and widely differing representations of Beethoven in the light of these indisputable sentences, the biographer finds himself in much the same situation as when he was asked which of the many German editions of the master's piano works was the most correct. He can answer this latter question confidently: the Haslinger edition is the most nearly correct, for it is the closest to the original editions.[345] Another excellent version is the famous calligraphic collection of Beethoven's complete works that Archduke Rudolph bequeathed to the GdMf. This might be likened to a portrait based upon a sketch that the master himself had approved, except that Beethoven wanted to proof-read the calligraphic collection again, which would have taken a whole year of his exclusive attention. And we know how driven he was to create new works.

Beethoven's portraits may be divided into two categories. First, there are those painted from life or sketched from life and used as the basis for engravings or lithographs. Secondly, there are the fantasy pieces and copies of pictures from one or the other category in which this or that feature was purposely altered so that it would not look like an absolute copy, to make it impossible for the publisher of the original to raise legal objections.

450

A. BEETHOVEN'S PORTRAITS

Although each day brings about changes in the appearance of the human countenance, so that the artist should reproduce only the unchanging principal features, there are still many heads that display such peculiarly characteristic lineaments that only a dauber or an inept artist could distort them. Of all the famous musical geniuses perhaps Beethoven had the head with the most distinctive features, starting with the thick mass of hair and continuing with the forehead, eyes, mouth, and chin in harmonious proportions, in which the only dissonance was the rather broad nose. It would be difficult to make a bad likeness of such strongly characteristic features, or even to make a caricature of them. Nevertheless, we have both. Up to his fiftieth year Beethoven's countenance presented a pleasing impression of physical well-being and the highest mental capacity. It was Jupiter who sometimes looked out from his face. In his fifty-first year intestinal troubles brought on the beginning of his decline, although until the middle of his fifty-sixth year there were many intervals reminiscent of his earlier vigour. We shall hear another witness speak of this.

It is worthy of notice that there are only three oil portraits of Beethoven for which he posed. The first is a three-quarter-length portrait showing the master, about thirty years of age, seated.[346] It is in the possession of his family, and has not been copied because of its mediocrity. The second is a bust by Schimon, painted in the autumn of 1819 when the master was forty-nine years old.[347] The original, which unfortunately has darkened greatly, was at first in my possession. It is now in the Royal Library in Berlin, and I have a considerably improved copy by Professor Schmid of Aachen. The third portrait dates from 1822 and was painted by Stieler of Munich.[348] It shows Beethoven dressed in his grey indoor coat standing in a grape-arbour; in his left hand is a sheet of paper with the words 'Missa Solemnis', and his right hand holds a pencil. The startling difference between the Schimon portrait and that by Stieler is explained by the long illness that had intervened.

We should mention in passing the engraving by Scheffner that was reproduced in the sixth volume (1804) of the AmZ.[349]

It has often been asked which of the various later portraits is the most faithful representation of the composer. The answer is without a doubt the engraving by Höfel after the drawing by Letronne, made in 1814 and published by Artaria & Co.*[350] It shows the master at the peak of his fame (as we have seen in the biographical portion), with brilliant, sharply observant eyes, full cheeks, a countenance bursting with good health. The title-page of the nineteenth volume of the AmZ bore a copy of this likeness, though on a somewhat larger scale that damaged the

* Editor's note. This is reproduced in the present edition as Plate II.

fidelity of the expression. This version was also reproduced and sold by Breitkopf & Härtel.

In time the Höfel engraving was followed by a lithograph by Klöber of Berlin.[351] On the sheet is written, 'Drawn from nature in Mödling, 1817'. The contrast between this life-sized head and the 1814 engraving is so great that one who knew no better would be thrown into much confusion, for the two are as opposite as the poles. In the Klöber drawing even the contours of the face are wrong, and the uncouth features show no trace of intelligence. It is the countenance of a worthy brewer, not that of an artist, and it certainly is not Beethoven. Of all the poor likenesses of our master, this one must be considered the most plebeian. In both northern and western Germany it is the one most generally known.

Then followed Schimon's oil portrait. It is worthwhile relating how this picture came to be. At my request the painter, who was still very young, was granted permission to set up his easel next to the master's study and to work there as he wished. Beethoven categorically refused a sitting, for he was then hard at work on the *Missa Solemnis* and protested he could not spare a single hour's time. But Schimon had already followed him on his walks in the country; he had already made quite a collection of sketches, and was entirely satisfied to be allowed to paint as the master worked. When the portrait was finished but for the most important feature, the expression of the eyes, it seemed advisable to do this most difficult task perfectly, for in Beethoven's face the eyes were remarkable, registering a whole gamut of emotions, from wild and defiant to tender and loving, just like the whole gamut of his states of mind. For the painter this feature constituted the most dangerous precipice. It was the master himself who came to his aid. The hardy, unaffected nature of the young academician, his forthright bearing as if he were in his own studio, his coming without saying 'Good day' and his departure with no 'Adieu' made more of an impression on Beethoven than what was on the easel. In short, the young man began to interest him, and he invited him to coffee. Sitting thus opposite the composer at the coffee-table, Schimon was able to do the eyes. A second invitation to take a cup of coffee 'with sixty beans' was sufficient for the painter to complete his work, with which Beethoven was well pleased.

From an artistic point of view, Schimon's portrait is not a significant work of art, yet it is faithful to Beethoven's character. No other likeness succeeded so well in portraying the characteristic expression of the eyes, the majestic brow, that domicile of so many powerful and lofty ideas, his colouring, the firmly closed mouth and the muscular chin. Its close relation to the engraving of 1814 is unmistakable.

The engraving that is used for the frontispiece of this book is taken from the Schimon oil portrait.* The best-known engravers in Frankfurt compared the work of their colleague in Berlin with the original painting and were outspoken in their praise of it, though they realized that all this head contained (according to Schimon's representation) could never be fully reproduced by any engraver's tool.

In the autumn of 1821 the painter Stieler from Munich presented himself to Beethoven. He was highly recommended and was already an artist of repute. His personality and appearance added to his popularity. He had the knack of making the temperamental master conform to his wishes. Sitting after sitting was granted, without a single complaint about loss of time. As a work of art, Stieler's portrait is significant. Although it is brilliant according to the modern convention which was already in vogue at that time, it shows little superficial virtuosity. The whole painting seems to be executed in a style of simplicity. As for natural, characteristic expression, the moment was well captured and the reaction has been favourable. On the other hand, the attitude the painter so loves to depict in men of genius, with the head inclined, is contradictory to Beethoven's character, for the master in his middle years was never known to bear himself otherwise than with his head proudly erect, even in moments of physical suffering. A painter personally acquainted with Beethoven would not have painted him in this attitude. The first lithographic reproduction of this portrait, published by Matthias Artaria, was good, but the current one put out by Spina is quite flat, making the subject look even more sickly than in the original.[352]

The next oil painting is a bust by Waldmüller. I have already had occasion to speak of the worthlessness of this painting and the strange story of its genesis in AmZ XXXVII (1835) No. 8, and I refer the reader to this article. At the beginning of 1823 the publishing firm of Breitkopf & Härtel wanted to own a portrait of our master, and chose Waldmüller, professor at the Academy, to paint it. But there were obstacles; Beethoven felt the pressure of work, his eyes were giving him constant trouble, and he was almost always in a bad temper. After much wrangling, an appointment was made for the first sitting. Waldmüller's behaviour on this occasion was reverential and far too self-effacing, a bearing that Beethoven generally found most irritating. We have just seen how both previous painters had succeeded in their work by taking the opposite approach. No matter how much Waldmüller hurried with sketching the head and roughing out the portrait, the preoccupied master was impatient to get back to his work, and would

---

* Editor's note. For the 1860 edition of the *Biographie*, Schindler had a reproduction of the Schimon painting prepared by Eduard Eichens, 'one of the most significant German engravers of his period'. This is reproduced as the frontispiece in the present edition too.

repeatedly stand up, pace the floor irritably, and go to his writing-table in the next room.

The under layer of paint had not yet been completed when Beethoven made it clear that he could tolerate the procedure no longer. When the painter had left, the master gave vent to his spleen and called Waldmüller the worst artist in the world because he had made him sit with his face towards the window. He obstinately refused to hear any argument in the man's defence. No further sittings took place and the artist completed the portrait from memory because, as he replied to my suggestions to the contrary, he could not afford to give up the fee of twenty ducats that had been agreed upon. Whether the matter was handled in a manner both artistic and honourable, I leave to the reader. In a word, the Waldmüller portrait is, if possible, further from the truth than any other. It is the likeness of a venerable pastor whose thoughts are occupied with elaborating a homily for the edification of his congregation. Even in its outlines, it has nothing in common with the head of Beethoven, the composer in whose mind there was evolving at that time the ninth symphony. One cannot help wondering how the publishing firm of Breitkopf & Härtel could recently have offered music-lovers an engraving made from it.[353]

If the author has been careful to give proof or cite witnesses to most of the important events he has related, or if circumstances have forced him merely to relate them from hearsay, as is the usual case in the writing of history, if it has always been for him an easy matter to choose the testimony closest to the truth because of his many years' association with the great musician, the situation is identical in the case of the portraits. A personal description, now long forgotten, by an unprejudiced observer is worth quoting here, for it will serve admirers of Beethoven as the best guide in selecting a portrait. We are indebted to Friedrich Rochlitz for this faithful description, which he wrote to his friend Härtel in Leipzig after repeated visits to Beethoven in the summer of 1822 at Baden near Vienna, and which he later incorporated into his book *Für Freunde der Tonkunst* (IV 350). Let us hear what he says:

> If I had not been prepared for it, the sight of him would have disturbed me, as it has so many others. It was not the distracted, almost savage exterior, not the thick black hair that hung shaggily around his face, nor any other single feature, but the whole impression of his presence. Picture to yourself a man of about fifty years,* somewhat shorter than the average yet of powerful, stocky build. His bone structure is compact and very strong, something like Fichte's but heavier, especially in the full face. His complexion is ruddy and healthy. His eyes are restless, glowing, and, when his gaze is fixed, almost piercing; if they move at all, the movement is darting, abrupt. The expression of his

---

* Beethoven **was** at the time almost fifty-two years old.

countenance, especially of his eyes, so full of intelligence and life, is a mixture or a vacillation, sometimes in a flash, between shyness and the most sincere kindness. His whole bearing bespeaks that tension, that restless, careful listening of the deaf, that is so deeply touching. Now a cheerful word flung out carelessly, then immediately a lapse into brooding silence.* And, whatever the observer may say on the subject, whatever others have said to the same effect, this is the man who has given happiness to millions—pure, spiritual happiness.

When one compares this description with the portraits painted at the same time, the only one that agrees with Rochlitz' picture is Schimon's. Stieler's painting bears no resemblance to it, while Waldmüller's, which on the canvas is dated less than a year later than Rochlitz's description, is entirely beyond consideration.

To supplement this subject of Beethoven portraits, let us quote another passage from Rochlitz' letter. He relates how Beethoven received his suggestion concerning music for *Faust*, and says:

He [Beethoven] read what I had written. 'Ha!', he exclaimed, and flung up his hand. 'That would be a piece of work! That might be worth doing!' He went on a while in this manner, and began at once to think out ideas, and not at all bad ones, all the time with his head thrown back, gazing at the ceiling.

This attitude was one of Beethoven's most frequent ones, as we have already said. Often his eyes, which ordinarily seemed rather small, would protrude and look large, and he would gaze up either at the ceiling or at the sky, for a long time, either in meditation or when he was especially affected by something said in conversation. Schimon alone was successful in catching such a moment; Stieler only approached it. The illness of 1825 dimmed the fire in his eyes so that, like so much of his internal and external being which at that time had begun to undergo a metamorphosis, the strange look in his eyes was no longer to be seen. It is with this external transformation that Stieler's portrait is in full accord.

Soon after Beethoven's death the commerce of artists and publishers began to throw itself into the business of duplicating his portraits. These copies were bad, but they were sold in great quantities. The prototype for many of these was Steinmüller's lithograph, published by Artaria & Co.354 The blatant contrast between this bit of fantasy and the lithograph made from Stieler's portrait and published by Matthias Artaria is sufficient to condemn it. To present the master with short hair is like painting a lion with its mane cut off. Moreover, this likeness shows Beethoven as much too old, while the expression of his character has nothing in common with the creator of great works of art. A repro-

* It seems almost superfluous to mention that the master comported himself very differently in the presence of his friends. Then he was 'unbuttoned', but with strangers he would 'button up', and was often at a loss for words.

duction made by Kriehuber, that master of convention and flattery, was published by Haslinger.[355] This lithograph shows Beethoven with a black cravat. With no thought whatsoever, Kriehuber included this article of modern dress. The white cravat, which had been in vogue for a full century and which our Beethoven always wore, apparently was to the lithographer an affront to aesthetic propriety of dress.

Another copy of Steinmüller's lithograph was published by Johann André in Offenbach. Schott in Mainz, too, decided to put out its own Beethoven portrait. The lithographer in this case had stood for a moment before Schimon's painting in my apartment, and his version showed that he retained the memory of the contours of Beethoven's head. Everything else was forgotten. Laruelle in Aachen also published a lithograph that is not one of the worthless ones. It has a certain physical similarity, though none of the intellectual expression that characterized the composer up to his forty-fifth year.

The Schlesinger music firm has committed repeated offences with pictures of our master. The first, published with two pieces of music, one of which even bore the inscription, 'Dernière pensée musicale de Louis van Beethoven', is a caricature, the likeness of a money-changing Jew who with scowling face seems to be counting up his losses. The other, a lithograph by Mittag, is a contender for the distinction of being worst and ugliest. Truly, Berlin has not been fortunate in the matter of Beethoven portraits. If only the publishers felt any sense of devotion to accuracy concerning historical persons, even in respect to their portraits, these two and the one by Klöber would be removed immediately from circulation out of respect for our master. We live in an unhappy day, however, when poor wares are considered good business. It is one of the many unfortunate features in the commerce of art products.

Nor do most of the sculptured busts of Beethoven bear close examination. Most of them are coarse masses.[356] Recently the young sculptor in Frankfurt, G. Schierholz, made a bust based upon the death-mask. It distinguishes itself favourably from the others, and is deserving of attention. The artist is now developing the bust in beautiful marble.

In selecting the clothing for the portrait of a historical person, one has much to consider—whether it should be everyday dress or Sunday best, and even the time of year. A man like Beethoven, who always dressed well for the street or the salon, requires the utmost attention. In this connection one must say of the master that right up to the last days of his life he liked to dress with care, and would always choose garments that went well together. A coat of a fine blue material (the favourite colour of that day) with metal buttons was very becoming to him. He always had in his closet one of these, as well as a dark green one. In summer, when the weather was fine, he always wore white trousers and white shoes and stockings, according to the fashion of the day. His vest and cravat were white in all seasons, and his were remarkable for their spotlessness, even on weekdays. Add to this apparel the master's light step, erect bearing, and graceful movements, and you have before your eyes Beethoven's person. With this picture in mind, one would do well to avoid the statue in Bonn made after Hähnel's model, for there is nothing to be seen there that conforms to reality.[357]

B.

BEETHOVEN AND HIS LAST PHYSICIAN, DR. WAWRUCH

When we spoke of Beethoven's final illness, we mentioned in passing an article written by Dr. Wawruch entitled, 'Medical Review of L. van Beethoven's Last Days', in which our master was made out to be a drunkard.[358] The article was first published in the issue of the *Wiener Zeitschrift* for 30 April 1842, then immediately reprinted in the *Frankfurter Conversationsblatt* and in other German papers and even in Paris. The publication in Vienna did not take place upon this author's initiative, but on that of Aloys Fuchs, in the following manner—that he did not confess to me until 10 February 1852. After the death of Dr. Wawruch, Fuchs tried to acquire some of his musical papers. 'On this occasion,' went his explanation to me, 'the widow showed me her husband's manuscript about the matter in question and asked me to help her to have it printed so that she might get something for it. I showed it to my friend Witthauer, who published it in his *Zeitschrift* and gave me a considerable sum for the widow. She was very grateful. My only intention in this whole matter was to be of some service to a widow left with a large family.' The musical antiquarian, who was so concerned with Beethoven, had no thought of keeping Beethoven's memory unsullied!

I was in duty bound to take immediate steps against Wawruch's report, which was both false and damaging. When the editor of the *Wiener Zeitschrift* returned my protest without comment, I had it printed in the *Frankfurter Conversationsblatt* of 14 July 1842.[359] Those who cherish the master will with justice require that this important question be given space in this book as well.

At the very beginning of his article, Dr. Wawruch says, 'Persons of rare talent, like Beethoven, are frequently rich in interesting moments right up to their death, and no one is better able to collect these rich moments than the attending physician, with whom the patient was on an intimate footing.'

We can evaluate the validity of this sentence if we remember the circumstances that brought Dr. Wawruch to the master's bedside. Beethoven's comments at the time prove that Wawruch was in no way on an intimate footing with him: 'someone had sent him a doctor, but he did not know who or how, and this doctor knew nothing of Beethoven or his temperament.' Moreover, we know from the history of Beethoven's illness that the master's one-time friend Malfatti, when he had finally consented to hear his plea and had undertaken to care for him in consultation with Dr. Wawruch, had prescribed frozen punch in order to restore some tone to his sluggish organs. Wawruch had the audacity to report this treatment in the following manner: 'As a friend of many years' standing, Malfatti was aware of Beethoven's compelling desire for spirituous liquors.' Further on the doctor adds, 'sedebat et bibebat',[360] and other such defamatory remarks, all of which were calculated to gloss over his own poor treatment and its bad effects, and to make the public believe that the dropsy of which Beethoven died was the inevitable consequence of his intemperate enjoyment of spirits.

We have already spoken about Beethoven's drinking habits. The single fact that he liked treated and fortified wines, even though he sometimes declaimed against them, proves that he was no connoisseur of wines. But anyone who knew him well in the years before 1826 will have to affirm that he always drank in moderation. In that year there were some isolated exceptions on the instigation of strangers, as we saw in the last chapter of the biographical section. But we also saw that they came to an end. Dr. Gerhard von Breuning should also make his voice heard on this question, for undoubtedly he must have heard his father speak on the subject, as the various events at our friend's sickbed and throughout the last period in general were often the topic of conversation in the circle of his family.

There is an incident that proves the extent of Beethoven's drinking habits better than my words can do. In June 1823 a music-lover sent our master six bottles of genuine Tokay wine in the hope that it would help fortify him against his intestinal disorders. Since I was alone in the apartment, I wrote to Beethoven in Hetzendorf to tell him what a rare gift had come to him. A few days later I received a letter from him, with the following postscript: 'As for the Tokay, it is not for the summer but for the autumn, and indeed for a fiddler who is able to respond to its noble fire and who can keep his footing in stormy weather.'

The housekeeper who brought me the letter had been instructed to tell me I might do as I wished with the wine. I sent Beethoven one bottle and disposed of the others. A facsimile of this postscript was included in my protest in the *Conversationsblatt*. I still have the original. It was very disconcerting to me to be asked so often in Paris if it was

C. BEETHOVEN AND PRINCE GALITSIN

true that Beethoven and Schubert were given to drink and found their inspiration in strong liquors. The question shows that even before the appearance of Wawruch's article, this damaging rumour had been spread. What support was given to this false belief by a doctor's report —a doctor, moreover, who claimed that he was on an intimate footing with the master!

C.

BEETHOVEN AND PRINCE NICOLAI BORISSOVITCH GALITSIN[361]

(see pp. 240, 296–302 *supra*)

Upon reading through once more what we said in the third period about the relationship between Beethoven and Prince Galitsin, we find that all that remains, if we are to keep our account brief, is to reproduce the letters from the musical scholar Berthold Damcke to this author that have already been mentioned. Enclosed with the first letter was the Prince's promissory note of November 1826 to Beethoven that I had tried in vain to find while in Vienna. Furthermore, the letter informed me that the object of the dispute, 125 ducats, had already been paid to the nephew of the great master, but not until twenty-five years after the debt had been incurred!

The Prince had appointed Herr Damcke of St. Petersburg as his representative in the dispute with Beethoven and Beethoven's biographer, so that it was Damcke who assumed responsibility for the correspondence with Beethoven, and with his nephew and heir. Among the nephew's letters to the Prince, Herr Damcke found the promissory note for which I had been searching as well as a demand for payment of the 125 ducats.* Damcke concluded that the Prince's position was not honest and gave up all further responsibility in the affair. In order to clear Beethoven's honour, however, he wrote and told me the main facts of the case, using an assumed name. When he was in Frankfurt in 1854, he identified himself before witnesses as the author of the two letters,

* The reader will remember that in the discussion of this matter it was mentioned that Seyfried makes note of this debt in the 1832 edition of *Beethovens Studien* (Appendix, page 12). This footnote appears in connection with the information on the evaluation of Beethoven's estate: 'Not included is the sum of 125 ducats which the deceased never received for compositions commissioned by and delivered to a foreign prince.' It was not necessary for Seyfried to give the name of this princely debtor, for he was writing only notes and not a biography in which the unfortunate consequences of the Prince's broken promise and all that it involved had to be presented. Had the Prince kept his word, no request for aid would have been made to the Philharmonic Society of London, and there would not have been the ensuing ugly gossip so harmful to our master. These last considerations constitute the most deplorable aspect of the affair.

and gave me further details regarding the dispute that he had gleaned from the papers that had been entrusted to him. Here follows then, the resolution of a mystery which a few years ago had the musical world of both hemispheres in such suspense.

I.

St. Petersburg, 7 January 1853

Esteemed Sir:

A good many years ago I had the honour of making your acquaintance in Berlin. I was at that time only an insignificant young student, and perhaps you barely remember me. You showed me, however, the utmost friendliness, which I have not forgotten and for which I shall now attempt to demonstrate my gratitude. I have some information to communicate to you concerning Prince Galitsin and his relationship to Beethoven. It will surely be of interest to you; perhaps you may even find it useful.

Galitsin bases his defence against the accusation expressed in your book on the affirmation that he did not receive the last two quartets until his return from Persia, and that he was therefore unable to pay for them during Beethoven's lifetime. He might be forgiven if this statement were true, for one cannot reasonably expect a person to pay for goods he has not received. Galitsin's statement, however, is false, like so many other things he said.

Karl Beethoven, whose present address is 221 Josephstadt, Vienna, has in his possession about twenty letters that Galitsin himself wrote to Beethoven. Among them is one that contains the following:

Charkoff, 10/22 November 1826

'My dear and esteemed Hr. Beethoven:

You must think me quite capricious and inconsiderate to have neglected to answer your letter for such a long time, especially after I received from you two new masterpieces of your immortal and inextinguishable genius. But there have been misfortunes. . . . I now live at the other end of Russia, and before many days I shall leave for Persia to take part in a war. Before leaving I shall surely send Messrs. Stieglitz & Co. the sum of 125 ducats, and all I can do is offer you my thanks for your masterpieces and my excuses for not having written to you for such a long time. . . .'[362]

The last two quartets had therefore been received before the Prince's departure, and Beethoven was promised explicitly that 125 ducats were to be made over to him *absolument* (immediately).[363] Beethoven was thus fully justified in writing his letter of 11 March 1827 to Stieglitz. You presumably knew only Beethoven's last letter; you were in error when you inferred from it that the 125 ducats were payment for the first three quartets and that Beethoven never received anything from Galitsin, yet what you said is basically entirely correct; Galitsin cheated poor Beethoven out of 125 ducats.*

* This expression was never used by the present author.

C. BEETHOVEN AND PRINCE GALITSIN

He received the compositions he had ordered and thus was obliged to pay for them. He did not pay, and instead went to Persia and stayed there for several years. Later he paid fifty ducats to Beethoven's heir, but only when the heir's guardian, Herr Hotschevar, protested to the embassy, and Count Nesselrode forced Galitsin to pay.[364] It was a dishonest and fraudulent affair. At any rate, Karl Beethoven last summer received the remaining seventy-five ducats, which only proves that Galitsin wanted to win the heirs to his side in order to be able to wipe out his debt falsely.

But apart from the 125 ducats, he owed Beethoven for several other compositions that had been sent at his explicit request. Many of these have been published; others remain in Galitsin's possession. Of this latter category I know of a quintet for string instruments, a weak piece, probably from the master's youth.[365] Galitsin boasts of owning it, but has never paid for it. Karl Beethoven can testify to all this from the Prince's letters.

You naturally wish to know the basis on which I make these allegations. I shall tell you. Galitsin deposited all his papers having to do with Beethoven, including the letters from Karl Beethoven, with a musician of this city whom he hoped to employ in his literary dispute. The musician, however, has since renounced Galitsin. I have seen all the papers several times and was able to copy out from a letter in Karl Beethoven's writing dated Vienna, 29 March 1852, the letter from Galitsin given above that Karl quoted in order to show the Prince he still owed him seventy-five ducats.

What I said about works, other than the quartets, that Galitsin received from Beethoven without paying for them is also taken from Karl's letters, which repeatedly quote from the Prince's letters to substantiate his claims. The Prince's letter given above seems to me to be of particular significance, for it disproves the claims the Prince is now making and shows clearly that you were quite right in saying that Beethoven was cheated out of 125 ducats. Neither Galitsin nor Karl Beethoven would be able to deny the authenticity of the letter of 10/22 November 1826 if you were to publish it.

I have the honour to remain, etc.

II.

St. Petersburg, 13 February 1853

Esteemed Sir:

Surely you will not let Galitsin's shameful article in the Paris musical journal, No. 3, go unanswered, for if its accusations were true, people would believe that the dying Beethoven was demanding a payment that was not his due. I have already sent you, in my last letter, Galitsin's letter to Beethoven which says that the Prince received the three quartets before leaving, and that he undertook to pay the debt of 125 ducats immediately. This, however, was a deception, and he did not do it. The letter entirely destroys his false plan of defence.

Moreover, his defence contains contradictions which prove that he is standing on untenable ground. He paid fifty ducats in advance. Beethoven then sent

461

him the mass with the request that he accept it for the sum already paid. Galitsin agreed. Now he wants to say that he paid for the first two quartets, leaving the mass unpaid for. Actually, all he has paid for are the mass and the first quartet, as Holz agrees, leaving a debt, as you so rightly say, of 125 ducats.[366] As for his statement that he was never so petty as to require that he be named in the dedications of the quartets, ask him if on 5 May 1823 he did not write to Beethoven from St. Petersburg: 'All I ask for myself is the dedication and a copy of the manuscript when you have finished.'[367]

He has even used for his own ends the letter from Karl Beethoven, making of it the last piece of his 'justifying evidence'. In the letter Karl Beethoven demands money, but is willing to do anything asked of him. He offers to clear the Prince in a newspaper article, but then adds, 'as soon as Your Highness has paid me', a phrase that the noble Prince wisely left out. Later he told the Prince he would be willing to give the bankers, Henickstein & Co., who wanted to have nothing to do with the matter, certain documents which, he claimed, he had just found, so that it would appear that the bankers had given these possibly false letters to those requesting them.

At any rate you, worthy sir, have an obligation to yourself and to Beethoven's memory to pursue this matter further. Your error concerns only a minor detail. You thought that Beethoven had never received any payment from the Prince, whereas he was paid for the first quartet. (If we count the mass, then all the better for the Prince, but here we are speaking of the quartets alone.) In the principal consideration, that there is an outstanding debt of 125 ducats, you speak the absolute truth, and it is your responsibility to defend this truth and clear it of all doubt. Galitsin's reputation here is very bad. Everyone who knows him, and that is almost the whole of musical society, has not the least doubt of the truth of your allegation.

If there is any way that my information can help you, I am entirely at your service.

With the highest regard. . . .

Undoubtedly the reader is amazed that a person so highly placed should behave in such a dishonourable manner. The behaviour, in itself despicable, the debate with this author through which he hoped to exonerate himself, so ill-advised and mean, everything we read in Damcke's letters—all this is nothing compared to the outrageousness of Galitsin's accusations against Beethoven. The behaviour of the Russian Prince has throughout the matter been marked by boorishness such as has never before shown itself in a person of noble blood. We have already seen in the biographical section how the whole reading public was won over to the Prince's side by his very first publication against his 'pamphleteering' opponent. Such blind partisanship on the part of the public may be explained by the Prince's high title and by the dazzling halo that people of all classes are just as prone to see around any aristocratic head as they were fifty years ago. But I cannot refrain from reporting here that even the *Gazette Musicale* of Paris took the

C. BEETHOVEN AND PRINCE GALITSIN

Prince's part, giving absolute credence to his diatribes even after I had proved them invalid. That periodical was so base as to censor my second rejoinder, and so bold as to cut out the Prince's promissory note that I had quoted. Moreover, the *Gazette* acquiesced in all the Prince's invectives against Beethoven and recorded them in such a way as to mislead the reader into believing that the Prince was the deceived and Beethoven the deceiver.

To conclude this unprincely tale on a final harsh note, we must introduce a man who some years ago made himself known to the French and German musical-literary world as a Beethoven scholar and interpreter. Everything that Herr Damcke, the Hanoverian, felt it was beneath his dignity to report after examining all the papers on the subject, was dared without any such research by a man half German, half Russian. This man had the boldness to take up the cudgels for the Prince despite the promissory note that I had published in a rejoinder appearing in the NZfM. This daring knight was none other than Wilhelm von Lenz, the Livonian, the great virtuoso of conjectural criticism. A few lines from his defence of the Prince, contained in the first section of his book, *Beethoven, eine Kunststudie*, will be sufficient to show the character of the man. On pp. 275 ff. he says:

If the German press feels called upon to champion the ghost of a man whom it practically ignored during his lifetime, then Vienna, the city in which Beethoven was for 35 years martyred for his art, will champion him all the more ardently. Vienna is inseparable from Beethoven's life and from its veneration of him. What is to be gained, though, from passionately accusing a foreigner of being somewhat in Beethoven's debt? Especially today, when all sorts of pains are being taken to present Beethoven as a man like any other? The avid analysis of all such matters, as well as the animosity that grows out of the situation, seem to pervade German life. [!] The Prince would hardly have been exposed to attack if a certain man of letters had not wished to vent his insolence on someone of noble estate. It would have been better if the Prince had not taken up the gauntlet, thus avoiding a vulgar dispute in the newspapers, which have more important matters to consider than the microscopic object of this argument.

Herr von Lenz had the audacity to write this in 1855, at a time when he was in almost constant correspondence with the 'certain man of letters', as we may see from twenty letters from him to me, mostly containing a series of questions on Beethoven's work so that he might advance his own literary endeavours. He had moreover the audacity to incorporate into his publications more material from my book on Beethoven than anyone else has, as I pointed out in the Foreword.

It is painful for an injured party to have to obtain its own satisfaction. Herr von Lenz might have had it otherwise if he had given me the satisfaction that I asked and that he repeatedly promised. He might have explained away the injury with any plausible excuse, but he failed to do so. Instead, he continued his questioning of me, frequently with the intention of using my answers in a way quite different from what I had specified and what he had promised. Readers of his *Kritischer Katalog sämmtlicher Werke Beethovens* please note!

(Written a full year after the above paragraphs)

Unfortunately the writer finds it necessary to announce in this supplement that Prince Galitsin refuses to remain quiet, despite all that has taken place. The contents of a letter directed to me and dated 7 December 1858 testify to this restiveness. First he reviews the object of the dispute in a long diatribe; then he threatens that his son will take the father's slanderers to court. He adds that for the 125 ducats he might have had all the Beethoven works; he goes on to say that Beethoven sent him the useless (!) score of the *Missa Solemnis* without his foreknowledge, and that five months later he could have bought a printed copy for five thalers.* (The reader remembers the enthusiastic letter of praise that the Prince wrote Beethoven after this work had been performed in St. Petersburg.) He next complains that I might have made public his generosity and nobility instead of slandering him. Finally, he closes with these words: 'In brief, if you want me to restrain my son from executing his purpose, you will recant immediately. Otherwise I shall press my suit. This offer is an act of my generosity.' The reader of such expostulations finds it difficult to believe his eyes. The only explanation is that the writer of the letter is a Russian prince accustomed to absolute power. Needless to say, this author made no reply to these most recent signs of generosity and nobility, and would not reveal them here if Beethoven's interests did not require a full disclosure.

D.

'BEETHOVEN'S STUDIES IN THOROUGHBASS,
COUNTERPOINT, AND COMPOSITION'
OR
IGNAZ RITTER VON SEYFRIED
AND TOBIAS HASLINGER

Seldom, or never perhaps, has the world of music been so misled by a piece of musical literature as it has been by the work whose title appears

---

* This passage in the Prince's letter deserves to be reproduced verbatim. It reads: 'Think a moment: who acted more nobly, Beethoven or I? He sends me without warning a useless score for which I had not asked. He then asks me to pay fifty ducats for it, when I could have bought a printed copy a few months later for only five thalers.'

above. For years much has been written about this book. It was this author himself who took the initiative in 1835. He undertook to weaken the well-constructed edifice by removing one of its foundation stones but with no effect. In recent years another person has succeeded in toppling it to the ground by proving conclusively that *Beethovens Studien* is a spurious work. We shall in this supplement name the person who is honoured with this discovery. First of all, however, we must relate the historical development of the situation in all its ramifications. This is done by simply setting forth the pertinent facts.

In November 1827 Beethoven's musical *Nachlass* was sold at an auction. The correspondent of the AmZ writes of the occasion:

Domenico Artaria and Tobias Haslinger entered into a regular contest. By outbidding everyone else, these two practically divided the priceless *Nachlass*, and each acquired, if not a half, at least a third of it.[368] There are about forty unknown works, largely composed in the bloom of the composer's youth, works that would surely promise great pleasure to the admirers of the great master. Yet it is to be feared that under the circumstances these works will become the object of commercial speculation and disorder.

Among other items, Haslinger acquired for a few kreutzer a note-book of counterpoint exercises written in an unknown hand. A short time later the publisher Diabelli, who had also been present at the auction, asked me if I had ever seen among Beethoven's possessions a notebook fitting a certain description. By chance I had held the notebook in my hands just a few days before Beethoven's death. When I asked the master where it came from, he answered, 'It is examples of Albrechts-berger's exercises for his pupils'. He kept the notebook for several days, and it awakened many memories of his own years as a student. Further investigation convinced both Diabelli and me that this was indeed the notebook about which he had questioned me. Towards the end of 1831 Diabelli heard that Seyfried was engaged in editing the papers bought at the auction of Beethoven's *Nachlass*, which were to appear in a single volume to be published by Haslinger. We thought of the notebook.

In 1832 the long-announced work appeared. It was preceded by a list of the names of 1,293 subscribers; the title-page included the statement: 'Compiled from his [Beethoven's] handwritten *Nachlass* and edited by Ignaz Ritter von Seyfried'. A cursory leafing through the pages showed me some of the familiar fugues for three voices from the Albrechtsberger notebook, and I immediately apprised Diabelli of my discovery. We could do no more, however, until an opportune time should present itself. In the meantime the book sold like hot cakes, since from the wording of the title everyone thought it to be a textbook of composition or something of the kind prepared by Beethoven himself. The newspapers proclaimed it to be an authentic work; the editor himself, who stood in high public esteem, said specifically in the Foreword: 'I have made every attempt to reproduce this work conscientiously, exactly, and in the same order as that in which I found it. Even the composer's own words and expressions have in large part been retained.'

In issue No. 2 of the AmZ for 1835 there was a flowery advertisement for a lithographed 'head of Beethoven, only one inch high', made by Kriehuber of Vienna and available at Haslinger's.[369] It was proclaimed the 'best likeness of Beethoven'. This lithographer, who was a clever artist otherwise, had only seen the master in the street, and had not made his drawing until seven years after the composer's death. One may then imagine how accurate the likeness was! This new evidence of commercial speculation gave me the opportunity to inveigh loudly in the AmZ for 1835, issue No. 8, against the activity of this Viennese publishing firm, all of which had been carried on in the name of its alleged 'friendship' with the great deceased. I took the occasion to declare myself 'an unbeliever' in the matter of the Beethoven studies.

I immediately received three letters on a single page dated Vienna, 28 February 1835, from Haslinger, Seyfried, and Castelli, who is still living and who was at that time in charge of publicity for Haslinger's musical publications. Each in his own way ordered me to withdraw my statement about the *Studien*. Haslinger threatened that if I refused, he would publish original letters from Beethoven in which I was 'branded in a damaging way'.[370]

The wording of these three letters made me certain that my shot had hit its mark. On only one point was I unsure, and that was whether all three were equally implicated in the fraud. Since Haslinger himself did not possess sufficient knowledge to distinguish the authentic from the spurious, provided anything in Beethoven's own hand was included in the Seyfried edition, he might easily have been a dupe in the enterprise. As for the poet Castelli, he knew nothing about music and could even more easily have been duped. The irrefutable guilt thus concentrated itself on Seyfried who, as an experienced teacher of counterpoint, familiar moreover with all styles of composition, must be solely responsible. With this in mind I related the situation to Dr. Bach in a letter, enclosing an unsealed letter to Haslinger in which I declared myself prepared to withdraw my accusation provided the entire contents of the *Studien* was written in Beethoven's own hand as confirmed by several men known to me, one of whom must be Dr. Bach.

It was in vain that I awaited this confirmation or, indeed, a reply of any kind. The 'foxes' lair'* was silent, even when in 1841 I answered

---

* Beethoven sometimes used to call the music firm in the Paternoster-Gässchen a 'foxes' lair'.

an inquiry in the *Wiener Theater-Zeitung* concerning the first version of *Fidelio* and at the same time made a vigorous reference to the *Studien*. However, the accused found other means of revenge. After the publication of my book on Beethoven, Haslinger took the trouble of writing to his business friends, casting suspicion on its entire contents and dismissing its author as 'Beethoven's valet'. Two such letters were shown me by their recipients. Do not ask about the effects of this intrigue. Haslinger was connected with all the music publishers in Germany, and almost all the composers and virtuosi were his clients. The virtuosi on tour did him the service of carrying this rumour to places not reached by his letters. Nevertheless, my book and its author continued to go their way, and I am now in a position to present in this new edition an account of all these endeavours.

In 1851 the music publisher Schuberth & Co. in Hamburg announced a second edition of *Beethovens Studien*. In the public interest and the interest of truth I felt obliged to allude to this audacious undertaking in the NZfM, No. 16, of that year. I openly declared the work an enigma or a fraud (which amounts to the same thing), and included some of the information that appears above. The publishing firm was not in the least disturbed by my accusations, and perhaps they even contributed to the market success of the edition. The halo around Beethoven's name darkens everything surrounding it. This halo profited the music publisher Maurice Schlesinger in Paris 30,000 francs, as he himself has said, for a French translation of the *Studien*. However, my intervention had another effect: it prompted an erudite musician in Cologne to get to the bottom of this mystery. The results of his research appeared in the *Rheinische Musik-Zeitung*, II (1852) 572.* This musical journal, at that time still very new, had only a small circulation, so that this most important discovery by Franz Derckum remained unknown to almost the entire musical world, even to those who were concerned with musical literature.

It is especially to be regretted that even A. B. Marx had no knowledge of all these circumstances dating from various times, as his book, *Ludwig van Beethoven: Leben und Schaffen*, clearly shows. (A journalist's work is like the work of the Danaides!) This scholar, gifted with such sharp intelligence, nevertheless failed to sense the counterfeit in Seyfried's work and quotes it widely in his own book. He placed belief and trust in this tainted spring, thus strengthening its acceptance, just as Oulibicheff had done a short time before. We now see how speculation can deceive with a thrice-published book! It is my hope that the following will erect a secure dam against any further speculation and will once

* This was the predecessor of the *Niederrheinische Musik-Zeitung*, which started in July 1853. Both were edited by Professor Ludwig Bischoff.

and for all paralyse the harmful effects of such gullible trust on the part of renowned musical authorities.

This is Derckum's disclosure:

Beethovens Studien:

a demonstrably spurious work

Some years after Beethoven's death, Haslinger in Vienna published a book entitled: *L. van Beethovens Studien im Generalbasse, Contrapuncte und in der Compositionslehre. Aus dessen handschriftlichem Nachlasse gesammelt und herausgegeben von J. Ritter von Seyfried.* (Beethoven's Studies in Thoroughbass, Counterpoint, and the Art of Composition. Compiled from his handwritten *Nachlass* and edited by J. Ritter von Seyfried.) As long ago as 1835 Anton Schindler challenged the authenticity of this work, but the voice of truth's guardian was partly ignored, partly suppressed by those who had an interest in the publication. The musical public is like the world, of which it is said: *Mundus vult decipi* (The world wants to be deceived.) It bought the book and its money flowed into the pockets of the speculators who had dishonourably exploited the sacred name of Beethoven.

'How, on what grounds, can you make such a claim? Is it not possible that Schindler was mistaken? Does not a highly estimable man assure us on the title-page of the book that these studies were compiled from Beethoven's handwritten *Nachlass*? Read the editor's Foreword!' Such will be the reaction of many. But I say that Schindler was entirely right and that we ought to thank him for again bringing the matter to public attention, now that the world is about to be hoodwinked by a second edition. Yet he has only exposed the historical and external condition of this mysterious manuscript. He himself, and the whole musical world as well, will be astounded when they read the results of my research into the contents of the book, which makes every assertion on the title-page a lie and the whole Foreword a mockery. Never has a more thoroughgoing or a longer-lasting deception been worked upon the public, for the book is nothing but a compilation of textbooks already published in the last century.

Such a statement must be proved. Here is the proof.

When I read in this journal (No. 70) the report of Schindler's renewed protest, I recalled that years ago when I was looking through these so-called Beethoven studies, I noticed a fugue that I seemed to remember from the days of my own lessons. I now took the book in my hand and to my joy found the old familiar piece. The more I looked through the book and the more examples of counterpoint I read, the more clearly I remembered that I had already been in this same Rococo society with some great master of the past. Since the whole value of the book in question rests on the assumption that the examples and exercises are really Beethoven's,* that we have here the interesting attempts of a young genius to master the rules and to solve the problems given him by his teacher, my doubts, once excited, gave me no rest.

* This is vouched for by Seyfried's advertisement in the AmZ.

D. BEETHOVEN'S STUDIES IN COMPOSITION

As I paced up and down in front of my bookshelves, trying to remember, it suddenly seemed to me that two great, familiar eyes were staring at me from the title of an old quarto volume. *Gradus ad Parnassum* was what I read there, and in the same moment the thought flashed through my mind, 'That's it!' I seized the book and held none other than the work of that old demigod, Johann Joseph Fux: *Gradus ad Parnassum sive Manuductio ad Compositionem regularem* (Introduction to the Rules of Composition) as translated from the Latin by Lorenz Mizler (published in Leipzig, 1797, by J. S. Heinsius).[371]

I thereupon summoned the ghost of the worthy Kapellmeister to their Imperial Majesties Leopold I, Joseph I, and Karl VI, for a friendly chat, and showed him the examples from *Beethovens Studien*. How can I describe my amazement when with a hollow, ghostly voice he replied, 'All of it has already appeared. I wrote it all myself; it was given birth in print with my Emperor's blessing in the year 1725.' 'What!' I cried, 'Is it possible?' Apparently Albrechtsberger who, in the three volumes of Seyfried's edition, stood beside Fux on the shelf, had heard our conversation. He looked over my shoulder at *Beethovens Studien* and whispered, 'Hm! Hm! I know all of that well; it's all appeared before. That, and that, and that is mine. It was published in my third volume several years ago by my dear pupil, Ritter Seyfried.'

I jumped up in a rage, banged my fist on the table so violently that the two ghosts disappeared, and swore that I would avenge the desecrated memory of Beethoven by publicly denouncing those who had sold us the powder from the wigs of those estimable old masters under the pretence that it was the first shoot of Beethoven's sprouting genius!

I therefore proceed to a legal confrontation of the malefactors with Fux and Albrechtsberger, and present the documented evidence. I use the edition of Fux named above, and Albrechtsberger's complete writings on thoroughbass, harmony, etc., edited by his pupil Ignaz Ritter von Seyfried, in three volumes, as published in Vienna by Anton Strauss (no date).

The first section of the *Studien*, 'Instruction in Thoroughbass', will not be considered here. It comprises 74 pages, and we shall speak of it later. The second section, 'Theory of Composition', is the portion of the book that we wish to examine more closely. The contrapuntal exercises begin on page 87. I pass over the minor plagiarisms before this point; I also mention in passing that in the first examples there is here and there a note that seems to be altered from the original. Among the studies we find:

Studien: Page	In Fux: Plate	Fig.
87	Plate II,	Fig. 13
88	Plate II,	Fig. 16, 17
89	Plate III,	Fig. 1, 3
90	Plate III,	Fig. 12, 15
91	Plate III,	Fig. 13, 14
92	Plate IV,	Fig. 6
103	Plate VII,	Fig. 22, 23
104	Plate VIII,	Fig. 1, 2
106	Plate IX,	Fig. 4, 2

SUPPLEMENTS

I believe that this list of comparisons is sufficient to prove my point. There may be still more, but I am tired of this unpleasant research. What little remains outside this register of shame is also very unlikely to be of Beethoven's composition. Schindler's allegation that the whole thing is a notebook of Albrechtsberger's is more probable, or perhaps it is a notebook of one of Albrechtsberger's pupils. He used Fux's text, from which, in addition to musical examples, he had copied the passages that followed. Fux's book is written in dialogue form, and the teacher speaks to his pupil in this manner: 'You have done your lesson well. One can achieve much through thought and work. Remember the proverb: "Drops of water can bore a hole in a stone, not by force but by repetition." This proverb teaches us that knowledge can be acquired only through untiring effort, so that we may not let a single day go by without having done our stint.' The passage is found with insignificant modifications on page 92 of the *Studien*. It is also to be noted that although Fux's name is mentioned twice, his text is referred to only once in the *Studien*, on page 96, where it reads: 'In this cadence one passes from the seventh to the fifth. This is the well-known Fux change-note [*Nota cambiata*], named after its inventor, the royal and imperial Principal Kapellmeister, Johann Fux,* author of the first textbook of musical theory under the title *Gradus ad 'Parnassum,* that famous work whose publication was commissioned by his noble patron, Emperor Karl VI.'

When I told Professor Bischoff about this striking proof of the falseness of the Beethoven studies, he asked me not to weaken in my search for the truth, and to make a closer examination of the first chapter, which deals with thoroughbass, and to compare it with Albrechtsberger's thoroughbass text. I did so, but with no result so far as Albrechtsberger was concerned. I did, however, find in D. G. Türk's *Anleitung zum Generalbassspielen* (Introduction to the Playing of Thoroughbass), which first appeared in 1791, the source of the so-called *Beethovens Studien* and the original of the whole thoroughbass instruction included there, all but a few pages! I refer now to the third edition of Türk, published in Halle in 1816. The plagiarism is apparent right at the beginning of the first chapter of the *Studien,* where it says, 'All the signs that apply to accompaniment are called signatures'. Türk, page 23, says, 'The numbers and signs that refer to the playing of thoroughbass are all called signatures'. It continues in this manner; most of the musical examples are exact copies of Türk's. Compare the following places:

	Page		Page	Section
Studien:	5 (lower half)	In Türk:	49	26
	6		47	30
			48	31
	7		46	28
	8 and 9		46	29
	9 (lower half)		48	32
	10		49	34
	11		50	
	12 (lower half)		51	
	13 and 14		52 and 54	

I have not been able to find the source of the second chapter, which is seven pages long, except for a few minor instances (e.g., page 21 is from Türk, page 59, sec. 42).

In the third chapter, compare:

	Page		Page
Studien:	21	In Türk:	57
	22		61, 62, 63, 65
	23		65, 102, 103
	24		104

Ten pages follow whose source is still a mystery. Then comes page 56, which is Türk, pp. 322–3, and page 58, which is Türk, page 128, sec. 88, 89.

---

* This, by the way, is erroneous, as one may read in Fux's text itself.

From the sixth chapter on the plagiarism is obvious. The whole sixth chapter is a mangled version of the sixth chapter of Türk. Admittedly it takes a practised eye to stay on the track. Here are some guides that will help anyone who is interested to go through and compare the other chapters. Take, for instance, the first line of music on page 59 of the *Studien*. The first measure appears on page 264 of Türk (c, d), the second measure is on page 265 (e), the third on page 265 (f), the fourth on page 265 (g), and the fifth under (h). It is confused, but it is all there. Just as Chapter 6 of the *Studien* is made from Chapter 6 of Türk, the same is true of Chapters 7, 8, and 9, which are derived from the corresponding chapters in Türk. For the tenth chapter, compare Türk, pp. 139 ff.

Finally, the chapter 'On recitative' in the *Studien* is borrowed from J. G. Schulzer's chapter, 'Recitative' in his *Theorie der schönen Künste* (Theory of the Fine Arts), Part IV, page 4 of the second edition, published in Leipzig in 1799. This chapter comprises 17 pages and 6 music plates. Anyone may easily find in them the plagiarized sources of the *Studien*.

I have pursued the unscrupulous smugglers through bog and mire long enough. I have thoroughly demolished the 'foxes' lair'; it has been an unpleasant, tiresome task, and I am weary of it. Perhaps others will dig up all the rest of the sources. I was driven to do it by my feeling of outrage at the double guilt of those who sinned both against Beethoven and against the readers of musical literature. How many young musicians went hungry in order to save the money to buy a true relic of Beethoven! And what has the poor wretch left, now that we have cruelly toppled his faith? I refrain from any further comment, though there is much more that one could say, for as a poet of antiquity wrote:

> Si natura negat, facit indignatio versum.
> (When nature refuses, indignation makes the verse.)

So here, too, righteous anger at a wanton offence against a great name has dictated to my pen.

Cologne

F. Derckum[372]
Teacher at the Rhine School of Music

The fears of the Viennese reporter that we heard at the beginning of this chapter regarding commercial speculation and disorder have, according to the foregoing evidence, been fulfilled to a monstrous degree.

There remains one more matter to discuss. Again and again Seyfried calls our master his friend, and makes the reader believe that between Beethoven and Seyfried there were ties of intimate friendship, so that everything he claims may bear the appearance of first-hand authenticity. In the interests of truth I must answer this claim and affirm that at no time did there exist between the two musicians any sort of relationship.[373] On the contrary, Beethoven had conceived a profound dislike for Seyfried, and pronounced him unworthy of anyone's respect. The basic reason for such animosity was the Kapellmeister's immoral conduct regarding his marital relations, for as a prominent public figure he presented a bad example.* Even if no one else in the morally lax Babel on the Danube took offence at this conduct, our incorruptible Cato did. How could Beethoven have publicly excluded the musically worthy Kapellmeister from the post of music director in 1824 (as we have seen in the third period) if he had felt even the slightest regard for him? This aspect of his private life put Seyfried in difficult circumstances after his dismissal from the Theater an der Wien in 1825, and he was forced to give lessons and to do odd jobs for publishers, a situation that was far removed from the status of a highly placed scholar that he had occupied. It was this circumstance that finally induced him to commit the deed that has just been laid bare before the reader.

It may be confidently assumed that after the year 1806 and the re-hearsals and performances of the revised *Fidelio* at the Theater an der Wien, Beethoven and Seyfried did not exchange another word. If anyone doubts the truth of this statement, let him ask the man who is now director of the Stadt-Theater in Aachen, Michael Greiner, who in 1822 and 1823 all too often had the opportunity of observing these two men eating at the same time in the restaurant next to the Josephstädter Theater. In addition to the above-mentioned reasons for their deep-rooted mutual animosity, there was another. Beethoven believed that Seyfried was the author of all the reviews of his dramas in music that appeared in the AmZ, each one extending over five or six columns and including a detailed formal analysis. During a visit to Baden in 1822, Friedrich Rochlitz personally attempted to disabuse Beethoven of this belief, without saying who actually was the author of these extrava-gantly laudatory articles. Beethoven replied, 'Say what you will, I know it is he and no other!' This author was a witness to the conversation.

If, then, Seyfried's account of Beethoven's life and activities was mostly based upon hearsay, this was not the case with the master's music, which he heard performed with his own ears. Therefore his evaluations deserve our full attention, provided they are not based on the performance of a prejudiced musician, and provided they are not read out of context. But as for the criticisms of Handel, Mozart, Cheru-bini, and Weber attributed to our master, Seyfried gleaned some of them from here and there, and invented others. It is true that Beethoven had pronounced Handel the 'unrivalled master of all masters'; among the old composers he was the one best known to him. We have already seen elsewhere how little he knew of Johann Sebastian Bach. The reasons were twofold: first, the time, and second, the fact that in Vienna no one would have anything to do with 'Lutheran music'. It is also true

* For many years Seyfried lived in sin with a woman who had deserted her lawful husband, and regularly appeared with her in public places.

that Beethoven considered *Die Zauberflöte* the greatest of all German operas. His appreciation, however, was chiefly based on its inclusion of every musical form, from the *Lied* to the fugue, each in its ultimate perfection. When Seyfried makes Beethoven say of *Don Giovanni*: 'The sacred arts should never demean themselves to the folly of such a scandalous subject', he must have derived this from Beethoven's often-repeated remark that he could never have composed on such a subject.

Beethoven's statement that if he were ever to write a requiem he would copy much of Cherubini's note for note is an invention of Seyfried's. To think that Beethoven would take any foreigner's work as a model! Beethoven was not even acquainted with Cherubini's *Requiem*;[374] the only religious work by his great contemporary that he knew was the *Mass in D*. Otherwise he could not have expressed himself as he did in his letter of 1823 to Cherubini, the original of which is in the Royal Library in Berlin: '. . . for I value your works above all others for the theatre . . .' There is no mention in this letter of religious music. Everything Beethoven is supposed to have said about Carl Maria von Weber is absurd and of Seyfried's invention. 'Weber started to learn too late, and his art could never develop naturally of itself; instead, his whole efforts seemed to be bent upon appearing to be a genius.' Beethoven was fully aware that Weber had started composing operas at the age of twenty. All this evidence taken together is sufficient to show the worth of every aspect of Seyfried's efforts regarding Beethoven.

E.

BEETHOVEN AND KARL HOLZ

(See page 303)

When in the third period the relationship between Beethoven and Karl Holz was discussed, we referred to this Supplement and to two documents reproduced here that would help to clarify the position of both men. Before these documents are presented, however, a brief introduction is necessary.

Shortly after the reconciliation with his old friend Stephan von Breuning in 1826, Beethoven confided to him that he had recently complied with a request from Holz that he sign a letter entrusting to Holz the task of writing his biography. In all the confusion about him, he had not given the matter thoughtful consideration, he had been surprised by the request, etc.[375] When he had finished, Beethoven begged Breuning to go to Holz and retrieve the letter. Breuning refused categorically;

the matter was dropped until, at the time of the master's illness, he spoke with Breuning and this author about his biography, as was mentioned in the Introduction. Then Beethoven referred again to the letter and expressed doubt whether it was valid, since it had been written in pencil and in Holz's hand. He himself lacked the courage to approach Holz for the return of the letter.

Time and circumstances have worked in such a way that this document has come before this author's eyes. It happened in the following manner. While spending the summer months of 1850 in Heidelberg, I received a visit from the music director to the court of the Grand Duke, Dr. Gassner from Karlsruhe, a man whose acquaintance I had made at the Beethoven festival in Bonn in 1845. I had read in the papers that Gassner was intending to write a biography of Beethoven. The purpose of his visit was to discuss this proposed biography. He told me that he had collected material in Vienna, including papers acquired from Karl Holz. One of Holz's papers was Beethoven's authorization. He had, however, encountered great difficulties, for the material he had found concerned only isolated episodes in the great master's life and, as he lacked the information to fill in the gaps, he doubted that he would ever complete his task. Gassner showed me the original document of Beethoven's authorization to Holz, written on a sheet with a six-kreutzer stamp.[376] He also showed me the article of transfer from Holz to himself, written on the third page of the document. Dr. Gassner gave me permission to make a copy of each document. This estimable musician and writer died in 1851, having barely begun the project he had undertaken. All his papers, including the documents I have just mentioned, remained the property of his family.

A declaration made by Beethoven regarding his biography is so important that we cannot merely let the document lie ignored. We must bear in mind the time when this document was drawn up. It was at the end of the third period, about the same time as his nephew's catastrophe occurred; the master's whole life was in chaos, and he was deeply shaken and depressed. Because of this situation, it is the author's duty to quote this important document verbatim, since otherwise one would not know how to interpret it. In the same spirit we must include the article of transfer to Dr. Gassner, but in this case the reader must evaluate it as best he may. Let us remember two circumstances as we read these documents: first, Beethoven's oft-repeated complaint that he did not have a single friend in Vienna; and second, that his intimate friendship with Holz did not begin until 1825—as we can see from the Conversation Books that are in the Berlin Royal Library. And now the documents:

SUPPLEMENTS

It is with pleasure that I comply with the wishes of my friend Karl Holz by declaring that I consider him the person best qualified to undertake the eventual writing of my biography, assuming that anyone should want it, and I have the utmost confidence that he will convey to future generations, without distortion, what I have told him concerning my life.

Vienna, 30 August 1826   Ludwig van Beethoven

The original, which had been drawn up by Holz in pencil, had been written over in ink. Beethoven's signature is unquestionably authentic. How Holz had endeavoured to give this letter the appearance of truth, and how he had helped to document his qualifications as Beethoven's biographer, can be seen in the article of transfer written seventeen years later:

In relinquishing to my friend Dr. Gassner of Karlsruhe the enclosed declaration and the rights therein conferred upon me, I am confident that with his well-ordered fund of material he will at last be able to give the great master's admirers, who grow more numerous with each passing year, the most authentic and best documented biography possible. To this purpose I engage myself to put at Dr. Gassner's disposal for the writing of this work the not inconsiderable amount of data that I possess. Moreover, I shall use my influence with any of Beethoven's friends still living here who ever came into any kind of close contact with him, to the end that only new, hitherto unknown original data from the most reliable sources will be used, and that the errors in the deficient biographies already published will at last be corrected. I pledge my support all the more willingly, as Dr. Gassner has stated that he is prepared to give his completed manuscript to the publisher by the end of August 1844. I consider this to be easily feasible, for his two visits to Vienna have already put him in personal contact with most of the people who can be of service to him in this undertaking.

Vienna, 4 November 1843   Karl Holz
                                           Director of the *Concerts spirituels*

What would the master's old friends, Stephan von Breuning, Dr. Bach, Schuppanzigh, and others, say to Beethoven's declaration, no matter what circumstances had induced it, be it overhaste or surprise, as Beethoven claimed! If one considers it together with the fact that the dying master entrusted all his documents and family papers to Breuning and all his other letters to me (as we have seen in the Introduction); if, moreover, one compares the statements made in the above two documents with Gassner's remarks quoted earlier, then the whole situation seems as complex and as puzzling as all the other circumstances described in the biographical section for the year 1826, unless we can assume that 'what [Beethoven] had told him concerning [his] life' was an anticipation of fact.

There is another circumstance that is no less puzzling. We know that

E. BEETHOVEN AND KARL HOLZ

Holz was a member of the Schuppanzigh Quartet during its second period; that is, between its first rehearsal on 12 June 1823, after Schuppanzigh's return from Russia, and his death in March 1830. This period of seven years was sufficient to put Holz in possession of the tradition that was best preserved by this quartet in the performance of both Beethoven's and Haydn's works. What both masters themselves did in their own interest was stated in the biographical section (see pages 59 ff. *supra*). Of the members of the quartet who survived Schuppanzigh, Holz was the only one with the means to write down these traditions (in regard to tempo in general, changes of tempo in specific passages or whole sections, particular emphasis, etc.) and to save them—or at least their most important elements—from being lost. The unreasonable behaviour of the new generation of musicians as early as the beginning of the 1830's showed that it would soon destroy the spiritual character of all chamber music. This behaviour should have prompted those initiated in traditions of classical chamber works to use their better knowledge by constructing a dam against such a tendency.

In the quartets of Haydn and Beethoven, no one was equipped to do this more thoroughly or more comprehensively than Holz. He, however, remained silent. He did not even react to the appearance in Vienna of the Brunswick Quartet,[377] whose interpretations often completely negated the inherent character of the works performed, because they were ignorant of all information having to do with the classical tradition in general and with the works of their repertoire in particular. How was it possible for Holz to keep silent in the face of such performances? At that time his word could still have carried weight, for it would have found support among the many intelligent musicians of Schuppanzigh's time who were still alive then. But who would support it today, after a deluge of errors, now that we have come to the place where emancipation from the domination of tradition is regarded as the feat of a powerful spirit secure in the knowledge of its own superiority? In my own struggles against the ever more threatening evil—virtuosity for its own sake among instrumentalists and conductors—I publicly called upon Holz again and again to let his voice be heard. But he ignored my plea, was insensitive to the obligation that was his to intervene in this vital matter and thus to make manifest his memory of Beethoven. Truly a puzzling silence!

(Supplementary Remarks)

After the death of Karl Holz on 9 November 1858, the Viennese papers took great pains to publish wholly erroneous information concerning his relationship with Beethoven, and other particulars pertaining

477

to the two men. It is important that some of these reports should be refuted and others corrected. For instance, we read in the *Presse* of 16 November:

> It was Holz who, when Beethoven wrote the famous sonata opus 101 for the *Hammerklavier*,[378] helped him to devise the German musical expressions about which the reader might be interested to hear. Instead of 'aria' they used the word 'air-song' (Luftsang) or 'single-voice' (Einsang); 'bass' became 'bottom voice' (Grundsang); 'canon', 'running-in-circles piece' (Kreisfluchtstück); 'fantasy', 'mood-piece' (Launenspiel), etc.'

When the sonata opus 101 was published in 1816[379] (see Beethoven's letter to Frau von Ertmann, page 211), the eighteen-year-old Karl Holz was still sitting on the school benches of the university, and certainly had no notion that nine years later he would become a close friend of the man who had composed the sonata. Public journals as well as individual musicians had started long before 1816 to translate Italian musical terms into German, sometimes seriously, sometimes in jest. In Beethoven's Conversation Books for 1825 or 1826 there are notations of similar translations, which both Holz and the master's nephew claimed to have made up. Their only purpose was to amuse the master. But now the popular thing is to suppose that these jokes were really a serious endeavour, and even to parody Beethoven as an accomplice to this absurdity, forgetting that if he did give his assent it was merely to take part in a joke.[380]

The same Viennese paper published, accompanied by a commentary, an angry letter from Beethoven to Holz written from Baden on 24 August 1825 and having to do with business affairs. The following is an excerpt:

> It is all the same to me which hell-hound licks or gnaws my brain, since admittedly it must be so, but let us hope that the answer is not delayed too long. The hell-hound in Leipzig can wait, and meanwhile amuse himself in Auerbach's cellar with Mephistopheles, the editor of the Leipzig *Musikalische Zeitung*, who soon will be seized by the ears by Beelzebub, the chief of all devils.

The commentator explains that Mephistopheles was intended to mean Hofrat Rochlitz. But Beethoven had too much respect for Rochlitz (see Chapter III of the third period)[381] for him to have used such an epithet to designate this learned man, even considering the deviations he made in 1825 and 1826 from his usual estimations of persons and things. Moreover, in 1822 Rochlitz told Beethoven in my presence (we were in Baden at the time) that he expected to resign from the editorship of the musical journal, which in actual fact he did soon thereafter.[382]

F. WEBER AS A CRITIC OF BEETHOVEN

And finally the same Viennese paper refers to a notebook left by Holz:

that contains highly valuable information about music in Vienna and about Beethoven in particular. Yet we fear that not much public use can be made of the notebook, for most of it is written in a jargon and in a system of abbreviations known only to its author.

Can it be that this was the only object among Holz's possessions that had reference to Beethoven? If so, the puzzle we mentioned before is all the more difficult to solve. The solution must be left for time to discover.

F.

CARL MARIA VON WEBER AS A CRITIC OF BEETHOVEN

(See page 139)

In our discussion of the *Eroica* symphony we referred the reader to the present chapter of the supplement. In order to have the right perspective, the reader must bear in mind here that it is not of Carl Maria von Weber, the composer of the great operas *Freischütz, Euryanthe,* and *Oberon,* that we are speaking, but a young man of twenty-three who had just left the instruction of Abbé Vogler. Though his talent could be discerned in a few compositions, his name was entirely unknown beyond his own circle. We can be sure that even before Weber there had been apprentice musicians who found fault with great masters crowned with glory and who went so far as to ridicule them in their own particular manner; just as we can be sure that there have been lieutenants who have found fault with their general though he should be the victor in many battles. These young critics are always sure that they could have done the job better. Weber was not alone in his audacity, and we would be wrong if we thought ill of him for it. But the circumstances surrounding his criticism make it interesting and give it historical value, apart from the fact that the criticism itself represents the general reaction of the time to our master, or at least the reaction of a considerable proportion of his contemporaries. Let the facts, therefore, speak for themselves.

Among the papers left at the death of the music publisher Hans Georg Nägeli of Zürich there was a letter to him from Weber written from Mannheim on 21 May 1810. It was published by August Hitzschold of Zürich in the 20th issue of the *Niederrheinische Musik Zeitung* for 1853. The principal section reads as follows:

Sir:

Now that my situation has changed and I may once more devote myself solely to art, I am taking the first opportunity to act on Herr von Wangenheim's introduction and at the same time to thank you for your favourable opinion of my compositions. Yet I cannot refrain from touching on one point that is so important to me that I cannot allow it to pass without comment. You seem to find that in my quartet and *Caprice* I am an imitator of Beethoven, and though this might strike many as flattering, it is not at all pleasing to me. First of all, I detest everything that bears the stamp of imitation, and secondly, my views differ so radically from Beethoven's that I do not think I could ever stand on common ground with him. The fiery, indeed almost incredible, inventiveness of which he is possessed is accompanied by such confusion in the organization of his ideas that only his early compositions appeal to me, while the later ones seem to me nothing but utter chaos, an incomprehensible striving for novelty, from which there shines forth an occasional lightning-like bolt of genius, showing how great he might be if he would only rein in his exuberant fantasy.

Since I can naturally never boast of Beethoven's great genius, I believe that in respect to logic and rhetoric at least I can defend my music, and that every piece of music I write will make its own specific impression. For it seems to me that the only purpose of a musical performance is to spin a single idea into a coherent whole in which, even amidst the greatest complexity, unity and cohesiveness are maintained through a primary principle or theme. A rather amusing sidelight on this subject appeared in the *Morgenblatt*, No. 309, of 27 December 1809. It may serve to clarify further my position.

As luck would have it, along with the quartet that I had the honour of sending to you, only the *Caprice* had been copied out, so that you must think all my compositions bear the stamp of eccentricity. I hope, however, that if I may have the pleasure of sending you more of my work, you will not misconstrue my efforts for clarity, restraint, and feeling. . . .

Weber's reference to the 'amusing sidelight' in the *Morgenblatt*, which he had written himself though he did not acknowledge it, put me on the scent of at least one of his criticisms of Beethoven, of which I had already spoken in the first edition of this book. I did not have at hand the information with which to defend my statements against the flood of complaints and accusations that came from Dresden (see NZfM, 1840, No. 47), for all my efforts to find conclusive evidence had been in vain. Weber himself indicated the place where one of the objects of my search was to be found—and indeed, there it was! Here is yet another instance of how time is the best discoverer of hidden things and facts. No fewer than three similar discoveries concerning Beethoven followed one another in quick succession: Beethoven's authorization to Karl Holz in 1826, Prince Galitsin's promissory note to Beethoven from the same year, and Carl Maria von Weber's criticism, written in 1809, which reads as follows:

Fragment of a Musical Journey
Which Will Perhaps Take Place

Full of contentment over a symphony I had just finished to my satisfaction,

480

and with an excellent noon meal under my belt, I fell quietly asleep and in my dream found myself suddenly transported to a concert hall where all the instruments had come to life and were holding a great assembly under the chairmanship of the emotional and naïvely impertinent oboe. On my right was a group consisting of a viola d'amore, a basset horn, a viola da gamba, and a recorder, who were lamenting the good old days in plaintive tones; on my left Dame Oboe was conversing with a circle of young and old clarinets and flutes with and without the countless modern keys; in the middle sat the gallant pianoforte surrounded by a few sweet violins who had cultivated the style of Pleyel and Gyrowetz. Trumpets and horns caroused in one corner, while the piccolos and flageolets pierced the hall with their naïve, childish cries, in which Mama Oboe consistently discovered true, Jean-Paul-like artistic ability, raised to the highest expression of nature along the lines prescribed by Pestalozzi.

Everyone was enjoying himself thoroughly when all of a sudden the morose doublebass burst in at the door in the company of a couple of cellos, his cousins. He flung himself on to the conductor's stool so violently that the pianoforte and all the stringed instruments present let out an involuntary discordant gasp. 'No!' exclaimed the contrabass, 'The devil take anyone who makes us listen to compositions like that every day! I have just come from the rehearsal of a symphony by one of our newest composers, and though, as you know, I have a very strong and resilient constitution, I could stand it no longer, for within another five minutes my sound post would have fallen over and my life strings would have snapped. Rather than be forced to jump about like a rabid wild goat, rather than be turned into a violin to execute the non-ideas of the worthy composer, I will become a dance-band fiddle and earn my bread with Müller and Kauer dance pieces.'

First Cello (wiping the perspiration from his brow): *Cher père* is right. I am so fatigued! I can't remember being so provoked since we played the Cherubini operas.

All the instruments: Tell us! tell us!

Second Cello: Something like this can hardly be told, let alone listened to. For according to the principles with which my divine master, Romberg, imbued me, the symphony we have just played is a musical monstrosity, suited neither to the nature of any instrument nor to the execution of an idea nor to any other purpose except novelty and the desire to appear original. We were made to climb high like violins . . .

First Cello (interrupting): As if we couldn't do it just as well as they can!

(We will omit here the various speeches by the other instruments, almost every one of which contributed a sarcastic joke or a vulgar comment, and resume the text at a further point.)

All of a sudden the property man entered the hall, and all the instruments separated in fear, for they knew the rough hand that packed them up and took them to the rehearsals. 'Wait!' he shouted, 'Are you rebelling again? Just wait! Pretty soon they are going to set out the *Eroica* symphony by Beethoven, and after that I'd like to see which one of you can move a limb or a key!'

'Oh, no! Not that!' begged all the instruments.

'Give us an Italian opera; then at least one can get twenty winks from time to time,' said the viola.

'Fiddlesticks!' retorted the property man. 'You'll soon learn. In these enlightened times when all traditions are flung aside, do you think that a composer is going to deny his divine, his herculean inspiration just to please the likes of you? God forbid! It is no longer a question of clarity, preciseness, restraint, and emotion, as in the old days of artists like Gluck, Handel, and Mozart. No; listen to the recipe from the newest symphony that I have just received from Vienna, and then tell me what you think. First there is a slow section, full of short, disjointed ideas, none of which has anything to do with any other. Every quarter of an hour we hear three or four notes. It's exciting! Then there is a muffled roll of drums and a mysterious viola phrase, all adorned with the right number of rests and empty measures. Finally, after the audience has given up all hope of ever surviving the tension and arriving at the Allegro, everything bursts forth in a break-neck tempo, but care is taken that no principal theme emerges, and it is up to the listener to try and make one out. Modulations from one key to another abound, but they need not give you any trouble. Just remember Paer in *Fidelio*: all you have to do is make a chromatic run and stop on any note you like, and there is your modulation. Above all, every rule must be disregarded, for rules only fetter genius.'*

Suddenly a string snapped on the guitar hanging over my bed. I woke up terrified, for in my dream I was on the way to becoming a great composer of the new school—or a great fool.

Carl Marie

Such was the opinion that the apprentice artist Weber had conceived of the master Beethoven, just as the latter was climbing to the very peak of his artistic renown. At the time when 'Carl Marie' wrote this bit of satire for the *Morgenblatt*, our master had already published six symphonies, nine quartets, a long series of sonatas (up to and including the A major cello sonata opus 69), and other works of equal stature. The reader, having read the above specimen of conceit and malice, will not be surprised to hear of a second, far worse pronouncement in which Weber, after hearing our master's A major symphony, declared its composer ready for the madhouse. This evaluation, too, appeared in print, and sooner or later it will turn up as the others have. This is indeed a clear example of an apprentice artist's transcendental consciousness (to use Kant's phrase), which precedes all experience and leads to erratic fantasies like the ones we have just seen.

As I said in the earlier editions, the great composer of Vienna was not oblivious to these critical lucubrations and fantasies which their author referred to as 'amusing'. For a long time Baron von Lannoy, the

---

* This satire undoubtedly refers to the Introduction and the first movement of symphony No. 4 in B flat major.

well-known composer and writer, was suspected of having written the pieces, and it was not until 1820 that Weber was credited with all of them. Nevertheless, in October 1823 Beethoven received Weber cordially, as we related in the correct chronological context, and the only complaint that Weber could make about Beethoven was that he refused his request to make such changes in the score of his opera *Euryanthe* as he thought advisable, in order to redeem it from the unfortunate reception that its first performance had elicited. After looking at the score, Beethoven declared that Weber should have made his request before the opera had been performed, and that it was now too late for anyone but Weber himself to revise the opera; he should do as Beethoven himself had done with his *Fidelio*. We should remark in passing that later such revisions actually were made in *Euryanthe* by other persons.

Weber's criticisms become far more interesting when we compare the development of the principles of Weber the composer, as they are revealed in his great operas, with the statements he had made some ten years earlier. There emerges from such a comparison the moral that young musicians should avoid publishing their opinions of works they do not understand, lest sooner or later they themselves practise what once offended them, or that they even surpass others in this practice—as we can see, not always to our satisfaction, when we compare Weber's works, especially his operas, with the works of our master (with the exception of some of his later compositions).

G.

TWO MEASURES IN THE SCHERZO OF THE C MINOR SYMPHONY THAT ARE THE SUBJECT OF CONTROVERSY AND CONTINUING DISAGREEMENT

At the Lower Rhine Music Festival held at Aachen in 1846, the conductor, Felix Mendelssohn, announced the discovery of a letter from Beethoven to the publisher of the C minor symphony, Breitkopf & Härtel, which referred to two redundant measures in the orchestral parts of the Scherzo that had just been printed, and called them 'a great blunder'.[383] The two measures occur at the return of the principal theme after the section in C major. The passage in question is found on page 108 of the score and, with the preceding measures on page 107, reads as follows:

Ex. 22

The two questioned measures are those marked with dots. We see that at this point the master did not want the notes held but separated as in the following two measures. Thus the two measures with half notes should not be there at all. This is the great blunder!

It was inevitable that Mendelssohn's information, announced thirty-six years after the symphony had been published, should arouse great excitement. The first reaction on the part of most musicians was disbelief; some conductors even replied immediately that the two measures were no error, and that they had no intention of deleting them. I was asked many times if I had ever heard Beethoven himself say anything on the subject. I could only answer that I never had.

Even the musical press took sides for and against the two measures. Although no one had objected to them before, proof of their falsity was now presented. The story excited no less interest in Paris. Hector Berlioz declared himself for the correctness of the passage in the *Journal des Débats*. Director Habeneck told me he was not going to give up the denounced measures; in fact, that he could not give them up without stirring up a storm in the Conservatoire orchestra. The most amazing reaction was that the price of cotton in America went up considerably as a result of this international controversy. At any rate, no announcement has ever caused such consternation in the musical world, for an open revolt broke out against the noble creator of the work for having put a curse on these two measures. In short, this battle, waged so obstinately on all sides, had much in common with battles among philologists concerning such all-important matters as the correct reading of a particular word, the placing of a comma, or the like. Let us then give the necessary amount of space to a discussion of this difficulty.

There can be no doubt about the existence of Beethoven's letter, probably written in 1809, to the publisher of the symphony, though it has been questioned and a published facsimile has been demanded.[384] Perhaps the master later, or even immediately, changed his mind and decided to accept the 'blunder'; perhaps he decided that it produced a humorous effect, and therefore should be retained. At any rate, he forgot to make any further protest to the publishers. Between the time of this symphony's publication and the master's death—a full eighteen years— it was often rehearsed and performed in his presence without his ever saying a word about the passage,[385] just as in the case of the General Pause in the first movement (page 36 of the score), which is also the subject of much debate at present. Yet we heard Seyfried say how Beethoven required everything to be performed 'precisely, within a hair's breadth of what he had written'. How could he have allowed the measures in question to remain intact if he had not changed his mind about them?

He spoke with exceptional clarity about his intentions when he reviewed this and other works with the directors of the *Concerts spirituels,* which were to give new life to several of his works. He did the same with me in 1823 for the C minor symphony and others as well, but he never mentioned the two measures. Tradition makes it evident that in this case the master simply changed his mind. How could his sharp scrutiny pass over this 'great blunder' as he read through the full score which had just then (at the beginning of the 1820's) been published for the first time? This circumstance is especially significant.

And finally, the question can be decided once and for all if the reader will consider the following. If one examines Beethoven's manuscripts, especially those of major works, one is aware not infrequently of the composer's difficulty in working out the rhythm of certain passages. One may find one, two, four, or even more measures crossed out, and in the middle of the page or at the very top comments written in such as 'omit', or 'good—leave in'. If one compares these corrected manuscripts with the printed versions, one sees that the phrases that were crossed out and then recognized as good were adopted note for note. I have such manuscripts in my possession. Knowing that this was his method of working, and considering the two critical measures, it does not seem at all unlikely that the composer originally wrote them, then doubted that they should be there, but finally decided that they were good and that the rhythm of this phrase should remain in its original form.

When critics say that apart from the violation of rhythmic regularity there is another error here, for the raised seventh F sharp in the fourth measure is not resolved at once but must wait for the seventh measure to go to G, a violation of the rules of harmony—to such critics we may answer: as for the rhythm in general, it constitutes one of the particular attractions of Beethoven's music. What delightful handling of rhythm we find, for instance, in the first movement of the C minor symphony! What a wealth of variety in the rhythmic patterns throughout the whole work! And yet this variety is far surpassed in several of the sonatas for piano solo.

In addition to the rhythmic imbalance of the phrase in question, the extension of the phrase has been offered as a reason for its not having been intended by the master, but for its being a copyist's mistake. But we see the motif that first occupied eight measures extended to ten when it is repeated after the *fermata* on the dominant. Moreover, the tonic at the beginning of this excerpt is held for a full measure, producing a phrase with an odd number of measures (11), an intentional variation of the motif. Extended rhythms developing a fragment of the melody are in fact commonplace with Beethoven. What but rhythmic extension is the passage that forms the transition between the Scherzo and the Finale of the C minor symphony, which Oulibicheff calls 'a kind of frightful caterwauling and dissonance that tears at even the least sensitive ear' (!!)? As for the so-called mistaken leading note F sharp, the strict grammarian may find it correct if it is possible for his ear to retain through the flow of conversation the sound of the first F sharp.

Perhaps to quiet the doubters completely, it should be added that immediately after the incident in Aachen, the critic Lewinsky, who had for many years followed musical events in Vienna, began to question musicians of Beethoven's era who were still alive. His investigation, the findings of which were published in the *Wiener Zeitschrift* in 1846, disclosed that not one musician who had taken part in the *Concerts spirituels* could remember any change made in the printed orchestral parts. This is borne out by copies dated from that time that are still in existence.

H.

PAPERS WITH REFERENCE TO THE LEGAL CONTROVERSY WITH THE MECHANIC MAELZEL

(See page 206)

1.

Deposition

Of my own volition I composed for Maelzel, without honorarium, a composition for his panharmonicon, the *Battle* symphony. After he had had this for a while he brought me the score, the engraving[386] of which had already been started, and asked that it be arranged for full orchestra. I had already conceived the idea of a battle piece that would not be adaptable for his panharmonicon. We agreed to give this work and several others I had written in a concert for the benefit of the veterans.[387]

At this time I was beset by severe financial embarrassments. I was alone here in Vienna, abandoned by the whole world, awaiting a change for the better, and Maelzel offered me fifty gold ducats. I took them and told him that I would repay him here or, if I did not go with him to London, I would give him the work to take along and would direct an English publisher to pay him the fifty ducats.

The concerts took place, and meanwhile Herr Maelzel's plan and character first showed themselves. Without my permission, he caused to be placed on the posters the statement that the work was his property. Though indignant, he was forced to have these posters taken down. Then he placed upon them, 'Out of friendship, for his journey to London'. I consented to this, since I believed that I still retained the freedom to stipulate the conditions under which I would let him have the work. I remember having quarrelled violently with him during the printing of the posters, but the time was too short—I was still writing the work. In the heat of inspiration, wholly absorbed in my work, I gave little thought to Maelzel.

Immediately after the first concert at the University Hall, I was told from all sides by trustworthy men that Maelzel was broadcasting the word that he had lent me 400 ducats in gold. I forthwith had the following statement inserted in the newspapers, but the writers for the papers did not insert it, since Maelzel stood well with all of them. Immediately after the first concert I gave Maelzel back his fifty ducats and told him that since I had come to know his character here, I would not travel with him—righteously angered at the fact that without asking me he had placed on the placards the statement that all arrangements for the concert had been badly handled, and also that his own unpatriotic character had shown itself in the following statement: 'I [obscenity] upon L[ondon?] if only they say in London that people here paid ten gulden; I did this not for the wounded but for ——'; also, that I would give him the work for London only upon conditions that I would communicate to him.

Then he asserted that it was a gift of friendship, and had this statement published in the newspapers after the second concert, without in any way asking me about it. Since Maelzel is a crude fellow, entirely without education or culture, one can imagine how he comported himself towards me during this time and thus constantly increased my wrath. And who would force a gift of friendship upon such a person?

I was now offered the opportunity of sending the work to the Prince Regent. It was thus wholly impossible to give Maelzel the work unconditionally. He then came to you and made proposals. He was told on what day he should appear to receive the answer, but he did not come, left the city, and had the work performed in Munich. How did he obtain it? Theft was impossible. Thus, Herr Maelzel had some of the parts at his house for a few days, and from these he had the whole work reconstructed by a vulgar musical craftsman, and is now hawking about the world with it.

Herr Maelzel promised me some ear-trumpets. To encourage him, I arranged the *Victory* symphony for his panharmonicon. His ear-trumpets were finally ready, but they were of no use to me. For this slight service Herr Maelzel would have one believe that after I had arranged the *Victory* symphony for full orchestra and composed the *Battle* for it, I should make him sole owner of this work. If we assume that I was in some small degree obliged to him for the ear-trumpets, this obligation is cancelled by the fact that with the *Battle*, compiled from parts stolen from me or made up in a mangled condition, he has made for himself at least 500 gulden CM. Thus he has paid himself off.

He had the audacity to say here that he had the *Battle*; indeed, he showed it in writing to a number of people, but I did not believe it, and was correct to the extent that the whole work was not by me but had been assembled by someone else. Moreover, the honour that he claims for himself alone might be reward enough. The War Council did not refer to me in any way, yet everything that was presented at the two concerts was by me.[388] If, as Herr Maelzel says, he delayed his journey to London because of the *Battle*, this was said only in jest: Herr Maelzel stayed here until he had completed his job of patchwork [?], since the first attempts were unsuccessful.

Beethoven m. p.

2.

*Explanation and Appeal to the Musicians
of London by Ludwig van Beethoven*
(See page 207)

Herr Maelzel, who is at present in London, on his journey thither performed my *Victory* symphony and Wellington's *Battle at Vittoria* in Munich, and according to reports will also give it in London, just as he planned to do in Frankfurt. This induces me to declare publicly that I never and in no way made over or surrendered the above-mentioned works to Herr Maelzel, that no one possesses a copy of them, and that the only one that I gave out I sent to His Royal Highness the Prince Regent of England.

The performance of these works is accordingly either a fraud upon the public, since according to the explanation given herein he does not possess them, or if he does possess them it is an encroachment upon my rights since he acquired them in an illegal manner.

But even in the latter case the public will be deceived, since what

Herr Maelzel offers it under the title 'Wellington's Victory at Vittoria and Victory symphony' must obviously be a spurious or mutilated work, since he never received anything of these works from me except a single part for a few days.

This suspicion becomes a certainty when I add the assurance of musicians of this city, whose names I have been authorized to give if necessary, that at the time of his departure from Vienna he told them that he possessed this work and that he showed them parts for it, which however, as I have already proved, could only be mutilated and spurious.

Whether Herr Maelzel is capable of doing me such an injury is ascertained by the fact that he announced himself in the public papers as the sole entrepreneur for my concerts that took place here in Vienna for the benefit of the soldiers wounded in the war, at which only my works were performed, without mention of my name.

I therefore call upon the musicians of London not to allow such an injustice to me, their colleague in art, by a performance of the 'Battle of Vittoria and the Victory symphony' arranged by Herr Maelzel, and to keep the London public from being deceived in the aforementioned manner.

Vienna, 25 July 1814

3.

Certificate

We, the undersigned, certify in the interests of truth (and can if necessary testify under oath) that there were several conferences between Herr Louis van Beethoven and the Court Mechanic Herr Maelzel, both of this city, at the home of the undersigned Dr. Carl v. Adlersburg, at which the first of the musical compositions, the *Battle of Vittoria*, and the journey to England were discussed. At these conferences, Herr Maelzel made various proposals to Herr van Beethoven to secure for himself the above-named work or at least the rights for its first performance. Since, however, Herr Maelzel did not appear at the last appointed meeting, nothing came of the matter, the proposals that he made to the former not having been accepted. In witness thereof, our signatures.

Vienna, 20 October 1814

> Joh. Freiherr v. Pasqualati,
>   k. k. patented wholesaler
>
> Carl Edler von Adlersburg
>   Court and trial attorney and
>   k. k. patented notary

SUPPLEMENTS

I.

THREE LETTERS FROM BEETHOVEN TO BETTINA
(See page 157)

1.

Vienna, 11 August 1810

Dearest Bettine:[389]

No lovelier spring than this one: that I say and feel too, for I have made your acquaintance. You yourself must have seen that in company I am like a frog on the sand, that flounders about this way and that and cannot get away until a kind-hearted Galathea puts it back into the mighty sea. I was indeed high and dry, dearest Bettine: you surprised me at a moment when ill-humour had complete control of me, but truly it vanished upon your appearance: I realized that you were from another world than this absurd one to which, with the best of wills, one cannot give a hearing.

I am a wretched fellow, and yet I complain about others!! Surely you can forgive me, with your good heart that can be seen from your eyes and your good sense that resides in your ears—at least, your ears know how to flatter when they listen. My ears, alas, are unfortunately a barrier through which I cannot easily have friendly communication with others. Otherwise, perhaps, I might have had more confidence in you. As it is, I could understand only the wide, understanding look of your eyes, which made upon me an impression I shall never forget. Dear Bettine, dearest girl! Who understands Art? With whom can one converse about this great goddess? How dear to me are the few days when we were chatting together, or rather, corresponding! I have preserved all the bits of paper that bear your wise, dear, dearest replies.[390] Thus I have to thank my bad ears that the best part of this fleeting conversation is written down.

Since you have gone I have had melancholy hours, dark hours in which nothing can be done. After you were gone, for fully three hours I paced the Schönbrunn Walk and the Bastion, but no angel met me there who seized me as you have, my Angel. Forgive me, dearest Bettine, for this deviation from the usual key, but I must have intervals of this kind to unburden my heart.

You have written to Goethe about me, haven't you? Would that I might put my head in a bag so that I might hear and see nothing of what goes on in the world, for you, dearest Angel, will hardly meet me there. But may I not receive a letter from you? Hope sustains me—indeed, it sustains half the world—and all my life I have had hope as my neighbour; otherwise, what would have become of me?

I send you herewith a copy in my own hand of *Kennst du das Land* as a remembrance of the hour in which I first met you.[391] I am also sending the other song, which I composed after I parted from you, dear, dearest heart:

> *Heart, my heart, what now will happen?*
> *What distresses you so sore?*
> *I would think you were a stranger,*
> *Hardly know you any more.*[392]

Yes, dearest Bettine, reply to this letter. Write me what it is that is going to happen to me, since my heart has become such a rebel. Write to your most faithful friend

Beethoven

2.

Vienna, 10 February 1811[393]

Dear, dear Bettine:[394]

I have already received two letters from you, and see from your letter to Toni[395] that you still remember me, indeed much too favourably. I carried your first letter around with me throughout the summer, and it often made me happy. Even if I do not write to you often and although you never see me, I write a thousand, a thousand times a thousand letters in my thoughts. Even if I had not read what you said about it, I could imagine how you are getting along in Berlin with that cosmopolitan rabble: talk and chatter about art, but without deeds!!!!! The best description of this is in Schiller's poem *Die Flüsse*, where the River Spree is speaking.[396]

You are getting married, dear Bettine, or already have been,[397] and I have not been able to see you even once beforehand. May all the happiness with which marriage blesses the married flow upon you and your husband. What shall I tell you about myself? 'Pity my fate,' I cry with Johanna.[398] If a few more years of life are spared to me, I shall thank the all-encompassing Deity on high for that as well as for all else, weal or woe.

If you write to Goethe about me, seek out all the words that will tell him of my deepest reverence and admiration. I am just on the point of writing to him myself regarding *Egmont*, which I have set to music purely out of love for his poems which make me happy.[399] But who can sufficiently thank a great poet, the most precious jewel of a nation?

491

No more now, dear, good B. This morning I did not get home until four o'clock from a bacchanal at which I really was forced to laugh much, so that today I shall have to weep almost as much. Boisterous jollity often drives me powerfully back within myself.

Many thanks to Clemens for his kindly interest. As regards the cantata, the matter is not of sufficient importance to us here; it is different, however, in Berlin.[400] As for affection, the sister has so large a share of it that not much will be left for the brother. Will that do for him?

Now farewell, dear, dear B. I kiss you [illegible word] on the forehead, and thus impress upon it as with a seal all my thoughts for you. Write soon, soon and often, to your friend

Beethoven

[on the outside of the letter] Beethoven lives on the Mölkerbastei in the Pasqualati house.

3.

Teplitz, August 1812[401]

Dear, kind Bettine:

Kings and princes, it is true, can make professors and privy councillors, and can hang on ribbons of titles and orders, but they cannot make great men, spirits that rise above the rabble of the world. That they should not try to do, and accordingly such men must be held in respect. When two men like Goethe and me come together, then these great gentlemen must perceive what greatness means in such as we.

On the way home yesterday we met the entire imperial family. From a distance we saw them approaching, and Goethe slipped away from me to stand to one side; say what I would, I could not induce him to advance a step further. I pulled my hat down on my head, buttoned my overcoat, and with folded arms pushed through the thickest part of the crowd. Princes and sycophants drew up in line; Archduke Rudolph took off his hat; the Empress was the first to greet me. Persons of rank know me. To my great amusement, I saw the procession file past Goethe; hat in hand, he stood at the side, bowing deeply. Afterwards I gave him a thorough dressing-down; I showed him no mercy and reproached him for all his sins, most of all against you, dearest Bettine. We had just been talking about you. God! had I been able to spend as much time with you as he has, I know that I could have produced many, many more great works. A musician is also a poet; by a pair of eyes he can feel himself suddenly transported into a lovelier world where greater minds join in company with him and set him mighty tasks.

All kinds of ideas came into my mind when I came to know you in the little observatory during the splendid May rain that was also so fruitful for me. Then the most beautiful themes glided from your eyes into my heart, themes that will enchant the world when Beethoven can no longer conduct.

If God will only spare me a few more years, I must see you again, dear, dear Bettine: so calls within me the voice that never errs. Even spirits can love one another, and I shall always pay court to yours. Your praise is to me the most precious in the whole world. I gave Goethe my opinion of how praise affects people like ourselves—and that we wish to be listened to with the intellect by our equals. Emotion is only for womankind (forgive me for saying this); with a man, music must strike fire from his mind. Ah, dearest child! how long it has been that we are of one mind about everything!!!

There is nothing so good as possessing a beautiful, kind soul that is recognized in every action, and in the presence of which nothing need be concealed. One must be what one is if one wishes to be recognized as such: the world must recognize one; it is not always unjust. To me, that is of no importance, for I have a higher goal.

I hope to find a letter from you in Vienna. Write soon, soon—a long letter. I shall be there in a week; the court leaves tomorrow, and today there is one more performance.[402] The Empress rehearsed her role with him.* He and his duke want me to perform some of my music. I have refused them both. They are both mad about Chinese porcelain; hence, there is need for indulgence, since common sense has lost the upper hand. I shall not conform to their silly whims; I shall not take part in absurdities at public cost with princes who never pay debts of that kind.

Farewell, farewell, darling. Your last letter lay for a whole night on my heart and comforted me there. To a musician, everything is permitted.

God! how I love you!

Your most faithful friend and deaf brother,

Beethoven

K.†

DRAFT OF A LETTER TO CHERUBINI (1823)[403]
(See pp. 241, 345)

Most highly esteemed Sir:

With great delight I take this opportunity of approaching you in writing. I have often done so in spirit, for I value your works above all others for the theatre. The world of art must lament that for a long

* Editor's note. This presumably means Goethe.
† Editor's note. There was no supplement J in the original text.

time, at least in our Germany, no new theatrical work of yours has appeared. However highly your other works are treasured by true connoisseurs, it is still a great loss to art not to possess any new product of your great spirit for the theatre. True art is immortal, and the true artist finds deep satisfaction in the great products of genius. Thus I too am delighted whenever I hear of a new work of yours, and I take even more interest in such a work than I do in my own—in short, I honour and love you. Were it not that my persistent ill-health makes it impossible for me to see you in Paris, with what extraordinary joy would I discuss matters of art with you! . . . Do not think that because I am about to ask a favour of you, this is merely an introduction to it. I hope and am confident that you would not attribute such petty sentiments to me.

I have just completed a great solemn mass, and it is my intention to send it to the courts of Europe, since for the time being I shall not publish it in engraved form. Accordingly, I have sent through the French embassy here an invitation to His Majesty the King of France to subscribe to this work, and I am convinced that the King himself would certainly accept it upon your recommendation.[404] My critical situation demands that I do not direct my prayers to heaven alone as one usually does, but that I must direct them here below as well to secure the necessities of life. Whatever may come of my request to you, I shall always love and honour you, and you will always remain the contemporary that I most admire. If you wish to give me extreme happiness, I would ask you to write me a few lines, which would be a great comfort to me. Art unites all the world—how much more, true artists—and perhaps you will do me the honour of counting me among that number.

With the greatest esteem,

Your friend and servant,
Beethoven[405]

L.

THE THEME OF THE FINALE OF THE QUARTET IN C SHARP MINOR, OPUS 131

(See page 265)

In the third period we spoke of the many experiments Beethoven often had to make before he was satisfied that his themes or melodies were correct and perfectly suited to all his intentions in the working out of a particular movement. An example of this has been provided in a facsimile: the principal theme (on Schiller's ode) of the fourth movement of the ninth symphony.

L. FINALE OF THE QUARTET IN C SHARP MINOR

An even more interesting one is the following, the theme of the Finale of the quartet in C sharp minor opus 131, which is given exactly as it stands in his sketchbook for this work. Like so many others, this sketchbook is preserved in the Royal Library in Berlin. There are no fewer than seven sketches of this theme, perhaps more than for any other one of the master's compositions. He even tried it in different rhythms: No. 5 shows the theme in $\frac{2}{4}$ time. The correctness of individual notes and even of bar lines cannot be guaranteed, for all Beethoven's sketches are evidence of the great haste in which he jotted down his ideas. Other marks and signs also appear, sometimes more, sometimes fewer than necessary.

Ex. 23

Nº 1 "Finale C# minor"

Nº 2

SUPPLEMENTS

Nº 7

M.

THE *SONATE PATHÉTIQUE*

(See pages 69, 72)

Ex. 24

The opening chords in the first, second, and third measures should be struck firmly, then allowed to die away almost completely. The long and short notes that follow are played with a light touch and in a free rhythm. The dotted sixteenth-note rest in the bass in all these measures should be given somewhat more than its full value. The last three chords of the third measure are the first to be played in a firm, even tempo, which continues to the *fermata* in the fourth measure. The last three notes of this measure are to be played freely, in the way that an Italian singer treats every *fermata*. The composer's directions merely ensure a definite measure length without imposing on the performer the duration of the notes any more than the poet will dictate to the orator or actor the metre of his lines. Both are determined only by the cultivated taste of the singer, musician, or orator.

The tender *cantilena* that begins in the fifth measure and its sharply contrasting *fortissimo* move for four measures in strict rhythm. The octave F in the ninth measure and the C in the tenth are to be held somewhat longer, and the groups of notes that follow them are to be breathed out gently, rounding out the phrase gracefully. The short notes must be given special significance in these *cantilena* phrases in order not to spoil their character. They must, therefore, be played softly and rather broadly. Obviously, this does not apply to the opposing *fortissimo* phrases.

Repeated experience has taught me that it is difficult even for well-trained musicians not to play any piece of music like clockwork, no matter how deeply the composer felt it, no matter what indications he has given for a correct understanding of its meaning. The $\frac{4}{4}$ time signature has thus misled performers by making it impossible for them to give uninhibited expression to their feelings. The change of the time signature in this introduction to $\frac{2}{4}$ has sometimes had beneficial results, for it entirely removes the thirty-second notes from the pampered eye.[406] We saw in the preceding supplement on the theme of the C sharp minor quartet how Beethoven attempted various metres to achieve the desired rhythmic and thematic pattern for the whole movement. The performing artist, therefore, should not shrink from making similar experiments, at least with certain passages, to achieve a correct rendering of a great work. To find a perfect version of difficult passages, he may in his preparation sometimes have to make quite bizarre experiments.

M. THE *SONATE PATHÉTIQUE*

Subsidary Theme of the First Movement Allegro

Though in the introduction the two principles (or opposites) were only hinted at, they appear in this subsidiary theme in a more urgent form, repeated together in close succession. Even the most humdrum piano teacher cannot fail to recognize a particular significance in this theme, once he has heard it played by an artist who has thought it through carefully. The markings in the version given above make the necessary shadings of tone unmistakable. The frequently repeated mark, **V**, indicates not merely a stronger accent but also a short pause on the note so marked, a pause not be be observed by the left-hand accompaniment, which moves along in strict rhythm to the last measure of the phrase. (See the concluding chapter of C. P. E. Bach's textbook, II 227.)

In the second movement (Adagio) of the *Pathétique*, many dynamic markings are lacking in all editions. In the principal theme, the opening *piano* rises to a *mezzo forte* in the sixth measure, and falls back in the eighth measure with a *diminuendo* to *piano*. The emotional sensitivity of the performer will enable him to fill in the missing markings with no difficulty. A holding back of the tempo, for instance, in the lyrical section in F minor between the 17th and 23rd measures, and the stepping up of the tempo from the 37th measure until the return of the principal theme in A flat major are, as in every other *adagio* movement, among the most important requirements if the performance is to carry out the spirit of the composition (see pp. 68, 78, 417). Only cultivated musical taste will determine the degree of holding back and acceleration, and even then only after repeated experiments. Emotion alone is not reliable. Moreover, this Adagio has many examples of both the rhetorical pause and the caesura. Such a pause is essential before the beginning of the F minor Cantilena, and there must be a caesura before the A flat major section in the 37th measure.

In the third movement, the Rondo, none of the necessary performance markings are missing, if one thinks only of the usual signs. But the thoughtful pianist will find additional places where he will use special devices to enhance the musical expressiveness. To give directions for a humorous playing of the principal theme of this movement, as Beethoven himself used to play it, resists all efforts with words and signs.

Probably the honourable 'piano masters' will continue to regard this and all the sonatas of the first period and most of the second as 'minor sonatas' simply because they contain no passages calculated to break the pianist's fingers, and for this reason they will continue to give them to their pupils to murder whether they have any talent or not. I have no

Ex. 25

illusions that all I have said will improve the situation, for anyone who does not want to learn, or who does not have the capacity to do a thing better, is beyond the reach of even the most conclusive proof. I have had plenty of opportunity to observe the results of their blowing the way the wind blows, both in my own experience and from the experience of others. Let me just remark that the world has not yet had to witness Schiller's great lyrical poems taught to primary-school pupils. But in the case of musical compositions that are as lofty and as difficult as those poems and that make the greatest demands on the performer, the situation is different. Of course it is, for here one sees only symbols that stand for notes. In this practice we see not only the deplorably low education of most of those dealing with teaching the young; it throws a heavy shadow over the intelligence, so highly acclaimed by our would-be critics, of our entire musical generation.

N.

THE INTRODUCTION OF BEETHOVEN'S MUSIC IN PARIS[407]

This historical outline is based on comments made in the Musical Section, page 431. Once again we must realize that without the Paris Conservatoire the whole body of our master's piano music, which had already begun to disappear from concert programmes by about 1815 owing to the advancing flood of the modern style, would never have been revived. The supplement to the earlier edition of my book contained a detailed article devoted to this event so important in the history of music. The article included a critical appraisal of the extraordinary services performed by this Paris institution. Here, however, I shall limit my comments to historical facts and show the phases through which Beethoven's music passed until the establishment of the Société des Concerts became a reality.

I should like first to name the men who, after many years of efforts against all sorts of obstacles, succeeded in obtaining the acceptance of Beethoven's instrumental music in the Conservatoire. This contribution was made above all by three Germans who enjoy a good reputation in the world of music: Urhan, Sina, and Stockhausen. The first, a native of Montjoie in the administrative district of Aachen, was taken to Paris as a boy by the Empress Josephine and placed in the Conservatoire because of his exceptional talent. The reader has heard Sina's name as one of the members of the Rasumovsky Quartet in Vienna. Stockhausen was a harp virtuoso and, like Sina, had taken up permanent residence in Paris.

It is to these three men that the author owes his knowledge of the following information, which has been corroborated by Habeneck, Tulou, Philipp, and other co-founders of the Société des Concerts.

Until 1806 Beethoven's name was unknown in Paris except to a few players of quartets, including Habeneck and Philipp. What Cherubini had to say in Paris about the German composer's orchestral works, with which he had become acquainted in Vienna, did nothing to further their reputation as we have already said. Yet even these uncomplimentary remarks led to an experiment with the first symphony, which was in itself of benefit to the work. In 1807 the AmZ (IX (1807) 516) carried a brief report from Paris about the Conservatoire. It read:

Since his return from Vienna, Cherubini, with the collaboration of several faithful and highly estimable teachers, has imparted to the zeal of the Conservatoire students not only new impetus, but a whole new direction—towards a more earnest, a greater, a more rigorous character. . . . The Mozart symphonies had been tried before, but they had never found favour with the public. Now Cherubini has sought to make them more familiar by giving them the introduction they deserve. They have been tried again, and this time they are beginning to please the public, especially since the young musicians playing these symphonies, having studied them with their teachers, performed them admirably.

A few weeks ago a similar attempt was made with the Beethoven symphonies, and the first received a masterly performance. Since this work is very lively and easy to understand and since it is so pleasing in mood, some applause was to be expected, but no one anticipated such a huge success as this. . . . Now we are looking forward to more Mozart symphonies, and also to Beethoven's second, though this will certainly offer more difficulties because of its harmonic complexity and because it is considerably longer than the works that one is accustomed to hearing here. Nevertheless, once our enthusiasm has been aroused, to what heights will it not aspire!

The correspondent had been right in anticipating problems. The enthusiasm generated by the first symphony foundered when it came to the length of some movements of the second, and the work was dropped. For a time no one thought of trying any of the others.

The occupation of Paris by the Allied Powers in 1815 brought to the French capital a Prussian commissariat officer by the name of Paris who gave the next impetus in the direction of Beethoven's instrumental music. An ardent music-lover and a performer himself, this officer made the acquaintance of a number of German musicians, including Urhan and Stockhausen. At his recommendation, Stockhausen ordered the *Eroica* symphony to be sent from Germany and, accompanied by Urhan, took it to Habeneck,* who by then was conductor of the students'

* Habeneck's father had come from Mannheim, but Habeneck himself was born in Paris and did not know a word of German.

concerts at the Conservatoire. It was a long time before he decided to rehearse the new work. At the end of the first movement everyone burst out laughing. After the second it was the same thing, and it took no little persuasion to induce the orchestra to play through the remaining movements. Thus Beethoven's music seemed to be condemned to death as far as Paris audiences were concerned; and since Habeneck himself had lost heart, and may have had too little insight in the matter, all further attempts were abandoned. Time had to wait for a more cultured society or for another foreign impulse before renewed efforts could be dared. In the meantime the works already introduced were made the subject of ridicule, though it happened occasionally that one movement or another was used as a kind of filler in a programme. Beethoven heard that in Paris his music had been turned into quadrilles and dances.

In about 1820 Sina came to Paris and decided to make his home there. The outrageous position of all Beethoven's music prompted him, after long deliberation with Urhan, to make another, perhaps final approach to Habeneck. In his opinion the next attempt should be made with the C minor symphony, the existence of which was unknown, even to the most prominent men of the Conservatoire. A devious means was suggested in order at least to arouse Habeneck's curiosity about the work. An anonymous letter was sent to him giving various comments about the C minor symphony which could have been written only by Sina, who had studied this work under the master's personal supervision. Habeneck caught fire and wished to see the score, which Urhan fortunately found in the Royal Library. After considerable hesitation, the symphony was rehearsed. Its reception was favourable! It was not until one of the subsequent rehearsals that the truth began to dawn in the minds of the musicians. Without losing any time, other symphonies that had likewise remained unknown were tried, and lo! to everyone's surprise they were as well received as the C minor!

This is how Beethoven's instrumental music was introduced into the Paris Conservatoire. As it became more familiar, its success grew, until it produced in all the musicians a degree of enthusiasm and excitement never before experienced. The musicians who took part in this discovery still remembered it with noble pride in 1841 when I heard them say: 'Beethoven taught us the poetry of music. His compositions awakened in us the first consciousness of the dignity and significance of our profession, and when we had gained some understanding of him, we recognized our obligation to make his music heard and known. He is our joy, but also our despair, if we hope to emulate him.'

Everyone sensed the necessity of forming a permanent society for the realization of so high a purpose, yet obstacles of all kinds delayed its establishment until the news of Beethoven's death eliminated them all. In January 1828, nine months after the master's passing, the Société des Concerts met for the first time. The world-wide fame of its performances makes any words in its praise superfluous. Even since the death of Habeneck, who was the soul of the organization, this creation of his remains in spirit the foremost institution in the world.

At this point it will be of interest to the reader to learn how it has gone with our master's music in England. As early as 1812 the first six symphonies were taken into the repertoire of the Philharmonic Society in London, and all of them enjoyed an equally enthusiastic reception. As for the *Pastoral*, it is noteworthy that this symphony aroused less offence in England than anywhere else, and after a few performances it was fully appreciated. It is not so surprising that there were some who criticized the third, fourth, fifth, and sixth symphonies, and valued only the first two, when we consider the time, for as late as the 1850's Oulibi-cheff recognized only the first symphony as worthy of praise. In his biography of Mozart he calls this symphony 'admirable' for the reason that he finds in it Mozart's style. In 1816 an English general by the name of Ham was in Vienna, supposedly on behalf of the Philharmonic Society, and offered our master a commission to compose for this society two symphonies in the style of his first and second. I leave it to the reader to guess with what distaste this message was received.[408] Very soon, however, after personal enquiries had been made in London, Beethoven received a message saying that the general had only expressed his personal wish, and that he was known as a Mozart enthusiast exclusively.

O.

A REVIEW OF BEETHOVEN'S PRIVATE LIBRARY AND THE PUBLIC AUCTION OF HIS MUSICAL *NACHLASS* IN NOVEMBER 1827[409]

Anyone who has read what we said on page 378 about the master's library and compared it with what was said on page 41 of *Beethovens Studien* under 'Legal inventory and evaluation of the musical effects and books left by the deceased composer' will, as regards the music that is listed, find a striking contradiction and will wonder where to turn to find the truth. Whereas this biographer says, 'He had nothing by Haydn or Cherubini', the legal inventory includes under the heading of 'manuscript music' the score of Cherubini's *Faniska* and twenty-one assorted pieces, as well as various works by Haydn and Mozart. Similarly, there appear under the heading of 'engraved music' three works by Haydn and several by Mozart, Reicha, Salieri, Cherubini, Méhul, Paisiello, Johann Sebastian Bach, and others.

When this author saw this list in Vienna, he immediately expressed his utter amazement at such a wealth of musical works, especially considering that the master never had even a small music rack or bookcase in his little apartment. He could say with complete confidence that Beethoven did not own these and other works on the list, and that they must have been illegally smuggled in by someone in order to sell them for better prices at the auction. It is no secret that this has often been done when the effects left by famous people have been auctioned off. Nothing would have been easier than smuggling foreign material of this sort into the *Nachlass* of our master, for his executor had entrusted the handling of this important business to a man who was close to the principal auctioneers, a man, moreover, of very dubious scruples where the legality of his actions were concerned. Let us say no more.

From Supplement D, discussing *Beethovens Studien*, and from the notes on pages 392, 393, the reader has already gained some idea of what happened to the musical effects at that auction. The musical antiquarian Aloys Fuchs gave some information to this author that will serve to clarify this typical circumstance. On 30 September 1851 this worthy, widely renowned man wrote:

From my own experience, I can tell you the following regarding the original score of Beethoven's mass in D sharp.[410]

In the autumn of 1828, when G. Pölchau, the famous musical historian from Berlin with whom you are no doubt acquainted, was visiting me, he asked me if I could get him a good Beethoven autograph, for we had long been in the practice of exchanging autographs. Since I had been present at the Beethoven auction and had seen how the publishers Artaria and Haslinger bought up everything without letting a poor Christian soul get a thing,[411] I suggested to Herr Pölchau that he go to one of these gentlemen and see if he could find something there.

He decided on Artaria and asked me to take him there. We were shown several Beethoven original manuscripts that we examined with the greatest interest. Among them was the score of the second mass in D sharp in a huge folio format, and Pölchau bought the entire Kyrie for four gold ducats. I still remember that at the beginning of the piece there was written in Beethoven's hand, 'It came from the heart; may it go to the heart'.[412] But it was a piece of mercantile vandalism to sever the Kyrie from such a work, to cut up the whole, selling the portions by the pound as if it were a slaughtered lamb. I learned myself how Beethoven's *Nachlass* had been picked over when, among other original manuscripts, I bought the Kyrie from the first mass in C, and it was not until years later that I found the Gloria of the same mass at Artaria's. I had to buy it at a great sacrifice in order to bring together at least two of the fragments of this beautiful work. Unfortunately, the Gloria is complete only as far as 'Quoniam', and where the rest may be, only the gods know. All my attempts to find it have been fruitless. Do you know anything about it?

Unfortunately I was not able to give the excellent man the answer he wanted, for I had been in Pesth at the time of the auction. It gives me an additional reason for being grateful that I was away from the scene of such outrageous proceedings, for surely I would have fought alone against the scoundrels, as I so often did in subsequent years. Yet the above letter awakened so many memories that now, through the friendly intervention of Aloys Fuchs, could be pursued further. I also remembered that the itemized list of the Beethoven *Nachlass* contained nothing of the *Missa Solemnis*, and that I had tried in vain to find out what had become of this large volume which until the master's dying hours had been among his books. Fuchs obtained permission to look at this list in the office of Dr. Bach and, sure enough, the score of the *Missa* was not there. On 28 October 1851 he wrote me the following letter on the subject:

. . . I am not able to say how Herr A . . . gained possession of the original manuscript of Beethoven's mass in D sharp. I only hope that he did not get it in any way other than by buying it at the auction. The absence of this work from the list is just one more illustration of the ignorance of the men who organized and listed Beethoven's *Nachlass*. I have in my hands proof of what speculative absurdities have been committed with these treasures. . . .

With this, let us bring to a close the chapter on the publishers' outrages against the person of the great master as well as against the products of his genius, although the subject is by no means exhausted. Every honest, right-thinking man will have to devise his own punishment for these outrages. Perhaps their literary accomplices will get hold of this significant chapter and adorn it so prettily that the scoundrels are made to look like patrons of the arts to whom the whole musical world owes its thanks. This is what happened when the semi-official guardians of music put their hands over their eyes so as not to see the reprehensible deeds of certain publishers in the early 1830's, when the domination of virtuosity and its offspring, 'salon music' had their beginnings. This disloyal silence was an injustice to the better-minded publishers, for one was inclined to lump them all together.

A notable exception was the Hirschbach *Repertorium für Musik* during the two years of its existence, 1844 and 1845. It fought in vain against the effects of something whose causes it could not eliminate, for they had already infected the whole body like a pernicious poison. As for the present situation, the business has long ceased to be an 'art establishment', for it has become the business of music merchants, whose ideas

P. EXISTING PERSONAL EFFECTS OF BEETHOVEN

and goals are quite different, and it would be hopeless for even an unbiased and independent critic to try to bring about an improvement in the publishing situation in the interests of true art and worthy, promising young artists. One swallow does not make a summer, even if one could point out one or two encouraging examples of young composers of this sort who did not have to have their more significant works printed at their own expense. Dealing in names that are already famous with no consideration whatsoever for the inner worth of their compositions is in no branch of art so conspicuous a sign of the times as in music.

P.

EXISTING PERSONAL EFFECTS OF BEETHOVEN
(See page 516)

Articles that great men have used constantly in their daily affairs, such as garments, household utensils, and similar things which were once part of their lives, have always been cherished and honoured as valuable mementoes. For this reason, Stephan von Breuning, Dr. Bach, and this writer have wished to keep for themselves certain articles left by Beethoven, of little or no monetary value in themselves, as keepsakes of the great musician. Our choice concerned mostly the articles on his worktable, which in former years had been a repository of all kinds of objects, some of which had been reminiscent of Greek and Roman antiquity while others were reminders of contemporary events. Some may have looked like toys, but were something quite different to the master's serious nature. Unfortunately, most of these objects were lost during his lifetime, as we have already said elsewhere.

Among the effects preserved by this writer there are:

(a) A pendulum clock in the form of an inverted pyramid, with the small head of a woman in alabaster. (A gift from Princess Lichnowsky.)

(b) A copy in Beethoven's hand of the inscription from the temple of the goddess Neith in Egypt. (Framed and under glass.)

(c) A small landscape fashioned from Beethoven's hair, under glass.

(d) A brass candlestick with a shade. It shows a cupid sitting in a boat, supporting the shade with both hands.

(e) Two bronze Cossacks, used as paperweights.

(f) A little table bell.

(g) A large pair of paper scissors.

(h) Two seals with Beethoven's initials. He used to call the large one his 'state seal'.

507

SUPPLEMENTS

(i) Two pairs of spectacles in individual cases. On one of them is written in Beethoven's hand 'old'; on the other 'short distance'.

(j) A monocle which for many years he wore hanging from a black ribbon around his neck.

(k) A statuette representing Brutus.

(l) A steel quill and a goose-quill in a black case. It was with the latter that he wrote his second will, the last thing he wrote himself.

(m) A razor.

(n) A walking-stick of bamboo with a silver plate on top, on which his name is engraved.

I am still undecided about the eventual resting-place of this small yet interesting Beethoven collection. At any rate, it should not and will not be separated from the considerable number of existing written effects, autographs, and documents, as well as books and musical scores, that have already been mentioned.[413]

EDITOR'S NOTES (344–413)

Supplements

[344] The most extensive study of the portraits, statues, and medallions of Beethoven has been made by Theodor von Frimmel. His *Beethoven-Studien: I. Beethovens äussere Erscheinung—seine Bildnisse* (1905) is a revision, copiously illustrated, of a lengthy monograph that formed a part of his *Zweite Beethoveniana* (1887), pp. 191–324. Shorter discussions of the same subject are found in his *Beethoven in zeitgenössischen Bildnissen* (1923), with 28 plates, and in the article 'Bildnisse' in his *Beethoven-Handbuch* (1926). Beethoven's young friend Gerhard von Breuning, writing in 1874, gives his evaluation of some of the better-known portraits in BaF, p. 176n. The B. & H. *Verzeichnis* (1851), p. 154, and the Nottebohm *Verzeichnis* (1868), p. 195, contain lists of the most significant portraits and busts available at the time of publication. The special 'Beethoven' issues of *Die Musik* from 1902 to 1927 contain in all more than fifty reproductions of Beethoven portraits and statues, with brief discussions of each.

[345] Many recent studies—e.g., Mies, *Textkritische Untersuchen bei Beethoven* (1957); Unverricht, *Die Eigenschriften und die Originalausgaben von Werken Beethovens in ihrer Bedeutung für die moderne Textkritik* (1960); Carse, 'The sources of Beethoven's Fifth Symphony' (M. & L. XXIX [1948] 249)—have shown that an edition that exactly duplicates the original edition may be (and probably is) far from a true representation of the composer's intentions.

EDITOR'S NOTES

346 This is the portrait painted in 1804 by the talented dilettante Willibrord Joseph Mähler. It was considered by contemporaries and by Frimmel (BStud I 28) as an excellent likeness, drawn with care and accuracy, though not of great artistic worth (Frimmel, 1923, *op. cit.*, p. 18). A reproduction may be found in BStud I 29. According to Gerhard von Breuning (BaF, p. 164), this portrait hung in Beethoven's apartment at the Schwarzspanierhaus in 1826; it was later owned by nephew Karl, then by his widow, and then by his daughter. This portrait is not to be confused with a less satisfactory one made by Mähler in 1814 (BStud I 60), of which three copies by the artist are known.

347 A reproduction of the portrait by Schimon (1797–1852) is used as the frontispiece of BStud I; an enlarged detail from the portrait appears in BStud I 84.

348 The Stieler portrait, which dates from 1820 (not 1822) is reproduced in BStud I 90.

349 A reproduction of the Scheffner engraving appears as a *Beilage* to the first *Beethoven-Heft* of *Die Musik* (2nd March issue, 1902; see also p. 1141 of that issue).

350 At the time of the Vienna Congress in 1814, the artist in pastels, Louis Letronne, made a drawing of Beethoven which Höfel was engaged to engrave. The original drawing was not satisfactory, and Höfel was obliged in effect to redraw it on his copper plate (BStud I 53). Beethoven gave him two sittings of an hour each, and the result was one of the most popular portraits of the composer, considered by contemporaries as an excellent likeness, though slightly idealized. This drawing was also used by Riedel for the engraving that Schindler refers to. The original crayon drawing by Letronne does not seem to have been preserved. A fantastically bad engraving was made in 1877 by Hillemacher. This appears as a *Beilage* to the first *Beethoven-Heft* of *Die Musik* (2nd March issue, 1902; see also p. 1142 of that issue). Frimmel conjectures (BHdb I 341) that Hillemacher may have worked directly from Letronne's drawing, thus indicating the poor quality that Höfel complained about, but Unger (SBSK–Bi 8) disagrees.

351 A contemporary description of Klöber's work describes a full-length oil painting of Beethoven with a bit of Mödling landscape in the background, in which Nephew Karl is shown lying under a tree. This portrait, if it ever existed, has disappeared (TK II 399; TF 702; BStud I 72). The lithograph that Schindler describes was made in 1841 by Theodor Neu after a pastel drawing by Klöber that until World War II was in the possession of C. F. Peters & Co. in Leipzig (BStud I 74). Stargardt Auction Catalogue No. 495 (Item 146) describes and gives in facsimile a pencil drawing, found in Klöber's *Nachlass*, that was presumably a study, drawn from life, for both the painting and the pastel Klöber's date '1817' is certainly a year or more too early: Beethoven spent the summer of 1817 in Heiligenstadt and Nussdorf, but was in Mödling in the summers of 1818, 1819, and 1820.

352 The lithograph published by Matthias Artaria in 1826 was by Stieler's nephew, Friedrich Dürck, then only seventeen years of age (BStud I 96). A reproduction of this lithograph is used as a frontispiece in BaF (1927). Frimmel describes the Spina lithograph as 'by an unknown hand, after the lithograph by Kriehuber' (BStud I 99).

353 Frimmel remarks that at least three versions of this portrait are known, and points out that Waldmüller's *forte* was genre and landscape painting rather than portraiture. He continues, 'If a painter of significant ability should have made a portrait entirely from memory, the result would be of more value, in my judgement, than the work of a dauber who for weeks on end had laboured before the subject. I am of the opinion that we may accept the Waldmüller portrait as a means of bringing before our eyes Beethoven as he actually looked in the 1820's' (BStud I 119). A reproduction of this portrait in colour appears as frontispiece to *Der Bär*, 1927. A letter from Waldmüller to Breitkopf & Härtel dated 3 May 1823 (*Der Bär* 1927, p. 36) shows that the artist's fee for the portrait was twelve gold ducats, not twenty as stated by Schindler.

354 Joseph Steinmüller prepared an engraving of a lithograph made in 1824 by Stefan Decker (TK III 176; TF 913); the engraving was published by Artaria & Co. in the autumn of 1827 with a dedication to Archduke Rudolph. A facsimile of the engraving is given in *Die Musik* XIX (1927) after p. 400; a facsimile of Decker's lithograph may be found in BStud I 134. Czerny referred to the Decker-Steinmüller portrait as 'the only correct likeness that has been published' of Beethoven (BStud I 139), but Frimmel says that this evaluation must be considered with scepticism.

355 Kriehuber, who is considered 'one of the masters of Viennese portrait lithography' (Thieme-Becker), made reproductions of the first Mähler portrait (facsimile in *Die Musik* II$_1$ [1902], No. 6), the Stieler portrait (see BStud I 99), the Dietrich bust (facsimile in *Die Musik* II$_1$ [1902], No. 6), and at least two versions of the Decker-Steinmüller portrait, one of which was published as a separate issue by Haslinger in 1827 and the other, in an engraving by Lämmel, used as a frontispiece for Seyfried's *Beethovens Studien* (1832), (see also *Die Musik* IX$_3$ [1910], No. 14). The Lämmel engraving shows the black cravat that Schindler mentions; BStud I 139 says that the Haslinger issue shows a white cravat.

356 It should be noted that the bust made by Klein in 1812 for the Streicher piano salon, based upon the life-mask that Klein took for this purpose, may be accepted as a model of fidelity for evaluating all other busts and portraits. Photographs of the mask and the bust are given in BStud I 40, 41, 44, and 46.

357 An engraving showing the Hähnel monument erected in Bonn in 1845 may be found in the second edition (1852) of Seyfried's *Beethovens Studien* and, as a reproduction of a rather unsatisfactory lithograph, in Bory, p. 221.

358 See p. 304 and Note 237.

359 Excerpts from this article are given in TK III 284, 286, and in TF 1031–32.

360 As stated in Note 237, the phrase 'sedebat et bibebat' ['he sat and drank'] does not appear in any of the transcriptions or translations of Wawruch's report that the present editor has seen.

361 See also TDR V 576, KBr I 161, and Note 221.

362 See p. 301 *supra*.

[363] 'Absolument' means 'surely' or 'without fail', not 'immediately' (sofort) as translated by Damcke or Schindler.

[364] See TDR V 571.

[365] Hess 39 is a string quintet, now apparently lost, that was described by Lenz (*Beethoven et ses trois styles* [1909] 438) as follows: 'Original manuscript quintet for 2 violins, 2 violas, and cello, F major, in the possession of Prince N. Galitsin, to whom Beethoven sent it in 1824. This quintet, without scherzo or minuet, dates from Beethoven's youth, and is of only historical value. It is desirable, nevertheless, that it be published: its authenticity is beyond question.'

[366] Note 227 summarizes these transactions in another way but with the same result.

[367] Actually, the Prince received the dedication of the three quartets that he had commissioned (opp. 127, 130, 132) and the dedication of opus 124.

[368] As nearly as can be determined from published information, the purchasers of the various items in the musical *Nachlass*, which was divided into six classes, were as shown below. Class IV was of course potentially the most valuable and important. Regarding this auction, see BStud II 185 and NBJ IV (1935) 66.

	Artaria	Haslinger	Others	Unknown	Total
I. Sketchbooks	26	7	13	5	51
II. Autograph sketches and fragments	12	1	5	1	19
III. Autograph MSS of published works	28	20	22	8	78
IV. Autograph unpubd. MSS*	15	11	15		41
Subtotal	81	39	55	14	189
V. Manuscript parts	6	3		18	27
VI. Engraved music		2		34	36
Total	87	44	55	66	252

[369] See Note 355.

[370] See TDR III ix.

[371] The first edition of Mizler's translation was published in 1742. The original work was published in Latin in 1725, and within the next fifty years translations in German, Italian, French, and English had appeared. The durability of Fux's works is shown by the fact that abridged editions in English and in German were published during and immediately before World War II.

[372] This exposé by Derckum in 1852 was followed eleven years later by an even more detailed and devastating analysis of Seyfried's book by Nottebohm, appearing in eleven instalments in AmZ from NF I (1863) 685 to NF II (1864) 169 and reprinted in *Beethoveniana* (1872), pp. 154–203.

---

* Lot 149 was described as 'Exercises in counterpoint, probably by other masters, with Beethoven's own markings: 5 bundles'. This lot was purchased by Haslinger for 74 florins, the highest single price paid at the auction except for the 40 volumes of Handel's works (102 florins). These 'exercises' served as the basis for Seyfried's book.

373 See Note 180.

374 Both Jahn and Nohl quote Holz to the effect that Beethoven valued the Cherubini *Requiem* highly, preferring it even to Mozart's *Requiem* (TDR V 329).

375 See Note 274.

376 In Austria during Beethoven's day no document was legally binding unless it bore a revenue stamp.

377 This was the quartet of the four Müller brothers of Brunswick, which during the winter of 1833–4 gave eight concerts in Vienna. Hanslick (p. 305) and Mahaim (p. 71) describe this quartet as the first to dedicate its entire activity to giving concerts as a travelling quartet. Although the Gebrüder Müller gave the world première of opus 131 in Halberstadt on 5 June 1828 (Mahaim, pp. 70, 74), they otherwise limited their playing of Beethoven to the earlier quartets. These, with the quartets of Haydn and Mozart, formed the mainstay of their programmes. This group is not to be confused with the Gebrüder Müller of Meiningen, a quartet formed by the four sons of Karl Friedrich Müller, first violin of the Brunswick quartet.

378 Only opus 106 was published with this terminology, but in the autograph opus 101 was designated as 'Neue Sonata für Ham . . .' (KHV 279), and several letters to the publisher (And. 737, 742; MM 209, 210) show that, at least for a time, Beethoven wished the word 'Hammerklavier' to be used instead of 'pianoforte'. Opus 109 was also designated in the autograph as 'Sonate für das Hammerklavier' (KHV 311).

379 Actually, in February 1817 (KHV 280).

380 Beethoven's efforts to supplant Italian with German in musical terminology are discussed in KBr V 181 and in ZfM LXXX (1913) 520. An article on this subject by Gottschalk (*Muttersprache* XLII [1927] 65) may be summarized as follows:

Explanatory notations in German appear in opp. 68, 81a, 115, 123, 132, and 135. Statements of tempo or expression in German in addition to or instead of in Italian are found in opp. 48, 90, 98, 101, 110, 123, and 130. Beethoven used the word *Hammerklavier* instead of *pianoforte* in opp. 101 and 106 [and in the manuscript title-page but not the published version of opus 109—see NBJ VII (1937) 163], and the word *Veränderungen* instead of *Variationen* in WoO 74 (1805) and opus 120 (1823).

With Holz, Beethoven worked out a considerable number of Germanic substitutes for words of non-Germanic origin, and discussed the general idea in his letter to Holz of 24 August 1825 (And. 1415). In thinking that Beethoven was less than completely serious in this project, the author agrees with Schindler and disagrees with Kalischer (Kal 1105).

A further sidelight on Beethoven's coining of words to avoid loan-words is given by Henk in the same journal, p. 233 (MM 205), and in the letters bearing on the 'Life of Tobias' fantasy for *Cäcilia* (And. 1345, 1411; MM 414).

381 The portion of the *Biographie* that Schindler refers to mentions meetings of Beethoven and Rochlitz (pp. 244, 473, 478), but does not comment on Beethoven's opinion of Rochlitz. The reference to Rochlitz as 'Mephistopheles'

was probably based on a remark by Holz that appeared in a Conversation Book used in September 1825: 'When will Mephistopheles Rochlitz arrive from Leipzig?' (BJ II [1909] 166.)

382 Actually, Rochlitz gave up the editorship of the AmZ in 1818 (Grove 7–195).

383 Beethoven's request appeared at the end of the postscript to his letter of 21 August 1810 to the publishers (And. 272), and reads as follows:

I have found the following mistake in the symphony in C minor (specifically, in the third movement in $\frac{3}{4}$ time), where after the major ♮ ♮ ♮, the minor comes in again. I quote only the bass part: [as in the music example in the text]. . . . The two measures that are crossed out [those indicated in the text by dots] must be deleted, together with the corresponding rests in all the other parts.

Beethoven referred to the mistake merely as a 'mistake' (Fehler); the term 'great blunder' (grosser Bock) is Schindler's.

In an earlier letter to B. & H. (And. 204 of 28 March 1809) Beethoven said: 'You stated that you had found another mistake in the third movement of the C minor symphony; I don't recall what it was'. Might it be that B. & H. had questioned the two disputed measures at that time?

384 Schindler apparently was not aware that a facsimile of Beethoven's request had been published in AmZ XLVIII (1846) 461, together with the explanation by B. & H. that Beethoven had apparently originally intended to have a *da capo* at this point, with the questioned two measures as a *prima volta* and those following as a *seconda volta*. These pairs of measures were marked in Beethoven's manuscript with '1' and '2', but when the parts were engraved this marking was overlooked. The explanation by B. & H. as published is given in KBr I 331 (KS I 202).

This gives a definite No to the question as to whether both pairs of measures should be played, but raises the new (and unanswerable) question: is it due only to an engraver's oversight that at this point in the movement we do not have a *da capo*?

385 There seems to be no record of Beethoven having conducted the C minor symphony subsequent to the date of his complaint to B. & H.

386 TK II 272n makes the very logical suggestion that the 'engraving' referred to was the preparation of the cylinder for the panharmonicon.

387 The reference is to the concerts of 8 and 12 December 1813, at which the seventh symphony and *Wellington's Victory* received their first performances.

388 According to TK II 257 and TF 566, the second number at each of the concerts was 'Two Marches played by Maelzel's Mechanical Trumpeter, the one by Dussek, the other by Pleyel'.

389 The Beethoven literature includes three letters from Beethoven to Bettina. Of these, the authenticity of the second, dated 10 February 1811, cannot be challenged, since the autograph is known and is accepted as genuine. The first and third letters, however, are generally considered to have been written by Bettina herself, who published them as having been received from Beethoven but who would never produce the autographs for scrutiny. And. 1355n comments: 'Doubtless the two spurious letters were based on reminiscences of conversations between Beethoven and Bettina and on certain events reported to her later.' See also MR XIX (1958) 16.

390 As an indication that this letter was written by Bettina long after 1810, And. 1356 notes that not until years after 1810 was Beethoven forced to depend upon written replies in his conversations. The earliest known Conversation Book dates from February and March 1818.

391 Beethoven's setting of this poem by Goethe was written in 1809, and was published as opus 75 No. 1 in October 1810. No autograph copy of it is known (KHV 200).

392 Beethoven made two settings of this poem by Goethe, *Neue Liebe, neues Leben*. The earlier version, composed in 1798–9 and published by Simrock in 1809, is identified in KHV (589) as WoO 127 and is published in Vol. V of the *Supplemente zur Gesamtausgabe* (1962) as No. 8. The later version was composed in 1809 and was published as opus 75 No. 2 in October 1810. MM 81 describes a copy in an unidentified hand of the first nine measures of opus 75 No. 2, with an inscription by Beethoven to Bettina, dating probably from May (not August) 1810. The translation used here is by Henry S. Drinker.

393 This is the date shown on the autograph. Schindler gives the date '11 February 1811'.

394 This letter was first published in the *Nürnberger Athenäum für Wissenschaft, Kunst und Leben* for January 1839 in a transcription that at many points made minor deviations from the autograph (e.g., the salutation in the autograph reads *Liebe, liebe Bettine!* and in the *Athenäum* transcription *Geliebte, liebe Bettina!*). Schindler used the *Athenäum* transcription, but the translation given here is from Frimmel's transcription in KFr II 1, in which the discrepancies between *Athenäum* and autograph are stated in detail. A facsimile of the autograph is given in Marx: *Ludwig van Beethoven*, 5th ed. (1901), Vol. II, Beilage G.

395 'Toni' was Bettina's sister-in-law Antonia, wife of Franz von Brentano.

396 *Die Flüsse* was a series of distichs by Schiller and Goethe, published in 1797 under the title *Xenien* as satires against their literary opponents. See And. 312n.

397 Bettina married Ludwig Achim von Arnim on 11 March 1811.

398 'Pity my fate' (Bedaure mein Geschick) is a misquotation from Act IV, Scene 2 of Schiller's *Jungfrau von Orlean* (line 2658): 'Beklage mich! Beweine mein Geschick!', though Schindler-Moscheles I 270n says that the quotation refers to Goethe's poem *Johanna Sebus*.

399 In Beethoven's letter of 12 April 1811 to Goethe (And. 303) he expressed his admiration for *Egmont*.

400 In January 1811 Bettina's brother Clemens sent Beethoven a long poem on the death of Queen Luise of Prussia as a possible text for a cantata. Beethoven made a few sketches but did not carry the work further.

401 Various details demonstrate beyond argument that this letter is spurious.

(1) The letter is dated 'Teplitz, August 1812', but Beethoven was not in Teplitz at any time during that month: 'on the 27th of July, Beethoven went to

Karlsbad on the advice of his physician, Dr. Staudenheimer [sic], and he did not return to Teplitz until after 8 September' (TK II 223; see also TF 537).

(2) The list of guests in Teplitz during the 1812 season (TK II 222; TF 532) shows in great detail the arrival of many noble persons. The absence of the name of Archduke Rudolph from this list may be taken as conclusive evidence that he was not in Teplitz during this summer.

(3) A letter that Bettina wrote to Prince Pückler-Moskau, perhaps about 1832 (Sonneck, Impr, p. 84) says that immediately after the incident of pushing his way through the royal procession, at some time that is not stated, Beethoven 'came running to us and told us everything'. 'Therefore, if the letter to Pückler is true—and it bears all the marks of being so—and if the other is authentic, Beethoven is made to relate the story one day and write a long letter containing it to the same person the next. It follows: when such a letter in Beethoven's well-known handwriting shall be seen and accepted as authentic by competent judges, its genuineness may be conceded but, henceforth, until then, never' (TK II 227).

[402] Regarding the 'one more performance', TDR III 330 explains that at the request of the Empress, Goethe wrote a farce, *Die Wette*, and rehearsed it with the court.

[403] And. 1016n says that according to Beethoven's calendar this draft, written in a mixture of German and French, was dated 15 March 1823. The fair copy was presumably sent to Maurice Schlesinger in Paris for delivery but, as mentioned in Note 176, Cherubini told Schindler in 1841 that he never received it.

[404] And. 1017n says that the two previous sentences, given by Schindler, do not appear in the autograph draft of this letter in the Staatsbibliothek in Berlin.

[405] And. 1017n says that on the fourth and last page of the draft that is in the Berlin Staatsbibliothek there is a brief note to Schindler that reads in part, 'I don't know whether the other copy has been corrected, so I am sending this one' (And. 1155). This intimation that there were two copies of the draft may explain the added sentences referred to in Note 404.

[406] The meaning of this last clause—'wodurch dem verwöhnten Auge die dreigeschwänzten Noten entzogen werden'—is not clear.

[407] The general subject matter of this section is treated at length in the book by Schrade, *Beethoven in France* (1942).

[408] This story is told in more detail in TK II 344 and TF 647, where the visitor is identified as a General Kyd.

[409] The auction of Beethoven's musical *Nachlass* is discussed in considerable detail by Kinsky in NBJ VI (1935) 66.

[410] During the first half of the nineteenth century, the key of D major was often referred to as D sharp—see, for example, the manuscript shown in Stieler's portrait.

[411] Regarding the extent to which Artaria and Haslinger dominated the auction, see Note 368. Fuchs's reference to 'poor Christian souls' should not be taken as an intimation that either Artaria or Haslinger was Jewish: each was brought up in the Roman Catholic faith.

[412] A facsimile of the first page of the Kyrie, with the inscription, 'Von Herzen—Möge es wieder—zu Herzen gehn!', is given in Bory, p. 187.

[413] The articles that Schindler describes, with the exception of the inscription from the Temple of Neith (see p. 507), are now in the Beethovenhaus in Bonn (see Schmidt & Knickenberg, *Das Beethovenhaus in Bonn* [1927], pp. 42, 75). Most of them are illustrated in Ley: *Beethovens Leben in Bildern*, pp. 126–8, and in Bory, p. 204.

Reviews of Beethoven Works in the 'Allgemeine Musikalische Zeitung'

During its first fifty years(1798–1848) the *Allgemeine musikalische Zeitung* (AmZ) was in effect a musical newspaper. Its contents consisted principally of reviews of newly published music and of letters from various cities discussing concerts, personalities, and other matters of musical interest. The number of signed articles was relatively small.

The tables below are an attempt to list all reviews of *newly published* works by Beethoven that appeared in this journal. Those reviews marked with an asterisk are actually extended analyses, usually with examples in musical notation.

A. Reviews in Chronological Order

Composition	Review	Schindler—MacArdle reference, if any
Opus 66, WoO 72	I (1799) 366	Page 76
Opus 11	I (1799) 541	76, 86
Opus 12	I (1799) 570	76–7
WoO 73	I (1799) 607	76
Opus 10	II (1799) 25	77
Opus 13	II (1800) 373	78, 111
WoO 76	II (1800) 425	76
Opp. 23, 24	IV (1802) 569	93
Opp. 26, 27	IV (1802) 651	93–4
WoO 46	V (1802) 188	94
Opus 28	V (1802) 188	94
Opus 34	V (1803) 556	99
Opus 30	VI (1803) 77	100
Opus 35	VI (1804) 338	100
Opus 48	VI (1804) 608	
Opus 88	VI (1804) 626	
WoO 129	VI (1804) 642	
Opus 45	VI (1804) 643	

Opp. 36, 55 (score)	XXV (1823) 408	
Opp. 109, 110, 111	*XXVI (1824) 213	231, 232, 233
Opus 123	XXVI (1824) 439	286
Opp. 121b, 122	XXVII (1825) 740	
Opus 108	XXVII (1825) 866	
	XXX (1828) 283	
Opus 126	XXVIII (1826) 47	
Opus 130 (B flat Qnt.)	XXVIII (1826) 310	
Opus 116	XXVIII (1826) 494	
[WoO 30]	XXIX (1827) 749	
Opus 118	XXIX (1827) 797	
Opus 137	XXIX (1827) 835	
Opus 114	XXX (1828) 331	
Opus 131	*XXX (1828) 485, 501	
LvB's sämmtliche Werke		
(Haslinger)	XXXIII (1831) 30	
Opus 84	XXXIV (1832) 109	
Opus 136	XXXIX (1837) 617	
	XL (1838) 84	

B. Reviews in Opus Number and WoO Order

Composition	Review	Schindler—MacArdle reference, if any
Opus 10	II (1799) 25	Page 77
11	I (1799) 541	76
12	I (1799) 570	76–7
13	II (1800) 373	78
20	VII (1805) 769	
21 (score)	XXIV (1822) 756	
23	IV (1802) 569	93
24	IV (1802) 569	93
26	IV (1802) 651	93–4
27	IV (1802) 651	93–4
28	V (1802) 188	94
30	VI (1803) 77	77
32	VIII (1806) 815	
34	V (1803) 556	99
35	VI (1804) 338	100
36 (trio)	IX (1806) 8	
36	XXV (1823) 408	
37	*VII (1805) 445	
38	VII (1805) 769	
45	VI (1804) 643	
47	VII (1805) 584, 769	119

48	VI (1804) 608	
52	VII (1805) 769	
53	VIII (1806) 261	
54	VIII (1806) 639	
55	*IX (1807) 321	117, 138–9
55 (score)	XXV (1823) 408	
57	IX (1807) 433	138
60	VIII (1806) 670	139, 417
62	*XIV (1812) 519	
66	I (1799) 366	76
67	*XII (1810) 630, 652	156
68	*XII (1810) 241	
70	*XV (1813) 141	156 n.
74	XIII (1811) 349	
75	XIII (1811) 593	
76	XIII (1811) 152	
77	XIII (1811) 548	
78	XIII (1811) 548	
80	XIV (1812) 307	142
82	XIV (1812) 16	
84	XV (1813) 473	
	XXXIV (1832) 109	
85	XIV (1812) 3, 17	
86	*XV (1813) 389, 409	
87	XI (1808) 108	
	XIV (1812) 67	
88	VI (1804) 626	
90	XVIII (1816) 60	
91	*XVIII (1816) 241	168
92	*XVIII (1816) 817	
93	*XX (1818) 161	
96	XIX (1817) 228	
97	XXV (1823) 192	286
98	XIX (1817) 73	
99	XIX (1817) 135	
100	XIX (1817) 52	
101	*XIX (1817) 686	213
102	XX (1818) 792	
107	XXIII (1821) 567	
108	XXVII (1825) 866	
	XXX (1828) 283	
109	*XXVI (1824) 213	231–3
110	*XXVI (1824) 213	231–3
111	*XXVI (1824) 213	231–3
112	XXIV (1822) 674	
114	XXX (1828) 331	

Index of Compositions

(with dates of performance and publication)

Period 1, 69–73
Period 2, 175–81
Period 3, 332–7

522

INDEX OF COMPOSITIONS

INDEX OF COMPOSITIONS

INDEX OF COMPOSITIONS

Index of Names

B. is used throughout for Beethoven himself.

COMPOSITIONS

(*see* Index of Compositions for individual works)

A CATALOG OF SELECTED
DOVER BOOKS
IN ALL FIELDS OF INTEREST

A CATALOG OF SELECTED DOVER
BOOKS IN ALL FIELDS OF INTEREST

CONCERNING THE SPIRITUAL IN ART, Wassily Kandinsky. Pioneering work by father of abstract art. Thoughts on color theory, nature of art. Analysis of earlier masters. 12 illustrations. 80pp. of text. 5⅜ × 8½.   23411-8 Pa. $3.95

ANIMALS: 1,419 Copyright-Free Illustrations of Mammals, Birds, Fish, Insects, etc., Jim Harter (ed.). Clear wood engravings present, in extremely lifelike poses, over 1,000 species of animals. One of the most extensive pictorial sourcebooks of its kind. Captions. Index. 284pp. 9 × 12.   23766-4 Pa. $12.95

CELTIC ART: The Methods of Construction, George Bain. Simple geometric techniques for making Celtic interlacements, spirals, Kells-type initials, animals, humans, etc. Over 500 illustrations. 160pp. 9 × 12. (USO)   22923-8 Pa. $9.95

AN ATLAS OF ANATOMY FOR ARTISTS, Fritz Schider. Most thorough reference work on art anatomy in the world. Hundreds of illustrations, including selections from works by Vesalius, Leonardo, Goya, Ingres, Michelangelo, others. 593 illustrations. 192pp. 7⅛ × 10¼.   20241-0 Pa. $9.95

CELTIC HAND STROKE-BY-STROKE (Irish Half-Uncial from "The Book of Kells"): An Arthur Baker Calligraphy Manual, Arthur Baker. Complete guide to creating each letter of the alphabet in distinctive Celtic manner. Covers hand position, strokes, pens, inks, paper, more. Illustrated. 48pp. 8¼ × 11.
24336-2 Pa. $3.95

EASY ORIGAMI, John Montroll. Charming collection of 32 projects (hat, cup, pelican, piano, swan, many more) specially designed for the novice origami hobbyist. Clearly illustrated easy-to-follow instructions insure that even beginning papercrafters will achieve successful results. 48pp. 8¼ × 11.   27298-2 Pa. $2.95

THE COMPLETE BOOK OF BIRDHOUSE CONSTRUCTION FOR WOOD-WORKERS, Scott D. Campbell. Detailed instructions, illustrations, tables. Also data on bird habitat and instinct patterns. Bibliography. 3 tables. 63 illustrations in 15 figures. 48pp. 5¼ × 8½.   24407-5 Pa. $1.95

BLOOMINGDALE'S ILLUSTRATED 1886 CATALOG: Fashions, Dry Goods and Housewares, Bloomingdale Brothers. Famed merchants' extremely rare catalog depicting about 1,700 products: clothing, housewares, firearms, dry goods, jewelry, more. Invaluable for dating, identifying vintage items. Also, copyright-free graphics for artists, designers. Co-published with Henry Ford Museum & Greenfield Village. 160pp. 8¼ × 11.   25780-0 Pa. $9.95

HISTORIC COSTUME IN PICTURES, Braun & Schneider. Over 1,450 costumed figures in clearly detailed engravings—from dawn of civilization to end of 19th century. Captions. Many folk costumes. 256pp. 8⅜ × 11¾.   23150-X Pa. $11.95

EARLY NINETEENTH-CENTURY CRAFTS AND TRADES, Peter Stockham (ed.). Extremely rare 1807 volume describes to youngsters the crafts and trades of the day: brickmaker, weaver, dressmaker, bookbinder, ropemaker, saddler, many more. Quaint prose, charming illustrations for each craft. 20 black-and-white line illustrations. 192pp. 4⅜ × 6. 27293-1 Pa. $4.95

VICTORIAN FASHIONS AND COSTUMES FROM HARPER'S BAZAR, 1867-1898, Stella Blum (ed.). Day costumes, evening wear, sports clothes, shoes, hats, other accessories in over 1,000 detailed engravings. 320pp. 9⅜ × 12¼. 22990-4 Pa. $13.95

GUSTAV STICKLEY, THE CRAFTSMAN, Mary Ann Smith. Superb study surveys broad scope of Stickley's achievement, especially in architecture. Design philosophy, rise and fall of the Craftsman empire, descriptions and floor plans for many Craftsman houses, more. 86 black-and-white halftones. 31 line illustrations. Introduction. 208pp. 6½ × 9¼. 27210-9 Pa. $9.95

THE LONG ISLAND RAIL ROAD IN EARLY PHOTOGRAPHS, Ron Ziel. Over 220 rare photos, informative text document origin (1844) and development of rail service on Long Island. Vintage views of early trains, locomotives, stations, passengers, crews, much more. Captions. 8⅞ × 11¾. 26301-0 Pa. $13.95

THE BOOK OF OLD SHIPS: From Egyptian Galleys to Clipper Ships, Henry B. Culver. Superb, authoritative history of sailing vessels, with 80 magnificent line illustrations. Galley, bark, caravel, longship, whaler, many more. Detailed, informative text on each vessel by noted naval historian. Introduction. 256pp. 5⅜ × 8½. 27332-6 Pa. $6.95

TEN BOOKS ON ARCHITECTURE, Vitruvius. The most important book ever written on architecture. Early Roman aesthetics, technology, classical orders, site selection, all other aspects. Morgan translation. 331pp. 5⅜ × 8½. 20645-9 Pa. $8.95

THE HUMAN FIGURE IN MOTION, Eadweard Muybridge. More than 4,500 stopped-action photos, in action series, showing undraped men, women, children jumping, lying down, throwing, sitting, wrestling, carrying, etc. 390pp. 7⅞ × 10⅝. 20204-6 Clothbd. $24.95

TREES OF THE EASTERN AND CENTRAL UNITED STATES AND CANADA, William M. Harlow. Best one-volume guide to 140 trees. Full descriptions, woodlore, range, etc. Over 600 illustrations. Handy size. 288pp. 4½ × 6⅜. 20395-6 Pa. $5.95

SONGS OF WESTERN BIRDS, Dr. Donald J. Borror. Complete song and call repertoire of 60 western species, including flycatchers, juncoes, cactus wrens, many more—includes fully illustrated booklet. Cassette and manual 99913-0 $8.95

GROWING AND USING HERBS AND SPICES, Milo Miloradovich. Versatile handbook provides all the information needed for cultivation and use of all the herbs and spices available in North America. 4 illustrations. Index. Glossary. 236pp. 5⅜ × 8½. 25058-X Pa. $6.95

BIG BOOK OF MAZES AND LABYRINTHS, Walter Shepherd. 50 mazes and labyrinths in all—classical, solid, ripple, and more—in one great volume. Perfect inexpensive puzzler for clever youngsters. Full solutions. 112pp. 8⅛ × 11. 22951-3 Pa. $4.95

PIANO TUNING, J. Cree Fischer. Clearest, best book for beginner, amateur. Simple repairs, raising dropped notes, tuning by easy method of flattened fifths. No previous skills needed. 4 illustrations. 201pp. 5⅜ × 8½. 23267-0 Pa. $5.95

A SOURCE BOOK IN THEATRICAL HISTORY, A. M. Nagler. Contemporary observers on acting, directing, make-up, costuming, stage props, machinery, scene design, from Ancient Greece to Chekhov. 611pp. 5⅜ × 8½. 20515-0 Pa. $11.95

THE COMPLETE NONSENSE OF EDWARD LEAR, Edward Lear. All nonsense limericks, zany alphabets, Owl and Pussycat, songs, nonsense botany, etc., illustrated by Lear. Total of 320pp. 5⅜ × 8½. (USO) 20167-8 Pa. $6.95

VICTORIAN PARLOUR POETRY: An Annotated Anthology, Michael R. Turner. 117 gems by Longfellow, Tennyson, Browning, many lesser-known poets. "The Village Blacksmith," "Curfew Must Not Ring Tonight," "Only a Baby Small," dozens more, often difficult to find elsewhere. Index of poets, titles, first lines. xxiii + 325pp. 5⅜ × 8¼. 27044-0 Pa. $8.95

DUBLINERS, James Joyce. Fifteen stories offer vivid, tightly focused observations of the lives of Dublin's poorer classes. At least one, "The Dead," is considered a masterpiece. Reprinted complete and unabridged from standard edition. 160pp. 5³⁄₁₆ × 8¼. 26870-5 Pa. $1.00

THE HAUNTED MONASTERY and THE CHINESE MAZE MURDERS, Robert van Gulik. Two full novels by van Gulik, set in 7th-century China, continue adventures of Judge Dee and his companions. An evil Taoist monastery, seemingly supernatural events; overgrown topiary maze hides strange crimes. 27 illustrations. 328pp. 5⅜ × 8½. 23502-5 Pa. $7.95

THE BOOK OF THE SACRED MAGIC OF ABRAMELIN THE MAGE, translated by S. MacGregor Mathers. Medieval manuscript of ceremonial magic. Basic document in Aleister Crowley, Golden Dawn groups. 268pp. 5⅜ × 8½. 23211-5 Pa. $8.95

NEW RUSSIAN-ENGLISH AND ENGLISH-RUSSIAN DICTIONARY, M. A. O'Brien. This is a remarkably handy Russian dictionary, containing a surprising amount of information, including over 70,000 entries. 366pp. 4½ × 6⅛. 20208-9 Pa. $9.95

HISTORIC HOMES OF THE AMERICAN PRESIDENTS, Second, Revised Edition, Irvin Haas. A traveler's guide to American Presidential homes, most open to the public, depicting and describing homes occupied by every American President from George Washington to George Bush. With visiting hours, admission charges, travel routes. 175 photographs. Index. 160pp. 8¼ × 11. 26751-2 Pa. $10.95

NEW YORK IN THE FORTIES, Andreas Feininger. 162 brilliant photographs by the well-known photographer, formerly with *Life* magazine. Commuters, shoppers, Times Square at night, much else from city at its peak. Captions by John von Hartz. 181pp. 9¼ × 10¾. 23585-8 Pa. $12.95

INDIAN SIGN LANGUAGE, William Tomkins. Over 525 signs developed by Sioux and other tribes. Written instructions and diagrams. Also 290 pictographs. 111pp. 6⅛ × 9¼. 22029-X Pa. $3.50

ANATOMY: A Complete Guide for Artists, Joseph Sheppard. A master of figure drawing shows artists how to render human anatomy convincingly. Over 460 illustrations. 224pp. 8⅜ × 11¼. 27279-6 Pa. $10.95

MEDIEVAL CALLIGRAPHY: Its History and Technique, Marc Drogin. Spirited history, comprehensive instruction manual covers 13 styles (ca. 4th century thru 15th). Excellent photographs; directions for duplicating medieval techniques with modern tools. 224pp. 8⅜ × 11¼. 26142-5 Pa. $11.95

DRIED FLOWERS: How to Prepare Them, Sarah Whitlock and Martha Rankin. Complete instructions on how to use silica gel, meal and borax, perlite aggregate, sand and borax, glycerine and water to create attractive permanent flower arrangements. 12 illustrations. 32pp. 5⅜ × 8½. 21802-3 Pa. $1.00

EASY-TO-MAKE BIRD FEEDERS FOR WOODWORKERS, Scott D. Campbell. Detailed, simple-to-use guide for designing, constructing, caring for and using feeders. Text, illustrations for 12 classic and contemporary designs. 96pp. 5⅜ × 8½. 25847-5 Pa. $2.95

OLD-TIME CRAFTS AND TRADES, Peter Stockham. An 1807 book created to teach children about crafts and trades open to them as future careers. It describes in detailed, nontechnical terms 24 different occupations, among them coachmaker, gardener, hairdresser, lacemaker, shoemaker, wheelwright, copper-plate printer, milliner, trunkmaker, merchant and brewer. Finely detailed engravings illustrate each occupation. 192pp. 4⅝ × 6. 27398-9 Pa. $4.95

THE HISTORY OF UNDERCLOTHES, C. Willett Cunnington and Phyllis Cunnington. Fascinating, well-documented survey covering six centuries of English undergarments, enhanced with over 100 illustrations: 12th-century laced-up bodice, footed long drawers (1795), 19th-century bustles, 19th-century corsets for men, Victorian "bust improvers," much more. 272pp. 5⅝ × 8¼. 27124-2 Pa. $9.95

ARTS AND CRAFTS FURNITURE: The Complete Brooks Catalog of 1912, Brooks Manufacturing Co. Photos and detailed descriptions of more than 150 now very collectible furniture designs from the Arts and Crafts movement depict davenports, settees, buffets, desks, tables, chairs, bedsteads, dressers and more, all built of solid, quarter-sawed oak. Invaluable for students and enthusiasts of antiques, Americana and the decorative arts. 80pp. 6½ × 9¼. 27471-3 Pa. $7.95

HOW WE INVENTED THE AIRPLANE: An Illustrated History, Orville Wright. Fascinating firsthand account covers early experiments, construction of planes and motors, first flights, much more. Introduction and commentary by Fred C. Kelly. 76 photographs. 96pp. 8¼ × 11. 25662-6 Pa. $8.95

THE ARTS OF THE SAILOR: Knotting, Splicing and Ropework, Hervey Garrett Smith. Indispensable shipboard reference covers tools, basic knots and useful hitches; handsewing and canvas work, more. Over 100 illustrations. Delightful reading for sea lovers. 256pp. 5⅜ × 8½. 26440-8 Pa. $7.95

FRANK LLOYD WRIGHT'S FALLINGWATER: The House and Its History, Second, Revised Edition, Donald Hoffmann. A total revision—both in text and illustrations—of the standard document on Fallingwater, the boldest, most personal architectural statement of Wright's mature years, updated with valuable new material from the recently opened Frank Lloyd Wright Archives. "Fascinating"—*The New York Times*. 116 illustrations. 128pp. 9¼ × 10¾. 27430-6 Pa. $10.95

PHOTOGRAPHIC SKETCHBOOK OF THE CIVIL WAR, Alexander Gardner. 100 photos taken on field during the Civil War. Famous shots of Manassas, Harper's Ferry, Lincoln, Richmond, slave pens, etc. 244pp. 10⅝ × 8¼.
22731-6 Pa. $9.95

FIVE ACRES AND INDEPENDENCE, Maurice G. Kains. Great back-to-the-land classic explains basics of self-sufficient farming. The one book to get. 95 illustrations. 397pp. 5⅜ × 8½. 20974-1 Pa. $7.95

SONGS OF EASTERN BIRDS, Dr. Donald J. Borror. Songs and calls of 60 species most common to eastern U.S.: warblers, woodpeckers, flycatchers, thrushes, larks, many more in high-quality recording. Cassette and manual 99912-2 $8.95

A MODERN HERBAL, Margaret Grieve. Much the fullest, most exact, most useful compilation of herbal material. Gigantic alphabetical encyclopedia, from aconite to zedoary, gives botanical information, medical properties, folklore, economic uses, much else. Indispensable to serious reader. 161 illustrations. 888pp. 6½ × 9¼. 2-vol. set. (USO) Vol. I: 22798-7 Pa. $9.95
Vol. II: 22799-5 Pa. $9.95

HIDDEN TREASURE MAZE BOOK, Dave Phillips. Solve 34 challenging mazes accompanied by heroic tales of adventure. Evil dragons, people-eating plants, bloodthirsty giants, many more dangerous adversaries lurk at every twist and turn. 34 mazes, stories, solutions. 48pp. 8¼ × 11. 24566-7 Pa. $2.95

LETTERS OF W. A. MOZART, Wolfgang A. Mozart. Remarkable letters show bawdy wit, humor, imagination, musical insights, contemporary musical world; includes some letters from Leopold Mozart. 276pp. 5⅜ × 8½. 22859-2 Pa. $7.95

BASIC PRINCIPLES OF CLASSICAL BALLET, Agrippina Vaganova. Great Russian theoretician, teacher explains methods for teaching classical ballet. 118 illustrations. 175pp. 5⅜ × 8½. 22036-2 Pa. $4.95

THE JUMPING FROG, Mark Twain. Revenge edition. The original story of The Celebrated Jumping Frog of Calaveras County, a hapless French translation, and Twain's hilarious "retranslation" from the French. 12 illustrations. 66pp. 5⅜ × 8½. 22686-7 Pa. $3.95

BEST REMEMBERED POEMS, Martin Gardner (ed.). The 126 poems in this superb collection of 19th- and 20th-century British and American verse range from Shelley's "To a Skylark" to the impassioned "Renascence" of Edna St. Vincent Millay and to Edward Lear's whimsical "The Owl and the Pussycat." 224pp. 5⅜ × 8½. 27165-X Pa. $4.95

COMPLETE SONNETS, William Shakespeare. Over 150 exquisite poems deal with love, friendship, the tyranny of time, beauty's evanescence, death and other themes in language of remarkable power, precision and beauty. Glossary of archaic terms. 80pp. 5³/₁₆ × 8¼. 26686-9 Pa. $1.00

BODIES IN A BOOKSHOP, R. T. Campbell. Challenging mystery of blackmail and murder with ingenious plot and superbly drawn characters. In the best tradition of British suspense fiction. 192pp. 5⅜ × 8½. 24720-1 Pa. $5.95

THE INFLUENCE OF SEA POWER UPON HISTORY, 1660–1783, A. T. Mahan. Influential classic of naval history and tactics still used as text in war colleges. First paperback edition. 4 maps. 24 battle plans. 640pp. 5⅜ × 8½.
25509-3 Pa. $12.95

THE STORY OF THE TITANIC AS TOLD BY ITS SURVIVORS, Jack Winocour (ed.). What it was really like. Panic, despair, shocking inefficiency, and a little heroism. More thrilling than any fictional account. 26 illustrations. 320pp. 5⅜ × 8½. 20610-6 Pa. $8.95

FAIRY AND FOLK TALES OF THE IRISH PEASANTRY, William Butler Yeats (ed.). Treasury of 64 tales from the twilight world of Celtic myth and legend: "The Soul Cages," "The Kildare Pooka," "King O'Toole and his Goose," many more. Introduction and Notes by W. B. Yeats. 352pp. 5⅜ × 8½. 26941-8 Pa. $8.95

BUDDHIST MAHAYANA TEXTS, E. B. Cowell and Others (eds.). Superb, accurate translations of basic documents in Mahayana Buddhism, highly important in history of religions. The Buddha-karita of Asvaghosha, Larger Sukhavativyuha, more. 448pp. 5⅜ × 8½. 25552-2 Pa. $9.95

ONE TWO THREE . . . INFINITY: Facts and Speculations of Science, George Gamow. Great physicist's fascinating, readable overview of contemporary science: number theory, relativity, fourth dimension, entropy, genes, atomic structure, much more. 128 illustrations. Index. 352pp. 5⅜ × 8½. 25664-2 Pa. $8.95

ENGINEERING IN HISTORY, Richard Shelton Kirby, et al. Broad, nontechnical survey of history's major technological advances: birth of Greek science, industrial revolution, electricity and applied science, 20th-century automation, much more. 181 illustrations. ". . . excellent . . ."—Isis. Bibliography. vii + 530pp. 5⅜ × 8¼.
26412-2 Pa. $14.95

Prices subject to change without notice.

Available at your book dealer or write for free catalog to Dept. GI, Dover Publications, Inc., 31 East 2nd St., Mineola, N.Y. 11501. Dover publishes more than 500 books each year on science, elementary and advanced mathematics, biology, music, art, literary history, social sciences and other areas.